GERMANY

Executive Editorial Director   David Brabis
Chief Editor   Cynthia Clayton Ochterbeck

THE GREEN GUIDE GERMANY

Editor   Gwen Cannon
Principal Writer   Amy S. Eckert
Production Coordinator   Allison M. Simpson
Cartography   Peter Wrenn
Photo Editor   Lydia Strong
Layout & Design   Tim Schulz
Cover Design   Laurent Muller; Ute Weber

Contact Us: The Green Guide
                            Michelin Maps and Guides
                            One Parkway South
                            Greenville, SC 29615
                            USA
                            ☎ 1-800-423-0485
                            www.michelintravel.com
                            Michelin.guides@us.michelin.com

                            The Green Guide
                            Michelin Maps and Guides
                            Hannay House
                            39 Clarendon Road
                            Watford, Herts WD17 1JA
                            UK
                            ☎ (01923) 205 240
                            www.ViaMichelin.com
                            Travelpubsales@uk.michelin.com

Special Sales: For information regarding bulk sales,
                            customized editions and premium sales,
                            please contact our Customer Service
                            Departments:
                            USA   1-800-423-0485
                            UK   (01923) 205 240
                            Canada 1-800-361-8236

Note to the reader

One Team ...
A Commitment to Quality

There's just one reason our team is dedicated to producing quality travel publications—you, our reader. We want you to get the maximum benefit from your trip—and from your money. In today's multiple-choice world of travel, the options are many, perhaps overwhelming.

In our guidebooks, we try to minimize the guesswork involved with travel. We scout out the attractions, prioritize them with star ratings, and describe what you'll discover when you visit them.

To help you orient yourself, we provide colorful and detailed, but easy-to-follow maps. Floor plans of some of the cathedrals and museums help you plan your tour.

Throughout the guides, we offer practical information, touring tips and suggestions for finding the best views, good places for a break and the most interesting shops.

Lodging and dining are always a big part of travel, so we compile a selection of hotels and restaurants that we think convey the feel of the destination, and organize them by geographic area and price. We also highlight shopping, recreational and entertainment venues, especially the popular spots.

If you're short on time, driving tours are included so you can hit the highlights and quickly absorb the best of the region.

For those who love to experience a destination on foot, we add walking tours, often with a map. And we list other companies who offer boat, bus or guided walking tours of the area, some with culinary, historical or other themes.

In short, we test and retest, check and recheck to make sure that our guidebooks are truly just that: a personalized guide to help you make the most of your visit. After all, we want you to enjoy traveling as much as we do.

The Michelin Green Guide Team

PLANNING YOUR TRIP

INTRODUCTION TO GERMANY

SYMBOLS

- 🐝 **Tips to help improve your experience**
- 🐝 **Details to consider**
- 🐚 **Entry Fees**
- 🚶 **Walking tours**
- ⚮ **Closed to the public**
- 🕐 **Hours of operation**
- 🕐 **Periods of closure**

CONTENTS

DISCOVERING GERMANY

HOW TO USE THIS GUIDE

Orientation

To help you grasp the "lay of the land" quickly and easily, so you'll feel confident and comfortable finding your way around the region, we offer the following tools in this guide:

- Detailed table of contents for an overview of what you'll find in the guide, and how it is organized.
- Map of Germany at the front to the guide, with the principal sights highlighted for easy reference.
- Detailed maps for major cities and villages, including driving tour maps and larger-scale maps for walking tours.
- Map of Germany Regional Driving Tours, each one numbered and color coded.

Practicalities

At the front of the guide, you'll see a section called "Planning Your Trip" that contains information about planning your trip, the best time to go, different ways of getting to the region and getting around, basic facts and tips for making the most of your visit. You'll find driving and themed tours, and suggestions for outdoor fun. There's also a calendar of popular annual events. Information on shopping, sightseeing, kids' activities and sports and recreational opportunities is also included.

LODGINGS

We've made a selection of hotels and arranged them within the cities, categorized by price to fit all budgets (see the Legend at the back of the guide for an explanation of the price categories). For the most part, we selected accommodations based on their unique regional quality. So, unless the individual hotel embodies local ambience, it's rare that we include chain properties, which typically have their own imprint. If you want a more comprehensive selection of accommodations, see the red-cover *Michelin Guide Deutschland*.

RESTAURANTS

We thought you'd like to know the popular eating spots in the country. So we selected restaurants that capture the German experience—those that have a unique regional flavor and local atmosphere. We're not rating the quality of the food per se. As we did with the hotels, we selected restaurants for many towns and villages, categorized by price to appeal to all wallets. If you want a more comprehensive selection of dining recommendations, see the red-cover *Michelin Guide Deutschland*.

Attractions

Principal Sights are arranged alphabetically. Within each Principal Sight, attractions for each town, village, or geographical area are divided into local Sights or Walking Tours, nearby Excursions to sights outside the town, or detailed Driving Tours—suggested itineraries for seeing several attractions around a major town. Contact information, admission charges and hours of operation are given for the majority of attractions. Unless otherwise noted, admission prices shown are for a single adult only. Discounts for seniors, students, teachers, etc. may be available; be sure to ask. If no admission charge is shown, entrance to the attraction is free.

If you're pressed for time, we recommend you visit the three- and two-star sights first: the stars are your guide.

STAR RATINGS

Michelin has used stars as a rating tool for more than 100 years:

★★★	Highly recommended
★★	Recommended
★	Interesting

SYMBOLS IN THE TEXT

Besides the stars, other symbols in the text indicate tourist information 🚹; wheelchair access ♿; on-site eating facilities ✗; camping facilities △; on-site parking 🅿; sights of interest to children Kids; and beaches ⚓.

See the box appearing on the Contents page for other symbols used in the text.

See the Maps explanation below for symbols appearing on the maps.

Throughout the guide you will find peach-coloured text boxes or sidebars containing anecdotal or background information. Green-coloured boxes contain information to help you save time or money.

Maps

All maps in this guide are oriented north, unless otherwise indicated by a directional arrow. See the map Legend at the back of the guide for an explanation of other map symbols. A complete list of the maps found in the guide appears at the back of this book.

Addresses, phone numbers, opening hours and prices published in this guide are accurate at press time. We welcome corrections and suggestions that may assist us in preparing the next edition. Please send your comments to:

Michelin Maps and Guides
Editorial Department
P.O. Box 19001
Greenville, SC   29602-9001
Email: michelin.guides@us.michelin.com
Web site: www.michelintravel.com

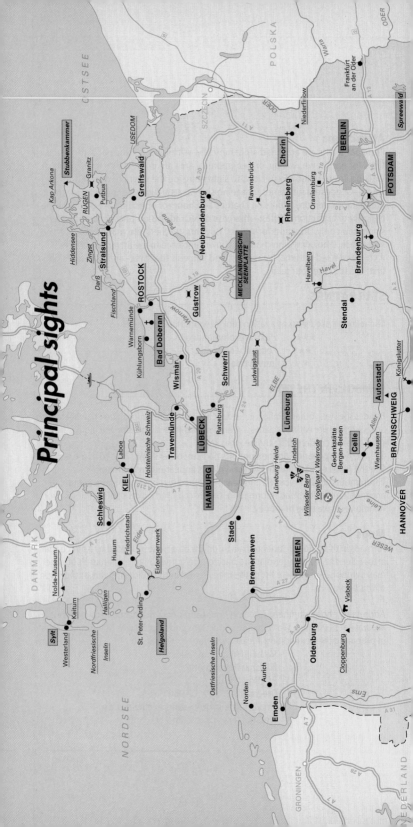

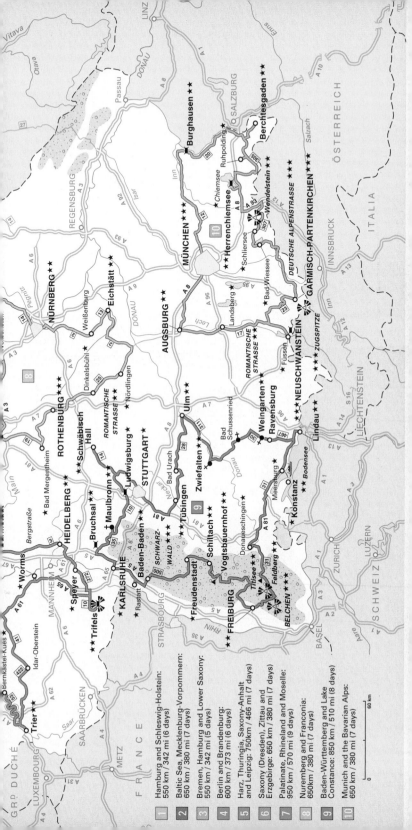

1 Hamburg and Schleswig-Holstein:
   550 km / 342 mi (6 days)

2 Baltic Sea, Mecklenburg-Vorpommern:
   650 km / 380 mi (7 days)

3 Bremen, Hamburg and Lower Saxony:
   550 km / 342 mi (5 days)

4 Berlin and Brandenburg:
   600 km / 373 mi (6 days)

5 Harz, Thuringia, Saxony-Anhalt
   and Leipzig: 750km / 466 mi (7 days)

6 Saxony (Dresden), Zittau and
   Erzgebirge: 650 km / 380 mi (7 days)

7 Palatinate, Rhineland and Moselle:
   950 km / 570 mi (9 days)

8 Nuremberg and Franconia:
   650km / 380 mi (7 days)

9 Baden-Württemberg and Lake
   Constance: 850 km / 510 mi (8 days)

10 Munich and the Bavarian Alps:
   650 km / 380 mi (7 days)

Beach at Fischland peninsula

T. Krieger/MICHELIN

WHEN AND WHERE TO GO

Driving Tours

For those who would like to tour by car over several days, we suggest ten itineraries (👣 *see the Driving Tours map on pp 11-13*). You can also refer to the map of principal sights (👣 *pp 8-10*) and read in-depth descriptions in the "Discovering Germany" section.

HAMBURG AND SCHLESWIG-HOLSTEIN ①

550km/342mi-tour leaving from Hamburg.

This tour through the Länder of Hamburg and Schleswig-Holstein provides an opportunity to explore the far north of Germany, a region with a glorious Hanseatic past. The country's second largest city, **Hamburg** is a bustling port set on the banks of the Elbe estuary; its central districts are ideal for a stroll, and the particularly well-stocked museums will be much appreciated by art lovers. A mere 70km/43mi from Hamburg is **Lübeck**. This delightful town in northern Germany has been on UNESCO's World Heritage list since 1987. Remarkably preserved, it boasts an exceptional collection of houses and monuments from many different periods. Not far from Lübeck, **Travemünde**, on the shores of the Baltic Sea, is renowned for its sandy beach, its very long seafront promenade and its casino. The tour continues northwards with the next port of call **Kiel, the gateway to Scandinavia**. Capital of Schleswig-Holstein, Kiel is an old maritime town steeped in a cheerful yet stylish atmosphere. The route then takes a northwesterly direction along the Baltic coast to **Schleswig**, an ideal place to relax and explore. Heading westwards, from one sea to the other, you will soon reach the island of **Sylt** and the North Frisian islands. The fragile sandy shores of these wild islands are pitted against the North Sea in a constant battle against marine erosion. Lastly, the peaceful seaside town of **Husum**, birthplace of the writer Theodor Storm, offers all the attractions of a modern tourist resort.

BALTIC SEA, MECKLENBURG-VORPOMMERN ②

650km/380mi-tour leaving from Neubrandenburg.

This itinerary will give you a glimpse of a little-known Germany that is both wild and captivating. The town of **Neubrandenburg has a surprise in store with its** imposing medieval ramparts, miraculously spared by the Second World War. The journey continues westwards through the **Mecklenburg lake district, a well-preserved region and** one of the least populated in Germany. With countless lakes and a wide range of activities on offer, it will certainly appeal to nature lovers. **Schwerin** is without a doubt one of the most pleasant towns in northern Germany. Its refined architecture and the majestic charm of its castle set atop an island facing the old town add to the appeal of this city full of character. Our itinerary takes us north out of Schwerin and up to the coast. **Wismar**, with its red-brick buildings, provides an excellent introduction to the Baltic coast. The town's historic centre was classed a UNESCO World Heritage site

Salzspeicher in Lübeck

J. Bouraly/MICHELIN

in 2002. Dotted along the coast, the towns of **Bad Doberan**, **Rostock** and **Stralsund** are all worth a visit on your way to the island of **Rügen** with its surprising variety of landscapes; bands of dunes, land reclaimed from the sea, salt meadows, cultivated fields, endless mudflats (Watt, or Wadden) and prehistoric tumuli. It is, like the neighbouring island of **Usedom**, a very popular holiday destination, with pleasant seaside, health and spa resorts. Last stop on the itinerary is **Greifswald, whose very old** architecture reveals a Scandinavian influence.

BREMEN, HAMBURG AND LOWER SAXONY ④③

550km/342mi-tour leaving from Bremen.

The bustling town of **Bremen is a true delight.** A large port and city of artistic interest where the Weser Renaissance style flourished, it has a number of parks and a charming riverside promenade. After a stop in **Hamburg**, 125km/78mi to the northeast (⚫ *see description in itinerary* ①), we invite you to explore **Lüneburg**, which owes its long-standing prosperity to salt. The town constitutes the gateway to the vast expanse of the **Lüneburg Heath**. In the face of the increasing advances of agriculture, attempts are being made to preserve this wild environment with its picturesque copses of birch, pine and juniper; from mid-August to mid-September, the carpet of heather in bloom is a magnificent sight. To the south of the Lüneburg Heath stands the aristocratic city of **Celle**. There are many reasons to stop here; treasures from the old city, a magnificently restored ducal palace, and a folklore and history museum to name but a few. For car fanatics, a trip to **Autostadt** – a vast automobile complex set up by Volkswagen about 60km/37mi from Celle – is a must. Here you will find generously landscaped areas of park and water, dotted with architecturally striking buildings. A stop in **Braunschweig** is followed by a leisurely look around the beautiful city of **Wölfenbuttel** with its exceptional collection of Renaissance houses. Further west, after **Hildesheim**, **Hannover** awaits with its **waterways** *(Maschsee)*, city forest and famous Herrenhausen gardens.

BERLIN AND BRANDENBURG ④

600km/373mi-tour leaving from Neubrandenburg.

After a look around **Neubrandenburg** (⚫ *see description in itinerary* ②), head south to explore Schloss **Rheinsberg** where Frederick the Great, by his own admission, spent the best years of his life. Germany's vibrant capital is located 90km/56mi further south. The buzzing city of **Berlin** offers a wealth of culture and a very lively night-life. This amazing metropolis – one of the most extensive and among those with the largest number of parks and gardens on the Old Continent – seems to be experiencing a new golden age. Another town marked by the personality of Frederick the Great, who held a brilliant and cosmopolitan court here, **Potsdam** is a genuine "Rococo treasure" of universal appeal. Carry on westwards and, after the small town of **Brandenburg** set in the heart of the Havelland (an area of scattered lakes), stop off at **Tangermünde** enclosed within its late 14C ramparts. **Stendal**, just a few kilometres away, was until the mid-16C the most important town

Partner für Berlin/FTB-Werbefotografie

Schloß Sanssouci, Potsdam

in the Brandenburg March, before the ravages of the Thirty Years' War dealt it a fatal blow. Several monuments typical of Gothic brick architecture from this period of prosperity can still be seen. Further north you can admire the beautiful cathedral of **Havelberg**, a pretty town set on the banks of the River Havel. The itinerary ends with a foray into the picturesque **Mecklenburg lake district.**

HARZ, THURINGIA, SAXONY-ANHALT AND LEIPZIG ⑤

750km/466mi-tour leaving from Leipzig.
This route will take you back into Germany's past, where – particularly in the 18C – literature and music flourished. **Leipzig** is a city of artistic interest that can be proud of its exceptional musical heritage; Bach, Wagner and Mendelssohn all lived here at one time and it remains very much in the foreground of the German music scene. Around 60km/37mi south, **Naumburg** stands among hills cloaked in vineyards and forests. The town is renowned in particular for its exceptional Romanesque-cum-Gothic cathedral. **Weimar**, **Jena**, **Erfurt** and **Eisenach** are all names with strong connotations in German culture, through their association with figures such as Luther, Goethe and Schiller. Offering a pleasant distraction from the "cultural pilgrimage", the Thuringia Forest and, farther north, the Harz mountains take you right to the very heart of nature. The countless activities on offer here include hiking, mountain biking, canoeing, skiing and rock climbing.

SAXONY (DRESDEN), ZITTAU AND ERZGEBIRGE ⑥

650km/380mi-tour leaving from Dresden.
Saxony is one of the regions which have played a key role in Germany's history. A city of art and culture, **Dresden** attracts an ever increasing number of visitors. A long and ongoing reconstruction effort has restored its Baroque treasures, making it once

again "the Florence of the Elbe". **Swiss Saxony** stretches out to the south of Dresden; with its impressive sandstone cliffs and long gorges gouged from the rock, this region is one of Germany's most spectacular natural wonders. The towns of **Görlitz** and **Bautzen** provide an opportunity to stop off in Sorbian country. An ethnic minority in Germany, occupying the region of Lusace which straddles the Länder of Saxony and Brandenburg, the Sorbians have long belonged to the kingdom of Bohemia. Not only do they still speak their language, but they have also kept alive many traditions, such as the decoration of eggs at Easter and the wearing of the Sorbian national costume and tall embroidered headdresses. Heading northwards, you will come to **Branitz**, a stone's throw from Cottbus where Prince Hermann von Pückler-Muskau built a palace and – indulging his passion for garden design – a fabulous park. Covering an area of 90ha/222 acres, the park alternates open spaces, groups of trees, individual specimens, ditches and pools. Heading back down to Dresden, you will stop at **Schloss Moritzburg** and **Meissen**, renowned for its porcelain. Further south, near the Czech border, **Annaberg-Buchholz** boasts one of the most impressive examples of Flamboyant Gothic style in Saxony: St Annen-Kirche.

PALATINATE, RHINELAND AND MOSELLE ⑦

950km/570mi-tour leaving from Cologne.
Not far from the borders with Belgium, Luxembourg and France, this very long route from Cologne to Heidelberg encompasses some of the major sights of western Germany. The Rhine valley is full of surprises; alternating vineyards and rocky outcrops dominated by lofty castles, the route from **Koblenz** to **Rüdesheim** or **Bingen** affords some magnificent views. Take a stroll around the historic centre of **Mainz** with its maze of little alleyways and old houses, some of them inhabited by craftsmen. After **Darmstadt**,

take the **Bergstrasse** southwards to the fascinating town of **Heidelberg**, a symbol of German Romanticism, whose hillside castle leaves a lasting impression. One of Germany's great forest regions, the Palatinate mountains are also a remarkable zoological and botanical reserve. The eastern part is blessed with an incredibly mild microclimate enabling the cultivation of exotic fruits. Some of the region's towns, such as **Speyer**, **Worms** and **Trier** are former Roman colonies and the oldest towns in Germany. From Trier to Koblenz, the winding course of the **Moselle** takes you on a journey dotted with picturesque villages, castles and vineyards. Cruises, hiking and cycling are among the activities on offer during this part of the tour. **Monschau**, on the road to **Aachen** in the northwest, is next on the agenda. This charming village, which went by the name of Montjoie until 1919, nestles at the end of a winding gorge of the River Rur. As for **Cologne**, with its two black spires reaching skywards, its multitude of churches, colourful little houses, numerous museums, trade fair and exhibition venues etc, it has a great deal to offer.

NUREMBERG AND FRANCONIA 8

650km/380mi-tour leaving from Nuremberg.
This itinerary provides a chance to explore the age-old sights of northern Bavaria. It begins with **Nuremberg**, an old bronze casters' and gold-beaters' town and one of the most beautiful medieval cities in Germany. Farther south, **Eichstätt** is now a "Mecca" of uncompromising contemporary architecture, exemplified by the new *Pädagogische Hochschule* and the university's summer residence. Passing through river valleys and fertile hills, the Romantic Road recalls at every stage some aspect of the past that could only belong to the history of Germany. As the route unfolds, it evokes life in the great medieval cities (**Nördlingen**, **Dinkelsbühl**, **Rothenburg**). In Würzburg, what remains

of the grandeur acquired in the mid 17C under three prince-bishops of the Schönborn family can be seen in the town's Baroque churches and the splendid Residenz Palace. After **Bamberg**, the town with which, according to the results of a survey, the Germans feel the strongest connection, our Bavarian route touches the region of Thuringia and passes through **Coburg**, where a stop at the **Vierzehnheiligen Church** is recommended. This pilgrimage church is a Baroque masterpiece which may surprise even those who are least enamoured of this style. The interior layout reflects the boldness of the architect Balthasar Neumann, and the wealth of decoration is truly captivating. **Bayreuth**, last stop on the tour, will be a high point for fans of Wagner's music and admirers of the Rococo style.

BADEN-WÜRTTEMBERG AND LAKE CONSTANCE 9

850km/510mi-tour leaving from Freiburg.
Southeast Germany has an astonishing number of remarkable tourist attractions. It is hard to remain untouched by the relaxed atmosphere of **Freiburg**, an old university town whose paved alleyways beg to be explored. The **Black Forest** is steeped in legend and offers a surprising variety of scenery for such a small region. Add to that its picturesque villages, a passion for cuckoo clocks and the possibilities of hiking in summer and skiing in winter, and it is easy to see why this mountainous region has become one of Germany's most popular tourist destinations. Passing through towns such as the elegant spa resort of **Baden-Baden**, which attracts a wealthy clientele all year round, and **Karlsruhe**, the route takes you up to **Bruchsal**. This town has inherited a sumptuous 18C palace which houses an original museum entirely devoted to mechanical musical instruments. A few kilometres southeast of Bruchsal stands **Maulbronn Abbey**; built in 1147, it was one of the earliest Cistercian foundations in Germany.

The school established here since the Reformation (1557) has seen the flowering of such diverse scientific, literary and philosophical talents as those of Kepler, Hölderlin and Hermann Hesse. The road south leads to **Tübingen** and **Ulm**. Tübingen's labyrinth of narrow sloping streets lined with old half-timbered houses combined with its animated student life create a relaxed and happy atmosphere away from the throng of tourists. In Ulm, you can take a stroll between the canals and the Danube and admire the town's extraordinary cathedral. The Upper Swabian Plateau is dotted with Baroque churches whose dazzling decoration and architecture combining light effects and symmetry are in perfect harmony with the landscape. **Zwiefalten** and **Weingarten** are two superb illustrations of the Baroque style that flourished so extensively in southern Germany. The tour ends with the magnificent **Lake Constance**, regarded by the Germans as their very own "Riviera".

Kloster Bebenhausen, Tübingen

visit such famous monuments as the castles of Ludwig II – including **Neuschwanstein** – and the Wieskirche. At **Füssen**, the Alpine Road joins up with the Romantic Road, plunging the traveller into the Baroque splendour of the episcopal courts and imperial towns such as **Augsburg**.

Historic Routes

Very clearly signposted, these "thematic" itineraries provide an original means of crisscrossing the country and getting to know it better. They include:

+ **Baden Wine Route (Badische Weinstraße)**, from Baden-Baden to Lörrach.
+ **Castle Road (Burgenstraße)**, from Mannheim to Bayreuth and then on to Prague (975km/605mi in total).
+ **Franconian Wine Route (Bocksbeutelstraße):** five different routes leaving from Würzburg.
+ **German Avenues (Deutsche Alleenstraße)**, from Sellin on Rügen Island to Goslar.
+ **German Holiday Route (Deutsche Ferienstraße Ostsee-Alpen)**, which links the Baltic Sea (Puttgarden) with the Alps (Berchtesgaden).
+ **German Wine Road (Deutsche Weinstraße)**, from Bockenheim/Palatinate to Wissembourg/Alsace.
+ **Half-timbered Buildings (Deutsche Fachwerkstraße)**, six

MUNICH AND THE BAVARIAN ALPS ①⓪

650km/380mi-tour leaving from Munich. A tour through this region, with its magnificent alpine scenery and wealth of culture, will undoubtedly be a high point in your exploration of Germany. The country's second most popular tourist destination after Berlin, **Munich** – Bavaria's vibrant capital – is a prosperous and lively city. Art lovers will delight in its fabulous museums and Baroque churches. A little over 100km/62mi to the east, on the Austrian border, **Burghausen** was the biggest fortress in Germany in the Middle Ages. Its defence system, reinforced at the beginning of the 16C in the face of a threatened invasion by the Turks, stretches for around 1km/0.6mi. The much-travelled **German Alpine Road** starts at **Berchtesgaden**, whose basin forms a salient on the German border that penetrates deeply into Austria. This route allows travellers not only to enjoy the superb Bavarian mountain scenery but also to routes through Lower Saxony and Hessen.

- **Old Salt Road (Alte Salzstraße)**, from Lüneburg to Lübeck.
- **Romanesque Road (Straße der Romanik)**, circuit leaving from Magdeburg.
- **Romantic Road (Romantische Straße)**, from Würzburg to Füssen.
- **Silver Route** (Ferienstraße Silberstraße), from Zwickau to Dresden.
- **Thuringian Classical Route (Klassikerstraße Thüringen)**, circuit from Meiningen.
- **Upper Swabian Baroque Route (Oberschwäbische Barockstraße)**, from Ulm to Lake Constance.
- **Weser Renaissance Route (Straße der Weser-Renaissance)**, from Hann. Münden to Bremen.

Seasons

Whatever the season, the weather in Germany is subject to enormous variation. The period when you are most likely to find good weather extends from May to October (and it may even be too hot during high summer in Baden-Württemberg and Bavaria). Autumn and spring, when tourist sights are less crowded, can be the perfect time to discover the country. In any case, it is sensible to pack some waterproof clothing whenever you plan to go. Before you leave, don't forget to find out about any festivals, fairs or other events which may considerably increase the number of visitors in certain towns and make finding a room difficult (*see Calendar of Events*). Skiers will find snow-covered slopes from the end of November until the end of February.

KNOW BEFORE YOU GO

Useful Web Sites

GENERAL INFORMATION

One of Germany's most popular tourist destinations is the *Romantischestraße*, the Romantic Road. Half-timbered houses, medieval fortresses and city walls, Alpine vistas and flower-filled balconies stretch along the route. **www.romantischestrasse.de** offers detailed travel information and maps for each of the cities along the route. Germany's most romantic castles are located along the *Burgenstraße*, Castle Road, that stretches across the country. For maps and details about the route, visit **www.burgenstrasse.de**. The German *Weinstraße*, or Wine Road, Web site is **www.deutsche-weinstrasse.de**. The site offers information about each of Germany's wines and wine regions and a listing of the nation's wine festivals. Germany is home to 13 national parks, 14 wildlife preserves and 80 regional parks. **www.europarc-deutschland.de** offers detailed information and maps for each of Germany's parks. Spas and wellness centers have long been considered by Germans an important part of healthy living. A visit to The German Spa Association's Web site, **www.deutscher-heilbaedervband.de**, provides links to spas nationwide, including lists of those with English-speaking therapists. Parents traveling with young children may want to visit **www.zoos.de** prior to traveling in Germany. This comprehensive Web site includes information about and links to all of the zoos and animal parks in the country. Oktoberfest is one of the world's most famous festivals. Visitors to Munich interested in up-to-date festival information can visit **www.oktoberfest.de**.

CULTURAL ORGANISATIONS

The Goethe-Institut Web sites for each of the cities below can be accessed via www.goethe.de

- **Goethe-Institut Johannesburg**, 119 Jan Smuts Ave, Parkwood 2193, Johannesburg, ☎ (011) 442 3232, fax (011) 442 3738.
- **Goethe-Institut London**, 50 Princes Gate, Exhibition Road, London SW7 2PH, ☎ (020) 7596 4044, fax (020) 7594 0230.
- **Goethe-Institut New York**, 1014 Fifth Avenue, New York, NY 10028, ☎ (212) 439-8700, fax (212) 439-8705.
- **Goethe-Institut Ottawa**, 47 Clarence Street, Suite 480, Ottawa, ON, K1N 9K1, ☎ (613) 241-0273, fax (613) 241-9790
- **Goethe-Institut Sydney**, 90 Ocean Street, Woollahra, NSW 2025, ☎ (02) 8356 8333, fax (02) 8356 8314.

Tourist Offices

TOURIST ORGANISATIONS

Information on travel arrangements and accommodation and a variety of brochures are available from the **German National Tourist Office**. For on-line information refer to www.germany-tourism.de, the German National Tourist Office website. Most German cities have Web sites, the addresses of which are generally composed of the city name, for example www.karlsruhe.de is the Web site for Karlsruhe.

Chicago
German National Tourist Office Chicago PO Box 59594, Chicago, IL 60659-9594 ☎ (773) 539-6303, fax (773) 539-6378, heike.pfeiffer@gntoch.com, www.cometogermany.com

Johannesburg
German National Tourist Office, c/o Lufthansa German Airlines, PO Box 412246, Craighall, 2024 Johannesburg ☎ (011) 325 1927, fax (011) 325 0867

London
German National Tourist Office, PO Box 2695, London W1A 3TN ☎ (020) 7317 0908, ☎ 09001 600 100 (24hr brochure line, calls cost 60p/min), fax (020) 7317 0917 gntolon@d-z-t.com, www.germany-tourism.co.uk

New York
German National Tourist Office, 122 East 42nd Street, New York, NY 10168-0072 ☎ (212) 661-7200, toll-free (800) 651-7010, fax (212) 661-7174, gntonyc@d-z-t.com, www.cometogermany.com

Sydney
German National Tourist Office, GPO Box 1461, Sydney NSW 2001 ☎ (02) 8296 0488, fax (02) 8296 0487, gnto@germany.org.au

Toronto
German National Tourist Office, 480 University Avenue, Suite 1410, Toronto, ON, M5G 1V2 ☎ (416) 968-1685, fax (416) 968-0562, info@gnto.ca, www.cometogermany.com

TOURIST INFORMATION ON SITE

Tourist offices
Tourist offices are marked on the town plans in this guide by the 🄑 symbol. The address and telephone number of the tourist office are found in *Discovering Germany* and indicated by the 🄑 symbol.

International Visitors

GERMAN EMBASSIES AND CONSULATES

In Australia
- Embassy of the Federal Republic of Germany 119 Empire Circuit, Yarralumla ACT 2600

☎ (02) 6270 1911, fax (02) 6270 1951,
info1@germanembassy.org.au
www.germanembassy.org.au

- Consulate General of the Republic
of Germany, Sydney,
13 Trelawney Street,
Woollahra NSW 2025,
☎ (02) 9328 7733,
fax (02) 9327 9649,
info@sydney.diplo.de,
www.sydney.diplo.de

In Canada

- Embassy of the Federal Republic
of Germany, 1 Waverley Street,
Ottawa, ON, K2P 0T8
☎ (613) 232-1101,
fax (613) 594-9330,
germanembassyottawa@on.aibn.
com, www.ottawa.diplo.de

  Postal address: PO Box 379, Postal
Station "A", Ottawa, ON, K1N 8V4

- Consulate General of the Federal
Republic of Germany,
77 Bloor Street West, Suite 1703,
Toronto, ON, M5S 2T1
☎ (416) 925 28 13,
fax (416) 925 28 18,
mail@germanconsulatetoronto.ca,
www.toronto.diplo.de

  Postal address: Consulate General
of the Federal Republic of Germany Postal Station "P" Box 523
Toronto, ON, M5S 2T1

In South Africa

- Embassy of the Federal Republic
of Germany, 180 Blackwood Street,
Arcadia, Pretoria 0083,
☎ (012) 427 89 00,
fax (012) 343 94 01,
germanembassypretoria@gonet.
co.za, www.pretoria.diplo.de

  Postal address: PO Box 2023,
Pretoria 0001

- Consulate-General of the Federal
Republic of Germany, 19th Floor,
Safmarine House, 22 Riebeek
Street, Cape Town 8001

☎ (021) 405 30 00,
fax (021) 421 04 00, info@german-
consulatecapetown.co.za

Postal address: PO Box 4273, Cape
Town 8000

In the United Kingdom

- Embassy of the Federal Republic
of Germany, 23 Belgrave Square,
London SW1X 8PZ,
☎ (020) 7824 1300,
fax (020) 7824 1449,
www.london.diplo.de

- Consulate General of the Federal
Republic of Germany,
16 Eglinton Crescent, Edinburgh
EH12 5DG, Scotland,
☎ (0131) 337 2323,
fax (0131) 346 1578

In the United States

- Embassy of the Federal Republic
of Germany, 4645 Reservoir Road
NW, Washington, DC 20007-1998
☎ (202) 298-4000,
www.germany.info

- Consulate General of the Federal
Republic of Germany, 871, United
Nations Plaza (1st Avenue @ 49th
Street), New York, NY 10017
☎ (212) 610-9700,
fax (212) 610-9702,
www.germanconsulate.org/
newyork

FOREIGN EMBASSIES AND CONSULATES IN GERMANY

◆ **American Embassy,** Neu-
städtische Kirchstraße 4-5, 10117
Berlin, ☎ 030-8 30 50 (emergen-
cies only), fax 030-8305-1215,
www.usembassy.de

◆ **American Consulate-General,**
Willi-Becker-Allee 10, 40227 Düsseldorf, ☎ 0211-7 88 89 27, fax
0211-7 88 89 38

◆ **Australian Embassy,** Wallstraße
76–79, 10179 Berlin, ☎ 030-88 00

Wannsee

J. Gläser/Presse- und Informationsamt des Landes Berlin

88-0, fax 030-88 00 88-210, www.
australian-embassy.de

- **Australian Consulate-General,**
  Neue Mainzerstr. 52-58, 60322
  Frankfurt am Main, ☎ 069-90 55
  80, fax 069-90 55 81 19

- **British Embassy Berlin,** Wilhelmstraße 70-71, 10117 Berlin,
  ☎ 030-20 45 7-0, fax 030-20 45
  7-579, www.britischebotschaft.de

- **British Consulate-General,**
  Yorckstraße 19, Düsseldorf 40476,
  ☎ 0211-94 48-0, fax 0211-48 81 90

- **Canadian Embassy,** Friedrichstraße 95, 10117 Berlin, ☎ 030-20
  31 20, fax 030-20 31 25 90, www.
  kanada-info.de

- **Consular Services Section,**
  Canadian Embassy, Leipziger Platz
  17, 10117 Berlin, ☎ 030-2031-2470,
  fax 030-2031-2457

- **South African Embassy,** Tiergartenstraße 18, 10785 Berlin,
  ☎ 030-22 07 30, fax 030-22 07 31
  90, www.suedafrika.org

- **South African Consulate-General,** Sendlinger-Tor-Platz 5, 80336
  München, ☎ 089-2 31 16 30, fax
  089-23 11 63 63

DOCUMENTS

Passport
Visitors entering Germany must
be in possession of a valid national
passport. Citizens of European Union
countries need only a national identity
card. In case of loss or theft, report
to the embassy or consulate and the
local police.

Driving licence
A valid national or international
driving licence is required to drive in
Germany and third-party insurance
cover is compulsory; it is advisable to
obtain an International Insurance Cer-
tificate (Green Card) from your insurer.
If you are bringing your own car into
the country, you will need the vehicle
registration papers.

HEALTH

Make sure before you leave that you
have adequate health insurance
cover. The cost of medical treatment
given in Germany is reimbursed for
all European Union citizens (pick up
an **E111** from any main post office or
travel agent).
Medication for minor problems can
be obtained from a **pharmacy** (signs
with a red **A** for *Apotheke*). When they
are closed, the pharmacies display
the names of doctors on duty and
emergency pharmacies.
It is also advisable to check whether
you have **repatriation** insurance
cover (check whether this is included
in your car insurance or with your
bank card).
British citizens should apply to their
local post office for an E111 Form
(application form available from the
post office), which entitles the holder
to emergency treatment for accidents
or unexpected illness in EU countries.
Non-EU residents should check that
their private health insurance policy
covers them for travel abroad, and if
necessary take out supplementary
medical insurance with specific
overseas coverage. All prescription
drugs should be clearly labelled, and

we recommend that you carry a copy of the prescription with you.

Accessibility

Many of the sights described in this guide are accessible to people with special needs. Sights marked with the symbol ♿ offer access for wheelchairs. However, it is advisable to check beforehand by telephone. A book entitled *Handicapped-Reisen Deutschland* (€14.80, plus postage) is published by FMG-Verlag GmbH, Postfach 2154, 40644 Meerbusch, ☎ 02159-815622, fax 02159-815624, www.fmg-verlag.de. It lists 890 wheelchair-friendly hotels, apartments and youth hostels with wheelchair facilities, giving detailed information for wheelchair users. A similarly helpful publication is Reise-ABC (€5, plus postage) published by Bundesverband Selbsthilfe Körperbehinderter e.V., Postfach 20, 74236 Krautheim, ☎ 06294-4281-0, fax 06294-4281-79, www.bsk-ev.de.

Disabled motorists should take note that a disabled car badge/sticker does not entitle them to unrestricted parking, as it does in the UK (local disabled residents are granted special parking permits only in exceptional circumstances). Apart from this, Germany is on the whole a well-equipped country for disabled visitors.

GETTING THERE

By Air

Various international airline companies operate regular services to one or all of Germany's international airports (Berlin, Bremen, Dresden, Düsseldorf, Frankfurt/Main, Hamburg, Hannover, Köln/Bonn, Leipzig, München, Münster/Osnabrück, Nürnberg, Saarbrücken, Stuttgart). The international German airline **Lufthansa** can be contacted on the following numbers:

* **Australia**, ☎ 1300 655 727
* **Canada**, ☎ 1-800 563 5954
* **South Africa**, ☎ 0861 842538
* **UK**, ☎ 0870 8377 747
* **USA**, ☎ 800 399-5838, 800 645-3880

Information about flights to and in Germany can also be obtained, and reservations made, on their website at www.lufthansa.com.

Budget airlines **Ryanair** and **easyJet** also fly to several destinations in Germany from various cities in Europe. They are both ticketless airlines. Ryanair serves Berlin, Hamburg, Düsseldorf, Leipzig, Erfurt, Friedrichshafen and Karlsruhe/Baden from London Stansted airport. For information and reservations, visit www.ryanair.com or contact one of their European call centres. They can be contacted on ☎ 0871 246 0000 (£0.10/min) from within the UK, on ☎ 01 90 170 100 in Germany (€0.62/min), and on ☎ +353 1 249 7700 from the rest of the world. Web-based airline **easyJet** flies to Berlin, Cologne/Bonn, Dortmund and Munich from various airports in the UK. Fares are quoted one way and discounts granted for online booking. For information and reservations, visit www.easyjet.com, or call ☎ 0871 7500 100 in the UK for departures within two weeks.

By Car

When driving to the Continent the ideal ports of entry for Germany are Cuxhaven (from Harwich, 19hr sailing), Rotterdam (from Hull, 11hr sailing), the Hook of Holland (from Harwich, 3hr 40min by fast ferry), Zeebrugge (from Hull, 11hr sailing) and Calais (from Dover, 1hr 15min sailing; or Folkestone via the Channel Tunnel, 35min crossing). From these ports there is a wide choice of routes using motorway or national roads into Germany.

Michelin offers motorists and motor-cyclists a free route planning service on the Internet, at www.ViaMichelin. com. For a proposed journey, you can determine possible stopovers between departure point and destination, and define your required route using various criteria (such as time, distance, use of motorways, road tolls etc). You are given information on mileage, journey time, hotels and restaurants along the way (selected from the *Michelin Guide Germany*), and map extracts that can be printed out.

Railway Station

G. Schneider/Press- und Informationsamt des Landes Berlin

Distances

- ◆ Cuxhaven to Berlin 404km/251mi.
- ◆ Rotterdam to Berlin via Hannover 698km/434mi.
- ◆ Hook of Holland to Munich via Bonn, Mainz, Stuttgart and Augsburg 845km/525mi.
- ◆ Zeebrugge to Munich via Karlsruhe, Stuttgart and Augsburg 853km/530mi.
- ◆ Calais to Cologne via Aachen 417km/259mi.

By Coach

Eurolines serves many cities in Germany from the UK. The coaches are all well-equipped for maximum comfort, with air conditioning, WC, TV/video, reclining seats etc. Journey times can be quite long (from London Victoria it takes around 18hr to Berlin, 19hr to Munich and 13hr to Cologne), but tickets are inexpensive, especially when booked in advance (a 30-day advance return to Berlin costs around €76). The **Eurolines Pass**, valid for 15, 30 or 60 days allows you to travel for a set price between a choice of 35 cities across Europe, with internal connections in Germany available between Frankfurt and Munich (low/high season prices for adults from €219/€287

for a 15-day pass to €390/€490 for a 60-day pass). A **Mini Pass** is also available for travel between London, Cologne and Paris (cost from €107). There are discounts for children, youths (under 26) and senior citizens. Children under 4 travel free. For information and reservations, call ☎ 08705 143219 in the UK, or visit the Eurolines Web site at www.eurolines. co.uk.

By Train and by Sea

The principal travel routes by rail and sea are from:
- ◆ London Victoria or Charing Cross Station, via Dover and Calais (sailing: 1hr 15min);
- ◆ London Liverpool Street Station, via Harwich and the Hook of Holland (sailing: 7-9hr) or Cuxhaven (on the mouth of the River Elbe, sailing: 19hr);
- ◆ London to Brussels via Folkestone and Calais (the Channel Tunnel), travel time to Brussels 2hr 20min;
- ◆ Hull to Rotterdam (sailing: 11hr).

⚅ *For details of rail tickets, see Getting Around – By Train opposite.*

GETTING AROUND

By Car

DRIVING REGULATIONS

Traffic in Germany drives on the right. Drivers in cities with trams should be especially careful before crossing tramlines. The maximum speed in built-up areas is 50kph/31mph. On the open road the maximum increases to 100kph/62mph. There is no official limit on motorways (Autobahnen), but drivers are recommended not to exceed 130kph/81mph. There is a compulsory speed limit of 80kph/50mph on roads and motorways for vehicles with trailers. In Germany careless or reckless driving is considered a serious offence and fines can be stiff. The maximum limit for alcohol in the blood is 0.5ml/g. German motorways (signposted 'A' for Autobahn) are toll-free and well equipped with service areas, usually open round the clock and providing:

petrol, spare parts and accessories, washrooms, toilets, public telephones, refreshments, accommodation and first-aid equipment.

City centres are often reserved for pedestrians. It is possible to park in one of the many covered car parks (Parkhaus).

Seatbelt usage is compulsory in the back as well as the front of the car. Children under age 12, or less than 1.5m/4ft 11in tall, are required by law to be fastened in a suitable child car seat; there are fines for non-compliance. It is a legal requirement to carry the regulation red emergency triangle, for warning other motorists of a breakdown or enforced roadside halt, and a first-aid box (including disposable gloves and rescue blanket). In Germany emergency services are always given priority and drivers should pull over to the side of the road.

EMERGENCY TELEPHONE NUMBERS:

Police: 110
Fire brigade: 112

BREAKDOWN SERVICE

For 24-hour service on motorways and main roads, call ☎ 01 80/2 22 22 22 (or ☎ 22 22 22 from mobile phones). Service is provided on main roads and motorways by the ADAC (www.adac.de), and by the Auto Club Europa in the eastern part of Germany (☎ 01 802/34 35 36). Roadside breakdown services can be called from one of the emergency phones – small arrows on the roadside posts indicate the direction of the nearest emergency phone. On-the-spot repairs are free, as only the cost of replacement parts or towing is charged. Motorists ringing this service should ask specifically for the "Straßenwachthilfe" (road patrol assistance). The Michelin Guide Deutschland lists the numbers to use to contact the ADAC service in all big towns.

Important Warning Signs:	
Anfang	beginning
Ausfahrt	exit
Baustelle	roadworks, building site
Einbahnstraße	one-way street
Einfahrt	entrance
Ende	end
Gefär	danger
LKW	HGV; truck
PKW	private car
Rechts einbiegen	turn right
Links einbiegen	turn left
Rollsplitt	gravel chippings
Stau	hold-up, traffic jam
Unfall	accident
Umleitung	diversion
Verengte Fahrbahn	road narrows
Vorfahrt	priority
Vorsicht	Look out!

PETROL

The following grades of petrol (gas) are available in Germany:

- *Super Plus Bleifrei*: Super unleaded (98 octane)
- *Normal Bleifrei*: Standard unleaded (95 octane)
- Diesel

Leaded petrol is no longer available. A lead substitute can be added to the fuel tank of those vehicles that require it; the additive can be purchased at petrol stations.

CAR HIRE

Cars may be hired only if the driver is over 23 and has held a driving licence for more than one year.

The major car hire firms have offices at airports and main stations and in large towns, but it is generally cheaper to arrange car hire before travelling to Germany. Some useful numbers include:

- **Avis**: ☎ 0 18 05 55 77 55, fax 0 18 05 21 77 11, www.avis.com
- **Europcar**: ☎ 0 18 05 80 00 00, fax 0 40 52 01 82 610, www.europcar.com
- **Hertz**: ☎ 0 18 05 33 35 35, fax 0 61 96 93 71 16, www.hertz.com
- **Sixt**: ☎ 0 18 05 25 25 25, www.e-sixt.com

By Train

TICKETS AND FARES

Deutsche Bahn (DB), Germany's leading transportation provider, is also the country's quickest and most reliable option. Most cities are served by DB's high-speed train, the InterCityExpress, or InterCity/EuroCity (IC/EC) services; regional centres are connected by a fleet of Regional Express trains.

Special offer tickets: **Euro Domino** – for 3-8 days' unlimited travel all over Germany (available for adults, youths and senior citizens); **Bahncards** – 25% or 50% discount for frequent travellers to Germany; **InterRail** – the classic

European rail pass for unlimited rail travel for 16 days (1 zone), 22 days (2 zones) or 1 month (global pass). Savertickets and discounted fares for groups and mini groups are also available.

Children under fourteen may travel free, if accompanied by their parents or grandparents. NightTrain and Motorail bookings are also available. For further information and reservations, apply to: Deutsche Bahn UK Booking Centre, ☎ 0870 243 5363 (🕓 *Mon-Fri 9am-5pm*), sales@bahn.co.uk, www.bahn.co.uk.

Information can also be obtained from Deutsche Bahn's website, www.bahn.de (for English text, select the "Int. Guests" option).

Rail Europe, 178 Piccadilly, London W1, ☎ 08705 848 848 (brochure hotline: ☎ 08708 30 60 30), www.raileurope.co.uk

DER Travel Service, 18 Conduit Street, London W1R 9TD, ☎ 020 7290 1111, fax 020 7629 7501, sales@dertravel.co.uk, www.dertravel.co.uk

By Bus

The bus can be invaluable travelling throughout Germany, especially in areas where there is no train service. Bus stations are generally found near railway stations. For prices and timetables, contact **Deutsche Touring GmbH**, Am Römerhof 17, 60486 Frankfurt am Main, ☎ 01805 7903 03 (€0.12/min), www.deutsche-touring.com.

By Air

There are numerous internal flights in Germany, most of them operated by **Lufthansa** (☎ 0180 5 83 84 26, www.lufthansa.com). Local airports are served by smaller airlines. **Deutsche BA** (☎ 0180 5 35 93 22, www.flydba.com), Lufthansa's main competitor and the German wing of British Airways, often has more competitive rates than the national carrier. Children up to age 11 enjoy 33% to 50% price savings.

WHERE TO STAY AND EAT

Where to Stay

Hotels are described in the **Address Books** within the *Discovering Germany* section. Room rates are indicated according to the following key:

⛁⛁⛁⛁	Over €100
⛁⛁⛁	€65 to €100
⛁⛁	€40 to €65
⛁	Less than €40

ADDRESSES IN THE GUIDE

We have selected accommodations for their value, location or character, trying to cater to all budgets. However, popular tourist regions, resorts and big cities are more expensive than others. Likewise, there is often a significant price difference between high and low season. During festivals and other cultural events last-minute accommodations are very hard to find. Tourist information offices offer lists of local lodging, including apartment accommodations, rural guesthouses and castle hotels and are able to reserve rooms on your behalf.
The **ADZ (Allgemeine Deutsche Zimmerreservierung)**, Corneliusstraße 34, D-60325 Frankfurt am Main. ☎ (069) 74 07 67, fax (069) 75 10 56, is a German room reservation service, able to reserve rooms in hotels, guesthouses and hostels throughout Germany. Reservations can be made up to 5 weeks in advance. A deposit may be required. English spoken.

BED AND BREAKFAST

The sign *Zimmer frei* outside private houses indicates that guestrooms are available. Final prices quoted usually include tax, service charges, breakfast etc.

CAMPING

With around 2 200 campsites, Germany has plenty of scope for camping. Most are closed between November and April, but 400 remain open all year. Allow around €2.50 to €5 to pitch a tent. More information is available from **Deutscher Camping-Club**, Mandlstraße 28, 80802 München, ☎ (089) 380 14 20, www.camping-club.de, or from **ADAC**, Am Westpark 8, D-81373 München, ☎ (089) 76 76 70, www.adac.de

YOUTH HOSTELS – JUGENDHERBERGEN (JH)

Germany has almost 600 youth hostels, many located in converted castles and manor houses. In fact, many of Germany's finest Rhine River castles have become popular hostelling destinations; book space at these popular sites up to six months in advance. With the exception of Bavaria, German hostels are not restricted only to the youth; many have private or family rooms and offer an affordable alternative for travelers of all ages.
The **Deutsches Jugendherbergswerk**, Hauptverband, Bismarckstraße 8, D-32756 Detmold, ☎ (052 31) 740 10, www.djh.de, offers a complete list of German youth hostels; it is possible to search for and book accommodations or to obtain a membership online.
A bed in a dormitory averages €15, including breakfast. Non-members are welcome to book lodging in German hostels, but should expect to pay slightly more.

APARTMENT LIVING

Renting a flat for a short period of time is common practice in Germany. Local tourist information offices normally have information on availability.

FARMS

This type of accommodation is particularly well developed in Bavaria and in the wine-growing regions. A guide to farms with accommodation, *Urlaub auf dem Bauernhof* (price €9.90), is edited by DLG-Verlag, Eschborner Landstrasse 122, 60489 Frankfurt, ☏ 069/24 788-451, www.dlg-verlag.de

CASTLE HOTELS

A list of hotels and restaurants in castles and other historic buildings is available from **European Castle Holidays GmbH**, Erika Köther Str. 56, D-67435 Königsbach, ☏ (06321) 96 84 87, www.european-castle.com or from **Gast Im Schloss**, Schillerstr. 17, 99423 Weimar, ☏ (0180) 589 17 91(0.12/min), www.gast-im-schloss.de

THE MICHELIN GUIDE DEUTSCHLAND

For a more exhaustive list of hotels and restaurants consult *The Michelin Guide Deutschland* which provides a whole host of details on Germany's hotels and restaurants.

Where to Eat

Restaurants are described in the **Address Books** within the *Discovering Germany* section. Meal prices are indicated according to the following key:

⊜⊜⊜⊜	Over €40
⊜⊜⊜	€25 to €40
⊜⊜	€14 to €25
⊜	Less than €14

GERMAN CUISINE

German food is more varied and balanced than is generally supposed. Breakfast **(Frühstück)** – and there is plenty of it – includes cold meats and cheese. Lunch **(Mittagessen)** usually begins with soup, followed by a fish or meat course with salad (lettuce, cucumber, shredded cabbage). **Imbisse**, small fast-food concerns,

Bremer Touristik-Zentrale

are found everywhere, in town or at the roadside. These offer traditional **Bratwurst** (grilled sausage), sometimes accompanied by a potato salad, and usually washed down with beer (often on draught, **Bier vom Fass**). In the afternoon, you can take a break in a coffee-house, which typically offers a large selection of cakes, such as **Schwarzwälder Kirschtorte** (Black Forest cherry cake) or **Käsekuchen** (cheesecake). They also serve the somewhat lighter fruit tarts and the famous **strudel**, a mixture of fruit wrapped in crisp pastry. The coffee served with these pastries is always accompanied by cream **(Kaffee-sahne)**. For the evening meal **(Abendessen)**, there will be a choice of cold meats **(Aufschnitt)** and cheeses served with a variety of breads.

Although each region has its own specialities, certain dishes are served all over the country: **Wiener Schnitzel** (veal cutlet fried in breadcrumbs), **Eisbein** (salted knuckle or shin of pork), **Sauerbraten** (beef in a brown

Ph. Gajic/MICHELIN

sauce) and **Gulasch** (either in the form of soup or as a stew).

Beer and Wine

Germans are justifiably proud of their national beverage, produced by nearly 1 200 breweries throughout the country. Brewing techniques respect a purity law *(Reinheitsgebot)* decreed in 1516, whereby nothing but barley, hops and plain water may be used in the fabrication of beer (with the addition, today, of yeast).

German vineyards cover 69 000ha/170 500 acres, extending from Lake Constance to the Siebengebirge, and from Trier to Würzburg. Growers produce a variety of wines from a wide range of grapes. Notable among the **white wines** – 80% of production – are the vigorous Rieslings of the Middle Rhine and of the Moselle, Saar and Ruwer rivers, aromatic and refreshing; the delicate wines of the Rheingau; full-bodied and elegant Nahe wines; the potent, dry wines of Franconia; and the varied wines of Baden and Württemberg. Among the **red wines**, choice examples come from Rheinhessen and Württemberg. The Palatinate and the Ahr are known for their well-balanced reds, especially the Spätburgunder. You can easily compare Germany's wines in bars, restaurants and **Weinstuben** (wine cellars or wine bars), sampling the various offerings by the glass *offene Weine).*

Regional specialities

Bavaria and Franconia
- **Leberknödel:** Dumplings of liver, bread and onion in a clear soup.
- **Leberkäs:** Minced beef and pork (no liver), cooked in the form of a loaf.
- **Knödel:** Dumplings of potato or soaked bread.
- **Schlachtschüssel:** Breast of pork, liver sausage and black pudding, served with cabbage and dumplings.
- **Rostbratwürste:** Small sausages grilled over beechwood charcoal.

Baden-Württemberg
- **Schneckensuppe:** Soup with snails.
- **Spätzle:** Egg-based handmade pasta in long strips.
- **Maultaschen:** Pasta stuffed with a mixture of veal and spinach.
- **Geschnetzeltes:** Thinly sliced veal in a cream sauce.

Rhineland-Palatinate
- **Sauerbraten:** Beef marinated in wine vinegar, served with potato dumplings.
- **Reibekuchen:** Small potato pancakes with apple or blueberry sauce.
- **Saumagen:** Stuffed pork belly with pickled cabbage.
- **Schweinepfeffer:** Highly seasoned pork ragout, thickened with blood.
- **Federweißer:** Partially fermented new wine accompanied by an onion tart.

Hessen and Westphalia
- **Sulperknochen:** Pork ears and tail served with cabbage and pease pudding.
- **Töttchen:** Ragout of brains and calf's head, cooked with herbs.
- **Pickert:** Sweet potato cakes with raisins.

Thuringia
- **Linsensuppe mit Thüringer Rotwurst:** Lentil soup with Thuringian sausages.

Saxony
- **Rinderzunge in Rosinen-Sauce:** Calf's tongue in a grape sauce.
- **Dresdener Stollen**: Dense butter cake with dried fruits.

Lower saxony and Schleswig-Holstein
- **Aalsuppe:** Sweet-and-sour eel soup with prunes, pears, vegetables and bacon.
- **Labskaus:** Favourite sailor's dish, beef, pork and salted herrings with potatoes and beetroot, served with gherkins and fried egg.
- **Buntes Huhn:** Salt beef on a bed of diced vegetables.

WHAT TO DO AND SEE

Outdoor Fun

PARKS

National Parks

Germany's 13 national parks will certainly appeal to travellers who prefer nature to culture. Further information is available from **Europarc Deutschland**, Friedrichstraße 60, D-10117 Berlin, ☎ (030) 28 87 88 20, fax (030) 288 78 82 16, www.europarc-deutschland.de

- ◆ **Bavaria:** Bavarian Forest (Bayerischer Wald), Berchtesgaden.
- ◆ **Schleswig-Holstein:** Schleswig-Holstein mudflats (Wattenmeer).
- ◆ **Lower Saxony:** Lower Saxon mudflats (Niedersächsisches Wattenmeer), Harz.
- ◆ **Hamburg:** Hamburg mudflats (Wattenmeer).
- ◆ **Saxony-Anhalt:** Hochharz.
- ◆ **Mecklenburg-West Pomerania:** Jasmund, Müritz, Vorpommersche Boddenlandschaft.
- ◆ **Saxony:** Swiss Saxony (Sächsische Schweiz).
- ◆ **Brandenburg:** Lower Oder valley (Unteres Odertal).
- ◆ **Thuringia:** Hainich.

Theme Parks

The list on page 33 includes some of the best known and most popular of Germany's amusement parks.

SPORTS

For nature lovers and outdoor sports fans alike, Germany's varied landscapes provide an ideal setting for all sorts of activities. Some very useful information in this respect can be found at www.germany-tourism.de (under Travel Tips, Outdoor Vacation).

Hunting

For information on hunting in Germany, contact **Jagdschutz-Verband**, Johannes-Henry-Straße 26, 53113 Bonn, ☎ (02 28) 94 90 620, www.jagd-online.de

Cycling

Cycling can be a very practical, economic and pleasant way to explore some of the regions of Germany. Information is available from the **Bund Deutscher Radfahrer e.V.**, Otto-Fleck-Schneise 4, 60582 Frankfurt am Main, ☎ (069) 967 80 00, www.bdr-online.org. The German National Tourist Office also publishes a brochure containing 30 tourist routes for cyclists.

Horseriding

Lists of equestrian centres can be obtained from regional tourist offices. You can also contact the **Deutsche Reiterliche Vereinigung**, Freiherr von Langen-Straße 13, 48231 Warendorf, ☎ (02581) 636 20, www.pferd-aktuell.de

Golf

There is no shortage of golf courses in Germany. For information, contact the **Deutscher Golf Verband e.V.**, Viktoriastraße 16, 65189 Wiesbaden, ☎ (0611) 99 02 00, www.golf.de. Prices are from €25 to €50 for a one-day pass during the week, and from €30 to €70 on Saturdays and Sundays.

Fishing

Information from the **Verband Deutscher Sportfischer e.V.**, Siemensstraße 11-13, 63071 Offenbach, ☎ (069) 85 50 06, www.vdsf.de

Walking

The Federation of German Mountain and Walking Clubs can provide details on hikes organised by regional associations and also publishes guides and maps. Contact details: **Verband Deutscher Gebirgs- und Wandervereine e.V.**, Wilhelmshöher Allee 157-159, D-34121 Kassel, ☎ (0561) 93 87 30, www.wanderverband.de. **The German Alpine club (Deutsche Alpenv-**

Park/Place	☎/Web site	Nearest motorway exit (number)
Bavaria-Filmstadt/Geiselgasteig (Bayern)	(089) 64 99 20 00 www.bavaria-filmtour.de	A 99: Oberhaching (4)
Churpfalzpark Loifling/ Cham (Bayern)	(099 71) 303 40 www.churpfalzpark.de	A 3: Straubing (106)
Erlebnispark Schloß Thurn/ Heroldsbach (Bayern)	(091 90) 92 98 98 www.schloss-thurn.de	A 73: Baiersdorf Nord (10)
Erlebnispark Tripsdrill/ Cleebronn-Tripsdrill (Baden-Württemberg)	(071 35) 99 99 www.tripsdrill.de	A 81: Mundesheim (13)
Erlebnispark Ziegenhagen/ Witzenhausen (Hessen)	(055 45) 246 www.erlebnispark-ziegenhagen.de	A 75: Hann.-Münden (75)
Europa-Park/Rust (Baden-Württemberg)	(01805) 77 66 88 www.europapark.de	A 5: Ettenheim (57
Fränkisches Wunderland/ Plech (Bayern)	(092 44) 98 90 www.wunderland.de	A 9: Plech (46)
Freizeit-Land/Geiselwind (Bayern)	(095 56) 92 11 92 www.freizeit-land.de	A 3: Geiselwind (76)
Filmpark Babelsberg/Potsdam (Brandenburg)	(0331) 721 27 50 www.filmpark.de	A 115: Potsdam-Babelsberg (5)
Fort Fun Abenteuerland/ Bestwig-Wasserfall (Nordrhein- Westfalen)	(029 05) 811 23 www.fortfun.de	A 46: Bestwig (71)
Hansa-Park/Sierksdorf (Schleswig-Holstein)	(045 63) 47 40 www.hansapark.de	A 1: Eutin (15)
Heide-Park/Soltau (Niedersachsen)	(01805) 91 91 01 www.heidepark.de	A 7: Soltau-Ost (44)
Holiday Park/Haßloch (Rheinland-Pfalz)	(018 05) 00 32 46 www.holidaypark.de	A 65: Neustadt-Süd (13)
Phantasialand/Brühl (Nordrhein-Westfalen)	(022 32) 362 05 www.phantasialand.de	A 553: Brühl-Süd (2)
Potts Park/Minden-Dützen (Nordrhein-Westfalen)	(0571) 510 88 www.pottspark-minden.de	A 2: Porta Westfalica (33)
Ravensburger Spieleland/ Weitnau (Bayern)	(075 42) 40 00 www.spieleland.com	A 96: Wangen-West (5)
Safari- und Hollywood-Park/Schloß Holte-Stukenbrock (Nordrhein- Westfalen)	(052 07) 95 24 25 www.safaripark.de	A 2, then A 33: Stukenbrock-Senne (23)
Legoland (Günzburg)	(082 21) 70 07 00 www.legoland.de	A 7, then A 8: exit Günzburg
Serengeti-Safaripark/ Hodenhagen (Niedersachsen)	(051 64) 979 90 www.serengeti-park.com	A 7: Westenholz (7)
Taunus-Wunderland/ Schlangenbad (Hessen)	(061 24) 40 81 www.taunuswunderland.de	A 66: Wiesbaden-Frauenstein (2)
Vogelpark Walsrode/ Walsrode (Niedersachsen)	(051 61) 60 440 www.vogelpark-walsrode.de	A 27: Walsrode-Süd (28)
Warner Bros. Movie World/Bottrop-Kirchhellen (Nordrhein- Westfalen)	(020 45) 89 90 www.movieworld.de	A 31: Kirchhellen-Feldhausen (40)

erein, DAV), Von-Kahr-Straße 2-4, 80997 München, ☎ (089) 14 00 30, fax (089) 1 40 03 23, www.alpenv-erein.de, gives useful information on routes and accommodation in the mountains. Their Alpine information centre (Alpine Auskunft), at the same address, can be contacted ☎ (089) 29 49 40, Mon-Fri 8am to noon, Mon-Wed 1pm to 4pm and Thurs 1pm to 6pm for details on mountain refuge opening times, weather reports, guides and maps. For the Alpine weather forecast, call ☎ 0 9001 29 50 70.

Canoeing and Kayaking

Those interested in canoeing and kayaking or rafting can contact the **Deutscher Kanu-Verband e.V.**, Ber-taallee 8, 47055 Duisburg, ☎ (0203) 99 75 90, www.kanu.de.

Winter Sports

Although the Alps and the Black Forest remain the most popular skiing areas in Germany, there are a large number of upland sites where, depending on the snow cover, skiing is possible. These include the Harz mountains, the Thuringian Forest, and the Eifel, Sauerland and Swabian Alp (Schwäbische Alb) ranges.

Sailing

Sailing is a widely practised sport in Germany; over 180 sailing schools are scattered along the shores of the North Sea, Baltic Sea and many inland lakes. Information can be obtained from the **Verband Deutscher**

Sailing on the Aussenalster, Hamburg

Hamburg Tourismus GmbH

Sportbootschulen, Varlar 86, 48720 Rosendahl, ☎ (06322) 95 62 80, www.sportbootschulen.de or from the German Sailing Federation, the **Deutscher Seglerverband**, Gründgens-straße 18, 22309 Hamburg. ☎ (40) 632 00 90. www.dsv.org.

Spas

Since Roman times spa treatments have been considered by Germans an important component of a healthy lifestyle. And the frantic pace of modern life is driving an increasing number of visitors to follow suit at one of Germany's spa resorts. Not only are **spas** used for the treatment or prevention of certain illnesses, they are also an ideal place to recharge your batteries.

Spas have access to mineral water with medicinal properties – a declared public utility – and they also have health services and proper facilities for applying the necessary treatments. They are usually found in beautiful natural settings and are an interesting alternative for those wishing to have a quiet holiday, enjoy nature and get back into shape.

Information on all of the country's spa resorts can be found on on www.deutscher-heilbaederverband.de or www.baederkalender.de.

Activities for Children

In this guide, sights of particular interest to children are indicated with a KIDS symbol. Some attractions may offer discount fees for children.

Calendar of Events

Listed below are the main events and festivals which take place in Germany. More details can be obtained from tourist information centres.

See also under 'Festivals' in certain blocks in the Address Book section.

1 JANUARY

New Year's Day International Ski Jump, part of the Four Jump Tournament — **Garmisch-Partenkirchen**

SUNDAY BEFORE SHROVE TUESDAY

"München narrisch" Carnival — **Munich**

SHROVE MONDAY

Rosenmontagszug: procession and street carnival — **Cologne, Düsseldorf, Mainz**

SHROVE MONDAY AND TUESDAY

Narrensprung Carnival: elaborate traditional costumes and expressive wooden masks; Dance of the Fools — **Rottweil**

MAUNDY THURSDAY TO EASTER MONDAY

Traditional Sorbian Easter Egg Market — **Bautzen**

EASTER

Sorbian Easter Egg market — **Oberlausitz**

30 APRIL/1 MAY

Walpurgisnacht: Witches' Sabbath Festival — **Various towns in the Harz region**
Marburg townspeople and students sing in the month of May — **Marburg**

END OF APRIL TO END OF MAY

International May Festival: theatre, music — **Wiesbaden**

MID-MAY TO MID-SEPTEMBER EVERY SUNDAY AT NOON

Rattenfängerspiel: pageant retracing the legend of the Pied Piper — **Hameln**

FRIDAY AFTER ASCENSION

Blutritt: mounted cavalcade in honour of the Holy Blood — **Weingarten**

EARLY MAY TO EARLY JUNE

Classical Music Festival — **Schwetzingen**

SECOND HALF OF MAY

International horse racing at Iffezheim — **Baden**-Baden

WHITSUN

Kuchen und Brunnenfest: dance of the salt-workers in traditional 16C costume — **Schwäbisch Hall**
Meistertrunk: performance of the legend of the "Long Drink" and re-enactment of the Thirty Years War by locals in period costume — **Rothenburg ob der Tauber**

WHIT MONDAY

Pfingstritt: mounted cavalcade — **Kötzting**

WHIT TUESDAY

Historische Geißbockversteigerung: auctioning of a goat (period costumes; folk dancing; local fair) — **Deidesheim**

CORPUS CHRISTI

Solemn procession through the decorated town — **Munich**
Mühlheimer Gottestracht: procession of boats along the Rhine — **Cologne**
Procession through flower-decked street — **Hüfingen**

LAST SATURDAY OF MAY

Wildpferdefang: capture and auction of young stallions — **Merfelder Bruch**

14 DAYS AFTER WHITSUN, FROM FRIDAY TO MONDAY

Salatkirmes: Salad Fair commemorating the introduction of the potato to the Hessen region; traditional local costumes — **Schwalmstadt**

1ST WEEKEND IN JUNE AND SEPTEMBER, 2ND WEEKEND IN JULY

Castle illuminations (firework displays) — **Heidelberg**

JUNE-AUGUST

Summer Music Festival: concerts of classical music in the Cistercian abbey — **Chorin**
Festival of Drama and Opera in the abbey ruins; theatre, opera — **Bad Hersfeld**

JUNE TO SEPTEMBER (EVERY 5 YEARS, NEXT: 2007)

Documenta: world's largest international exhibition of contemporary art — **Kassel**

LAST WEEK OF JUNE

Kiel Week: international sailing regatta; local festival — **Kiel**

LAST WEEKEND OF JUNE

Bergparade in historical costumes — **Freiberg**

FOUR SUNDAYS FROM END OF JUNE TO MID-JULY (EVERY 4 YEARS, NEXT: 2009)

Fürstenhochzeit (Landshut Royal Marriage): historical pageant in period costume — **Landshut**

DURING SUMMER MONTHS

Mecklenburg-Vorpommern Summer Music Festival, held in historic houses, castles and churches — **Various places in Mecklenburg-Vorpommern**

JULY TO AUGUST

Schleswig-Holstein Music Festival — **Various places in Schleswig-Holstein**

1ST WEEKEND IN JULY

Spreewald Festival: Sorbian folklore and traditions — **Lübbenau**

EARLY JULY

Archers' Festival: procession of archers — **Hannover**

MID-JULY (EVERY 4 YEARS, NEXT: 2008)

Fischerstechen (Fishermen's Festival) — **Ulm**

3RD WEEKEND IN JULY (SATURDAY, SUNDAY, MONDAY)

Kinderzeche: commemorating the saving of the town by a deputation of children (historical costumes) — **Dinkelsbühl**

PENULTIMATE MONDAY IN JULY

Schwörmontag: river procession on the Danube — **Ulm**

3RD SUNDAY AND MONDAY IN JULY

Tänzelfest: historical procession by schoolchildren — **Kaufbeuren**

Tourist-Information Rottweil

The Dance of the Fools, Rottweil

LAST SATURDAY IN JULY AND 1ST SUNDAY IN AUGUST

Summer music festival — **Hitzacker**

END OF JULY TO END OF AUGUST

Bayreuther Festspiele: Wagner Opera Festival — **Bayreuth**

JULY-AUGUST

Festival on the cathedral steps — **Erfurt**
Der Rhein in Flammen (The Rhine Ablaze): illumination of the river valley from Braubach to Koblenz — **Koblenz-Oberwesel, St Goar**

2ND SATURDAY IN AUGUST

Seenachtsfest: evening lakeside festival — **Constance**

2ND WEEK IN AUGUST

Der Drachenstich (Death of the Dragon): pageant of the legend of St George, in period costumes — **Furth im Wald**

SATURDAY AFTER 24 AUGUST

Schäferlauf: shepherds' race (barefoot over a field of stubble) — **Markgröningen**

LAST WEEK IN AUGUST

International horse racing at Iffezheim — **Baden-Baden**

SEPTEMBER

Festival with firework display — **Rothenburg ob der Tauber**

END OF SEPTEMBER TO BEGINNING OF OCTOBER

Cannstatter Volksfest: popular local fair — **Bad Cannstatt**

Oktoberfest

THE TWO WEEKS LEADING UP TO THE FIRST SUNDAY IN OCTOBER

Oktoberfest: Beer Festival. The largest popular festival in the world attracts nearly 6 million people to the Bavarian capital every year. — **Munich**

1ST AND 2ND WEEKEND IN OCTOBER

Weinlesefest: Wine Fair and election of the Queen of Wine — **Neustadt an der Weinstraße**

LAST 10 DAYS IN OCTOBER

Bremer Freimarkt: largest popular fair in northern Germany — **Bremen**

SUNDAY BEFORE 6 NOVEMBER

Leonhardifahrt: similar celebration to that at Bad Tölz (⚭ *below*) — **Benediktbeuern**

6 NOVEMBER (ST LEONARD)

Leonhardifahrt: prior to a Mass in honour of St Leonard, gaily decorated horse-drawn carts process through town to the church — **Bad Tölz**

ADVENT

Christkindlesmarkt: Christmas market (Christmas tree decorations and gifts); seasonal performances by children — **Nuremberg**

24 DECEMBER AND NEW YEAR'S EVE

Weihnachtsschießen und Neujahrss-
chießen: Christmas and New Year
shooting matches — **Berchtesgaden**

Sightseeing

The *Discovering Germany* section gives
the opening times and admission
charges for monuments, museums,
churches etc. On account of the ever-
increasing cost of living and frequent
variations in the opening times of these
monuments, this information should
only be used as a rough guide. It is
intended for tourists who are travelling
on their own and are not entitled to
any reduction. With prior agreement,
groups can obtain special conditions
as regards both times and charges.
Enquire at the ticket office before
purchasing your tickets; age-related
reductions, in particular, are available.
It is always a good idea to make
enquiries by phone before setting
off since certain monuments may be
temporarily closed for restoration.
Visiting conditions for churches are
only specified if the interior is of particular interest, if there are set opening
times or if there is an admission
charge. Churches can generally not
be visited during services. If a church
is open only during services, visitors
should behave with all due respect.

MUSEUMS

Museums are usually closed on
Mondays. Art museums often have a
late-night opening one evening per
week. But remember, ticket offices
close between 30min to 1hr before
closing time.

Discounts

For budget accommodation, refer
directly to the Address Book for each
town; these list addresses divided
into four price categories, including
a budget category (⊖, rooms for less
than €40).

By Train

👃 See *Getting Around* for information
on reductions offered by Deutsche
Bahn.

By Air

Often purchasing a ticket in advance
will give you a cheaper fare. Several
airlines, including Lufthansa, operate
Frequent Flyer programmes that
entitle passengers to free tickets
once they have accumulated a certain
number of air miles. Lufthansa's website lists special offers and discounts
are given for online bookings. For flying between European cities, easyJet
and Ryanair offer very low fares.

DISCOUNTS FOR YOUNG
PEOPLE UNDER THE AGE OF 26

By Air

Many airlines give discounts for
children and adults under 26. Children
under the age of 2 usually travel free.

By Train

See the Getting around – By train
section above.

Books

HISTORY AND BIOGRAPHY

- **A Concise History of Germany**
  – Mary Fulbrook (Cambridge Uni-
  versity Press)
- **A History of Germany 1815-1985**
  – W Carr (Edward Arnold)
- **Hitler, A Study in Tyranny** – A Bul-
  lock (Perennial)
- **The Last Days of Hitler** – HR Trevor-
  Roper (Macmillan)

THE ARTS

- **Bauhaus** – F Whitford (Thames &
  Hudson)
- **Early Medieval Art: Carolingian,
  Ottonian, Romanesque** – J Beck-
  with (Thames & Hudson)
- **The Expressionists** – WD Dube
  (Thames & Hudson)
- **The Weimar Years:** *A Culture Cut
  Short* – J Willett (Abbeville Press)

LITERATURE

- **The Lost Honour of Katharina Blum** – Heinrich Böll
- **The Caucasian Chalk Circle; Threepenny Novel; Mother Courage** – Bertolt Brecht
- **The Riddle of the Sands** – Erskine Childers
- **The Tin Drum; The Flounder; From the Diary of a Snail;** *Mein Jahrhundert* – Günter Grass
- **The Glass Bead Game; Narcissus and Goldmund; Steppenwolf** – Hermann Hesse
- **Die Architekten** – Stefan Heym
- **Tales of Hoffmann** – Ernst Theodor Amadeus Hoffmann
- **Buddenbrooks; The Magic Mountain** – Thomas Mann
- **The Adventures of Baron Münchhausen** – Rudolph Erich Raspe
- **All Quiet on the Western Front** – Erich Maria Remarque
- **Kindheitsmuster** – Christa Wolf
- **Goethe the Poet and the Age: Revolution and Renunciation (1790-1803)** – Nicholas Boyle

TRAVEL AND MODERN GERMAN SOCIETY

- **A Time of Gifts** – P Leigh Fermor (Penguin)
- **A Traveller's Wine Guide to Germany** – K Brady Stewart et al (Interlink Publishing Group)
- **A Tramp Abroad** – M Twain
- **Deutschland: A Winter's Tale** – H Heine
- **Germany and the Germans** – J Ardagh (Penguin)
- **Goodbye to Berlin** – C Isherwood (Hunter Publishing)
- **The Simon & Schuster Guide to the Wines of Germany** – I Jamieson (Simon & Schuster)
- **The Germans** – GA Craig (Plume Books)
- **The Origins of Modern Germany** – G Barraclough (WW Norton & Company)
- **Vanishing Borders** – M Farr (Penguin)

BASIC INFORMATION

Business Hours

BANKS

Banks are closed on Saturdays and Sundays. They are open during the week from 9am to 12pm and from 1pm to 3.30pm (sometimes to 6pm). Bureaux de change *(Wechselstuben)* are usually open longer.

SHOPPING

On the whole, shops open between 9am and 10am, and close between 6.30pm and 8pm. On Saturdays they close at 4pm (except for grocer's, butcher's and baker's shops, which close between 1pm and 2pm). Some bakeries open on Sunday mornings.

Electricity

Voltage is 220 V and appliances use two-pin plugs.

Public Holidays

1 Jan, **6 Jan** (in Baden-Württemberg, Bayern and Sachsen-Anhalt only), **Good Fri**, **Easter Day**, **Easter Mon**, **1 May**, **Ascension**, **Whit Sun** and **Mon**, **Corpus Christi** (in Baden-Württemberg, Bayern, Hessen, Nordrhein-Westfalen, Rheinland-Pfalz, Saarland, Sachsen, Thüringen and those communities with a predominantly Roman Catholic population only), **15 Aug** (in Roman Catholic communities in Saarland and Bayern only), **3 Oct** (Day of German Unity), **31 Oct** (Reformation

Day, celebrated in the new Federal States, i.e. Brandenburg, Mecklenburg-Vorpommern, Sachsen, Sachsen-Anhalt and Thüringen only), **1 Nov** (in Baden-Württemberg, Bayern, Nordrhein-Westfalen, Rheinland-Pflaz and Saarland only), **Buß- und Bettag** (Day of Repentance and Prayer, usually third Wed in Nov, observed in Sachsen only), **24** (afternoon), **25**, **26** and **31** (afternoon) **Dec**.

Mail

Yellow is the trademark colour of the post office in Germany. Most post offices are open Mondays to Fridays from 8am to 6pm and on Saturdays from 8am to 12pm. Some of them, particularly at stations and airports in the big cities, are open longer. They are generally indicated in the Address Book sections in this guide. Domestic postal rates apply to all of the countries in the European Union as well as to Turkey and Switzerland.

Money

The euro has been the unit of currency in Germany since the beginning of 2002. Citizens of countries that are not part of the euro zone can change currency at airports and banks, as well as in some stations and hotels.

CREDIT CARDS

Traveller's cheques and the main international credit cards (especially Visa and Eurocard-Mastercard) are accepted in most shops, hotels and restaurants. You can also use these cards to withdraw money at cash dispensers.

In the event of loss or theft of your card, call the following numbers immediately: **Visa** ☎ (0800) 81 49 100, **Eurocard-Mastercard** ☎ (069) 79 33 19 10, **American Express** ☎ (069) 97 97 10 00

Newspapers

Regional daily newspapers are widely read in Germany. The conservative *Frankfurter Allgemeine* and Munich's liberal *Süddeutsche Zeitung* have a broad readership throughout Germany. Berlin's most popular daily paper is the *Tagesspiegel*, but the *Berliner Zeitung* and the *Tageszeitung* are also popular with readers in the capital. Among the national newspapers, the sensation-seeking daily *Bild* has a print run of over 5 million copies. *Die Welt* offers better quality news, *Focus* and *Der Spiegel* are excellent weeklies, and *Stern* and *Bunte* belong more to the tabloid category.

The main foreign newspapers are, of course, available at airports, stations and the larger newspaper kiosks.

Telephone

The international dialling code for Germany is **49**, so from the UK, for example, you would dial 00 49 + local dialling code **omitting** the initial 0 + subscriber's number.

International dialling codes from Germany:
- ☎ 00 44 for the UK
- ☎ 00 353 for Ireland
- ☎ 00 1 for the USA and Canada
- ☎ 00 61 for Australia
- ☎ 00 27 for South Africa.

National directory enquiries
☎ 11 833

International directory enquiries
☎ 11 834

Public telephones: phonecards *(Telefonkarten)* for the increasingly card-operated public telephones can be bought at post offices and newspaper kiosks. Some phones also take bank cards.

☺ Note that phone calls from hotel rooms are generally expensive.

Mobile phones with a Europe or World package are very handy for making calls within the country (the GSM 900 and GSM 1800 networks ensure global roaming). Please note that it is illegal to use your phone while driving.

Tipping

A service charge of 15% is already included in the bill at German restaurants and cafes, so no additional tip is required. However, it is common to round your bill up to the nearest €. If the service has been especially good, an additional 5% tip may be given, 10% if the service was exceptional. Don't leave the tip on the table; pay the waiter in person. Taxi drivers typically receive a 5% tip. Porters and others assisting with your luggage expect €1 per bag.

Emergencies

✚ **Medical emergencies/First aid**
☏ 112

✚ **Traffic accidents** ☏ 110

Emergency telephones are available along the hard shoulder on motorways. There are also alarm buttons on S-Bahn and U-Bahn platforms.

Time

In winter, standard time is Greenwich Mean Time + 1 hour. In summer the clocks go forward an hour to give Summer Time (GMT + 2 hours) from the last weekend in March to the last weekend in October.

Television

Germany has two national state television channels, **ARD** and **ZDF**. There are also regional channels such as Cologne's Westdeutscher Rundfunk (WDR) and Munich's Bayrischer Rundfunk (BR), and the Franco-German cultural television channel **Arte**. Numerous private channels have schedules that include soap operas, sitcoms and game shows. Although most of them target the general public (RTL 2, PRO 7, SAT 1 etc), there are some theme channels, such as the music channel VIVA – the German equivalent of MTV – and the sports channel DSF.

The Chiemsee

INTRODUCTION TO GERMANY

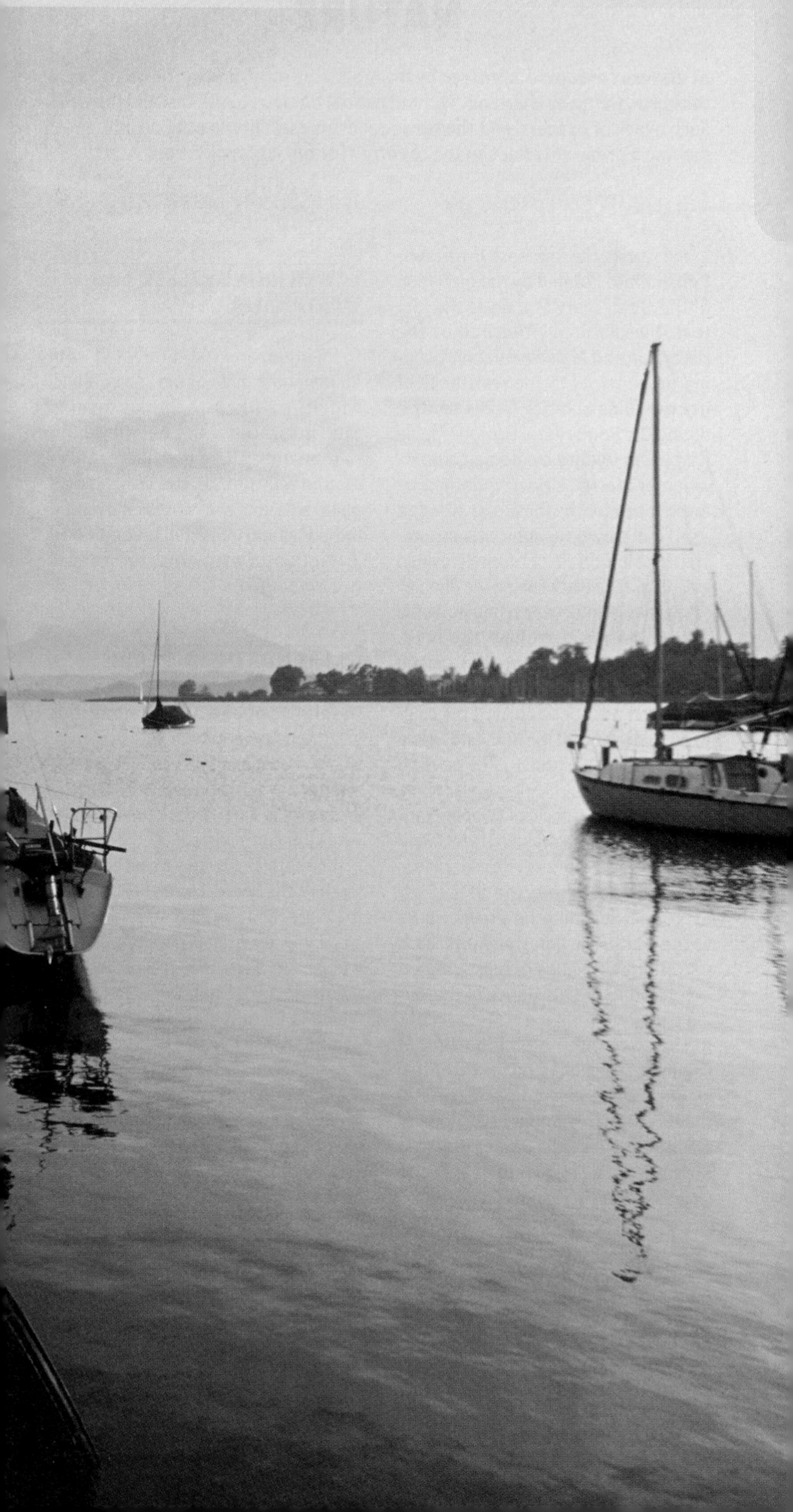

NATURE

At the heart of Europe, bordered by the Alps to the south and by the Baltic Sea to the north, Germany is virtually without natural frontiers to the east and the west. Such a lack of barriers, and the subsequent accessibility to outside influences has had a profound effect on the country's history and civilisation.

Germany's Geology

In the **north**, the immense **Germano-Polish Plain**, formed by the glaciation of the Quaternary Era, owes the fact that it was scarcely touched by the Hercynian and Alpine mountain-building movements to the resistance of its crystalline bedrock. In the **centre**, during the Primary Era, the formidable Hercynian folding created a complex of minor massifs – now smoothed by erosion and for the most part wooded – separated by geographic depressions. The most important of these Hercynian massifs are the Black Forest, the Rhenish schist massif, and – encircling Bohemia – the Böhmerwald, the Bavarian Forest, the Erzgebirge (Ore Mountains) and the Sudeten Mountains. On the edges of this Hercynian zone accumulated the coal-bearing deposits of the Ruhr and Silesia which led to the industrial expansion of the 19C.

The sedimentary basin of Swabia-Franconia, its vast area drained by the Main and the Neckar, offers a less dramatic landscape; abutting the Black Forest to the west and the Swabian Jura to the south, the limestone plateau is patterned with lines of hills sculpted according to the resistance of the varied strata.

In the **south**, the Alpine portion of Germany is delimited by the **Pre-Alps**, where the debris torn up and crushed during the final exertions of Quaternary glaciation formed the Bavarian plateau – a huge area stretching in a gentle slope as far as the Danube.

Northern Germany

LOWER RHINE VALLEY AND WESTPHALIA

Lush, green and flat, protected from flooding, the plain of the Lower Rhine, with its cosy houses, brings to mind the landscape of the neighbouring Netherlands. There is similar scenery around Münster, on the Westphalian plain, where the farmlands patterned by hedges and trees offer the additional attraction of many moated castles (Wasserburgen).

GREAT NORTHERN PLAIN

Despite its apparent monotony, this enormous area (which extends eastwards into Poland but is confined, so far as Germany is concerned, between the Ems and the Oder) does offer a certain variety of landscapes.

In the south, below the Weser and Harz foothills, the Börde country lies between the Weser and the Elbe – a region covered by an alluvial topsoil whose fertility is legendary. Farms and market gardens flourish in this densely populated zone, which is favoured also with mineral deposits rich in iron and potassium. Farther north, on either side of the Elbe, is the Geest – a region of glacial deposits (sand, gravel, clay) with little to recommend it geographically, since it was covered by the Scandinavian glaciers right up to Paleolithic times. This has resulted in poor drainage and soils that are too sandy; between Berlin and the Baltic, the Mecklenburg plateau is scattered with shallow lakes interspersed with morainic deposits that bear witness to the prolonged glacial presence. The Spree and the Havel, meandering through the flatlands, supply the lakeland regions

The red-sandstone cliffs of the island of Helgoland

of the Spreewald and Potsdam. West of the Lower Weser, and in the Worpswede neighbourhood north of Bremen, peat bogs (Moore) alternate with very wet pastureland. Most of the peat moors are now under cultivation, after drainage using Dutch methods. The nature reserve south of Lüneburg, however, has preserved for all time a typical stretch of the original moorland.

THE BALTIC COAST

The German section of the Baltic Coast, which stretches from Flensburg all the way to the Stettin Haff, is a murrain landscape, which, in addition to very flat parts also has a few elevations that rise above the 100m/320ft mark. Because of the relatively limited tidal differences of the on average 55m/180ft deep Baltic Sea, the coastline has only been subject to little change. That's why numerous cities with long traditions have evolved here. Between the bays of Lübeck and Kiel lies the Holsteinische Schweiz (Holstein Switzerland), the hilly and lake-dotted remainders of a ground and end moraine from the Ice Age. The arms of the sea, which are the fjords and bays left over from the glaciers of the

last Ice Age, cut deep into the land and form excellent natural harbours. Their banks are lined with beaches, forests and little fishing villages. Further to the east, the Baltic Coast is marked by shallow, water-filled inlets from the post-Ice Age period. Four islands lie offshore, the largest is the water-washed Rügen.

NORTH SEA COAST

Because of the winds and waves, the North Sea Coast between the Netherlands and Denmark is constantly undergoing change. The tides (every 12hr 25min 53s) raise and lower the water level by 2m/6.4ft to 3m/9.6ft. Several island groups lie out off shore in the «Watt», a 5x30km/3x18mi strip of land that is washed by the sea when the tide is in, but is above sea level at ebb times. The Watt ecosystem is home to nearly 2 000 species, from sea lions to almost invisible creatures 1/10 of a millimetre in size. A strip of marshland created over centuries lies along the coast. Once upon a time, the tides used to bring in animal and plant particles together with fine sand, which formed a fertile base for agriculture in the marshlands. Behind this is the less fertile, hilly "Geest". Broad

Lindau in Bavaria

moors have formed in the depressions, some of which have been turned over to farming. Germany's two largest seaports, Hamburg and Bremen, lie at the inner ends of the funnel-shaped Elbe and Weser estuaries.

Central Germany

THE RHENISH SCHIST MASSIF

This ancient geological mass, cut through by the Rhine – the only real channel of communication between the north and south of the country – the Lahn and the Moselle, comprises among others the highlands known as the Eifel, the Westerwald, the Taunus and the Hunsrück. They share the same inhospitable climate and the same evidence of volcanic activity as the crater lakes, known as the Maare, of the Eifel plateau. The Eifel will be familiar to motoring enthusiasts as the home of the Nürburgring Grand Prix race circuit. The Upper Sauerland, a thickly wooded, mountainous region (alt 841m/2 760ft), with its many dams, acts as a water reserve for the Ruhr industrial area.

MOUNTAINS OF UPPER HESSEN AND THE WESER

Between the Rhenish schist massif and the forest of Thuringia (Thüringer Wald)

lies a confused amalgam of heights, some of them volcanic (Vogelsberg, Rhön), and depressions which have been used as a highway, linking north and south, by German invaders throughout the ages.

Between Westphalia and the north, the Weser Mountains – extended westwards by the Teutoburger Wald – form a barrier that is breached at the Porta Westfalica, near Minden. Farther to the east, the Erzgebirge (Ore Mountains) form a natural frontier with the Czech Republic.

HARZ MOUNTAINS

This relatively high range (alt 1 142m/ 3 747ft at the Brocken) has a typical mountain climate, characterised by heavy snowfalls in winter.

Southern Germany

PLAIN OF THE UPPER RHINE

Between Basle and the Bingen Gap, a soil of exceptionally fertile loess, accompanied by a climate which combines light rainfall, an early spring and a very hot summer, has produced a rich agricultural yield (hops, corn and tobacco) and a terrain highly suitable for the cultivation of vines. The whole of this low-lying, productive tract has become a crossroads for the rest of Europe, which is why certain towns – Frankfurt, for instance – have profited internationally from their development.

BLACK FOREST

This crystalline massif (alt 1 493m/4 899ft at the Feldberg), which overlooks the Rhine Gap, is relatively well populated. The region's healthy climate and many thermal springs, with their attendant, highly reputed spa resorts, draw large numbers of tourists here every year.

SWABIAN-FRANCONIAN BASIN

Franconia, formed by vast, gently undulating plateaux, is bordered to the south-east by the small limestone massif of the Franconian Jura which produces Germany's building stone, and to the north and north-east by the wooded crystalline ranges flanking Bohemia and Thuringia. Swabia, once ruled by the kings of Württemberg, offers a variety of landscapes – barred to the south by the blue line of the Swabian Jura, which rises to 874m/2 867ft. Small valleys, enlivened by orchards and vineyards, alternate here with the gentle slopes of wooded hillsides.

THE ALPS AND THE BAVARIAN PLATEAU

The Bavarian Alps and the Alps of Allgäu offer contrasts between the sombre green of their forests and the shades of grey colouring their rocks and escarpments, an impressive sight when seen against the backdrop of a blue sky. The Zugspitze, the highest point in Germany, reaches an altitude of 2 962m/9 720ft. Torrents such as Isar, Lech, Iller and Inn, have over time carved out corridors with broad, flat floors suitable for the cultivation of the land and the development of towns (Ulm, Augsburg and Munich).

HISTORY

Long divided into a number of autonomous states, Germany was slow to achieve unity. This nation of great diversity, which was for a long time marked by feudalism and whose regions still hold considerable powers, is today one of the main spearheads of European unity.

Time Line

GERMANS AND ROMANS

The earliest evidence of human life on German territory today is the lower jaw bone dating back over 500 000 years of the so-called Homo heidelbergensis, which was discovered near Heidelberg in 1907. The Middle Palaeolithic Age (200 000-40 000 BC) is considered the age of the Neanderthal Man (🕯 see *DÜSSELDORF: Excursions).* The first "modern people", the Homo sapiens, who lived from fishing, hunting and gathering, lived during the Late Palaeolithic, an epoch of the Stone Age within the last Ice Age. During the Neolithic Era, people began to settle in village-like communities, where they lived for a while, grew plants and began raising animals.

The last prehistoric period, the Iron Age, began around 1000 BC, following the Bronze Age, thus named because that material was widely used to make implements, weapons and jewellery. The Iron Age is divided up into the La Tène Culture and the Hallstatt Culture. Economic and political power started becoming more concentrated, evidence from graves suggests a stratified social system.

In the first millennium before Christ, Germanic tribes began resettling towards Central Europe. The occurrence and extent of this movement was under the auspices of numerous population groups of various origins and cultural levels living in the area between the northern German flatlands and the central mountain ranges. The first written reference to "Germania" is in the works of the Roman author Poseidonius (1C BC). Julilus Caesar, too, used this term in his *De Bello Gallico* to describe the non-Gallic regions north of the Alps.

The wars conducted by the Kimbers and the Teutons against the Romans around 100 BC were the first military conflicts between German tribes and the Roman civilisation. The expansion of the western German tribes was stopped by Caesar's conquest of Gaul (58-55 BC). The aims of foreign policy until Emperor Augustus also covered the inclusion of Germania into the Roman Empire all the way to the Elbe, an objective that was never met.

During the 1C AD, the **Limes** was built, a 550km/330mi fortified line that sealed the Roman sphere of influence from the Rhine to the Danube. Skirmishes did break out every now and then, but there were also alliances, trade and cultural exchanges. New towns arose where Roman camps stood and at river crossings (eg Cologne, Koblenz, Regensburg).

In the 2C-3C AD, large tribes like the Franks, the Saxons and the Allemanni joined forces. The military kingdoms of the age of mass migration gave way to early medieval states.

La Tène Culture

The name for this cultural epoch supported by Celtic tribes (5C-1C BC) originated at an excavation site on Switzerland's Neuenburg Lake. Over 2 500 objects were found, including grave furnishings and treasures. The La Tène Culture was located primarily in southwestern Germany, along the northern edge of the Alps and in the Main-Moselle area. Fortifications expanded into settlements, the first north of the Alps. The advance of Germanic tribes and the expansion of the Roman Empire brought the La Tène Culture to an end.

AD 9 Three Roman legions under General Varus are annihilated by Germanic troops under prince **Arminius**, resulting in Roman relinquishment of bastions on the Rhine.

314 One year after announcing the Edict of Tolerance, Emperor Constantine establishes the first German bishopric, in Trier.

375 Beginning of the *Völkerwanderung*, the "movement of the peoples": The Huns drive the Goths (eastern Germans) to the west. The former *Imperium Romanum* breaks into partial empires.

800 End of the West Roman Empire brought about by German general Odoaker, who is in turn murdered by the Ostrogoth Theodorich.

THE FRANKISH EMPIRE

The tribal union of the Franks expanded slowly south. Their king, Clovis I, eliminated the remains of the West Roman Empire and adopted Christianity. In the 7C, the Merovingians lost their hegemony to the Carolingians, formerly the highest royal officials under the Merovingians.

Since the 8C, the general term *thiutisk* developed from a derivation of the word for tribe to describe the peoples speaking Germanic languages. There was still no supra-regional language spoken to the east of the Rhine, the area of the Franks, until the 11C. In the 10C, the term *Regnum Teutonicorum* appeared for the first time in relation to the Eastern Frankish tribes. During the 11C and 12C it slowly established itself as a term.

751 Pope Zacharias agrees to the deposition of the last of the Merovingian kings, Childeric III, in favour of the palatine Pippin. Three years later the Pope places Rome under the protection of the Frankish kings.

768 Charlemagne becomes ruler. He conquers, among others, the Lombards, divides up Bavaria and defeats the Saxons after a long war.

800 Coronation of Charlemagne in Rome. The emperor legally assumes sovereignty over the former empire.

843 The Treaty of Verdun divides the Carolingian Empire among Charlemagne's grandchildren. The East Frankish Kingdom is given to Ludwig the German. The final division, determined by the treaties of Mersen (870) and Verdun/Ribemont (879-80), would evolve into Germany and France

911 The East Franks elect the Frankish duke Konrad to become their king, separating themselves from the West Franks.

THE HOLY ROMAN EMPIRE

The Roman-German Empire consisted of an elective monarchy in which the king was crowned emperor by the Pope. From the 11C onwards, the emperor could rely on being king of not only Germany and Italy, but also of Burgundy. An especially "German" Imperial concept gave way to a Roman-universal idea of an emperor, a fact underscored in 1157 by the additional title *sacrum Imperium*. During the time of the Staufer dynasty, in the mid 13C, the claim to rule in Italy came to an end. In the 15C, the term "Holy Roman Empire of the German Nation" was finally established, implying the politically active community of the German Imperial estates, who acted as a counterweight to the emperor.

Ruling this empire, which during the High Middle Ages stretched from Sicily to the Baltic, was difficult without central administration and technical, financial and military wherewithal. By granting land and privileges (e.g. customs rights), administrative responsibility, security and imperial expansion were domains of the aristocracy.

Beginning in the second half of the 11C, the **Investiture Controversy** pitted the Pope against the Emperor on the issue of the right to invest bishops. This weakened the empire and shook up Christianity. The dispute ended with the Concordat of Worms (1122), declaring that ecclesiastical dignitaries had to be separated from worldly goods. The position of the bishops became similar to that of the princes, since they became vassals of the empire.

These vassals gradually accumulated more power owing to the heredity laws of the fiefs and regalia. In the long term this weakened the empire, paving the way to the rise of numerous territorial states. The regional princely territorial states replaced the personal union state resulting in Germany's current federal structure .

962 In Rome, Otto the Great, having been crowned king in 936, is crowned emperor by the Pope. The Otto dynasty rules until the death of Henry II in 1024, and is followed by that of the Salians (Franks).

Charlemagne's Empire

After being crowned Emperor in St Peter's Cathedral in Rome in 800, Charlemagne followed the lead of the Roman emperors. His empire stretched from Spain to the Elbe, from Rome to the English Channel. Charlemagne's reign introduced the "Carolingian Renaissance" as well as a new administrative structure. The emperor instituted a county constitution, disposing of independent duchies and tribal states. Each administrative district was governed by an officer chosen from the Frankish aristocracy, thus ensuring the coherence of the empire. Vulnerable borders were secured by border marches under authorized margraves. And emissaries with royal powers watched over the Imperial administration. The king constantly travelled his empire, visiting the "Pfalzen", which grew into major economic and cultural centres, and overnighting in Imperial monasteries.

Emperor Charles IV and seven prince electors (armorial, c 1370)

1073 Pope Gregory VII elected. The reformer disputes the role of secular power in the church. The crux of the conflict was the penitent journey to Canossa (1077) by King Heinrich IV to receive absolution from the Pope, who had excommunicated him.

1152-90 Rule of the Staufer emperor Frederick I Barbarossa, who strengthened Imperial power *(Restauratio Imperii)* and captured the duchies of Bavaria and Saxony from the Guelph duke Henry the Lion (👁 *see BRAUN-SCHWEIG*). He also strove to limit papal power.

1212-50 Frederick II stays in southern Italy and Sicily for much of his reign, holding little interest in the area north of the Alps. Two Imperial edicts (1220-31) confirm the power over the territories of the secular and religious princes.

1254-73 The years extending between the death of Konrad IV and the election of Rudolf of Habsburg are known as the Interregnum. It was a time of lawlessness under "foreign" kings and anti-kings, finally eliminating the empire's power in the High Middle Ages.

THE LATE MIDDLE AGES

After the Interregnum, the power of the Habsburgs grew, buildiing up and consolidating family power by the 15C though the Luxembourg, Nassau and Wittelsbach families occasionally won the throne. The emperors tried to have a son elected king during their lifetime in order to maintain the ranking of their own dynasties. But during the Renaissance, the Imperial crown surrendered its holiness.

In the Late Middle Ages, the "Hoftage", or Imperial meetings, became the **Reichstag**, a meeting of 350 secular and religious Imperial estates, foreshadowing a sharp dualism between the emperor and his estates. At the Reichstag in Worms (1495), fundamental reforms created the preconditions for transforming the Reich into a unified legal and pacified territory. The proclamation of the *Ewiger Landfrieden* (Eternal Peace in the land) prohibited personal feuds, favoring a new legal basis. A Permanent Imperial Chamber Court ensured compliance. After a long debate, financial reform was pushed through raising the *Common Penny*, a combination of wealth tax, income tax and poll tax. Later Reichstags divided up the empire into administrative units – the Reichskreise, or Imperial districts. In 1663, the Permanent Reichstag was set up in Regensburg.

Bildarchiv Preussischer Kulturbesitz

Inspired by the Humanists, the concept of a "German nation" began to arise politically as well as culturally, legitimised thanks to the rediscovery of literary monuments such as "Germania" by Tacitus. Until around 1500, Europe ans spoke of the *deutsche Lande* (German lands); after 1500 the term "Deutschland" in the singular became common.

1273 After a warning from the Pope, electors chose as king Count Rudolf of Habsburg (dynastic power in the Breisgau, Alsace and Aargau).

1346-78 Charles IV of Luxembourg emerges as the most important ruler of the Late Middle Ages.

1386 Founding of the University of Heidelberg, Germany's first.

1414-18 Council of Constance; the largest church meeting of the Middle Ages to date.

1438 After the death of the last Luxembourg emperor, the electors chose the Habsburg duke Albrecht V to become King Albrecht II.

c 1450 Invention of movable type printing by Johann Gutenberg from Mainz; flourishing and spread of Humanism.

1452 During a military campaign by Frederick III, the last imperial coronation takes place in Rome.

1493 Maximilian I becomes king. As of 1508 he is the "elected Roman Emperor". His successors adopt the Imperial title immediately after the royal coronation in Aachen, avoiding the difficult and dangerous journey to Rome.

1519-56 – Emperor Charles V, Maximilian's grandchild, gathers more power during his term than any ruler since the Carolingians.

THE REFORMATION AND THE THIRTY YEARS WAR

In 1503, **Martin Luther** (1483-1546) entered the Augustinian monastery of Erfurt. A dedicated cleric, he was tormented by the problem of salvation. Appointed Professor of Theology, he found in the Holy Scriptures (c 1512-13) his answer: "We cannot earn forgiveness for our sins through our deeds, only God's mercy justifies us in our faith in it." Man's salvation, Luther argued, lies entirely within the grace of God. This concept led him to attack the Church's dealing in indulgences. On 31 October, 1517, he nailed to the doors of Wittenberg Church 95 "theses" condemning such practices and reminding the Faithful of the importance of Christ's sacrifice and the Grace of God.

Luther was denounced in the court of Rome, refused to recant, and in 1520 burned the Papal Bull threatening him with excommunication. Subsequently he attacked the institutions of the Church. He objected to the primacy of the clergy in spiritual matters, arguing the universal priesthood of Christians conferred by baptism.

Refusing again to recant before the Diet of Worms (1521), where he had been summoned by Charles V, he was

The Golden Bull

Beginning in the 10C, the number of electors for the king began to decline. At the same time the election process became more regulated and formalised. In 1356, the Golden Bull promulgated an Imperial law regulating royal election, defining an institutional framework and limiting the power of the empire. Thenceforth, the king would be elected by three religious electors (the Archbishops of Mainz, Cologne and Trier) and four secular ones (the Kings of Bohemia, the Margrave of Brandenburg, the Duke of Saxony and the Palatine of the Rhine), and then crowned emperor. The election was set in Frankfurt/Main, and the coronation in Aachen; papal confirmation was no longer necessary. This law, announced by the Luxembourg emperor **Charles IV,** is considered the empire's first constitution and a basis for a federal system of state.

The Hanseatic League

The Hanseatic League existed between the 12C and the 17C. Its basic structure was established by about 1300. Thirty larger and numerous smaller cities joined to safeguard their shipping and trade interests. This union went through its Golden Age in the 14C: Over 100 cities, under Lübeck's leadership, formed the most significant economic force in northern Germany. After the Thirty Years War, the Hanseatic tradition only continued in Hamburg, Lübeck and Bremen.

placed under a ban of the Empire and his works were condemned.

The patronage of Frederick the Wise, Duke of Saxony, enabled him to complete a Bible translation considered the first literary work in modern German. The Edict of Worms was confirmed in 1529 and hardened by an additional ruling forbidding any religious reform.

The Council of Trent (1545-63) resulted in the renewal of Catholicism and the Counter Reformation, which was resolutely supported by the Emperor. The internal struggles of the Protestants and the feud between Rudolf II and his brother Matthias ended the Peace of Augsburg. The Protestant Union led by the Electorate of the Palatinate now faced the Catholic League with the Duchy of Bavaria at its head. The Bohemian Rebellion of 1618 led to the outbreak of the Thirty Years War, which began as a religious conflict and soon engulfed all of Europe.

The war, which was almost exclusively fought on German territory, devastated the land, caused general havoc, left cities in rubble and ruined economic life in the countryside. By the end of the war, only individual territorial states showed some gain in authority; the empire's significance dwindled.

1530 Invited by Charles V to Augsburg, theologians of the opposing faiths fail to agree. Luther's assistant, Melanchthon, draws up the "Confession of Augsburg," the charter of Protestantism.

1555 The Peace of Augsburg establishes a compromise, and Lutheran Protestantism is recognised as equal to Catholicism. The empire lost its sovereignty over religious matters to the territories.

1618 The Bohemian estates refuse to recognise Archduke Ferdinand, the successor of Emperor Matthias, as the Bohemian king. Instead, they elect the Protestant Elector Frederick V from the Palatinate to be their ruler. After the Defenestration of Prague in May (when the Bohemian king's representatives were thrown out of a window by nobles protesting reduced privileges), the situation intensified and led to the Thirty Years War.

1618-23 The first phase of the war (Bohemian-Palatinate War) is decided by the defeat of Frederick V at the battle of Weißer Berg in 1620 against an army commanded by Tilly.

1625-29 Phase two (the Danish-Dutch War) ends with Denmark's Protestant soldiers defeated by Imperial troops under Wallenstein.

1630-35 Sweden enters the war on the Protestant side (Swedish

Luther's Bible, 1534

Bildarchiv Preussischer Kulturbesitz

Prussian Reforms: The Revolution from Above

The reforms already prepared by the General Land Law of 1794, were initially set in motion by Baron von Stein, and, after his dismissal, by Baron von Hardenberg. The two men went about installing new structures for government and society virtually by decree and with almost revolutionary energy. Abolition of serfdom by the Edict of 1807 was of particular importance, as was the lifting of guild compulsion and the introduction of a free crafts market. Educational reforms followed, resulting in the founding of the University in Berlin by Wilhelm von Humboldt (1810) and a military reform. Other reforms included the emancipation of the Jews and the modernisation of the administration.

War). King Gustav Adolph II dies in battle near Lützen.

1635-48 France, under the leadership of Richelieu, participates in the alliance with Bernhard von Weimar (French-Swedish War).

1648 Peace of Westphalia: peace treaty in Münster and Osnabrück after five years of negotiations (see MÜNSTER).

1688-97 Palatinate War of Succession. Louis XIV lays claim to the left bank of the Rhine; French troops under Louvois devastate the Palatinate.

THE RISE OF PRUSSIA

In 1415, Burgrave Frederick of Hohenzollern was granted the Electorate of Brandenburg. The Duchy of Prussia, 203 years later, also came under the authority of his dynasty. Frederick William (1640-88), the Great Elector, turned the small country into the strongest, best-governed northern German state thanks to successful power policies, deprivation of the estates' power, a centralised administration and the creation of a standing army. He also expanded the country, adding eastern Pomerania which he received in the Peace of Westphalia. After the revocation of the Edict of Nantes in France, thousands of Huguenots fled to Brandenburg and built up the economic basis of Berlin.

His grandson, King Frederick William I continued his efforts by laying the foundations to a Prussian military and official state. Fulfilment of one's duty, industriousness, economy and strict discipline were aspects inspired by the "Soldier King".

His son, **Frederick the Great** (1740-86), took the throne in a country with an exemplary administration, and within a few years turned it became the second imperial power. The Silesian War and the Seven Years War won him Silesia, and the division of Poland extended his power eastwards. This connoisseur of music and literature, the friend and correspondent of Voltaire, was considered an "enlightened ruler" and had a high reputation among European scholars. The rule of "Old Fritz" left Prussia with a well organised administration and a close relationship between the king and the nobles, all cornerstones of Prussian power.

1701 Elector Frederick III is crowned Frederick I King of Prussia in Königsberg.

1740-48 War of Austrian Succession/ Silesian Wars: The legality of the Pragmatic Sanction (1713) pronounced by Charles VI is disputed. The war is triggered by Frederick II's troops marching into Silesia.

1756-63 Prussia joins forces with England against the Emperor during the Seven Years War. By the end of the war, Prussia was the fifth European power; the system of power will guide Europe until the First World War.

The Deutscher Bund

The Deutscher Bund, or German Confederation, a loose federation with little authority, was founded in 1815. The confederation included 39 politically autonomous states; four free cities; the kings of Holland, Denmark and the Low Countries; and portions of Prussia and Austria. The Bundestag (Parliament) included 11 governmentally-appointed representatives who met in Frankfurt and were led by Austria. Prince Metternich, who came from the Rhineland, played a decisive role in this union after he became the Austrian chancellor. In collaboration with Prussia, he mercilessly crushed the libertarian and national movements. The restoration policies of the Bundestag gave rise to a period of extreme calm (Biedermeier period).

THE WAY TO A GERMAN NATIONAL STATE

Since 1792, war had raged between France and the other powers of Europe. The Peace of Lunéville, signed in 1801, resulted in the loss of German territories on the left bank of the Rhine. The Decision of the Deputation of German Estates (1803) destroyed the political and legal foundations of the old Empire. Bavaria, Prussia, Baden and Württemberg benefitted, gaining territory, while the latter two received Elector ranking. Sixteen of the southern and western German states left the Imperial Union and founded the Confederation of the Rhine in 1806 in Paris under the protection of France.

At the **Congress of Vienna** (1814-15), leaders discussed the geographical reorganisation, including restoration of the political status quo of 1792, legitimisation of the Ancien Régime, and solidarity of the princes in combating revolutionary ideas and movements.

Since the 18C, literature, philosophy, art and music had melded, giving rise to a single German culture that preceded patriotism. The ideals of the French Revolution, the end of the Holy Roman Empire, the experience of French occupation and other reforms led to the growth of a 19C movement toward a free, unified German national state. One important stage on the way to unity was an economic one: the foundation of the German Zollverein (Customs Union) at the behest of Prussia.

On 31 March 1848, a pre-Parliament met in Frankfurt and held a National Convention, which opened on 18 May in the Paulskirche in Frankfurt. The aim was passing a liberal constitution and consideration of the future German state. On the table were the greater German solution, with the Habsburg empire under Austrian leadership; and the smaller German solution, ie without Austria, but with a Hohenzollern emperor at the top. The latter was finally voted in. However, the Prussian king Frederick William IV refused the Imperial crown brought to him by a delegate from the Paulskirche Parliament.

Otto von Bismarck, appointed Minister-President of Prussia in 1862, needed only eight years to bring about unification under Prussian rule. With the loyalty of an elite bourgeoisie born through the advances of industry and science, and aided by the neutrality of Napoleon III, he aggressively pursued a policy of war. After joining Austria in defeating Denmark in 1864, Prussia declared war on her German ally and defeated the Imperial troops at the battle of Sadowa, thus ending Austrian-Prussian dualism for good. A year later, Bismarck created the North German Alliance, including all German states north of the River Main; Hannover, Hessen and Schleswig-Holstein already belonged to Prussia. The Franco-Prussian War of 1870-71 completed the task of unification.

Napoleon at Regensburg, 23 April 1809

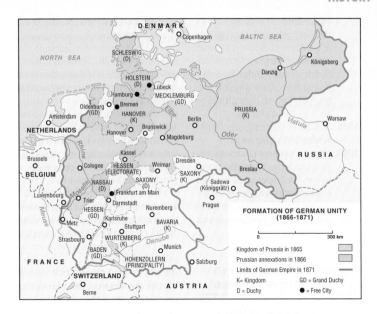

FORMATION OF GERMAN UNITY
(1866-1871)

0 ————————— 300 km

Kingdom of Prussia in 1865
Prussian annexations in 1866
Limits of German Empire in 1871
K= Kingdom   GD = Grand Duchy
D = Duchy   ● = Free City

1806 Napoleon marches into Berlin. Emperor Francis II of Austria surrenders the Roman-German Imperial Crown ending the Holy Roman Empire of the German nation going back to Charlemagne.

1813 Prussia commands the Coalition in the Wars of Liberation against Napoleon, who is defeated in the Battle of Nations at Leipzig.

1814-15 Congress of Vienna establishes the German Confederation; Holy Alliance between Russia, Prussia and Austria.

1819 The Decisions of Karlsbad include press censorship, prohibitions of fraternities, monitoring of universities.

1833-34 Founding of the German Customs Union (Zollverein), an economic unification of most German states – except Austria – led by Prussia.

1835 First German railway line is opened between Nuremberg and Fürth.

1848 Unrest in France in February spreads to Mannheim and then, in March, to all German states. But the "March Revolution" quickly turns into a bourgeois reform movement.

THE GERMAN EMPIRE (1871-1918)

The immediate cause of the Franco-Prussian War of 1870 was the claim by the House of Hohenzollern (Leopold von Hohenzollern-Sigmaringen) to the Spanish throne. Bismarck succeeded in kindling national pride on both sides of the border. France then declared war on Prussia. The southern states united with the states of the North German Union led by Prussia. The German princes all stood against France as they had signed secret alliances with Prussia. After the victory of Sedan (2 September), the southern states opened negotiations with Prussia on the issue of German unification.

The first years following the founding of the German Reich in 1871 were marked by an exceptional economic boom, the **Gründerzeit**, financed in part by the receipt of 5 billion francs in French reparations. The advantages of the larger boundary-free economic area and measures to standardise coins, measures and weights combined for rapid growth in the financial, industrial, construction and traffic sectors.

1871 On 18 January, William I is crowned German Emperor in the

Mirror Room of Versailles. Imperial Germany, enlarged by the acquisition of Alsace-Lorraine, remains in theory a federation, but is in fact under Prussian domination. Germany is transformed from an agricultural to an industrial economy.

1888 William II succeeds his father Frederick III's brief reign.

1890 After numerous altercations, the Emperor forces Bismarck's resignation. The Emperor's unabashed expansionary policies and dangerous foreign policy provokes the enmity of England, Russia and France.

THE FIRST WORLD WAR AND THE WEIMAR REPUBLIC

The assassination of the Austrian Archduke Ferdinand and his wife at Sarajevo on 28 June 1914 unleashed an intense international reaction. Austria-Hungary's declaration of war against Serbia mobilised the great powers of Europe. Germany launched into wars on two fronts. German troops moved into France, halting only once they reached the River Marne. In the east, German troops invaded large sections of Russian territory.

1914 Germany declares war on France and Russia on 3 August.

1917 An armistice is agreed with Russia, shattered by Revolution. The USA enters the war, after Germany declares indiscriminate submarine warfare.

1918 On 28-29 October, the sailors of the German naval fleet at Wilhelmshaven mutiny. Revolution erupts in Germany, with workers' and soldiers' councils springing up throughout the land. The revolution was suppressed by the provisional government under Friedrich Ebert with the support of military supreme command. On 9 November, William II abdicated and Philipp Scheidemann proclaimed the republic. Two days later, Matthias Erzberger signed the armistice at Compiègne.

After the November revolution, which dwindled in early 1919 due to the unrest caused by the Spartacists, the model of a liberal democratic state with a strong president was established. On 11 August 1919, Germany adopted a Republican Constitution in Weimar, where the National Convention was meeting. This "republic without republicans" shouldered the burden of the Treaty of Versailles, which took effect in 1920: acceptance of responsibility for the war, diminution of national territory (including important agricultural and industrial areas), loss of colonies, demilitarisation and high reparations.

The only truly republican parties accepting the constitution, the SPD (Social Democrats), the Centre Party and the DDP (German Democratic Party) had a parliamentary majority after 1920. The Weimar Republic had 16 government changes, an average of one every eight and a half months. Galloping inflation erupted, brought about by economic crisis, difficulties in relaunching the industrial sector and by high government debt: the bourgeoisie was ruined, and all financial assets exceptreal estate were worthless.

Germany experienced an economic upswing and relative tranquility from 1924 to 1929, in spite of major economic burdens and high unemployment. The Dawes Plan can be credited with those successes; it managed German reparations, ended the French occupation of the Ruhr and committed to capital investment. Germany was even accepted into the League of Nations (1926) during the incumbency of Chancellor and Foreign minister Gustav Stresemann. A year earlier in Locarno, Germany and France signed a pact pledging not to use violent means to revise borders – a corresponding agreement could not be signed for the eastern borders.

However, the world economic crisis hit the Weimar Republic in 1929. High foreign debt, sharp export declines, inflation and dramatic unemployment all led to the rise of radical political parties, especially the German National

Socialist Worker's Party, after 1930. They presented a theory that solving social problems would require a people's community, or "Volksgemeinschaft," based on race. Nazi storm-troops and Communist groups increasingly fought in the street. Social elites and the business community saw in **Adolf Hitler** a bulwark against Communism: on 30 January 1933, Hitler was named Chancellor of the Reich by President Von Hindenburg; it was the end of the Weimar Republic.

1919 The National Convention meets in Weimar, Friedrich Ebert (SPD) is named its first President (11 February); Versailles Peace Treaty is signed (28 June).

1923 Occupation of the Ruhr region on 11 January by France, because of Germany's failure to make reparation payments. The NSDAP (the National Socialist German Workers' Party) attempts a coup in Munich on 8-9 November led by Adolf Hitler, who had joined the party in 1919. The coup is foiled, Hitler is jailed, but released in 1924.

1925 After the death of Friedrich Ebert, the former Field Marshall General Paul von Hindenburg is elected President of the Republic.

1930 An electoral defeat in the Reichstag (Parliament) ushers in several presidial cabinets (Brüning, Von Papen, Von Schleicher), ie governments without parliamentary majorities.

1932 At the Reichstag elections in July, the NSDAP assumes leadership with almost 38% of the votes. Together with the Communists, the Nazis have an absolute majority, which lets the radical parties block all other parliamentary minorities.

THE NAZI DICTATORSHIP AND THE SECOND WORLD WAR

No sooner had the NSDAP taken power under Hitler than it began to organise a totalitarian dictatorship and eliminate all democratic rules. In a climate of propaganda, intimidation and terror on the part of the SA, SS and Gestapo, all parties, associations and social organisations were liquidated or dissolved, with the exception of the churches. The NSDAP was declared the sole legal party. Opponents were thrown into concentration camps and murdered. Their power and societal control allowed the party to penetrate every level of state government. Competing authorities and rivalries quietly coexisted, but art and literature were subjected to censorship, forcing numerous artists into exile.

The Nuremberg Laws promulgated at the Reich party rally (September 1935) codified Jewish persecution on racist grounds; prohibitions, loss of civil rights and mass arrests were the instruments of the anti-Semitic ideology. As early as 1 April 1933, the NSDAP had ordered a "boycott of the Jews," initiating the gradual exclusion of Germany's 500 000 Jews from public life. In the night of 9-10 November 1938, the Nazis organised a pogrom, "Reichskristallnacht"; synagogues, Jewish apartments and shops were damaged or destroyed.

The improved worldwide economic situation helped reduce unemployment as did a programme of public works (motorways, drainage schemes), a policy of rearmament, and the recruitment of youth into para-governmental organisations. In 1942, the National Socialist Reich stood at the zenith of its power: materially speaking and otherwise, many Germans had profited up until that point.

The assault on Poland on 1 September 1939 launched the **Second World War**. German preparations for an annihilation war had been underway since 1936 in the hopes of eliminating other peoples and creating a European area dominated by *Aryan* Eurasians. But the war reached German civilians as soon as the British and the Americans began dropping explosive and incendiary bombs on war-related and residential targets. By the end of the war, Germany lay in ruins, the bulk of the inhabitants suffered from under-nourishment and millions had been driven out of the eastern regions. With the liberation of the concentration camps, the world discovered with what

Dresden in ruins, 1949

cruelty and meticulousness the Nazis had carried out their policy of genocide against the Jews.

GERMANY FROM POST-WAR 1945 TO THE PRESENT

1945 Germany and Berlin are divided into four zones of occupation. According to the agreement, American and British forces pull out of Saxony, Thuringia and Mecklenburg and redeploy in the western sector of Berlin. At the Potsdam Conference (*see POTSDAM*) the victorious powers decide to demilitarise and democratize Germany and administer it jointly.

1946 Amalgamation of the British and American zones.

1948 End of the Four-Power administration of Germany after the Soviet delegate leaves the Allied Control Council (20 March). Soviet blockade of the western sectors of Berlin, the city is supplied by the airlift.

1949 Creation (23 May) of the Federal Republic in the three western zones. The Soviet zone becomes (7 October) the German Demo-cratic Republic. Under Konrad Adenauer, Chancellor until 1963, and Ludwig Erhard, Minister of Economic Affairs, the Federal Republic enjoys a spectacular economic rebirth and re-establishes normal international relations.

1952 Soviet leadership offers to create a single, neutral, democratic Germany, a reunification initiative which fails.

1961 Construction of the "Berlin Wall" (12-13 August).

Willy Brandt in 1966

1972 Signature of a treaty between the two Germanies, a milestone in Chancellor Willy Brandt's policy of openness towards the East (*Ostpolitik*).

1989 Citizens of East Germany occupy West German embassies in Prague, Budapest and Warsaw with the aim of travelling to West Germany. The opening of the border between Austria and Hungary launches a mass East German mass migration. On 4 November, the largest demonstration ever takes place in East Berlin, involving over one million people. On the night of 9-10 November, the internal German border is opened, the Wall is breached. On 7 December, the Round Table meets for the first time as an institution of public control, with representatives from the political parties and the citizens' movements.

1990 Treaty of reunification drawn up; on 3 October the German Democratic Republic joins the Federal Republic of Germany according to Article 23 of the Basic law. On 2 December, the first joint German parliamentary elections take place.

2005 Angela Merkel is elected German Chancellor. She becomes Germany's first female chancellor and its first East German chancellor since reunification.

Keen to achieve rapid reunification, on 28 November 1989 West German Chancellor **Helmut Kohl** put forward a ten-point plan providing for the initial constitution of a confederation. On 3 October 1990 (now a public holiday) the Parliament sitting in the Reichstag in Berlin ratified the treaty of reunification. Helmut Kohl won the elections in December 1990, and, in 1991, the Bundestag chose Berlin as capital of the reunified country. With the withdrawal of the last occupying troops in 1994, Germany became a sovereign state. It set its sights on the construction of a unified Europe. After the Federal President's move to Berlin, the Parliament followed suit in 1999. On 19 April the new Plenary Room of the Reichstag building, crowned by a dome designed by British architect Sir Norman Foster, was inaugurated.

The reunification, which had been carried out at great speed on the political level, caused considerable problems in the economic and social domains; a drop in competitiveness, high rates of unemployment in the new Länder, and increased taxation in the West to finance the modernization of the East fuelled growing discontent. These problems partly explain the poor performance of Helmut Kohl's CDU-CSU party in the 1998 legislative elections; it was Social Democrat **Gerhard Schröder** who claimed victory and formed a coalition government with the Greens.

The modern German state under Gerhard Schröder succeeded in reclaiming a post-World War leadership role within Europe and on the international stage. Germany is considered a leading political and economic force within the European Union, enjoying equal footing with France and Great Britain. The German military took an active peace-keeping role in war-torn Kosovo as part of the KFOR in 1999.

But while the country has reemerged as a positive force internationally, economic stresses continued to take its toll in the early 2000s. High unemployment and increased taxation as a result of reunification, and decreased competitiveness due to economic globalization helped to oust Schröder's SPD from office. In its place, the CDU-CSU coalition regained a parliamentary majority in the 2005 federal election, and the coveted role of Chancellor went to **Angela Merkel**. Merkel's election to the head of government reflected several historical milestones for Germany. She was the first female Chancellor of Germany; the first former citizen of East Germany to head a reunified German government; and she was the youngest person to be chancellor since the Second World War. On January 1st, 2007, Merkel will become only the third woman to chair the G8.

ART AND CULTURE

Religious architecture

Plan of a church

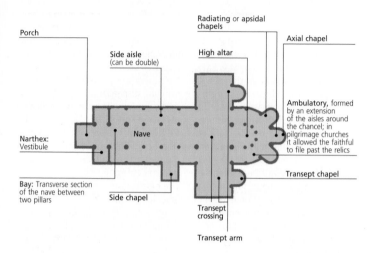

Porch

Side aisle
(can be double)

Radiating or apsidal
chapels

Axial chapel

High altar

Nave

Ambulatory, formed
by an extension
of the aisles around
the chancel; in
pilgrimage churches
it allowed the faithful
to file past the relics

Narthex:
Vestibule

Bay: Transverse section
of the nave between
two pillars

Side chapel

Transept chapel

Transept
crossing

Transept arm

Cross section of a church

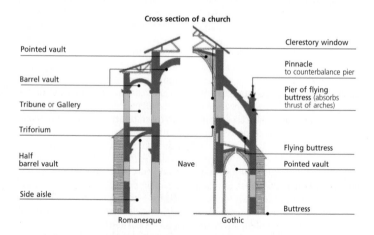

Pointed vault

Clerestory window

Pinnacle
to counterbalance pier

Barrel vault

Pier of flying
buttress (absorbs
thrust of arches)

Tribune or Gallery

Triforium

Half
barrel vault

Nave

Flying buttress

Pointed vault

Side aisle

Buttress

Romanesque

Gothic

Hall Church

Unlike a basilica, a hall church has aisles the same height as the central nave and covered with one roof;
their windows let light inside the edifice.

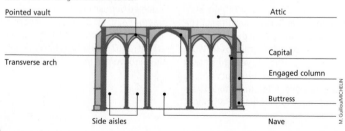

Pointed vault

Attic

Transverse arch

Capital

Engaged column

Buttress

Side aisles

Nave

M. Guillou/MICHELIN

SPEYER – East End of the Cathedral (11C)

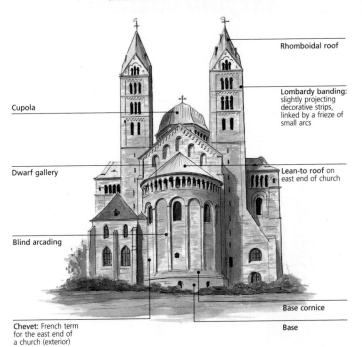

Rhomboidal roof

Lombardy banding: slightly projecting decorative strips, linked by a frieze of small arcs

Cupola

Dwarf gallery

Lean-to roof on east end of church

Blind arcading

Base cornice

Chevet: French term for the east end of a church (exterior)

Base

FREIBURG – Cathedral Altar (14C-16C)

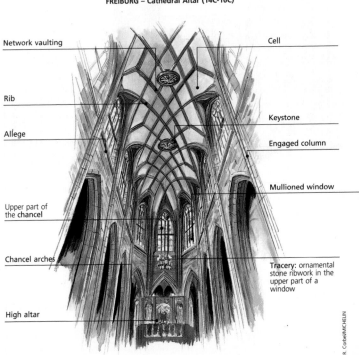

Network vaulting

Cell

Rib

Allège

Keystone

Engaged column

Upper part of the chancel

Mullioned window

Chancel arches

Tracery: ornamental stone ribwork in the upper part of a window

High altar

R. Corbel/MICHELIN

COLOGNE CATHEDRAL (1248 to 1880), South façade

The construction of the cathedral began in 1248 and took more than 600 years to complete. It was the first Gothic church in the Rhineland and the original design was based on those in Paris, Amiens and Reims. The twin-towered western façade marks the peak of achievement in the style known as Flamboyant Gothic. Stepped windows, embellished gables, slender buttresses, burst upwards, ever upwards, slimly in line with the tapering spires that reach a height of 157m/515ft.

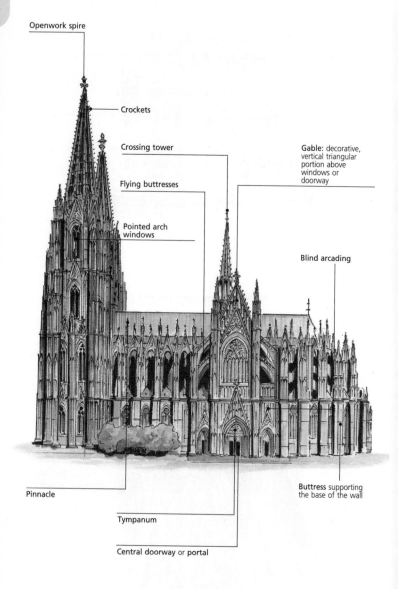

Openwork spire

Crockets

Crossing tower

Flying buttresses

Pointed arch windows

Gable: decorative, vertical triangular portion above windows or doorway

Blind arcading

Pinnacle

Tympanum

Central doorway or portal

Buttress supporting the base of the wall

R. Corbel/MICHELIN

Schloß BRUCHSAL – Garden façade (18C)

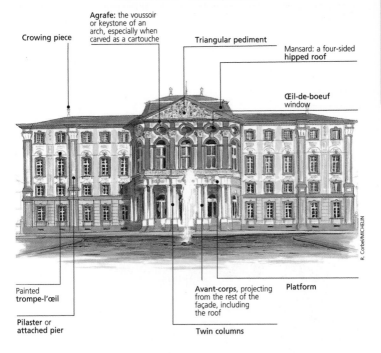

Crowing piece

Agrafe: the voussoir or keystone of an arch, especially when carved as a cartouche

Triangular pediment

Mansard: a four-sided hipped roof

Œil-de-boeuf window

Painted trompe-l'œil

Pilaster or attached pier

Avant-corps, projecting from the rest of the façade, including the roof

Twin columns

Platform

R. Corbel/MICHELIN

POTSDAM – Sanssouci Palace and Park
(Georg Wenzelaus von Knobelsdorff and Friedrich II, 1745-47)

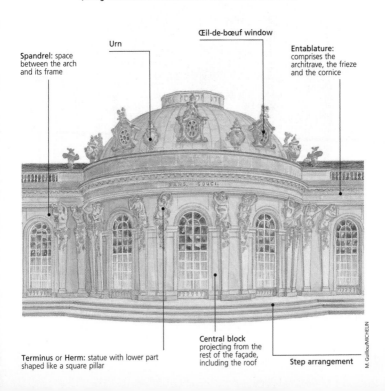

Œil-de-bœuf window

Urn

Spandrel: space between the arch and its frame

Entablature: comprises the architrave, the frieze and the cornice

Terminus or Herm: statue with lower part shaped like a square pillar

Central block projecting from the rest of the façade, including the roof

Step arrangement

M. Guillou/MICHELIN

OTTOBEUREN Abbey Church (18C)

Ottobeuren is characteristic of other Bavarian churches with its dazzling ornamentation and plays of light and symmetry.

Painted vaulting

Spandrel: triangular space between the curve of an arch and the frame in which it is set

Stuccowork

Cornice with projecting ornamental motifs

Retable or **altarpiece**

Tabernacle

Pulpit (or ambo): elevated stand from which sermons were preached

Sounding board

R. Corbel/MICHELIN

"Uncle Tom's Cabin" estate
(Bruno Taut, Hugo Häring, Otto Rudolf Salvisberg, 1926-32)

Designed to house 15 000 people, this estate built under the supervision of Martin Wagner, does not convey an impression of monotony. There is a U-Bahn Station in its centre as well as a shopping centre and a cinema.

Terraced roof

All the buildings are of a moderate size

The simplicity of the façades painted with bright colours, hence the nickname of "parrot estate", is due to a rational building plan and the use of standard, relatively cheap, materials.

The natural surroundings are in keeping with the concept of **garden cities** at the beginning of the century.

Individual houses have re-entrant angles and tall windows characteristic of the style of Salvisberg who designed the buildings along Riemeisterstraße.

Philharmonie (Hans Scharoun, 1960-63) and Chamber Music Hall
(Edgar Wisniewski, from a drawing by Scharoun, 1984-88)

In 1957, during a congress, H Scharoun expressed his wish to build "an adequately shaped hall for music making, where listening to music would be a common experience". The audience sits round the orchestra, which occupies the very heart of the arena.

Aluminium sheeting: perforated, it was only added in 1978-81. Before that time, the concrete roof was painted in an ochre colour.

Philharmonie

The internal structure and the outside appearance are closely related. The place occupied by the orchestra determines the type of structure (three imbricated pentagons in the case of the Philharmonie, a hexagon in the case of the Chamber Music Hall): the tent-shaped roof provides good acoustics and adds a dynamic element to the visual aspect.

Chamber music hall

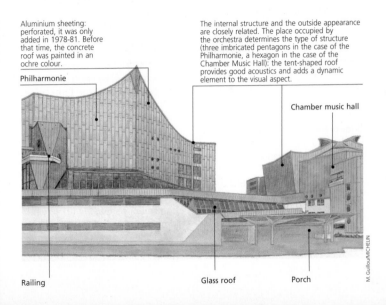

Railing

Glass roof

Porch

M. Guillou/MICHELIN

Glossary of Architecture

Absidiole or **apsidiole chapel**: small apsidal chapel opening on the ambulatory of a Romanesque or Gothic church.

Aisles: lateral divisions running parallel with the nave.

Ambulatory: formed by an extension of the aisles around the chancel; in pilgrimage churches it allowed the faithful to file past the relics.

Apse: rounded or polygonal end of a church; the outer section is known as the chevet.

Archivolt: ornamental moulding around the outside of an arch.

Atlantes (or **Telamones**): male figures used as supporting columns.

Atrium (or **four-sided portico**): court enclosed by colonnades in front of the entrance to a early Christian or Romanesque church.

Basilica: rectangular religious building, built on the Roman basilica plan with three or five aisles.

Bossage: architectural motif or facing made of bosses, uniformly projecting blocks on the outer wall. They are surrounded by deep carving or separating lines. Bossage was in vogue during the Renaissance.

Buttress: external mass of masonry projecting from a wall to counterbalance the thrust of the vaults and arches.

Capital: crowning feature of a column, consisting of a smooth part, connecting it to the shaft, and a decorated part. There are three orders in classical architecture: Doric, Ionic (with double volute), and Corinthian (decorated with acanthus leaves). The latter is often found in 16C-17C buildings.

Chancel: part of the church behind the altar set aside for the choir, furnished with variously decorated wooden stalls.

Chevet: French term for the east end of a church (exterior).

Choir screen or **rood screen**: partition separating the chancel from the nave.

Ciborium: canopy over an altar.

Console (or **corbel** or **bracket**): element of stone or wood projecting from a wall to support beams or cornices.

Corbelling: projecting course of masonry.

Corbie gable: triangular section crowning a wall, with steps on the coping.

Cornice: in classical architecture, projecting ornamental moulding along the top of a building. Also designates any projecting decoration around a ceiling.

Cross (church plan): churches are usually built either in the plan of a Greek cross, with arms of equal length, or a Latin cross, with shorter transept arms.

Crossing: central area of a cruciform church, where the transept crosses the nave and choir. A tower is often set above this space.

Crypt: underground chamber beneath a church, where holy relics were placed. Often a chapel or church in its own right.

Diagonal arch: diagonal arch supporting a vault.

Drum: circular or polygonal structure supporting a dome.

Embrasure: recess for a window or door, splayed on the inside.

Entablature: in classical architecture, the section above the columns consisting of architrave, frieze and cornice.

Gable: decorative, triangular section above a portal.

Gallery: in early Christian churches, an upper story opening on the nave. Later used in exterior decoration.

Grotesque: fanciful ornamental decoration inspired by decorative motifs from Antiquity. The term comes from the old Italian word *grotte*, the name given to the Roman ruins of the *Domus Aurea*, uncovered in the Renaissance period.

Hall-church: church in which the nave and aisles are of equal height and practically the same width, communicating right to the top.

High relief: sculpture with very pronounced relief, although not standing out from the background (half-way between low relief and in-the-round figures).

Jamb or **pier**: pillar flanking an opening (doorway, window etc) and supporting the lintel above.

Keystone: wedge-shaped stone at the crown of an arch.

Lantern: turret with windows on top of a dome.

Lesene: slightly projecting pilaster used for decoration.

Lintel: horizontal beam connecting pilasters or columns and constituting the lower part of the entablature (in classical buildings such as temples).

Lombard strips: Romanesque decoration consisting of vertical bands in slight relief or lesenes joined at the top by an arched frieze.

Low relief: bas-relief, carved figures slightly projecting from their background.

Misericord or **miserere**: bracket on the underside of a hinged choir stall used for support by canons or monks.

Modillion: small console supporting a cornice, beginning of an arch etc.

Moulding: ornamental shaped band which projects from the wall.

Mullion window: window with two arches divided by a central post.

Narthex: portico preceding the nave of a church.

Nave: central main body of a church, flanked by aisles.

Oriel window: window projecting from a wall on corbels.

Ovolo moulding: egg-shaped ornamentation.

Pediment: usually triangular ornament above buildings, doors, windows, recesses.

Pendentive: triangular section of vaulting rising from the angle of two walls enabling the transition from a square space to an octagonal or circular dome.

Polyptych: painted or carved work consisting of more than three folding leaves or panels.

Predella: base of a polyptych or altarpiece.

Pulpit (or **ambo**): elevated stand in various locations from which sermons were preached in a church.

Retable or **altarpiece**: vertical structure, either painted or carved, above or set back from the altar. Monumental altarpieces are often found in Baroque churches.

Rib: projecting band on the surface of a dome or vault that disperses the weight onto the structures below.

Rococo: type of decoration in the late Baroque period typified by abstract combinations of shells and volutes.

Rose window: circular window usually inserted into the front elevation of a church, decorated with delicate fan-shaped stone tracery (small columns, volutes, patterns).

Spandrel: triangular space between the curve of an arch and the frame in which it is set.

Squinch: arches placed diagonally across the internal corner angles of a square tower, converting the square into an octagonal form, thus enabling it to support a drum.

Stalls: wooden seats reserved for the clergy, grouped together in the chancel.

String course: ornamental, horizontal band on an exterior wall marking the division between storeys.

Stucco: form of plaster widely used from the Renaissance period for decoration in relief on walls and ceilings.

Transept: transverse arms set at right angles to the nave and giving the church a cruciform shape.

Tribune: upper platform in a church, overlooking the interior.

Triforium: in a Gothic church, a wall-passage above the aisles, opening on the nave, often via a blind arcade.

Triptych: work comprising three painted or carved panels, whose outer sections can be folded over the central section.

Tympanum: in buildings, doors and windows, the triangular section between the horizontal entablature and the sloping sides of the pediment.

D. Scherf/MICHELIN

Mainz Cathedral

Vault: arched structure forming a roof or ceiling.

Westwerk or **westwork**: the west end of a church containing a second chancel. A massive structure, often flanked by two stair turrets, typical of Carolingian and Ottonian architecture, sometimes reserved for the emperor.

Architecture

Germany's geographical location and history have left it open to the influence of artistic currents from the rest of Europe – mainly French in the Gothic period and Italian in the Renaissance period. Each style has been interpreted and adapted according to regional tastes. This inventiveness has allowed Germany to develop an originality that is reflected in the sumptuous decoration of the Baroque abbeys in Bavaria and in the Expressionism of the interwar years.

ROMANESQUE ARCHITECTURE

Carolingian Architecture (9C and early 10C)

Under the impetus of the emperor and the great prelates, a large number of religious buildings were built in Germany on a basilical or central plan (Palatine chapel at Aachen), both inherited from Antiquity. Carolingian architecture is marked by the building of churches with two chancels: at the west end, a particular form emerged, the **Westwerk**, a tall square structure attached to the nave and often flanked by two towers, like at Corvey, for instance. The Westwerk constitutes almost a church in itself, where the emperor may have worshipped and where a special liturgy developed. It had a long-lasting effect on German Romanesque architecture.

Ottonian Architecture (10C and early 11C)

The restoration of Imperial power by Otto I in 962 was accompanied by a revival of religious architecture in Saxony and in the regions of the Meuse and Lower Rhine. The huge churches of this period, characterised by deeply projecting transepts and wide aisles, feature wooden roofs that were usually painted. The alternation of piers and columns broke up the uniformity of the central portion, and east and west choirs were linked by the nave, with a skilful use of proportion giving a harmonious effect. The churches of St Michaelis at Hildesheim and St Cyriacus at Gernrode date back to this period.

Rhineland Romanesque Style

At Cologne and in the surrounding countryside, several churches feature a distinctive ground plan with a triple apse designed in the form of a cloverleaf, a style dating back to the 11C. A fine example can be seen at the church of St Maria im Kapitol in Cologne. These trefoil extensions are adorned on the outside with blind arcades and a "dwarf gallery" (Zwerggalerie) – a motif of Lombard origin.

In the Middle Rhine region, the style achieves its full splendour in the majestic "Imperial" cathedrals of Speyer (the first church to be entirely vaulted), Mainz and Worms. Typical of these cathedrals are floor plans with a double chancel and no ambulatory, but sometimes a double transept. The exterior features numerous towers, blind arcades and Lombard bands. A characteristic of these Rhineland towers is a pointed roof in the form of a bishop's mitre, the base decorated with a lozenge pattern.

The churches of Limburg and Andernach and the cathedral at Naumburg, which were built early in the 13C, mark the transition between two periods. They are built in a style which combines Romanesque aesthetics and Gothic structures, with pointed rib vaulting and triforia.

GOTHIC ARCHITECTURE

The gradual emergence of the Gothic style (13C)

The French style of Gothic architecture, which attempted to free itself of Romanesque austerity, did not flourish in Germany until the mid 13C. Architecture then reached new heights of refinement,

producing such masterpieces as the cathedral in Cologne with its vast interior, two tall slender towers framing the façade in the French style and its soaring pointed vaulting. Also inspired by the French Gothic style are the cathedrals of Regensburg, Freiburg im Breisgau, Magdeburg and Halberstadt. A further manifestation of the predominance of French architecture can be seen in the establishment of Cistercian monasteries between 1150 and 1250. Their churches, usually without towers or belfries and often later modified in the Baroque manner, were habitually designed with squared-off chancels flanked by rectangular chapels. The abbey of Maulbronn is one of very few Cistercian complexes preserved in almost its entirety still extant in Europe.

The originality of German architecture

The German imprint first emerged in the use of brick. In the north of the country the most imposing edifices were brick, complete with buttresses and flying buttresses. Typical of this brick Gothic style (known in German as Backsteingotik) are the Nikolaikirche at Stralsund, the Marienkirche in Lübeck, the town halls of those two cities, Schwerin Cathedral and the abbey church at Bad Doberan. Also unique to Gothic German architecture is the adoption of a new layout inspired by Cistercian architecture and manifested in the **hall-churches** (Hallenkirche). In these buildings, the aisles are now the same height as the nave, which therefore has no clerestory windows, and separated from it only by tall columns. In the Elisabethkirche in Marburg, the three aisles are separated by thin supports, giving an impression of space and homogeneity.

Late Gothic Architecture
(Spätgotik)

The lengthy Late Gothic period (14C, 15C and 16C) witnessed the widespread construction of hall-churches, including Freiburg cathedral, the Frauenkirche in Munich and the Georgskirche, Dinkelsbühl. The vaulting features purely decorative ribs forming networks in the shape of stars or flowers in stark

Zwiefalten Church

M. Hertlen/MICHELIN

contrast to the austerity of the walls. St Annenkirche at Annaberg-Buchholz epitomises this artistic virtuosity, free of all constraints. **Secular Architecture in the Late Middle Ages** – Commercial prosperity among merchants and skilled craftsmen in the 14C and 15C led to the construction in town centres of impressive town halls and beautiful gabled and half-timbered private houses, frequently adorned with painting and sculpture. Examples of such architecture are still to be seen in the old town centres of Regensburg, Rothenburg ob der Tauber, Goslar and Tübingen.

THE RENAISSANCE

The Renaissance (1520-1620) is no more than a minor episode in the history of German architecture. Long held at bay by the persistence of the Gothic style, it was finally eclipsed by the troubles of the Reformation. Renaissance-style buildings are therefore rare in German towns. Augsburg is the lone exception. Its beautiful mansions lining Maximilian-staße and its town hall were designed by **Elias Holl** (1573-1646), Germany's most important Renaissance builder.

Southern Germany shows a marked Italian influence: elegant Florentine arcading was used by Jakob Fugger the Rich as decoration for his funerary chapel at Augsburg (1518); the Jesuits, building the Michaelskirche in Munich

(1589), were clearly inspired by their own Sanctuary of Jesus (Gesù) in Rome; and in Cologne, the town hall with its two-tier portico reflects Venetian influence.

Northern Germany, on the other hand, was influenced by Flemish and Dutch design. In the rich merchants' quarters, many-storeyed gables, such as those of the Gewandhaus in Brunswick, boast rich ornamentation in the form of obelisks, scrollwork, statues, pilasters etc. The castles at Güstrow and Heidelberg and the old town of Görlitz are important examples of Renaissance architecture, while the buildings of Wolfenbüttel, Celle, Bückeburg and Hameln are steeped in the particular charm of the so-called "Weser Renaissance" (*see HAMELN*).

THE SPLENDOURS OF BAROQUE ARCHITECTURE

After the disruption of the Thirty Years' War (1618-48), the ensuing revival of artistic activity provided an opportunity for the principalities to introduce Baroque architecture by welcoming French and Italian architects. Characterised by an irregularity of contour and a multiplicity of form, the Baroque style seeks, above all, the effect of movement and contrast. Taken to its extreme, it was soon saturated by Rococo decoration, which originated in the French *Rocaille* style; this style was originally secular and courtly but subsequently used in religious buildings.

From the mid 17C, Baroque influence was felt in southern Germany, encouraged by the Counter-Reformation's exaltation of dogmatic belief in Transubstantiation, the cult of the Virgin Mary and the saints, and in general all manifestations of popular piety. The aim was to achieve an emotional response from the spectator. This exuberance did not spread to Protestant Northern Germany.

The Masters of German and Danubian Baroque

There were exceptionally talented individuals in Bavaria who displayed equal skill across a variety of techniques, and who tended to prefer subtle ground plans, such as a round or elliptical focal shape. **Johann Michael Fischer** (Dießen, Zwiefalten and Ottobeuren), the **Asam brothers** (Weltenburg and the Asamkirche in Munich) and **Dominikus Zimmermann** (1685-1766, Steinhausen and Wies) were the virtuosi of this Bavarian School; their vibrant creations are covered by a profusion of Rococo decoration.

The Baroque movement in Franconia, patronised by the prince-bishops of the Schönborn family, who owned residences in Mainz, Würzburg, Speyer and Bamberg, was closely linked with the spread of similar ideas in Bohemia. The Dientzenhofer brothers decorated the palaces in Prague as well as the one in Bamberg. Perhaps the greatest of all Baroque architects was **Balthasar Neumann** (1687-1753), who worked for the same prelates, and whose breadth of cultural knowledge and creativity, enriched by his contact with French, Viennese and Italian masters, far surpassed that of his contemporaries. One of his finest creations was the Vierzehnheiligen Church near Bamberg, where he managed to combine the basilical plan with the ideal of the central plan. In Saxony, the Zwinger Palace in Dresden – joint masterpiece of the architect **Matthäus Daniel Pöppelmann** (1662-1736) and the sculptor Permoser – is a consummate example of German Baroque with Italian roots. The refinement of the Rococo decor in Schloss Sanssouci at Potsdam is even more astonishing given the reputed Prussian tendency towards austerity, but is explained by the periods of study undertaken in France and Italy by **Georg Wenzeslaus von Knobelsdorff** (1699-1753), official architect and friend of Frederick the Great.

Churches

A sinuous movement, generally convex in line, animates the façades, while the superposition of two pediments, different in design, adds vitality to the whole. They are additionally adorned with twin domed towers. Inside, huge galleries stand above the lateral chapels, at the height of pilaster capitals with jutting abaci. Chapels and galleries stop at the level of the transept, giving it a much greater depth. Clerestory windows at gallery level allow plenty of light to enter.

Bohemian and Franconian Baroque is typified by **complex vaulting**, round or oval bays being covered by complicated structures in which the transverse arches bow out in horse-shoe shape, only to meet in their keystones.

Illusion is the keyword as regards the often **Rococo** decoration, using the effects of the white stucco, coloured marble and gilding. The numerous paintings and sculptures enhance this celebration of the sacred.

The monumental altarpiece or reredos

Reminiscent of a triumphal arch, in carved wood or stucco, the reredos became the focal point of the church, framing a large painting and/or statuary (Ottobeuren Abbey Church). Columns twisted into spiral form accentuate the sense of movement which characterises Baroque art, and back lighting from a hidden source, with its striking contrasts of brightness and shadow, is equally typical of the style.

Palaces

The one-storey construction of these country residences was often lent additional importance by being built on a raised foundation. The focal point was a half-circular central bloc with the curved façade facing the garden.

Monumental stairways with several flights and considerable theatrical effect are often the centrepieces of the larger German castles and palaces built in the 18C. The staircase, embellished with arcaded galleries and a painted ceiling, leads to the first floor state room which rises majestically to a height of two storeys. Such elaborate arrangements characterise many of the great abbeys of this period, often complemented by that other ceremonial room, the library.

FROM NEO-CLASSICISM TO NEO-GOTHIC

The ideal of an original austerity

From 1750 on, Winckelmann's work on the art of Antiquity, and the excavations taking place at Pompeii, threw a new light on Greco-Roman architecture. At the same time, the example of Versailles inspired in Germany a new style of court life, particularly in the Rhineland and the Berlin of Frederick II. Many French architects were employed by the Electors of the Palatinate, of Mainz, of Trier and of Cologne; mainly, they produced plans for country mansions with names such as Monrepos ("my rest") or Solitude. Other German architects, such as **Carl Gotthard Langhans** (1732-1808), were instrumental in the transition from the Baroque to the neo-Classical style (Brandenburg Gate and the Charlottenburg theatre in Berlin).

Features such as unadorned pediments, balustrades at the base of the roofs, columned porticoes at the main entrance, all indicate a desire for unobtrusive elegance. A new fashion arose, in which architects favoured the Doric style coupled with a preference for the colossal – pilasters and columns of a single "order" no longer stood one storey high but always two.

The interior decoration, carried out with a lighter touch, confined itself to cornucopias of flowers mingled with Rococo motifs that were now a little more discreet (garlands, urns, vases and friezes of pearls).

Architecture was now responding to a demand for rationality that had emerged in reaction to the Late Baroque and Rococo styles.

Karl-Friedrich Schinkel (1781-1841)

Appointed state architect by Frederick William III in 1815, he designed many buildings, including the Neue Wache, Altes Museum and Schauspielhaus in Berlin. In a refined approach using elements inspired by Antiquity, this great exponent of Romantic Classicism constantly sought to blend his constructions in with their surroundings. The grandiose style of his buildings with their long neo-Classical colonnades, the dramatic contrasts of light and the use of Gothic elements are typical of the Romantic trend.

The 19C and the neo-Gothic

19C architecture was characterised by a great diversity of styles. By 1830, the neo-Classical movement had become sterile; it was superseded, except in Munich, by a renewed interest in the Gothic, emblematic for the Romantics of "the old Germany".

At the same time, the **Biedermeier** style – lightweight, cushioned furniture with flowing lines, glass-fronted cabinets for the display of knick-knacks – corresponding perhaps with the later Edwardian style in England, was popular in middle-class homes between 1815 and 1848.

1850 marks the beginning of the **Founders' Period** *(Gründerzeitstil)* with E. Ludwig and A. Koch pursuing an up-to-date style. But the wealthy industrialists fell for pretentious medieval or Renaissance reproductions, also to be found in public buildings such as the Reichstag in Berlin.

20C MOVEMENTS

In the late 19C, artists began exploring new avenues in a desire to move away from past styles and into the modern age. **Art nouveau** or **Jugendstil**, a European movement, became the vogue in Germany. The architects' idea was to create a complete work of art accessible to all, combining structure, decoration and furniture. This ideal, based on cooperation with industry, its methods of production and the use of its newest building materials (glass, iron, cement), resulted in the fundamental concept of an industrial aesthetic, brought to the fore by such pioneers as Peter Behrens, **Ludwig Mies van der Rohe** and **Walter Gropius**.

This style flourished mainly in Munich, Berlin and Darmstadt (with the Mathildenhöhe artists' colony). The artists' commitment, expressed within the Secessions (Munich 1892, Berlin 1899), was coupled with a political demand for independence.

The Bauhaus

In 1919, Walter Gropius founded the **Bauhaus** (Weimar: 1919-25, Dessau: 1926-32), a school of architecture and applied arts which radicalised the movement for modernisation, displaying an even greater interest in industrial production. The quest for unity between art and technique was a fundamental element. Architecture remained, in principle at least, the preferred form of expression since it combined structure and decoration and enabled application of the principles of functionality and rationality (& see DESSAU and WEIMAR). The movement instigated modern reflections on architecture and habitat and lent its vocabulary to modern design.

The school, which was critical of society, was closed in 1933 by the Nazis, who adopted a pompous and monumental style of architecture intended to reflect their power. It was, in most cases, to be destroyed.

At the end of the war, the reconstruction effort inspired a wide variety of architectural creations. Architects such as Dominikus Böhm and Rudolf Schwartz were among the craftsmen who were brought to light by this renewal of interest in sacred work, many of their designs being markedly austere.

New concepts, too, characterised the construction of municipal and cultural enterprises such as Hans Scharoun's Philharmonia in Berlin and the Staatsgalerie in Stuttgart by British architect James Stirling – buildings of an architectural audacity only made possible by the development of entirely new materials and construction techniques. Architectural creation is still very much alive in Germany today, particularly in Berlin with centres such as Friedrichstrasse or Potsdamer Platz – showcases of the avant-garde – and creations such as the Jüdisches Museum, completed by Daniel Liebeskind in 1998.

Art

GERMANY'S GREAT PAINTERS AND SCULPTORS

15C

In the fields of painting and architecture, Germany remained for a long time attached to the Late Gothic tradition, which denied the realism so sought after in Italy. The country was divided into a large number of local schools under Dutch influence. Now came the time to seek an outlet for emotional expression and give vent to the religious concerns that marked the end of the Middle Ages.

Stefan Lochner (c 1410-51)

This leading master of the Cologne School perpetuated the tradition of international Gothic, giving it a lyrical and refined touch with his sweet expressions and an exquisitely delicate palette. The use of gold backgrounds afforded him a certain amount of leeway as regards the requirements of perspective. (*Adoration of the Magi*, Cologne cathedral; *Virgin and Rose Bush*, Wallraf-Richartz-Museum, Cologne).

© Wallraf-Richartz-Museum, Cologne

Mary Magdalene by Cranach

Veit Stoß (c 1445-1533)

Sculptor, painter and engraver with a distinctive, powerful style; one of the greatest woodcarvers of his age. His figures were generally of a pathetic nature (*Annunciation*, Lorenzkirche, Nuremberg; *Reredos of the Nativity*, Bamberg Cathedral).

Tilman Riemenschneider (c 1460-1531)

Sculptor of alabaster and wood, he was master of an important studio where he created many altarpieces. His intricate works are executed with great finesse and richness of expression (*Tomb of Henry II the Saint*, Bamberg Cathedral; *Adam and Eve*, Mainfränkisches Museum, Würzburg; *Altarpiece to the Virgin*, Herrgottskirche, Creglingen).

The Master of St Severinus (late 15C)

The intimacy and iridescent colours of his works reflect Netherlandish influence (*Christ before Pilate*, Wallraf-Richartz-Museum, Cologne).

© Wallraf-Richartz-Museum, Cologne

The Fife Player and The Tambourine Player by Dürer

The Master of the Life of the Virgin (late 15C)

Painter of original works, influenced by the Flemish artist Van der Weyden (*Scenes from the Life of the Virgin*, Alte Pinakothek, Munich; *Vision of St Bernard*, Wallraf-Richartz-Museum, Cologne).

Engraving

First emerging in Germany around 1400, engraving was espoused by the greatest German masters. One pioneer was the unidentified engraver **Master E.S.**, known by the monogram with which he signed his engravings, whose work dates from between 1450 and 1467. Copperplate engraving techniques were later perfected and best demonstrated by virtuosi such as **Martin Schongauer** (c 1450-91), whose designs were later followed by Albrecht Dürer.

16C

The German Renaissance did not emerge until the 16C with Dürer. The observation and idealising of nature resulted in works of increasing refinement. The Danube School showed a new interest in landscape, encouraging its development as a genre, while Holbein breathed new life into the art of portrait painting with his striking realism.

Matthias Grünewald (c 1480-1528)

An inspired painter of the Late Gothic period, producing works of great emotional intensity capable of expressing the pain of humanity (*Crucifixion*, Staatliche Kunsthalle, Karlsruhe; *Virgin and Child*, Stuppach parish church).

Albrecht Dürer (1471-1528)

The greatest artist of the German Renaissance, he was fascinated by the art of Antiquity and the Italian Renaissance, with which he was able to lend Nordic gravity. Based in Nuremberg, Dürer produced woodcuts achieving some magnificent light effects and a broad range of greys (*The Apocalypse*). His religious scenes and portraits are of an extraordinary intensity (*The Four Apostles*, *Self-Portrait with Cloak*, Alte Pinakothek, Munich; *Charlemagne*, Germanisches Nationalmuseum, Nuremberg).

Lucas Cranach the Elder (1472-1553)

Official painter to the prince-electors of Saxony and master of an important studio, he was the portraitist of the most eminent men of the Reformation, most notably of his friend Luther. His works reflect a strong sense of the wonders of nature, allying him with the painters of the Danube School. As court painter in Wittenberg, he produced Lutheran-inspired religious paintings. The more Expressionist works of his youth gave way to paintings full of grace and nobility, typical of the refinement towards which 16C German art was heading. (*The Electors of Saxony*, Kunsthalle, Hamburg, *The Holy Family*, Städel museum, Frankfurt; *Portrait of Martin Luther*, Germanisches Nationalmuseum, Nuremberg).

Albrecht Altdorfer (c 1480-1538)

Leading member of the Danube School and one of the founders of landscape painting, his use of chiaroscuro creates dramatic and moving works, with the focus on landscapes shrouded in mystery (*Battle of Alexander*, Alte Pinakothek, Munich).

Hans Baldung Grien (c 1485-1545)

His complex compositions feature dramatic lighting effects, unusual colours and tortured movement (Altarpiece: *The Coronation of the Virgin*, Freiburg Cathedral).

Hans Holbein the Younger (1497-1543)

Painter of German merchants and subjects from court circles and the high aristocracy, he breathed new life into the art of portrait painting. His subjects are depicted with incredible precision in skilfully composed settings that illustrate their office. His compositions, both solemn and realistic, mark a definitive departure from the Gothic tradition (*Portrait of the Merchant Georg Gisze*, Museum Dahlem, Berlin).

17C and 18C

Italian influence remained evident during these two centuries. Court circles played host to many French and Italian

Atlantes in the Zwinger Palace, Dresden

R. Mattes/MICHELIN

artists who introduced an increasingly exuberant Baroque style.

Adam Elsheimer (1578-1610)

Elsheimer's often small scale mythological and biblical paintings reflect a combination of Italian influence and a concept of landscapes peculiar to Flemish and German painting. At the same time as Caravaggio, he experimented with the power of light in the evocation of nature, notably in his dramatic nocturnal landscapes (*The Flight into Egypt*, 1609, Alte Pinakothek, Munich).

Andreas Schlüter (c 1660-1714)

This master of Baroque sculpture in northern Germany and talented architect produced some very powerful works (*Statue of the Great Élector*, Schloss Charlottenburg, Berlin; *Masks of Dying Warriors*, Zeughaus, Berlin).

The Merians (17C)

A family of engravers specialising in plates illustrating German towns.

Balthasar Permoser (1651-1732)

Sculptor to the Court of Dresden, Permoser studied in Rome, Vienna and Venice. His masterful works reflect the exuberant style of the Italian Baroque, particularly at the Zwinger (*Wallpavillon* and *Nymphenbad*, Zwinger, Dresden).

Antoine Pesne (1683-1757)

This French-born painter in the service of the Prussian court became the portraitist of Frederick II, who admired his colouristic talent. He produced a great number of portraits and some mythological ceiling paintings and murals (*Portrait of Frederick II and his sister Wilhelmina,* apartments of Schloss Charlottenburg, Berlin).

Joseph Anton Feuchtmayer (1696-1770) and Johann Michael II Feichtmayr (1709-72)

These members of a family of German painters and sculptors helped to perpetuate the Rococo style with their fanciful compositions (decoration of the abbey churches of Ottobeuren and St Gall).

Matthäus Günther (1705-88)

A pupil of CD Asam, master of Rococo painting in southern Germany, Günther is famous for his decoration of many churches in Swabia and Bavaria (Amorbach, Rott am Inn).

19C

The 19C was first of all dominated by the **Biedermeier style** (1815-48) which glorified middle-class values and way of life, as perfectly illustrated by the genre painting of GF Kersting. Then came the time for rebellion. Romanticism called the classical values into question, launching a dialogue between reason and feeling. Realism and Impressionism, which both originated in France, allowed German artists to express certain budding socialist ideas. All of these various forms of artistic expression came in response to the moral crisis of modern Europe.

Caspar David Friedrich (1774-1840)

German Romantic painter whose landscapes were represented as manifestations of the divine and places of wonderment ideal for meditation (*The Monk by the Sea, The Cross on the Mountain, Alte Nationalgalerie,* Berlin; *Rambler Above a Sea of Clouds,* Kunsthalle, Hamburg).

Friedrich Overbeck (1789-1869)

Member of the Lucas Brotherhood, he was the most important member of the group of **Nazarenes** who occupied the abandoned monastery of San Isidoro in Rome in 1810. Advocating a form of painting that glorified moral values in a reaction against neo-Classicism, they revived medieval art and sought the purity of the early Italian and Flemish masters of the 15C. (*Italia and Germania,* Neue Pinakothek, Munich).

Adolf von Menzel (1815-1905)

Representative of German Realism, initially illustrating anecdotal themes and later producing powerful portrayals of the industrial world, tempered by the influence of Impressionism (*Rolling Mill,* Nationalgalerie in Berlin).

Wilhelm Leibl (1844-1900)

Master of German Realism, he was influenced by Courbet and mostly painted scenes of village life (*Three Women in Church,* Kunsthalle, Hamburg; portrait of *Mina Gedon,* Neue Pinakothek, Munich).

Adolf von Hildebrand (1847-1921)

German sculptor based in Munich, whose measured taste in monumental sculpture, inspired by the most austere Greek style, was in contrast to the excesses of most 19C artists. (*Wittelsbach Fountain,* Munich).

Max Liebermann (1847-1935)

Greatly influenced by French Realism and Naturalism, he painted the universe of peasants and workers in all its harsh reality. Later, under the influence of Impressionism, he allowed light to suffuse his already rich palette. He led the Berlin "Sezession" movement in 1899, advocating freedom and realism as opposed to the patriotic insipidness of the court painters (*Jewish Street in Amsterdam,* Wallraf-Richartz-Museum, Cologne).

20C

The Expressionism which marked the beginning of the century gave way to a new form of revolt and glorification of subjective feeling. The shock of the First World War and the ensuing social crisis plunged art into a period of darkness and disillusionment. Political and social

Bayerische Staatsgemäldesammlung, Collection d'Art moderne de la Pinakothek der Moderne Múnich

Kämpfende Formen by Franz Marc

dissent were embodied in a succession of new avant-garde movements. More than ever before, art was driven by a desire to change society and expose its failings.

Expressionism

German Expressionism introduced an emotionally charged, often violent or tragic vision of the world to modern painting. The movement owed much to Van Gogh and the Norwegian painter Edvard Munch (1863-1944), whose work had a marked influence in Germany. In Dresden and then in Berlin, the **Brücke (Bridge) Group** united from 1905 to 1913 such painters as Erich Heckel, Ernst Ludwig Kirchner and Karl Schmidt-Rottluff, whose work, with its use of pure colour, recalls that of the Fauves in France. See the works of **Emil Nolde** (1867-1956) at Seebüll, and of Expressionism in general at the Brücke-Museum, Berlin.

Der Blaue Reiter (The Blue Rider Movement)

Association of artists founded in Munich in 1911 by **Wassily Kandinsky** and **Franz Marc**, later to be joined by **August Macke** and **Paul Klee**. Although the work of the artists involved differed widely, they were united by a general aim to free art from the constraints of reality, using bold colours and untraditional forms, thus opening the way to abstraction (*Deer in the Forest* by **Franz Marc**, Orangerie Staatliche Kunsthalle, Karlsruhe; *The Dress Shop* by **August Macke**, Folkwang-Museum, Essen). The movement broke up during the war.

The Bauhaus

This movement, which united all art forms, attracted a host of avant-garde painters and sculptors including Klee and Kandinsky, Oskar Schlemmer, Laszlo Moholy-Nagy, **Lyonel Feininger** and **Joseph Albers**.

Neue Sachlichkeit (New Objectivity)

An artistic movement affecting all the arts which grew up in the early 1920s, aiming to produce a realistic illustration of social facts and phenomena. It corresponds to the harshness of the post-war period. Pioneers of this movement were **Otto Dix** and **George Grosz** (*War* by **Otto Dix**, 1932, Albertinum in Dresden). The Dada movement, present in Cologne and Berlin, and in Hannover with **Kurt Schwitters**, used art for political ends. On the sidelines of these movements, **Max Beckmann** (1884-1950), who was also deeply affected by the war and its consequences, shared his very bleak view of humanity.

Second half of the 20C

The Nazi regime brought an abrupt end to these artistic experiments labelled as "degenerate art", replacing them with a neo-Classical style glorifying race, war and family. This "Nazi art" died out at the end of the Reich in 1945.

Social Realism, an official art form which served the regime's ideology, was predominant in East German painting until the 1960s-70s. The painters of Leipzig in particular won international acclaim, among them Bernhard Heisig, Wolfgang Mattheuer, Willi Sitte and Werner Tübke. In East Germany in the years leading up to reunification, non-conformist artists were also given the opportunity to express themselves.

The 1960s saw a turning point in German artistic creativity. **Gruppe Zebra** took up the credo of New Objectivity against German Abstract art, while the members of **Gruppe Zero** (Heinz Mack, Otto Piene, Güntheb Uecker) concentrated on using kinetic art to transform thoughts into material objects. In the 1970s, **Joseph Beuys**, together with the artists of the school of **Constructivist Sculpture** in Düsseldorf, strove to create a direct relationship between the artist and the viewing public in his Happenings and Performances, and to redefine the role of art and the artist in contemporary society (**Neue Nationalgalerie** in Berlin; **Hessisches Landesmuseum** in Darmstadt; **Staatsgalerie** in Stuttgart).

From the 1980s, a new generation of German artists managed to break through onto the international scene with "new Fauves" *(Neue Wilde)* **Georg Baselitz** and **Markus Lüpertz** developing a new form of Expressionism, **Sigmar Polke**, closer to pop art, and **Anselm Kiefer**, with his focus firmly on German history.

Literature and Philosophy

German literature, from the reign of Charlemagne up to the present day, has demonstrated an enduring vitality, constantly breaking with tradition and inventing new forms of expression. In the wake of Goethe's monumental influence in the 18C, the best authors have been guaranteed international renown.

FROM THE MIDDLE AGES TO THE 17C

German literature in the Middle Ages was written in a great variety of dialects. Largely drawing on the oral tradition, it was characterised by lyrical poetry and genres that can be described – not in any pejorative way – as popular: plays, ballads, songs and epics. One of the earliest works, dating back to Charlemagne's reign, is the **Lay of Hildebrand** (820), of which only a 68-line fragment has survived. The national folk saga of the **Nibelungen**, an anonymous work from the late 12C, draws on the sources of Germanic mythology and celebrates the heroic spirit that faces up to trials and tribulations without ever giving up. One of the big names in courtly epics was **Wolfram von Eschenbach;** his poem *Parzifal* (c 1200), which **recounts the** quest for the Holy Grail, revolves around religious and chivalrous themes. The 14C was an age of mystic literature, with writers such as **Meister Eckhart**. In a departure from the dryness of scholastic teaching, he sometimes forsakes Latin to discuss religious topics in powerful and eloquent German.

Satire took centre stage in the 16C (*The Ship of Fools* by **Sebastian Brant** appeared in 1494) along with folk songs and the poetry of the Meistersingers. **Hans Sachs** (1494-1576), a poet-cum-cobbler from Nuremberg, was a prominent figure in the latter genre, which provides the theme of Wagner's opera *Tannhäuser*. **Luther**'s contribution during this period also marked a turning point; his hymns and translation of the Bible (1534) paved the way for the writing of literary works in a common, modern German language. The late 16C witnessed the publication of the *Faust Book* (1587) by **Johann Spies**, a work of remarkable depth which draws the captivating portrait of a man driven by an unquenchable thirst for knowledge which distances him from God.

The ravages of the Thirty Years' War (1618-48) profoundly marked the collective psyche; 17C literature bears echoes of this traumatic time. Among the recurrent themes of these often edifying works is the vanity of human things and man's need to find God in order to ensure his salvation. *Adventurous Simplicissimus* (1669) by **Grimmelshausen** (1622-76) is a picaresque novel whose hero, having experienced the suffering of war, finally chooses a life of retreat and meditation.

Jakob and Wilhelm Grimm

J. P. Anders/Bildarchiv Preussischer Kulturbesitz

"AUFKLÄRUNG" (AGE OF ENLIGHTENMENT)

The 18C marked the beginning of the golden age of German literature, as its influence began to extend well beyond the German-speaking countries. The spotlight was now on philosophical and moral themes, the flourishes of language belying a pursuit of the natural. The influence of **Leibniz** (1646-1716), whose Theodicy in French and Latin uses rational arguments to justify evil and show that we live in "the best of all possible worlds", still remains strong. Rationalism, apparent in the works of **Christian Wolff** (1679-1754), coexisted with the tenacious survival of Pietism, which highlights the emotional experience in any religious phenomenon. This explains how **Lessing** (1729-81), in his writings on religion (*The Education of the Human Race*, 1780), strives to combine a rationalist deism with a belief in revelation. In the purely literary field, Lessing also set the principles of new German theatre by creating middle-class drama *(Emilia Galotti)*. His contemporary, **Immanuel Kant** (1724-1804), endeavoured to define the limits of what can be known; only that which is determined by pure forms of understanding can be the subject of rational

knowledge. Whatever eludes such determination (the soul, God etc) can, of course, be "thought" and give rise to "belief", but cannot be "known". In the practical field, Kantianism defines the balance between liberty and the "moral law" that governs every rational being: man finds liberty by submitting to the "categorical imperative" and renouncing the influence of his "sensitivity".

"STURM UND DRANG" AND CLASSICISM

In reaction to the strict rationalism of the Aufklärung, the **Sturm und Drang** (Storm and Stress) movement, encompassing authors such as **Herder** (1744-1803) and **Hamann** (1730-88), exalts freedom, emotion and nature. Poetry, "the mother tongue of the human race", takes pride of place and the past is revisited, with particular emphasis placed on folk songs. The works of the young **Goethe** (1749-1832), such as *The Sorrows of Young Werther*, bear witness to the influence of Sturm und Drang. However, Goethe – poet and universal genius – soon tempered this fashionable enthusiasm with a move towards the **classical humanist** tradition. As the leading light of German literature prior to the emergence of the Romantic trend, in which he never became involved, he penned a great number of works. Classical dramas (*Iphigenie auf*

Tauris, Egmont, and *Torquato Tasso*), novels (*Elective Affinities, Wilhelm Meister's Apprenticeship*) and *Faust (Parts I and II,* 1808 and 1832) contain the quintessence of Goethe's philosophy. After settling in Weimar in 1775, Goethe was joined by Herder, **Wieland** and **Schiller** (1759-1805). The historical dramas of the latter, a poet and dramatist of genius, are undisguised hymns to liberty (*Don Carlos, Wallenstein, Wilhelm Tell*).

Two major literary figures emerged during the transitional period between Weimarian Classicism and actual Romanticism: **Hölderlin** (1770-1843), a tragic, lyric author (*Hyperion, The Death of Empedocles*) with a passion for Ancient Greek civilisation, produced some powerful odes before sinking into madness at the age of 36. The novelist Johann Paul Friedrich Richter (1763-1825), better known as **Jean Paul**, had a creative imagination although a somewhat laboured style.

19C: BETWEEN ROMANTICISM AND REALISM

The **Romantic movement** charts the individual soul's quest for the infinite in all its forms. Besides literature, it incorporates the fine arts, philosophy, politics and religion. First Jena, then Heidelberg and Berlin were centres from which the movement blossomed. After initially being theorised by the **Schlegel brothers**, the Romantic doctrine was put into powerful poetic form by **Novalis** (1772-1801); a poet and mystic, Novalis exalts the art and religion of the Middle Ages and his "Blue Flower" symbol comes to represent the Absolute, or object of Romantic longing (*Heinrich von Ofterdingen*). While in the process of theoretical elaboration, budding Romanticism was exposed to the influence of post-Kantian idealist philosophers, in particular **Fichte** (1762-1814), **Schelling** (1775-1854) and **Hegel** (1770-1831). It also reflects a heightened interest in popular literature, often seeking inspiration in the sources of myths and legends, as can be seen in the tales of the **Brothers Grimm** (1812) or the more disturbing tales of **Hoffmann** (1776-1822). On the sidelines of the Romantic movement, the playwright **Heinrich von Kleist**, who tragically committed suicide in 1811, wrote some remarkable plays, notably *The Prince of Homburg* (1810), a play about a man of action led away by his dreams.

The exuberant idealism of Romanticism was succeeded by a search for greater realism. An outstanding figure and "defrocked Romantic" poet of the *Loreley*, **Heinrich Heine** (1797-1856), treats the naivety of his age with bitter irony and enthuses about St Simonian ideals. **Hebbel** (1813-63), a fine psychologist, wrote plays often inspired by biblical or mythical subjects, focusing on conflict between the individual and the existing moral order (*Judith, Herodes und Mariamne, Agnes Bernauer*). Toward the mid 19C, a number of writers sought to bring literature closer to life and everyday experience; novelists such as **Stifter** (1805-68) and **Keller** (1819-90) were among the main exponents of this "Realist" trend. Some of them, such as **Fontane** (1819-98) and **Raabe** (1831-1910), focus on the social and political conditions of human existence. Social drama is brilliantly illustrated by **Hauptmann** (1862-1946), a prolific author whose Naturalist writing is at times allegorical and symbolic, drawing inspiration from legend and mythology (*The Atrides Cycle*).

In the field of philosophy, **Schopenhauer** (1788-1860), pessimistic theorist of the will to live, describes the will as reality's true inner nature, and this will as suffering (*The World as Will and Idea*, 1819); he had a crucial influence on the thinking of authors such as Nietzsche, Freud and Wittgenstein. Political thought, moreover, took a new direction with **Karl Marx** (*The Communist Manifesto* was published in 1848); rejecting Hegelian idealism, Marx, who was both a philosopher and an economist, developed the theory of "historical materialism", a powerful conceptual tool enabling the analysis of human societies according to their historical development. Together with **Engels**, Marx cofounded "scientific socialism", in opposition to so-called "utopian"

Ernst Jünger in 1949

socialism, and launched the modern international workers' movement.

THE MODERN PERIOD

Friedrich Nietzsche, who died in 1900, belongs as much to the history of philosophy as to the history of literature. His tremendous influence over the history of literature and western thought is still in evidence today. His fundamentally life-affirming philosophy called, with great lyricism, for mankind to surpass itself (*Thus Spoke Zarathustra*, 1886).

Focusing on the often irreconcilable duality of the mind and the senses, the irrational and the rational, the works of **Thomas Mann** (*Buddenbrooks*, *The Magic Mountain*) and **Hermann Hesse** (*Der Steppenwolf*) bear the stamp of Nietzscheism; the sanatorium in Davos in *The Magic Mountain* symbolises the "disease" that runs rife in decadent European societies. In this struggle between life and morbid instincts, the shadow of Thanatos hangs over our western civilisations. The Czech-born German language writer **Franz Kafka** (1883-1924) differs from these authors in both style and thought; his nightmarish novels (*The Trial*, *The Castle*, *America*) contain a vision of a dehumanised world dominated by anxiety and the absurd. The works of Vienna-born **Stefan Zweig**, one of Kafka's contemporaries, were of a less

tortured nature. This highly cultivated man, citizen of the world, traveller and translator proved in his best short stories (*Amok, Conflicts, The Royal Game*) to be a remarkable story teller with humanist sympathies.

The early 20C also witnessed a revival in poetry. **Stefan George** (1868-1933) published poems which, in their formal perfection, ally him with the French Symbolists, while the Austrians **Rainer Maria Rilke** (1875-1926) and **Hugo von Hoffmannsthal** (1874-1929) reach the peak of lyrical impressionism.

The 1930s and 40s were marked by an intensified search for the meaning of life; spurred on by Husserlian phenomenology, **Heidegger** and, to a lesser degree, **Jaspers**, put the question of being back at the heart of philosophy. Based on our essential finiteness, Heideggerian existentialism distinguishes between an existence marked by a sense of being and an "inauthentic" existence, led astray into the impersonal self.

The world of theatre was dominated by **Bertolt Brecht** (*The Threepenny Opera*, *Mother Courage*, *Galileo*). A committed socialist, he rejected the "theatre of illusion", advocating the alienation effect: the spectator must observe the action on stage with a critical eye and be able to decipher the methods by which the strong exploit the weak.

National Socialism forced numerous poets and writers into exile (Walter Benjamin, Alfred Döblin, Lion Feuchtwanger, Else Lasker-Schüler, Thomas and Heinrich Mann, Carl Zuckmayer, Stefan Zweig). **Gottfried Benn** (1886-1956) withdrew into silence, while **Ernst Jünger** (1895-1998) courageously published his novel *On the Marble Cliffs* in 1939: "...Such are the dungeons above which rise the proud castles of the tyrants... They are terrible noisome pits in which a God-forsaken crew revels to all eternity in the degradation of human dignity and human freedom."

POST-1945 LITERATURE

Twelve years under National Socialist rule had broken the flow of literary creation in Germany, necessitating repair work in this domain too. The association of authors known as **Gruppe 47** (after the year of its founding), which centred upon **Hans Werner Richter** and **Alfred Andersch**, was instrumental in putting Germany back onto the map as far as world literature was concerned. This loosely associated group of writers served as a forum for reading, discussion and criticism, until its last conference in 1967, exerting a lasting and formative influence on the contemporary German literary scene. Authors associated with Gruppe 47 included **Paul Celan**, **Heinrich Böll** (Nobel Prize winner in 1972), **Günter Grass** (Nobel Prize winner in 1999), **Siegfried Lenz**, **Peter Weiss** and **Hans Magnus Enzensberger**. By the end of the 1950s, works of international standing were being published: Günter Grass' masterpiece *The Tin Drum* is an extraordinary novel in the tradition of Celine; **Uwe Johnson**'s *Speculations about Jacob*, **Heinrich Böll**'s *Billiards at Half Past Nine* and **Martin Walser**'s novel *Marriages in Philippsburg*. Increasing politicisation was what finally put an end to Gruppe 47's activities. Authors not associated with Gruppe 47 were hard at work also; **Arno Schmidt** developed a very original and high-quality body of work, while **Wolfgang Koeppen** produced some wickedly satirical novels on contemporary society. The literature of the 1960s was characterised by a wave of criticism, but, by the following decade, German literary concerns were withdrawing to a newly discovered "inner contemplation". A particularly prolific amount of good writing was produced by women during the 1970s and 1980s (**Gabriele Wohmann**, **Karin Struck**, **Verena Stefan**).

In the world of theatre, dominated initially by the dramatic theory of Bertolt Brecht, a new band of writers began to emerge, with works by **Tankred Dorst** (*Toller*, 1968), **Peter Weiss** (*Hölderlin*, 1971) and **Heinar Kipphardt**. **Rolf Hochhuth** was particularly successful with his "documentary dramas" in which he examines contemporary moral issues (*The Representative*, 1963), and **Botho Strauß**, the most widely performed modern German dramatist, has won international acclaim with plays such as *The Hypochondriac* (1972), *The Park* (1983) and *Final Chorus* (1991).

The political division of Germany was also reflected in German literature. In the old East German Republic, the leadership viewed literature's *raison d'être* as the contribution it might make to the socialist programme for educating the masses. The Bitterfelder Weg, a combined propaganda exercise and literary experiment launched at the Bitterfeld chemical factory in 1959 as part of the East German Republic's cultural programme under Walter Ulbricht, was intended to unite art and everyday life and break down class barriers. Factory visits were organised for writers, so they could observe workers and then portray them glowingly in their novels, poems or plays, while the workers themselves were encouraged to write about their lives. The results of the project were mixed, and although it gave authors a clearer idea of the primitive conditions that most East German workers were obliged to tolerate, those who wrote too honestly about what they saw found their works censored. Poetry was the literary form least easily subject to Communist censorship, and poets such as **Peter Huchel**, **Johannes Bobrowski** and **Erich Arendt** produced some remarkable work. From the early 1960s the prose work of **Günter de Bruyn**, **Stefan Heym** (d 2001) and **Erwin Strittmatter** was widely appreciated. **Anna Seghers**, who returned from exile in America after the war, was considered the greatest East German writer of the older generation, while rising star **Christa Wolf** won acclaim in both Germanies. Important contributions to the theatre were made by playwrights **Ulrich Plenzdorf**, **Peter Hacks** and above all **Heiner Müller** (*The Hamlet Machine*, 1978).

Any overview of German-language literature since the Second World War must, of course, acknowledge the enormous contribution made by **Max Frisch** and **Friedrich Dürrenmatt**, of Switzerland, and **Ilse Aichinger**, **Ingeborg Bachmann** and **Thomas Bernhard** of Austria.

Music

Germany and the German-speaking world have made a considerable contribution to western music. After reaching an initial high point in the 18C with the Baroque period, German music was propelled back into the limelight by the genius of composers such as Beethoven and Wagner. Modern experimentation since the emergence of the twelve-tone system testifies to the continuing vitality of German music.

FROM MINNESINGERS TO MEISTERSINGERS

In the 12C and 13C, feudal courts constituted the main forum for musical expression. The **Minnesänger**, who were often noble knights, such as **Wolfram von Eschenbach** and **Walther von der Vogelweide**, drew inspiration for their songs from French lyric poetry. They would perform their love songs before the nobility, accompanying themselves on the lute.

The Meistersingers or Mastersingers of the 14C-16C preferred a more sedentary lifestyle and organised themselves into guilds. They introduced polyphony to German music and clearly set the musical forms of their art. Anyone wanting to become a Meistersinger had to prove himself in a public contest. Among the prominent figures of the time was **Heinrich von Meißen** (1250-1318) who marked the transition from Minnesang to the poetry of the Meistersingers. **Hans Sachs** (1494-1576), a cobbler by trade and an ardent supporter of Luther, was also a prolific poet; many of his compositions were turned into Protestant chorales. Sachs later became the subject of Wagner's opera *The Mastersingers of Nuremberg*.

FROM THE RENAISSANCE TO THE 17C

In the wake of the Reformation, German music began to develop an individual identity with the emergence of the chorale, the fruit of the collaboration between **Luther** and **Johann Walther** (1496-1570). *"Ein' feste Burg ist unser Gott"* (*A Mighty Fortress is Our God*) composed by the two men in 1529 was reworked by Bach. Originally a hymn with a simple melody, the chorale – sung in the vernacular – soon opened up to the secular repertoire, embracing popular genres of music. It subsequently gave rise to the German cantata and oratorio.

Religious music maestro, **Heinrich Schütz** (1585-1672) managed to produce a skilful combination of German and Italian elements. He composed the first German opera, *Dafne*, a work which was sadly lost. *The Seven Words of Christ* (1645) shows the influence of Monteverdi who, along with Gabrieli, was one of Schütz's masters.

The second half of the 17C witnessed a proliferation of organ schools, one of the most famous of which was in Nuremberg. An inspiration for Bach who is said to have walked hundreds of kilometres to hear him play in Lübeck, **Dietrich Buxtehude** (1637-1707) organised the first concerts of sacred music. **Johann Pachelbel** (1653-1706) was the great master of the organ school in southern Germany; the only surviving piece of his work is the *Canon in D Major*.

BACH AND BAROQUE MUSIC

His consummate skill as a composer, his genius for invention and his mastery of counterpoint enabled **Bach** (1685-1750) to excel in every kind of music he wrote. Based in Weimar until 1717, he spent several years at the court of Köthen, during which he composed *The Brandenburg Concertos*. In 1723, he was appointed "Cantor" at St Thomas' School, Leipzig. Bach's duties included the composition of a cantata for every Sunday service, as well as the supervision of services at four other churches. He also taught Latin and voice and still found time to write his own instrumental and vocal works. His masterpieces include *The Well-Tempered Clavier* (1722 and 1744) and the *St Matthew Passion* (1727).

A brilliant court composer, influenced by his travels in Italy, **Georg Friedrich Händel** (1665-1759) excelled in both

Munich Philharmonic Orchestra in concert

opera and oratorio (*The Messiah*, 1742). Born in Halle, he was organist at the town's cathedral before pursuing his career at the Hamburg opera. Based in England from 1714, he spent most of the last forty years of his life in London, and even obtained British nationality.

Händel's friend, **Georg Philipp Telemann**, (1681-1767) was influenced by French and Italian composers, and was himself a particularly prolific composer. He turned from counterpoint to harmony and composed chamber music and church music as well as operas. Telemann was godfather to Bach's second son, **Carl Philipp Emmanuel** (1714-88), who popularised the sonata in its classic form.

FROM THE MANNHEIM SCHOOL TO BEETHOVEN

In the mid 18C, the musicians of the **Mannheim School**, under the patronage of Elector Palatine Karl Theodor, helped establish the modern symphonic form, giving a more prominent role to wind instruments. Influenced by the innovations from Mannheim, **Christoph Willibald Gluck** (1714-87) undertook a "reformation of opera", producing refined works where the lyrics took pride of place; he provoked the enthusiasm of the innovators – and the horror of fans of traditional, Italian-inspired opera – by staging, in Paris, his *Iphigenia in Aulis* and *Orpheus*. This period was also marked by the appearance in Germany of the **Singspiel**, a popular opera in which dialogue is interspersed with songs in the form of Lieder. Mozart's *Magic Flute* (1791) and Beethoven's *Fidelio* (1814) are excellent examples of this genre later identified with operetta.

The contribution of Viennese Classicism during the second half of the 18C proved to be crucial. **Joseph Haydn** (1732-1809) laid down the classical form of the symphony, the string quartet and the piano sonata. **Wolfgang Amadeus Mozart** (1756-91) perfected these forms and created some truly immortal operas (*The Marriage of Figaro, Don Juan*).

Born in Bonn, **Ludwig van Beethoven** (1770-1827) went to Vienna to study under Haydn and Antonio Salieri. With his innovative harmonisations, he developed a highly individual style and transformed existing forms of music, heralding the Romantic movement. The depth of his inspiration, ranging from pure introspection to a wider belief in the force and universality of his art, emanates from his work with extraordinary power, perhaps most particularly in his symphonies. It was in 1824, when he had already been suffering from total and incurable deafness for five years, that Beethoven's magnificent *Ninth Symphony* – inspired by one of Schiller's odes – was performed for the first time.

ROMANTIC MUSIC AND WAGNER

Franz Schubert (1797-1826) brought Romantic music to its first high point. He focused much creative energy on the Lied (song), blending folk and classical music in a unique style.

Carl Maria von Weber (1786-1826), created Germany's first Romantic opera, *Freischütz* (1821), paving the way for the characters of Wagnerian drama. It was a resounding success when first performed in Berlin, due in part to the use of folk songs. As for the lofty world of **Felix Mendelssohn-Bartholdy** (1809-79), it was far removed from the forces of evil that inhabit the *Freischütz*. Although espousing classical music forms, Mendelssohn, who was a conductor, pianist and founder of the Leipzig Conservatory, also reveals a Romantic influence.

Robert Schumann (1810-56), passionate and lyrical in turn, but brought up in the Germanic tradition, strives to reconcile a classical heritage with personal expression. A talented music critic (he founded the *Neue Zeitschrift für Musik* newspaper in 1834), he initially wrote for piano alone (*Carnival, Scenes from Childhood*). Then, spurred on by his admiration for Schubert and the advice of his friend Mendelssohn, he began to compose Lieder *(Dichterliebe)*, subsequently turning his attention to symphonies and chamber music. A close friend of Schumann whose wife Clara he loved with a passion, **Johannes Brahms** (1833-97) exemplified a more introverted style of German Romanticism. After long being accused of formalism, he was rediscovered in the 20C, notably thanks to the influence of Schönberg (*Brahms the Progressive*). Crowning glory of the German Romantic movement, the work of **Wagner** (1813-83) revolutionised opera. Wagner claimed that music should be subservient to drama, serving as "atmosphere" and a "backdrop of sound" without which the opera's message could not be fully conveyed. Orchestration thus becomes of paramount importance. Libretto and plot unfold continuously, preserving dramatic reality. Wagner introduces the use of "leitmotifs" – musical phrases used recurrently to denote specific characters, moods or situations – making them essential to the continuity of the action. *Lohengrin* was first performed in 1850 in Weimar, under the supervision of **Franz Liszt**.

Designed by Wagner himself as a stage for the performance of the entire work (Gesamtkunstwerk), the Bayreuth Theatre was inaugurated in 1876 with *The Ring of the Nibelung (Rheingold, Walküre, Siegfried* and *Götterdämmerung*). The fruit of 22 years' work, the magnificent first public performance of *The Ring* lasted 18 hours. Although its artistic success was undeniable, the Bayreuth episode ended in financial ruin for the composer. *Parsifal*, Wagner's last opera, revolves around the theme of redemption through sacrifice, and was first performed in Bayreuth in 1882.

At the end of the 19C, **Gustav Mahler** (1860-1911), Czech-Austrian composer and creator of the symphonic Lied, and **Hugo Wolf** (1850-1903) developed a new musical language which forms a bridge between Romanticism and dodecaphony.

Richard Strauss (1864-1949) excelled in orchestra music (*Thus Spoke Zarathustra*), uniting a certain harmonic audacity with a dazzling and multifaceted style.

CONTEMPORARY MUSIC

Contemporary musical experimentation is derived principally from the Austrian school of atonal, or serial (especially 12-note systems) music, represented by **Arnold Schönberg** and his two main disciples **Alban Berg** and **Anton von Webern**. Introducing a new method of composing music, the twelve-tone system was first revealed to the public by Schönberg in 1928 in the *Variations for Orchestra*. Berg applied his master's innovation to lyrical drama *(Lulu)*, while Webern, turning his back on Romanticism, focused on the concision of form. The brilliant **Paul Hindemith** (1893-1963), initially influenced by Romanticism, remained untouched by Schönberg's innovations; in a break with German tradition, he forged a path of his own between atonality and dodecaphony.

Carl Orff (1895-1982), creator of the Orff Schulwerk, propounded innovative ideas about music education. His highly original theatrical compositions combine drama, speech and song in a fascinating rhythmic framework: his powerful collection of secular songs with infectious rhythms, *Carmina Burana* (1937), soon gained international renown. The compositions – mainly opera and ballet music – of **Werner Egk** (1901-83), a student of Carl Orff, reveal the influence of Igor Stravinski and Richard Strauss. As for **Kurt Weill** (1900-50), influenced at the beginning of his career by the atonal composers, he returned under the impact of jazz to tonal music, and composed *The Threepenny Opera* (1928) in collaboration with Brecht.

Although **Wolfgang Fortner** (1907-87) was influenced initially by Hindemith, he nonetheless later turned to modal 12-tone serial music. His mature works introduce electronic elements into his musical compositions.

Bernd Alois Zimmermann (1918-70) perceived past, present and future as one, and the multiple layers of reality are reflected in his composition technique. Quotations and collage were particularly important to him. His major work is the opera *The Soldiers*.

From 1950, a younger generation of musicians developed the potential of electronic music under the aegis of **Karlheinz Stockhausen** (b 1928). **Hans Werner Henze** (b 1926) created expressive operas, in which modernity and tradition, and atonality and tonality are combined. **Wolfgang Rihm** (b 1952), a student of Fortner, like Henze, also mixes traditional stylistic elements with new techniques in his extremely complex musical language.

Cinema

After producing a number of masterpieces during the Expressionist period of the 1920s, German cinema fell into a decline from which it did not emerge until the 1960s. Although now struggling to make its mark in the face of the American productions, it has managed to produce some remarkable international award-winning works.

THE GOLDEN AGE OF EXPRESSIONISM

The creation in 1917 of UFA (Universum Film Aktiengesellschaft), a production company of considerable means which, from 1921, was directed by producer **Erich Pommer**, led to some lavish productions. The Expressionism that was apparent in literature, theatre and painting also seeped into film production in the troubled post-war political and social scene. Deliberately turning its back on Realism, it often revelled in angst-ridden atmospheres, cultivating an exaggeration of forms and contrasts; it was typified by the use of chiaroscuro lighting effects and the geometric stylisation of the decor. Very few works could actually be classed as purely Expressionist, but among them is **Robert Wiene**'s masterpiece *The Cabinet of Dr Caligari* (1919), which was well-received in the United States and France. Nevertheless, Expressionism was a great source of inspiration for German cinema in the 1920s; this period was dominated by the films of **FW Murnau** (*Nosferatu the Vampire*, 1922; *The Last Laugh*, 1924; *Faust*, 1926) and **Fritz Lang** (*Dr Mabuse*, 1922; *Metropolis*, 1925). Lang's German work reached its high point in 1931 with *M*, the director's first talking picture. Initially entitled *Murderers Among Us* (the title was changed under pressure from the Nazis), *M* paints the picture of a diseased society which, unable to cure its own ills, seeks scapegoat sinners on whom to place the blame. *The Last Will of Dr Mabuse* in 1932 attracted Nazi censure. Soon after being invited by Goebbels to supervise the Reich's film production, Lang went into exile, first moving to

Paris and then to California, where he pursued his film-directing career.

The 1920s in Germany also witnessed a shift towards Realism and away from the dominant Expressionist trend. Examples of this new trend include the films of **GW Pabst** (*The Joyless Street*, 1925; *Diary of a Lost Girl*, 1926; *Lulu*, 1929) and **Josef von Sternberg**'s *The Blue Angel* (1930) starring **Marlene Dietrich** and **Emil Jannings**.

AN ABRUPT HALT

The promising surge of German cinema after the First World War was sadly stopped in its tracks with the arrival of the Third Reich. Many actors and directors went into exile. The Nazis turned cinema into a tool to serve the regime's ideology. Filmmaker **Leni Riefenstahl** (1902-2003) stands out in the generally disappointing and inartistic genre of propaganda films, with her productions of amazing cinematic beauty, such as *The Gods of the Stadium*, a glorification of the 1936 Berlin Olympics.

The period immediately after the Second World War was a cultural desert. While "Socialist Realism" prevailed in East Germany, film production in the Federal Republic of the 1950s was of poor quality. Only a few films, such as *The Last Bridge* (1954) and *The Devil's General* (1955) by **Helmut Kaütner**, managed to escape the pervasive mediocrity. The 1962 **Oberhausen Manifesto**, signed by 26 young filmmakers, signalled the birth of a new cinematographic language; the long-awaited revival was here at last.

THE REVIVAL OF THE 1960s AND BEYOND

In the 1960s and 1970s makers of "New German cinema" rose up in the wake of the French *nouvelle vague*, seeking to distance themselves from old-style cinema with its run-of-the-mill commercial superficiality. Films made by **Werner Herzog**, **Volker Schlöndorff** (*Young Törless*, 1966) and **Alexander Kluge** (*Artists at the Top of the Big Top:*

Disorientated, 1968) quickly met with success. It was not long – the mid 1970s – before this younger generation had reestablished German cinema on an international scale. **Volker Schlöndorff** made *The Lost Honour of Katharina Blum* (in collaboration with **Margarethe von Trotta**, 1975), and *The Tin Drum* (1979). **Werner Herzog** went on to explore a fantastic, often quite exotic world in *Aguirre, Wrath of God* (1972), *Nosferatu the Vampyre* (1979), and *Fitzcarraldo* (1982). Prominent figures in the **Munich School** include **Rainer Werner Fassbinder** (1945-82), who also worked in television, and who was responsible for a considerable number of excellent films (*Fear Eats the Soul (Angst essen Seele auf)*, 1973; *The Marriage of Maria Braun*, 1978; *Berlin Alexanderplatz*, a 14-part television series, 1980), and **Wim Wenders** (*The American Friend*, 1977; *Paris, Texas*, 1984; *Wings of Desire*, 1987; *Buena Vista Social Club*, 1999). Important and innovative women film directors include **Margarethe von Trotta** (*Rosa Luxemburg*, 1986; *Das Versprechen*, 1995). Wolfgang Peterson's fantasy world in *The Neverending Story* (1984) was a resounding commercial success. **Edgar Reitz** won international acclaim with his film epic *Heimat* (1984) and its sequel *Heimat 2* (1993). However, West German cinema has been characterised by a strongly individual narrative feel which perhaps makes it less approachable to outsiders. One refreshing filmmaker worthy of note is **Doris Dörrie** who, with *Men... (Männer)* (1985) and *Bin ich schön?* (1998), reduced the Zeitgeist to a humorous point. Other successful films include **Caroline Link**'s 1996 *Jenseits der Stille* and **Tom Tykwer**'s 1999 *Lola rennt (Run Lola Run)*. However, German film today rarely crosses the borders of the German-speaking world, and hits such as **Wolfgang Becker**'s *Goodbye Lenin*, which won the Best European Film award at the 2003 Berlin Film Festival, remain few and far between.

CINEMA IN THE FORMER EAST GERMAN REPUBLIC

East German cinema, like all other art forms was compelled by the state to fulfil a didactic function. Thus a number of films used literary classics as a theme, since directors felt unable to confront issues relevant to contemporary East Germany. **Konrad Wolf** made his mark on three decades of East German filmmaking, with films such as *Sterne* (1958), which won him recognition worldwide. In *Solo Sunny* (1979), he put the case for individualism, thus paving the way for a breakthrough in the East German film industry. **Egon Güntheb** made the highly successful *Der Dritte* (1971),

while the greatest hit of the East German Film Industry Cooperative (DEFA) was **Heiner Carow** with *Die Legende von Paul und Paula* (1973). 1984 was a particularly fruitful year, with **Hermann Zschoche**'s *Hälfte des Lebens*, **Iris Gusner**'s *Kaskade Rückwärts*, and **Helmut Dzuiba**'s *Erscheinen Pflicht*. One of the leading East German filmmakers of the 1970s and 1980s was **Rainer Simon** (*Das Luftschiff*, 1982; *Die Frau und der Fremde*, 1985). Finally, **Lothar Warneke** studied the problems of everyday life, and endeavoured to dismantle rigid ideological points of view (*Bear Ye One Another's Burdens (Einer trage des anderen Last)*, 1988).

THE COUNTRY TODAY

Germany is a highly decentralised federal state whose human, political and administrative facets reflect very individual traits that are rooted in its history. This brief, factual portrait highlights some of the aspects peculiar to the German nation and to life in Germany today.

Population

With over 82 million inhabitants, Germany is the most highly populated country in the European Union. It has been in demographic decline for about 25 years and is experiencing an accelerated ageing of the population (the average age – over 42 – is the highest in Europe). Nearly 90% of Germans live in towns with more than 2 000 inhabitants, and the western part of the country has by far the highest population densities. Although immigration has, since the 1970s, provided a significant additional source of labour, the tightening of legislation has considerably reduced the influx of people from abroad. Over 7 million foreigners have now settled in Germany, including at least 2 million Turks and 1 million people from the former Yugoslavia.

A Federal State

Subdivided throughout history into largely autonomous regions, owing allegiance to no single capital (prior

to 1945 Berlin was only capital of the Reich for just over 70 years), Germany has naturally gravitated towards a federal governmental structure. Today it is a highly decentralised state whose Länder or regions enjoy considerable powers. The **Basic Law** established in 1949 guarantees individual liberties and defines the institutions of a republic founded on democratic principles. The Federal Parliament is composed of two chambers: the **Bundestag**, a national assembly of 656 members elected by universal suffrage, is invested with legislative power, chooses the Chancellor, and controls the

The Reichstag in Berlin

© Partner für Berlin/FTB-Werbefotografie

government; the **Bundesrat**, a federal council comprising members drawn from the local governments administering the Länder, is concerned with certain aspects of legislative power, particularly when they affect the Länder. The Bundesrat also exercises certain control over the government, with the government being required to submit all bills to it.

The **Chancellor** holds executive power and is elected by the Bundestag, to whom he is accountable. He is invested with wide-ranging powers and defines the broad lines of government policy. The government introduces laws (adopted by the Bundestag) and is responsible for their implementation. The role of the Federal President **(Bundespräsident)** is essentially representative. It is he who concludes treaties with foreign states, and appoints or removes judges, federal functionaries and federal ministers suggested by the Chancellor. Lastly, the supreme judicial authority of the Federal Republic is the **Constitutional Court,** based in Karlsruhe. It ensures compliance with the Basic Law, guards constitutional principles, and acts as arbitrator in disputes between the Federal Government and the Länder.

The Länder Regions

The Federal Republic comprises 16 Länder, 11 of which formed the old West Germany and 5 of which were added in 1990, re-constituted from the 15 districts of the former East German Democratic Republic. Each Land organises its constitution within the terms of the Basic Law. The Länder have a legislative assembly **(Landtag)** elected by universal suffrage and an executive body consisting of a council of ministers with a President **(Ministerpräsident)**. Areas involving the sovereignty of the state, such as foreign affairs, defence or monetary policy, fall under the responsibility of the Federal Government alone, but the Länder possess broad powers; they have exclusive jurisdiction over education and culture, and are actively involved in the areas of justice and the economy.

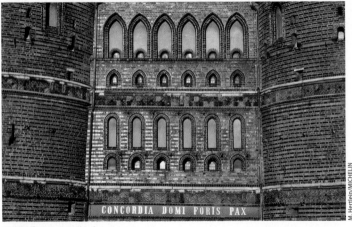

The Holstentor at Lübeck

Economy

After the Second World War, the economy of West Germany made a spectacular recovery, generally referred to as an **"economic miracle"** *(Wirtschaftwunder)*. Indeed, the considerable reconstruction effort coupled with judicious fiscal and monetary policy propelled the West German economy to third place worldwide, behind the United States and Japan. Good relations between employers and trade unions and a powerful banking system helped maintain this growth. The **"social market economy"** (state intervention to correct the perverse market effects) long provided the context of this development, which was also stimulated by a favourable economic climate.

Despite the strong development of service-sector activities, industry remains the cornerstone of Germany's economic strength. The industrial sector, which represents around one third of Gross Domestic Product, consists of large international groups with varied activities (Thyssen-Krupp, Bayer, Hoechst, Siemens, Bosch, BMW, Volkswagen etc) and countless small but dynamic companies.

The **reunification** of the two Germanies in 1990 was an enormous challenge; the high cost of the economic integration of the former German Democratic Republic severely impacted the competitiveness of the Federal Republic. The modernization of the new Länder and social support for employees in the East put a great strain on the federal budget. However, the massive investments made by the Federal Government, increased taxation, and structural aid from Europe finally allowed the East to make the transition from a planned economy to a market economy. The cost of the reunification partly explains why, in spite of an effective policy of restraint, **budget deficits** remain high in Germany and are still a sore spot with Brussels. And although Germany's economy remains the fifth largest in the world, the nation's **high unemployment** (11.7% in 2005) and **slow growth rate** (+0.9% in 2005) have left most Germans worried about their nation's economic future.

Politics

THE BIPARTITE SYSTEM

Since 1949, two parties – the CDU and the SPD – have dominated political life in the Federal Republic. A rare alliance between these two groups arose in 1966 with the formation of the "great coalition" (Große Koalition). One of the most significant recent developments in German politics is, without a doubt, the rise of the ecology party, Die Grünen.

The conservative Christian Democratic Union **(CDU)** and their Bavarian counterpart, the CSU, joined with liberal allies from the FDP in 1949 to elect **Adenauer** Chancellor. The party returned to power under the aegis of **Helmut Kohl**, who was elected Chancellor four times (1983, 1987, 1991 and 1994).

The Social Democrat Party **(SPD)** left Marxist theory behind and came to power for the first time in 1969 led by **Willy Brandt.** The SPD allied with the liberals again in 1974 under **Helmut Schmidt**. More recently, they claimed victory in the 1998 elections under the leadership of **Gerhard Schröder**.

RECENT DEVELOPMENTS

Chancellor Schröder owed his 2002 reelection to the SPD's alliance with the Greens.

The liberal **FDP** party, capable of making alliances with either of the two main parties, has for a long time acted as referee on the political chessboard. Chairman of the party, **Guido Westerwelle**, is the archetypal dynamic young politician.

Successor of the SED, East Germany's former communist party, the Party of Democratic Socialism **(PDS)** has a considerable following in the new Länder. It did, however, suffer a considerable setback after the 2002 elections, when it dropped below the 5% mark.

In 1983, **Die Grünen** entered the Bundestag. Their 1998 alliance with the SPD enabled their leader, **Joschka Fischer**, to take up office as Foreign Secretary in Schröder's government.

Continued frustration with high unemployment, high taxes and slow economic growth (due in part to Germany's reunification in 1990, and in part to the economic globalization that has affected Western industrial nations worldwide) led to an impatience with the liberal SPD -Green coalition in federal elections in 2005. The more conservative coalition between the CDU and CSU regained majority status in the Bundestag in 2005, resulting in the naming of **Angela Merkel** as German Chancellor. Merkel serves as Germany's first female chancellor; its first East German chancellor since reunification; and its youngest chancellor since World War II.

Schloss Moritzburg to the north of Dresden
R. Mattes/MICHELIN

AACHEN★

POPULATION 260 000

The hot springs of Aachen were already famous in the time of the Celts, but they were transformed into thermal baths by the Romans. Charlemagne transformed Aachen into the capital of the Frankish Empire; thirty princes were crowned King of Germania in the cathedral. Today, the city is an important industrial centre.
🔲 *Elisenbrunnen, Friedrich-Wilhelm-Platz, D, 52062 Aachen, ☎ 0049-241/1802960 and 1802961; www.aachen.de.*

- ▶ **Orient Yourself:** Situated among the northern foothills of the Ardennes (Hohes Venn), near the Belgian and Dutch borders, Aachen is Germany's most westerly town, easily accessible by road from Cologne, Düsseldorf or Liège, Belgium.
- 🅿 **Parking:** Public parking is available in lots near the main train station, near the market, near the cathedral, and near Kaisersplatz. Electronic signs throughout town indicate lot availability and free spaces.
- 🚬 **Don't Miss:** The Cathedral, a UNESCO World Heritage Site, and its Treasury.
- 🕐 **Organizing Your Time:** Allow at least 1/2 day for the Cathedral District.
- 🐾 **Also See:** *MONSCHAU (38 km to the south), KÖLN (70 km to the east by A4), EIFEL (Bad Münstereifel is 74 km to the southeast).*

A Bit of History

Charlemagne (747-814) – King of the Franks from 768, Charlemagne (known to Germans as Karl der Große) chose Aachen as the Frankish Court. After being crowned Holy Roman Emperor in 800, he conquered the Saxons and Bavarians and cultivated

Address Book

WHERE TO EAT

🍴 **Ratskeller** – *Markt 40.* ☎ *(0241) 350 01. www.ratskeller-aachen.de.* ♿ This restaurant occupies a groined vault in the historic town hall near the marketplace. Friendly hosts and a pleasant atmosphere make a perfect environment for sampling traditional food.

🍴 **Zum Schiffgen**–*Hühnermarkt 23.* ☎ *(0241) 335 29 www.zum-schiffgen. de.* A clean, well-run establishment welcoming both locals and newcomers. Enjoy traditional regional specialities from the menu, and charming views of the town hall from the terrace on the pedestrian zone.

WHERE TO STAY

🛏 **Haus Press** – *Trierer Straße 842-844.* ☎ *(0241) 92 80 20. fax (0241) 9280211. www.haus-press.de.* 🅿 *15 rooms.* 🍴 *Restaurant.* Unpretentious family hotel. Functional rooms with interesting furniture, some with up to 3 beds. Regional cuisine on offer in the restaurant.

🛏🍴 **Forsthaus Schöntal** – *Kornelimünsterweg 1 (southeast of town centre, toward Kornelimünster Abbey).* ☎ *(0241) 55 94 30. fax (0241) 559 43 24. www.forsthaus-schoental.de.* 🕐 *Closed Wed.* 🅿 *10 rooms* 🍴 *Restaurant.* Clean, well-maintained brick guest-house, its functional rooms furnished in pine. The Biergarten behind out back is pleasant in summer.

GOING OUT

Café Molkerei – *Pontstr. 141 (northeast of Markt).* ☎ *(0241) 489 82.* 🕐 *Open daily, 10am-2am, Fri-Sat until 3am.* This student café sits in a former dairy in working-class Aachen. Breakfast is served daily; in the evening the delicious cocktails attract aficionados.

Magellan – *Pontstr. 78 (northeast of Markt).* ☎ *(0241) 4 01 64 40.* 🕐 *Open Sun-Thu, 10am-1am, Fri-Sat, 10am-2am.* This café-bar/restaurant is particularly pleasant in the summer for its shady terrace. Weekdays between 11am and 3pm Turkish dishes and set menus are served. At the bar, choose from 40 cocktails.

Van den Daele Alt Aachener Kaffee- und Weinstuben – *Büchel 18/ Körbergasse (near the Couven-museum).* ☎ *(0241) 3 57 24. www.van-den-daele.de.* 🕐 *Open Mon-Thur, Sat, 9am-6:30pm, Fri, Sun 11am-6:30pm.* This unusual café restaurant was built at the intersection of four old buildings. The establishment's varied rooms are worth exploring. Try the town's speciality, *Printen* (gingerbread), or *Milchreisfladen* (rice biscuits).

a court marked by its culture and Christianity. Charlemagne was buried in Aachen's Palatine chapel (Pfalzkapelle). Between 936 and 1531, thirty princes were crowned King of Germania in Aachen's cathedral; in 1562 the town lost the status of Coronation City to Frankfurt am Main (♿ *see FRANKFURT AM MAIN*).

Cathedral District

Cathedral★★ (Dom)

♿ 🔊 *Guided tours daily 11am-7pm, Sun, from 12.45pm. Treasury (Domschatzkammer) (access via Klostergasse):* 🕐 *Open Mon 10am-1pm, Tue-Sat 10am-6pm, Sun 10am-9pm.* 🕐 *Closed 1 Jan, Mon before Shrove Tuesday, Good Friday, 24, 25, 31 Dec.* 🎫 *€4* ☎ *(0241) 47 70 90; www.aachendom.de.*
The 74m/242ft high cathedral tower is at the heart of Aachen. Charlemagne's Palatine chapel (Pfalzkapelle), ca 800, an octagonal structure surrounded by a 16-sided Byzantine gallery. The Gothic chancel was consecrated in 1414. The Aachen cathedral was the first German inclusion in UNESCO's World Heritage Sites.

Exterior

Starting at the Katschhof (north side), walk around the cathedral.

Exterior chapels of note include those of St Nicholas (pre-1487) and of Charles-Hubert (1455-74). From the Münsterplatz *(south side)*, the Carolingian church is visible, crowned with a 17C 16-sided cupola. The Carolingian entrance hall on the courtyard features bronze doors embellished with lions' heads (c 800).

Interior

Aachen's cathedral is remarkable for its Carolingian elements, as is its two-story ambulatory. Other works of historical significance include the 11C **Ambo of Henry II**★★★ above the sacristy door, a copper pulpit decorated with precious stones; a magnificent 12C copper **chandelier**★★ donated by Emperor Frederick I Barbarossa; the 13C **Shrine of Mary**; the 14C Virgin of Aachen statue; and the Carolingian high altar adorned with a **Pala d'Oro**★★★, a gold altar with scenes from the Passion and Christ in Majesty (c 1020). Behind the altar is the **Shrine of Charlemagne**★★★ (Karlsschrein: 1200-15), a hand-worked gold and silver reliquary containing the Emperor's bones. On the upper floor is the **Throne of Charlemagne**★ *(visible during the guided tour; meet in the treasury)*, the marble throne that seated 30 Roman-German kings following their consecration. Over time, thousands of pilgrims have participated in the Aachen Shrine Pilgrimage (Aachener Heiligtumfahrt), held every seven years since 1349 (next pilgrimage is 2007).

Domschatzkammer★★★

Access via Klostergasse.

The Treasury is one of the most important north of the Alps, with over 100 outstanding artworks in five thematic sections. Highlights include: the silver and gold Bust Reliquary of Charlemagne (post-1349); the Cross of Lothair (c 1100); the Aachen Altarpiece (c 1520); and a unique ivory situla (c 1000) for holy water.

Rathaus

♿ ⏱ *10am-1pm, 2-5pm.* ⏱ *Closed 1 Jan, Carnival, Good Friday, 1 May, Ascension, 1 Nov, 24-26 and 31 Dec, and special events.* ✆ *€2*☎ *(0241) 180 29 60. www.aachen-tourist.de.*

The 14C town hall stands on the site of Charlemagne's palace. The tower façade overlooks the market with its **fountain** and **statue of Charlemagne**. The Peace Treaty of 1748 ending the War of Austrian Succession was signed in the **White Room** *(Weißer Saal);* the **Council Chamber** *(Ratssaal)* is clad with panelling crafted in 1730.

Excursion

Kornelimünster

10km/6mi SE. The slate-roofed, blue and grey stone houses in Kornelimünster are typical of small towns in the Eifel region. The old **Abbey Church**★, dating back to the Carolingian period, is unusual with five naves (14C-16C) . The galleries above the chancel were added in the 17C, the octagonal Kornelius chapel in the early 18C.

DEUTSCHE ALPENSTRASSE★★★

GERMAN ALPINE ROAD

The splendours of mountain scenery combined with renowned sites like the Wieskirche and the castles of Ludwig II of Bavaria make the Alpenstrasse an unforgettable journey. When passing through the region's villages, where life goes on much as it has for centuries, stop to sample local culinary or cultural traditions, or head off for a walk among the alpine flowers. ⧉ *Deutsche Alpenstraße, Mühlbachweg 6, 83700 Rottach-Egern.* ☎ *08022/92737-0. www.deutsche-alpenstrasse.de.*

▶ **Orient Yourself:** From Lake Constance (Bodensee) to Salzburg, this scenic route runs through high mountain country dotted with pristine alpine lakes. The route crosses the foothills of the Allgäu and the Bavarian Alps, passing such heights as the Zugspitze (2 964m/9 724ft) and the Watzmann (2 712m/8 898ft). The trip follows the southern German border in an area dominated by ski resorts, traditional villages with flower-filled balconies and churches and castles perched atop mountains. To cover the whole itinerary of 310mi/500km, allow three days.

⊙ **Don't Miss:** Beautiful panoramas appear around every corner, but the best lie atop the Wendelstein and along the final part of tour ④ below.

🕑 **Organizing Your Time:** Allow at least 3 days to explore this alpine region.

Kids Especially for Kids: Hohenschwangau and Neuschwanstein castles; cable car rides up the Wendelstein.

Ⓒ **Also See:** *ROMANTISCHE STRASSE (meets the German Alpine Road at Füssen), KONSTANZ, CHIEMSEE (to the north of the final part of tour ④ below).*

Driving Tours

The Allgäu★ ①

▶ *From Lindau to Füssen 112km/70mi – half a day*

It is Alemannic civilisation, not Bavarian, that pervades the Allgäu. The farmers of this region have made this region Germany's great cheese manufacturing area.

Hindelang seen from the Jochstrasse.

T. Krieger/MICHELIN

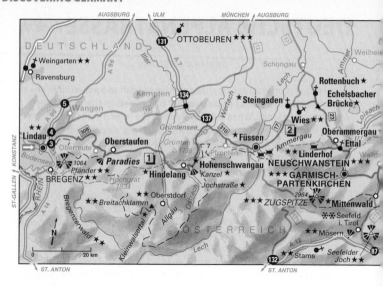

Lindau★★ 🌙 see LINDAU

Paradies
Engineers gave this name to a viewpoint between Oberreute and Oberstaufen, along a sweeping curve, from which the distant Swiss Appenzell Alps can be seen.

Oberstaufen
This charming ski resort sits at the foot of the Hochgrat massif (1 834 m/6 017ft).

▶ *The road now climbs the alpine valley of the Iller, which runs to the foot of Grünten, the "guardian" of the Allgäu.*

Hindelang★
Together with its neighbour, Bad Oberdorf, this flower-decked village is a holiday centre and spa perfectly suited for mountain walks in summer and skiing in winter. Above Hindelang, the climb of the **Jochstraße**★ affords idyllic views over the jagged summits of the Allgäu Alps. From the **Kanzel**★ viewpoint, near the summit, admire the panorama embracing the Ostrach Valley and surrounding mountains.

▶ *Descending on the far side, the road crosses the Wertach valley, skirts the Grüntensee and passes near the large Pfronten ski resort before arriving at Füssen.*

Füssen★ (🌙 see FÜSSEN)

The Ammergau★ 2

▶ *From Füssen to Garmisch-Partenkirchen. 95 km/59mi – a day.*

The road bypasses the Ammergau Alps to the north, then crosses countryside seamed and broken by the moraines deposited by the ancient Lech glacier. This rolling land is punctuated by the "onion" domes of village churches.

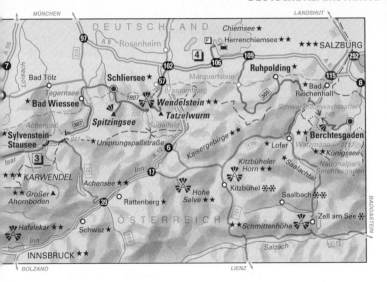

Kids Hohenschwangau and Neuschwanstein★★★ – 🍂 *See NEUSCHWANSTEIN*

Steingaden

The former 12C abbey of the Steingaden Premonstratensians still boasts its remarkable minster, though the **abbey church**★ received an 18C Baroque makeover. Only the exterior reveals its original Romanesque appearance.

The Gothic entrance bears a painted genealogy of the House of Welf, the abbey's founders. The chancel stuccowork contrasts sharply with the brightness of the nave and its finely painted motifs. Baroque and Rococo furnishings – pulpit, organ loft, altarpieces, statues – overpower the church's modest architecture.

Wieskirche★★ 🍂 *See WIESKIRCHE*

Rottenbuch

First built as an Augustinian monastery, the **Mariä-Geburts-Kirche**★ (Church of the Nativity of the Virgin) was remodelled in Baroque and Rococo styles in the 18C. The School of Wessobrunn, of which Joseph and Franz Schmuzer were masters, crafted the magnificant stucco. Frescoes by Matthäus Günther harmonise perfectly with the extravagantly sculpted decor. The pulpit, organ loft and altars by Franz Xaver Schmädl are heavily adorned with statues and giltwork in pure Rococo tradition.

Echelsbacher Brücke★ (Echelsbacher Bridge)

Since 1929, this concrete structure has spanned the Ammer gorge, at this point 76m/250ft deep. Walk to the middle of the bridge for an impressive view.

Oberammergau★

This small town of peasants and craftsmen, encircled by the wooded foothills of the Ammergau, owes its fame to the internationally-renowned Passion Play, performed only once every 10 years (next performance: 2010). The play, involving 1 100 amateur local actors, lasts an entire summer's day. The tradition derives from a vow made by the inhabitants in 1633, after a plague epidemic was miraculously cut short.

Address Book

WHERE TO EAT

⊜ **Ratskeller** – *Rathausstraße 1a, 83727 Schliersee.* ☎ *(08026) 47 86.* 🕑 *Closed Mon.* 🍴 ♿ Reasonably-priced traditional food in a pleasant rustic restaurant.

⊜⊟ **Obere Mühle** – *Ostrachstraße 40, 87541 Hindelang.* 🕑 *Closed Tue.* ☎ *(08324) 28 57 www.obere-muehle.de.* This country-style restaurant was built in 1433 in a former windmill. Regional cuisine and wood-fired dishes are the rule. Check out the cheese dairy next door.

⊜⊟⊟ **Freihaus Brenner** – *Freihaus 4, 83707 Bad Wiessee.* ☎ *(08022) 820 04. www.freihaus-brenner.de.* This restaurant's setting leaves nothing to be desired. Views include mountains and Lake Tegernsee; dining rooms bear wooden ceilings, exposed beams and curtained windows.

WHERE TO STAY

⊜ **Gästehaus Weißes Rössl** – *Dorfstraße 19, 83242 Reit im Winkl.* ☎ *(08640) 982 30. fax (08640) 5297. www.weissesroessl-riw.de.* 🕑 *Closed 3 weeks after Easter and mid Oct to 20 Dec.* 🍴 ▣ 🍴 *20 rooms* ▭ ⊜ *Restaurant.* This well-kept and centrally-located hotel offers clean and comfortable rooms, a sauna and a gym. The dining room has a country feel.

⊜ **Gasthaus Zum Stern** – *Dorfstraße 33, 82487 Oberammergau.* ☎ *(08822) 867. fax (08822) 7027* 🕑 *Closed Wed.* ▣ *13 rooms.* ▭⊜⊟ *Restaurant.* A typical 17C Bavarian hotel, this inn has modest, well-tended rooms. A simple dining room offers light meals as well as three-course dinners. The *Biergarten* is recommended in summer.

⊜⊟ **Gasthof Fischerwirt** – *Linderhofer Straße 15, 82488 Ettal.* ☎ *(08822)*

63 52. fax (08822) 3568. www.zum-fischerwirt.de. 🕑 *Closed Nov to mid-Dec and 2 weeks at Easter.* ▣ *10 rooms* ▭ ⊜⊟ *Restaurant.* A traditional, pleasant hotel with charming, simply-decorated guestrooms. The restaurant serves reasonably-priced regional favorites.

⊜⊟⊟ **Alpengasthof Hirsch** – *Kurze Gasse 18, 87541 Hindelang-Bad Oberdorf* ☎ *(08324) 308. fax (08324) 8193. www.alpengasthof-hirsch.de.* 🕑 *Closed 3 weeks in Nov.* ▣ 🍴 ♿ *25 rooms* ▭ ⊜ *Restaurant.* A centrally-located, family-run hotel with modern guestrooms, some with a kitchenette or lounge area. The country-style restaurant is always pleasant and lively.

⊜⊟⊟ **Alpengasthof Winkelmoosalm** – *Dürrnbachhornweg 6, D-83242 Reit im Winkel.* ☎ *(08640) 974 40 fax (08640) 974444. www.winkel-moosalm.com.* 🕑 *Closed Nov-Dec.* ▣♿ *18 rooms* ⊜⊟ *Restaurant.* Tourists and skiers alike flock to this inn's well-maintained rustic guestrooms. A bright restaurant features panoramic views and organic dishes.

⊜⊟⊟ **Terrassen Hotel Isnyland** – *Alpenblickweg 3, 88316 Isny-Neutrauchburg.* ☎ *(07562) 971 00 fax (07562) 971040. www.terrassenhotel.de.* ▣🍴 *28 rooms.* ▭ ⊜⊟⊟ *Restaurant.* A peaceful hillside establishment with bright, themed guestrooms. All rooms have balconies; the dining areas look out on the valley.

⊜⊟⊟⊟ **Hotel Lederer am See** – *Bodenschneidstraße 9, 83707 Bad Wiessee.* ☎ *(08022) 82 90. fax (08022) 829200. hotel@lederer.com.* 🕑 *Closed Nov to mid-Dec.* ▣🏊 *104 rooms.* ▭⊜⊟ *Restaurant.* Four traditional-style houses make up this pleasant hotel in the heart of a lakeside park. The inn's bright country-style restaurant also enjoys lake vistas.

Linderhof★★ ☾ *See Schloss LINDERHOF*

Ettal

A blossoming of the Benedictine tradition and the local veneration of a Virgin statue explain the vast dimensions of Ettal Abbey, founded by the Emperor Ludwig IV "the Bavarian" in 1330. The **abbey church** was a Gothic building with a polygonal floor plan. The present 17C construction was by Baroque architect Enrico Zucalli; Joseph Schmuzer of the School of Wessobrunn *(see above)* added the dome after a fire in 1774. The Rococo **frescoes** inside the dome are the work of Johann Jakob Zeiller.

▶ *The road rejoins the Loisach Valley. To the south, the Wetterstein range features the peaks of the Zugspitze, Alpspitze and Dreitorspitze. Continue to Garmisch-Parten-kirchen.*

The Upper Isar Valley and the Lake District★ 3

▶ *From Garmisch-Partenkirchen to Schliersee. 105 km/65mi – 1 day.*

Mittenwald★ 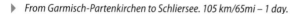 *See GARMISCH-PARTENKIRCHEN excursions*
At Wallgau, the route joins the upper valley of the Isar *(toll road as far as Vorderriß)*, a wild, bleak stretch of open country.

▶ *The road crosses the wooded Achenpaß (going 2km/1.2mi into Austria) and then plunges down towards the Tegernsee.*

Bad Wiessee★
An elegant resort, a fashionable holiday centre and a major spa, Bad Wiessee is pleas-antly set on the shores of Lake Tegernsee in cultivated, semi-Alpine surroundings.

Schliersee
Beside the lake of the same name, this small community – together with Fischhausen, Neuhaus and Spitzingsee *(see itinerary below)* – offers interesting day trips. The **St Sixtus Parish Church★** (Pfarrkirche) was rebuilt in the Baroque between 1712 and 1714. The interior frescoes and delicate stucco were executed by Johann Baptist Zimmermann (1680-1758), brother of the architect of the Wieskirche *(see WIESKIRCHE).*

The Sudelfeld and the Chiemgau Mountains★ 4

▶ *From Schliersee to Berchtesgaden. 172km/107mi – one day*

Spitzingsee
Less than 1mi from the summit the steep access road offers views of the Fischhausen-Neuhaus plain and Lake Schliersee. Soon after, the road stops at the Spitzingsee.

▶ *Shortly (3km/2mi) before Bayrischzell, the road passes the lower terminal of a cable-way leading to the summit of the Wendelstein.*

Tatzelwurm-Wasserfall
15min there and back on foot.
From the "Naturdenkmal Tatzelwurm" car park, a footpath leads to this cascade.

Wendelstein★★
To climb the Wendelstein, take the cableway from Bayrischzell-Osterhofen ter-minal *(about 7min)*, or the **rack-railway**, Wendelstein-Zahnradbahn, from the lower station at Brannenburg-Inntal *(about 25min)*. Ruggedly grinding its way up increas-ingly steep slopes, the little train reaches an altitude of 1 738m/5 702ft. The rest of the climb is via a footpath carved out of the bedrock. a A solar observatory and a 18C chapel crown the summit (1 838m/6 030ft). The **panorama★★** from the top is unforgettable. *(From the valley station at Brannenburg.* ◐ *Summer: 9am–5pm; Winter: 9am-4pm. Departures every hour. Journey time: 30min.* ◐ *Enquire about closure peri-ods.* ⇆ *Return fare (round trip) €22.50.* ☎ *(08034) 30 80; www.wendelsteinbahn.de)*

Four geological trails (Geo-Wanderwege) crisscross the peak, each marked with explanatory panels. We recommend the Gipfelweg, which circles the summit in about 2hr 30min.

▸ *From the Wendelstein terminal, our route winds down the Inn valley and along the Munich-Salzburg motorway, skirting the shore of the* **Chiemsee**★. *After Marquartstein a succession of tortuous, steep valleys finally end at the foot of the Zahmer Kaiser. Heading east, the Alpenstraße cuts through a long corridor of Alpine lakes.*

Ruhpolding★

This popular resort houses its most precious artwork in the parish church of **St George:** a 12C Romanesque statue of the Virgin Mary.

▸ *The Schwarzbachwacht pass reveals the contrast between the austere wooded Schwarzbach valley and the open pastures on the Ramsau slopes. The drive offers* **panoramas**★★ *of the Watzmann peak and the Hochkalter with its Blaueis glacier. The German Alpine Road ends at Berchtesgaden.*

Berchtesgaden★★ 🕭 *See BERCHTESGADEN*

ANNABERG-BUCHHOLZ★

POPULATION 23 000

After the discovery of silver and tin ore in 1491 and 1496, Annaberg and Buchholz experienced an economic boom; at its peak, 600 mines enriched the capital of the Erzgebirge (Ore Mountains). In the 16C, as the silver diminished, lace production became Annaberg's most important industry. Today the town's principal attraction is its Gothic cathedral. 🗐 *Markt 1, 09456 Annaberg-Buchholz,* ☎ *(037 33) 42 51 39.*

▸ **Orient Yourself:** Annaberg-Bucholz lies in the Erzgebirge region of Saxony, about 60 mi/100km southwest of Dresden, near the border with the Czech Republic.
- **Don't Miss:** St-Annen-Kirche
- **Organizing Your Time:** Annaberg-Buchholz's sites can be seen in a single day.
- **Also See:** *Chemnitz (20mi/32km to the north; see DRESDEN excursions), Freiberg (32mi/51km to the northeast; see DRESDEN excursions), DRESDEN (106 km to the northeast), SÄCHSISCHE SCHWEIZ (tour departing from DRESDEN), ERZGEBIRGE.*

Visit

St-Annen-Kirche★★

Built between 1499 and 1525, this church is one of the most impressive examples of Saxony's Flamboyant Gothic style. Twelve thin pillars soar into the vaulting, each yoke covered by a "blossom baldaquin." This composition was the work of Jakob Heilmann from Schweinfurt. The gallery parapets display Old and New Testament scenes. At the far end of the church is the **Schöne Tür**★★ ("beautiful door"), a multicoloured portal designed by Hans Witten in 1512. References to Annaberg's mining past can be seen in the **pulpit**★★ (1516), with the relief figure of a miner, and in the painted panels behind the **Miners' Reredos**★ (Bergmannsaltar, c 1520), depicting various stages of mine work in that period.

Erzgebirgsmuseum mit Besucherbergwerk

🕐 *Museum: open Jan to Nov Tue–Sun 10am–5pm; in Dec open also on Mon. Mine: opening times as for museum;* 🚶 *guided tours only (1hr; last tour of mine at 3.30pm).* 🕐 *Closed 24 Dec.* 💶 *€5.50 (museum and mine).* ☎ *(037 33) 234 97.*

This museum retraces local history with an emphasis on mining. Annexed to the museum is the **Im Gößner** mine, which opened at the height of Annaberg's prosperity ca 1498. *The entrance shaft is in the museum courtyard.*

Technisches Museum Frohnauer Hammer

🚶 *Guided tours (50min) daily 9am–12pm and 1–4pm.* 🕐 *Closed 1 Jan, 24, 25 and 31 Dec.* 💶 *€3.* ☎ *(037 33) 220 00; www.annaberg-buchholz.de*

Once a flourmill, this old building was turned into a coin mint when silver was discovered in the region, and later transformed into a **forge**. Hydraulically-operated bellows and power-hammers (100, 200 and 300kg/220, 440, 660lb) can be seen there today.

Excursion

Erzgebirge★ 👣 *see ERZGEBIRGE*

AUGSBURG★★

POPULATION 276 000

In the 17C and 18C, Augsburg's reputation for excellent crafts reached throughout Europe. But the city has long been affiliated with first-rate artists: Martin Schongauer (1448-1491), the son of Augsburg-born goldsmith Konrad Peutinger; Hans Burgkmair (1473-1531); and Hans Holbein the Elder (d 1525). Mozart's father Leopold (1719) was born here, as was the dramatist Bertolt Brecht (1898). The city of the German Renaissance continues to enchant visitors with its artistic beauty today. 🛈 *Bahnhofstraße 7, 86150 Augsburg,* ☎ *(0821) 50 20 70*

▶ **Orient Yourself:** Augsburg is one hour from Munich by the A 8 and 30 minutes by train. The river Lech, a tributary of the Danube, crosses the town and feeds into a canal in the lower town. Augsburg is the third largest town in Bavaria and an important industrial and communications centre.

🅿 **Parking:** Public lots and garages are located throughout the city; several are near the main train station and the Rathaus. Electronic signs indicate lot availability and the number of free spaces.

👁 **Don't Miss:** Maximilianstraße and the Cathedral

🕐 **Organizing Your Time:** Allow at least one full day to see Augsburg.

👣 **Also See:** *ROMANTISCHE STRASSE, MÜNCHEN (41mi/66km to the east), ULM (46mi/74km to the west), OTTOBEUREN (56mi/89km to the southwest).*

A Bit of History

Roman origins – Founded in 15 BC by Drusus and Tiberius, stepsons of Emperor Augustus, Augsburg is, along with Trier and Cologne, one of Germany's oldest cities. It became a trading centre en route to Italy and, at the fall of the Roman Empire, an Episcopal See. By the late 13C it was a Free Imperial City and the seat of the Diet.

The Fuggers – At the end of the 15C, Augsburg (already with a population of 50 000) became a centre of high finance due largely to the Fuggers and the Welsers. History

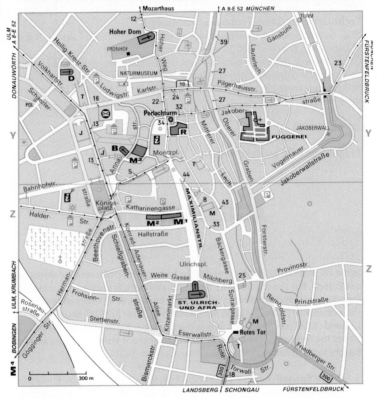

AUGSBURG		Grottenau	Y	16	Maximilianstr.	Z	
		Haunstetter Str.	Z	18	Mittlerer Graben	Y	27
Annastr.	Y	Hoher Weg	Y		Perlachberg	Y	32
Bahnhofstr.	YZ	Karlstr.	Y		Predigerberg	Z	33
Bgm.-Fischer-Str.	Y 5	Karolinenstr.	Y	22	Rathauspl.	Y	34
Dominikanergasse	Z 8	Lechhauser Str.	Y	23	Unterer Graben	Y	39
Frauentorstr.	Y 12	Leonhardsberg	Y	24	Vorderer Lech	Z	43
Fuggerstr.	Y 13	Margaretenstr.	Y	25	Wintergasse	Y	44

Heilig-Kreuz-Kirchen	Y D	Schaezlerpalais	Z M¹	Staatsgalerie	
Maximilianmuseum	Y M³	St. Anna-Kirche	Y B	In der Kunsthalle	Z M⁴
Rathaus	Y R	Staatsgalerie alter Kunst	Z M²		

has preserved the name of Jakob Fugger the Rich (1459-1529), renowned as the Empire's banker and the financier of the Habsburgs. He was powerful enough to rebuke Charles V, reminding him: "It is well known that, without my help, Your Majesty would no longer wear the crown of the Holy Roman Empire." The unpaid debt of the Habsburgs to their Augsburg bankers has been estimated at four million ducats.

The Augsburg Confession – In 1530 Charles V, disturbed by the growing strength of the Reformation, called an Imperial Diet at Augsburg with the hope of dissipating the religious troubles. The Protestants, inspired by Luther, thereupon proclaimed a "Confession" of the basic tenets of their beliefs. The statement was rejected, and it was not until the **Peace of Augsburg** in 1555 that German Protestants won freedom of worship.

The town hall and the Perlachturm

Sights

Rathausplatz

The **town hall** is a vast Renaissance edifice built by Elias Holl between 1615 and 1620, and rebuilt from original plans after damage in 1944. Two onion-domed towers frame a pediment adorned with the traditional pine cone. Inside, the Golden Room *(Goldener Saal)*, with its restored coffered ceiling, can be visited. (🕐 *Open 10am-6pm*, 👁 *€2)*. The **Perlachturm** was originally a Romanesque watchtower expanded three times over the centuries. When the Alps are visible from the top, a yellow flag is flown *(tower visits in high season)*.

St Anna-Kirche

When Luther came to Augsburg in 1518 to defend his reformed thesis he stayed in this 14C Carmelite monastery. The church became Protestant in 1525 and the rooms where Luther stayed are a museum *(Lutherstiege)*. The **Fugger Funeral Chapel**★ *(Fuggerkapelle)* at the heart of the church is exceptional: a Catholic enclave in an otherwise Protestant church, it is the first example of Renaissance architecture in Germany. Note the three works by Lucas Cranach the Elder in the east chancel.

Fuggerei★

In 1519 this quarter was founded by Jakob Fugger the Rich to house the town's poor. the first of its kind in the world. The Fuggerei still operates with its own church and administration, welcoming the city's neediest. and charging them a token rent in exchange for their promise to pray for the souls of the founders.

Dom

The 14C Gothic cathedral features a noteworthy **Virgin's Door**★★ *(Jungfrauen-Portal)*, as well as 11C Romanesque bronze door **panels**★ *(Türflügel)*. Four of the nave altars are adorned with **paintings**★ *(Tafelgemälden)* by Holbein the Elder. In front of the cathedral are remains of the Roman city.

Address Book

WHERE TO EAT

@@ **Zur alten Feuerwache** – Zeug-platz 4 ☎ (0821) 51 16 85 - zuraltenfeuer-wache@t-online.de ♿ This pleasant restaurant sits opposite the 16C arsenal of Augsburg. A large Biergarten offers a relaxing bite out front.

@@ **Die Ecke** – Elias-Holl-Platz 2 ☎ (0821) 51 06 00 - restaurant.dieecke@t-online.de This historic restaurant melds rustic and modern styles. Bertolt Brecht was a regular here at one time.

WHERE TO STAY

@@ **Unterbaarer Hof** – Ulmer Straße 218 🅿 2 ☎ (0821) 43 13 00 fax (0821) 4866540 - www.unterbaarer-hof.de 6 rooms 🛏 @ Restaurant A good hotel with modern guestrooms and a huge self-catering apartment. Modest wooden furnishings give the dining room a country feel. Traditional reasonably-priced meals are served as well.

@@ **Hotel Garni Georgsrast** – 🅿 2, Fischertor. ☎ (0821) 50 26 10. fax (0821) 5026127. 🕐 Closed Christmas to Twelfth Night Georgenstraße 31. 24 rooms 🛏. A clean and simple guesthouse on a quiet side street about 1km from the town-centre. Small guestrooms are well maintained with plain, light-coloured furnishings.

TAKING A BREAK

Caféhaus Eber – Philippine-Welser-Str. 6 (opposite the town hall). ☎ (0821) 3 68 47. www.cafe-eber.de. 🕐 Open Mon-Sat, 8am-6pm. Just try to choose just one confection at this shop: delicious tarts vie with chocolates in the window. Try your goodies in the first-floor tearoom or, in good weather, on the Rathausplatz terrace. Lunch is available 11am to 2pm.

Stadtmarkt – Annastr. 16 (accessible also from Fuggerstr. 12). ☎ (0821) 3 24 39 22 . 🕐 Open Mon-Fri 7am-6pm, Sat 7am-2pm. Pick up a snack or meal from the city's market stalls: cold cuts from the meat stall (Fleischhalle); groceries from the Viktualienhalle. You'll also find a morning farmers' market, cafés, restaurants and a crêperie.

GOING OUT

Der Weinbäck (Laxgangs Wein-stuben) Spitalgasse 8. ☎ (0821) 3 79 11 (Reservations: ☎ 50 26 80). www.weinbaeck.de. 🕐 Mon-Sat 5pm-1am. 🕐 Closed Fri, Sun and bank holidays and 25 Dec to 1 Jan. 16C wine cellars and a charming summertime courtyard set the scene in this wine bar. Sample German wines by the glass with com-plimentary homemade bread or with a seasonal set menu.

Maximilianstraße★

Lined by mansions and private houses built by wealthy Renaissance-era Augsburgers, this street offers one of the most majestic vistas of Old Germany. Many façades have been extensively restored. Three bronze Renaissance fountains adorn the street.

Städtische Kunstsammlungen★ (Municipal Art Gallery)

Entrance: Maximilianstraße 46. ♿ 🕐 Open every day except Mon, 10am-5pm. Art collections: Wed, 2pm-4pm. 🕐 Closed 24, 25 and 31 Dec. 🎫 €3, no charge on the first Sun of the month. ☎ (0821) 324 41 02.

German Baroque master paintings are displayed in the museum's **Schaezler-Pal-ais Galleries**. The enormous **banqueting hall**★★ (Festsaal) is noteworthy for its lavishly-adorned ceiling and wall panelling, decorated with Rococo frescoes and stuccowork. A second **gallery**, the Staatsgalerie Alter Kunst exhibits paintings by 15C and 16C Augsburgan and Swabian masters, including works by Hans Holbein the Elder and Albrecht Dürer.

Münster St Ulrich und Afra ★

This former Benedictine abbey lies adjacent to a Protestant church of the same name. The two churches, one Catholic, one Protestant, each with the same name, is characteristic Augsburg. The basilica of Münster St Ulrich und Afra (1474) is of late-Gothic style with Renaissance and Baroque additions. Notice the fine Baroque screen and three Baroque altars. At the transept crossing the bronze *Crucifixion* dates from 1607. St Simpert's chapel features a lovely balcony surmounted by terracotta **Statues of the Saints** ★.

BADEN-BADEN★★

POPULATION: 54 000

From Brahms to Queen Victoria, some of the richest and most famous people of the 19C enjoyed the baths and casinos of Baden-Baden. A spa resort since Antiquity, a gambling centre for the last 150 years, and a World Cup venue in 2006, the town still attracts visitors from around the world. *Kaiserallee 3, 76530 Baden-Baden, ☎ (072 21) 27 52 00, www.baden-baden.de*

▶ **Orient Yourself:** Situated between the Black Forest and the Baden vineyards, in a sheltered position in the Oos Valley, Baden-Baden is 60km/37mi from Strasbourg on the A 5-E 52.

⊙ **Don't Miss:** The parks and promenades: Lichtentaler Allee, Gönneranlage, and the Kurhaus gardens.

⊙ **Organizing Your Time:** Reserve half a day to relax in the city's numerous parks and gardens; relaxation is, after all, what made Baden-Baden famous.

⚙ **Also See:** *RASTATT (8km/5mi to the north), KARLSRUHE (40km/25mi to the north), or one of the tours in the SCHWARZWALD.*

A Bit of History

Spa – The restorative powers of Baden-Baden were already known in Roman times. By the Middle Ages the wealthy folks were hooked, including the Margraves of Baden. Today, two spa complexes offer treatments *(each open daily, price varies with length*

Baden-Baden

T. Krieger/MICHELIN

of stay and treatment): the **Friedrichsbad**, a neo-Renaissance style palace; and the **Caracalla-Therme**, a more modern complex geared to relaxation and leisure.

Sights

Lichtentaler Allee★★

This riverside promenade has been the place to see and be seen for over a century. Napoleon III, Queen Victoria, Bismarck and Dostoevsky all whiled away the hours here, and in 1861, the King of Prussia, (later Kaiser Wilhelm I) was very nearly assassinated here. The adjacent **Gönneranlage**★ is a pretty park, perfect for a stroll.

Kurhaus

Guided visits of the casino every 30min until 11:45am. €4. To use the Casino, you must show your passport, pay an entrance fee and be suitably dressed.

Address Book

GETTING AROUND

Baden-Baden is linked to Karlsruhe's public transport by city line S 4 or regional line R 3. Network info and ticket prices from **Baden-Baden-Linie** *(Beuernerstraße 25;* ☎ *(072 21) 27 77 0)* or from the town hall office *(Jesuiten-platz;* ☎ *(072 21) 27 73 52).*

Airport – Baden-Baden Airport (10 km southeast of town) has several flights daily to and from Berlin. ☎ *(072 29) 66 20 00 or www.baden-airport.de.*

SIGHTSEEING

An English guided tour of the main sites is available. ☎ (072 21)27 52 81

Tourist bus – City-Bahn Baden-Baden tours year round *(45min,* €4.50).

WHERE TO EAT

Yburg – *Burgruine 1.* ☎ *(07223) 95 75 43 - www.burggaststaette-yburg.de.* *Closed Jan-Feb except weekends.* This popular tourist haunt offers pleasant Rhine River views. Expect a good selection of traditional dishes.

Hildegard's – *Am Verfas-sungsplatz.* ☎ *(07221) 337 55. www. hildegards.de.* Richly-coloured paintings adorn the walls of this restaurant-bistro. After a hearty meal, enjoy a drink at the longest bar in town!

WHERE TO STAY

Haus Rebland – *Umwegerstraße 133, 76534 Baden-Baden-Varnhalt.* ☎ *(07223) 95 11 880. fax (07223) 95 11 88*

88. www.haus-rebland.de. *Closed mid-Nov to mid-Dec.* 24 rooms *Restaurant.* Set amid the vineyards of Varnhalt, this family-run establishment features balconies in all its guestrooms. The rustic restaurant has a country feel and pretty views over the Rhine valley.

Hotel Bayrischer Hof – *Lange Straße 92.* ☎ *(07221) 935 50. fax (07221) 935555. www.hotel-bayr-ischerhof.de.* 201 38 rooms . It would be difficult to find a more convenient hotel – the town's sights are all virtually on the doorstep. The Festival Theatre *(Festspielhaus)* is across the street.

TAKING A BREAK

Café König – *Lichtentaler Straße 12.* ☎ *(07221) 2 35 73. www.chocolatier.de.* *Café open 8:30am-6:30pm; confec-tionery: 9:30am-6:30pm.* Try cakes and sweets from the neighbouring confectionery; savoury snacks or a full lunch. In summer, enjoy the terrace, shaded by a giant lime tree.

GOING OUT

In der Trinkhalle *Kaiserallee 3 (west aisle of the Trinkhalle, entrance at rear of building).* ☎ *(07221) 30 29 05. www.in-der-trinkhalle.de.* *Open 10am-2am.* Very chic café-bar with leather armchairs and a large selection of drinks and snacks. The tranquil terrace offers relaxing views of the spa park.

Despite its name, the 19C Kurhaus no longer bathes its guests; instead, the Corinthian-style hall treats them to glittering balls, concerts and games of chance. The casino's 19C **gaming rooms**★ were designed by Bénazet to resemble French chateaux.

Stadtmuseum im Baldreit★ (Town Museum)

Lichtentaler Allee 10. ◷ *Open Tue to Sun, 10am-6pm (-8pm, Wed).* ◷ *Closed 1 Jan, Easter Mon, Whit Mon, 24, 25 and 31 Dec.* ◌ *€1.* ☎ *(072 21) 93 22 72, stadtmuseum@ baden-baden.de.*
Two thousand years of town history are presented using archaeological documents and historical artifacts. Note the locally-produced 18C porcelain and religious art.

Neues Schloss (New Castle)

The New Castle was built in the 16C by the Margraves of Baden, but several remodeling efforts added their own touches. Until 1918, this was the summer residence of the Margraves of Baden. The castle is private property, but you can visit the gateway building which houses a Stadtmuseum annex. The terrace provides pleasant views of the town and the Stiftskirche.

Stiftskirche (Collegiate Church)

From the 14C to the 18C all of the Margraves of Baden were buried in this church. The chancel contains several beautifully-decorated tombs from the Late Gothic to the

Rococo period. Take special note of the sandstone **Crucifix**★, a 1467 masterpiece by Nicolaus Gerhaert von Leyden and a fine example of late medieval sculpture.

Driving Tours

Baden Vineyards★

▶ *34km/21mi, 2hr. Leave town on Kaiser-Wilhelm-Straße then Fremersbergstraße. Follow the signposts marked 'Badische Weinstraße'.*

The **Badische Weinstraße**★★★ winds sinuously from village to village through the vineyards on the lower slopes of the Black Forest.

▶ *At Altschweir, leave the Wine Road to get to Altwindeck.*

Burg Altwindeck★
This ancient fort, built on a circular plan, has been transformed into a restaurant with panoramic views. From its precincts there is a wide **view**★ of the plain.

▶ *Rejoin the Wine Road and head towards Kappelrodeck.*

Oberkirch★
This beautiful town is surrounded by orchards, vineyards and forests and retains charming half-timbered houses dating from the 17C.

Schwarzwald-Hochstraße (Black Forest Crest Road)
 See SCHWARZWALD.

BADENWEILER★

POPULATION: 3 500

A pleasant village of orchards and vineyards, Badenweiler has long been known for its thermal waters and gentle climate. This spa town attracts people seeking relief from a variety of physical ailments, as well as those who simply crave peace and quiet. *Ernst-Eisenlohr-Straße 4, 79410 Badenweiler. ☏ (076 32) 79 93 00.*

▶ **Orient Yourself:** Badenweiler lies on a slope on a valley in the foothills of the Black Forest, within view of the Rhine Valley and the Vosges.
 Don't Miss: Badenweiler's pleasant Kurpark.
 Also See: *FREIBURG IM BREISGAU (36 km/22mi to the north), Bad SÄCKINGEN (46 km/29mi to the southeast) or SCHWARZWALD.*

Visit

Kurpark★★ (Spa Park)
The rolling parkland abounds in sub-tropical plants and trees: cedars and cypresses mingle with enormous sequoias. The largest, best-preserved **Roman baths** north of the Alps also lie within the park. A climb up to the ruins of the old fort offers a fine **view**★ of the resort, the Rhine Valley and the Vosges.

Excursions

Schloss Bürgeln★
10km/6mi S.
Set in beautifully terraced gardens, this 18C palace of the abbots of St Blasien over-looks the edge of the Black Forest, the Rhine, and the outskirts of Basel. ☞ *Guided tour (40min),* ⏱ *Mar-Nov: Wed-Mon, 10:30am-6pm.* ☞ *€3.* ☎ *(076 26) 237.*

Burg Rötteln★★
27km/17mi S.
The ruins of this fortress extend are all that remains of a 14C fortress destroyed in the 17C. The fortress Oberburg is reached via a drawbridge. For stunning vistas, ascend the Green Tower (Grüner Turm) to view the Wiese Valley, the Black Forest and, on the horizon, the Swiss Alps.

BAMBERG★★

POPULATION: 71 000

Established in the Middle Ages, transformed in the 17C and 18C and spared war-time bomb-raids, Bamberg recalls Germany's past with 2 300 buildings spanning the Romanesque and Baroque periods. UNESCO honored Bamberg by giving it World Heritage status in 1993. Among Bamberg's many gastronomic speci-alities are traditionally prepared carp (Karpfen), and smoked beer (Rauchbier).
🛈 *Geyerswörthstraße 3, 96047 Bamberg, ☎ (0951) 87 11 61, www.stadt.bamberg.de*

▶ **Orient Yourself:** Bamberg lies within seven hills in the heart of Franconia. The River Regnitz and the Main-Danube Canal bisect the town, with the historic centre in the upper part of town.

🅿 **Parking:** Garages are in the Old Town, at Geyerswörtherstr. 5; on the south side at Schützenstr. 2; and on the north side at Am Georgendamm and Hornthalstr.

⊘ **Don't Miss:** The Old Town, especially the Kaiserdom.

🕐 **Organizing Your Time:** Plan to spend 2 hours at the Kaiserdom.

⚲ **Also See:** *Wallfahrtskirche VIERZEHNHEILIGEN (32 km/20mi to the north), BAY-REUTH (65 km/40mi to the east), NUREMBERG (63 km/39mi to the south), or take the ROMANTISCHE STRASSE to Volkach (66 km/41mi to the west).*

M. Herlein/MICHELIN

Bamberg

The Old Town

Kaiserdom★★

The Cathedral of St Peter and St George, completed in 1237, is transitional Gothic in style. The older of its two apses, the Georgenchor, stands upon a raised terrace, its cornices worked in a chequered pattern; the Peterschor is entirely Gothic. Four towers quarter the two choirs. The design stems from the original Ottonian edifice (see Architecture).

The finest of the cathedral entrances is the *Fürstenportal* (**Princes' Doorway**) on the Domplatz. It comprises 10 recessed arches supported on fluted, ribbed

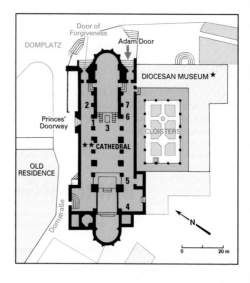

or chevroned columns with statue-columns representing prophets with apostles on their shoulders. The *Adamspforte* (**Adam's Doorway**) is decorated with diamond and dogtooth carving. Underneath the choir nearest the entrance is the huge crypt. Beneath the second choir *(at the rear of the church)* is the tomb of the Bamberg archbishops.

Among the masterpieces of German Gothic sculpture on view are the 13C equestrian statue of **(1) The Knight of Bamberg**★★★ *(Bamberger Reiter)*, and the statuary group, **(2) The Visitation**. The **(3) tomb**★★★ of Henry II the Saint and Cunegunda *(St Heinrichs Grab)* stands in the centre of the nave, at the entrance to the eastern choir. It took native son Tilman Riemenschneider 14 years to complete the tomb. The **(4) Reredos of The Nativity**★ was created in 1523 by Veit Stoß. The **(5)** funerary statue, **(6)** statue representing the church, and the **(7)** statue symbolising the Synagogue in the form of a blindfolded woman are also worthy of note.

The Bamberg Christmas Crèche Tour

Bamberg is a popular destination during Advent and up to January 6 for its Christmas Crèche Tour (Bamberger Krippenweg), featuring about 30 churches, museums and squares with unique, decorative Nativity scenes.

The route begins in the cathedral with the altar to the Virgin Mary and continues to the *Maternkapelle* and the *Obere Pfarre*, portraying scenes from the Annunciation to the Wedding at Cana. An astonishing variety of crèches is on display: the enormous manger in Schönleinsplatz with life-size figures in traditional local costume; 200 figures in the Nativity scene at St Martin's; and the tiny crib in the church of St Gandolf, seen through a viewer.

Brochures on the Bamberg Christmas Crèche Tour are available from the Bamberg Tourismus und Kongreß Service, Geyerswörthstraße 3, 96047 Bamberg.

Alte Hofhaltung (Old Residence)

🕐 *The courtyard is open until dusk.*

This was formerly the episcopal and Imperial palace (10C-11C). Its doorway and façade, with carved gables, oriel window and corner turret, date from the Renaissance. The delightful inner **courtyard**★★ *(Innenhof)* is bordered by half-timbered Gothic buildings. It houses the Historical Museum (art and culture in the town's history).

Neue Residenz (New Residence)

🦽 📷 *Guided tour (45min).*🕐 *Apr-Sep: 9am-6pm; Oct-Mar: 10am-4pm.* 📷 €4.
📞 *(0951) 51 93 90; www.schloesser.bayern.de*

This palace, the largest building in Bamberg, includes two early-17C Renaissance wings *(on Obere Karolinenstraße)*; and two late-17C Baroque wings *(on the Domplatz)*, by local architect Leonard Dientzenhofer. On the first floor are displayed works of the German masters. On the second floor are the Imperial apartments, with beautiful parquet floors, Baroque furniture and authentic Gobelins tapestries. The **Emperors' Hall** *(Kaisersaal)* is outstanding for its portraits and allegorical frescoes.

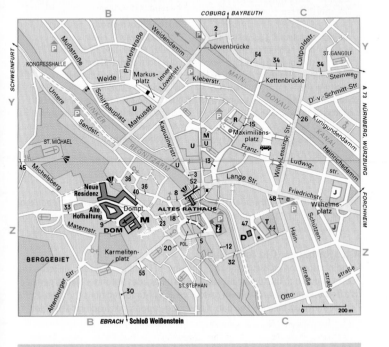

Address Book

WHERE TO EAT

☞ **Historischer Brauereiausschank Schlenkerla** – *Dominikanerstraße 6.* 🚌 *26.* ☎ *(0951) 560 60. www.schlenkerla. de.* ⏰ *Closed Tue.* 🍴 This beautiful half-timbered building is a little piece of Bamberg's history: Franconian specialities are served here, including smoked beer *(Rauchbier)*, brewed on-site and drawn directly from the barrel, in the traditional manner.

☞☞☞ **Würzburger Weinstube** – *Zinkenwörth 6 (west of Schönleinsplatz).* ☎ *(0951) 2 26 67.* ⏰ *Closed Tue evening and Wed.* This *Weinstube* is located in a half-timbered building in the town centre. Franconian wines and food specialties are served here. In the summer, enjoy refreshments on the terrace in the shade of hundred-year-old chestnut and lime trees.

WHERE TO STAY

☞☞ **Romantik Hotel Weinhaus Messerschmitt** – *Lange Straße 41.* ☎ *(0951) 29 78 00. fax (0951) 29 78 029. www.hotel-messerschmitt.de.* ⏰ *Closed 17-23 Feb.* 🍴 *19 rooms* ☞ ☞☞☞ *Restaurant.* This yellow and white-fronted hotel sits at the start of the main shopping street. Guestrooms are equipped with rustic or modern furniture. The hotel's restaurant has a charming terrace looking out on a courtyard and fountain.

☞☞ **Barock-Hotel am Dom** – *Vorderer Bach 4.* ☎ *(0951) 540 31. fax (0951) 54021* ⏰ *Closed Feb and 24-27 Dec.* ♿

19 rooms. ☞ This hotel has been in operation since 1520 and was given an elegant Baroque façade in 1740. Located right next to the cathedral, breakfast is served under a Gothic vault.

TAKING A BREAK

Café im Rosengarten – *Domplatz (in the Neue Residenz).* ☎ *(0951) 98 04 00.* ⏰ *Open Easter to mid-Oct, 10am-6pm.* Delicacies from the Graupner pastry shop at Lange Str. 9 are served in the formal pavilion or on the pleasant rose garden terrace.

GOING OUT

Lots of bars are located on Austr. (west of Grüner Markt) and Obere Sandstr.

Klosterbräu – *Obere Mühlbrücke 1-3 (to the southeast of Judenstr.).* ☎ *(0951) 5 77 22. www.klosterbraeu.de.* ⏰ *Mon-Fri, 11am-10pm, weekend, 11am-9pm.* Choose from a large selection of speciality beers in the oldest brewery in town, with beautiful country-style rooms. Local cuisine is also available, as is a terrace in summer.

Palais Schrottenberg – *Kasernstr. 1 (between Dominikanerstr. and the Regnitz).* ☎ *(0951) 95 58 80. www. palais-schrottenberg.de.* ⏰ *Sun-Fri, 9am-1am, Sat, 9am-3am.* Built in the 18C by Johann Dientzenhofer, the café-bar offers a choice of style and ambience: Baroque-style lounge, modern winter garden, sushi bar (Fri-Sat from 6pm) or an interior courtyard.

▶ *Follow the Karolinenstraße to the lay quarter of the old town, built on the banks of the River Regnitz. Take time to explore some of the adjoining streets, particularly around Judenstraße (note the statues of the Virgin Mary on the house corners).*

Altes Rathaus★ (Old Town Hall)

Standing alone on an islet in the river, this unusual building was remodelled in the 18C. In addition to the town hall proper, with its façades decorated with a perspective fresco, there is a bridge tower and a small half-timbered house, known as the Rottmeisterhaus, balanced on one of the bridge's pontoons leading to the islet.

The Noble Dynasty of Saxe-Coburg

In a history of intrigue and diplomacy spanning centuries, the noble dynasty of Saxe-Coburg was related either directly or through marriage to nearly every royal family of Europe: Belgian, Portuguese, Russian, Swiss and Bulgarian. The marriage between Edward, the Duke of Kent, and the Coburg Princess Victoire produced Queen Victoria; she, in turn, married a cousin: Prince Albert of Saxe-Coburg.

Excursions

Schloss Pommersfelden★

21km/12mi south. ○ *Open daily, 10am-5pm.* ○ *Closed Good Fri, 24, 25 and 31 Dec.* ○ *€6.* ☎ *(09548) 981 80; www.pommersfelden.de.*

Also known as **Weißenstein**, this building designed by Dientzenhofer and Hildebrandt in the 18C quickly became one of Germany's finest Baroque palaces. A brief tour reveals the **galleried state staircase**★. On the ground floor, an artificial grotto opening onto the garden perpetuates a Renaissance tradition. The marble hall on the first floor features frescoes by Rottmayr. A lengthier tour encompasses the Elector's apartments with their small painting gallery and a hall of mirrors.

Coburg★

46 km/29mi north.

The brilliant beginnings of the dukes of Saxe-Coburg resulted in an indelible Renaissance mark on Coburg. The townscape, surmounted by a mighty fortress (⌘ *see below*), dates to this period. Coburg is rich with beautiful façades on the Marktplatz. The **Gymnasium Casimirianum**★ *(opposite the Moritzkirche)* dates from 1605.

Veste Coburg (Fortress)★★

○ *Open daily, 10am-5pm (Apr-Oct) and Tue-Sun, 1-4pm (Nov-Mar).* ○ *Closed Shrove Tue, 24, 25 and 31 Dec.* ○ *€3.30.* ☎ *(095 61) 87 90; www.kunstsammlungen-coburg.de.*

This is the best-preserved large medieval fortress in Germany, with a triple ring of fortified walls. The original castle from the 11C was replaced in the 16C. Martin Luther famously sought refuge in Veste Coburg during the Augsburg Confession; his apartment is preserved as a small Luther Museum. Elsewhere in the fortress are the **art collections**★ *(Kunstsammlungen)*, including paintings by Albrecht Dürer and Lucas Cranach. In the central wing *(Carl-Eduard-Bau)* a decorative arts display includes the largest Venetian glassware collection in Europe.

Schloss Ehrenburg

🚶 *Guided tour (50min – hourly), Tue-Sun, 9am-5pm (Apr-Sep) and 10am-3pm (Oct-Mar).* ○ *Closed 1 Jan, Shrove Tue, 1 Nov, 24, 25 and 31 Dec.* ○ *€4.* ☎ *(095 61) 80 88 32; www.sgvcoburg.de.*

This castle was the residence of the dukes of Coburg from 1547 to 1918. Today the Renaissance palace features a Baroque interior with an early 19C English neo-Gothic façade. Castle rooms house sumptuous Empire and Biedermeier furniture. An art gallery contains works by German and Dutch masters.

BAUTZEN★

POPULATION: 42 000

Built on a rocky outcrop skirted by the Spree River, Bautzen has managed to retain its old-fashioned charm despite wars and the deprivations of the East German Iron Curtain. *Hauptmarkt 1, 02625 Bautzen. ☎ (035 91) 420 16. www.bautzen.de.*

▸ **Orient Yourself:** Bautzen developed along a bend in the Spree river. The town is reached by the A4 motorway linking Dresden and Görlitz.

🕐 **Organizing Your Time:** Allow at least four hours to see the cathedral, Ortenburg Castle and to wander along the ramparts.

👒 **Also See:** *GORLITZ (40 km/25mi to the east), DRESDEN (64 km/40mi to the west), SÄCHSISCHE SCHWEIZ.*

A Bit of History

Sorbian Town – There are many **Sorbian** families in Bautzen, descendants of a Slavic people who settled here in the 6C. Sorbian, a Slavic language related to Czech and Polish, is still taught in local schools. Numerous folk traditions, like the decoration of eggs at Easter and the wearing of tall embroidered headdresses, promote the identity of this ethnic minority.

Sights

Hauptmarkt

The old market square is surrounded by fine burghers' houses and a three-story 18C town hall built by Johann Christoph Naumann. Reichenstraße leads from the market square to the **Reichenturm** (Tower of the Rich), a 56m/179ft leaning tower that offers an excellent view of the city. 🕐 *Open from Apr-Oct, 10am-5pm.* ⊛ *€1.20* ☎ *(035 91) 46 04 31. www.bautzen.de. Tourist information available at the Fleischmarkt, behind the Town Hall.*

Dom St-Peter★

This hall-church (1213-1497) is used both by Roman Catholics and Protestants (Catholic Masses in the chancel; Protestant services in the main nave). Construction began early in the 13C, with the southern section enlarged in the 15C. In 1664, the 85m/279ft tower was crowned with a Baroque cupola. Inside the cathedral, note the large **Crucifix** (1714) by **Balthazar Permoser**; the **Baroque high altar** (1722-24) by G Fossati in the chancel; an **altar painting** by GA Pellegrini; and the Princes' Loggia (1674) in the Protestant section.

▸ *Follow the road that runs past the cathedral as far as the monastery.*

Those parts of the **monastery** that remain date from 1683. The southern façade with its imposing portal dates from 1755.

▸ *Now follow the Schloßstrasse.*

This charming street with restored Baroque houses leads to Ortenburg Castle.

Schloss Ortenburg

Where Ortenburg stands today was once a fortified complex completed ca AD 600 and expanded in 958 by Heinrich I. Two early-15C fires destroyed the construction, but in the late 15C, when the region fell under Hungarian rule, Hungarian king Matthias

Corvinus rebuilt in Late Gothic style. A portrait of the king is still visible on the tower of the north wing. The Thirty Years War left profound scars, removed by renovations after 1648. In 1698, three Renaissance gables were added.

Sorbisches Museum / Serbski Muzej

 🚾 🕐 *Open Apr-Oct, Mon-Fri, 10am-5pm, Sat-Sun, 10am-6pm; Nov-Mar: 10am-4pm, Sat-Sun, 10am-5pm.* 🕐 *Closed 24 and 31 Dec.* 💶 *€2.50.* ☎ *(035 91) 424 03.*

Situated in the former Salt House, an annex of Ortenburg castle added in 1782, the **Sorbian Museum** illustrates the history, culture and way of life of the Sorbians from the 6C to the current day.

Town ramparts★

The medieval ramparts are very well maintained and shape the silhouette of the town. A walk along the town walls provides visitors with an idea of what it must have been like in the Middle Ages. The ruins of the **Nikolaikirche** and the cemetery of the same name are worth a visit.

Alte Wasserkunst★

🕐 *Apr-Oct: 10am-5pm; Feb-Dec: 10am-4pm; Jan: Sat-Sun, 10am-4pm.* 💶 *€1.50.* ☎ *(035 91) 415 88.*

This formidable defensive and water tower has been standing since 1558. Testament to its sturdiness is the astonishing fact of its having supplied the town's water until 1965. The workings of this technical monument are extremely interesting.

BAYREUTH★

POPULATION: 74 400

Bayreuth is the Holy Grail to Wagner fans, and the Bayreuth Festival attracts many of them every August. Wagner was not the only one to leave his mark on the town: The Margravine Wilhelmina, one of the most cultivated women of the 18C, transformed Bayreuth into the cultural centre it remains. 🅸 *Luitpoldplatz 9, 95444 Bayreuth.* ☎ *(0921) 885 88. www.bayreuth.de.*

▶ **Orient Yourself:** Bayreuth is located in northern Bavaria, between the wooded heights of the Fichtelgebirge and the, desolate landscape of Swiss Franconia. The A 9 motorway linking Munich and Berlin runs near the town.

🅿 **Parking:** Parking garages are located throughout the city of Bayreuth.

😊 **Don't Miss:** The Bayreuth Festival if you're an opera fan, but make your plans well in advance (👤 *see A BIT OF ADVICE*).

🕐 **Organizing Your Time:** Bayreuth's highlights can be seen in half a day unless you plan to enjoy the city's musical performances.

Kids **Especially for Kids:** Cave explorations in Excursions ① and ③.

👤 **Also See:** *Oberes SAALETAL (80 km/50mi to the north along the A 9), Wallfahrtskirche VIERZAHNHEILIGEN (56 km/35mi to the west), NUREMBERG (80 km/50mi to the south along the A 9).*

A Bit of History

Princess Wilhelmina – The Margravine Wilhelmina, daughter of the King of Prussia and sister of Frederick the Great, was paired with a rather dull husband: Margrave Friedrich of Brandenburg-Bayreuth. As compensation, Wilhelmina created as stimulating an environment as possible, surrounding herself with the most cultivated figures

Address Book

WHERE TO EAT

🍽🍽 **Oskar – Das Wirtshaus am Markt** – *Maximilianstr. 33.* ☎ *(0921) 516 05 53. www.oskar-bayreuth.de.* 🕐 *8 am (Sun 9am) -1am.* This restaurant is in the former town hall, divided into small rooms with varying styles and varying degrees of intimacy. There are also a pretty winter garden and a terrace. Bavarian specialties dominate the menu.

🍽🍽🍽 **Zur Sudpfanne** – *Oberkon-nersreuther Straße 6 – 95448 Bayreuth-Oberkonnersreuth (southeast along Nürnberger Str.)* ☎ *(0921) 528 83. www. sudpfanne.com.* The façade of this establishment mixes old brick with modern glass. Inside, the restaurant has rustic-style décor.

WHERE TO STAY

🍽🍽🍽 **Grunau Hotel** – *Kemnather Str. 27 (east of Wieland-Wagner-Str and Königsallee).* ☎ *(0921) 7 98 00. fax (0921) 7 98 01 00 www.grunau-hotel.de.* 🅿 ✂ ♿ 🛏 On the upper floor of a commercial complex east of town centre, guestrooms are modern, spacious, quiet and comfortable. Guests can use the fitness centre at a discount.

🍽🍽🍽🍽 **Goldener Anker** – *Opern-straße 6.* ☎ *(0921) 650 51. fax (0921) 655 00. www.anker-bayreuth.de.* 🕐 *Closed Nov-mid-Jan 35 rooms.* 🛏 🍽🍽🍽🍽 *Restaurant.* Each guestroom

in this traditional hotel has its own style, but all are large and spacious. Traditional cuisine is served in the restaurant.

TAKING A BREAK

Café Funsch – *Sophienstr. 9.* ☎ *(0921) 6 46 87. www.funsch.de.* 🕐 *8.30am-6.15pm, Sun 10am-6pm* 🕐 *Closed for 2 weeks after Whit Sun and at Christmas.* This tearoom has a terrace on the pedestrian zone and a varied menu. The shop sells little marzipan figures that make good souvenirs.

Café Orangerie – *Eremitage 6 (east of town along Wieland-Wagner-Str.).* ☎ *(0921) 79 99 70. www.eremitage-gastro.de.* 🕐 *Apr/May-Oct (depending on weather): 11am-6pm.* This tea room's magnificent terrace is ideal for relaxing after exploring the castle park, just 5 minutes' away by foot. There is also a restaurant with a *Biergarten* on-site.

GOING OUT

Sinnopoli – *Badstr. 13.* ☎ *(0921) 6 20 17. www.sinnopoli.de.* 🕐 *Mon-Sat, 8-1am, Sun and bank holidays, 9-1am.* Tastefully decorated bar with more than 40 cocktails, alcoholic and non-alcoholic, and lots of home-made pastas. "Happy hour" is 5-7pm. A beautiful garden is open in the summer.

of the age. Her lifetime (1709-58) marked the most brilliant period in Bayreuth's history. A gifted artist, writer, composer and patroness of the fine, the Princess helped Bayreuth bloom.

Wagner and the festival – Wagner moved to Bayreuth in 1872, attracted by Princess Wilhelmina's famous opera house. His wife Cosima, daughter of the Hungarian composer **Franz Liszt**, came along. Wagner's music was stimulated by admiration for his father-in-law, who is said to be indirectly responsible for many of Wagner's masterworks. The writer and composer of *Parsifal* and *Tannhäuser*, Richard Wagner searched far and wide for the ideal music venue. With the support of Ludwig II of Bavaria, he had built to his own design the Festival Theatre *(Festsplielhaus)*, revolutionary in its day for its generous audience space as well as its outstanding acoustics. Wagner held the first festival of his lyrical pieces here in 1876. After his death in 1883, the tradition continued under Cosima and, subsequently, his son Siegfried, his grandson Wieland (d 1966) and Wolfgang Wagner, the current director.

Sights *Map p 121*

Markgräfliches Opernhaus★

 ♿ 🕐 *Apr-Sep: 9am-6pm; Oct-Mar: 10am-4pm.* 🕐 *Closed 1 Jan. Shrove Tue, 24, 25 and 31 Dec.* 👓 *€5.* ☎ *(0921) 759 69 22.*

The Margravine Wilhelmina built this theatre in 1748 as a venue for the opera and ballet performances of the troupe under her patronage. The austere façade gives no clue to the exuberance of the **interior decoration**★ by Giuseppe Galli Bibiena of Bologna. The reds, greens and browns harmonise perfectly with the gilded stuccowork on the columns; the interior is constructed entirely of wood. This was the largest opera house in Germany until 1871.

Neues Schloss (New Palace)

 ♿ 🕐 *Open Tue-Sun, Apr-Sep: 9am-6pm; Oct-Mar: 10am-4pm.* 🕐 *Closed 1 Jan, Shrove Tue, 24, 25 and 1 Dec.* 👓 *€4.* ☎ *(0921) 75 96 90.*

The sumptuous Markgräfliches Opernhaus in Bayreuth

Wilhelmina created this palace between 1753 and 1754 from a number of existing buildings. The elegance of the **interior decoration**★ owes much to the stucco-master Pedrozzi, greatly influenced by the Princess, who clearly loved the airy, flowery Rococo style. Wilhelmina, whose private apartments were on the first floor of the north wing. On the ground floor of the north wing is a **museum of Bayreuth porcelain** *(Museum Bayreuther Fayencen)*.

Richard-Wagner-Museum ★

 🕐 *Open every day, Apr-Oct: 9am-5pm, (8pm Tue and Thu); Nov-Mar: 10am-5pm.* 🕐 *Closed 24 and 25 Dec.* 👓 *€4.* ☎ *(0921) 757 28 16; www.wagnermuseum.de.*

Haus Wahnfried (House of Supreme Peace), in which the composer lived from 1874 onwards, and which was owned by his family until 1966, is still one of the main stops on a Wagnerian pilgrimage. The only remaining original feature of the house is the façade. Collections on display in the museum evoke the maestro's life and work (furniture, manuscripts, pianos and death mask) and the history of the Bayreuth Festival. Richard Wagner and his wife Cosima lie buried in the garden. The tomb of Liszt, Wagner's great friend and father-in-law, who died during one

---

🙂 A Bit of Advice 🙂

Bayreuth Festival: From 25 July until 28 August, Bayreuth reverberates to the sound of Wagner. Hotels within 10 km of the town tend to be fully booked, and many of the 60 000 hotel rooms are reserved seven years in advance. Bookings can only be made by post and the lucky few who get a room endure poor seating and stifling heat while listening to the marathon operas. But each year the exceptional program mesmerizes opera enthusiasts.

Write to Bayreuther Festspiele, Kartenbüro, Postfach 100262, 95402 Bayreuth. Information and program (in German) is posted on www.festspiele.de. Prices vary year to year but are comparable to the usual cost of opera tickets. At 6am of performance day queuing begins for sales of any unused tickets.

of the first festivals in 1886, is in the Bayreuth cemetery (Stadtfriedhof – *entrance on Erlanger Straße*)

Schloss Eremitage (Hermitage Palace)★

4 km/2.5mi east by ② on the town plan.   *Guided tour (25min) Apr-Sept, 9am-6pm, 1-15 Oct, 10am-4pm.* €3. ☎ (0921) 759 69 37.

The Hermitage was the pleasure palace of the Margraves of Brandenburg-Bayreuth, a gift from her husband to the Margravine Wilhelmina, who couldn't wait to remodel it. The **old castle** (*Altes Schloss*), surrounded by geometric flowerbeds, was built in 1715 and remodelled by the Margravine in 1736. The **Schloßpark**★ is laid out in the manner of an English garden. The **new palace** (*Neues Schloss*), designed on a semicircular plan, was rebuilt after 1945.

Excursions *Map p 122*

Swiss Franconia★★ (Fränkische Schweiz) and Sanspareil ①

Round-trip tour of 105km/65mi – allow one day

Pottenstein

The castle, a former residence of the elector-bishops of Bamberg, overlooks the town. Natural wonders, like gorges and caves, mark the local countryside.

Teufelshöhle

Kids   *Guided tour (45min).* ⊙ *Apr-Oct: daily, 9am-5pm; Nov-Feb: Tue and Sat-Sun, 10am-3pm (26 Dec-6 Jan: daily).* ⊙ *Closed 24 and 25 Dec.* €3.50 ☎ (092 43) 708 41; www.teufelshoehle.de.

The stalactites and stalagmites of the Devil's Caves are impressive, particularly in the *Barbarossadom* (Cathedral of Barbarossa).

Gößweinstein★

The Circuit of **Marienfelsen** (*about 45min round trip on foot, following from the castle the signposts: Marienfels-Schmitt-Anlagen*) leads to several fine **vistas**★★ over the deep valley of the Wiesent. In the village, the Pilgrimage Church (Wallfahrtskirche) was built between 1730 and 1739 by Balthasar Neumann.

Sanspareil★

After completion of Bayreuth's Hermitage, Margravine Wihelmina and Margrave Friedrich converted an old hunting estate into an impressive **rock garden**★ named Sanspareil ("without equal").

Burg Zwernitz

North of Sanspareil.

From 1338, this 12C fortress was the property of the Hohenzollern before falling to Bavaria in 1810. It contains furnishings, and a selection of 16C-18C weapons. The keep offers good **views**. & ⊙ *Open Apr-Sep, daily except Mon, 9am-6pm.* €2.50. ☎ (0921) 759 69 0.

The Franconian Mountains★ ② (Frankenwald)

Round-trip tour of 125km/78mi – allow 5hr

Döbraberg★

45min round-trip on foot. Climb to the look-out tower (795m/2 608ft).

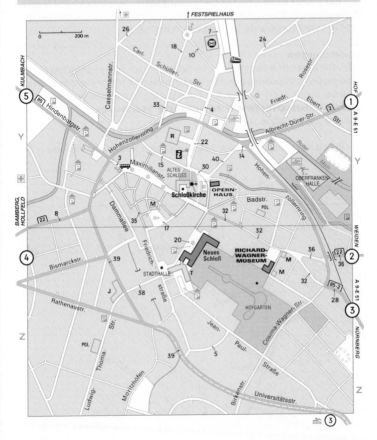

The majestic **panorama**★ extends as far as the Thuringian Mountains in the north, and the Fichtelgebirge in the south.

Kronach
Festung Rosenberg (16C-18C), one of the largest medieval fortresses in Germany, towers over the small town of Kronach and the wooded heights of the Franken-wald. The fortress houses the Franconian Gallery, a branch of the Bavarian National Museum. Medieval and Renaissance Franconian art is displayed, including works by **Lucas Cranach the Elder** who was born in Kronach ca 1472.

Kulmbach
Once the seat of the Hohenzollern Margraves, Kulmbach is famous today for its strong beers *(Echt Kulmbacher, Bayrisch Gfrorns)*. **The Plassenburg**★, a well-preserved medieval fortress, melds a strong, defensive exterior with an elegant **Renaissance courtyard**★★. Various collections on display in the apartments include 300 000 **tin**

soldiers★ from the Deutsches Zinnfigurenmuseum, the largest collection of its kind in the world. ♿ 🕐 *Apr-Oct: 9am-6pm; Nov-Mar: 10am-4pm.* 🕐 *Closed 1 Jan, 24, 25 and 31 Dec.* 🎫 *€4.* ☎ *(092 21) 95 88 20. www.kulmbach.de.*

The Fichtelgebirge★ ③

Round tour of 92km/57mi – allow about 5hr

The **panoramic route**★ follows the Steinach Valley, penetrating into the granite massif of the Fichtelgebirge. Above Fleckl, a cable car climbs the **Ochsenkopf** (1 024m/3 360ft), one of the highest peaks in the massif.

Luisenburg★★

🧒 This labyrinth of enormous granite boulders makes for a pleasant hike along a pine-shaded, hilly path *(blue arrows indicate the way up, red the way down)*. Several look-out points along the way afford views of the Fichtelgebirge. Goethe, then minister to the court of Weimar and a geology enthusiast, was the first to explore the cave scientifically in 1785.

▶ *Return to Bayreuth on road n° 303, which passes through the small spa of Bad Berneck.*

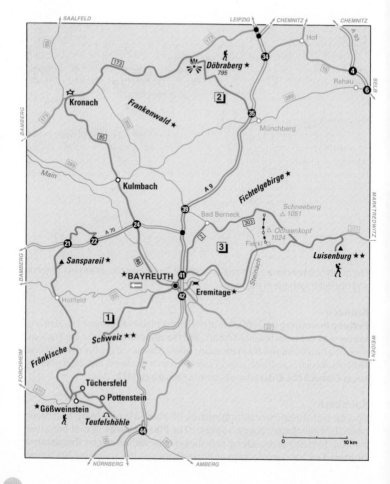

BERCHTESGADEN★★

POPULATION: 7 800

Journey's end on the German Alpine Road (Deutsche Alpenstraße) and departure point for many tourist excursions, Berchtesgaden is intensely beautiful in the summer, if also intensely busy. Berchtesgaden was chosen as a holiday retreat by Adolf Hitler, who built his notorious "Eagle's Nest" sanctuary on the Kehlstein. *Königseer Straße 2, 83471 Berchtesgaden, ☎ (086 52) 96 70. www.berchtesgaden.de.*

▶ **Orient Yourself:** The basin of Berchtesgaden is enclosed on three sides by the mountain chains of the Watzmann, the Steinernes Meer and the Hagengebirge. The town is dominated by the Watzmann peak (2 712m/8 900ft).

◉ **Don't Miss:** Berchtesgaden's mountain peaks and lakes are its highlights. Get out and enjoy them, whether by foot or by car.

◔ **Organizing Your Time:** Allow a full day to enjoy this region's outstanding natural beauty.

Especially for Kids: The Berchtesgaden Salt Mines.

◔ **Also See:** *Deutsche ALPENSTRASSE (Berchtesgaden is the last stop on this tour), CHIEMSEE (67 km/41mi northwest), BURGHAUSEN (76 km/48mi north).*

Sights

Schlossplatz★

This triangular-shaped square is the heart of Berchtesgaden. On the western side is the Getreidekasten, the former granary furnished with an arcade in the 16C. Lombard influence is evident in the façade of the **Church of St Peter and St John** *(Stiftskirche St Peter and Johannes)*, decorated with multicolored stones.

Schloss (Palace)

🐾 *Guided tour (50min).* ◕ *From Whit Sun to mid-Oct: daily except Sat, 10am-noon, 2pm-4pm; from mid-Oct until Whit Sun: Mon-Fri at 11am and 2pm.* ⌘ *€7.* ☎ *(086 52) 94 79 80; www.haus-bayern.com.*

Once a monks' priory, this sumptuous palace was home to Crown Prince Rupert, Commander-in-Chief of the Bavarian forces during the First World War. The palace museum displays weapons, religious art, French tapestries and Nymphenburg por-

Berchtesgaden Tourismus

Winter in Berchtesgaden

Address Book

WHERE TO STAY

Neuhäusl – *Wildmoos 45, 83471 Berchtesgaden (7 km east).* ☎ *(08652) 94 00. fax (08652) 64637. www. neuhaeusl.de.* ○ *Closed 20 Apr-1 May, 15 Nov-15 Dec.* 🅿 *26 rooms.* ☐ ☺☺ *Restaurant.* A well-cared-for, rustic hotel. Enjoy magnificent alpine countryside by day, and at night, the comfort of well-furnished guestrooms and apartments.

Alpenhotel Denninglehen – *Am Priesterstein 7, 83471 Berchtesgaden (7 km east).* ☎ *(08652) 978 90. fax (08652) 64710. www.denninglehen.de* ○ *Closed 1-18 Dec, 15-30 Jan.* 🅿 🏊 *24 rooms.* ☐ ☺☺ *Restaurant.* Remotely situated and surrounded by mountains,

this country-style hotel is appointed with rustic painted furniture. Winter sports are available locally.

Hotel Fischer – *Königsseer Straße 51, 83471 Berchtesgaden.* ☎ *(08652) 95 50. fax (08652) 95 52 55. www.hotel-fischer.de.* ○ *Closed Mar and late-Oct to mid-Dec.* 🅿 🏊 *54 rooms* ☐ ☺☺ *Restaurant.* A few minutes on foot from the town centre, this hotel is a practical option for those interested in leisure activities. Guestrooms are simple and well presented, and most of them have a balcony or terrace. Ski instruction is available by reservation.

celain. A **guided tour** allows a close-up look at the palace. Visit the highest terrace for unforgettable views of the Watzmann.

Kids Salzbergwerk (Salt Mines)★★
Guided visit (1hr). ○ *From May to mid-Oct: daily, 9am-5pm; from mid-Oct to Apr: Mon-Sat, 12.30-15.30pm.* ○ *Closed 1 Jan, Shrove Tue, Good Fri, 24-26 and 31 Dec.* ☺☺ *€12.50.* ☎ *(086 52) 600 20. www.salzwelt.de.*

The Berchtesgaden salt mines, begun in 1517, brought prosperity to a once very poor region. The salty rock is washed by water and the resulting brine (*Sole*) is piped to Bad Reichenhall to be refined. In the salt museum **tour**★★, visitors wear miner's overalls, take a small train, raft across an illuminated underground lake, and cruise down wooden slides within the earth.

Excursions

Obersalzberg and the Kehlstein ★★
4km/2.5mi. A shuttle service runs between Obersalzberg and the Kehlstein mid-May to mid-Oct. ☺☺ *€13.50 round-trip. For details* ☎ *(086 52) 96 70; www.obersalzberg.de.*

After the Putsch of 1923, **Adolf Hitler** settled in Obersalzberg. When the Nazis seized power in 1934, the new Chancellor enlarged and enhanced his chalet (Berghof), and the sanctuary of "the lonely man of Berchtesgaden" became centre stage for diplomatic receptions.

Most of the Berghof buildings were destroyed in an American air raid on 25 April, 1945; they were captured on 4 May by French and American military units.

Obersalzberg
Except for the Platterhof, where Hitler's faithful lodged for the nominal sum of a single mark, the buildings comprising the Nazi sanctuary have been razed. A **Documentation Centre on the History of National Socialism** opened here in 1999 (*Dokumentationszentrum zur Geschichte des Nationalsozialismus*).

Kehlstein★★

An impressive ascent along a narrow **road**★★★ leads up the Kehlstein. At the end of the road *(reserve seats for the return journey)*, a lift ascends the final 100m/328ft. On the summit is the old Eagle's Nest *(Adlerhorst, now a Tea Room)*, which Hitler was given by the Nazi party as a 50th birthday present. The **panorama**★★ includes the neighbouring peaks and, on the far side of Salzburg, the rolling peaks of the Salzkammergut.

Königssee★★

5 km/3mi south. ⏱ *Boat trips year round, leaving approx every 30min. Allow 1hr45, plus at least 1hr for possible short trips ashore. Cruises stop at St Bartholomä in low season.* ☞ *€12.* ☎ *(08652) 96 360; www.bayerische-seenschifffahrt.de.*

This long, narrow lake is one of the most romantic sites in Bavaria. Dominated by the Watzmann and the Steinernes Meer, the lake narrows at St Bartholomä, where visitors go ashore to admire the **Chapel of St Bartholomä**. From the landing at Salet, it's a 15min walk to the **Obersee** and the 400m/1 312ft Röthbach falls. The **cable car** from Jenner to Königssee *(30min climb,* ☞ *€13.50)* offers views of the lake and surrounding peaks.

The Königssee natural park tourist centre, in the former station next to the car park, has information about numerous local hikes.

Roßfeld-Höhenringstraße★★

Round trip of 29km/18mi E of Berchtesgaden (anti-clockwise) – about 1hr 30min. Toll: ☞ *€1.50 per person.* ☎ *(086 52) 28 08; www.berchtesgadener-land.com.*

The **Roßfeld Road**, open year-round, ascends the crest of the Austrian valley of the Salzach and overlooks the Tennengebirge. The Dachstein, recognisable by its glittering glaciers, fills in the background. On the other side of the ridge is a view of the countryside around Berchtesgaden and Salzburg and of the Hoher Göll, Kehlstein and Untersberg peaks. From the Hennenkopf car park, it is only a few minutes' climb to the beacon and the Hennenkopf Cross at 1 551m/5 089ft. The road plunges down from the crest after the Roßfeldhütte (Inn) and winds through the charming valleys of the Oberau region.

Hintersee★

12km/8mi west. The road climbs the narrow Ramsau Valley to reach this lake framed by the domes of the Reiteralpe and the Teeth of Hochkalter. The eastern shore, the "enchanted forest" *(Zauberwald)* bordering it, and the shady lake banks make this a popular destination for hikers.

BERGSTRASSE

The Bergstraße, or Mountain Road, was an ancient trading route used and named by the Romans *(strata montana)*. Gentle forest- and vineyard-covered hills and sunny escarpments slope toward the Rhine River. Castles and half-timbered villages invite exploration; orchards and wineries offer opportunities to sample the region's produce; and the idyllic landscape appeals to hikers, cyclists and others who crave more active pursuits.

▶ **Orient Yourself:** The Bergstrasse runs north from Heidelberg to Darmstadt following a course parallel to the A 67 motorway, which intersects it at Frankfurt.

Don't Miss: The scenic town of Heidelberg.

Organizing Your Time: If you want to explore Heidelberg, plan to spend a full day on the Bergstraße.

Also See: *HEIDELBERG, DARMSTADT, WORMS (50km/31mi to the northwest of Heidelberg), FRANKFURT AM MAIN (32km/20mi to the north of Darmstadt), MAINZ (34km/21mi to the northwest of Darmstadt).*

Driving Tour

From Heidelberg to Darmstadt   *58km/36mi – about 3hr.*

Heidelberg★★ – *see HEIDELBERG*

Weinheim

Weinheim is the first town on the Bergstraße to see springtime. The 13C agricultural community is today the seat of local government. The **old town** is charming, with a 16C Altes Rathaus (old town hall) on Marktplatz and the Büdinger Hof *(Judengasse 15-17)*. The Schloss (castle), which serves as the town hall, abuts an English-style park. Adjacent is the 19C **Exotenwald**★ (Exotic Forest), with a wonderful variety of trees. The ruins of castles **Burg Windeck** and **Wachenburg** stand watch over the town.

Heppenheim an der Bergstraße

The **Marktplatz**★, or *Großer Markt*, is charming, with the medieval Liebig pharmacy, the 16C town hall, and the vast neo-Gothic "Bergstraße Cathedral".

Lorsch

An 8C Carolingian abbey once dominated Lorsch; only the church narthex and the **Torhalle**★, a Carolingian triumphal arch, remain. The abbey, now a UNESCO World Heritage site, houses a **museum** *(Museumszentrum Lorsch)* which details its history and that of the town.   *Guided tour (1hr).*   *Open Tue-Sun, 10am-5pm.*   *Closed 1 Jan, Shrove Tue, 24 Dec.* *€3.* *(062 51) 10 38 20; www.kloster-lorsch.de.*

Bensheim

This "town of flowers and wine" is proud of its **old town**. Quaint half-timbered houses line the Marktplatz, the Haupstraße and Wambolterhofstraße. In a sheltered valley is the **Fürstenlager**★★, once the summer residence of the Landgraves of Hessen, now surrounded by a park. To the north, **Auerbacher Schloss** commands a view of the whole region.   *10am-5pm.* *(062 51) 729 23; www.schloss-auerbach.de.*

Darmstadt – *see DARMSTADT*

BERLIN★★★

POPULATION: 3 700 000

The vibrant, ever-changing city of Berlin never ceases to amaze with its enduring capacity for innovation and reinvention. Its dynamism is visible in the urban landscape, where avant-garde structures are creating a new city of stone, glass and concrete. This metropolis, which also features more parks and gardens than nearly any other on the Old Continent, is experiencing a new golden age. Its central European location, its restored status as capital city and its exciting artistic growth make this an exceptionally city. *Europa-Center, Budapester Straße, 10787 Berlin. ☎ (030) 25 00 25. www.berlin.de.*

▶ **Orient Yourself:** Berlin lies on the banks of the River Spree on the great Brandenburg plain, and stretches 45km/28mi east to west and 38km/24mi north to south. The outer districts are residential (Dahlem, Grunewald, Pankow) or industrial (Charlottenburg/Spandau, Köpenick, Tempelhof).

🅿 **Parking:** Parking garages lie throughout the city of Berlin. Visit http://wap.parkinfo.com for a complete listing of locations and charges.

🅿 **Don't Miss:** Charlottenburg Castle, the Gemäldegalerie, and the "Historic Centre" Walking Tour.

🕐 **Organizing Your Time:** You could spend a week in Berlin and not see everything. Prioritize your visit. To do the city justice, allow 1 day for Charlottenburg; 1 day for the Gemäldegalerie, and half a day for the historic sites near the Reichstag.

Especially for Kids: The Berlin Zoo, Großer Müggelsee, and the TV towers: the Fernsehturm in Alexanderplatz and the Funkturm.

👆 **Also See:** *POTSDAM (30km/19mi southwest), the SPREEWALD (Lübbenau is 93km/58mi southeast via the A 13), Lutherstadt WITTENBERG (107km/67mi southwest via the A 9), WÖRLITZER PARK (114km/71mi southwest, also via the A 9), the MECKLENBURGISCHE SEENPLATTE (Röbel is 141km/88mi northwest), MAGDEBURG (152km/95mi west).*

A Bit of History

Early History – The German capital originated from two 13C villages: Cölln and Berlin, small towns built respectively on a sandy island and on the Spree's east bank, each inhabited by fishermen and travelling merchants. The Hohenzollern Electors of Brandenburg were responsible for Berlin's evolution as a capital city. The first castle constructed on Cölln was completed in 1451. Nineteen years later it became the permanent residence of the Hohenzollern family.

The Great Elector (1640-88) – **Frederick-William of Brandenburg** constructed quays along the banks of the Spree and established laws making Berlin a healthy and well-governed town. Frederick-William's most important contribution was opening Berlin to the French Huguenots in 1685. The arrival of approximately one Huguenot for every five Berliners transformed the city with an influx of craftsmen, theologians, doctors and scholars.

Berlin in the Age of Enlightenment (18C) – The first King of Prussia, Frederick I, was succeeded by **Frederick-William I (1713-40)**, the **Soldier-King,** who laid the foundations of Prussian military power. He also laid out a new town, Friedrichstadt, beyond the old city bastions. Draconian measures accelerated the development of the district, which is cut by Leipziger Straße, Friedrichstraße and Wilhelmstraße (now Toleranzstraße).

Frederick II the Great (1740-86) continued this civic effort, adding monuments along Unter den Linden and the Forum Fridericianum (Bebelplatz). He enlisted the aid of architect Knobelsdorff (1699-1753), and the evolution toward neo-Classicism continued until 1835. The monuments of Berlin were finally completed with the Brandenburg Gate (1789) and the *Neue Wache* (1818).

19C Berlin – Berlin found its soul when the high patriotism following the King of Prussia's call to arms against Napoleon. The city benefited from the growing prestige of Prussia and led its Industrial Revolution. Although official architectural projects produced prestigious buildings like the Reichstag, green spaces also increased. By 1871, Berlin had become the capital of the Empire and numbered almost one million inhabitants.

Greater Berlin – In 1920 the city united six urban suburbs, seven towns, 59 villages and 27 demesnes under a single administration of four million inhabitants. Despite the upheavals following the First World War, the 1920s saw immense intellectual and artistical growth in Berlin. In 1928 Bertolt Brecht and Kurt Weill's *The Threepenny Opera* premiered, bringing together the best artistic and cultural spirits of the city. The blossoming of this talent was violently interrupted by Hitler regime, when, along with the persecution of the Jews, a wealth of German artistic and literary heritage was banned or destroyed in the campaign against "degenerate art."

The Taking of Berlin – The Yalta Conference concluded with Berlin's post-war occupation by the major powers. From 21 April to 3 May, the German capital was a battlefield. The Red Army marched against the remnants of the German army, destroying everything above ground, including 120 of Berlin's 248 bridges. At last, on 30 April 1945, the Reichstag was captured and Hitler committed suicide.

Berlin Divided – After the German surrender on 8 May, the four victorious allies – Great Britain, the United States, France and the Soviet Union – took over administration of greater Berlin. But political developments in the Soviet Sector hindered the municipal administration until, in 1948, the eastern sector found itself isolated. The Berlin Blockade, provoked by Russian opposition to currency reform in the western sectors, was beaten by an airlift of supplies from the west (26 June 1948 to 12 May 1949). Berlin's split was deepened by the introduction of the German Democratic Republic in 1949. In 1961 eastern authorities constructed a concrete and barbed wire Wall along the Soviet borderline.

Großer Müggelsee

Sir Norman Foster's lofty Reichstag dome

The "Fall" of the Wall – A night of wild celebration, especially around the Branden-burg Gate, followed the official "opening" of the Berlin Wall on 9 November 1989: the eastern authorities, bowing to increased public pressure, agreed to re-establish free passage between the two Germanies. In June 1991, the Bundestag selected Berlin as the capital of a reunited Germany. The two halves of the once-divided city still have their differences. What to change, and how much to change it, remain controversial questions. The traces of the Wall, in the mind and on the ground, will fade slowly.

An Outdoor City – Berlin, the biggest city in Germany, covers an area eight times the size of Paris. Devastated by the war, the capital lost much of its historical heritage, but thanks to the famous architects (Le Corbusier, Scharoun, Jean Nouvel, Liebeskind and others) involved in its reconstruction, a modernistic city, its quarters separated by vast green belts, has emerged from the ruins of 1945. The River Havel has been widened to form lakes (Tegeler See, Stößensee, Großer Wannsee). More than one third of the city's surface is covered by forests, parks and waterways.

A Lively Cultural Scene – Berlin justly enjoys a reputation for the quality and diversity of its cultural scene, particularly for its music, theatre and film festivals. The action today is found near the Kurfürstendamm ("Ku'Damm"), the Gedächtniskirche (Memorial Church) and the Alexanderplatz. Night-life on the **Kreuzberg** has a cos-mopolitan, anti-establishment flavour, while the Prenzlauer Berg, alive with bars, shops and cultural events, has a cool, alternative atmosphere. 300 years of immigrant influences have contributed to the character of a "typical" Berliner: lively, tolerant and with a sardonic sense of humour. This multiculturalism is also evident in Berlin's restaurants, which offer a great variety of cuisines alongside Brandenburger pig's knuckles (*Eisbein*) with sauerkraut and pease-pudding.

Walking Tours

Historic Centre★★

The itinerary starts from the Reichstag and then follows the celebrated Unter den Linden ("Under the Lime Trees"), which runs from Schlossplatz to Pariser Platz. Most of the great monuments of the former Prussian capital are set around this avenue, once a path taken by the Prince-Electors to the Tiergarten hunting reserve.

Reichstag★★

This massive neo-Renaissance palace was inaugurated in 1894. It was gutted by fire in 1933, heavily damaged in 1945 and its famous cupola was dynamited in 1954. The building was restored during the 1970s without the cupola. Building work began again in 1995 based on the design of British architect **Sir Norman Foster**. His glass cupola stands in sharp contrast to the massive building beneath it. Supported by twelve columns, it draws light into the Plenary Hall by way of a mirrored spindle. Access the cupola via a ramp leading to a **Panorama Platform**★★, always popular with visitors. In 1999, the Parliament convened in plenary session in the new Reichstag for the first time.

▶ *From the Reichstag go along Eberstraße towards the Brandenburg Gate.*

Holocaust Memorial ★★ (Holocaust-Mahnmal)

Built to honour the memory of the six million Jews exterminated by the Nazis, this powerful memorial was designed by Jewish German-American architect Peter Eisenman. The memorial stretches over two hectares (five acres) near the Brandenburg Gate and the Reichstag, and consists of 2 700 concrete pillars of differing heights. An attached underground Information Centre *(Ort der Information)* lists by name all known Jewish Holocaust victims, obtained from the Israeli museum Yad Vashem. The inauguration took place on 10 May 2005, 60 years after the German capitulation.

Brandenburg Gate★★ (Brandenburger Tor)

This triumphal arch, the very emblem of Berlin, was for almost three decades the symbol of the city's division: the structure was integrated into the Wall. Inspired by the Propylaea of the Parthenon, the gate was built by Carl Gotthard Langhans in 1788-91 and surmounted by the famous Victory Quadriga of Gottfried Schadow (1793). The original group was removed to Paris after one of Napoleon's campaigns and returned to Berlin in 1814.

Unter den Linden★★

The famous avenue "Under the Lime Trees", conceived by the Great Elector Frederick William in 1647, is bordered from the Friedrichstraße intersection onwards by monuments of the 17C and 19C. The original lime trees that shaded Unter den Linden were cut down in 1658. Four rows were replanted in 1820.

▶ *Take the Charlottenstraße southwards to the Gendarmenmarkt.*

Brandenburg Gate, symbol of Berlin

Ph. Gajic/MICHELIN

Address Book

PRACTICAL INFORMATION

TELEPHONE PREFIX: 030

TOURIST INFORMATION

Berlin Tourismus Marketing GmbH,
Am Karlsbad 11, ☎ *25 00 25* (room
reservations) or *0190 01 63 16* (Info
Hotline), Mon-Fri 8am-7pm, Sat-Sun
9am-6.30pm. Offices: Europa-Center,
Budapester Straße 45, Mon-Sat
8.30am-8.30pm, Sun 10am-6.30pm;
Brandenburg Gate, south wing, Mon-
Sun 9.30am-6pm; Tegel airport, gate
0, Mon-Sun 5am-10.30pm; KaDeWe,
Reisecenter (Travel Centre) ground
floor, Mon-Fri 8.30am-8pm, Sat 9am-
4pm.

City magazines *Zitty* and *Tip* and the
monthly *Berlin-Programm* (available
at the bookshops and kiosks) provide
event information. Berlin's major dai-
lies have weekly calendars of events,
and every other month Berlin Tourismus publishes the *Berlin Kalender*,
available for €1.20 at their offices at
the Brandenburg Gate, KaDeWe and
the Europa-Center (👆 *see above*).
Tickets are available up to three weeks
before performances at *Berlin Tourismus Marketing*. Theatre box offices
are the best place to buy tickets when
in town.

POST OFFICES WITH LATE HOURS

Post office 120 at Joachimstaler Straße
8 is open Mon-Sat 8am-midnight and
Sun 10am-midnight; post office 519 at
Tegel airport, main hall, is open Mon-
Fri 8.30am-6.30pm, Sat 9am-2pm.
(Deutsche Post AG, ☎ *62 78 10)*

DAILY PAPERS

*Berliner Morgenpost, Tagesspiegel,
Berliner Zeitung, Die Tageszeitung*

INTERNET

www.berlin.de
www.berlinonline.de
www.berlin-info.de
www.d-berlin.de
www.berlinculture.de
www.gotoberlin.de
www.city-berlin.com

TRANSPORT

AIRPORT

For general flight information ☎ 0180
500 01 86. **Tegel (TXL)**, northwest
of Berlin, handles most international
traffic. Bus nos. 109 and X9 (going to
Zoologischer Garten) travels to the
city centre from the airport. The Jet
Express Bus TXL runs between Tegel
and the Mitte district (notably Potsdamer Platz, Friedrichstraße and Unter
den Linden).

PUBLIC TRANSPORT

The BVG (Berliner Verkehrs-Betrieb)
manages trams, buses and underground trains in Berlin, ☎ 1 94 49 or
24hr hotline ☎ 0180 599 66 33 (offices
open Mon-Fri, 5.30am-8.30pm and
Sat, 8.45am-4.15pm).

Transportation for the region around
Berlin and the S-Bahn are operated by
the VBB (Verkehrsverbund Berlin-
Brandenburg) and the BVG, ☎ 25
41 41 41 Mon-Fri 8am-8pm, Sat-Sun
9am-6pm. Information is available at
the BVG-Pavillon on Hardenbergplatz
(Bahnhof Zoo) 6.30am-8.30pm and
at many U-Bahn and S-Bahn stations.
Berlin and its environs (eg Potsdam)
are divided into three fare zones (A, B
and C). For rides within the city, buy a
ticket for Zone AB. Tickets are available in all U-Bahn and S-Bahn stations,
in trams, at ticket vending machines
and from bus drivers. Tickets must be
stamped to be valid.

Normal fare (valid 2hr) €2.60 (for the
3 zones ABC); day ticket (valid from
tpunching until 3am next morning)
€6 and the 7-day ticket (7 Tage Karte)
€25.40 for 2 zones, €31.30 for 3 zones.
The **Welcome Card** (valid 72hr) costs
€35 and lets an adult with up to
three children under 14 use the entire
VBB network; it also gives discounts
for selected theatres, museums,
attractions and city tours. The card is
available at BVG outlets and at information offices of the *Berlin Tourismus
Marketing*.
Construction in Berlin can lead to
delays and detours in local transport.

SIGHTSEEING

Useful Tip: Bus number 100 that shuttles between Bahnhof Zoo and Alexanderplatz passes by many of Berlin's sights.

Internet – www.bvg.de; www.vbbon-line.de; www.berliner-verkehr.de

CITY TOURS

Severin & Kühn (☎ 880 41 90), *Bus-Verkehr-Berlin* (☎ 885 68 00), *Berliner-Bären-Service* (☎ 35 19 52 70; *www.sightseeing.de*) and *Berolina* (☎ 88 56 80 30; www.berolina-berlin. com) all drive the City-Circle. 2hr tours with explanations via headphones and on-off service leave every 30min beginning at 10am. Departure from Kurfürstendamm (between Joachim-sthaler Straße and Fasanenstraße) and Alexanderplatz in front of the Forum-Hotel. Severin & Kühn run the Große Berlin-Tour: 3-4hr tours at 10am and 2pm.

City walking tours with historical, topical and contemporary themes are offered by: *Kulturbüro* (☎ 444 09 36; *www.stadtverfuehrung.de), art:Berlin* (☎ 28 09 63 90, www.artberlin-online. de) and *Stattreisen* (☎ 455 30 28; www. stattreisen.berlin.de).

BOAT TOURS

Stern- und Kreisschiffahrt (☎ 536 36 00) offers rides through the city's historic centre beginning in the Nikolaiviertel (1hr); tours through the inner city by way of the Spree and Landwehr canals (3hr 30min) beginning at the Jannowitzbrücke and Schloßbrücke; and rides on the Havel from Wannsee to Potsdam/Lange Brücke (1hr 15min).

EATING OUT

◎◎ **Diekmann** – *Meinekestraße 7 10719. Berlin-Charlottenburg* ☎ (030) 883 33 21. www.j-diekmann.de. ◷ *Closed Sun lunchtime. Reservation necessary.* With its wooden flooring, simple chairs and old-style décor this restaurant resembles a colonial boutique. Quick lunch menus available.

◎◎ **Marjellchen** – *Mommsen-straße 9.* ☎ (030) 883 26 76. ◷ *Closed Sun.* Pleasant, homey Berlin restaurant serving substantial dishes from eastern Prussia and Silesia. The Marjellchen has inherited its grandmother's recipes.

◎◎ **Mutter Hoppe** – *Rathausstraße 21.* Tram *Alexanderplatz.* ☎ (030) 24 15 62 5. www.prostmahlzeit.de/mutter-hoppe. This old-style restaurant is near the Nikolaiviertel, rebuilt in historic style. The rustic layout, with old bars and photographs, is nostalgic. Traditional live music Fri and Sat from 8pm.

◎◎ **Nußbaum** – *Bundesplatz 5.* Tram *Bundesplatz.* ☎ (030) 854 50 20. ◷ *Closed Christmas Eve. Reservation recommended.* Nußbaum serves robust traditional cuisine in the Wilmersdorf district, on the lively Bundesplatz.

◎◎◎ **Bamberger Reiter** – *Regens-burger Straße 7.* ☎ (030) 218 42 82. ◷ *Closed Sun and Mon.* Delicious dishes delight fans of Austrian food. The rustic décor adds elegance with beautiful wood and sparkling mirrors.

◎◎◎ **Borchardt** – *Französische Straße 47.* ☎ (030) 20 38 71 10. ◷ *Closed Sun.* With impressive gilded columns, stuccoed ceilings and refined furniture, this is one of the most chic restaurants in town. People come here to see and be seen, and to enjoy seasonal French cuisine.

◎◎◎ **Zander** – *Kollwitzstraße 50 10405 Berlin-Prenzlauer Berg.* Tram *Senefelderplatz.* ☎ (030) 44 05 76 78 - www.gourmetguide.com/zander. ◷ *Closed Sun. Reservation recommended.* This simple restaurant spreads over two storeys. Its charm lies in its wooden flooring and dark wooden chairs. Modern cuisine with varying weekly menus.

The Turkish market in Kreuzberg

H. Champollion/MICHELIN

Harlekin – *Lützowufer 15.* ☎ *(030) 254 78 86 30 - www.esplanade. de.* ⓒ *Closed 1-6 Jan, Aug, Sun and Mon.* Markus Lüpertz's Harlekin dominates the dining area in this creative restaurant. The glass-fronted kitchen enables diners to watch the team of chefs and the pots.

Kaiserstuben – *Am Festungsgraben 1.* ☎ *(030) 20 61 05 48. info@kaiserstuben.de.* ⓒ *Closed 3 weeks in Jul/Aug, Sun and Mon.* This little restaurant, with its simple elegance, high white-stucco ceilings and classic menu, is on the first floor of a magnificent palace.

WHERE TO STAY

Am Wilden Eber – *Warnemünder Straße 19, 14199 Berlin-Zehlendorf.* 🚋 *Podbielskiallee.* ☎ *(030) 89 77 79 90. Fax (030) 897779999. www.hotel-am-wilden-eber.de.* 🅿 🏊 *15 rooms*. A simple hotel with well-kept and quiet rooms, and a small swimming pool and sauna in the basement.

Hotel Am Anhalter Bahnhof – *Stresemannstraße 36, 10963 Berlin-Kreuzberg.* ☎ *(030) 251 03 42. Fax (030) 2514897. www.hotel-anhalter-bahnhof.de.* 🅿 *33 rooms* A no-frills establishment in a central location near Potsdamer Platz, a bus stop on its doorstep. Basic rooms, some with showers, but clean and cheap.

Hotel Econtel – *Sömmeringstraße 24* 🚋 *Mierendorffplatz* ☎ *(030) 34 68 10. Fax (030) 34681163. www. econtel.de.* 🅿 ♿ *205 rooms* *Restaurant.* This establishment near the city centre is great for groups and offers three room categories: Economy, Business or Comfort. Mickey Mouse face painting available for children. Schloß Charlottenburg is a stone's throw away.

Hotel Künstlerheim Luise – *Luisenstraße 19.* ☎ *(030) 28 44 80 Fax (030) 28448448. www.kuenstler-heim-luise.de.* ♿ *Reservation necessary. 47 rooms.* *Restaurant.* This classical municipal palace built in 1825 today houses a unique hotel where artists have had a hand in the room decoration. Basic, cheaper rooms

with showers are also available. The Wein Guy restaurant is adjacent to the hotel.

Hotel Berlin-Plaza – *Knesebeckstraße 63.* ☎ *(030) 88 41 30. Fax (030) 88413754. www.plazahotel. de.* 🅿 *Reservation recommended. 131 rooms.* *Restaurant* This hotel stands in a central location near the Ku'damm. Rooms are modern and functional.

Hotel Hackescher Markt – *Große Präsidentenstraße 8.* ☎ *(030) 28 00 30. Fax (030) 28003111. www.hackescher-markt.com.* *31 rooms* A modern building with an old-style façade in Berlin's new Szeneviertel (theatre district). Despite the hotel's central location, the spacious rooms with terrace are very quiet as they face a small inner courtyard.

Grand Hotel Esplanade – *Lützowufer 15, 10785 Berlin-Tiergarten.* ☎ *(030) 25 47 80. Fax (030) 254788222. www.esplanade.de.* *386 rooms* This big hotel has been engulfed by the cultural life of the district and features edgy modern interior decoration, including paintings by the "Berliner Wilden." Very modern, luxurious rooms.

Hotel Adlon – *Unter den Linden 77.* ☎ *(030) 226 10. Fax (030) 22612222. adlon@kempinski. com.* ♿ *336 rooms.* In 1997, it once again became possible to stay in this legendary, luxuriously-restored building near the Brandenburg Gate and Unter den Linden.

CAFÉS

Café am Schiffbauerdamm – *Albrechtstraße 13 (Mitte).* 🚋 *Friedrichstraße* ☎ *(030) 28 38 40 49.* ⓒ *from 10am.* A pleasant atmosphere suffuses the bright rooms and terrace of the Café am Schiffbauerdamm, set in a quiet street in Friedrich-Wilhelm-Stadt. Cakes and tarts, sandwiches and meals are served.

Café Ephraim's – *Spreeufer 1 (Mitte, near Mühlendamm)* 🚋 *Klosterstraße* ☎ *(030) 24 72 59 47. www.ephraims.de* ⓒ *from 12pm.* A real gem of a café in the Nikolaiviertel, with Berlin specialities, homemade cakes and tarts, 19C "Gründerzeit" furniture and a warm atmosphere. Customers can sit outside on the banks of the Spree.

Telecafé – *Panoramastraße 1a (Mitte, near Alexanderplatz).*  *Alexanderplatz.* ☏ *(030) 2 42 33 33. www.berlinerfernsehturm.de. Panorama: Mar-Oct: 9am-1am; Nov-Feb: 10am-midnight . Telecafé: Mar-Oct: 9am-1am; Nov-Feb: 10am-midnight.* This café in the television tower rotates full-circle in 30min, allowing customers full views of the whole of Berlin.

Café terrace on the banks of the Spree

GOING OUT

Useful Tips – The "scene" in Berlin is decentralised: in Charlottenburg visit Savignyplatz and the Ku'Damm; in Schöneberg around Winterfeldplatz; in Kreuzberg around Chamissoplatz, on Oranienstraße and Wiener Straße and along the Landwehrkanal; in Berlin-Mitte at Friedrichstraße, in the Nikolaiviertel and the Hackescher Markt, and in Prenzlauer Berg around Kollwitzplatz and Kastanienallee.

Clärchen's Ballhaus – *Auguststraße 24-25 (Mitte).* *Weinmeisterstraße.* ☏ *(030) 2 82 92 95.* This traditional dance hall in the Spandauer Vorstadt district has belonged to the same family since 1913. The music ranges from old classics to the latest hits. Wed there are beginner's tango classes.

925 Loungebar – *Taubenstraße 19 (Mitte).* *Hausvogteiplatz, Stadtmitte.* ☏ *(030) 20 18 71 77.* ⏰ *Open from 5pm.* A cocktail bar at the Gendarmenmarkt, with rooms, furniture and lighting all in red. This place is named after its bar made of 925 sterling silver.

Die Tagung – *Wühlischstraße 29 (east of Warschauer Straße) , 10245 Berlin-Friedrichshain* *Frankfurter Tor.* ☏ *(030) 29 77 37 88.* ⏰ *Open from 7pm.* The appeal of this dark and slightly dilapidated bar lies in its abundant East German décor: busts, signs and posters of all kinds.

Universum Lounge – *Kurfürstendamm 153,10709 Berlin-Charlottenburg* *Adenauerplatz.* ☏ *(030) 89 06 49 94.* ⏰ *from 3pm.* A bar in the Ku'damm, in the same building as the Schaubühne. Coloured leather seats, teak panelling

and pictures of the universe. The copper bar and slightly rounded room hug the curves of Erich Mendelssohn's building.

Zillemarkt – *Bleibtreustraße 48a, 10623 Berlin-Charlottenburg.* ⓢ *Savignyplatz.* ☏ *(030) 8 81 70 40- www.zillemarkt.de.* ⏰ *10am-1am.* Traditional décor with small tables of undressed wood, a bar lit by old lamps and a charming little beer garden.

SHOPPING

USEFUL TIPS

Berlin's main shopping streets are Kurfürstendamm, Tauentzienstraße (with department stores Europa-Center and KaDeWe), Friedrichstraße, and Fasanenstraße in the city centre. The most prestigious shopping arcades are Leibnizkolonnaden (between Leibniz- and Wielandstraße), Potsdamer Platz Arkaden, Friedrichstadtpassagen (with Galeries Lafayette) and the Hackesche Höfe.

DEPARTMENT STORES

Kurfürstendamm, Tauentzienstraße and the Potsdamer Platz arcades are where the most famous department stores are found: *KaDeWe*, Tauentzienstraße 221, a gigantic selection in a luxurious setting; *Galeries Lafayette*, Friedrichstraße 207, good variety in amazing architectural surroundings. Exclusive shops are located on Fasanenstraße and Friedrichstraße.

A special shopping address is the **Hackeschen Höfe** (Rosenthalerstraße/ Sophienstraße, www.hackeschehoefe.com), with eight courtyards containing galleries, boutiques, antiques shops, restaurants and bars, a cinema and even a cabaret.

Art galleries – In the west half of the city galleries are on Savignyplatz (Charlottenburg), on Fasanenstraße (Charlottenburg), and on Pariser Straße (Wilmersdorf); in the east part of the city between Oranienburger Straße and Rosa-Luxemburg-Platz.

Antiques – Antique dealers are on Eisenacher Straße, Kalckreuthstraße and Fasanenstraße, around Bleibtreustraße,

Pestalozzistraße, and Knesebeckstraße, and around Friedrichstraße station.

Flea markets – Großer Berliner Trödel- und Kunstmarkt (flea and art market), Straße des 17. Juni (Charlottenburg), Sat-Sun 11am to 5pm; flea market in Wilmersdorf, Fehrbelliner Platz, Sat-Sun 7am to 4pm; art and antiques market on Museumsinsel, Sat-Sun 11am to 5pm.

Markets – Market on Winterfeldplatz, Wed and Sat 8am to 1pm; weekly Turkish market, Maybachufer (Neukölln), Tues and Fri noon to 6:30pm.

Gendarmenmarkt★★

This is undoubtedly the most beautiful square in Berlin, named after Frederick William I's "Gens d'Armes" regiment. In this square, the Schauspielhaus, an elegant theatre built by Schinkel in 1821, is bounded on the south by the German cathedral, **Deutscher Dom**★, and on the north by the French cathedral, **Französischer Dom**★, both early-18C churches.

Schauspielhaus★★ (Theatre)

Karl Friedrich Schinkel's principal inspiration for this theatre was Greek Antiquity: Notice the portico supported by six pillars. The theatre was rebuilt between 1980 and 1984, after its destruction in the 1940s, following the rules of classicist architecture. The interior is not an exact reproduction, but the concert halls are truly magnificent.

▶ *Take Französischestraße up to St Hedwigs-Kathedrale, set back from Bebelplatz.*

Forum Fridericianum★★ (Bebelplatz)

The Forum Fridericianum (also called Friedrichsforum or Lindenforum) was designed by Knobelsdorff to hold an opera house, a science academy and a castle. The opera house was the only building completed; the king lost interest and set his sights on Potsdam. In the 18C, the Forum was one of the most beautiful squares in the world. More recent changes include an imperial palace and a Dresdner Bank building. In 1994, Micha Ullman created the **Versunkene Bibliothek** (sunken library), a glass-fronted, empty-shelved room which commemorates the book-burning on Bebelplatz on 10 May 1933.

St Hedwigs-Kathedrale

Knobelsdorff drafted the plans for this 18C Catholic church, closely modelled on the Pantheon in Rome. Since Frederick II had been victorious in capturing Silesia, the church was dedicated to St Hedwig, the patron saint of Silesia. It was badly damaged during the Second World War and largely rebuilt between 1952 and 1963.

Staatsoper Unter den Linden★

Opposite St Hedwig's cathedral on Bebelplatz.

Built by Knobelsdorff between 1740 and 1743 on the "Forum Fridericianum", the Opera House burned down in 1843; Langhans' reconstruction follows the original plans. Destroyed again during the Second World War, the State Opera House was rebuilt by Richard Paulick between 1951 and 1955.

The Huguenots, France's Contribution to Berlin

In 1685, in response to Louis XIV's Revocation of the Edict of Nantes, the Great Elector Frederick William of Brandenburg issued the Edict of **Potsdam** granting asylum to French Calvinists.

These Protestants, or Huguenots, came in droves. 100 000 passed through Frankfurt-am-Main alone in 20 years' time. 15 000 Huguenots settled in Brandenburg, including 6 000 in Berlin, representing one quarter of the population. The Frenchmen developed the Friedrichstadt area, as well as some fifty trades, a textile industry and fruit and vegetable husbandry. They also introduced several popular new dances: the cotillon, the gavotte and the minuet. Until the 19C, the French community had its own ecclesiastical and legal organisation.

Humboldt-Universität
On Unter den Linden, opposite the Opera House.
The palace of Frederick II's brother, Prince Heinrich, built in 1753, became a university in 1810 and now enrolls 20 000 students. Left of the entrance, a statue of founder Wilhelm von Humboldt faces that of his brother, geographer Alexander von Humboldt. A few of the university's prestigious figures include: Fichte (the first rector); Hegel, Einstein and Planck taught here; and Heine and Marx were students.

Alte Bibliothek★ (Old Library)
Opposite Humboldt-Universität. Designed by Georg Friedrich Boumann in Viennese Baroque style for the royal book collection, this library was inaugurated in 1780.

▷ *Take Charlottenstraße southwards to the Gendarmenmarkt.*

Neue Wache (New Guardhouse)
This memorial, designed by Schinkel in 1818, was consecrated in 1966 as a Monument to the Victims of Fascism and Militarism. Since 1993, it has been designated Germany's leading memorial, a "place of remembrance for the victims of war and violence." The interior houses a sculpture by Käthe Kollwitz: *Mother with Dead Son.*

Zeughaus★★ (Arsenal)
&. ⊙ *Open daily, 10am-6pm.* ⊙ *Closed 24-26 and 31 Dec.* ⊛ *€4.* ☎ *(030) 20 30 40; www.dhm.de.*
Berlin's most important Baroque edifice, erected between 1695 and 1706, the Zeughaus houses the **Deutsches Historisches Museum**★★ *(German Historical Museum),* which reopened after extensive renovations in 2006. The comprehensive exhibition uses multimedia and artifacts to examine over 2 000 years of history: the upper floor, covering the period from the first century AD to the end of the empire in 1918; and the lower floor, with the Weimar Republic, the Nazi and Post-War years, the divided Germany and modern reunification.

Friedrichswerdersche Kirche★ (Friedrichswerdersche Church)
&. ⊙ *Open daily, 10am-6pm.* ☎ *(030) 20 90 55 77. www.smb.spk-berlin.de.*
This impressive brick church was built from 1824 to 1830 following the designs of Karl Friedrich Schinkel, who left his mark on the cityscape like none other. The church houses the **Schinkelmuseum**★, with sculptures by its namesake.

▷ *Cross the Spree and carry on to the Museumsinsel (described below in "Special Features"). On the left stands Berlin Cathedral.*

Berliner Dom★

 ♿ ◷ *Open Apr to Sep, 9am-8pm, Sun 12 noon-8pm; Oct to Mar, 9am-7pm, Sun, 12 noon-7pm.* ☎ *(030) 20 26 91 19. www.berliner-dom.de.*

This late-19C Italian Renaissance cathedral features a magnificent **interior**★★, capable of seating congregations up to 1 500. In the southern part of the church is the sarcophagus of Frederick I and his second wife Sophie Charlotte, by Andreas Schlüter. Part of the cathedral **crypt** is open to the public, with over 90 sarcophagi and the remains of the Prussian-Brandenburg Hohenzollerns.

▶ *At this point you can prolong your walk to see the modern districts via Karl Liebknechstraße.*

Alexanderplatz★

The name of this square derives from Tsar Alexander's 1805 visit to Berlin. The square – known as "Alex" by locals – acts as a city hub in the eastern sector. It was completely destroyed in the Second World War and rebuilt in the austere socialist style. The **Marienkirche** (late 14C: 15C Danse Macabre fresco in the tower) stands beside the 365m/1 198ft 🅺🅸🅳🅂**Fernsehturm**★ (Television Tower). The revolving sphere at the top houses a restaurant and viewing platform. South of the square stands the **Rotes Rathaus**★ (Red Town Hall), built from 1861 to 1869 entirely of bricks.

Nikolaiviertel★ (St Nicholas Quarter)

With its narrow cobbled streets and old taverns, this quarter teems with restored period houses like the **Knoblauch house**★ (Knoblauchhaus – *Poststraße 23;* ◷ *open Tue-Sun, 10am-6pm.* ◷ *Closed 24 and 31 Dec.* ⚅ *€1, free on Wed.* ☎ *(030) 27 57 67 33; www.stadtmuseum.de)* and the **Ephraim Palace**★ (Ephraim-Palais – *between Poststraße and Mühlendamm;* ♿ ◷ *Open Tue-Sun, 10am-6pm.* ◷ *Closed 24 and 31 Dec.* ⚅ *€3, free on Wed.* ☎ *(030) 24 00 21 21; www.stadtmuseum.de).* The Nikolaiviertel is dominated by the bell-towers of the **Nikolaikirche**★, the oldest church in Berlin. The Romanesque basilica, with its Gothic chancel (1379), was transformed into a brick Gothic hall-church after a city-wide fire in 1380.

Tiergarten District★

The oldest park in the city stretches almost 3km/2mi from Ernst-Reuter-Platz to the Brandenburg Gate. Originally a royal hunting reserve, then a military exercise area, it was transformed into a delightful English-style park by landscape architect Peter Joseph Lenné (1789-1866).

Siegessäule (Victory Column)

◷ *Open Apr to Oct, 9.30am-6.30pm, Sat-Sun, 9.30am-7pm; Nov to Mar, 9.30am-5.30pm.* ◷ *Closed 23 and 24 Dec.* ⚅ *€2.20.*

All of 67m/220ft high, this landmark monument, surmounted by Victory, commemorates the Prussian campaigns of 1864, 1866 and 1870 against Denmark, Austria and France. From the top (285 steps), there is an aerial **view**★ of the Spree, the Hanse complex, the Tiergarten, the Brandenburg Gate, Unter den Linden, the Berlin Rathaus and a view to the shores of the Havel.

Schloss Bellevue

Built in the neo-Classical style by Boumann in 1785, this was the summer palace of Frederick the Great's younger brother, Prince Augustus-Ferdinand. Today it is the official residence of the President of the Republic. Behind the castle is a 20ha/50-acre park.

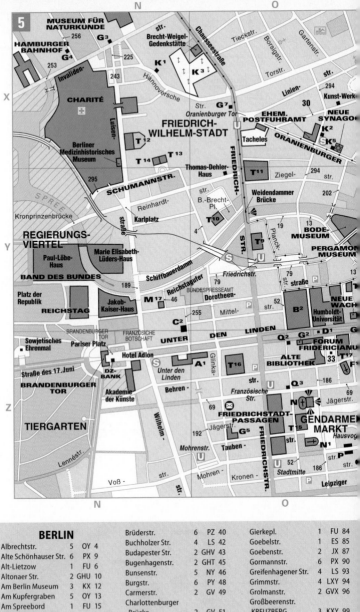

BERLIN

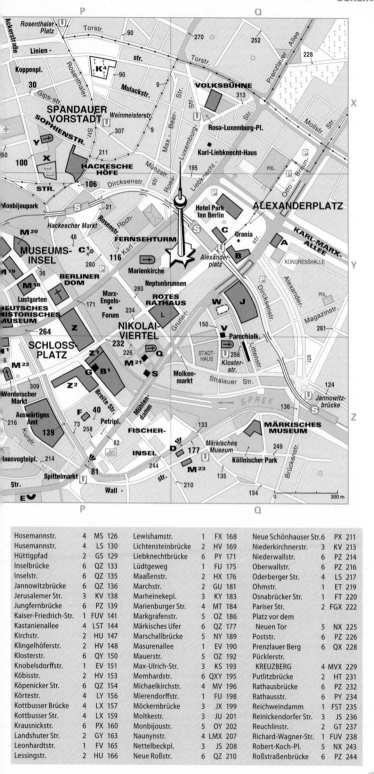

Zoologischer Garten★★★
(Zoological Gardens)

Kids *Main entrance: Hardenbergplatz.* ♿
🕐 *Summer: 9am-6.30pm; winter: 9am-5pm.* ▭ *€11.* ☎ *(030) 25 40 10; www.zoo-berlin.de.* Situated in the heart of Berlin, this zoo, with 14 000 creatures, is one of the largest in the world. The Aquarium *(entry via the zoo or from Budapester Straße)* displays a collection of approximately 650 species. On the first floor are the popular crocodile hall and the terrarium. ♿ 🕐 *Open 9am-6pm.* ▭ *€11.* ☎ *(030) 25 40 10; www.aquarium-berlin.de.*

Knautschke the Survivor

The end of the war was a difficult time for the animals at the zoo; the locals used them for food, just as they used trees from the Tiergarten for heat. One writer, Stefan Reisner (*Stadtfront, Berlin West Berlin*, 1982), recalls his father melting a camel's hump in a frying pan. However, the hippopotamus Knautschke was more fortunate. He stayed underwater during the conflict, re-emerging a true hero once the bombardments were over.

Kurfürstendamm District★

Kurfürstendamm★★

In the 16C, the Kurfürstendamm was a simple path allowing the Prince Electors to reach the Grunewald hunting lodge. Bismarck transformed it, between 1882 and 1886, into the prestigious thoroughfare known to Berliners today as the "Ku'Damm." Along its 3.5km/2mi length, the boulevard teems with cafés, restaurants, theatres, galleries and boutiques, making this the centre of cosmopolitan life in the capital.

Kaiser-Wilhelm-Gedächtniskirche★ (Kaiser Wilhelm Memorial Church)

♿ 🕐 *Open 9am-7pm.* ☎ *(030) 218 50 23; www.gedaechtniskirche.com.*
This neo-Romanesque church was built between 1891 and 1895 as a memorial to the Emperor Wilhelm I. It was badly damaged during the Second World War, but its ruins are preserved as a reminder of the horrors of war and have become a symbol of Berlin. The shattered tower is incorporated in a modernistic complex (1959-61) of pierced concrete modules, lit by 20 000 blue glass windows made in Chartres. The former entrance beneath the tower is now a **Memorial Hall**, tracing the history of the church, recalling the victims of the war, and pleading for peace.

Tauentzienstraße

This is the fashionable shopping street where Europe's largest department store, **"KaDeWe,"** is situated. The abbreviation stands for Kaufhaus des Westens: Big Store of the West. Behind the Gedächtniskirche is the **Europa-Center**, a shopping complex with restaurants, cinemas and the famous cabaret "Die Stachelschweine" (The Porcupines). From the roof of this building, 100m/328ft above the street *(lift to the 20th floor then staircase for the last two storeys)* is a fine **view**★ over the city. The fountain in the square between the Gedächtniskirche and the Europa-Center, with its bronze sculptures and exotic figures, symbolises the terrestrial globe. Berliners call it "**Wasserklops**" (the "water meatball").

Museumsinsel★★★ (Museum Island)

The brainchild of Frederick William III, this 19C museum complex between the Spree and the canal occupies the site of Berlin's former sister town, Cölln. A competition launched for a redesign of the Museumsinsel will refashion the Neues Museum (destroyed during the Second World War) by English architect David Chipperfield, and will incorporate the Egyptian Museum collections. German architect Oswald Mathias Ungers will extend the Pergamonmuseum, and all museums on the island (except the Alte Nationalgalerie) will be combined in an Archaeological Promenade by 2010.

Pergamonmuseum★★★ (Pergamon Museum)

Entrance Kupfergraben. 🚻 🕐 *Open daily except Mon, 10am-6pm, Thurs 10am-10pm.* 👓 *€12, free admission Thurs, 4 hours before closing.* ☎ *(030) 20 90 55 77; www.smb. spk-berlin.de.*

Built between 1909 and 1930, this is the island's most recent museum. The museum is divided into three sections. The **Collection of Antiquities**★★★ *(Antikensammlung)* features the **Altar of Pergamon**★★★, a masterpiece of Hellenistic art (2C BC); a gateway to the Milet market★★ (2C AD); and Greek and Roman sculptures. The **Middle East Museum**★ *(Vorderasiatisches Museum)* includes the **Processional Way and Ishtar Gate**★★ from ancient Babylon, 580 BC; Plinth of Asachadon, 7C BC; façade of the Temple of Irmin at Uruk (Sumerian period); and bas-relief sculptures of the Temple of Assurnasirpal II at Kalchu, 9C BC. The **Museum of Islamic Art**★★ *(Museum für Islamische Kunst)* features the Façade of Omayyade Castle, Mchatta (8C), east Jordan; painted panelling from Aleppo (early 17C); and miniatures (15C-17C).

Alte Nationalgalerie★★ (Old National Gallery)

Entrance Bodestraße. 🚻 🕐 *Open daily except Mon, 10am-6pm, Thurs 10am-10pm.* 👓 *€12, free admission Thurs, 4 hours before closing.* ☎ *(030) 20 90 55 77; www.smb. spk-berlin.de.*

This museum exhibits paintings and sculptures from the 19C. In the upper exhibition gallery are works from the time of Goethe until Late Romanticism (among others: **Caspar David Friedrich**, Waldmüller, Schinkel). The middle floor displays works by Feuerbach, Böcklin, Liebermann, the French Impressionists, and German and Flemish historical scenes. The lower floor exhibits focus on Berlin artists (**Adolph Menzel**, Krüger, Schadow) and Realist landscapes (Constable, Courbet).

Bode-Museum★★

Entrance Monbijoubrücke.

This splendid 1904 neo-Baroque edifice at the tip of Museumsinsel has been closed since mid-1999 for a thorough renovation. It is scheduled for a late-2006 reopening, housing the reunited **Sculpture Collection;** the **Museum of Late Antique and Byzantine Art** (Museum für Spätantike und Byzantinische Kunst); and the **Numismatic Collection**, displaying the history of coins and money.

The Museums of Berlin

The Altes Museum, the first museum in Berlin, was built in 1830 by Karl Friedrich Schinkel. It was followed under Frederick William IV by the Neues Museum and Nationalgalerie on the Museumsinsel. Wilhelm von Bode, director of the Berlin museums from 1906 onward, painstakingly organized the city's collections, bringing them to the attention of connoisseurs worldwide.

Reconstruction of the destroyed museums began after the Second World War – no small task considering collections had to be gathered from storage or reacquired from victorious pillagers. Post-war Germany further divided the museum collections between East and West. The Stiftung Preußischer Kulturbesitz (Foundation for Prussian Cultural Property) preserved the collections in the west while eastern artifacts gathered at the traditional spot: the "Museumsinsel".

In 1992, soon after Germany's reunification, Berlin's museums rejoined under the umbrella of the Stiftung Preußischer Kulturbesitz – Staatliche Museen zu Berlin.

The Altes Museum on Museumsinsel, Berlin's first public museum.

Altes Museum★★ (Old Museum)

   Open Tue-Sun, 10am-6pm. *Closed Easter and Pentecost, 24, 25 and 31 Dec.* *€12, free admission Thurs, 4 hours before closing.* *(030) 20 90 55 77; www.smb.spk-berlin.de.*

Berlin's first public museum, the main entrance is a masterpiece of neo-Classical art, with 18 Ionic columns. Inside, the ground floor houses the smaller works of the **Antikensammlung** (Collection of Antiquities – the monumental works are in the Pergamonmuseum). Ancient Greek art includes artifacts from the Cyclades (3rd millennium BC), the Archaic Period (7C-5C BC), Hellenism and the Roman Empire. The **Antiker Schmuck** (Antique jewelry) is fascinating as well, including gold discoveries from Vettersfelde (c 500 BC), from Tarent (3C BC) and the **Hildesheimer Silberfund**★★★ (Hildesheim Silver Hoard) from the Roman era.

Kulturforum im Tiergarten and surrounding Area

The Kulturforum was designed, in the late 1950s, to become the cultural centre of West Berlin, a counterpart to the Museumsinsel in the eastern part of the city.

Gemäldegalerie★★★ (Picture Gallery)

   Open daily except Mon, 10am-6pm, Thurs 10am-10pm. *Closed Easter and Pentecost, 24, 25 and 31 Dec.* *€8, free admission Thurs, 4 hours before closing.* *(030) 20 90 55 77. www.smp.spk-berlin.de.*

This collection was born of the passion of the Great Elector (1620-88) and Frederick the Great (1712-86). But it was **Wilhelm von Bode**, director of the Gemäldegalerie beginning in 1890, who tirelessly acquired European paintings from the 13C to the 18C. In spite of war losses (400 paintings were destroyed), the collection is still considered one of the finest in the world.

The modest building's 53 rooms are arranged in a horseshoe around a foyer and provide space for over 1 100 paintings. Works are presented in chronological order and arranged by school:

Rooms I-III, Galleries 1-4: German School, 13C-16C (Late Gothic/Renaissance), notably illustrated by Martin Schongauer (The Birth of Christ), Lucas Cranach the Elder (Venus und Amor, Adam

5-7-9

The three-naved foyer of the Gemäldegalerie, a wonderfully designed space, boasts a single work of art: a sculpture by the American conceptual sculptor Walter De Maria entitled *The 5-7-9 Series*. It consists of 27 polygonal, highly polished steel staffs ordered in three rows in a granite water basin. The geometric staffs are assembled according to various mathematical combinations. This artwork is a good conclusion to a visit to the Gemäldegalerie: It brings the viewer back to earth, tests his or her imagination and simply permits a rest.

and Eve), Hans Holbein the Younger *(The Merchant Georg Gisze)*, Albrecht Dürer *(Portrait of Hieronymus Holzschuher)*.

Rooms IV-VI, Galleries 5-7: Dutch School, 15C-16C (Late Gothic/Renaissance: Gérard David, Hans Memling, Hugo Van der Goes, Jan Gossaert, Jan Van Eyck, Quentin Metsys and Pieter Bruegel the Elder, including his famous painting *The Netherlandish Proverbs*).

Rooms VII-XI, Galleries 8-19: Flemish and Dutch Schools, 17C (Baroque). This extremely impressive section includes Peter Paul Rubens *(Child with a Bird, Virgin and Child)*, his pupil Anthony van Dyck *(Portrait of a Wealthy Genoan Couple)*, Matthias Stomer *(Esau Sells his Birth Right)*, Rembrandt *(Self-portrait, Moses Shatters the Decalogue, Susanna and the Two Old Men, The Man with the Golden Helmet)*, Jacob van Ruisdael *(Oaks by the Lake with Water Lilies)*, Jan Bruegel the Elder *(Flower Bouquet)*, Frans Hals *(Singing Child with Flute)*, Jan Vermeer van Delft *(The Glass of Wine)*.

Galleries 20-22: English, French and German Schools, 18C (Rococo/Neo-Classicism) Artists include Thomas Gainsborough *(The Marsham Children)*, Antoine Watteau *(The Dance)*, Jean-Baptiste-Siméon Chardin *(The Painter)*, Antoine Pesne *(Frederick the Great as Crown Prince)*.

Rooms XII-XIV, Galleries 23-26, 28: Italian School, 17C-18C (Baroque/Mannerism); French School, **17C; Spanish School, 16C-17C** (Mannerism/Baroque). Exhibits here include Francesco Guardi *(Canal Grande in Venice)*, Canaletto *(Canal Grande with View of the Rialto Bridge)*, Velázquez *(Portrait of a Lady)*, Caravaggio *(Amor as Victor)*, Claude Lorrain *(Ideal Roman Landscape)*, Nicolas Poussin *(Self-portrait)*, Georges de La Tour *(Peasant Couple Eating Peas)*.

Rooms XV-XVII, Galleries 29-32: Italian School, late 15C-16C (Late Renaissance/Mannerism). This part of the museum contains works by Correggio *(Leda with the Swan)*, Parmigianino *(Christ's Baptism)*, Titian *(Venus with the Organist, Portrait of a Bearded Young Man)*, Tintoretto *(Virgin and Child)*, and several paintings by Raphael (including the *Madonna Terranuova*).

Gallery 34: miniatures, 16C-18C, including *Katharine of Bora* (Martin Luther's wife) by Lucas Cranach the Elder.

Room XVIII, Galleries 35-41: Italian School, 13C-late 15C (Gothic/Early Renaissance), including Botticelli *(Saint Sebastian, Virgin Enthroned)*, Giovanni Bellini, Andrea Mantegna *(Representation of Christ in the Temple)*, Fra Angelico *(The Day of Judgement)*, Lorenzo Monaco *(The Last Supper)*.

Study Gallery: Top-quality paintings from all schools are also exhibited here, including still-life paintings: Jan Fyt: *Still-life with Fish and Fruit*; Jan Davidsz de Heem: *Still-life with Fruit and Lobster*; Pieter Claesz: *Still-life with a Drinking Vessel and Fruit*.

Kunstgewerbemuseum★★ (Museum of Decorative Arts)

Matthäikirchplatz. ♿ 🕐 *Open daily except Mon 10am-6pm, Sat-Sun 11am-6pm.* 🕐 *Closed Easter and Pentecost, 24, 25 and 31 Dec.* ▣ *€8, free admission Thurs, 4 hours before closing.* ☎ *(030) 266 29 02. www.smb.spk-berlin.de.*

This is the Kulturforum's oldest museum, housing a magnificent collection of works in silver and gold.

Gallery I *(ground floor)* is devoted to the Middle Ages. Inside the entrance is the Enger-Herford (Westphalia) **Treasure of Dionysius**★, with a remarkable reliquary purse with precious stones (late 8C). In the centre of the gallery is the **Guelph Treasure**★★★, including a reliquary resembling a Byzantine church (Cologne c 1175).

Gallery II *(ground floor)*: Italian furniture and majolica from the 14C to the 16C, Venetian glassware from the 16C to the 17C; Gallery III *(ground floor)*: **Lüneburg's municipal silver**★★★ (Late Gothic and Renaissance) and jewelry from Nuremburg; Gallery IV *(first floor)*: the splendid **Pommern Cabinet**★ and its contents; Gallery V *(first floor)*: 17C-18C porcelain from China and Germany, Gallery VI *(first floor)*: Biedermeier and Jugendstil objets d'art, panelled glass cabinet from Schloss Wiesentheid in Franconia (1724); Gallery VII *(first floor)*: porcelain, earthenware (glazed) and glass from the Jugendstil (Art Nouveau) and Art Deco periods. Galleries IX and X *(basement)* exhibit the largest existing permanent collection of international design in Germany, including furniture.

Kupferstichkabinett und Sammlung der Zeichnungen und Druckgraphik★ (Prints and Drawings Collection)

Matthäikirchplatz. ♿ *Exhibition:* ⏰ *open daily except Mon, 10am-6pm (8pm Thu), Sat-Sun 11am-6pm. Study room:* ⏰ *open daily except Mon, 9am-4pm.* ⏰ *Closed 24, 25 and 31 Dec. Prices vary by exhibition, free admission Thurs, 4 hours before closing. Study room: free admission* ☎ *(030) 266 20 02; www.smb.spk-berlin.de.*

In 1652 the Great Elector purchased 2 500 drawings and watercolours. So began the internationally renowned **Museum of Prints and Drawings**, now boasting 1 100 000 drawings, watercolours, gouaches and pastels from the 14C to the 20C and 540 000 prints from the late Middle Ages to the present. The drawings by old German and Dutch masters – including 80 Rembrandts– is a highlight. The museum's location, the Matthäikirchplatz, is home to the Kunstbibliothek, a richly stocked art library which frequently hosts special exhibitions.

Neue Nationalgalerie★★ (New National Gallery)

Potsdamer Straße 50 ♿ ⏰ *Open daily except Mon, 10am-6pm, Thurs 10am-10pm, Sat-Sun 11am-6pm.* 🎟 *€8, free admission Thu, 4 hours before closing.* ☎ *(030) 20 90 55 66; www.smb.spk-berlin.de.*

This steel and glass structure, designed in 1968 by Mies van der Rohe, houses paintings and sculptures from the 20C. Collections include works from the European Classical Modern art movements and American art of the 1960s and 1970s representing **Expressionism**, artists of the **Brücke**, French Cubism (Picasso and Juan Gris), **Bauhaus** (Schlemmer, Kandinsky) and Surrealism **(Max Ernst)**. Sculptural highlights are *The Washerwoman* by Renoir and Calder's *Heads and Tails*.

Philharmonie★★★

Herbert-von-Karajanstraße 1. ♿ 🚶 *Guided tour (1hr) at 1pm. Meeting point: stage door.* ⏰ *Closed 24-26 and 31 Dec.* 🎟 *€3* ☎ *(030) 25 48 89 99; www.berliner-philharmoniker.de.*

The roof of this asymmetrical building by **Hans Scharoun** (1963) resembles a giant wave. The Berlin Philharmonic Orchestra plays here, directed by **Sir Simon Rattle,** and surrounded by tiered seats accommodating up to 2 200. The **Chamber Music Hall** (1988), beside the Philharmonia, seats up to 1 150 under a tent-shaped roof. The **Musical Instruments Museum**★ *(Musikinstrumenten-Museum)* is housed in an annex *(Tiergartenstraße 1)*. Keyboards, strings and percussion dating to the 16C are on display *(♿⏰ Open daily except Mon, 9am-5pm, Sat-Sun 10am-5pm.* ⏰ *Closed 1 Jan, 1 May, 24, 25 and 31 Dec.* 🎟 *€8* ☎ *(030) 25 48 11 78; www.sim.spk-berlin.de).*

Gedenkstätte Deutscher Widerstand (Monument to German Resistance)

Stauffenbergstraße 13-14. ⏰ *Open daily, 9am-6pm (Thurs 8pm), Sat-Sun 10am-6pm.* ⏰ *Closed 1 Jan, 24-26 and 31 Dec. Free admission,* 🚶 *free guided tour Sun at 3pm.* ☎ *(030) 26 99 50 00. www.gdw-berlin.de.*

The monument stands where Claus Schenk, Count of Stauffenberg, had his office, the planning centre for an attempted overthrow of Hitler on 20 July 1944. An exhibition describes German resistance to the Nazis.

Potsdamer Platz★★

Legendary in inter-war Berlin, Potsdamer Platz was, for a long time, the busiest crossroads in Europe. Split in two by the Wall when the city was divided, it was abandoned until private investors restored it after the reunification. In 1990, Sony became the second largest investor in Potsdamer Platz after Daimler-Chrysler.

Dahlem Museums –
International Art and Culture★★★

The former seigneurial domain of Dahlem, strewn with English-style villas, adapted by **Hermann Muthesius** (1861-1927), remains a leafy residential suburb. Endowed with a vast university, whose buildings are contrast sharply with the villas, this district is of particular interest for its remarkable museums. The great space left after the Gemäldegalerie moved to the Kulturforum and the Museum of Islamic Art was united with the Pergamonmuseum was ideal for the Ethnographic Museum, the Museum of Far Eastern Art and the Museum of Indian Art. These three museums, along with the Museum of European Cultures, are now officially dubbed **Museen Dahlem – Kunst und Kulturen der Welt** (Dahlem Museums – International Art and Culture).

Ethnologisches Museum★★★ (Museum of Ethnography)

Lansstraße entrance. &. ◷ *Open daily except Mon, 10am-6pm, Sat-Sun 11am-6pm.* ◉ €8, *free admission Thurs, 4 hours before closing.* ☎ *(030) 830 14 38; www.smb. spk-berlin.de.*
This museum is home to 400 000 outstanding ethnographic objects.

Ancient American Cultures Section★★★

On display are **religious and secular Aztec statuary**, pre-Inca cloths and anthro-pomorphic ceramics from Peru. **The Gold Room**★★★ displays magnificent jewels and exquisitely engraved cult objects from the 7C BC to the 11C AD.

Oceania Section★★

Among the items gathered during sea voyages since the 18C, some by Captain James Cook, note the painted **masks** and **wooden sculptures** from New Guinea, the spectacular **Oceanian boats**, and the feathered cloak of the king of Hawaii.

Southern Asia★

Exhibits come from south-east Asia, India and Sri Lanka, including masks, puppets and Chinese shadow theatre figures. Indonesia is represented by a sizeable collection of textiles and carved and painted figures used in religious ceremonies.

North and West Africa Section★★

The most interesting objects in this collection include **terracotta heads from Ife** (Nigeria), **bronzes** from the ancient kingdom of Benin, and Berber jewellery. There are also some interesting wooden sculptures from Cameroon.

A showcase of Berlin's avant-garde archi-tecture: the Sony Center on Potsdamer Platz

H. Champollion/MICHELIN

Museum für Indische Kunst★★ (Museum of Indian Art)

Lansstraße entrance.

This museum's permanent exhibition is divided into three sections: the Indian subcontinent, south-east Asia and the Silk Road. In addition to featuring India are artifacts from Pakistan, Afghanistan, Sri Lanka, Nepal, Tibet, Myanmar and Vietnam. The museum's highlight is the **Turfan collection**★★ (named after an oasis in Chinese Turkestan) with wall paintings, statues, fabrics, manuscripts and a reconstructed cave temple, the "Cave with the Ringbearing Doves."

Museum für Ostasiatische Kunst★ (Museum of Far-Eastern Art)

Lansstraße entrance.

Chinese, Japanese and Korean exhibits comprise this museum, including bronze, wood, ivory, lacquer and ceramic art from the third millennium BC to the present.

Museum Europäischer Kulturen★ (Museum of European Cultures)

Im Winkel 6/8. ♿ 🕐 *Open daily except Mon, 10am-6pm, Sat-Sun 11am-6pm.* 🎟 *€6, free admission Thurs, 4 hours before closing.* ☎ *(030) 830 14 38. www.smb.spk-berlin.de.*

Created in 1992 from the merging of East and West Berlin's respective Museums of Folklore, the Museum of European Cultures features items from the 16C to the present. *The tour starts on the upper floor.* The **1st floor's** exhibition traces the evolution of European images in religious art, personal portraits, furniture and household items, extending to modern mass commodities. **Ground floor** Images are presented first in the light of Judaism, Christianity and Islam, then in the context of religion's role in society in the 19C and 20C.

Schloss Charlottenburg★★★

Allow one day for the tour. ♿ *Silverware room (Silberkammer), crown gallery (Kronkabinett) and apartments of Frederick William IV:* 🕐 *open daily except Mon, 9am-5pm, Sat-Sun 10am-5pm.* 🎟 *€2.* ☎ *(0331) 969 42 02. www.spsg.de.*

Charlottenburg was the favourite retreat of Queen Sophie-Charlotte, wife of Frederick I. When the queen died in 1705, the palace at Liezenburg was renamed Charlottenburg in her honour. The small summer residence was enlarged and a dome added in 1710. Years later Frederick II added an east wing; later still, Queen Louise, wife of Frederick William III, lived in the palace. After sustaining serious damage during the Second World War, Schloss Charlottenburg has been rebuilt and most of the interior restored.

Historic Apartments★★

Ground floor of central block (Altes Schloss). Guided tours (1hr) ♿🕐 *daily except Mon, 9am-5pm, Sat-Sun, 10am-5pm.* 🕐 *Closed 24, 25 and 31 Dec.* 🎟 *€8.* ☎ *(0331) 320 91 440. www.spsg.de.*

After viewing models of the 18C palace and gardens, visitors approach three small rooms in the **Mecklenburg Apartment.** The official function rooms span 140m/460ft overlooking the gardens. They house family portraits of the Houses of Hohenzollern and Hanover, finely lacquered furniture and Sophie Charlotte's harpsichord. The famous **Porcelain Room**★★ (1706) features a magnificent collection of Oriental porcelain, reconstituted after the Second World War. The **Palace Chapel**★ (*Schlosskapelle* – 1706) is occasionally used as a concert venue. Above the royal pew an enormous crown carried by two allegorical figures bears the Prussian eagle. The fine freestanding **staircase** by Eosander, architect of the palace extension after 1702, was the first of its kind in Germany.

▶ *Climb the staircase to view the first floor of the central block.*

The Crown Prince's Silverware

This masterpiece of 20C German craftsmanship was a gift from 414 Prussian cities at the marriage of Crown Prince William to Duchess Cecilia of Mecklenburg-Schwerin in 1904. Completed in 1914, the dinner service never belonged to the couple. Following the Hohenzollerns' abdication, it became property of the Berlin Senate and is now on long-standing loan to Schloß Charlottenburg. The service originally contained 2 600 pieces for fifty at a 16m/53ft-long table. Terrines, plates and salad bowls are displayed on a magnificent sideboard. A group of six, including architects, sculptors and the director of the Museum of Decorative Arts, supervised the creation of the dinner service, which is in classical and *Jugendstil* style. The statuettes include elephants surmounted by an obelisk, equestrian statues and candelabra, all part of a long tradition of royal dinner services.

Following a pass through upper rooms looking out over the courtyard and gardens, the tour continues to the **apartments of Frederick William IV**, the last king to frequent the palace. The painting *Parade along Unter den Linden in 1837* by Franz Krüger features some of this avenue's most important buildings, still recognizable today. Adjoining rooms exhibit part of the East Prussian noble Schlobitten Collection, including paintings, tapestries, porcelain and metalwork. The **Crown Prince's silverware**★★ is particularly interesting, given by the Prussian cities to Crown Prince William at his betrothal to Cecilie of Mecklenburg-Schwerin in 1904. The Prussian crown jewels are on display in the **crown gallery** (Kronkabinett).

New Wing★★ (Knobelsdorff Wing)
East of the central block. ♿ 🕐 *Open daily day except Mon, 10am-6pm, Sat-Sun, 11am-6pm.* 🚌 *€5.* ☎ *(0331) 969 42 02. www.spsg.de .*
A staircase leads to the **White Room** *(Weißer Saal)* used by Frederick II as a dining and throne room. The ceiling painting is a modern work by Hann Trier which replaced a work by Antoine Pesne destroyed in 1943. The 42m/138ft long **Golden Gallery**★★ is a large music room and dance hall in "Frederician Rococo": it has been restored to its original glowing pale green, pink and gold colours. Frederick II's apartments, which follow, feature white and gold Rococo decor and important 18C French paintings by Watteau: **Gersaint's Signboard**★★★ (1720) in the concert hall and **Embarkation for Cythera**★★★.

Winter apartments★
Frederick II's successors, (Frederick William II and his daughter-in-law Louise, wife of Frederick William III) occupied these winter quarters in the late 18C and early 19C. These south-facing rooms display the disciplined elegance of early Prussian neo-Classicism. **Queen Louise's Bedchamber**★ is decorated in harmonious mauve tones and draped in white net. The final apartment room contains a fine collection of **portraits**★ by court painter Antoine Pesne, and the garden-side rooms feature magnificent Rococo decor.
On the ground floor a model shows **Berlin Palace**, blown up in 1950 on the orders of the East German authorities. In the adjoining room are Baroque tapestries and portions of Frederick the Great's **antique collection**. The **Chinese Gallery and Chinese Room**, part of Frederick William II's summer apartments, overlook the gardens.

West Wing (Great Orangery)
The Orangery wing was built by Eosander between 1701 and 1707; the old theatre (built 1788-91) was built by Langhans. Directly opposite, the Small Orangery is a café and restaurant.

Museum für Vor- und Frühgeschichte★ (Museum of Pre- and Early History)
♿ ⏰ *Open daily except Mon, 9am-5pm, Sat-Sun 10am-5pm.* ⏰ *Closed Easter and Pentecost, 24, 25 and 31 Dec.* €6, free admission Thurs, 4 hours before closing. ☎ (030) 32 67 48 40. www.smb.spk-berlin.de .

Excellent dioramas and archaeological exhibits overview European history. An entire floor is devoted to the Iron Age and the Hallstatt, Lausitz, La Tène and Ibero-Celt cultures. The Roman Empire, Late Antiquity, the Middle Ages and Eurasia's Ages of Bronze and Iron are also well represented.

Schlossgarten★★

This English-style park is an oasis of tranquillity amid the bustle of Berlin. To the west, at the end of a yew and cypress walk, a small **mausoleum**★ contains the tombs of Frederick William III, Queen Louise, the Emperor Wilhelm I and Queen Augusta.

The New Pavilion★ **(Schinkel Pavilion)** *(between the east end of the Knobelsdorff Wing and the castle bridge)* was built in 1824 as a summer residence for Frederick William III. The outstanding works of art, including paintings by Caspar David Friedrich, Blechen and Gaertner, testify to the importance of Schinkel, who built this residence, and his Berliner contemporaries.

North of the lake, in the direction of the Spree, is a **Belvedere**★ housing a **historic exhibition**★ of the Royal Berlin Porcelain Manufactory. It outlines the development of Berlin porcelain from Rococo to Biedermeier.

Around Schloss Charlottenburg

Stüler Buildings
Schloßstraße 1, opposite the palace.
The two domed buildings on Schloßstraße were erected by Friedrich August Stüler between 1851 and 1859 as royal guard barracks. The Berggruen Collection is housed in the western building; the Egyptian Museum in the eastern one.

Sammlung Berggruen★★ – Picasso und seine Zeit (Berggruen Collection – Picasso and his Times)
In the western Stüler Building. ♿ ⏰ *Open daily except Mon, 10am-6pm.* €6, free admission Thurs, 4 hours before closing. ☎ (030) 326 95 80; www.smb.spk-berlin.de.
The collection of Parisian art dealer Heinz Berggruen emphasizes Pablo Picasso. Works include tableaux (*The Yellow Pullover*, 1929), sculptures (*Head of Fernande*, 1909), drawings and gouaches. There are also works by Cézanne, Van Gogh, Matisse, Giacometti and others, as well as African tribal art. The second floor features over 50 works by **Paul Klee:** *Stadtartiger Aufbau (Urban Structure)*, *Betrachtung beim Frühstück* (1925, watercolour), and *Klassicche Küste* (1931).

Ägyptisches Museum und Papyrussammlung★★★ (Egyptian Museum and Papyrus Collection)
Eastern Stüler Building. ⏰ *Open Tue-Sun 10am-6pm,* ⏰ *closed Easter and Pentecost, 24, 25 and 31 Dec. Ticket valid in all Preußischer Kulturbesitz museums.* €12, free admission Thurs, 4 hours before closing. ☎ (030) 20 90 55 77. www.smb.spk-berlin.de.
Berlin's ancient Egypt collection, founded in 1828, is one of the best and most comprehensive in the world. The collections were shared between the Stüler Building in the west and the Bode-Museum on Museumsinsel in the east during Berlin's division. The two collections will be reunited in 2009, when the Neues-Museum reopens.
The exhibits from the time of Pharaoh Akhenaton, king of Egypt between 1353 and 1336 BC, are among the museum's highlights. The collection focuses on treasures from **Tell-el-Amarna**, **Amenhotep IV-Akhenaton's** capital. The Deutsche-Orient-Gesellschaft excavated the site between 1911 and 1914. A particularly large number of finds were made at the **workshop of Thutmose**, one of the king's temple and

Amenhotep IV's Revolution

Upon his accession to the throne, **Amenhotep IV** imposed the idea of a single god. Other gods were abandoned in favour of **Aton**, the disk of the sun whose rays terminate in human hands holding the hieroglyph for life *(Ankh)*. **Amenhotep** changed his name to **Akhenaton, "One Useful to Aton,"** set up court in Tell el-Amarna and banned worship, priests and temples of all other gods, offending a rich and powerful clergy. The reign of his son-in-law **Tutankhamen**, who abandoned Tell el-Amarna after two or three years, marked the end of the revolution.

palace sculptors. Exhibits reveal the working methods of an Egyptian artist and the uniqueness of this period in ancient Egyptian history.

Take special note of the ebony **head of Queen Teje**★★ (1355 BC), the **Green Head of a Priest**★ (c 300 BC) and the world-famous **Bust of Queen Nefertiti**★★★ (painted plaster over limestone – 1350 BC). This miraculously preserved bust was uncovered in Thutmose's workshop and served as a model for future effigies of the queen.

Bröhan Museum★ (Bröhan-Museum)
Schloßstraße 1a. ♿ 🕐 *Open daily except Mon, 10am-6pm.* 🕐 *Closed 24 and 31 Dec.* 💶 *€4.* ☎ *(030) 32 69 06 00. www.broehan-museum.de.*
This exhibition, based on a private collection, presents arts, crafts and industrial design, including Jugendstil and Art Deco. Note the French furniture of the 1920s, the French glassware, and the porcelain.

Gipsformerei der Staatlichen Museen
Sophie-Charlotten-Straße 17-18. ♿ *Exhibition-salesroom:* 🕐 *open daily except Sat-Sun, 9am-4pm, Wed 9am-6pm.* 🕐 *Closed on public holidays.* ☎ *(030) 326 76 90.*
The national museums' replica workshop, with some 6 500 figures, is located near Schloss Charlottenburg, and is one of the largest in the world.

Additional Sights

Museum für Kommunikation Berlin★
(Museum of Berlin Telecommunications)
An der Urania 15, Leipziger Straße 16. ♿ 🕐 *Open daily except Mon, 9am-5pm, Sat-Sun 11am-7pm.* 💶 *€3.* ☎ *(030) 20 29 40. www.museumsstiftung.de.*
Set in the historic former Reichspost Museum, this interesting museum presents the past, present and future of communications.

Berlin German Transport and Technical Museum★★
(Deutsches Technikmuseum Berlin)
Trebbiner Straße 9. ♿ 🕐 *Open daily except Mon, 9am-5.30pm, Sat-Sun 10am-6pm; Mon, Easter and Pentecost 10am-6pm.* 🕐 *Closed 1st May, 24, 25 and 31 Dec.* 💶 *€4.50.* ☎ *(030) 90 25 40. www.dtmb.de.*
Technical progress is presented as the cultural evolution of mankind in a series of vivid displays. Air and space travel, road traffic and maritime transport are represented, along with the application of technology to the media, photography and energy. A particularly impressive **Railway Section**★★ includes locomotives, some of them dating back to the very earliest rail transport.

Hamburger Bahnhof – Museum für Gegenwart Berlin★★
(Hamburg Station – Museum of Contemporary Art
Invalidenstraße 50-51. ♿ 🕐 *Open daily except Mon, 10am-6pm, Sat-Sun 11am-6pm.* 💶 *€6, free admission 1st Sun of each month.* ☎ *(030) 20 90 55 66. www.smb.spk-berlin.de.*

Hamburg Station, the oldest of Berlin's remaining first generation railway stations, was built in 1845-47. It was closed in 1884 and later became the home of the Transport and Construction Museum. The station and its recent addition now house artworks from 1960 to the present. The collection includes works by Anselm Kiefer (*Census*, 1991), Richard Long (*Berlin Circle*), Mario Merz and Günther Uecker. The long gallery features Cy Twombly, Robert Rauschenberg and Andy Warhol. A whole room is devoted to Joseph Beuys' installations (*Biennale-Installation Tramstop*, 1976).

Käthe-Kollwitz-Museum★ (Käthe Kollowitz Museum)
Fasanenstraße 24. ◷ *Open daily except Tue, 11am-6pm.* ◷ *Closed 24 and 31 Dec.* ⬤ *€5.* ☎ *(030) 882 52 10. www.kaethe-kollwitz.de.*
A broad survey of Berlin-born artist Käthe Kollwitz (1867-1945) is presented at her namesake museum. Highlights include engravings *The Weavers' Revolt* (1893-98) and *The Peasants' War* (1903-08), woodcuts titled *War* (1920-1924) and *The Proletariat* (1925), and self-portraits and lithographs labelled *Death*. 1920s-era posters such as *Nie wieder Krieg (No More War)* underline the artist's political and humanistic views; sculptures on the upper floor include *Muttergruppe (Mother Group*, 1924-37).

Martin-Gropius-Bau★★ (Martin Gropius Building)
Stresemannstraße 110. ♿ ◷ *Open daily except Tue, 10am-8pm.* ⬤ *€5-7 varies with exhibition.* ☎ *(030) 25 48 60. www.gropiusbau.de.*
This neo-Renaissance building was originally conceived by Martin Gropius (great uncle of Walter Gropius) and Heino Schmieden as a home for the Royal Museum of Decorative Arts. Its reconstruction, after heavy war damage, was begun in 1978, paved the way for a collection of ceramics, mosaics and friezes reminiscent of an Italian palace.

Topographie des Terrors (Topography of Terror)
♿ ◷ *May-Sep: 10am-8pm; Oct-Apr: 10am-6pm.* ◷ *Closed 1 Jan, 24 and 31 Dec* ☎ *(030) 25 48 67 03. www.topographie.de.*
Adjacent to the Gropius building lies the headquarters from 1939 on of Reich security and secret police, the SS, the Gestapo and the SD (*Sicherheitsdienst*, Security Service). In the 1980s, the foundations of the centre's prison building were unearthed. An international documentation centre is planned for the site in future years; until completion of the building, an open-air exhibition recalls the terror of the Nazi years and reveals portions of the Niederkirchnerstraße excavations.

The Wall

The Berlin Wall divided the city's western districts from the east and the surrounding area. Watchtowers, barbed wire and guns have all long gone; in their place are construction sites, parks or fallow land. Rare traces of the city's barrier remain, but there are some. The watchtower at the *Schlesisches Tor* is now a museum for "Forbidden Art;" the walled-in house entrances at Heidelberger Straße remain in the Treptow district.

The longest stretch of the wall is the "East Side Gallery" in Friedrichshain, its 1990s-era graffiti art in poor condition. More central is the bit of wall near the former Prussian House of Parliament between the Detlev-Rohwedder-Haus (built as Göring's Reichs Air Ministry) and the grounds of the "Topography of Terror". Bernauerstraße remains a symbol of the inhumanity of the wall. In 1998, the **Berlin Wall Memorial** (*Gedenkstätte Berliner Mauer*) was opened on cemetery land from the Sophie Community (corner of Bernauerstraße/Ackerstraße). Berlin's ugly recent past is visible here more than any other spot in the city.

Viktoria-Park★

Berlin's highest point (66m/216ft) is today Victoria Park, featuring nice city views and Karl Friedrich Schinkel's monument to the "Wars of Liberation."

Luftbrückendenkmal (Airlift Memorial)

In the Tempelhof district, Platz der Luftbrücke.
The three west-facing arcs of this memorial symbolise the three air corridors used by the Allies to supply the city with its necessities during the Berlin Airlift.

Jüdisches Museum Berlin★★ (Jewish Museum)

Lindenstraße 9-14. ♿ 🕐 *10am-8pm, Mon 10am-10pm.* 🕐 *Closed on Rosh Hashanah, Yom Kippur, 24 Dec.* 💶 *€5* ☎ *(030) 259 93 30. www.jmberlin.de.*
American architect Daniel Libeskind designed this spectacular lightning-shaped museum, which opened in 2001. This veritable labyrinth, with empty rooms that lead nowhere, symbolizes the annihilation of the Jewish-German culture. The exhibition traces the history of the Jews in Germany from the earliest documents to the present. The contributions of Berlin's Jews fom the 18C to the 20C is given special attention, with emphasis on the Nazi Holocaust. A special section examines the current growth of Berlin's Jewish community.

The Jewish Museum designed by Daniel Liebeskind

H. Champollion/MICHELIN

Museum Haus am Checkpoint Charlie (Berlin Wall Museum)

Kochstraße 6 at Friedrichstraße. 🕐 *Daily, 9am-10pm.* 💶 *€9.50.* ☎ *(030) 253 72 50. www.mauermuseum.de.*
The Berlin Wall Museum houses artifacts on the Wall and Germans' extraordinary attempts to cross it: aboard a tractor, hidden in the boot of a car, in a suitcase, even via chairlift suspended from a cable. Many attempts came to a tragic end. Displays also address modern movements for human and civil rights.

Märkisches Museum/Stiftung Stadtmuseum Berlin★ (March Museum/Foundation Museum of Berlin)

🕐 *Open daily except Mon, 10am-6pm; Wed, noon-8pm.* 🕐 *Closed 24 and 31 Dec.* 💶 *€4.* ☎ *(030) 24 00 21 62. www.stadtmuseum.de.*
This picturesque building complex was built between 1899 and 1908 taking its name from the Gothic and Renaissance architecture of the March of Brandenburg. The museum displays the historical and cultural development of Berlin from prehistory to the present. A copy of the larger-than-life 1474 figure of Brandenburger Roland, symbol of civic liberties and privileges, stands before the museum entrance.

Kunstgewerbemuseum★★ (Museum of Decorative Arts)

In Schloss Köpenick (Schloßinsel). www.smb.spk-berlin.de.
The Museum of Decorative Arts is situated in a Baroque 17C mansion in the provincial green Köpenick suburb, southeast of the city centre and far from its noise. The 16C-19C furniture is especially interesting, as are the **panelled room**★ from Haldenstein castle (Switzerland, 16C), the **Treasury**★, with jewelry and 16C Baroque gold- and silverware, and the silver **sideboard**★★ from the Knights' Room in the old Castle of Berlin (made by J Ludwig and A Biller, famous Augsburger silversmiths, in the 17C.

Großer Müggelsee★★

Kids *Leave by Lindenstraße.*
The largest of Berlin's lakes, the terrace at the top of the tower provides broad views of the surrounding lakes and woods.

Botanischer Garten★★ (Botanical Gardens)

Königin-Luise-Straße 6/8. ♿ 🕐 *Nov-Jan: 9am-4pm; Feb: 9am-5pm; Mar and Oct: 9am-6pm; Sep: 9am-7pm; Apr and Aug: 9am-8pm; May-Jul: 9am-9pm.* 🕐 *Closed 24 Dec.* ✆ *€5.* ☎ *(030) 83 85 01 00. www.bgbm.org/bgbm.*
At 43ha/106 acres, this botanical garden is one of the world's largest. Vegetation is arranged geographically from mountains to plains. Rare species of trees and shrubs are in the Arboretum, while 16 greenhouses display tropical and subtropical plants. The **Botanical Museum**★ *(Botanisches Museum)* shows the evolution of flora and common historical plant uses, such as funeral offerings from Ancient Egyptian tombs (♿🕐 *Daily, 10am-6pm;* 🕐 *Closed 24 Dec;* ✆ *€2;* ☎ *030 83 85 01 00).*

Brücke-Museum★

Bussardsteig 9. ♿ 🕐 *Open daily except Tue, 11am-5pm.* 🕐 *Closed 24 and 31 Dec.* ✆ *€4.* ☎ *(030) 831 20 29; www.bruecke-museum.de.*
This museum contains works by members of the **Brücke**, the most important school of German Expressionists. The movement was founded in Dresden in 1905 by four architecture students (Bleyl, Heckel, Kirchner, and Schmidt-Rottluff) who wished to create an expressive art by the deformation of lines and the use of violent colours. In 1911, the group moved to Berlin, where it disbanded two years later. Most of the work on display is that of **Karl Schmidt-Rottluff** and Erich Heckel. Max Pechstein, Otto Mueller, Ernst Ludwig Kirchner and Emil Nolde are also represented.

Grunewald★★

A hunting reserve of the prince-electors in the 16C, this mixed forest covers 3 100ha/745 acres, and is bounded by a chain of small lakes. Beside one of these lakes, the Lake of Grunewald, is the elegant **Jagdschloß Grunewald**★, a hunting pavilion built in 1542. The original Renaissance pavilion was converted some 160 years later into the Baroque style for King Frederick I of Prussia. The building overlooks a courtyard surrounded on three sides by outbuildings *(Jagdzeugmagazin)* and bordered by ancient beech trees. Inside the pavilion is a furniture collection and a gallery with German and Dutch art of the 15C to 19C. 🕐 *From mid May to mid Oct: open daily except Mon, 10am-5pm;* 👣 *guided tours only from mid Oct to mid May: Sun at 11am, 1pm and 3pm.* ✆ *€2.* ☎ *(0331) 969 42 02.*

The western boundary of the Grunewald is formed by **Lake Havel**★★. Beside this runs the picturesque Havelchaussee road, which leads south to the beaches of the **Wannsee**★★, a favourite with Berlin bathers in warm weather.

Pfaueninsel★★ (Peacock Island)

Access by boat, leaving from the landing-stage at the end of Nikolskoer Weg (service on demand).
Landscaped gardens studded with small, picturesque buildings offer a perfect example of late-18C taste on this isle on the Havel. The shaded park is an ideal place for a quiet stroll. The **castle**★ (1794-97) displays souvenirs of Queen Louise in salons panelled and floored with exotic woods. 🕐 *Apr-end Oct:* 👣 *guided tour (30min) daily except Mon, 10am-5pm.* ✆ *€3.* ☎ *(0331) 969 42 02.*

Funkturm★ (Radio Tower)

Kids ♿ 🕐 *Open daily except Mon, 10am-11pm.* 🕐 *Closed 1 Jan and 24 Dec.* ✆ *€3.60.* ☎ *(030) 30 38 29 96.*

This 150m/492ft structure, known to Berliners as the "Beanpole", is indissolubly linked to the city and has become its mascot. At a height of 126m/413ft there is a viewing platform, reached by a lift, which offers a **panorama**★★★ of Berlin.

Olympia-Stadion★ (Olympic Stadium)

☏ *(030) 30 06 33.* ◷ *Open daily; summer, 10am-7pm, winter 10am-4pm; restricted opening before and after match days and other events.* ◷ *Closed 23 Dec-1 Jan.* ⌕ *€2.* ☜ *Guided tours available.*

This stadium, which seats 120 000 spectators, is accessed via a vast avenue leading up to two towers. Monumental statues represent Nazi ideals. The architect **Werner March** sunk the stadium; although the exterior appears quite low (17m/56ft), 12m/39ft lie below ground level. Behind the building stood the May field *(Maifeld)* where 500 000 people gathered to hear Hitler's speeches.

Bauhaus-Archiv★ (Bauhaus Archives)

Klingelhöferstraße. ♿ ◷ *Open daily except Tue, 10am-5pm.* ◷ *Closed 24 and 31 Dec.* ⌕ *€6.* ☏ *(030) 254 00 20. www.bauhaus.de.*

The building housing this museum was constructed in 1979 after the designs of **Walter Gropius**, founder of the Bauhaus *(see "Art and Architecture" and DESSAU)*. The Bauhaus School is known predominantly for its architecture, but it also exerted influence too on the plastic arts. Through the everyday objects it designed, it was the precursor of contemporary design. In addition to practical items, museum visitors see sculptures and paintings by Schlemmer, Moholy-Nagy, Feininger, Kandinsky and Klee, as well as models, experimental typography and drawings.

Gedenkstätte Plötzensee (Plötzensee Memorial)

♿ ◷ *Mar-Oct: 9am-5pm; Nov-Feb: 9am-4pm.* ◷ *Closed 1st Jan, 23-26 and 31 Dec.* ☏ *(030) 26 99 50 00.*

The memorial to victims of the Nazi regime occupies the former execution chamber in Plötzensee prison. Between 1933 and 1945 over 3 000 prisoners were killed here by guillotine or hanging.

Spandauer Zitadelle★

The Spandau citadel was built in the 16C on the site of a medieval castle (12C) at the confluence of the Havel and the Spree. The sole example north of the Alps of this style of fortification, which incorporates a square, brick keep, Spandau is best-known as a state prison rather than a fortress. A drawbridge leads to the gateway. Armorial pediment paintings represent the provinces of Prussia.

Juliusturm (Julius Tower)

Skirt the right-hand side of the building. ◷ *Open daily except Mon, 9am-5pm, Sat-Sun 10am-5pm.* ◷ *Closed 1 Jan, 1 May, 3 Oct, 24, 25 and 31 Dec.* ⌕ *€2.50.* ☏ *(030) 354 94 42 00.*

Sole remnant of the original castle, this 32m/105ft keep has become the emblem of Spandau. Inside the tower, 145 steps lead to a lookout point with a panoramic view. A **museum of local history** *(Stadtgeschichtliches Museum Spandau)* is located inside the citadel *(entrance via the footbridge)*. To the north are 13C and 14C Jewish gravestones, salvaged from the Spandau Jewish cemetery sacked in 1510.

St-Nikolai-Kirche★

In Spandau. ♿ ◷ *From beginning of Jan to end Nov: open daily except Fri, noon-4pm, Sat 11am-3pm, Sun 2-4pm.* ☏ *(030) 333 56 39.*

This hall-church is one of the last brick Gothic buildings remaining in Berlin. Note the Crucifixion Group (1540) of polychrome wood at the entrance to the north chapel; the magnificent Renaissance **altar**★, the gilded Baroque pulpit, and the bronze baptismal fonts (1398).

Excursions

Potsdam★★★   *19km/12mi W.*   *See POTSDAM.*

Oranienburg

31km/19mi N.   *From mid Mar to mid Oct: open Tue-Sun, 8.30am-6pm; from mid Oct to mid Mar: open Tue-Sun, 8.30am-4.30pm.*   *Closed 1st Jan, 24, 25 and 31 Dec.* ☏ *(033 01) 20 02 00.*

The Concentration Camp of **Sachsenhausen**, now a memorial – *Gedenkstätte und Museum Sachsenhausen* – dates from 1936. More than half of the 200 000 people imprisoned there perished. The history of the concentration camp is shown in exhibitions at the original sites. The **Museum Baracke 28**, which opened in 1997, is a special exhibition on the fate of the Jewish prisoners. A tour of the camp *(follow the plan distributed at the entrance)* details the organisation of the Nazi concentration system, whose cynical approach is exemplified by the slogan still above the entrance gates: *"Arbeit macht frei"* (Work brings Freedom).

Frankfurt an der Oder

90km/56mi E via ① on plan.

This former Hanseatic city founded has been has been home to the **European University of Viadrina** since 1991. A third of enrollment consists of students from neighbouring Poland, close enough to visit on foot over the town's bridge. Nearly 70% of Frankfurt an der Oder was destroyed in the Second World War, but many monuments have been rebuilt: the Rathaus (town hall), St Marienkirche and the Carl Philipp Emanuel Bach concert hall (a former Franciscan abbey). In 2001 the Kleist-Forum, designed as a cultural and conference centre, was opened, named after the town's most famous son, author **Heinrich von Kleist** (1777-1811). There is also a museum *(at Faberstraße 7)* documenting his life and work.

Kloster Chorin★★ (Chorin Abbey)

71km/44mi north of Berlin.   *Apr-Oct: 9am-6pm; Nov-Mar: 9am-4pm.* €3. ☏ *(03 33 66) 703 77. www.kloster-chorin.com.*

The majestic ruins of Chorin Abbey stand beside the Amtssee lake, originally constructed in the 13C by Cistercian monks. The abbey was dissolved in 1542, and after centuries of neglect was saved by the architect Karl Friedrich Schinkel and the King of Prussia. Now partially restored, Chorin Abbey is one of the finest examples of a brick building in northern Germany. Visitors to the abbey can tour the abbey church and convent buildings. This peaceful site hosts a festival of classical music during the summer.

Schloss Rheinsberg★

87km/54mi northwest of Berlin.   *Apr-Oct: open daily except Mon, 9.30am-5pm; Nov-Mar: open Tue-Sun, 10am-12.30pm, 1pm-4pm.* €5. *Guided tour (50min), Nov-Mar: Tue-Sun, 10am-12.30pm, 1pm-4pm.* *Closed 24, 25 and 31 Dec.* *Guided tour of palace and grounds.* €7.50. ☏ *(0339 31) 72 60.*

Frederick the Great only lived in the 16C Schloss Rheinsberg for four years, but he called them the best four years of his life. Small wonder, then, that the castle is forever linked to him. Purchased by Frederick's father in 1734 and remodeled to meet his needs, the castle was the setting for Frederick's decision to rule as "chief servant of his country." In Rheinsberg, the architect Knobelsdorff, the painter Pesne and the sculptor Glume created a Rococo style which is epitomized at Charlottenburg and Sanssouci. Until German reunification, the palace was used as a sanatorium. Its complete restoration is currently in progress.

BERNKASTEL-KUES ★

POPULATION: 8 000

Bernkastel-Kues is formed of two towns straddling the Moselle in the largest single wine-growing region of Germany. The grapes are 95% of the Riesling variety. Many visitors come during the first week in September to celebrate the grape harvest. ⓘ *Gestade 66, 54470 Bernkastel-Kues, ☎ (065 31) 40 23. www. bernkastel-kues.de.*

▶ **Orient Yourself:** Bernkastel-Kues is in the heart of the Middle Moselle *(Mittelmosel)* around 50km/30mi northeast of Trier.

⊙ **Don't Miss:** The pleasant vineyard-covered vistas surrounding this Moselle River valley town.

⌚ **Also See:** *IDAR OBERSTEIN (37km/23mi south), MOSELTAL (tour includes Bernkastel-Kues), TRIER (49km/31mi southwest), EIFEL (Manderscheid is 73km/46mi north).*

Sights

Markt ★
Old, half-timbered houses surround this small, sloping square in the middle of which is the 17C **St Michael fountain** *(Michaelsbrunnen).*

Cusanusstift (St Nikolaus-Hospital)
On the Kues side of the river. Chapel and cloisters: ⓧ *Open Sun–Fri, 9am-6pm, Sat, 9am-3pm.* 🚶 *Guided library tours Fri at 3pm and Apr to Oct Tue at 10.30am.* ⊕ *€4.* ☎ *(065 31) 22 60. www.cusanus.de.*

Founded in 1447 by **Cardinal Nicholas of Kues** (or Nikolaus Cusanus), a humanist and theologian, the hospice was built to house people in need. The number of lodgers was restricted to a symbolic 33 – the age of Christ at his death – a tradition still respected today.

Admire the Late Gothic cloister, the chapel with its fine 15C reredos, and the bronze copy of the cardinal's tombstone (the original is in Rome, at San Pietro in Vincoli). Note the fresco depicting The Last Judgement *(to the left of the entrance)* and the **tombstone of Clara Cryftz**, the prelate's sister. The **library** houses almost 400 manuscripts, in addition to astronomical instruments used by the founder.

Excursion

Burg Landshut
3km/2mi southeast towards Longkamp and uphill to the right.
The **castle**, built on a rocky promontory, was the property of the archbishops of Trier from the 11C. It has been in ruins ever since the War of the Orléans Succession. From the ruin there is a panoramic **view** ★★ over the bend in the Moselle, above which even the steepest slopes are planted with vines.

BODENSEE★★

With its expansive horizons and a climate mild enough for tropical vegetation, Lake Constance (*Bodensee* in German) attracts a multitude of German vacationers who regard it as their local "Riviera". In addition to the vistas, which encompass the Alps to the south in clear weather, tourists love the lake's clear waters, medieval towns and boat cruises.

▶ **Orient Yourself:** The Bodensee is filled by the Rhine as it empties out of the Alps. The lake borders Switzerland and Austria, and due to its size (53 000ha/210sq mi with a maximum depth of 252m/827ft, only slightly smaller than Lake Geneva, the largest Alipine lake) the Bodensee creates its own microclimate conducive to the fruit cultivation. Boat services ply the lake's waters, the most frequent of which run from the ports of Constance, Überlingen, Meersburg, Friedrichshafen, Lindau and Bregenz (& see The Green Guide Austria). The islands of **Reichenau**★, on the Untersee, and **Mainau**★★, on the Überlingersee, are described under *KONSTANZ:* Excursions.

⊛ **Don't Miss:** Lake cruises from the port of Constance or Friedrichshafen.

🕓 **Organizing Your Time:** Allow half a day for a leisurely boat cruise, which may include lunch.

Kids **Especially for Kids:** Swimming or cruising on Lake Constance.

🕭 **Also See:** *KONSTANZ, SALEM (8km/4mi north of Birnau), SIGMARINGEN (72km/45mi north of Konstanz),SCHWÄBISCHE ALB (tour includes Sigmaringen).*

Driving Tour

From Überlingen to Lindau

56 km/35mi – allow 4hr

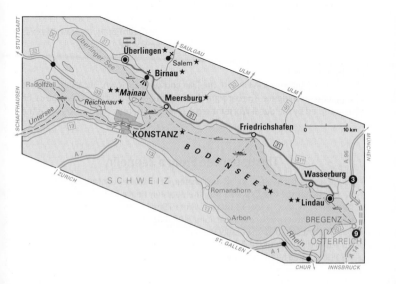

Boats on the lake with Uberlingen in the background

Überlingen★ ( see ÜBERLINGEN)

Birnau
The present 18C church overlooks the Bodensee, charming in its Rococo architectural design. Pilgrims venerate the 15C Virgin above the high altar.

Meersburg★
This former residence of prince-archbishops Meersburg is now a picturesque village among vineyards and orchards. The stylish upper town (Oberstadt) is centred on the **Marktplatz★**, from which the **Steigstraße★**, bordered by half-timbered houses, offers delightful views.

Annette von Droste-Hülshoff, a poet born in Westphalia in 1797, died in the Meersburg where she lived for 7 years. This massive medieval construction with circular room and dungeons dominates the little town. The two tower rooms where Annette wrote can be visited. The memory of the author of the *Judenbuche (The Jew's Beech)* is honoured here and in the Droste-Museum *(Fürstenhäusle, Stettener Straße)*.

▶ *The itinerary continues along the Grüne Straße (the Green Route), between orchards of apple trees, whose fruit is exported throughout Europe.*

Friedrichshafen
Kids Friedrichshafen is a lively port, the "Fair and Zeppelin town," recalling its role as birthplace of the dirigible. The Baroque **church** *(Schloßkirche)*, situated near the castle (still occupied by the ducal Wurtembergs), is worth a detour. Friedrichshafen is the

---

The Bodensee From a Zeppelin

Dirigibles are flying again in Friedrichshafen, having been reintroduced in 1997. 97 years after the first Zeppelin trip, the Zeppelin Neuer Technologie (NT) flew its maiden journey at speeds up to 130kmh/78mph. The new airship is small in comparison to its predecessors: At 75m/240ft long, the new aircraft is only about one third the length of the LZ 129 Hindenburg. The modern 12-seater is available for 1-hr flights over the Bodensee from March to September. The price is around €335, increased by 10% on weekends. It's wise to book ahead.

Address Book

WHERE TO EAT

⊖⊖▤ **Winzerstube zum Becher**
– *Höllgasse 4, 88709 Meersburg.*
☎ *(07532) 90 09. www.winzerstube-zum-becher.de.* ◷ *Closed 3 weeks in Jan and Mon.* This place has been welcoming thirsty visitors since 1610! Pleasantly rustic establishment with its own history: it has belonged to the same family for over 120 years.

WHERE TO STAY

⊖⊖ **Gasthof Auer** – *Stockacher Straße 62, 78359 Orsingen-Nenzingen.*
☎ *(07771) 24 97. Fax (07771) 87 50 86.*
◷ *Closed 1 week in late July.* ▣ *5 rooms.* A hotel typical of the village with painted façade and decorated shutters. The interior features simple, good taste.

⊖⊖ **Hotel Kreuz** – *Grasbeurer Straße 2, 88690 Uhldingen Mühlhofen.* ☎ *(07556) 933 60. Fax (07556) 933670. www.hotel-kreuz-bodensee.de* ▣ ⇝ *Reservation recommended .45 rooms* ⊠ ⊖⊖ *Restaurant.* This family-run hotel is on a quiet side street. Warm, rustic interior with well maintained guestrooms.

⊖⊖ **Landgasthof und Hotel Zum Sternen** – *Schienerbergstraße 23, 78345 Radolfzell, Moos-Bankholzen.* ☎ *(07732) 24 22 Fax (07732) 58910. www.zum-sternen.de.* ▣ ⇝ ♿ *Reservation recommended. 18 rooms* ⊠ ⊖⊖ *Restau-*

rant. The guestrooms of this renovated half-timbered hotel with modern extension contain light-coloured wooden furniture, some with kitchenettes. In the restaurant, expect country cooking and regional specialities.

⊖⊖▤ **Gästehaus Schmäh** – *Kapellenstraße 7, 88709 Hagnau.* ☎ *(07532) 62 10. Fax (07532) 1403. www.gaestehaus-schmaeh.de.* ⇝▣ *17 rooms* ⊠ This well-maintained guesthouse is situated in a quiet residential area, between the main street and the lake. Very clean guestrooms, all furnished in simple, rustic oak. Sun-worshippers will adore the lawn.

⊖⊖▤ **Seehof** – *Unterstadtstraße 36, 88709 Meersburg.* ☎ *(07532) 433 50. Fax (07532) 2406 www.hotel.seehof.mdo.de.* ◷ *Closed mid-Nov to mid-Mar.* ▣ *24 rooms.* ⊠ This hotel is located in the lower town, beside the lake. Modern, functional guestrooms are available. The perfect base for excursions into the surrounding area.

TAKING A BREAK

Strandcafé – *Strandbadstraße 102 78315 Radolfzell.* ☎ *(07732) 16 50.* ◷ *Open daily 11am-midnight.* This modern, glass-fronted building is made attractive by its lakeside location. Both from inside and from the terrace, expect superb lake views.

---

departure point for boat excursions to the Rhine falls in Schaffhausen, to the "flower island" of Mainau and to the stilt houses in Unteruhldingen (ℹ️ *see Überlingen*).

Zeppelin-Museum

♿ ◷ *Open May to Oct, Tue-Sun, 10am-6pm; Nov to Apr, Tue-Sun 10am–5pm.* ◷ *Closed 24 and 25 Dec.* ⊜ *€6.50.* ☎ *(075 41) 380 10. www.zeppelin-museum.de.*
This museum on the eastern end of the promenade in the former train station is devoted to Count Ferdinand Zeppelin (1838-1917) who developed his namesake dirigibles in Friedrichshafen. Part of the legendary "Hindenburg," which exploded in 1937, has been reconstructed, allowing a vision of the technology it represented.

Lindau★★ (ℹ️ *see LINDAU IM BODENSEE*)

BONN

POPULATION: 312 000

In 1949, Bonn was chosen as the capital of the new West German Federal Republic, to the surprise of many Germans given its modest size and provincial character. No longer a major European capital, Bonn has a calm and welcoming atmosphere. Bonn's most famous son, Beethoven, is highly celebrated, especially during the international Beethoven Festival. ▯ *Windeskstraße. 1 (Münsterplatz), 53103 Bonn.* ☏ *(0228) 77 50 00. www.bonn.de.*

▶ **Orient Yourself:** Bonn is at the gateway to the romantic Middle Rhine region. The town is accessible from Cologne by the A 555 or A 59 motorways. From the foot of the bastion, riverside promenades offer pleasant strolls and boat cruises.

▯ **Parking:** Garages are located throughout the city: near the train station, near Beethoven's Birthplace, and near the Old Cemetery on Oxfordstraße.

☺ **Don't Miss:** Beethoven's Birthplace and Bonn's Museum of Art.

🕓 **Organizing Your Time:** Allow half a day to enjoy the Siebengebirge.

Kids Especially for Kids: Museum of the Fedreal Republic of Germany and the Siebengebirge (☝ *see Excursions below*), especially the funicular.

☝ **Also See:** *BRÜHL (22km/14mi north), KÖLN (29km/18mi northwest), EIFEL (Bad Münstereifel is 39km/24mi south).*

A Bit of History

Origins – This site has been inhabited since Roman times, but it was in the 16C that Bonn became important as residence of the electors and archbishops of Cologne.

Capital of the Federal Republic of Germany – After **Konrad Adenauer** was nominated the first federal Chancellor in 1949, he pressed for Bonn to become provisional capital of West Germany. The town fulfilled that role for 50 years and became in the process a true seat of government. Since the reunification and transfer of government offices to Berlin in 1999, huge sums of money have been spent redefining the nature of the city.

Beethoven's formative years – Precursor of the Romantic music movement, **Ludwig van Beethoven** (1770-1827) was born and grew up near the Church of St Remigius *(St. Remigius-Kirche)*. At 13, Beethoven was already an accomplished musician, playing violin, viola and harpsichord in the Court of the Elector. At 22 the fervent admirer of Mozart and Haydn left Bonn for Vienna to follow in their footsteps. The **Beethovenhalle** hosts the annual international Beethoven Festival.

WHERE TO EAT

◔◔◔ **Bistro Kaiser Karl** – *Vorgebirgsstraße 50.* ☏ *(0228) 69 69 67.* 🕓 *Closed 1 week during Carnival and 2 weeks in August, Sat lunchtime and Sun.* This bistro attracts crowds for its *Jugendstil* decor: decorated ceilings, chandeliers, mirrored walls and brasserie windows leading to a terrace.

WHERE TO STAY

◔◔◔◔ **Sternhotel** – *Markt 8.* ☏ *(0228) 726 70. fax (0228) 7267125. info@stern-hotel-bonn.de.* 🕓 *Closed 24 Dec until early Jan.* ✎ *80 rooms* ☐. Located near the former town hall, this hotel is part of Bonn's history. Expect every convenience in a quiet, central location.

Walking Tour

Beethovenhaus (Beethoven's Birthplace)
Bonngasse 20. Open Apr-Oct: Mon-Sat, 10am-6pm, Sun, 11am-6pm; Nov-Mar: Mon-Sat, 10am-5pm, Sun, 11am-5pm. Closed 1 Jan, Mon before Shrove Tue, Good Friday, Easter Mon, 24-26 Dec. €4. (0228) 981 75 25. www.beethoven-haus-bonn.de.
In 1770 Beethoven was born in this house, which has been a museum since 1890. Documents highlight the life and opus of the great composer: portraits, original documents, musical instruments, listening horns and life and death masks.

▶ *Go down Bonngasse towards the Markt.*

Altes Rathaus (Town Hall)
Markt. A charming Rococo building (1738) with a pink and grey façade

▶ *Leave the Rathaus and head south.*

Kurfürstliche Residenz (Electors' Residence)
A few feet from the cathedral. The lawns of the Hofgarten make a fine setting for this Baroque building (1697-1702). Since 1818 the palace has housed the university.

Münster★ (Cathedral)
Münsterplatz. The former Stiftskirche St Cassius und Florentius melds 11C-13C Romanesque and Gothic eras beautifully. The Romanesque baptismal font and stone carvings are noteworthy, as are the drawings, ca 1200, and fresco, ca 1300, depicting the Madonna. The quiet Romanesque **cloister**★ (c 1150) is considered one of the best-preserved examples from the period in Germany.

▶ *From the Kurfürstliche Residenz, take the Poppelsdorfer Allee, a large chestnut-lined avenue.*

Poppelsdorfer Schloss
Meckenheimer Allee 171. This castle was built between 1715 and 1753, its outer façade reflecting a classical French influence, while the inner courtyard is more Italian in style. At the back, on level ground where a moat once flowed, are the university's **Botanical Gardens**.

Alter Friedhof
Bornheimer Strasse. Artists, scholars and celebrities are buried in the **old cemetery**, including Robert and Clara Schumann, Beethoven's mother, Ernst Moritz Arndt and August Wilhelm von Schlegel.

August Macke Haus
Bornheimer Strasse 96. August Macke (1887-1914) lived in Bonn from 1910 until 1914, where he produced impressive Impressionist and Fauvist artworks. Inside the neo-classical residence (1878) are examples of Macke's work and a history of Rhenish Expressionism.

Sights

Rheinisches Landesmuseum★
Colmanstr. 14-18. Open Tue-Sun 10am-6pm (Wed til 9pm). Closed Mon and Good Friday. €5. (0228)-2070-0. www.rlmb.lvr.de.
This museum offers an overview of the history, culture and art of the Middle and Lower Rhine, from prehistory to the present.

BONN

Am Alten Friedhof	BZ	2	Gerhard-von-Are-Str.	BZ	16	Rathausgasse	CZ 36
Am Hof	CZ		Kasernenstr.	BY	20	Remigiuspl.	CZ 38
Am Neutor	CZ	3	Markt	CZ	23	Remigiusstr.	CZ 40
Belderberg	CY	7	Martinspl.	CZ	24	Sternstr.	BCZ 43
Bertha-von-Suttner-Pl.	CY	9	Mülheimer Pl.	BZ	27	Sterntorbrücke	BY 45
Bottlerpl.	BZ	10	Münsterpl.	BZ	28	Thomas-Mann-Str.	BYZ 46
Brüdergasse	CY	12	Münsterstr.	BZ	29	Welschnonnenstr.	CY 48
Budapester Str.	BYZ	14	Oxfordstr.	BY	31	Wenzelgasse	CY 49
Fritz-Schroeder-Ufer	CY	15	Poppelsdorfer Allee	BZ	32	Wilhelmstr.	BY 50
			Poststr.	BZ	34		

Beethovenhaus	CY	M³	Rathaus	CZ	R	Rheinisches Landes-	
Kurfürstliche Residenz	CZ	U				museum	BZ M¹

The **Prehistoric Section** *(Urgeschichtliche Abteilung, 1st floor)* shows the skull of the celebrated Neanderthal Man, artifacts from the Stone and Bronze Ages and La Tène culture (weapons, metalwork, jewellery, etc).

Roman Antiquities★ *(Römische Abteilung)* is particularly well endowed, with Altars to the Matrons, a cult popular with Roman soldiers stationed in the Rhinelands. A masterpiece of Roman craft, the **Sun God Mosaic** (c 250 AD), shows the Sun God in his chariot, surrounded by the signs of the Zodiac.

The highlight of the **Frankish Section** is a reconstruction of a chieftain's tomb, ca 600 AD. The **Middle Ages to the Present** displays arts and crafts from the Romanesque to the 19C. Note the **Gothic and Dutch paintings** of the 16C and 17C.

Haus der Geschichte der Bundesrepublik Deutschland★ (Museum of the Federal Republic of Germany)

Kids *Adenauerallee 250.* & ⏲ *Open Tue-Sun, 9am-7pm.* ☎ *(0228) 916 50. www.hdg.de.*
Upon opening Germany's first museum of contemporary history, curators made great efforts to display materials engagingly, with multimedia screens and interactive exhib-

Deutsches Museum, Bonn

Rocket-carrier by Daimler-Benz, Deutsches Museum Bonn

its. Older visitors can retrace the historical events of their youth, while younger ones watch the past unfold before their eyes. The evolution of the former East German Republic (DDR) unfolds alongside that of the former West German Republic (BDR).

Kunstmuseum Bonn★ (Bonn Museum of Art)
Friedrich-Ebert-Allee 2. & ○ Open Tue-Sun, 10am-6pm, (-9pm, Wed). ● €5. ☎ (0228) 77 62 60. www.bonn.de/kunstmuseum.
Expressionism is well represented in Bonn's Museum of Art, particularly that of former resident August Macke. German art since 1945 is given prominence, with works by Uecker, Richter, Kiefer, Baselitz, Penck and Lüpertz. Three rooms are devoted to the installations of Joseph Beuys alone. The neighbouring **National Art Gallery and Exhibition Hall** *(Kunst- und Ausstellungshalle der Bundesrepublik Deutschland)* houses temporary exhibitions. & ○ *Open Tue-Sun, 10am-7pm, (until 9pm Tue and Wed).* ○ *Closed 24 and 31 Dec. ● €6.50. ☎ (0228) 917 12 00. www.bundeskunsthalle.de.*

Deutsches Museum Bonn
Ahrstraße 45. & ○ Open Tue-Sun, 10am-6pm. ○ Closed during Carnival period, Shrove Tue, Good Friday, 1 May, 24, 25 and 31 Dec. ● €4. ☎ (0228) 30 22 55. www. deutsches-museum-bonn.de.
This museum, which is an offshoot of Munich's famous museum of the same name, emphasizes "Research and Technology in Germany since 1945," a particularly exciting period in the history of technology. Technological advances in both the former West and East Germanies are covered in multimedia displays.

Excursions

Schwarz-Rheindorf★
▶ *Leave by the Kennedy bridge.*
This two-story Romanesque **chapel**★, consecrated 1151, features two chapels. The lower one features murals with scenes from the Book of Ezekiel; the upper has a replica imperial throne like that in the Pfalzkapelle in Aachen.

Bad Godesberg
Town plan in the Michelin Guide Deutschland.
This residential suburb south of Bonn was the seat of foreign embassies until the government moved to Berlin. The city's **riverside walk** between the Rhine ferry landing is popular. The Petersberg Hotel and the Drachenfels ruins overlook the river. The ruins of 13C Godesburg Castle stands on a basalt outcropping in the town

centre. From the keep is a fine panoramic **view**★ of the city and the Siebengebirge massif. ▯ *Telephone for information on opening times,* ☎ *(0228) 31 60 71.*

Siebengebirge★

[Kids] The Seven Mountains massif is the Rhine's northernmost wine-growing region on the eastern bank of the Rhine. Its name comes from the seven prominent summits once almost all crowned by castles. There's lots of romance in this region. At the foot of the range are **Bad Honnef-Rhöndorf** (house of Konrad Adenauer) and **Königswinter**, from where a funicular climbs to the [Kids] **Drachenfels**★ ruins, where legend has it that Siegfried slew the dragon and bathed in its blood to become invincible.

Funicular: ◷ *May to Sep 9am–7pm every 30min; Jan, Feb and Nov (up to and including Buß- und Bettag, or the third Wed in Nov) departures depending on demand Mon–Fri noon–5pm, Sat–Sun 11am–6pm (hourly); Mar and Oct 10am–6pm (every 30min); Apr 10am–7pm (every 30min).* ⌷ *Round-trip €8.* ☎ *(022 23) 920 90. www.drachenfelsbahn-koenigswinter.de.*

Remagen

23km/14mi south. Leave by the Adenauerallee.

Remagen began as a Roman fortified camp; associated archaeological finds are exhibited in the **Roman Museum** (Römisches Museum) at *Kirchstraße 9*, the former 16C Knechtstedener Chapel. Remagen became famous when its **bridge** across the Rhine fell into American hands in 1945 – the first time the Americans were able to establish a bridgehead east of the river. Days later, the bridge collapsed under the weight of armoured vehicles. The remaining towers are today the site of a **peace museum**, *Friedensmuseum*, tracing the history of the bridge and the battles of March 1945. ◷ *Open May to mid-Nov: daily, 10am–5pm; May-Oct: daily, 10am–6pm.* ⌷ *€3.50.* ☎ *(026 42) 201 59. www.bruecke-remagen.de.*

SCHLOSS BRANITZ

The former Branitz estate had belonged to the family since 1696 when Hermann von Pückler-Muskau took up permanent residence here in 1845. The prince was in dire financial straits, but was unable to abandon the great passion of his life, garden design. His talent is visible in Branitz Park a jewel of garden design.

▸ **Orient Yourself:** Branitz is less than 5km/3mi east of Cottbus, a merchant settlement near the Spree River.

◷ **Organizing Your Time:** Schloss Branitz and its park can be seen in half a day.

◔ **Also See:** *SPREEWALD (Lübbenau is 37km/23mi to the west), BAUTZEN (77km/48mi south).*

Visit

Schloss and Pückler-Park Branitz★★ *Tour: 3hr*

Schloss Branitz

◷ *Open Apr to Oct daily 10am–6pm; Nov to Mar Tue-Sun 11am–5pm.* ◷ *Closed 24 and 31 Dec; stables (Marstall) Nov to Mar.* ⌷ *€3.50.* ☎ *(0355) 751 52 25. www.pueckler-museum.de.*

The proceeds from the sale of Muskau enabled Prince Pückler to have the 18C **palace** sumptuously decorated. Large parts of the structure and furnishings remain, such

R. Chéret/MICHELIN

The terrace and park of the luxurious Branitz estate, laid out by the extravagant Hermann, Prince of Pückler-Muskau.

as the dining room furniture and the library. The palace features an art gallery with paintings by **Karl Blechen**, the Romantic painter born in Cottbus.

In front of the palace are the former Tudor-style royal **stables**, in which temporary exhibitions are housed, and the Cavalier's House, used today as a café. An attractive bower courtyard, with terracotta reliefs and cast zinc figures, extends between these buildings. On the garden side is a terrace featuring two bronze griffins.

Park

Hermann's garden park covers 90ha/222 acres. The soil from the excavation of lakes was used to form hills and pyramids. Pückler placed particular emphasis on the alternation between open spaces, tree groupings and individual specimens and pools.

Tumulus

Hermann's remains are interred in the 11m/36ft high tumulus in the pyramid lake.

Impoverished Prince Seeks Financial Backing

Hermann, Prince of Pückler-Muskau was born in Muskau in 1785. He was a spendthrift throughout his life, accumulating such debts as to threaten the family estate. His father even attempted to have his son legally declared incapable of managing his own affairs. Hermann discovered his true traveling through the magnificent parklands of England. He reacted by redesigning the Muskau estate park in 1815, a project that lasted 30 years.

His marriage for money to Lucie von Hardenberg was harmonious, but the Prince divorced her in order to marry for money again (a marriage that never actually took place). He had used up all his first wife's money for Muskau Park. Despite their troubles, the pair remained inseparable until Lucie's death in 1858.

When forced to leave Muskau at 60, Hermann took up a new project, Branitz Park, on which he worked for the remaining 25 years of his life.

BRAUNSCHWEIG

BRUNSWICK
POPULATION: 260 000

The second largest city of Lower Saxony, Brunswick has always been a thriving industrial town, and it remains so today. After its destruction in October 1944, the inner city was rebuilt according to modern urban concepts, but some noteworthy sights remain. ⓘ *Vor der Burg 1, 38100 Braunschweig.* ☏ *(0531) 27 35 50.*

▶ **Orient Yourself:** Located south of the Lüneburger Heath, the town of Brunswick is reached from the A 2 motorway which links Hannover and Berlin.

🅿 **Parking:** Garages are scattered throughout the town; a large facility is on Georg-Eckert-Straße near Museumpark and the Domplatz.

👁 **Don't Miss:** Altstadtmarkt, Herzog-Anton-Ulrich-Museum, and, if you're a car buff, Autostadt *(👶 see Excursions below).*

🧒 **Especially for Kids:** Volkswagen's automotive theme park, Autostadt *(👶 see Excursions).*

👶 **Also See:** *WOLFENBÜTTEL (11km/7mi southeast), CELLE (52km/32mi northeast), HANNOVER (63km/40mi west).*

A Bit of History

The Lion of Brunswick – In 1166, having boosted the House of Guelph to political power in Germany, Henry the Lion, Duke of Bavaria and Saxony, settled in Brunswick. Frederick I Barbarossa, jealous of his rise, ultimately stripped Henry of nearly all his personal and possessions. The lion sculpture on Burgplatz recalls his life.

Till Eulenspiegel Country – Memories of the famous Braunschweiger jester and buffoon, **Till Eulenspiegel**, spread far and wide through medieval storytellers and minstrels. He was born ca 1300 in Schöppenstedt, where a museum honours him.

Walking Tour

Town Centre

Brunswick grew up around 5 distinct districts **(Altstadt, Hagen, Altewiek, Neustadt and Sack)**, each with its own constitution, town hall and market. The majority of sights are best discovered on foot in the fully reconstructed town centre.

Altstadtmarkt

Municipal institutions of Brunswick's merchant quarter are visible in the Altstadt-markt. The **old town hall** *(Altstadtrathaus)* is built with stepped gables (13C-15C). The buttresses of buildings facing the square support statues of the princes of Saxony and the House of Guelph. In the middle of the Poststraße is the **Drapers' Hall** *(Gewand-haus)*, featuring the town's most decorated gable (Late Renaissance).

Dom★ (Cathedral)

The original Romanesque church was built in the 12C. at the time of Henry the Lion. Noteworthy artworks include the seven-branched 12C **candelabrum**★ *(Bronze-leuchter);* the impressive 12C **cross**★ in the northern side nave; the 12C **Marian Altar**; and the Saxon sculpting on the **tomb** of Henry and his wife, Matilda, in the nave.

Herzog-Anton-Ulrich-Museum★

 ♿ ⏱ *Open Tue-Sat, 10am-5pm (1pm-8pm, Wed).* ⏱ *Closed 1 May, 24, 25 and 31 Dec.* 🎟 *€2.50.* ☎ *(0531) 122 50. www.museum-braunschweig.de.*

Established in 1754, this art museum features a priceless collection of German, Flemish and Dutch masters, including Rembrandt, Rubens, Van Dyck, Vermeer, Cranach the Elder and Holbein.

Excursions

Autostadt★★

🧒 *32km/20mi northeast in Wolfsburg, north of town centre.* ♿ ⏱ *Open Apr to Oct, 9am-8pm; Nov to Mar: 9am-6pm.* ⏱ *Closed 24 and 31 Dec.* 🎟 *€15.* ☎ *(08 00) 288 67 82 38. www.autostadt.de.*

This 25ha/62 acre Volkswagen theme park was built beside the German auto maker's headquarters. Landscaped parkland forms a pleasant backdrop for all things automotive: its history, the values associated with it, and visions for its future. Brightly-waxed autos, science experiments and multimedia displays keep the topic interesting for all ages. Restaurants, cafes and a hotel are also on-site. VW offers guided factory tours Monday to Friday (☛ *1hr, included in admission fee, request tour when buying ticket*).

Helmstedt

41km/25mi E

Helmstedt-Marienborn was once the most important border crossing in Germany. Three monuments illustrate the border's history: the **Zonengrenz-Museum** in Helmstedt *(Südertor 6;* ♿ ⏱ *Open Mar: Wed, 10am-noon, 3-5pm, Thu, 3-6.30pm, Fri, 3-5pm, Sat-Sun, 10am-5pm.* ☎ *(053 51) 121 11 33; www.helmstedt.de;* the **Grenzdenkmal Hötensleben** *(16km/10mi S of Helmstedt via Schöningen)*, where original border installations are preserved; and the crossing itself, the **Gedenkstätte Deutsche Teilung Marienborn**★ *(access via A 2, towards Berlin)*, an archive and documentation centre. ♿ ⏱ *Open Tue-Sat, 10am-5pm. Donation.* ☎ *(0394 06) 920 90. www.grenzdenkmaeler.de.*

BREMEN★★

POPULATION: 546 000

Bremen, Germany's oldest maritime city, is famous for Beck's beer and popularised by the Brothers Grimm. Trade had always been important to this city, which enjoyed trade rights from 965, joined the Hanseatic League in 1358, and began trading directly with America in 1783. But Bremen is also a town of culture, where the Weser Renaissance architectural style blossomed. 🔲 *Am Bahnhofsplatz, 28195 Bremen.* ☎ *(0421) 30 80 00.*

▸ **Orient Yourself:** Bremen, at the interior of the Weser estuary, and Bremerhaven, its outer harbour 59km/37mi downstream, form an important port system.

🅿 **Parking:** Garages are located throughout Bremen. Visit http://wap.parkinfo.com for locations and fees.

🐾 **Don't Miss:** A stroll along the harbor that made this city what it is.

⏱ **Organizing Your Time:** Allow at least 2 hours to see Old Bremen.

👶 **Also See:** OLDENBURG *(48km/30mi west on the A 28)*, LÜNEBURGER HEIDE *(Undeloh is 62km/39mi east)*, HAMBURG *(126km/79mi northeast on the A 1)*.

Coffee bean city

Bremen's close links with coffee date back over three centuries. The first ever coffee house in German-speaking countries was built here in 1673, before those in Vienna and Hamburg. Half of all the cups of coffee drunk in Germany are brewed from beans imported via the port at Bremen.

A Bit of History

Die Bremischen Häfen (The Harbours) – The Bremen harbour group (including Bremen and Bremerhaven) directly or indirectly employs about a third of the city's population. These harbours are Germany's largest after Hamburg. Each year Bremen passes more than a million containers through the Wilhelm-Kaisen-Terminal, and over a million vehicles go through the docks.

&♿ 🕐 *River and harbour tours leave from the quay by the St Martinikirche. 1hr 15min. Departures Apr to Oct daily at 10.15am, 11.45am, 1.30pm, 3.15pm and 4.45pm; Mar, Sat-Sun at 11.45am, 1.30pm and 3.15pm. ☞ €8. ☎ (018 05) 10 10 30 or (0421) 33 89 89. www.bremen-tourism.de.*

Walking Tour

Old Bremen

Marktplatz★★
The market square, its wide expanse surrounded by the city's finest buildings, lies in the heart of the old town. The centre is marked by a giant 10m/33ft statue of **Roland** beneath a Gothic canopy (1404). The **Schütting**, an elegant 16C building, used to house Bremen's Guild of Merchants.

Rathaus★

Guided tour (45min) Mon-Sat, 11am, noon, 3pm and 4pm, Sun 11am and noon. ☞ €4. ☎ (018 05) 10 10 30. www.bremen-tourism.de.
The main building is Gothic, its upper floors crowned by decorative gables, part of a 17C transformation in the Weser Renaissance style.
The three-story façade rises above an arcaded gallery. Above this, tall windows alternate with statues of Charlemagne and the Seven Electors (copies: the Gothic

The market place in the heart of the old town, dominated by an immense statue of Roland

Bremer Touristik-Zentrale

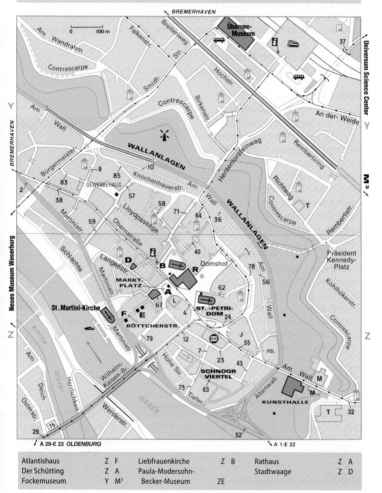

originals are in the Focke-Museum). At the corner of the west wing the modern bronze group represents the *Animal Musicians of Bremen* (a pyramid formed by an ass, a dog, a cat and a cockerel), characters from the popular Grimm fairy tale.
Inside, a splendid spiral **staircase**★★ *(Wendeltreppe)* in carved wood (1620) is worth making time for.
The Bremer Rathauskeller *(entrance on the west side)* serves exclusively German wines from 600 different vineyards.

St Petri-Dom★

St Petri-Dom was constructed in the 11C, and updated in the 16C and 19C. Inside notable religious artworks include a 16C **Virgin and Child**★, and, along the organ ballustrate, 16C carvings of Charlemagne and Willehad, the first Bishop of Bremen. Beneath the organ loft, the 11C western crypt houses Romanesque capitals and a magnificent bronze **baptismal font**★★ (*Taufbecken*, c 1220).

Pfarrkirche Unserer Lieben Frauen (Church of Our Lady)

The plain interior of this 13C hall church, bare of decoration except for the 1709 chancel, is relieved by rounded ogive vaulting dating to its construction. The four main stained-glass windows, on biblical themes, were executed between 1966 and 1979. The church's simple **crypt** dates from the preceding church (St Veit), which has been traced to 1020 and therefore represents the oldest construction in Bremen.

Stadtwaage (Weigh-House)

This simple 16C building features alternating layers of brick and embossed stone.

Böttcherstraße★

Running from the Marktplatz to the Weser, this narrow street was built in the 1920s by industrialist Ludwig Roselius, who made his fortune in the coffee trade. Bernhard Hoetger drew on the Expressionist style, using Jugendstil (Art Nouveau) and Art Deco overtones. The buildings house galleries, shops and museums. A porcelain carillon chimes at noon, 3pm and 6pm *(in summer, on the hour between noon and 6pm)*.

Along the Böttcherstraße is the **Paula-Modersohn-Becker-Museum**★ (*Böttcherstraße 6-10.* ○ *Tue-Sun, 11am-6pm.* ⊙ *€5.* ☎ *(0421) 336 50 66; www.pmbm. de)* built by Bernhard Hoetger. Inside are paintings, drawings and graphic work by Modersohn-Becker (1876-1907), a modern art pioneer.

Bremer Touristik-Zentrale

The richly-decorated Town Hall

Sights

Schnoorviertel★

The cottages in this quarter, once the homes of fishermen and their families, are all that remains of Old Bremen. Ranging in age from the 15C to the 19C, they have all been restored and are used as art galleries, antique shops, restaurants and boutiques. The narrow streets of the quarter, popular with tourists, are very busy after dark.

Kunsthalle★ (Art Gallery)

♿ ○ *Open Tue-Sun, 10am-5pm (Tue until 9pm).* ○ *Closed 24 and 31 Dec.* ⊙ *€5.* ☎ *(0421) 32 90 80. www.kunsthalle-bremen.de.*
An outstanding collection of 19C and 20C French and German art is the main attraction here. On display are works by: Courbet, Delacroix and the Barbizon School; Menzel, Leibl, Beckmann; the French Impressionists and their German counterparts; and artists of the Worpswede School (⚘ *see below).* Earlier periods of European art are illustrated by 15C Old Masters, and by Rubens, Rembrandt, Tiepolo, up to Picasso. In the print room (Kupferstichkabinett) are over 230 000 prints and drawings of exceptional quality from Dürer's day to the present.

Address Book

WHERE TO EAT

🍽 **Paulaner's** – *Schlachte 30* ☎ *(0421) 169 06 91 - www.paulaners.de. Reservations recommended.* A pleasant, riverside, country-style establishment with efficient, friendly service and Bavarian cuisine. The restaurant features a beautiful Biergarten.

🍽🍽 **John Benton Restaurant** – *Am Markt 1.* ☎ *(0421) 32 30 33* 🕐 *Closed 24 Dec.* ♿ This restaurant spans two floors in the heart of the old town. The terrace offers beautiful cathedral views.

🍽🍽 **Cargo** – *Schlachte 18* ☎ *(0421) 165 55 99 - www.cargo-bremen.de. Reservation required.* A trendy establishment on the promenade along the Weser. The restaurant covers two floors with modern, understated décor. Extensive variety on the menu.

WHERE TO STAY

🛏🛏 **Bölts am Park** – *Slevogtstraße 23* ☎ *(0421) 34 61 10 – fax (0421) 341227. www.hotel-boelts.de. 16 rooms.* 🍽 **Restaurant** This quiet little parkside guesthouse offers well-tended rooms; breakfast looks out over a small garden.

🛏🛏 **Hotel Buthmann** *Löingstraße 29* ☎ *(0421) 32 63 97. Fax (0421) 3398816 www.hotel-buthmann.de. 10 rooms* 🍽 This little inn is close to the station. Its guestrooms are clean, well-cared for and furnished with simple décor.

🛏🛏🛏🛏 **Park Hotel** – *Im Bürgerpark* ☎ *(0421) 340 80. Fax (0421) 3408602. www.park-hotel-bremen.de.* 🅿 🏊 ⊬ *150 rooms* 🍽 The luxury and exclusivity of this hotel are obvious as soon as you enter the sumptuous domed lounge of this former country house. The individually decorated suites are splendid and the fitness centre has a Turkish bath and heated outdoor pool.

TAKING A BREAK

F. L. Bodes – *Bischofsnadel 1-2 (alleyway leading from Wallanlagen to Domshof)* ☎ *(0421) 32 41 44. www.bodes.de.* 🕐 *Tue-Thu, 8am-6pm, Fri, 8am-6.30pm, Sat, 8am-3pm* 🕐 *Closed Sun, Mon, and bank holidays.* Fish shop and snack bar a stone's throw from the town centre.

Pannekoekschip Admiral Nelson

Try seafood and fish à la carte, choose from the blackboard menus or make your selection directly from the stalls. Between 11:30am and 2pm the shop is extremely busy.

Konditorei Knigge – *Sögestr. 42-44* ☎ *(0421) 13 7 13. www.knigge-shop.de* 🕐 *Mon-Sat 9am-6:30pm, Sun 12-6pm.* Bremen's classic tearoom. House specialities include the "Bremer Klaben", a fruitcake.

GOING OUT

Useful tip – In Bremen, most of the cafés, bars, restaurants and shops are in the historic Schnoor district, south of the cathedral. The Schlachte, on the Weser's right bank, features gourmet dining and plenty of bars here, many with river terraces.

Café Frei'tag – *Böttcherstr. 3-5.* ☎ *(0421) 32 09 95* 🕐 *Daily from 10am (food served: 11:30am-8.30pm).* This modern, elegant café-bar is situated in the Robinson-Crusoe House on the famous Böttcherstraße. In summer the terrace is perfect for people-watching.

Pannekoekschip Admiral Nelson – *Schlachte Anleger 1* ☎ *(0421) 3 64 99 84. www.admiral-nelson.de.* 🕐 *Food served: Fri-Sat, 12-10pm, Sun-Thu, 12-9.30pm; Nov-May: daily except Mon.* Ahoy there! Friendly "pirates" serve sweet or savoury pancakes on this three-masted ship.

Salomon's – *Ostertorstr. 11-13. ☎ (0421) 2 44 17 71. www.salomons-bremen.de.* ○ *10am-late.* The bar-restaurant is in a wing of the 19C Law Courts. Reasonably-priced dishes are served Mon - Sat 11:30am-3pm. In summer visit the terrace in the interior courtyard.

CULTURE

The monthly magazines *Mix* (free, available from restaurants and bookshops),

Bremer and *Prinz* (available for purchase from bookshops or newspaper stands) publish calendars of events.

SHOPPING

The elegant shopping thoroughfares of Lloydpassage, Domshof Passage and Katharinen-Viertel in the heart of town are great for a stroll. Independent boutiques are located in the historic Schnoor district (& *see Going Out*).

Focke-Museum★★

Leave via the Rembertiring. & ○ *Open Tue-Sun, 10am-5pm (9pm, Tue).* ○ *Closed 1 Jan, Easter Sun, Whit Sun, 1 May, Ascension, 3 Oct, 24, 25 and 31 Dec.* ☜ *€4. ☎ (0421) 361 35 75. www.focke-museum.de.*

This regional museum covers 1 000 years of Bremen history in four historic buildings and one modern main house. The newly opened **Main House** *(Haupthaus)* houses a virtual, chronological tour of the port city, as well as displays about modern Bremen. The prehistoric collections are displayed in a thatched annex. A **farmhouse** (from Mittelsbüren, 1586) on the museum grounds spotlights inland Bremen. The Tarnstedt Barn *(Tarnstedter Scheune)* shows the products of rural work.

Haus Riensberg also belongs to the museum This 18C house was once a summer residence for wealthy Bremen families and features decorative arts, Fürstenberg porcelain and European glass art.

Excursions

Worpswede

24km/15mi north – about 1hr 30min. Leave Bremen by the Rembertiring.
Isolated at one time in a desolate landscape of peat moors, the village of Worpswede attracted at the end of the 19C a colony of artists, notable among whom were Paula Modersohn-Becker, her husband Otto Modersohn and the poet Rainer Maria Rilke. Galleries, studios and workshops have sprung up since then. Asymmetrical buildings like the Worpswede Café and the Niedersachsenstein First World War Memorial represent the avant-garde ideas held by the group.

Bremerhaven

58km/36mi north.
Bremen's deep-sea port was founded at the mouth of the Weser estuary in 1827. Half of the German fishing fleet is based here, but Bremerhaven is first and foremost an important container port (& *see "The Harbours" above*).

SCHLOSS BRUCHSAL★★

Bruchsal, residence of the last four prince-bishops of Speyer, is blessed with a Baroque palace reconstructed after its destruction in March 1945. Theis vast complex was originally built in 1722 on the orders of the Prince-Bishop Damian Hugo von Schönborn.

▶ **Orient Yourself:** 20km/12.5mi north of Karlsruhe, on the edge of the rolling hills of the Kraichgau, the castle complex comprises 50 dwellings or annexes; the main road from Karlsruhe to Heidelberg runs through the grounds.

🕐 **Organizing Your Time:** Allow half a day to explore Schloss Bruchsal.

♿ **Also See:** *KARLSRUHE (20km/12.5mi south), Kloster MAULBRONN (24km/15mi east), SCHWARZWALD (the forest begins 30km/19mi south of Bruchsal), SPEYER (35km/22mi north), HEIDELBERG (38km/24mi north).*

Visit

Central Block

♿ 🕐 *Open daily except Mon, 9.30am-5pm.* 👓 *€4.50.* ☎ *(072 51) 74 26 61. www.schloesser-und-gaerten.de.*

Of all the architectural beauty of Schloss Bruchsal, its magnificent **staircase**★★ stands out, with an oval well designed by Balthasar Neumann in 1731. Rococo stucco decorates the dome above it. The **state apartments** have original furnishings on display: silver, porcelain tableware and portraits of the prelates.

The Gartensaal, a vaulted room with a marble floor, opens onto the park *(Hofgarten).*, a magnificent **garden** that once reached the river, 16km/10mi away.

Museum mechanischer Musikinstrumente★★

In the main building. 🔊 *Guided tour (1hr) with instrument demonstrations.* ♿ 🕐 *Open daily except Mon, 9.30am-5pm.* 👓 *€4.50, including castle visit.* ☎ *(072 51) 74 26 61. www.schloesser-und-gaerten.de.*

This department of the Regional Museum derives from a private collection and includes 200 18C-20C musical instruments, most of them worked by cylinders, pricked-out metal or cardboard, or rolls of paper. The guided tour features a recital performed on each instrument after an explanation of its function. Cinema organs, "Barbary organs", and pianolas (mechanical pianos operated by perforated "piano-rolls") are also represented. Note the "household" organs and orchestrions (in 19C England Aeolian Orchestrelles, machines resembling oversize upright pianos with manual keyboards and stops). Examples from Leipzig and the Black Forest are well represented.

Städtisches Museum

Southern part of the main block, on the attic floor. ☎ *(07251) 74 26 61.*

The museum is divided into five areas: the palaeontological collection, which also contains minerals from Bruchsal and its surrounding area; the prehistoric department, with regional finds from the Late Stone Age to the end of the Middle Ages; the Bruchsal penal system; the numismatic and medal collections of the former state of Baden, the Palatinate and the prince-episcopate of Speyer.

BRÜHL

POPULATION: 42 000

Brühl developed around a fortress which acquired municipal status in 1285. After the destruction of the fortress by foreign troops, its foundations were used for the 18C construction of the Augustusburg Palace. Brühl is widely known for this masterpiece of Rococo, part of UNESCO's World Heritage List. *Uhlstraße 1, 50321 Brühl. ☎ (022 32) 793 45.*

▶ **Orient Yourself:** Brühl is situated on route 265 a few miles to the south of Cologne (directly linked to Cologne by the B51)

⊘ **Don't Miss:** Schloss Augustusburg

⊙ **Organizing Your Time:** Allow at least one hour for Schloss Augustusburg.

Kids Especially for Kids: Phantasialand amusement park (⊙ *see Excursion below*).

⊙ **Also See:** *KÖLN (13km/8mi north), BONN (22km/14mi south), KOBLENZ (90km/56mi south).*

Sights

Schloss Augustusburg★★

& ◗ *Feb-Nov: Guided tour (1hr) daily except Mon, 9am-noon, 1:30-4pm, Sat-Sun, 10am-5pm. ◉ €4. ☎ (022 32) 440 00. www.schlossbruehl.de.*

The Rococo palace was built for Clemens August, illustrious member of the House of Wittelsbach. August became a bishop at 19, advancing to Archbishop and Elector of Cologne, when he converted his hunting lodge into a palace.

The castle's magnificent **staircase**★★ was designed by **Balthasar Neumann,** one of his most beautiful compositions. The marble stuccowork is in shades of greyish-green and yellowish-orange. The **ceiling fresco**★ by Carlo Carlone celebrates the prince and the House of Wittelsbach. About two dozen of the **interior**★★ rooms may be visited. Highlights include the **large new suite,** comprising a garden room with more Carlone frescos; the **summer suite,** with floors covered in blue and white tiles from Rotterdam; and the **yellow suite,** used principally by Clemens August as his private residence.

The French style **garden**★ designed by Lenôtre student Dominique Girardet features reflective lakes and elaborately decorative flower beds gradually yielding to a country park; the garden dates from 1840.

Schloss Falkenlust★

Some 2.5km/1.5mi from Schloss Augustusburg, past the lake and along Falkenluster Allee. A 20min slide show provides insight into the history of the castle. ⊙ Feb-Nov: Open Tue-Sun, 9am-noon, 1:30-4pm, Sat-Sun, 10am-5pm. ◉ €3. ☎ (022 32) 440 00. www.schlossbruehl.de.

This captivating little two-storey Rococo palace with its belvedere and lantern roof is designed in a perfectly symmetrical shape.

Inside, the small **japanned room**★ with its lacquered paintings is most impressive. The staircase is covered with blue and white tiles up to ceiling height. Particularly remarkable is the small **mirrored room**★, a miniature masterpiece with its blue-edged panels and gilded carved frames.

Excursion

Phantasialand★

Kids *On the southern edge of the town. & ⊙ Open Apr to mid-Oct: 9am-6pm; mid-Oct to early Nov: 11am-8pm. ◉ €24.50 child. ☎ (022 32) 362 00. www.phantasialand.de.*

The 28ha/69 acre leisure park, which is famous for its rides, offers many attractions within four themed areas: log flumes with drops of up to 16m/52ft, one of the world's largest indoor roller-coasters, a monorail jet, a Wild West stunt show, and a simulated space flight. The **Wintergarten-Show**★ *(reserve at the Wintergarten ticket office)* is magic in motion: one of the best attractions features illusions with white tigers.

BURGHAUSEN★★

POPULATION: 19 000

The dukes of Bavaria, who became lords of Burghausen in the 12C, converted its Burg into the biggest fortress in Germany: the defence system, reinforced in the early 16C, stretches for more than 0.8km/0.5mi. Above the old town is the castle, built on a long, narrow, rocky spur separating the Salzach from the Wöhrsee.
🛈 *Rathaus, Stadtplatz 112, 84489 Burghausen,* ☎ *(086 77) 88 71 40.*

▶ **Orient Yourself:** Burghausen lies within a curve of the River Salzach, where it forms the frontier between Bavaria and Austria.
😊 **Don't Miss:** The Burg from which Burghausen takes its name.
🕐 **Organizing Your Time:** Allow three hours for a visit of the Burg.
🕐 **Also See:** *PASSAU (83km/52mi northeast), LANDSHUT (75km/47mi northwest), CHIEMSEE (61km/38mi southwest), the eastern section of the Deutsche ALPENSTRASSE (Berchtesgaden is 76km/48mi south).*

Sights

Burg★★ (Castle)
Leave your car in the Stadtplatz and walk along the circular cliff road. Beneath the Wöhrenseeturm and beyond the lake, a steep path leads to the outer line of fortifications. From here, the ramparts are visible, stepped up the Eggenberg hill. The *Georgstor*, or **St George's Gate**, is set in the innermost ring of battlements,

Burghausen, dominated by its castle, for many years the largest fortress in Germany

Stadt, Verkehrs- u. Kulturamt, Burghausen

WHERE TO EAT

⊜⊜ **Fuchsstuben** – *Mautnerstraße 271.* ☎ *(08677) 627 24.* ◷ *Closed end of Aug to mid-Sep, Sun evenings and Mon.* Set in the heart of the old town, this tastefully-decorated dining room has a terracotta floor and is filled with German antiques.

WHERE TO STAY

⊜⊜⊜ **Bayerische Alm** – *Robert-Koch-Straße 211.* ☎ *(08677) 98 20. Fax (08677) 982200. www.bayerischealm.de.* ⅊ *23 rooms.* ⌁ ⊜⊜⊜ *Restaurant.* For a rural holiday with views of the Salzach, try this intimate, country-style establishment with Alpine-style balconies. Charming rustic restaurant covering two floors and with a pleasant garden terrace.

---

which protect the last small medieval courtyard at the castle's centre. Inside are two museums worth visiting

Staatliche Sammlungen (Municipal Collections)

The former ducal apartments house original 15C-17C furniture and an interesting collection of late Gothic panel paintings by the Bavarian School. From the observation **platform** *(62 steps, access from the second floor),* there is a splendid panoramic **view**★ of Burghausen, the Salzach and the surrounding hills. The Gothic **chapel** *(in the same wing)* has elegant star vaulting. ◷ *Open Apr to Sep, 9am-6pm, Oct to Mar, 10am-4pm.* ⊗ *€2.50.* ☎ *(086 77) 651 98.*

Stadtmuseum (Municipal Museum)

Once reserved for the duchess *(west side of the main block),* these rooms now house a Municipal Museum tracing the history of Burghausen. It includes collections of local folk art, craftwork and country furniture. ◷ *Open from mid-Mar to end Apr and Oct, 10am-4pm; May to Sep, 9am-6pm.* ⊗ *€2.* ☎ *(086 77) 651 98. www.burghausen. de/stadtmuseum.*

Excursions

Raitenhaslach

6km/4mi south.
Red marble tombstones recalling 15C-18C abbots can be seen in this 12C Cistercian church, modified in the Baroque style in the late 17C. The life of St Bernard of Clairvaux is illustrated in the fine **ceiling paintings**★★ (1739) by Johannes Zick of Lachen.

Tittmoning

16km/10mi south.
On the west bank of the Salzach, across the water from Austria, Tittmoning preserves the remains of its medieval fortifications and a castle, once the residence of the prince-bishops of Salzburg. Two old fortified gateways give access to the wide **Stadtplatz**. Brightly painted façades, some decorated with gilded figures, wrought iron signs, oriel windows and emblazoned fountains make this a charming stop.

Altötting

21km/13mi northwest.
This pilgrimage centre consecrated to the Virgin is one of the oldest in Bavaria and draws more than 700 000 people each year. The Miraculous Virgin, a black Madonna, is housed in the octagonal **Holy Chapel** *(Heilige Kapelle)*. In the late Gothic **Parish Church** *(Stiftskirche)*, there are two fine pieces in the Treasury *(Schatzkammer)*: a splendid Flemish ivory crucifix from 1580, and a masterpiece of goldsmith's work (c 1404) – a small gold horse, originally given to Charles VI of France by his wife, Isabella of Bavaria.

CELLE★★

POPULATION: 71 500

Formerly the official residence of the Dukes of Brunswick-Lüneburg, Celle retains the air of an aristocratic retreat. Its carefully preserved centre of half-timbered houses has miraculously escaped war damage over the centuries. Enjoy the old town, the restored ducal castle or the Folklore museum. *Markt 14-16, 29221 Celle. ☎ (051 41) 12 12.*

▶ **Orient Yourself:** Celle is located in the Lüneburg Heath, a region filled with charming villages and plenty of opportunities to explore the countryside.

🕑 **Don't Miss:** Celle's Old Town and its 13C castle.

🕐 **Organizing Your Time:** Allow one hour to explore Celle's Old Town.

🖑 **Also See:** *HANNOVER (41km/26mi southwest), BRAUNSCHWEIG (52km/32.5mi southeast), LÜNEBURGER HEIDE (89km/56mi north).*

Walking Tour

Old Town★★

The largely pedestrian-only old town of Celle has many half-timbered houses, particularly in the Neue Straße, the Zöllnerstraße, the Poststraße (note the richly carved Hoppenerhaus, dating from 1532) and the narrow Kalandgasse, near the church (**Alte Lateinschule**, 1602).

Rathaus

The pale roughcast town hall features varying Renaissance styles. The north gable, built in 1579 by craftsmen from the banks of the Weser, is heavily scrolled and bristles with fantastic pinnacles (🖑 *the Weser Renaissance style, see HAMELN*).

Sights

Schloss★

🖑 *Guided tour (50min).* 🕐 *Open Apr to Oct: Tue-Sun, 11am-3pm; Nov to Mar: Tue-Sun, 11am and 3pm.* 🕐 *Closed 24 and 25 Dec.* ☜ *€3. ☎ (051 41) 123 73.* Construction of Celle's castle began in 1292 and it initially served as fortification for the town. Modified in the Renaissance style in 1530, it was given a Baroque look at the end of the 18C.

This rectangular fortress is flanked by massive corner towers. The eastern façade, overlooking the town, features dormer windows topped by rounded pediments, characteristic of the Weser Renaissance style.

The castle **chapel★** *(Hofkapelle)* was modified in the 16C by Flemish painter Martin de Vos (1532-1603). Nearby is the 17C **Schlosstheater** said to be the oldest court theatre in Germany. It is still used by its own theatre company.

WHERE TO EAT

🍷🍴 **Weinkeller Postmeister von Hinüber** – *Zöllnerstraße 25. ☎ (05141) 284 44. www.weinkeller-celle.de.* 🕐 *Closed 3 weeks in Aug, Sun and Mon.* This historic half-timbered house surprises with its stylish interior. The Weinkeller is a beautifully rustic taverna in the brick cellar with huge wooden tables.

WHERE TO STAY

🛏🛏 **Hotel Am Hehlentor** – *Nordwall 62. ☎ (05141) 885 69 00. Fax (05141) 885 69013. www.hotel-am-hehlentor.de.* 🅿 ⚒ *16 rooms* 🍽. This wonderful half-timbered house is typical of the old town. The well-kept interior is modern and in summer, breakfast can be enjoyed in the interior courtyard, among the plants.

A permanent exhibition from the Bomann Museum in the eastern wing documents the history of the kingdom of Hanover.

Bomann-Museum★

Schloßplatz. ♿ 🕐 *Open Tue-Sun, 10am-5pm.* 🚫 €3. 🕐 *Closed 24, 25 and 31 Dec.* ☎ *(051 41) 123 72. www.bomann-museum.de.*
The rich collections in this museum cover the folklore of Lower Saxony, the history of Celle, and the history of the former kingdom of Hanover.

Stadtkirche★ (Church)

This dark and originally Gothic church was renovated in Baroque style by Italian stuccoworkers in the 17C. Especially noteworthy are the 1613 **altar**, which combines Renaissance and Baroque elements, the 16C Fürstenstuhl (Prince's Seat) beneath the organ and the 1610 baptismal font.

Excursions

Kloster Wienhausen★

10km/6mi south. ♿ 🔊 *Guided tour (75min).* 🕐 *Apr to Sep: Tue-Sun at 10am, 11am, 2pm, 3pm, 4pm and 5pm, Sun noon-5pm; beginning of Oct to mid-Oct: last tour, 4pm.* 🕐 *Closed Good Fri.* 🚫 €3.50. ☎ *(051 49) 186 60.*
This 13C Cistercian abbey has been occupied since the Reformation by a community of Protestant canonesses. Note the 13C wooden figures of the Virgin of Wienhausen and Christ Resurrected. The **Nuns' Choir** is embellished with early-14C **mural paintings**★. Every year, for 11 days starting on the Friday after Whitsun, the convent exhibits its famous tapestries (1300-1500), woven by the nuns in medieval times.

CHIEMSEE★

Known as the "Bavarian Sea", the Chiemsee is the largest of the province's lakes. Its calm waters embrace two islands, both worth a visit: Herreninsel (gentlemen's isle) and Fraueninsel (ladies' isle). On the former is an extraordinary palace, which took Versailles for inspiration; on the latter, an abbey.

Boats with the village of Seebruck in the background

T. Krieger/MICHELIN

▶ **Orient Yourself:** Summer resorts line the banks of the Chiemsee, especially **Prien**, the busiest, and **Seebruck**. The Salzburg-Munich motorway nears the lake's southern edge, but its northern bank, between Rimsting and Seebruck, offers alpine vistas.

Don't Miss: Schloss Herrenchiemsee, quiet walks or a picnic on Herreninsel.

Organizing Your Time: Allow at least half a day for queueing and tours of the castle.

Especially for Kids: Lake cruises, Schloss Herrenchiemsee.

Also See: Deutsche ALPENSTRASSE (itinerary along the south bank of the Chiemsee), WASSERBURG (27km/17mi northwest), BURGHAUSEN (61km/38mi northeast), and Ludwig II's other castles: LINDERHOF and NEUSCHWANSTEIN (134km/84mi and 154km/96mi southwest).

Visit

The Islands

From the motorway (Bernau exit), approach the lake from the west and head for the **Prien-Stock boat dock.** *Allow 15min for the trip to the Herreninsel,* €5.70 *round trip; for a combined ticket for Herreninsel and Fraueninsel, allow 75min,* €6.80. *Boats leave every half hour.*

Boat trips around the lake: all year leaving from the Prien-Stock dock: €6.80, *round trip* ☎ *(080 51) 60 90; www.chiemsee-schifffahrt.de.*

Herreninsel

The parks, woods and forests of the "Gentlemen's Isle" make this island an excellent place to explore on foot. Excavations reveal traces of an 8C monastery. The young **King Ludwig II of Bavaria** bought this island in 1873 to save it from deforestation, but he also planned to build a sumptuous palace there.

Schloss Herrenchiemsee★★

20min on foot from the dock. ♿ ⬤⬤ *Guided tours (30min, available in English). Visitors to Schloss Herrenchiemsee should prepare to queue for at least an hour in high season.* 🕐 *From Apr to beginning Oct daily 9am-6pm; mid-Oct to Mar 9:40am-3:40pm.* 🕐 *Closed 1 Jan, Shrove Tue, 24, 25 and 31 Dec.* ⬤ €7. ☎ (080 51) 688 70.

Construction of the **Neues Schloss** (New Palace) on Herreninsel lasted from 1878-1885. Ludwig II's visit to Versailles in 1867 inspired him to create an island palace to mimic it. The death of the king in 1886, after only one week in the palace, ended his dream, but not before 20 million DM were spent and the royal coffers emptied.

The resemblance between the Versailles and its copy is striking: the Latona fountain stands amid formal French gardens; the façade is adorned with columns and crowned by a flat roof in the Italian style; the apartments include a **State Bedroom**★ and a **Hall of Mirrors**★.

The southern wing of the building houses the **König Ludwig II Museum** *(entrance included in Schloss ticket)*, which documents the fairytale king's life. Spend some time here before the start of the guided tour.

Museum Augustiner Chorherrenstift

A chapter of Augustinian canons was installed on Herreninsel around 1130. It fell into decline during the Reformation, then enjoyed a revival in the 17C. Some of the monastery buildings house a **museum** tracing the island's history.

Fraueninsel

Although it is small, this islet boasts a charming fishing village and an ancient **Benedictine monastery** whose 13C church was rebuilt in the Gothic style in the 15C. The interior is decorated in Baroque style with a high altar from 1694. Note the church's free-standing octagonal bell-tower with 11C foundations.

DARMSTADT

POPULATION: 138 500

Darmstadt has long been renowned also as an intellectual and cultural centre, thanks to a succession of princes who were lovers of art, particularly Jugendstil. The tradition continues with the German Academy of Language and Poetry (Deutsche Akademie für Sprache und Dichtung), and the Institute of Industrial Design (Rat für Formgebung). 🚹 *Luisen-Center, Luisenplatz 5, 64283 Darmstadt.* ☎ *(061 51) 95 15 0 13 and opposite the central station, Hauptbahnhof.* ☎ *(061 51) 95 15 00.*

▸ **Orient Yourself:** The former capital of the Grand Duchy of Hesse-Darmstadt lies near the Odenwald massif, 30km/19mi south of Frankfurt on the A5.

🅿 **Parking:** Garages are located throughout Darmstadt, including near the main train station. http:// wap.parkinfo.com lists locations and fees.

👁 **Don't Miss:** Art lovers should allow time for the Hessisches Landesmuseum.

👃 **Also See:** *FRANKFURT (32km/20mi north), MAINZ (34km/21mi northwest), WIESBADEN (40km/25mi northwest), HEIDELBERG (64km/40mi south).*

Sights

Hessisches Landesmuseum★

♿ 🕐 *Open Tue-Sun, 10am-5pm, (-8pm, Wed); Sun, 11am-5pm.* 🕐 *Closed 1 Jan, Good Fri,1 May, Ascension, Corpus Christi, 24, 25 and 31 Dec.* ⬤ €2.50, no charge after 4pm (3pm Wed). ☎ (061 51) 16 57 03. www.hlmd.de.

The main block houses an outstanding selection of **medieval altar paintings** (Ortenberg and Reidberg), along with works by Stefan Lochner, Lucas Cranach the Elder and Dutch painters. Other exhibits include craftwork **(carved ivory)**, 19C German painting, a Jugendstil collection, a natural history collection and the famous **Werkkomplex of Beuys** (1949-69). The annex features German Impressionism and Expressionism and contemporary art.

Verkehrsamt Darmstadt

Mathildenhöhe
This is one of the most unusual places in the town, with its terraces, pergolas and Russian chapel. Typical of Art Nouveau architecture, this is the site on which the Grand Duke Ernst Ludwig founded, in 1899, a colony of artists known as the

Mathildenhöhe: A temple to Art Nouveau centred on a Russian chapel

Künstlerkolonie. It united painters, sculptors and architects who sought a "total art." Representatives included Joseph Maria Olbrich, Peter Behrens and sculptor Bernhard Hoetger. Dwellings and workshops were grouped near the Russian chapel.

Schloss
Guided tours (1hr) Mon-Thu, 10am-1pm and 2-5pm, Sat-Sun 10am–1pm. Closed Fri, 1 Jan, Easter Sun, Pentecost, 24, 25 and 31 Dec. €2.50. (061 51) 240 35. www.schlossmuseum-darmstadt.de.
The former residence of the Landgraves, in the town centre, comprises two separate buildings: the New Castle (*Neuschloß*, 1716-26), and the Old Castle (*Altschloss*, 16C and 17C). In the *Schlossmuseum*, family collections on view include splendid carriages, furniture, silver and Holbein the Younger's *Darmstadt Madonna*.

Prinz-Georg-Palais
Open Mon-Thu, 10am-1pm and 2-5pm, Sat-Sun 10am-1pm. Closed Fri, 1 Jan, Shrove Tue, Easter, 1 May, Pentecost, 24, 25 and 31 Dec. €2.50. 0 61 51/71 32 33. (061 51) 71 32 33. www.porzellanmuseum-darmstadt.de.
This former summer residence of the Landgraves (built in 1710) houses the priceless grand-ducal porcelain **collection★**, almost all gifts from the royal and imperial families of Europe. The table services and ornaments constitute one of the largest collections of porcelain from the ducal factory at Kelsterbach, as well as from other German and Russian factories.
The **Prinz-Georg-Garten** has been preserved as a work of landscape art. It is a unique example of a historical garden laid out in formal geometric patterns following late-18C principles of landscape gardening. The garden is roughly 2ha/5 acres and contains both useful and decorative plants arranged in formal flowerbeds divided by clipped yew borders. It features a number of charming ornamental elements (summer house, tea pavilion, ponds) and an orangery.

Jagdschloß Kranichstein
5km/3mi northeast. Open Apr to Oct Wed-Sat 1-6pm, Sun 10am–6pm; Nov to Mar Wed–Sat 2–5pm, Sun 10am–5pm. Closed 24 Dec-6 Jan. €2.70. (061 51) 71 86 13. www.jagdschloss-kranichstein.de.
The **hunting museum★** in this small hunting lodge has assembled an interesting collection of weapons, trophies and pictures.

DESSAU

POPULATION: 77 500

Dessau is famous for the Bauhaus, but the city was also the birthplace of neo-Classical architecture in the 18C, a style copied throughout Europe. Dessau was heavily bombed during the Second World War and was largely rebuilt in the socialist architectural style, with rather austere results. The town is not, however, without charm; Prince Leopold III's landscaped gardens are expecially enjoyable. *Zerbster Straße 2c, 06844 Dessau. ☏ (0340) 204 14 42.*

▶ **Orient Yourself:** Situated between the Elbe and the Mulde, Dessau is accessed by the A9 motorway which links Berlin and Munich.

DESSAU

Akazienwäldchen	BY	2
Bertolt-Brecht-Str.	CX	3
Carl-Maria-von-Weber-Str.	CX	5
Eisenbahnstr.	BY	8
Erdmannsdorffstr.	BY	10
Ferdinand-von-Schill-Str.	BCX	12
Flössergasse	CX	14
Friedrich-Naumann-Str.	CY	15
Friedrich-Schneider-Str.	CX	16
Hausmannstr.	BX	18
Humboldtstr.	CX	20
Johannisstr.	CX	
Kleiststr.	BX	21
Kornhausstr.	AX	23
Liebknechtstr.	ABX	25
Marktstr.	CY	26
Mendelssohnstr.	CX	28
Mozartstr.	CX	29
Richard-Wagner-Str.	CX	30
Schwabestr.	BX	32
Steinstr.	CX	33
Wallstr.	CY	34
Wörlitzer Str.	CX	37
Zerbster Str.	CXY	

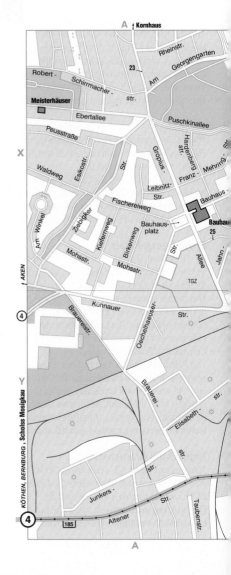

- 🎨 **Don't Miss:** The Bauhaus buildings, which put this city on the cultural map.
- 🕐 **Organizing Your Time:** Allow three hours to explore the Bauhaus sites.
- 👣 **Also See:** *WÖRLITZER PARK (Wörlitz is 17km/11mi east), WITTENBERG (32km/20mi northeast), MAGDEBURG (63km/39mi northwest), HALLE (53km/33mi south).*

Sights

The Bauhaus Legacy
UNESCO listed Dessau a World Cultural Heritage Site due to its Bauhaus buildings.

Bauhausgebäude (Bauhaus Buildings)
🕐 *Open daily, 10am-6pm.* 🕐 *Closed 24 and 31 Dec.* 💶 *€4.* ☎ *(0340) 650 82 51.*

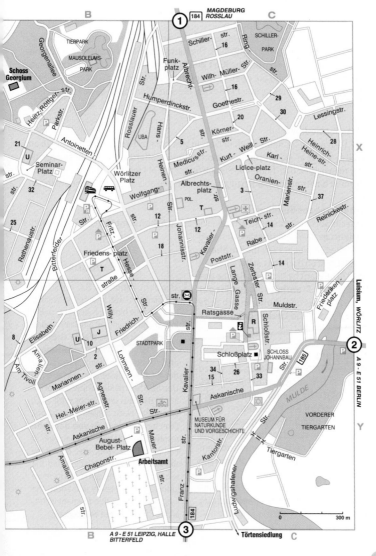

WHERE TO EAT

◒◒ **Das Pächterhaus** – *Kirchstraße 1, 06846 Dessau-Ziebigk.* ☎ *(0340) 650 14 47. www.paechterhaus-dessau.de.* 🕐 *Closed Mon.* This partially ruined, half-timbered house was built in 1743 and has been restored with enthusiasm. Pleasant cooking served in an unusual but elegant setting.

WHERE TO STAY

◒◒ **City-Pension** – *Ackerstraße 3a.* ☎ *(0340) 882 30 76. Fax (0340) 8825017. www. city-pension-dessau.de 24 rooms.* ⛉ This hotel is close to the town centre and has light and airy guestrooms. Watch the hustle and bustle of the town while enjoying breakfast.

The "Design Academy," built on plans by Walter Gropius, was opened in 1926 and displays all the features of the Bauhaus style: cubic blocks, absence of visible supports and glazed façades.

Meisterhäuser (Master Houses)

Walter Gropius drew up plans for a small development of houses for himself and his Bauhaus professors, built 1925-26. The **Kandinsky-Klee-Haus** and the **Feiningerhaus,** which now houses the **Kurt Weill Centre** (dedicated to the Dessau-born composer) remain and are open to the public. *Feiningerhaus:* 🕐 *Open mid Feb to Oct, Tue-Sun, 10am-6pm; Nov to mid Feb, Tue-Sun, 10am-5pm.* ⊛ *€4.10.* ☎ *(0340) 661 09 34.*

Törtenensiedlung

The Törten development south of Dessau was built by Gropius between 1926 and 1928 to relieve an existing housing shortage and to afford workers a cheap opportunity to own their own homes. Although few of the 314 terraced houses in this development have remained unchanged, the unmistakable Bauhaus style remains.

Other Bauhaus Buildings

Other important Bauhaus structures include the **Arbeitsamt** (*August-Bebel-Platz*), a semicircular flat-roofed building designed by Walter Gropius in 1928; the **Kornhaus,** a restaurant on the banks of the Elbe built in 1929 on plans by Hermann Baethe and Carl Fieger; **Stahlhaus, Haus Fieger** (*both on Südstraße*), **Konsumgebäude** (*Am Dreieck 1*) and **Laubenganghäuser** (*Peterholzstraße*).

Georgium

🕐 *Open Tue-Sun, 10am-5pm.* 🕐 *Closed 24 and 31 Dec.* ⊛ *€3.* ☎ *(0340) 61 38 74.* This palace by Friedrich Wilhelm von Erdmannsdorff for Prince Johann Georg lies in the broad George gardens. The Georgium houses a picture gallery, the Anhaltische Gemäldegalerie, an excellent collection of German paintings from the 15C to the 19C, with works by Lucas Cranach the Elder (princes' altar) and Hans Baldung Grien, Frankfurt painting from the 18C and Dutch artists from the 15C to the 17C.

Das Bauhaus

The most important 20C art school, the Bauhaus, was founded in Weimar in 1919, teaching architecture, painting, sculpture and all ancillary trades. Its first Director was **Walter Gropius**. The election of extreme Conservatives in 1924 ended the Weimar project, but the Bauhaus Masters began anew in Dessau. They molded a new style of living in Bauhaus workshops until 1932, when the Nazis closed the school. Director **Ludwig Mies van der Rohe** resolved to continue the Bauhaus in Berlin, but this, too, was closed by the Nazis in 1933. This act ended the institution for good, although its revolutionary ideas greatly influenced the world. It is impossible to imagine 20C architecture without the Bauhaus.

Excursions

Luisium

In Waldersee, via ②, 4km/2.5mi east of Dessau. 🚶 *Guided tours (1hr) May to Sep, Tue-Sun 10am-6pm; Apr and Oct, Tue-Sun 10am-5pm.* 🎫 *€4.50.* ☎ *(0340) 218 37 11. www.gartenreich.com.*

The attractive 18C neo-Classical palace by Friedrich Wilhelm von Erdmannsdorff was built for Princess Luise von Anhalt-Dessau. Rooms are decorated with ceiling paintings and murals amid a pleasant country park. The great house stands in the centre of the "garden kingdom;" its crowning glory is **Wörlitz Park**★★ *(👣 see WÖRLITZER PARK).*

Schloss Mosigkau★

On ④, B 185, around 5km/3mi southwest of Dessau. 🚶 *Guided tours (1hr) May to Sep, Tue-Sun 10am–6pm; Apr and Oct, Tue-Sun, 10am-5pm.* 🎫 *€4.50.* ☎ *(0340) 52 11 39. www.gartenreich.com.*

The 18C summer residence was home to Princess Anna Wilhelmine, daughter of Leopold I. The Rococo gem includes a lovely garden. Castle rooms are furnished with silk and damask hangings, panelling, white inlaying and stucco ceilings, affording a bright picture of the 18C. The **Gartensaal**★ features paintings by Flemish and Dutch masters.

Wörlitz Park★★ 👣 *see WÖRLITZER PARK*

BAD DOBERAN

POPULATION: 11 500

This small spa town developed between 1800 and 1825 for visitors of the neighbouring Baltic spa town of Heiligendamm. The oldest hippodrome in Germany is here and the town is famous for its horse races which take place in July and August. The principal sight is the superb Gothic brick cathedral (Münster).
🛈 *Alexandrinenplatz 2, 18209 Bad Doberan.* ☎ *(0382 03) 621 54.*

▶ **Orient Yourself:** Bad Doberan developed around a Cistercian monastery, a few kilometres from the Baltic. From Rostock, follow the 105 road; from the A 20, take exit 13.

😊 **Don't Miss:** The Münster

👣 **Also See:** ROSTOCK (16km/10mi east), WISMAR (75km/47mi west), MECKLENBURGISCHE SEENPLATTE (accessible by the A 19)

Münster★★

♿ 🕐 *Open May to Sep, Mon-Sat 9am-6pm, Sun 11am-6pm; Oct, Mar and Apr, Mon-Sat 10am-5pm, Sun 11-5pm; Nov to Feb, Mon-Sat 10am-4pm, Sun 11am-4pm.* 🕐 *Closed 1 Jan, Good Fri and 25 Dec.* 🎫 *€1.50.* ☎ *03 82 03/6 27 16.*

The former Cistercian monastery church, (1294-1368), is a prime example of northern German brick Gothic style and of Cistercian architectural mandates. Characteristic of the Order are a mighty window on the towerless western façade and friezes under the roof line. Inside, the Münster's sumptuous decor reflects the chapel's significance as the burial place for Mecklenburg dukes. 13C-14C artworks are worth examining, like the **high altar**★, a wood carving from 1310; the rood altar (1370), embellished with a

triumphal cross★ (depicted as the Tree of Life); and the Late Gothic needle-shaped oak **tabernacle**★, likely the oldest in Germany, from the same period.

Excursions

It is possible to get to the Baltic spa resorts of Heiligendamm and Kühlungsborn by means of the **"Molli Schmalspurbahn"**. This narrow gauge railway, affectionately referred to as the "Molli", has operated since 1886. *Allow 10min for the journey to Heiligendamm and 40min for Kühlungsborn.*

Heiligendamm
6.5km/4mi northwest.
Heiligendamm was founded by the Duke of Mecklenburg in 1793. The architecture is typical of period spa resorts; the 19C building and the elegant houses along Prof-Vogel-Straße attest to the town's luxurious past.

Kühlungsborn★
14 km northwest.
A beach resort and spa, Kühlungsborn has become one of the most popular holiday destinations on the Baltic coast, thanks to miles of beaches and pine forest.

DONAUESCHINGEN★

POPULATION: 21 300

The Danube starts in Donaueschingen where two streams unite, the Brigach and Breg. Donaueschingen owes its fame to the annual Festival of Contemporary Music, founded as the Donaueschingen Music Festival in 1921, drawing musicians and music-lovers worldwide. *Karlstraße 58, 78166 Donaueschingen. ☎ (0771) 85 72 21.*

▶ **Orient Yourself:** In the middle of the Baar, a fertile basin between the Black Forest and the Swabian Jura, Donaueschingen stands at the confluence of two rivers, the Breg and the Brigach, which form the Danube.

Don't Miss: The Source of the Danube *(Donauquelle).*

Also See: ROTTWEIL (31km/19mi north), FREIBURG IM BREISGAU (54km/34mi west), SCHWARZWALD.

Sights

Source of the Danube
The monumental fountain *(Donauquelle)* was built in the castle park in the 19C. It is considered the official source of the Danube, which travels another 2 840km/1 775mi after having flowed through 13 countries: Germany, Austria, Slovakia, Slovenia, Hungary, Croatia, Bosnia, Serbia and Montenegro, Bulgaria, Romania, Moldova and the Ukraine.

The source of the Danube

R. Chéret/MICHELIN

Fürstenberg-Sammlungen (Princely Collections)

🕐 *Open Mar-Nov, 10am-1pm, 2pm-5pm, Sun, 10am-5pm.* 🕐 *Closed 1 Nov.* 🎫 *€5.*
☎ *(0771) 865 63. Am Karlsplatz.*

The furnishings at this museum date to its founding (1868). The second-floor **Gemäldegalerie**★ (Picture Gallery) features works by 15C and 16C Swabian masters and the **Altarpiece of The Passion**★★ (*Passionsaltar*) by Hans Holbein the Elder. Also of interest are works by Cranach the Elder and contemporary art by Anselm Kiefer.

Schloss

🚶 *Guided tour (40min).* 🕐 *May to Aug: 11am and 2.30pm.* 🎫 *€10.* ☎ *(0771) 8 65 63.*

The home of the Fürstenbergs, a well-proportioned building of 1723 remodelled in the 19C retains the luxurious amenities of the period, enriched now with gold and silver plate, porcelain and fine Beauvais and Brussels Gobelins tapestries.

DRESDEN★★★

POPULATION: 491 000

Dresden's culture and art attract an ever increasing number of visitors. It was not so long ago, however, that the magnificent "Florence of the Elbe" was a scene of total devastation; on a night in February, 1945, just weeks before the armistice, the Allies carried out an air raid which killed at least 35 000 and almost completely destroyed the old Baroque town. The arduous reconstruction effort, has allowed Dresden to rise from its ashes and once again reveal an outstanding capital of culture. 🚇 *Prager Straße, 01069 Dresden.* ☎ *(0351) 49 19 20.*

▶ **Orient Yourself:** Dresden sits in the heart of Saxony, on the banks of the Elbe and at the gates of "Swiss Saxony" (*Sächsische Schweiz*). The Czech border is less than 50km/31mi away. The A 4, A 13 and A 14 motorways converge near the town.

🅿 **Parking:** Garages abound in this city, especially near the Frauenkirche and the Zwinger.

👁 **Don't Miss:** The Old City, the restored Frauenkirche and the Zwinger.

🕐 **Organizing Your Time:** Allow an entire day to do justice to the Zwinger.

👣 **Also See:** *SÄCHSISCHE SCHWEIZ (our suggested touring programme begins in Dresden), MEISSEN (23km/14mi northwest), BAUTZEN (64km/40mi northeast), GORLITZ (107km/67mi northeast), LEIPZIG (113km/70mi west).*

A Bit of History

"The Florence of the Elbe" – Dresden's major development took place in the early 18C, in the reigns of the Electors **Augustus II the Strong** and his son Augustus III. These powerful patrons of the arts drew artists from Italy, who were regular visitors at the court of Dresden. The magnificent Baroque ensemble of the Zwinger, the Japanese Palace and the Hofkirche (the Court church), and outstanding collections of paintings and objets d'art date back to this period. In addition to these treasures, Dresden boasts works by many 19C and 20C German Expressionist painters.

The Night of the Apocalypse – A few months before the end of the Second World War, on the night of 13-14 February 1945, Dresden was the target of one of the Allies' most destructive air raids. Three successive waves of Lancaster bombers left the blackened skeletons of the city's monuments emerging from a waste of smoking

The Elbe and the brilliantly reconstructed Baroque town

ruins, and a death toll of between 35 000 and 135 000. 75 per cent of the city was destroyed. Restoration of Dresden's historic sites, including the Zwinger, and the rebuilding of residential quarters have given the town a special quality marrying modern urbanism with ancient heritage.

Walking Tour

Historic Centre★★★ (Altstadt)

The Elbe runs through Dresden, dividing it into two very distinct parts. The old town *(Altstadt)* south of the river is dominated by the outlines of the Zwinger, Semperoper and Hofkirche; in the north, the new town stretches out around Albertplatz.

Semperoper★★ (Semper Opera House)
Built between 1871 and 1878 by **Manfred Semper**, a personal friend of Richard Wagner, the present opera house owes its form to the Italian Renaissance. The tiered façade comprises two storeys of arcades, surmounted by a third in recess. Each side wall is furnished with twin niches, occupied by statues of Shakespeare, Sophocles, Molière and Euripides. Nine operas premiered at the Semperoper, including *Der Rosenkavalier* by Richard Strauss.

▶ *Cross Theaterplatz eastwards towards the Hofkirche.*

Ehemalige Katholische Hofkirche★★ (Cathedral)
This enormous 18C basilica, the largest church in Saxony, was strongly influenced by the Italian Baroque, dominated by an 86m/282ft bell-tower and decorated with statues of the saints and apostles. Above the high altar, a painting (1765) by Anton Raphael Mengs depicts the Ascension. The pulpit was executed by Permoser in 1722, while the organ was the last work (1750-55) of the master craftsman **Gottfried Silbermann**. The crypt contains the tombs of several kings and princes

A Line of Organ Builders

Gottfried Silbermann (1683-1753) apprenticed in Strasbourg with his brother Andreas, famous for creating Alsace organs of Ebersmunster. In 1710, Gottfried settled in Freiberg, designing instruments with remarkable tone. Of the 51 organs attributed to him, those in Freiberg are the best. Gottfried's nephew Johann Andreas followed suit, and designed 54 organs in the Upper Rhine region.

DRESDEN

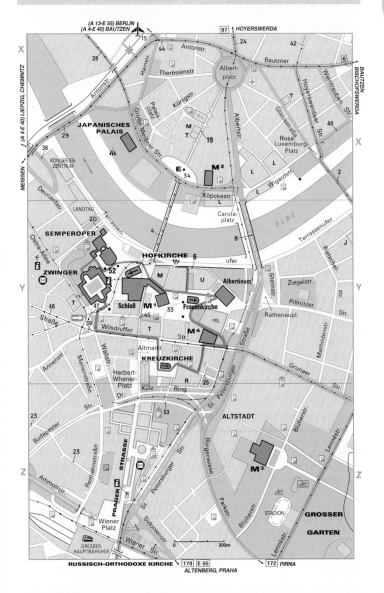

Address Book

PRACTICAL INFORMATION

TELEPHONE PREFIX: 0351

TOURIST INFORMATION

Dresden Werbung & Tourismus GmbH, ☎ 49 19 20, Fax 49 19 21 16, Mon-Fri 8am-7pm, Sat-Sun 9am-4pm. Information offices: Schinkelwache am Theaterplatz, Mon-Fri 10am-6pm, Sat 10am-4pm and Sun 10am-4pm; Prager Straße 2a, Mon-Fri 9am-7pm, Sat 9am-4pm. City magazines *SAX-Das Dresdner Stadtmagazin, Prinz* and *BLITZ! Dresden* (free) provide complete citywide calendars of events and are available at bookshops and newspaper kiosks. The *Kulturkalender* and *Dresdner Kulturmagazin* appear monthly and are available free in hotels, at tourist information offices and cultural venues. Tickets, maps and information available from *Dresden Werbung und Tourismus,* ☎ 49 19 22 33, www.dresden.de.

POST OFFICES WITH LATE HOURS

Postamt 1, Königsbrücker Straße 21-29, Mon-Fri 6.30am-7pm, Sat 6.30am-1pm. Another, more central post office can be found near the tourist information office at Prager Straße 72.

DAILY PAPERS

Sächsische Zeitung, Dresdner Neueste Nachrichten.

INTERNET

www.dresden-tourist.de; www. cityguide-dresden.de; www.dresden-online.de; www.dresden.de

GETTING AROUND

Dresden's historic centre is essentially a pedestrian and bicycle zone. Most sights and museums are concentrated within a limited area and easily accessible on foot. The city is served by a network of 18 tram lines and by buses and regional express trains *(S-Bahn DB).* Dresden has two railway stations: the *Hauptbahnhof* (Am Hauptbahnhof 4) south of the old town and the *Bahnhof Neustadt* (Schlesischer Platz 1). Most trains stop at both stations.

AIRPORT

☎ +881-33-60. Dresden's international airport is less than 10km/6mi north of the Elbe. An Airport City Liner runs to the city centre and central station every 30min (☎ €4). It is also possible to travel by S-Bahn (S2) to the city center and central station.

PUBLIC TRANSPORT

The *Dresdner Verkehrsbetriebe* (DVB) network is clear and well-structured, ☎ 857 10 11, Fax 857 10 10, round the clock. Information is available at the service centres at the main railway station *(Hauptbahnhof),* Mon-Fri 7am-7pm, Sat 8am-6pm, Sun 9am-6pm; Postplatz, Mon-Fri 7am-8pm, Sat 8am-6pm, Sun 9am-6pm; Pirnaischer Platz and Albertplatz, Mon-Fri 7am-6pm, Sat 9am-4pm. The DVB is integrated into the *Verkehrsverbund Oberelbe* (VVO), which also covers "Swiss Saxony" *(Sächsische Schweiz),* the eastern Erzgebirge mountains and parts of the Oberlausitz area, Info-Hotline ☎ 01 80/24 519 98, Mon-Fri 7am-8pm, Sat-Sun 8am-7pm. Tickets at service centres, station vending machines nd in tram stations and buses; normal fare is ☎ €1.50 (1hr). There are 4 geographical price zones. One-day passes *(Tageskarte)* are worthwhile if you plan to make several trips. Family/group tickets *(Familientageskarte)* are also available.

Internet – VVO: www.nahverkehr. sachsen.de, **DVB**: www.dvbag.de

The **Dresden-City-Card** for ☎ €19 (valid 48hr) lets an adult (plus any children under 6) use all buses, trams and Elbe ferries in Dresden, plus free entry to 12 museums of the State Art Collections and discounts for other museums; also includes discounts for certain coach and bus city tours.

The **Dresden-Regio-Card** for ☎ €29 (valid 72hr) includes free rides on the S-Bahn trains along the Elbe to eg Meißen, Pirna and Königstein, discounts for rides on various narrow-gauge trains, and discounts at the region's main museums. The two cards are available at tourist offices, in many hotels and in DVB service centres.

SIGHTSEEING

CITY TOURS BY COACH

Dresden Tour, ☎ 899 56 50; www. stadtrundfahrt.com: 1hr 30min tours, every 30min. First departure 9:30am, last one 5pm. Tickets cost ☺ €18 and are valid all day long. Departure Augustusbrücke/Schloßplatz and 11 other stops such as Königstraße, Frauenkirche and Dr.-Külz-Ring. The *Dresden Tour* ticket includes at no extra cost guided Zwinger and Grauenkirche tours and an evening city tour and night watchman's beat. The *Super Dresden Tour* includes, besides the bus tour, a guided walk through the city's historic centre (departure from Augustusbrücke daily 10.30am, 12pm, 1.30pm, Nov-Apr Sat only). Themed walking tours are organised by *igeltours* – *Dresdens andere Stadtführung*, ☎ 804 45 57, Fax 804 45 48, www.igeltour-dresden.de.

BOAT TRIPS

The *Sächsische Dampfschiffahrts GmbH und Co. Conti, Elbschiffahrts*, ☎ 86 60 90, fax 866 09 88, www.saechsische-dampfschiffahrt.de, offers Elbe cruises in authentic paddle-wheel steamers and in modern ships between Meißen and "Swiss Saxony." Tickets cost ☺ €9, half price for children. Trips last 1hr 30min, departing daily at 11am, 1pm and 3pm. Pick-up and drop-off point: Terrassenufer under the Brülsche Terrasse.

WHERE TO EAT

☺ **Alte Meister** – *Theaterplatz 1a.* ☎ *(0351) 481 04 26. www.altemeister.net.* This restaurant has bright, high-ceilinged rooms, one with frescoes. The atmosphere is casual; the terrace takes in the opera house and square.

☺ **Historisches Fischhaus** – *Fischerhausstraße 14 (5km/3mi northeast of city centre; follow Bautzner Str.)* ☎ *(0351) 89 91 00. www.fischhaus-dresden.de.* ⏰ *Mon-Fri noon-midnight, Sat 11am-midnight, Sun 11am-11pm* �& *Reservation recommended.* ☺☺ *8 rooms.* In a leafy setting on the outskirts of town, this has an establishment that menu varies with the catch of the day. Specialities include fish, naturally, but also game.

☺ **Kurhaus Kleinzschachwitz** – *Berthold-Haupt-Straße 128, 01259 Dresden-Kleinzschachwitz* 🚋 *1* ☎ *(0351) 200 19 96 www.kurhaus.net* ⏰ *Closed 2nd week in Jan to end of Jan* ✕ �& *Reservation recommended* This renovated restaurant is in the residential district and noted for its beautiful

architecture. Inside is a cozy dining room and a few comfortable rooms. A pleasant stop on the Elbe, opposite Schloss Pillnitz.

☺☺ **Le Maréchal de Saxe** – *Königstraße 15.* ☎ *(0351) 810 58 80.* �& This café-bar-restaurant occupies part of the Arts Centre *(Kulturrathaus)* in the heart of a shopping street lined with cafés in the new town. Dark wood, gleaming tables, a pleasant setting and friendly service. Fish and seafood specialities.

☺☺ **Luisenhof** – *Bergbahnstraße 8, 01324 Dresden-Weißer Hirsch.* ☎ *(0351) 214 99 60. www.luisenhof.org.* Set in a historic 19C building, this restaurant is called "Dresden's balcony" for its unique view. Distinctive modern decoration, large glass façade and pleasant, shady terrace.

☺☺ **Opernrestaurant** – *Theaterplatz 2 (1st floor).* ☎ *(0351) 491 15 21.* ⏰ *Closed 16 Jul-24 Aug.* Set in an annex to the Semperoper, this restaurant serves a variety of dishes. Before or after the opera, you can choose between the ground-floor café and the classic dining-rooms upstairs. Pleasant view.

☺☺☺ **Gourmet-Restaurant** – *Merbitzer Straße 53.* ☎ *(0351) 425 50. www.pattis.de.* ⏰ *Closed 2 weeks in Jan, 2 weeks in Aug, Sun and Mon.* Set behind the Jugendstil-style façade of the romantic Hotel Pattis, this restaurant features a magnificent interior. An intricately-worked ceiling, paintings and tastefully laid tables give this former ballroom an air of luxury.

☺☺☺ **Caroussel** – *Rähnitzgasse 19.* ☎ *(0351) 800 30. www.buelow-residenz. de.* Patrons can enjoy the tasteful decor – porcelain, an earthenware stove and paintings – and Stefan Hermann's excellent cuisine. You can also have a drink on the pleasant glass-roofed terrace.

WHERE TO STAY

☺ **Gästehaus Mezcalero** – *Königsbrücker Straße 64.* ☎ *(0351) 810770. Fax (0351) 8107711. www.mezcalero.de.* 🅿 *23 rooms.* ☒ Beautifully decorated Mexican-Aztec-style establishment. Rooms are personalised, some with loft beds. Dormitories for small groups.

⊝⊜ **Gasthof Coschütz** – *Kleinnaun-dorfer Straße 1.* 🚌 *72.* ☎ *(0351) 401 03 58. Fax (0351) 4013844. www.gasthof-coschuetz.de.* 🅿 ⨉ 🦽 *Reservations required 11 rooms.* 🍽 ⊝⊜ *Restaurant.* Four generations have run this well-furnished, comfortable hotel. The restaurant features authentic cuisine and two summer terraces.

⊝⊜ **Hotel Goldener Apfel** – *Schul-weg 3, 01326 Dresden-Pillnitz.* 🚌 *83* ☎ *(0351) 26 16 60. Fax (0351) 2616613. www.goldener-apfel.de.* ⨉ 🅿 ⨉ *12 rooms.* 🍽 Since 1999, this former 19C village school has housed a hotel with fitness centre. The accommodation is practical, polished and reasonably priced. Breakfast in the historic tea tavern.

⊝⊜ **Hotel Zum Nußbaum** – *Wirt-schaftsweg 13.* ☎ *(0351) 4273690. Fax (0351) 4210354. www.hotel-nuss-baum-dresden.de.* 🅿 *15 rooms.* 🍽 ⊝ *Restaurant.* A pleasant, intimate hotel. Functional, well-kept rooms with modern furniture, and a restaurant with terrace. Near bus and rail links to the town centre.

⊝⊜ **Landhaus Lockwitzgrund** – *Lockwitzgrund 100, 01257 Dres-den-Lockwitz.* ☎ *(0351) 271 00 10. Fax (0351) 27100130. www.landhaus-lockwitzgrund.de.* 🅿 ⨉ *12 rooms* 🍽 ⊝ *Restaurant.* The romantic Lockwitzgrund features comfortable rooms in country-house style with many original farmhouse features. Attractively decorated, friendly restaurant.

⊝⊜⊜ **Hotel Bayerischer Hof** – *Antonstraße 33.* ☎ *(0351) 82 93 70 .Fax (0351) 8014860. www.bayerischer-hof-dresden.de* 🕐 *Closed 23-27 Dec.* 🅿 ⨉ *50 rooms.* 🍽 ⊝⊜ *Restaurant.* This former library, now a chic hotel, offers spacious, elegant rooms with beautiful cherrywood furniture and old paintings.

⊝⊜⊜ **Hotel Schloss Eckberg** – *Bautzner Straße 134.* ☎ *(0351) 809 90. Fax (0351) 8099199. www.hotel-schloss-eckberg.de.* 🅿 ⨉ *84 rooms.* 🍽 ⊝⊜⊜ *Restaurant.* A grand park and comfortable rooms, some with antiques, others more modern, make this hotel, in a neo-Gothic castle and *Kavaliershaus*, an interesting stay. The classic restaurant fits perfectly with the historic rooms.

⊝⊜⊜ **Martha Hospiz** – *Nierizstraße 11.* ☎ *(0351) 817 60. Fax (0351) 8176222. www.marthahospiz.dresden.vch. de.* 🕐 *Closed 22-27 Dec.* 🦽 *50 rooms.* 🍽 Traditional evangelical church establishment, the Martha Hospiz offers elegant rooms with classic furniture, some in Biedermeier style. Some rooms reserved for disabled guests.

TAKING A BREAK

Café Schinkelwache – *Theaterplatz 2.* ☎ *(0351) 4 90 39 09 www.restaurant-dresden.de.* 🕐 *10am-midnight.* This old watchtower built by the German neo-Classical architect Friedrich Schinkel stands between the Zwinger, the castle and the opera house.

Café Toscana – *Schillerplatz 7 (5km/3mi east of old town on the Elbe).* ☎ *(0351) 310 07 44.* 🕐 *Mon-Sat 9am-7pm, Sun 11am-7pm.* This classic tea room with winter garden and terrace boasts views of the *Blaues Wunder* bridge and a 12m/39ft-long cake buffet.

Dresdner Molkerei Gebrüder Pfund – *Bautzner Straße 79* ☎ *(0351) 8 10 59 48.* 🕐 *Mon-Sat 10am-6pm, Sun and public holidays 10am-3pm, café-restaurant: 10am-8pm.* The dairy shop, serving dairy and cheese products, is entirely covered in hand-painted 19C tiles. Café-restaurant on the 1st floor.

GOING OUT

USEFUL TIPS

Cafés, bistros and restaurants abound in the old town and inner Neustadt, at Alaunstraße and Luisenstraße. The alternative/youth scene is mainly in Neustadt (east bank of the Elbe, north of Albertplatz).

Ballhaus Watzke – *Kötzschenbroder Straße 1 (west end of Leipziger Straße).* ☎ *(0351) 85 29 20. www.watzke.de.* 🕐 *11am-midnight.* Restaurant on the Elbe, set in a historical building 1st floor ballroom. The view of the old town from the beer garden is called "Canaletto's View" since it appeared in a painting by the master.

Brauhaus am Waldschlösschen – *Am Brauhaus 8b (2km/1.2mi east of Albert-platz; follow Bautzner Straße).* ☎ *(0351) 81 19 90. www.waldschloesschen.de.* 🕐 *11am-1am.* Probably the most attractive brasserie in town. Along with the three beers brewed here, cocktails and traditional dishes are served. Piano music Mon-Sat from 8pm. Splendid views of the Elbe from the beer garden.

Italienisches Dörfchen – *Theaterplatz 3 (Augustusbrücke at Terrassenufer).* ☎ *(0351) 498 160. www.italienisches-doerfchen.de.* 🕐 *10am-midnight (food until 11pm).* Tea room with a terrace on the Elbe, café on the ground floor, restaurant upstairs. Magnificent exposed beams, stuccowork and ceiling frescos.

Winzerstube Zum Rebstock – *Hauptstraße 17.* ☎ *(0351) 5 63 35 44. www.winzerstube-zum-rebstock.de.* 🕐 *Mon-Sat 12pm-10pm, Sun 2-10pm.* Both a Weinstube and shop, serving wines from Bad Kreuznach and Meißen and dishes to accompany them. Quiet, restful terrace.

SHOPPING

USEFUL TIPS

Dresden's main shopping streets are Prager Straße (department stores), Wilsdruffer Straße and Altmarkt in the old town, Königstraße (boutiques) and Hauptstraße.

Kunsthofpassage Dresden-Neustadt – *Alaunstraße 70 (north of Albertplatz between Rothenburger Straße and Königsbrücker Straße, and Görlitzer Straße 21-25).* ☎ *(0351) 8 02 67 04. www.kunsthof.com.* Between Alaunstraße and Görlitzer Straße are a series of rear courtyards, many with unusual façades, where you can browse craft shops or stop for a drink.

Neustädter Markthalle – *Metzer Straße 1 (level with Hauptstraße 36; access via Ritter- and Metzer Straße).* ☎ *(0351) 8 11 38 60 (museum). www.automobilmuseum-dresden.com.* 🕐 *Mon-Fri 8am-8pm, Sat 8am-6pm; museum: 10am-7pm.* ⊛ €3.80. Traditional fare and international specialities at the stalls in this historic covered market. An entertaining exhibition on the 1st floor presents the history automobiles in the GDR 1945-1990. Many vehicles on display.

Art galleries and antiques are mostly in Neustadt, on Königstraße and Hauptstraße, and between Bautzener Straße, Königsbrücker Straße and Alaunplatz.

Flea markets – *Elbemarkt, Käthe-Kollwitz-Ufer/Albert-Brücke,* May-Oct 9am-2pm; World Trade Center, Ammon/Freiberger Straße, second Sun every month, 8am-4pm.

Markets – Altmarkt, mornings from 8am, daily except Sun. The Spring Market *(Frühlingsmarkt)* is held here in May, the Autumn Market *(Herbstmarkt)* in Sep and the *Striezelmarkt* in Dec.

---

of Saxony, as well as the heart of Augustus the Strong, whose body lies in Cracow cathedral.

Schloss

The Renaissance palace, its restoration scheduled for completion in late 2006, bears an exterior façade covered by a colossal mosaic, The **Procession of Dukes**★ *(Fürstenzug,* 102m/335ft). Originally created by painter Wilhelm Walter, this monumental painting representing the dukes of the house of Saxe-Wettin was transferred in 1906 to 25 000 porcelain squares from Saxony. The work, which miraculously survived the 1945 bombardments, depicts 35 margraves, prince electors and kings over a period of 1 000 years.

The **Langer Gang**★ which connects the Johanneum to the George building, is a long gallery formed by a series of Tuscan arcades enclosing the stable courtyard. The **Johanneum** (left of the *Schöne Pforte* entrance, a gateway in the Renaissance style) was itself once used as the stables. It now houses a Transport Museum *(Verkehrsmuseum)*, where collections of vintage cars and motorcycles join a display outlining the evolution of public transport.

▶ *Leaving the Johanneum, cross the Neumarkt towards the Frauenkirche.*

The Procession of Dukes of Saxe-Wettin, an immense mosaic covering one of the palace façades

Frauenkirche★

This mighty building was built from 1726, the principal work of architect George Bähr. The famous 95m/312ft high 23.5m/77ft diameter dome, which so character-ises the silhouette of the town, was completed in 1738. When the air raids of 1945 hit the Frauenkirche, the heat burst the sandstone and caused the 5 800t stone dome to collapse. The ruin symbolised Dresden's destruction until its restoration in October, 2005.

▶ *Go onto the Brühlsche Terrasse on the site of ancient fortifications: this pleasant promenade offers* **views**★ *of the Elbe and the Neustadt quarter on the river's east bank. Then turn back and cross the Neumarkt heading toward the Stadtmuseum and cross Wilsdrufferstraße to reach the new Town Hall.*

Neues Rathaus (New Town Hall)

This early 20C neo-Renaissance building surmounted by a golden statue of Hercules stands behind the Kreuzkirche. *No organised tours.*

Kreuzkirche★

The city's original church, (early 13C), the Kreuzkirche was remodelled in the Baroque style after its destruction during the Seven Years' War. The damage inflicted during the Second World War has been repaired on the church's exterior; the interior has so far only been roughly plastered over. The Kreuzkirche is home to the Kreuzchor, a famous 400-voice male choir.

Neustadt★ (New Town)

This part of Dresden, spared by the air raids in 1945, stands on the site once occupied by *Altendresden* (Old Dresden), destroyed by fire in 1685. When the district was rebuilt in stone it was renamed New Town *(Neustadt).*

The **Hauptstraße** links the Albertplatz and the Neustädter Markt and is dominated by the gilded **equestrian statue**★ of Augustus the Strong. With its rows of plane trees and shops, it is one of the best places in town for a stroll.

The Neustadt quarter, where residences range from Baroque to neo-Classicism to the Gründerzeit, is increasingly popular among residents and tourists.

▶ *Approaching from the historic centre, reach the old town by the Augustusbrücke. Turn right into Köpckerstrasse to reach the Museum of Saxon Arts and Crafts.*

Museum für Sächsische Volkskunst★ (Museum of Saxon Arts)

🕐 *Open daily except Mon, 10am-6pm.* 🚌 *€3.* ☎ *(0351) 491 420 00. www.skd-dresden.de*

This collection is in the oldest Renaissance building in the city, the 1568 Jägerhof (Hunters Court). Works of Saxon folk art, furniture, pottery and basketry, as well as Saxon and Swabian costumes, lacework, toys and carvings.

▶ *Turn back along Köpckerstrasse and cross the Neustädtermarkt.*

Japanisches Palais★ (Japanese Palace)

Built between 1715 and 1737, this huge palace was designed to display Augustus the Strong's collection of Meißen tableware. It now houses the Museum of Ethnology and the Museum of Prehistory.

Pfunds Molkerei

Bautzner Straße 79.

This dairy, founded by the Pfund brothers in 1880, sells wine, milk and numerous cheeses. The shop is also interesting for its array of multicoloured ceramic tiles.

Sights

Zwinger★★★

A tour of this 18C Baroque palace, built by Augustus the Strong, is among the highlights of any trip to Dresden. After suffering severe damage in the 1945 bombardments, the building was painstakingly reconstructed and now houses five museums, including the Old Masters Gallery.

▶ *Enjoy the best view of the complex on the Glockenspielpavillon on Sophienstraße.*

Augustus the Strong's plan was to build, on the site of a former fortress, a simple orangery. His architect, **Matthäus Daniel Pöppelmann**

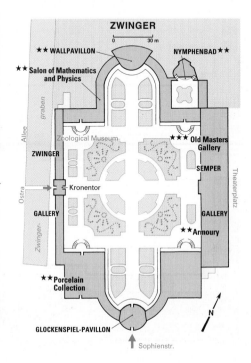

ZWINGER

0   30 m

★★ WALLPAVILLON   NYMPHENBAD ★★

★★ Salon of Mathematics and Physics

graben

Allee

Zoological Museum

★★★ Old Masters Gallery

ZWINGER

SEMPER

Theaterplatz

Ostra

Kronentor

GALLERY   GALLERY

Zwinger-

★★ Armoury

★★ Porcelain Collection

N

GLOCKENSPIEL-PAVILLON

Sophienstr.

(1662-1736), had grander ideas, resulting in an enormous esplanade surrounded by galleries and pavilions.

The huge rectangular courtyard has two extensions: the **Wallpavillon**★★ (Rampart Pavilion) and the **Glockenspielpavillon** (Carillon Pavilion). It is in the former that the relationship between sculpture and architecture expresses itself. Crowning the pavilion is **Hercules Carrying the World,** with which Augustus the Strong identified. The Wallpavillon leads to a terrace and the **Nymphenbad**★★ (Bath of the Nymphs).

The southwest side of the complex the elegant **Zwinger Gallery**, best seen from the outside passing beneath the **Kronentor** (Crown Gate). The **Semper Gallery** was built in 1847 by **Gottfried Semper**.

Gemäldegalerie Alte Meister★★★ (Old Masters Gallery)

Semper Gallery, west wing. ◷ *Open daily except Mon, 10am-6pm.* ◷ *Closed 25 Dec.* ◠ *€6.* ☏ *(0351) 491 420 00. www.skd-dresden.de.*

This collection of paintings is one of the best of its kind in the world. The most important masters from the Italian Renaissance and the Baroque period are represented, as are Dutch and Flemish painters from the 17C.

Ground floor:

Galleries 1-4 contain tapestries after sketches by Raphael and numerous townscapes by Bernardo Bellotto, otherwise known as Canaletto, who painted Dresden and Pirna with such extraordinary precision that many were used as guides during the post-war reconstruction.

Galleries 5-6 house paintings by Dresden masters.

1st floor:

Galleries 101-102: Works by Silvestre and Canaletto.

GEMÄLDEGALERIE

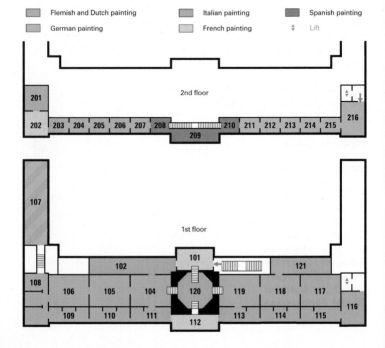

Galleries 104-106 and 108-111: Flemish and Dutch painting from the 16C-17C. Rembrandt's *Self-portrait with Saskia* (Gallery 106), Rubens' *Bathsheba*, and Vermeer's *Girl Reading a Letter by the Window* (Gallery 108).

Gallery 107: Paintings by the Early Netherlandish (Jan van Eyck) and Early German (masterpieces by Holbein, Cranach the Elder and Dürer) schools.

Gallery 112: 17C French painting (Claude Lorrain, Nicolas Poussin).

Galleries 113-121: 16C Italian painting. Works by Veronese, Tintoretto, Giorgione *(Sleeping Venus)*, Titian, in galleries 117-119. A highlight is Raphael's portrayal of the Virgin and Child, the *Sistine Madonna,* in gallery 117.

Gallery 116: Paintings by Botticelli, Mantegna and Pintoricchio *(Portrait of a Boy).*

2nd floor:

Gallery 201: pastel painting. Jean-Étienne Liotard's *Chocolate Girl*, world's largest collection of works by Rosalba Carriera (75 pastels).

Gallery 202: 18C French painting.

Galleries 203-207: 18C Italian painting with works by Tiepolo and Crespi.

Galleries 208-210: Spanish painting (El Greco, Murillo, Zurbarán, Velázquez).

Galleries 211-216: 17C and 18C German painting.

Porzellansammlung★★ (Porcelain Collection)

Entrance on Sophienstraße. ♿ 🕐 *Open daily except Mon, 10am-6pm.* 🕐 *Closed 25 Dec.* 🎟 *€5.* ☎ *(0351) 491 420 00. www.skd-dresden.de.*

This gallery displays porcelain from the famous factory at **Meißen**, as well as porcelain from Japan and China. Do not miss the "dragoon vases" for which the prince paid with 600 dragoon soldiers in 1717, or the life-size porcelain figures from Meißen on the upper floor (early 18C).

Rüstkammer★★ (Armoury)

Semper Gallery, east wing. 🕐 *Open daily except Mon, 10am-6pm.* 🕐 *Closed 25 Dec.* 🎟 *€3.* ☎ *(0351) 491 420 00. www.skd-dresden.de.*

Even those not particularly interested in armour will appreciate this exhibition of handcrafted armour, collected by the princely dynasty of the Wettiner. The inventory includes 1 300 objects from the 15C-19C. The **suits of armor** are most impressive, and include the work of famous Augsburg armorer Anton Peffenhauser. There is also a display of children's armor, worn by little princes during children's jousting tournaments.

Mathematisch-Physikalischer Salon★★ (Salon of Mathematics and Physic)

Northwest corner pavilion. 🕐 *Open daily except Mon, 10am-6pm.* 🕐 *Closed 25 Dec.* 🎟 *€3.* ☎ *(0351) 491 420 00. www.skd-dresden.de.*

The inventive genius of scientists is documented in the clocks and instruments of the 16C to 19C. The display includes sun, sand, oil, artistic and automatic clocks as well as many others.

Albertinum★★★

This neo-Renaissance building houses three museums: the Gallery of 19C and 20C Painters, the Green Vault Collections, and a sculpture collection.

Gemäldegalerie Neue Meister★★★ (Gallery of 19C and 20C Painters)

🕐 *Open daily except Thur, 10am-6pm.* 🕐 *Closed 25 Dec.* 🎟 *€6.* ☎ *(0351) 491 420 00. www.skd-dresden.de.*

This museum showcases German art of the Romantics (Casper David Friedrich), the Biedermeier (Carl Spitzweg), the Bourgeois Realists (Adolf von Menzel), the so-called "Deutsch-Römer" (Arnold Böcklin) and the Jugendstil. The German Impressionists are represented by Max Liebermann, and Lovis Corinth; the **Brücke** movement (spin-off of Fauvism and spearhead of German Expressionism, born in Dresden in the early 20C) is represented by Karl Schmidt Rottluff and Max Pechstein.

Grünes Gewölbe★★★ (Green Vault Collections)

🕐 *Open daily except Thur, 10am-6pm.*
🕐 *Closed 25 Dec.* 🎫 *€6.* ☎ *(0351) 491 420 00. www.skd-dresden.de.*

This treasury is a must-see on a tour of Dresden. The masterpieces of gold-smiths' work and jewelry were originally secured in the "Grünes Gewölbe" (Green Vault) at the Dresden palace, so named for the room's color. The name stuck in spite of the collection's transfer to the Albertinum.

Staatl. Kunstsammlungen Dresden

Green Vault Collections – Diana's Bath (1704)

Excursions

Schloss Moritzburg★

14km/9mi northwest, via Hansastraße. 🕐 *Open Apr-Oct: 10am-5.30pm; Nov-Mar: guided tours only (1hr) daily except Mon, 10am-4pm, Jan, Sat-Sun 10am-4pm.* 🕐 *Closed 24 and 31 Dec.* 🎫 *€6.* ☎ *(0352 07) 87 30. www.schloss-moritzburg.de.*

Built in the 16C by Duke Moritz, this simple hunting lodge was considerably refashioned in the 18C at the request of Frederick Augustus I (1670-1733), who longed for a Baroque château.

Freiberg★

37km/23mi south. Set at the foot of the Erzgebirge mountain range, Freiberg was the largest town in Saxony in the Middle Ages. For a long time its underground mineral resources were the source of its wealth (silver, copper, and lead, among others). Take time for Freiberg's **Cathedral**★★. The 15C Gothic hall-church includes several important religious artworks, including the **tulip pulpit**★★, a masterpiece by sculptor Hans Witten ca 1505; the **Gottfried Silbermann organ**★★; and the magnificent **golden entrance portal**★★, erected ca 1230 for the church's Romanesque predecessor. 🚹 ⏳ *Guided tour (45min). May-Oct, daily at 10am, 11am (11.30am Sun), 2pm, 3pm and 4pm; Nov-Apr daily at 11am (11.30am Sun), 2pm and 3pm.* 🎫 *€2.50.* ☎ *(037 31) 225 98. www.freiberger-dom.de.*

Chemnitz

80km/50mi southwest. Known as "Saxony's Manchester", Chemnitz became home to the first cotton mills from 1800 and also boasts some Gothic and Renaissance treasures. Between 1953 and 1990, the town was known as Karl-Marx-Stadt. While in Chemnitz, stroll along **Brückenstraße;** the city's impressive modern town centers around this street and the Straße der Nationen, which it crosses. The imposing 1971 **Karl-Marx monument** (12m/40ft high) stands before a plaque bearing in several languages the last words of the Communist Manifesto: *"Workers of the world, unite!"* Also worth visiting are the **Altes Rathaus (Old town hall),** painstakingly restored after 1945 (the 20C Neues Rathaus is just to the east); and the **Fine Arts Collection,** German painting and sculpture of the 19C and 20C (Dresden Romantic School, German Impressionism and Expressionism). 🕐 *Open daily except Mon, 12pm-7pm,*

Wed, 1pm-6pm. 🕐 Closed 24 and 31 Dec. 📷 €4. ☎ (0371) 488 44 24. www.chemnitz.
de/kunstsammlungen.

Swiss Saxony★★★ (👶 see SÄCHSISCHE SCHWEIZ)

Meißen★ (👶 see MEISSEN)

DÜSSELDORF★

POPULATION: 573 000

This onetime fishing village is today one of the country's most important economic centres. Capital of the Rhineland-Westphalia and fashion capital of
Germany, Düsseldorf is a place where people like to be seen, particularly on
Königsallee with its prestigious boutiques. 🚩 Immermannstraße 65b, 40210 Düsseldorf, ☎ (0211) 17 20 20.

▶ **Orient Yourself:** Düsseldorf stands on the Rhine's east bank, at its confluence
with the Düssel. The city is at the heart of a major motorway junction, linking it
to Cologne, Duisburg, Essen and Dortmund. Düsseldorf is only one hour away
from Paris by Thalys (daily service). The city also has an international airport.
🅿 **Parking:** Garages are plentiful, especially along Königsallee.
👶 **Don't Miss:** A stroll along the fashionable Königsallee, also called "The Kö."
🕐 **Organizing Your Time:** Allow two hours for the Fine Arts Museum.
👶 **Also See:** ESSEN (37km/23mi north), KÖLN (39km/24mi south), AACHEN (81km/50mi
southwest).

A Bit of History

City of the arts – Düsseldorf acquired city status in 1288 from the Count of Berg
after the Battle of Worringen; in 1380 it was chosen as the official residence of the
dukes of Berg. Four centuries later, Johann Wilhelm (1679-1716, also known as Jan
Wellem), of the prince-electors of Neuburg-Palatinate, surrounded himself with
brilliant court musicians, painters and architects who transformed Düsseldorf into
a true city of the arts.

Düsseldorf and the Rhine

Düsseldorf Marketing & Tourismus GmbH

Address Book

WHERE TO EAT

◎◎◎ **Rheinturm Top 180** – Strom-straße 20, 40221 Düsseldorf-Unterbilk. ☎ (0211) 863 20 00. www.guennewig.de. The lift takes less than a minute to reach this restaurant 172m/564ft in the air. It rotates slowly, allowing diners to enjoy superb views of the city.

◎◎◎◎ **Berens am Kai** – Kai-straße 16, 40221 Düsseldorf-Unterbilk. ☎ (0211) 300 67 50. www.berensamkai. de. ○ Closed 1-7 Jan, Sat lunchtime, Sun, public holidays. A modern restaurant in an office building beside the harbour. Concrete walls and columns and chrome chairs with black cushions highlight the refined decoration. Splendid view of the Rhine through the glass façade.

WHERE TO STAY

◎◎ **Fashion Hotel** – Am Hain 44, 40468 Düsseldorf-Stockum. ☎ (0211) 439 50. Fax (0211) 4395200. www.fash-ion-duesseldorf.de. ○ Closed 24-31 Dec P 38 rooms. ⊠ A haven of peace and quiet despite being right next to the centres of business and industry. Comfortable rooms with rustic furniture plus some brand new rooms in a private house.

◎◎ **Hotel Merkur** – Mörsenbroicher Weg 49, 40470 Düsseldorf-Mörsenbroich. ☎ (0211) 159 24 60. Fax (0211) 15924625 www.hotel-merkur.de ○ Closed Christmas to early Jan. P ⊱ 30 rooms. ⊠ A pleasant hotel with well-kept rooms, almost all with cherrywood furniture. The Hotel Merkur stands in a quiet loca-tion in a side street near the city centre, and has its own parking.

TAKING A BREAK

Eis-Café Pia – Kasernenstr. 1. ☎ (0211) 326 233. ○ 10am-11pm. ○ closed mid Oct to mid Feb. Probably the best Italian ice cream in town. You may have to queue, but it's certainly worth the wait. Hot and cold drinks also served in the café.

GOING OUT

USEFUL TIPS

The old town is known as the longest bar in the world on account of the succession of countless bars, pubs and restaurants between Ratinger Straße and Karlsplatz. But don't make the mistake of ordering a Kölsch in Düsseldorf; Here the beer that reigns supreme is the brown ale known as "Altbier".

Op de Eck – Grabbeplatz 5 (in the Kunstsammlung Nordrhein-Westfalen building). ☎ (0211) 32 88 38. www. op-de-eck.de. ○ Tue-Sun 11am-1am, Mon 5pm-1am.This café-restaurant has a concave glass façade and modern design interior. On the menu: international specialities, home-made cakes and sorbets, and a good selection of wines and cocktails. A good place for a snack at any hour of the day.

Uerige – Bergerstr. 1 (between Karlsplatz and Marktplatz). ☎ (0211) 86 69 90. www.uerige.de. ○ 10am-midnight. ○ Carnival Monday and 25 Dec. The place to come if you want to try Altbier – the atmosphere is unique. Casks serve as tables, and in summer patrons of all ages spill out into the street.

Head Office of the Ruhr – Seat of one of Germany's most important stock exchanges, Düsseldorf is a principal banking and financial centres and administrative capital for most of the Rhineland industries.

The World of Fashion – Exhibitions, fairs and collections of haute couture secure Düsseldorf's reputation as a "minor Paris" and fashion capital of Germany. The CPD (Collections Premiere Düsseldorf) is the world's largest fashion trade show, with over 2 000 exhibitors from over 40 countries. Everything elegant centres on the graceful **Königsallee**★, with boutiques and arcades on either side of the old moat.

The Far East – Düsseldorf plays an increasingly important role in economic relations linking Germany with the Far East. Japanese firms alone have 300 branches in

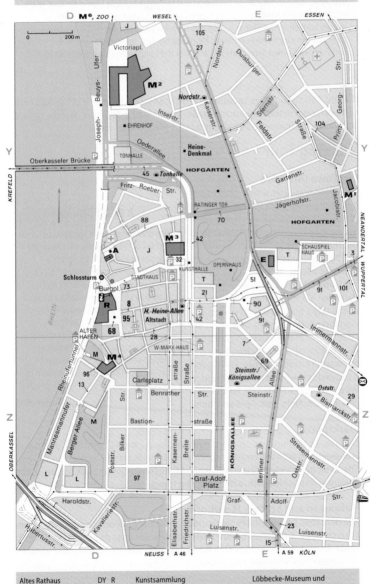

Poetry and Music in the 19C

Heinrich Heine (1797-1856), son of a Bolkerstraße merchant, spent his youth in Düsseldorf, deeply impressed with the French and Napoleon. A poet, pamphleteer, traveler, defender of liberalism and a Francophile, Heine described himself as "a German nightingale which would have liked to make its nest in Voltaire's wig."

Among the musicians who have given Düsseldorf its reputation as an artistic centre are Robert Schumann and Felix Mendelssohn-Bartholdy. **Schumann** (1810-56) was appointed conductor of the municipal orchestra in 1850. Living for four years in a house in the Bilker Straße, he neared nervous breakdown here, attempting to drown himself in the Rhine in 1854. His friend **Mendelssohn** (1809-47) brilliantly directed the city's Rhine Festival. He made his first journey to England in 1829, conducting his own *Symphony in C Minor* at the London Philharmonic Society.

the city. This strong Asian presence is reinforced by the existence of the Japanese Cultural Center in the Immermannstraße, the Taiwan Trade Center near the central station, and a Japanese cultural centre in the Niederkassel district.

Walking Tour

Old Town (Altstadt)

This riverside quarter, with its taverns and bars jam-packed from the earliest hours of the evening, is known as "the biggest boozer in Europe". It is here that you'll find the "Radschläger" – local street urchins and buskers who perform outdoor acrobatics for a few pennies.

The **Bolkerstraße**, birthplace of Heinrich Heine (no 53), is the busiest and liveliest of the city's pedestrian precincts. The neighbourhood is equally linked with the story of the tailor Wibbel, who attended his own funeral after switching identities to escape a prison sentence. This legend is recalled by the figures of the Schneider-Wibbel-Gasse carillon clock, which operates at 11am, 1pm, 3pm, 6pm and 9pm.

> 🍂 **A Bit of Advice** 🍂
>
> **Gastronomy:** It is in the taverns typical of the old town that regional specialities can best be appreciated: *Blutwurst mit Zwiebeln* (black pudding with onions); *Halve Hahn* (caraway cheese eaten with strong local mustard); and *Röggelchen* (small rye bread rolls). On Friday evenings, there is a tradition of eating *Reibekuchen*, a kind of savoury potato cake. *Altbier*, the still, dark brown ale of the region, is brewed in Düsseldorf.

Marktplatz

Separated from the Rhine only by the Altes Rathaus (late-16C town hall), this square is embellished with the bronze equestrian statue (18C) of the famous Jan Wellem. There is a good view of the river from the Burgplatz adjoining this square, in the shadow of the Schloßturm, a free-standing tower.

Hofgarten and Schloss Jägerhof★

The Hofgarten park is a shady continuation of the Königsallee. The park's Napoleon Hill is crowned with a small bronze titled *Harmony,* a modest monument to Heinrich Heine. The Schloss houses the **Goethe-Museum★**, with the author's manuscripts, autographs, drawings and engravings.

Sights

Museum Kunst Palast★ (Fine Arts Museum)

♿ 🕐 *Open daily except Mon, 11am-6pm.* 🎫 *€10.* ☎ *(0211) 899 24 60. www.museum-kunst-palast.de.*
Romantics of the Düsseldorf School dominate the important painting gallery in this museum. There is equal exposure for German Impressionists and Expressionists. The museum also houses a collection of medieval sculpture, and an outstanding collection of **glassware**★★, including glass from Roman times to the present, from Europe and the Far East, and lots of Jugendstil glassware.

Kunstsammlung Nordrhein-Westfalen★ (Rhineland-Westphalia Art Collection)

♿ 🕐 *Open daily except Mon, 10am-6pm, Sat-Sun 11am-6pm.* 🎫 *€6.50.* ☎ *(0211) 83 81 130. www.kunstsammlung.de.*
Designed by Danish architects Dissing and Weitling, this modern building houses a 20C art collection including works by Picasso, Chagall, Ernst, Beuys and 100 of **Paul Klee's** works. Klee was Fine Arts Professor in Düsseldorf from 1930 to 1933.

Excursions

Schloss Benrath★

10km/6mi southeast. Town plan in current Michelin Guide Deutschland. 🕐 *From mid Mar-end Oct: open daily except Mon, 10am-6pm, Wed 10am-8pm; from Nov to mid Mar: open daily except Mon, 11am-5pm.* 🕐 *Closed 24, 25 and 31 Dec.* 🎫 *€4.* ☎ *(0211) 892 10 03. www.schloss-benrath.de.*
This 18C Late Baroque building was designed by Nicolas de Pigage as a country palace for the Prince Elector of the Palatinate. The interior is decorated in transitional Rococo and Early Classicism.

Neandertal

14km/9mi east, via Am Wehrhahn.
The deep, steep valley of the Düssel owes its name to Calvinist poet Joachim Neander (1650-80), who used it as a retreat. It was here that the famous 60 000-year-old skeleton of Neanderthal Man was discovered in 1856. A plaque on a triangular rock *(right side of the road, 3km/2mi beyond the motorway underpass)* marks the site of the cave. The **Neanderthal Museum,** not far from the excavation site, gives an overview of human evolution. There is a striking reconstruction of our ancestor, created via computer re-creation from the skull. *Talstraße 300.* ♿ 🕐 *Open daily except Mon, 10am-6pm.* 🕐 *Closed 24, 25 and 31 Dec.* 🎫 *€6.50.* ☎ *(021 04) 97 97 97. www.neanderthal.de.*

KLOSTER EBERBACH★★

The former Cistercian abbey is the only sister foundation of Clairvaux in Germany apart from Himmerod in the Eifel. The abbey still emanates the peace and isolation characteristic of a Cistercian community.

▶ **Orient Yourself:** The abbey grew up at the bottom of a small valley, on the northern side of the Rheingau, on the edge of the vineyards.
🕐 **Organizing Your Time:** Allow two hours to tour the Abbey church and buildings.
🤸 **Also See:** *WIESBADEN, MAINZ, RHEINTAL.*

Sights

Abbey Church

 ♿ *Apr-Oct, 10am-6pm; Nov-Mar, 11am-5pm, Sat-Sun, 11am-4pm.* ♿ *Closed 24, 25, 31 Dec.* ✆ *€3.50.* ☏ *(067 23) 91 78 100; www.klostereberbach.net*

Built in two stages, in 1145-60 and in 1170-86, this is a Roman cross vaulted basilica, its austere appearance characteristic of Cistercian architecture. Gothic chapels with tracery windows were added in the 14C. Remarkable **tombs**★ dating from the 14C to the 18C.

Abbey Buildings

Outlying 13C-14C buildings center around the **cloister**★; only the portal remains of the 12C monks' refectory. Rebuilt in 1720, the latter is impressive, with a magnificent stucco ceiling by Daniel Schenk from Mainz (1738). The lay brothers' refectory contains a collection of mighty **winepresses**★★, documenting the 800-year-old wine-producing tradition of the abbey. The oldest press dates from 1668.

The **monks' dormitory**★, dates to ca 1250-70. The double-naved, ribbed vaulted room was built with a slightly rising floor and the columns shortened to give the appearance of length. The **chapter-house**, with beautiful 14C star-ribbed vaulting and stylised plant decoration dating back to 1500, was built prior to 1186. The dormitory leads to the **abbey museum** (*Abteimuseum*), with a history of the abbey and the Cistercian Order.

The Name of the Rose

The cameras began rolling at Eberbach in 1986 for the filming of the monastic whodunnit *The Name of the Rose*. Director Jean-Jacques Annaud allegedly chose the Cistercian abbey of Eberbach from a list of 300 abbeys as the primary setting for Umberto Eco's novel. The dispute between the papal envoy and the Franciscan monk William of Baskerville, played by Sean Connery, was filmed in the chapter-house, where monastic law was once laid down. The scriptorium was reconstructed in the monks' dormitory. In the film, sentences were passed by the Holy Inquisition where people now gather to taste wine, in the monastery cellar. The abbey church and hospice also feature in the film.

EICHSTÄTT★★

POPULATION: 13 000

Eichstätt, a small episcopal city and seat of a Catholic university, owes its Baroque character to its reconstruction after the Thirty Years War; only the cathedral survived the burning of the town by the Swedish army. But Eichstätt is also a centre of contemporary architecture, such as the new Pedagogical University.
▣ *Kardinal-Preysing-Platz 14, 85072 Eichstätt,* ☏ *(084 21) 988 00.*

▶ **Orient Yourself:** Eichstätt lies in the midst of the Altmühl Valley natural park. Many of the roofs are covered with limestone slabs unique to this region.

☞ **Don't Miss:** The cathedral and the Residenzplatz.

♿ **Organizing Your Time:** Half a day is sufficient to see Eichstätt's highlights, including the cathedral and the Residenzplatz.

☞ **Also See:** *ROMANTISCHE STRASSE, NÖRDLINGEN (65km/41mi west), NUREMBERG (79km/49mi north), REGENSBURG (99km/62mi east).*

Sights

Dom★

A mixture of architectural styles marks the 14C cathedral: Romanesque, Early Gothic or Baroque. The main entrance is via a Gothic door decorated with polychromatic statues. The west face is Baroque.

Inside, a highlight is the late-15C **Pappenheim Reredos**★★, almost 9m/30ft high and of Jura limestone. The *Crucifixion* is a masterpiece of religious sculpture; in the west chancel is seated a statue of **St Willibald** (8C Bishop of Eichstätt) , an early 16C work.

The **Mortuarium**★ *(through the south transept)* funerary chapel is a late-15C Gothic hall with handsome **tombstones** paving the floor. Four stained-glass **windows** in the east wall are by Hans Holbein the Elder (c 1500), and the 16C *Crucifixion* on the south wall is by Loy Hering.

Upstairs, above the chancel, the **Diözesanmuseum** outlines the long history of the diocese with pictures, maps, vestments and statues. In the Bishop's Room, note St Willibald's Chasuble, thought to be a Byzantine work dating from the 12C. Reliquaries, chalices, monstrances and other examples of religious art are on view in the **Treasury**. ⏰ *Wed-Fri 10.30am-5pm, Sat-Sun, 10am-5pm.* ⏰ *Closed Good Fri.* 💶 *€2, no charge Sun and bank holidays.* ☎ *(084 21) 502 66.*

The **Cloister**★ was a 15C addition to the cathedral.

Residenzplatz★

Lawns carpet the centre of the Residenzplatz (Residence Square). Rococo palaces surround it. The south side is bordered by four imposing houses with decorated gables and entrances guarded by atlantes. Facing them is the southern wing of the Residence and, on the west, the former Vicar-General's mansion. The **Virgin's Column** in the immediate foreground *(Mariensäule)* rises from a fountain surrounded by cherubs.

Willibaldsburg

Access via route B 13 and the Burgstraße.

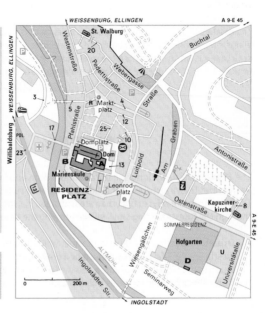

WHERE TO EAT

◉◉ **Schmankerlwirtshaus Gasthof Krone** – *Domplatz 3. ☎ (08421) 44 06. www.krone-eichstaett.de.* Located in the heart of the old town near the cathedral, this corner house has dark wooden furnishings and country-style décor. Regional specialities are on the menu.

WHERE TO STAY

◉◉ **Hotel Zum Hirschen** – *Brückenstraße 9, 85072 Eichstätt-Wasserzell. ☎ (08421) 96 80. Fax (08421) 968888. www.hirschenwirt.de. ◷ Closed in Jan. ⊡ 40 rooms.* ⌑ ◉◉ *Restaurant.* This well-kept hotel is an ideal hub for excursions into the Altmühltal natural park. Comfortable guestrooms, lawn and restaurant with winter garden serving Franconian specialities.

This 14C castle, unfinished until the early 17C, occupies a height overlooking the river in the western part of town. Inside the castle, note the **well** *(Tiefer Brunnen) (access through the courtyard).* From atop the crenellated tower *(98 steps)* is a view of the fortifications, the town and the river.

Jura-Museum★

♿ ◷ *Open Apr-Sep, Tue-Sun, 9am-6pm; Oct-Mar, Tue-Sun, 10am-4pm. ◷ Closed 1 Jan, Shrove Tue, 24, 25 and 31 Dec. ◈ €3. ☎ (084 21) 47 30.*
The geological history of the Franconian Jura is traced in this museum. Most of the fossils (ammonites, crustaceans, fish, reptiles and dragonflies) were discovered in the limestone beds of neighbouring Solnhofen. The museum's prize exhibit is the complete fossilised skeleton of an Archaeopteryx. An evolutionary link between reptiles and birds, this extremely rare example was found in 1951 near Workerzell, northwest of Eichstätt.

Excursion

Ellingen
3 km/2mi north of Weißenburg. This locality owes its fame to the Teutonic Knights, whose Commander for Franconia was based here from the 13C until Napoleon's dissolution of the Order in 1809.
The **castle** *(Schloss)* (1718-25) comprises an inner courtyard framed by four imposing wings, one of which is entirely occupied by the church. The huge twin-flight **main staircase★** is worth seeing, as is the small museum covering the history of the Teutonic Order. ♿ ⬝⬝ *(see the ticket office) Guided tours hourly. ◷ Apr to Sep, Tue-Sun 9am-5pm; Oct to Mar, Tue-Sun 10am-3pm. ◈ €3. ☎ (0981) 953 83 90.*

EIFEL★

The Eifel massif runs along the border of Belgium and Luxembourg between Aachen and Trier, a picturesque backdrop to dozens of quaint villages and towns. There are no motorways or big urban areas; instead, narrow roads snake their way through the forests passing small villages among the trees.

▶ **Orient Yourself:** Straddling the Länder of Rheinland-Pfalz and Rheinland-Westfalen, the Eifel massif is flanked by a great plain to the north, the Rhine to the East, the Moselle to the south and the Belgian border to the West.

☻ **Don't Miss:** The volcanic lakes called "Maare".

- 🕒 **Organizing Your Time:** Allow one day for the driving tour from Bad Münstereifel to Manderscheid.
- **Kids Especially for Kids:** Outdoor excursion at the Altenahr, the Hohe Acht and the Maare.
- 👜 **Also See:** *BONN (39km/24mi northeast), KÖLN (49km/31mi northeast), AACHEN (74km/46mi northwest), RHEINTAL, MOSELTAL.*

Driving Tour

From Bad Münstereifel to Manderscheid

145 km/90mi
This excursion follows the valley of the Ahr with its popular resorts, climbs to the forested immensity of the Upper Eifel, and then snakes between the volcanic lakes of the Maare.

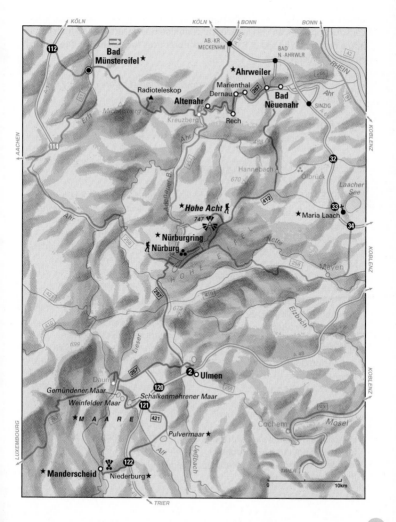

Bad Münstereifel

Surrounded by massive **ramparts**★ *(Stadtbefestigung)*, the town still boasts a quantity of old houses and monuments. The **Stiftskirche St Chrysanthus und Daria** is an outstanding abbey church, its twin towers flanking an 11C Romanesque front.

A few miles east of Münstereifel, the road passes a giant **radio-telescope**, rejoins the Ahr at Kreuzberg and continues along the winding valley. The telescope is 100m/328ft in diameter and its parabolic depth is 21m/69ft.

Altenahr

Kids On a site between two bends in the river, Altenahr is an excursion centre dominated by the scattered ruins of the 12C **Burg Are**. There is an attractive view from the upper terminal of the chair-lift.

The valley, in which vineyards now alternate with rock outcrops, plays host to a number of wine producing villages: Rech, on either side of its Roman bridge; Dernau with its "wine fountain"; Marienthal and its ruined convent.

Bad Neuenahr-Ahrweiler

Plan in the Michelin Guide Deutschland.

The old town of **Ahrweiler**★ still retains its medieval gates and fortifications. Half-timbered houses line narrow, pedestrian-only streets of the town centre. During road construction a Roman villa in excellent condition was unearthed and transformed into a museum. The spa at Bad Neuenahr produces the celebrated "Apollinaris" sparkling mineral water.

▶ *Leaving Ahrweiler, the road climbs toward the forest before reaching the highlands.*

Hohe Acht★

▶ *30min on foot round trip*

Address Book

WHERE TO EAT

⊖⊜🍽 **Weinhaus an der Rauschen** – *Heisterbacher Straße 1, 53902 Bad Münstereifel.* ☎ *(02253) 84 25.* 🕐 *Closed 2 weeks in Jul and Mon.* 🍴 This half-timbered house was built in 1553 and is in the historic town centre, next to the Erft waterfall *(Erftwasserfall).* Furnished in light wood and rattan, with a fireplace and exposed beams, this establishment has a decidedly rustic air.

WHERE TO STAY

⊖ **Pension Oos** – *Lieserstraße 16, 54550 Daun-Gemünden.* ☎ *(06592) 29 09. Fax (06592) 7890. www.pension-oos. de.* 🕐 *Closed Nov to mid-Mar.* 🍴 🅿 6 *rooms.* ⌗ As well as its simple, well-kept guestrooms, this pension has a living room and small kitchen with fridge for use of the guests. Leisure pursuits include swimming, sailing and visiting the volcanic craters nearby.

⊖⊜ **Hotel Seemöwe** – *Am Obersee 10, 52152 Simmerath-Einruhr.* ☎ *(02485) 271. Fax (02485) 1356. www.hotel-see-moewe.de.* 🕐 *Closed Jan and Feb.* 🅿 ⌗ ♿ *50 rooms.* ⌗ ⊖Restaurant. Good hotel on the edge of the lake (Obersee), with clean and well-cared for guestrooms and a terrace. Country-style restaurant offers traditional cuisine.

⊖⊜🍽 **Burg Adenbach** – *Adenbachhutstraße 1, 53474 Bad Neuenahr-Ahrweiler.* ☎ *(02641) 389 20. Fax (02641) 31714. www.burghotel-adenbach.com* 🕐 *Restaurant closed Mon* 🅿 ⌗ *Reservations recommended. 7 rooms.* ⌗ ⊖⊜🍽 *Restaurant.* This hotel is in a romantic medieval castle with beautiful, comfortable guestrooms and large bathrooms. The restaurant has its own attractions: Feasts worthy of a medieval gathering are served in the cellars.

Kids From the viewpoint at the top of the tower *(75 steps)* erected at the highest point of the Eifel (747m/2 451ft), there is a **panorama**★★ taking in deep valleys. Above, the only prominent points are Nürburg Castle to the southwest and, in the opposite direction, the ruins of Olbrück in front of the distant Siebengebirge (Seven Mountains).

Nürburg
▶ *30min on foot round trip*
A much-restored ruin in the middle of a rugged **landscape**★, best seen from the top of the keep.

Nürburgring★
♿ 🕐 *Open daily, 10am-6pm.* 💳 *€11.* ☎ *(026 91) 30 26 02. www.erlebnis-welt-nuer-burgring.de.*
The famous motor racing track is named after the Nürburg ruin, which lies inside its northern loop. Formula 1, motorcycle Grand Prix, International Touring and Super Touring races are held here. The Erlebnispark Nürburgring is entirely devoted to motor racing. The **Collection of Nürburgring Legends**★ is housed in one of the halls.

Ulmen
A pretty volcanic crater lake between the village and a ruined castle.

Maare★
Kids The ancient volcanic region of the Maare features small lakes resulting from volcanic activity in the Upper Eifel. Gas pressure produced explosions, forming craters with only a rim of cinders and pools of water: the **Gemündener Maar**, the **Weinfelder Maar** (also known as the **Totenmaar**), the **Schalkenmehrener Maar** and the almost perfectly circular **Pulver Maar**★.

▶ *Follow the brown signposts with the word "Maare".*

Manderscheid★
In Manderscheid go to the **Niederburg**★ ruins. From atop the castle keep is a **view**★ to the Oberburg ruins and the Lieser Valley. Drive to the Pension Burgenblick car park and from here take the footpath to the **viewpoint**★★, the so-called Kaisertem-pelchen (little Imperial temple) overlooking the Oberburg and Niederburg ruins.

EINBECK★

POPULATION: 28 400

In the Middle Ages, no less than 700 small breweries in this former Hanseatic town supplied the whole of Germany with "Einpöckisches Bier" (forerunner of Bock beer). Einbeck still retains part of its medieval fortifications, but a more attractive heritage is almost 400 half-timbered 16C houses, richly decorated with multicoloured carvings. 🏛 *Rathaus, Marktplatz 6, 37574 Einbeck.* ☎ *(055 61) 161 21.*

▶ **Orient Yourself:** Einbeck lies between the Harz massif and the Weser valley. The town is easily reached along the A 7 motorway which links Hannover to the north and Hann. Münden sits to the south.
🙂 **Don't Miss:** The Old Town.
🕐 **Organizing Your Time:** Allow one hour to see Einbeck's Old Town.
👣 **Also See:** *HILDESHEIM (54km/34mi north), HANN. MÜNDEN (69km/43mi south), THÜRINGER WALD.*

Walking Tour

Old Town★

There is a remarkable collection of half-timbered houses in the town centre of Einbeck, most near the old market place.

Marktplatz★★

Of special note are the two houses on the corner of the Münsterstraße: the Brodhaus (1552), and the Ratsapotheke (1590), an impressive building which, like most of the old houses, has ventilated attics which served as lofts for hops and barley. Opposite is the town hall *(Rathaus)*, its three projecting fronts crowned with unusual pointed roofs.

Tiedexerstraße★★

▶ *Start behind the church tower (Marktkirche).*
The gables and façades on this street are especially attractive.

Marktstraße

Note particularly the **Eickesches Haus**★★ *(no 13, on the corner of Knochenhauerstraße)*. Erected between 1612 and 1614, this wooden construction ignores the traditional local style and imitates the stone mansions of the Renaissance.

Excursion

Bad Gandersheim

Spa *22km//14mi northeast.*
The birthplace of Roswitha von Gandersheim, Germany's first (10C) poetess, is better known as a hot spring and salt-water spa. The twin octagonal towers of the **cathedral**★ overlook the town centre. Inside are two altars, one 15C and the other 16C. Around the market place well-preserved half-timbered houses date from the 16C.

EISENACH★★

POPULATION: 44 000

Martin Luther called Eisenach "my dear town." The town's Wartburg fortress is a place dear to many Germans, symbolising the very spirit of German civilisation and history. The town hosts Lutherans and Bach lovers from around the world, and is also famous for producing Wartburg cars, once popular in East Germany.
 *Markt 2, 99817 Eisenach. ☎ (036 91) 792 30..*

WHERE TO STAY

◻◻ **Hotel St. Peter** – *Am Petersberg 7.* ☎ *(03691) 87 28 30. Fax (03691) 872831. www.stpeter-eisenach.de.* 🄿 *13 rooms.* 🍽 ◻◻ *Restaurant.* This little hotel on the edge of the town has well-kept guestrooms and modern furnishings. Dark wood and neat décor give the restaurant a rustic feel. There is also a Biergarten.

◻◻◻◻ **Auf der Wartburg** – *at the Wartburg (shuttle to the hotel).* ☎ *(03691) 79 70 Fax (03691) 797100. info@wartburghotel.de.* 🕐 *Closed 6 Jan to 6 Feb.* 🄿 ✕ *35 rooms.* 🍽 Above and beyond its location, one night in this tastefully restored hotel is a never-to-be-forgotten experience. The Landgrafenstube restaurant has a rustic feel.

▶ **Orient Yourself:** A former East German town near the former West German border, Eisenach is on the northwestern edge of the Forest of Thuringia.

😊 **Don't Miss:** The Wartburg fortress.

🕐 **Organizing Your Time:** Allow at least two hours for the Wartburg.

⚖ **Also See:** *ERFURT (61km/38mi east), WEIMAR (77km/48mi east), HANN. MÜNDEN (96km/60mi northwest).*

A Bit of History

At the Heart of Germany – At the beginning of the 13C, the Minnesänger (troubadours) took part in legendary contests in the Wartburg, a custom which inspired Wagner's opera *Tannhäuser*. It was at Eisenach that **Martin Luther** studied and translated the New Testament into German, and here that **Johann Sebastian Bach** was born in 1685.

Sights

The Wartburg★★

Leave the car in one of the lots (fee payable) half-way up the hill for a 15min walk up to the fortress, or take the bus from the market place. 👣 *Guided tour (1hr).* 🕐 *Mar-Oct, 8.30am-5pm; Nov-Feb, 9am-3.30pm.* 🎟 *€6.* ☎ *(036 91) 25 00; www.wartburg-eisenach.de*

Since 2000, the Wartburg has appeared on the UNESCO World Heritage list. Perched on a rocky spur, the fortress welcomes visitors through a 12C entrance and into a 15C-16C **outer courtyard** *(Erster Burghof)* of half-timbered buildings. Inside the fortified complex is the **Palais★**, where the Landgraves lived. The fortified wall and south tower give a **view★** of Eisenach, the Forest of Thuringia and the Rhön foothills.

The one-hour guided tour *(available in English)* is worthwhile. It includes a visit to the **Hall of the Troubadours**, with Von Schwind's huge fresco illustrating the Minnesänger in the Wartburg. The tour ends in the **Wartburg Museum**, which displays selected works from the Wartburg foundation's collections.

Don't leave before seeing **Luther's Room** *(Lutherstube)*, where the New Testament of the Bible was first translated into German.

Wartburg Fortress where memories of the Troubadours mix with those of Luther

The Old Town★

Markt

The market place is bordered by administrative buildings and townhouses surrounding a fountain with a statue of the town's patron saint, St George.

Schloss

♿ 🕐 *Open Tue-Sun, 11am-5pm.* 🎟 *€2.60.* ☎ *(036 91) 67 04 50.*

This former residence of the dukes of Saxe-Weimar now houses the **Thuringian Museum**, with items ranging from the 18C- 20C.

EISENACH

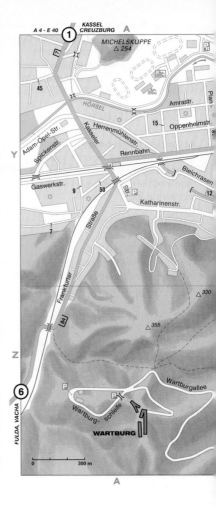

Georgenkirche

This triple-aisle 16C church contains the tombs of several Landgraves of Thuringia. Luther preached here on 2 May 1521 despite his being officially banned from the Holy Roman Empire. Johann Sebastian Bach was baptised here in 1685.

Predigerkirche

The church, a late-13C Early Gothic building, now houses the **wooden sculpture collection★** formerly in the Thuringian Museum. Carvings date from the 12C-16C.

Lutherhaus

🕐 *Open daily 9am-5pm.* 💶 *€3. (036 91) 298 30. www.lutherhaus-eisenach.de.*
It was in this late-14C house that **Luther** lived between 1498 and 1501 while he studied at the Latin School. Displays retrace the Reformation.

Bachhaus

From the Lutherhaus, return along the Lutherstraße as far as the Frauenplan. ♿ 🕐 *Open daily, 10am-6pm.* 💶 *€4.* ☎ *(036 91) 793 40. www.bachhaus.de.*
The house at no 21 Frauenplan is believed to be the **birthplace** of Bach. Manuscripts, scores and portraits recall Johann Sebastian Bach and several other family members, all of them composers.

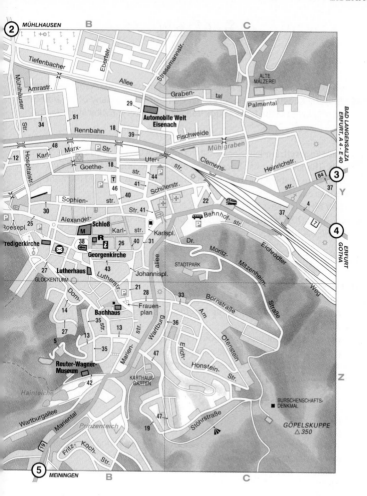

Automobile Welt

 ♿ ⏰ *Open Tue-Sun, 10am-5pm.* ⚀ *€2.10.* ☎ *(036 91) 772 12.*
Here a small exhibition documents the history of the Wartburg car, first manufactured here in 1955, while the last one rolled off the production line in 1991. On the Wartburg auto premises *(Friedrich-Naumann-Str 10)* is the exhibition, **Automobile Welt Eisenach**, presenting the history of car manufacture in Eisenach.

Excursion

The Forest of Thuringia★★ (✎ *see* THÜRINGER WALD)

EMDEN

POPULATION: 51 700

Emden is a pleasant town. Art lovers will enjoy Emden's remarkable museums, including the Kunsthalle, a gallery of contemporary art. Many of the inhabitants are employed at the town's huge Volkwagen factory. ▯ *Alter Markt 2a, 26721 Emden.* ☎ *(049 21) 974 00.*

▶ **Orient Yourself:** Emden is located at the mouth of the Ems and faces the Netherlands. The Ems River has been dyked and the Dortmund-Ems and Ems-Jade canals have enabled the town to regain its position as the chief maritime port of Lower Saxony.

☺ **Don't Miss:** Emden's port.

⚲ **Also See:** *OLDENBOURG (84km/52mi southeast), BREMEN (131km/82mi east), OSTFRIESISCHE INSELN.*

Sights

Ostfriesisches Landesmuseum★
(Museum of the East Frisian Islands)
In the former town hall. ⏲ *Open Tue-Sat, 10am-6pm.* ⊛ *€6.* ☎ *(049 21) 87 20 58. www.landesmuseum-emden.de.*
Items excavated in peat bog digs, models of the port and fishing boats and paintings by the Dutch School evoke the colourful history of the town. Pride of place is given to the collection of the former **Rüstkammer**★★: weapons and armour of the militia from 1500 to the 18C.

Port
Ratsdelf.
The oldest section is the **harbour gateway** *(Hafentor)* built in 1635 and bearing the Latin inscription *"God is Emden's bridge, harbour and sailing wind"*. In the historical harbour basin are several **museum ships** *(Museumsschiffe)*.

Pelzerhaus
Pelzerstrasse.
This 16C building is one of the few houses in the town centre that survived the bombs of the Second World War.

Kunsthalle in Emden – Stiftung Henri und Eske Nannen
Hinter dem Rahmen 13; northwest of town. ♿ ⏲ *Open Wed-Fri, 10am-5pm, Tue, 10am-8pm, Sat and Sun, 11am-5pm.* ⏲ *Closed 24 and 25 Dec.* ⊛ *€5, no charge on 3 Oct.* ☎ *(049 21) 97 50 50. www.kunsthalle-emden.de.*
The post-modern red-brick building houses the sizeable collection of works of art by the German Expressionists and Neue Sachlichkeit, gathered together during his lifetime by founder of *Stern* magazine Henri Nannen, who was born in Emden. The exhibition includes contemporary painting and sculpture.

ERFURT ★

POPULATION: 200 800

Erfurt is a peaceful, captivating town dominated by steeples and bell-towers. Its historic centre is one of the best preserved in Germany, with carefully restored half-timbered houses and Renaissance-style buildings. The city is a virtual who's who of German history, once home to Luther, Goethe, Schiller, Herder and Bach.
🔲 *Benediktsplatz 1, 99084 Erfurt,* ☎ *(0361) 664 00.*

▶ **Orient Yourself:** Erfurt is situated in the heart of Thuringia, between Gotha and Weimar, and has been its capital since 1990.

🅿 **Parking:** Garages are located near the Dom, the main train station and throughout town

🅟 **Don't Miss:** The Domplatz

🕚 **Organizing Your Time:** One day is sufficient to see Erfurt.

🕯 **Also See:** *WEIMAR (21km/13mi east), EISENACH (61km/38mi west), THÜRINGER WALD (itinerary leaves from Eisenach).*

A Bit of History

A trading town – In the year 742, St Boniface from England founded a bishopric at Erfurt, which was soon joined to that of Mainz. From the Middle Ages on, the town's position on the important trade route linking the Rhine with Russia lent it such commercial consequence that it was incorporated into the Hanseatic League in the 15C.

Spirituality and Humanism – The influential Christian mystic **Master Eckhart** was born near town and established in Erfurt as Provincial of Saxony. Two centuries later **Martin Luther** further shook the religious world. He studied philosophy at the local university, then entered the Augustine monastery before setting off for Wittenberg.

Address Book

WHERE TO EAT

🍽🍷🥂 **Alboth's Restaurant** – *Futterstraße 15.* ☎ *(0361) 568 82 07.* 🕚 *Closed Sun and Mon and 3 weeks in Jul and Aug.* This chic, well-presented restaurant is in one of the town's historic houses: dark wood ceilings and smart décor in the dining room. Varied menu with good wine list.

🍽🍷🥂 **Köstritzer "Zum güldenen Rade"** – *Marktstraße 50.* ☎ *(0361) 561 35 06. www.gourmetguide.com/koestritzer_zum_gueldenen_rade.* ♿ This restaurant is situated in the old town, not far from the town hall. Stone walls, plenty of wood and paintings form a pleasant ambience. In pleasant weather, there is a summer garden and interior courtyard. A separate building houses an old mill.

WHERE TO STAY

🍽🥂 **Hotel Erfurtblick** – *Nibelungenweg 20.* ☎ *(0361) 22 06 60. Fax (0361) 2206622. www.hotel-erfurtblick.de.* 🅿 ⬌ *11 rooms.* 🛏 Well-kept hotel-guesthouse with light and airy guestrooms and a pleasant atmosphere. Pleasant garden and views of the town from the breakfast room and terrace.

🍽🥂 **Der kleine Nachbar** – *Weimarer Straße 16, 99867 Gotha.* ☎ *(03621) 40 07 95. Fax (03621) 28841. www.derkleinenachbar.de.* 🅿 ⬌ *9 rooms.* 🛏 🍽 *Restaurant.* This small guesthouse has plain and simple rooms which are immaculately kept. Well served by public transport with quick and easy access to the historic centre of Gotha.

ERFURT		Fischmarkt	A	Regierungsstr.	A	34
		Löberstr.	B	22	Schlösserstr.	AB	36
Anger	B	Mainzerhofstr.	A	24	Schlüterstr.	A	37
Bahnhofstr.	B	Marktstr.	A	Walkmühlstr.	A	40
Dalbergsweg	A	13	Meienbergstr.	B	27	Wenigemarkt	B	42
Domstr.	A	15	Moritzwallstr.	A	28	Willy-Brandt-Pl.	B	43

Angermuseum	B	M¹	Rathaus	A	R

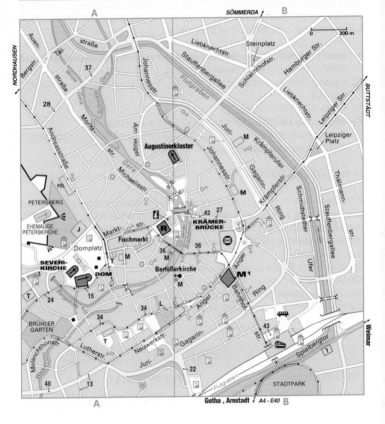

Walking Tour

Around the Domplatz

The Domplatz is dominated by the two imposing edifices of the Mariendom (Cathedral) and the Severikirche. In the centre, an obelisk commemorates a visit in 1777 by the Archbishop of Mainz.

Dom St-Marien★★

The original Romanesque basilica, built in 1154 on a hill occupied by the citadel, was renovated in the mid 14C: a portal at the north entrance, the so-called Triangle Portal; a soaring Gothic chancel at the east end. A century later, the Romanesque nave was replaced by a nave in the Flamboyant Gothic style.

The cathedral's **triangle portals**★★ at the north entrance consists of two doors set obliquely and supporting elegant statuary groups: on the northeast the Apostles at Work; on the northwest side, the Wise and Foolish Virgins.

Inside, the church's **interior** boasts several import artworks: the Romanesque Altar of the Virgin (1160); the **statue candelabra**★ known as "the Wolfram" (1160); and the intricately worked choir stalls (14C). The stained-glass **windows**★ above the choir (c 1370-1420) shed light on everyday medieval life through their depiction of episodes from Old and New Testament and the lives of various saints.

Severi-Kirche★

Formerly the Benedictine monks' abbey church of St Paul and of the Augustines, this Early Gothic building is of the hall type, with five naves. The **sarcophagus**★ of the saint (c 1365) is in the southernmost aisle.

▶ *Cross the Domplatz and take the Marktstraße.*

Around the Fischmarkt

Fischmarkt (Fish Market)

Inside the imposing neo-Gothic *Rathaus* are **frescoes**★ illustrating he lives of Luther, Faust and Tannhäuser. On the north of the square is a fine Renaissance building, *"Zum Breiten Herd"*.

Krämerbrücke★

This bridge, built in 1325, similar to the Ponte-Vecchio of Florence, is the only bridged street north of the Alps on which the houses are inhabited. The narrow, half-timbered houses date from the 16C to the 19C.

Angermuseum★

Anger 18. ⌚ *Closed for restoration work, but a few rooms open for temporary exhibitions.* ☎ *(0361) 55 45 611. www.angermuseum.de.*

This museum is located in a Baroque building dating from 1706. The focal point is the exhibition of medieval art from Thuringia. Among its highlights are 14C and 15C **altarpieces**★★; a **Pietà**★★ by the Master of St Severinus; and sarcophagus and paintings by Hans Baldung Grien. In the gallery is a collection of 18C-19C German landscape painting.

ERZGEBIRGE★

Known as the Ore Mountains, this medium-height massif owes its name to the many deposits of silver, tin, cobalt, nickel and iron, a natural wealth which brought prosperity to small towns like Zwickau, Annaberg and Schneeberg. The stretch of the range in Germany features the summit of the Fichtelberg. Landscapes include reservoir lakes, forests crisscrossed by footpaths and picturesque villages.

▶ **Orient Yourself:** The ridge of peaks marking the Czech frontier reaches a modest height above sea level of 750m/2 461ft.

🕐 **Organizing Your Time:** Allow at least three hours for the suggested driving tour.

🖝 **Also See:** *Oberes SAALETAL (Saalburg is 65km/41mi west of Klingenthal), DRESDEN (106km/66mi northeast of Annaberg-Bucholz), BAYREUTH (106km/66mi southwest of Klingenthal).*

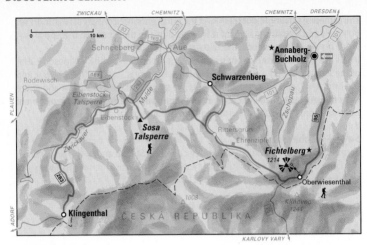

Driving Tour

From Annaberg-Buchholz to Klingenthal

81km/50mi (93km/58mi via Schwarzenberg). Leave Annaberg-Buchholz (🕭 see entry) on road no 95 in the direction of Oberwiesenthal.

Fichtelberg★

Towering above the health and winter sports resort of **Oberwiesenthal**, this peak is identifiable by the meteorological equipment atop its summit. The top is reached by ski lift or on foot *(30min round trip. Leave the car in the lot 455m/500yd after the lower ski-lift terminal)*. A **panorama**★ opens out when the top is reached, showing all of the surrounding country and the silhouette of Mount Klinovec in the Czech Republic. At 1 214m/3 950ft, this is the highest peak of the Erzgebirge.

▶ *From Oberwiesenthal to Ehrenzipfel is a pretty forest road which follows a riverbed. At Rittersgrün, take the detour via Schwarzenberg or continue on the direct route.*

Schwarzenberg

Resting on a crag, this officially protected town nestles around its castle and church. The 12C fortress became the elector's hunting lodge in 1555-58. Next to it stands the Baroque **St Georgenkirche**★ (1690-99).

Sosa-Talsperre

▶ *From the car lot, walk to the kiosk and then the promontory, passing this small lake and its dam. The road follows the northern reservoir bank before climbing (Road 283) the winding valley of the Zwickauer Mulde.*

Klingenthal

Built at the end of the 16C as a mining community, this town is better known for the musical instruments made here since the mid-17C. The Baroque church **Zum Friedenfürsten** is worth visiting.

FRANKFURT AM MAIN★★

POPULATION: 660 000

Financial and commercial capital of Germany, Frankfurt has more skyscrapers than any other city in Europe; many international companies, government organisations and financial institutions are based here, as are international trade fairs. But Frankfurt isn't all business. This is also Goethe country, and for over two centuries, the coronation site for kings and emperors of the Holy Roman Empire. ▯ *Hauptbahnhof, 60329 Frankfurt am Main. ☎ (069) 21 23 88 49.*

▶ **Orient Yourself:** Frankfurt stands at Germany's crossroads, literally and figuratively. Two major motorways join here: the A 3 (Cologne-Nuremberg) and the A 5 (Karlsruhe). The city is 2hr from Cologne, 2hr 30min from Nuremberg.

▯ **Parking:** Garages are located throughout the city. Visit http://wap.parkinfo.com for specific locations and fees.

⊘ **Don't Miss:** The Städelsches Kunstinstitut and Städtische Galerie, the Römerberg, and the cathedral.

⊙ **Organizing Your Time:** Allow half a day to explore the Old Town by foot.

▦ **Especially for Kids:** The Frankfurt Zoo, Senckenburg Natural History Museum.

⚭ **Also See:** *DARMSTADT (32km/20mi south), WIESBADEN (41km/26mi west), MAINZ (42km/26mi west) or RHEINTAL (Rüdesheim is 66km/41mi west).*

A Bit of History

The second coronation city – Built in the 8C on the site of an old Roman camp, Frankfurt became the emperor's residence and capital of Franconia one century later. In 1152, Frederick I Barbarossa engineered his election as Emperor of Germania at Frankfurt, thus setting the stage for the Golden Bull in 1356. Two centuries later, in 1562, the town replaced Aachen as the **coronation place** of the rulers of the **Holy Roman Empire** – a privilege it retained until the dissolution of the Reich in 1806.

The Young Goethe – Johann Wolfgang von Goethe was born in Frankfurt in 1749. It was here that he enjoyed his most prolific years, between 1772 and 1775, producing among other classics *Die Leiden des jungen Werthers* in only four weeks.

Capital of Finance and Economy – In the 16C Frankfurt was granted the right to mint money. The money market flourished and the **stock exchange** followed. German banks dominated the economy in the 18C; in the 19C they acquired a worldwide reputation thanks to financiers such as **Bethmann** and above all, **Rothschild,** whose sons, "the Five Frankfurters", established branches throughout Europe. Profiting from such a climate, industry quickly followed. The first Autumn Fair was held in 1240. The Spring Fair was added in 1330. Since the war the Fur Fair *(Pelzmesse)*, the Motor Show *(Automobilausstellung)* and the famous Book Fair *(Buchmesse)* have confirmed Frankfurt as the country's

A German Manhattan

G. Marth/Tourism + Congress GmbH Frankfurt a. M.

Address Book

PRACTICAL INFORMATION

TELEPHONE PREFIX: 069

TOURIST INFORMATION

For room reservations: *Tourismus + Congress GmbH.* ☎ 21 23 88 00, Fax 21 23 78 80, Mon-Fri 8.30am-5pm. Information offices: Tourist Information Hauptbahnhof, central station entrance hall, Mon-Fri 8am-9pm, Sat-Sun 9am-6pm, ☎ 21 23 88 49; Tourist Information Römer, Römerberg 27, Mon-Fri 9.30am-5.30pm, Sat-Sun 10am-4pm; City Info Zeil, Mon-Fri 10am-6pm, Sat 10am-4pm.

The city magazines *Journal Frankfurt* (in newsstands), *Fritz* (free) and *Welcome to Frankfurt* (in German) provide calendars of events. Tourist offices, the central station and the Römer also have a free calendar of events, the *Veranstaltungshinweise...* (followed by the month) The magazines *Prinz* and *Journal Frankfurt* are available from bookshops and newspaper kiosks. Information is at www.frankfurt-tourismus.de or www.frankfurt-rhein-main.de

POST OFFICES WITH LATE HOURS

The post office on the Zeil is open Mon-Fri 9.30am-8pm, Sat 9am-4pm; the branch office at the train station (Hauptbahnhof, 1st floor) is open Mon-Fri 7am-7.30pm, Sat 8am-4pm, and at the airport daily 7am-9pm.

NEWSPAPERS

Frankfurter Allgemeine Zeitung, Frankfurter Rundschau, Frankfurter Neue Presse.

INTERNET

www.frankfurt.de
www.rhein-main.net
www.frankfurt-am-main.de
www.frankfurt-online.net
www.frankfurt-tourismus.de

GETTING AROUND

Getting around Frankfurt is especially easy since much of the city centre is a pedestrian zone. The best way to get around is on foot.

PUBLIC TRANSPORT

The **RMV** (Rhein-Main-Verkehrsbund) is responsible for all public transport services, trams, buses, U-Bahns and S-Bahns, and regional trains in the greater Frankfurt region: ☎ (01805) 768 46 36 (€0.12/min) daily, 8am-midnight. The **VGF** (Verkehrsgesellschaft Frankfurt am Main) manages the local public transportation of the city of Frankfurt: ☎ 1 94 49 Mon-Thu 8am-5pm, Fri 8am-1pm. Information is at the traffic island of the Hauptwache, Mon-Fri 9am-8pm, Sat 9am-4pm; the Konstablerwache, Passage B level and underground (U-Bahn) and S-Bahn stations. The tariff rate 3 is for all rides inside Frankfurt. Normal fare is ☜ €2.10, between 9am-4pm €1.60, day ticket €4.90 (valid until the last ride of the day, and valid for travel to the airport). Tickets are available at vending machines or from the bus drivers. Tickets are not available in the U-Bahn, S-Bahn or tramcars.

Internet www.rmv.de; www.vgf-ffm.de

The **Frankfurt Card** costs ☜ €8 (valid for one day) and €12 (valid for two days) and can be used for the RMV network within city limits including the airport. It also gives a 50% discount to 15 museums and other attractions, such as the zoo and the airport terraces, and 25-30% off selected boat and coach rides. The Frankfurt Card is available at many travel agencies, at tourist information offices and in both airport terminals.

Ebbelwei-Express

Lechthaler/Tourism + Congress GmbH Frankfurt a. M.

Tip: For S-Bahn rides to the airport you need a ticket at tariff rate 4.

WHERE TO EAT

Bauer – *Sandweg 113.* ☎ *(069) 40 59 27 44. www.gebrueder-bauer.de.* ⏱ *Closed Sat and Sun lunchtime.* This fashionable establishment, in a residential quarter near the city centre, attracts people of all ages. The Bauer brothers serve varied dishes in a bistro-style setting.

Steinernes Haus – *Braubach-straße 35.* 🚋 *4+5.* ☎ *(069) 28 34 91. www.steinernes-haus.de.* ⏱ *Open 11am-11pm. Reservation necessary.* This pleasant, rustice establishment is some 500 years old, one of the oldest in Frankfurt. It is surrounded by art galleries. Typical Frankfurt cuisine and specialities grilled on lava stone can be sampled here.

Toan – *Friedberger Anlage 14.* ☎ *(069) 44 98 44.* Excellent Vietnamese restaurant in the Nordend district (next to the zoo), with a garden terrace.

Meyer's Restaurant – *Große Bockenheimer Straße 54.* ☎ *(069) 91 39 70 70 www.meyer-frankfurt.de.* ⏱ *Closed 1-5 Jan and Sun.* A little bistro-restaurant on the edge of the pedestrian zone near the old opera house. You can observe the kitchen at the back of the restaurant; dishes served here have a maritime flavour.

Restaurant-Café Zum Schwarzen Stern – *Römerberg 6.* ☎ *(069) 29 19 79. www.schwarzerstern. de.* ♿ *Reservation recommended.* Goethe once wrote that one could study the most varied styles of building in Frankfurt just by looking at this half-timbered house. This remains true today, since the restaurant was rebuilt after the war to resemble the original establishment. Pleasant, rustic decor.

Ernos Bistro – *Liebig-straße 15.* ☎ *(069) 72 19 97. www. ernosbistro.de.* ⏱ *Closed 20 Dec-4 Jan, 26 Jul-17 Aug, Sat-Sun (except fair days).* A friendly, bistro-style establishment in a villa in the bank district. High-quality French cuisine.

Tiger-Restaurant – *Heilig-kreuzgasse 20.* ☎ *(069) 92 00 22 0. www. tigerpalast.com.* ⏱ *Closed 14 Jul-26 Aug, Sun and Mon.* This restaurant, with walls covered in photographs of performers, offers creative cuisine which appeals to more than just the theatre crowd who gather after the show. The brick vaulting contributes to the atmosphere.

WHERE TO STAY

A Casa Bed&Breakfast – *Var-rentrappstraße 49.* Ⓢ *Messe.* ☎ *(069) 97 98 88 21. Fax (069) 97988822. www. hotel-acasa.de.* ⏱ *Closed end of Dec to beginning of Jan.* 🅿 ♿ *6 rooms.* A small English-style bed & breakfast set in an old villa. The charming rooms, each one personalised and tastefully decorated, have each been given a name, adding to the family atmosphere of the establishment.

Hotel-Pension Gölz – *Beethoven-straße 44 (south of Palmengarten, northwest of the central station).* ☎ *(069) 74 67 35. Fax (069) 746142. www. hotel-goelz.de.* ⏱ *Closed Dec.* 🅿 ☕ A stone's throw from the city centre and exhibition centre, this family-run hotel in a 19C villa has spacious double rooms and basic single rooms.

Hotel Wiesbaden– *Basler Straße 52* ☎ *(069) 36 50 75 80 Fax (069) 252845. 39 rooms.* ☕ A small, simple, clean and comfortable hotel next to the station. Rooms are well-kept and inexpensive.

Kolping Hotel Frankfurt – *Lange Straße 26* Ⓢ *Ostendstraße.* ☎ *(069) 29 90 60. Fax (069) 29906100. www.kolping-hotel-frankfurt.de.* 🅿 ✕ ♿ *41 rooms* ☕ ☕ *Restaurant* This simple, functional hotel is in the heart of the city centre, near the Allerheiligentor and under the same roof as the Kolping training institute and youth hostel. The exhibition centre, airport and central station are within easy reach by S-Bahn.

Hotel Hamburger Hof – *Poststraße 10.* ☎ *(069) 27 13 96 90. Fax (069) 235802 www.hamburgerhof. com.* ✕ *66 room.s* ☕ An inexpensive, comfortable hotel near the station.

Hilton – *Hochstraße 4.* ☎ *(069) 133 80 00. Fax (069) 133820. sales.frankfurt@hilton.com.* ⚑ ✕

342 rooms. ⚏ ⚌⚏Restaurant. Access to this modern hotel is via a spartan, atrium-style lobby. Transparent lifts lead to the rooms with all the modern conveniences. The city's old swimming pool has been tastefully incorporated into the establishment.

⚏⚏⚌⚏ **Liebig-Hotel**– Liebig-straße 45. ☎ (069) 241829 90. Fax (069) 24182991. www.hotelliebig. de. 🕐 Closed 22 Dec-2 Jan ⚎ 20 rooms. ⚏ Small hotel in a villa in the bank district with charming and luxurious rooms: Italian- and English-style furniture and beautiful fabrics.

⚏⚏⚌⚏ **Steigenberger Frankfurter Hof** – Bethmannstraße 33. ☎ (069) 215 02. Fax (069) 215900. www.frank-furter-hof.steigenberger.de. ⚎ ♿ 332 rooms. ⚏ This grand 19C hotel, traditional residence of the Steigenbergs, is truly magnificent. The Weißfrauenflügel wing has been superbly renovated. Luxury reigns throughout, from the elegant lobby to the rooms.

TAKING A BREAK

Useful Tips – Große Bockenheimer Straße (the Fressgass or "eatery alley") is a good place grab a quick bite to eat. It offers a wide selection of restaurants.

Kleinmarkthalle – Hasengasse 5-7. www.kleinmarkthalle.de. 🕐 Mon-Fri 7:30am-6pm, Sat 7:30am-3pm. It's hard to resist all the regional and international specialities on offer in the stalls of this covered market.

Sandwicher Fastgoodfood – Katharinenpforte 6 (north from the crossroads between Kleiner Hirschgraben and Bleidenstraße) ☎ (069) 71 03 40 67 www.sandwicher.de. 🕐 Mon-Fri 10am-11pm, Sat 10am-8pm. Here you can choose your own bread and sandwich filling. Ready-made sandwiches also available, to eat in or take out. This fast-food chain also has outlets at Reuterweg 63 and Westendstraße 27.

Wacker's Kaffee – Kornmarkt 9 (south of the crossroads between Kleiner Hirschgraben and Bleidenstraße). ☎ (069) 28 78 10. www.wackers-kaffee.de. 🕐 Mon-Fri 8am-7pm, Sat 8am-6pm. Over 30 roasted coffees and 60 teas are available at this establishment. Small

Krüger/Tourism + Congress GmbH Frankfurt a. M.

snacks also served. From Oct, almond "Frankfurter Bethmännchen" are available.

Zarges – Kalbächer Gasse 10. ☎ (069) 29 90 30. 🕐 8:30am-11pm (until 8pm in winter). Delicatessen where you can choose your own sandwich filling. The upstairs restaurant has a reasonably-priced "Fast Lunch" menu (11am-6pm) with 4 or 5 different dishes every day.

GOING OUT

USEFUL TIPS

One of the most lively quarters is Alt-Sachsenhausen on the south bank of the Main. Around "Große Rittergasse" (south of Deutschherrnufer), are many traditional restaurants serving the famous Äppelwoi (dry cider), and a great variety of bars.

Café Hauptwache – An der Haupt-wache 15. ☎ (069) 21 99 86 27. 🕐 Mon-Sat 10am-1am (food until 11pm). Frankfurt's main 18C guardhouse was entirely renovated after the Second World War. Since 1905 it has housed a café with a modern look; it also has a lovely terrace.

Harry's New-York Bar – Walther-von-Cronberg-Platz 1 (in the Main Plaza hotel) ☎ (069) 66 40 10 www.main-plaza.com 🕐 5pm-3am. This classic, quiet bar follows the tradition of Harry MacElhone, who, in 1911, inaugurated Europe's first cocktail bar in Paris. Piano music, summer terrace.

Jazzkeller – Kleine Bockenheimer Strasse 18a. ☎ (069) 28 85 37. www.jazzkeller. com. 🕐 Wed and Thu from 9pm, Fri and Sat from 10pm, Sun from 8pm – concerts from ⚏ €10; discotheque €5. A German institution. Since 1952, the greatest jazz legends, like Louis Armstrong and Frank Sinatra, have appeared here. Newcomers also perform.

SHOPPING

USEFUL TIPS

Frankfurt's **main shopping street** (department stores) is the Zeil, includ-

ing the passage called Les Facettes. This is near the exclusive shops in the Große Bockenheimer Strasse and Goethestraße. In Sachsenhausen interesting shopping is at Schweizer Straße; in Bockenheim at Leipziger Straße.

Antique dealers have settled in the Pfarrgasse in the vicinity of the cathedral.

commercial capital; the EU's decision to base the European Central Bank here confirmed its financial standing.

City Life – Despite its cosmopolitan character, this "metropolis on the Main" has preserved a typical Hessian atmosphere. It is around the **Hauptwache**, a square dating from 1729, that Frankfurt is busiest. The Zeil is said to be the most shopped street in Germany. To the north, the quarter known as the Westend fights to stave off encroaching office blocks of the commercial centre. Cafés, cabarets, bars, and restaurants, often exotic, are grouped around the central station, while the taverns of the Alt Sachsenhausen quarter, on the south bank of the Main, specialise in the celebrated **Äppelwoi** or **Ebbelwei** (slightly bitter cider), and *Handkäse mit Musik* (a small yellow cheese with onions and vinegar sauce).

A General View – The old town, almost entirely destroyed in 1943-44, lay within a green belt on the site of former fortifications razed in 1805. The Eschenheimer Turm (1428) still stands as a well-preserved example of the medieval defence system. Frankfurt's skyline is most striking when seen from the southern end of the bridge **Untermainbrücke**, contrasting historic buildings like the cathedral, the Römer, the Leonhardskirche and an Imperial Palace with the imposing skyscrapers of the Fair Tower, the Deutsche Bank and the Dresdener Bank.

Walking Tour

Old Town

Römer and Römerberg

The Römer is a collection of three medieval burghers' houses, reconstructed in the 1980s. The name derives from the **Haus zum Römer**, the oldest and the most richly decorated. From 1405 the block served as town hall, and later as the banquet hall for the election and coronation of the emperors. In the 19C, to celebrate the 1 000-year history of the Holy Roman Empire, 52 statues of emperors, from Charlemagne to Franz II (1806) were installed in niches hollowed from the walls of the Imperial Hall (*Kaisersaal*). ♿ 🕐 *Open 10am-1pm, 2pm-5pm.* 🕐 *Closed when being used by the Mayor.* 🎫 *€2.* ☎ *(069) 21 23 88 00.*

The **Römerberg** is ringed by several historic buildings: the 13C **Alte**

Election of the Emperors

In the Holy Roman Empire, the emperor was elected; hence the crown passed between Franconians (Salian dynasty), Saxons (Ottonians), Bavarians and Swabians (the Hohenstaufens). However, the emperors granted privileges to dukes, counts and high prelates in order to keep the title in their family. In 1356, the Golden Bull limited the number of Electors to seven, three from the clergy (the Archbishops of Mainz, Cologne and Trier) and four laymen (Duke of Saxony, Margrave of Brandenburg, Count Palatine, King of Bohemia).

Nikolaikirche; the half-timbered **Haus Wertheim;** the 1464 Italianate **Steinernes Haus**; and a row of half-timbered 15C-18C houses (all reconstructed). In the centre of the square is the **Gerechtigkeitsbrunnen** (Fountain of Justice, 1543). The restored sector of old Frankfurt is right next to the post-modern **Kunsthalle Schirn,** a stark edifice housing contemporary artworks.

Bartholomäuskirche★ (Dom)

This church was designated a cathedral after it was chosen as the election and then the coronation site of the emperors (1356 and 1562).

A Gothic hall-church, it was built between the 13C and the 15C on a hill previously occupied by a Carolingian edifice. Its outstanding feature is the tall **west tower**★★ *(Westturm)*, ornamented with a gabled polygonal crown and lantern.

Inside are several artworks worth noting: the 16C sandstone **Crucifixion** by Mainz artist Hans Backoffen; the 14C finely worked **choir stalls**★ crafted in the Upper Rhine; and **mural paintings** from 1427 of the Cologne School illustrating the legend of St Bartholomew. The Election Chapel *(Wahlkapelle,* early 15C) is where the seven Electors chose the Holy Roman Emperor.

In the north chancel is the **Altar of Mary Sleeping** *(Maria-Schlaf),* from 1434. Sole remaining altar from the original church, this too is the work of the Cologne School. The large **Descent from the Cross** on the west wall was painted by Anthony van Dyck in 1627.

Dommuseum★ (Cathedral Museum)

   Open daily except Mon, 10am-5pm, Sat-Sun 11am-5pm.   *Closed 1 Jan, 24, 25 and 31 Dec.*   *€2.*   *(069) 13 37 61 86. www.dommuseum-frankfurt.de.*

This small museum is installed in the remains of the Gothic cloister. Besides the cathedral treasure *(Domschatz),* preserving precious gold works and vestments from the high Middle Ages, the Late Merovingian tomb of a young girl merits special attention. West of the cathedral is an **Archaeological Garden** *(Historischer Garten),* with remains of Roman, Carolingian and Baroque fortifications.

Museum für Moderne Kunst★ (Modern Art Museum)

   Open daily except Mon, 10am-5pm, Wed 10am-8pm.   *€6, free admission the last Sat of each month.*   *(069) 21 23 04 47. www.mmk-frankfurt.de.*

The Viennese architect, Hans Hollein, designed this imaginative space for a mainly contemporary art collection. Artists of the New York School (Claes Oldenburg, Andy Warhol) are represented, as are German contemporary artists (Joseph Beuys, Mario Merz, Katharina Fritsch, and Gerhard Richter). There is also a photography collection. Every six months, six to eight of the museum's galleries are rehung, giving the collection the impression of perpetual motion.

Leonhardskirche

The outer aspect of this 15C Gothic church denies its Romanesque basilican origins. Two octagonal towers remain at the east end, along with the fine carvings of **Master Engelbert's Doorway**. The central nave is surrounded on three sides by a gallery. Fine stained-glass windows illuminate the chancel. Left of the chancel are a superbly carved reredos representing scenes from the life of the Virgin, and a painting by Holbein the Elder depicting the Last Supper. The baptismal chapel is in the north aisle.

Paulskirche

It was in this circular building that the German National Assembly, elected after the revolution of March, sat from 1848 to 1849. The church houses an exhibition devoted to the history of the German democratic movement.

FRANKFURT

Allerheiligenstr.	HY	3	Friedensstr.	GZ	24	Münzgasse	GZ	40
An der Hauptwache	GHY		Goethestr.	G		Rechneigrabenstr.	HZ	50
Bethmannstr.	GZ	7	Gr. Bockenheimer Str.	GY	27	Roßmarkt	GY	
Bleidenstr.	HY	9	Große Friedbergerstr.	HY	29	Schillerstr.	GY	54
Bockenheimer Landstr.	GY	10	Großer Hirschgraben	GZ	30	Stoltzestr.	HY	58
Domstr.	HZ	13	Kaiserstr.	GZ		Taunusstr.	GZ	62
Elisabethenstr.	GZ	16	Kalbächer Gasse	GY	32	Untermainanlage	GZ	65
Friedberger Anlage	HY	20	Kleiner Hirschgraben	GY	35	Weißfrauenstr.	GZ	68
Friedberger Landstr.	HY	22	Limpurgergasse	HZ	36	Weserstr.	GZ	69
			Münchener Str.	GZ		Zeil	HY	

Alte Nikolaikirche	HZ	A	Jüdisches Museum	GZ	M³	Museum für Völkerkunde	GZ	M⁸
Deutsches Architektur-			Kunsthalle Schim	HZ	M¹²	Naturmuseum		
Museum	GZ	M⁶	Liebfrauenkirche	HY	E	Senckenberg	GY	M⁹
Deutsches Filmmuseum	GZ	M⁷	Museum für Moderne			Römer und Römerberg	HZ	R
Goethe-Museum	GZ	M²	Kunst	HY	M¹⁰	Städtische Galerie		
Haus Wertheim	HZ	B	Museum für Post und			Liebieghaus	GZ	M⁴
Historisches Museum	HZ	M¹	Kommunikation	GZ	M⁵	Steinernes Haus	HZ	C

FRANKFURT
AM MAIN
0   300 m

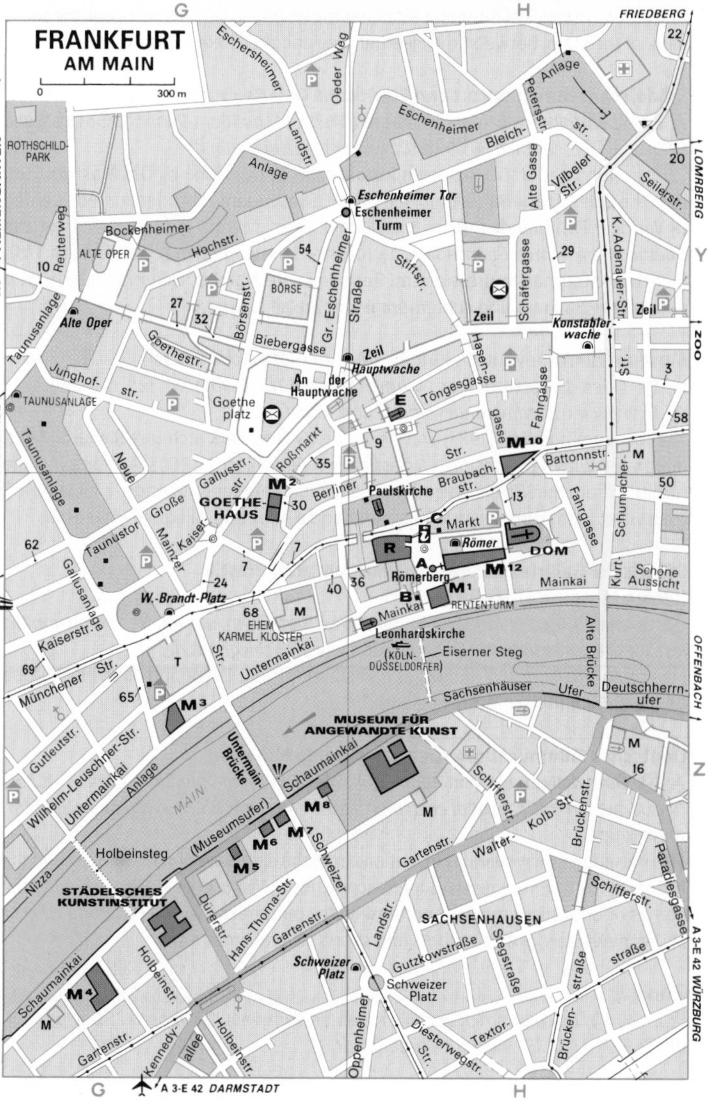

Goethe-Haus★ and Goethe-Museum

🕐 *Open daily 10am-6pm (5.30pm Sun).* 🕐 *Closed 1st Jan, 24, 25 and 31 Dec.* 🔗 *€5.*
☎ *(069) 13 88 00; www.goethehaus-frankfurt.de*

The German master writer Goethe lived at this home, reconstructed after 1945; the room in which he wrote is as it was in his lifetime; even a silhouette of Charlotte Buff, the object of his youthful passion, hangs there. A separate exhibition examines the lives of the Goethe family in 18C Frankfurt and has documents pertaining to Goethe's early work.

The **Museum** adjoining Goethe's birthplace has been arranged as a painting gallery of his era. The works include paintings by, among others, Tischbein, Graff, Hackert, Fuseli and Friedrich.

Sights

Museumsufer

An impressive series of museums stretches the length of the Schaumainkai, the south bank of the Main, between the Eiserner Steg and the Friedensbrücke.

Städelsches Kunstinstitut and Städtische Galerie★★

♿ 🕐 *Open daily except Mon, 10am-6pm, Wed and Thu 10am-9pm.* 🕐 *Closed 24 and 31 Dec.* 🔗 *€8.* ☎ *(069) 605 09 82 00 www.staedelmuseum.de*

This stronghold of art houses an important collection of works by **Old Masters** (Holbein the Elder, Grünewald, Altdorfer, Dürer). Subsequent centuries are represented by Vermeer, Rembrandt, Rubens and Tiepolo. German works include the memorable *Goethe in the Roman Countryside*, by Johann Heinrich Wilhelm Tischbein in 1787. French and German Impressionism, German Expressionism, Fauvism, Cubism, Surrealism, the Bauhaus and contemporary art are all featured.

Museum für Angewandte Kunst★ (Museum of Applied Arts)

♿ 🕐 *Open daily except Mon, 10am-5pm, Wed 10am-9pm.* 🔗 *€5.* ☎ *(069) 21 23 40 37; www.museumfuerangewandtekunst.frankfurt.de*

The museum building (1985) was designed by New York architect Richard Meier; integrated within the design is a classically styled villa from 1803. Artifacts include furniture from the Middle Ages, Renaissance, Baroque; and Jugendstil; 15C and 16C glassware; Islamic porcelain and carpets; and a book and calligraphy section.

Städtische Galerie Liebieghaus/Museum alter Plastik (Liebig Museum of Sculpture)

🕐 *Open daily except Mon, 10am-5pm, Wed 10am-8pm.* 🔗 *€4, free admission the last Sat of each month.* ☎ *(069) 21 23 86 15. www.liebieghaus.de.*

Fine sculpture from civilisations as diverse as Ancient Egypt and Medieval Europe fill the halls of this sculpture museum.

Deutsches Filmmuseum★ (German Cinema Museum)

♿ 🕐 *Open daily except Mon, 10am-5pm, Wed, Sun 10am-7pm, Sat 2-7pm.* 🔗 *€2.50, free admission the last Sat of each month.* ☎ *(069) 21 23 88 30. www.deutschesfilm-museum.de.*

This museum displays various inventions from the early days of photography and the history of the cinema (Edison's Kineto-scope, 1899). Visitors get a glimpse behind the scenes of both silent movies and those with soundtracks. A small working cinema shows newsreels, publicity shots and shorts several times a day.

Zoo★★

Kids ♿ 🕐 *Open summer: 9am-7pm; winter: 9am-5pm.* 🕐 *Closed 25 Dec.* 🔗 *€8.*
☎ *(069) 21 23 37 35. www.zoo-frankfurt.de.*

The Frankfurt zoo is famous for its rare species, encouraged, successfully, to repro-duce. The bird section, with its huge free-flight aviary, is particularly colourful. Penguins, reptiles, fish and insects inhabit the Exotarium. In the **Grzimek-Haus**, darkened by day, nocturnal animals such as the desert fox can be observed.

Naturmuseum Senckenberg★
(Senckenberg Natural History Museum)

[Kids]   *Leave by the Bockenheimer Landstraße.* ○ *Open 9am-5pm, Wed 9am-8pm, Sat-Sun 9am-6pm.* ⊜ *€6.* ☎ *(069) 754 20. www.senckenberg.de.*

Opened in 1821, this museum's **Department of Palaeontology**★★ *(ground floor)* is highly respected. Fossils from the Lower Jurassic are on display in the entrance hall, most discovered near Holzmaden, in Württemberg. In the **Hall of Dinosaurs**, the skeletons of huge beasts from the Secondary Era are on view.

There is a display of objects found in **Jurassic digs**, most of them near Solnhofen, on the banks of the Altmühl. The evolution of man is traced with the aid of numerous artifacts. An interesting collection of stuffed animals and slide shows complete this visit of Germany's largest natural history museum.

Palmengarten★ (Tropical Gardens)

Leave by the Bockenheimer Landstraße. ♿ ○ *Open Mar-Oct: 9am-6pm; Nov-Jan: 9am-4pm.* ⊜ *€5.* ☎ *(069) 21 23 66 89. www.palmengarten-frankfurt.de.*

These botanical gardens include a large number of greenhouses with tropical plants, palms, Alpine plants and also exotica. The 19C Palm House is the oldest botanical building in Europe.

Excursions

Offenbach

Town plan in the current edition of The Michelin Guide Deutschland. 7km/5mi east. Leave on the Deutschherrn-Ufer.

This town on the south bank of the Main is the centre of the German leather industry (International Leather Fair twice a year).

Deutsches Ledermuseum/Deutsches Schuhmuseum★★
(Leather and Shoe Museum)

Frankfurter Strasse 86. ♿ ○ *Open daily, 10am-5pm, Sat 10am-10pm.* ○ *Closed 1st Jan, 24, 25 and 31 Dec.* ⊜ *€4.* ☎ *(069) 829 79 80. www.ledermuseum.de.*

The Leather Museum contains some interesting collections of articles made from leather, especially vellum and hides, and the display covers the use of leather in various domains such as sport, travel and leisure.

The **Shoe Museum** in the same building presents a history of foot fashion in all its variety, from Ancient Egyptian and Roman sandals to modern footwear. The section on shoes as works of art is particularly interesting.

Friedberg★

28km/17mi north on the Friedberger Landstraße.

This is an attractive example of a medieval community with two distinct centres: the town enclosed within the Imperial castle and the bourgeois town grouped at the foot of the church, at either end of the main street *(Kaiserstraße)*.

The castle *(Stauferburg)* erected by Frederick Barbarossa in 1180 together with its outbuildings still has the air of a small, self-sufficient town. The ramparts, now a prom-enade, have been made even more attractive with bays of greenery and look-out points. **Adolf's Tower**★ *(Adolphsturm*, 1347) overlooks the assembled buildings.

The **Jewish Baths**★ *(Judenbad*, 13C) at Judengasse 20 in the bourgeois sector, con-sist of a deep, square well with a dome, which served originally for ritual ablutions required by Jewish law. The **church** *(Stadtkirche)* is a 13C-14C building with a typically

Hessian exterior: transverse attics with separate gables jutting from the roof above the aisles. Inside, an unusually tall **ciborium**★ (1482) stands in the chancel. On the left of the rood screen is the **Friedberg Madonna** (c 1280).

FREIBURG IM BREISGAU★★

POPULATION: 215 000

Set among the hills of the Black Forest, Freiburg is one of the most attractive cities in southern Germany, with its five-hundred year-old university and the little streets of its old town. Fortunately, successive wars have left intact the beautiful cathedral and historic sites. ℹ *Rotteckring 14, 79098 Freiburg, ☎ (0761) 388 18 80; www.freiburg.de*

▶ **Orient Yourself:** Mid-way between Basel and Strasbourg, on the Rhine plain, Freiburg is on the A 5 which leads to Karlsruhe *(130km/81mi north)*.
🅿 **Parking:** Garages are located throughout the city, including near the Old Town.
◉ **Don't Miss:** The Münster and the Augustinermuseum
🕐 **Organizing Your Time:** Allow at least two hours to appreciate the cathedral.
Kids **Especially for Kids:** Cable-car rides up the Schlossberg
🔆 **Also See:** *BADENWEILER (36km/22mi southwest), Bad SÄCKINGEN (71km/44mi southeast), SCHWARZWALD (tour leaves from Freiburg).*

A Bit of History

Freiburg was founded in the 12C by the dukes of Zähringen who conferred upon it a number of special privileges; this is the origin of its name, literally "free town". From 1368 to 1798 the city was under Habsburg rule. In the second half of the 19C, Freiburg won renewed importance as a place of research and learning thanks to its university.

Sights

Münster★★
Brochure in English available at the entrance.
All that remains of the original Roman-esque building, on which work began ca 1200, is the transept crossing and the two "Cockerel Towers" flanking it. In 1354, work started on a new chancel, but the grandeur of the design and the severity of the times were such that this huge addition was not finished until 1513.
The cathedral's **north side** features an interesting 14C tympanum over the door illustrating the theme of Original Sin. The **West Tower**★★★ is surmounted by a delicate spire of stone. Four sharply jutting projections form a star at the foot of the tower house, the Sterngalerie. On

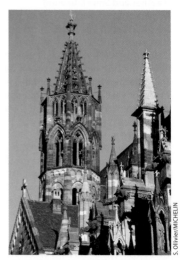

The cathedral tower and the finely worked masonry of its spire.

S. Ollivier/MICHELIN

the **south side,** statues of the Apostles and the Old Testament kings stand on the buttresses of this richly ornate façade.

Inside, the cathedral's **west porch and doorway** feature late-13C figures. On the left wall, Satan, disguised as "the Prince of this world", leads a procession. The doorway itself, flanked by statues representing the Church (left) and the Synagogue (with eyes covered, right) is entirely occupied by the mystery of the Redemption.

The **Nave** is embellished with graceful galleries and furnished with a variety of statuary: **(1)** the Virgin at the pillar (1270-80); **(2)** a Late Gothic pulpit (1560); **(3)** a statue of Berthold V, last of the dukes of Zähringen who founded the town; **(4)** the Holy Sepulchre, from c 1330; **(5)** 13C stained-glass medallions in the windows; and **(6)** a 1505 group sculpture, the Adoration of the Magi.

The **Chancel** includes many of its own works of note, including **(a)** a Rococo baptismal font and **(b)** a 1521 Oberried altarpiece in the Universität Chapel. The two side panels, the *Nativity* and *Adoration of the Magi*, are by Hans Holbein the Younger. Also worthy of note are **(c)** in the Second Kaiser Chapel; an altarpiece depicting *Rest during the Flight to Egypt* by Hans Wydyz on the central panel; **(d)** painting of the Crucifixion, reverse of the large Buldung Grien altarpiece; **(e)** the Romanesque Locherer Crucifix in beaten silver by Böcklin; and **(f)** an altarpiece in the Locherer Chapel by Sixt von Staufen (1521-24). The carved portion depicts the Virgin with her sheltering cloak.

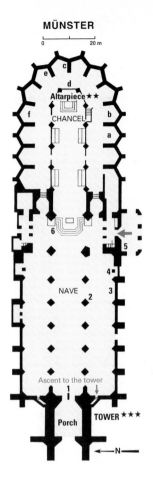

MÜNSTER

The **altarpiece**★★ *(Hochaltar)* by **Hans Baldung Grien** (1512-16) portrays the Coronation of the Virgin on the central panel. ♿ 🕐 *Open Apr to Oct, Tue-Sun, 10am-noon, 2.30-5pm; Sat 10am-noon only.* ⊜ €1. ☎ (0761) 20 27 90.

Ascend the West Tower *(Turmbesteigung)* along the stairway leading to the tower room. The upper platform beneath the beautiful spire offers **views**★ over the city, with the Kaiserstuhl and the Vosges visible in the distance. *Outside southern wall.*
🕐 *Open Apr to Oct, 9.30am-5pm, Sun, 1-5pm; Nov-Mar, Tue-Sun, 9.30am-5pm, Sun, 1-5pm.* ☎(0761) 290 74 47.

Münsterplatz

Facing the cathedral's south front on this square are buildings designed with municipal or ecclesiastical prestige in mind. They include the: **Archbishop's Palace** *(Erzbischöfliches Palais)* from 1756; the **Historical House of Trade**★ *(Historisches Kaufhaus),* centre of commercial life in the Middle Ages; and the **Wentzingerhaus,** built in 1761 by the famous local painter and sculptor Johann Christian Wentzinger as his own residence; it now houses the Museum of Local History *(Museum für Stadtgeschichte). Ticket includes entrance to the Augustinermuseum.* 🕐 *Open Tue-Sun, 10am-5pm.*
🕐 *Closed 24 and 31 Dec.* ⊜ €2. ☎ (0761) 201 25 15. www.museen.freiburg.de.

FREIBURG		Gerberau	Z	Salzstr.	YZ	38
		Grieffeneggring	Z 19	Schiffstr.	Y	40
Auf der Zinnen	Y 2	Habsburgerstr.	Y 20	Schuster	Z	43
Augustinerpl.	Z 3	Herrenstr.	YZ 24	Schwabentorpl.	Z	45
Bertoldstr.	Y	Holzmarkt	Z 26	Schwabentorrig	Z	47
Eisenbahnstr.	Y 7	Kaiser-Joseph-Str.	YZ	Schwarzwaldstr.	Z	49
Eisenstr.	Y 9	Münsterstr.	Y 30	Turmstr.	Y	5
Europapl.	Y 1	Oberlinden	Z 31	Universitätsstr.	Y	55
Fahnenbergpl.	Y 13	Platz der Alten Synagoge	Y 32	Unterlinden	Y	57
Franziskanerstr.	Y 14	Rathausgasse	Y 33	Werthmannpl.	Z	59
Friedrichring	Y 16					

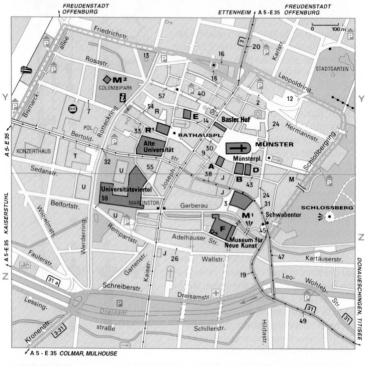

Adelhauser Neukloster	Z F	Erzbischöfliches Palais	Y A	Neues Rathaus	Y R¹
Augustinermuseum	Z M¹	Haus zum Walfisch	Y E	Wentzingerhaus	Y D
Colombischlöße	Y M²	Historisches Kaufhaus	Y B		

Rathausplatz★

The town hall square is a pleasant sight, with flowered balconies and a fountain featuring Berthold Schwarz, said to have invented gunpowder in Freiburg in 1350.

Augustinermuseum★★

🕐 *Open Tue-Sun, 10am-5pm.* 🕐 *Closed 24 and 31 Dec* ☏ *(0761) 201 25 31. www. museen.freiburg.de.*

The most interesting part of this museum is the **Medieval Religious Art Section**★★ *(Mittelalterliche Sakralkunst)*, housed in the church of an old Augustinian monastery and adjacent ground-floor galleries. Among the special treasures are the altarpiece panel (once at Aschaffenburg) depicting the miracle of the Virgin Mary and the Snow, painted in 1519 by Matthias Grünewald, and works by Lucas Cranach the Elder and Hans Baldung Grien.

Address Book

WHERE TO EAT

🍴 **Hausbrauerei Feierling** – *Gerberau 46.* ☎ *(0761) 24 34 80. www.feierling. de.* 🕐 *11am-midnight (-1am, Sat); Biergarten open 11am-11pm.* 🚭 Since 1989, this micro-brewery has produced its own organic beers. Check out the copper stills from the gallery. Regional cuisine is served here and in the biergarten, on the other side of the road.

🍴🍴🍴 **Schlossbergrestaurant Dattler** – *Am Schlossberg 1 (follow Wintererstraße or take the Schlossberg cable-car) 79104 Freiburg im Breisgau.* ☎ *(0761) 317 29. www.dattler.de.* 🕐 *Closed Tue.* This popular eatery is worth a visit if only for the altitude of its location. The view over the roofs of Freiburg is magnificent!

WHERE TO STAY

🏨🏨🏨 **Hotel Oberkirchs Weinstuben** – *Münsterplatz 22.* ☎ *(0761) 202 68 68. Fax (0761) 2026869. www. hotel-oberkirch.de* 🕐 *Closed Jan. 26 rooms.* 🛏 🏨🏨🏨 *Restaurant.* This establishment is in a 1738 house and a hotel; the rooms are furnished in a rustic-style. There is a good view of the cathedral from some rooms of the main building. The restaurant, furnished in dark wood, is particularly warm and welcoming.

🏨🏨🏨🏨 **Hotel Zum Roten Bären** – *Oberlinden 12* ☎ *(0761) 38 78 70 Fax (0761) 3878717 www.roter-baeren.de 25 rooms.* 🛏 🏨🏨🏨 *Restaurant.* This

is one of the oldest hotels in town (don't worry – it's been modernized) and is located in the heart of a lively district. For centuries, guests have enjoyed Swiss-influenced cusine in the restaurant.

TAKING A BREAK

Markthalle – *Kaiser-Joseph-Str. 233 (via Grünwälderstr. and Fressgässle).* ☎ *(0761) 38 70 00. www.freiburger-markthalle.de.* 🕐 *Mon-Fri 7am-7pm, Sat 7am-4pm.* A multitude of market stalls offer a range of international flavours – Afghan, Chinese, Portuguese and others. Take out or eat in. Fresh fruit, vegetables and fish are available.

GOING OUT

Kagan – *Bismarckallee 9 (in the building beside the central station; take the lift).* ☎ *(0761) 7 67 27 66. www.kagan-lounge.de.* 🕐 *Café: 10am-1am; club: Thur-Sat, 10-5am, Wed, 9pm-3am.* From the café-bar on the 17th floor is an exceptional panorama of the town. The club was designed by German-American designer Valdimir Kagan. Large choice of drinks and snacks available (Fri is sushi day). The club on the 18th floor has salsa evenings on Sun from 9pm.

UC-Café – *Niemensstr. 7 (between Bertoldstr. and Kaiser-Joseph-Str.).* ☎ *(0761) 38 33 55. uc-cafe@t-online.de.* 🕐 *8-1am, Sun from 10am.* 🕐 *Closed 1 Jan.* A maple shades the terrace of this popular café in Freiburg's pedestrian zone, where visitors stop for coffee and snacks.

Schlossberg★

Kids On this last foothill of the Black Forest, woods have taken over Zähringen Castle. The climb, either in the cable-car *(from Stadtgarten cable-car station)* or on foot *(pathway starts from the Schwabentor)*, offers panoramic views from the summit *(20min on foot from the cablecar station).* Cable-car: summer, 11am-7pm; winter: Wed-Sun, 11.30am-5pm. 🎫 €3.60 return trip. ☎ (0761) 398 55.

Excursions

The Kaiserstuhl★

Round tour of 73km/45mi – allow 3hr. Leave Freiburg on Lessingstraße and go to Breisach via Gottenheim.

A small volcanic massif rising in the Baden plain, the Kaiserstuhl (the Emperor's Throne: 538m/1 765ft) enjoys on its lower slopes a warm, dry climate particularly suitable for orchards and vineyards. The wines of Achkarren, Ihringen, Bickensohl and Oberrotweil are considered among the finest in the region. The tour goes past charming wine-growing villages such as **Endingen**★, with its fine old market square, and **Burkheim**★, in its picturesque site on the south-west slope of the Kaiserstuhl

Upper Black Forest★★★ ( See SCHWARZWALD)

FÜSSEN★

POPULATION: 14 400

The old town of Füssen, dominated by its castles, is surrounded by the remains of its fortified wall and watchtowers. The town attracts a lively number of tourists: it is on the Romantische Strasse and near the castles of Neuschwanstein and Hohenschwangau. ▪ Kaiser-Maximilian-Platz 1. 87629 Füssen, ☎ (083 62) 938 50.

▸ **Orient Yourself:** Located in the Königswinkel ("royal corner"), near the Austrian border, Füssen is surrounded by lakes (Forggensee, Hopfensee, Weißensee) and has beautiful views over the Tyrol peaks.

⊘ **Don't Miss:** Quiet strolls in a picturesque alpine setting.

◔ **Organizing Your Time:** Allow a full day for exploring Füssen's outdoor attractions.

Kids **Especially for Kids:** Viewing the Lechfall, swimming in the Forggensee.

⌖ **Also See:** Schloss NEUSCHWANSTEIN (4km/1mi east), Deutsche ALPENSTRASSE, ROMANTISCHE STRASSE, WIESKIRCHE (25km/16mi north).

Address Book

WHERE TO EAT

⊖⊖ **Zum Schwanen** – Brotmarkt 4. ◔ Closed Mon, from Nov to mid-Dec, Sun and Mon from Jan to Apr. ☎ (08362) 61 74. ⊱⊰ This well-run hotel is in the old town. The welcoming hosts serve specialities from the Allgäu in a simple environment with a slighty rustic feel.

WHERE TO STAY

⊖⊖ **Hotel Eiskristall** – Birkstraße 3. ☎ (08362) 50 78 12. Fax (08362) 507810. www.hotel-eiskristall.de. ▣ Reservations recommended. 32 rooms. ▭ ⊖⊖ Restaurant. Travellers will find this plain and well-maintained establishment on the outskirts of Füssen, next to the skating rink. Functional guestrooms feature light-coloured wood. The town centre is easily accessible on foot.

⊖⊖ **Hotel Geiger** – Uferstraße 18, 87629 Füssen-Hopfen am See. ☎ (08362) 70 74. Fax (08362) 38838. www.hotel-geiger.de. ◔ Closed Nov to mid-Dec. ▣ 24 rooms. ▭ ⊖⊖ Restaurant. This hotel has been in the same family for many years. It is on the lakeside promenade, an ideal place for exploring the idyllic Hopfensee. The country-style restaurant has a winter garden and beautiful views over the lake.

⊖⊖⊖ **Hotel Sonne** – Reichenstraße 37. ☎ (08362) 90 80. Fax (08362) 908100. www.hotel-sonne.de. ▣ ⊱⊰ 32 rooms ▭ This family hotel with pretty façade is in the heart of the old town. Expect comfortable, modern rooms and wonderful views of the Kaiser-Maximilian-Platz from the café-restaurant on the 1st floor.

Sights

Ehemaliges Kloster St Mang
🕐 *Open all year, Tue-Sun, 11am-4pm (2-4pm, Nov to Mar).* 👓 €*3. Ticket valid for the chapel, abbey buildings and the museum collections (free entry to the parish church).*
A Benedictine foundation, St Mang recalls the work of St Magnus (who died in 750) in Füssen. It was rebuilt in the Baroque style during the 18C and secularised in 1802.

Parish Church (Stadtpfarrkirche)
Rebuilt between 1701 and 1717, this church displays the harmony you would expect of a church designed, painted and plastered by the same man, native Johann-Jacob Herkomer. The Romanesque crypt in front of the high altar has frescoes from AD 1000 portraying Magnus and Gallus.

Abbey Buildings
🕐 *Open all year, Tue-Sun, 11am-5pm (1-5pm, Nov to Mar).* 👓 €*2.50.* ☎ *(083 62) 90 31 46.*
Like the Parish Church, the abbey buildings were planned by Herkomer as a grandiose symmetrical Baroque complex in Venetian Baroque style. The Museum der Stadt Füssen, reached across the main quadrangle, is housed in the former state apartments of the abbey and contains displays on the history of the abbey

Hohes Schloss
The ramp leading up to the castle entrance starts behind the parish church.
In the late 15C, the castle was the summer residence of the prince-bishops of Augsburg. The apartments housing the local museum, in particular the Knight's Hall (Rittersaal) with its sumptuous octagonally coffered ceiling, display a collection of Swabian painting from the 15C to the 18C. The surrounding property has been transformed into a public park (Baumgarten).

Lechfall
Kids *0.5km/550yd south.*
The river Lech leaves the Alps in Füssen and hurls itself tumultuously over a ledge in a small, rocky gorge. The falls are spanned by a footbridge.

Forggensee
Kids This reservoir lake, as well as the many other little lakes to be found on the outskirts of Füssen, is a pleasant place to walk and swim.

FULDA

POPULATION: 64 000

The town's name is closely connected to Christian history in Germany. But Fulda is not so much dominated by its medieval buildings as by its Baroque core, with the cathedral, palace and mansions of the nobility recalling a time when prince-bishops guarded the tomb of St Boniface. 🛈 *Schloßstraße 1, 36037 Fulda.* ☎ *(0661) 10 23 46.*

▶ **Orient Yourself:** Fulda is the economic and cultural centre of eastern Hessen, a few kilometres from the borders of Thuringen and Bavaria.
👁 **Don't Miss:** The cathedral and St. Michaelskirche.

🕙 **Organizing Your Time:** Allow at least four hours for the driving tour (🚶 *see below*).

🚶 **Also See:** *EISENACH (100km/62mi northeast), FRANKFURT AM MAIN (102km/64mi southwest), WURZBURG (108km/66mi south), THÜRINGER WALD (tour starts in Eisenach).*

A Bit of History

St Boniface, the Apostle of Germany – Wynfrith, an English missionary from a monastery in Exeter, was sent by Pope Gregory II in the 8C to preach the gospel to the heathen Germans. The Pope gave him the Latin name "Bonifatius", meaning "he who does good deeds". The result was a monastery in Fulda, Boniface's favourite. In 754, Boniface was murdered in Friesland. His corpse was brought back to Fulda, rendering the abbey a centre of religious devotion, art and scholarship which was responsible for the production of Germany's earliest literary works.

Sights

Dom (Cathedral)

From the beginning of 1704, this church was rebuilt in a style inspired by Italian Baroque by the architect Johann Dientzenhofer. Pilgrims still worship the tomb of St Boniface, which lies in a crypt (Bonifatiusgruft) beneath the high altar. At the base of the **funerary monument**★, an 18C alabaster bas-relief represents St Boniface. The reliquaries of the saint are conserved in the museum (**Dommuseum**). *Access to the left of the cathedral* 🚶 🕙 *Open Apr to Oct, Tue-Sun, 10am-5.30pm, Sun 12.30-5.30pm; Nov-Mar, Tue-Sun, 10am-12.30pm, 1.30-4pm, Sun, 12.30pm-4pm.* 🕙 *Closed mid-Jan to mid-Feb, from Good Fri to Easter Sun and Pentecost, 24 and 25 Dec.* 👓 *€2.10.* ☎ *(0661) 872 07. www.bistum-fulda.de.*

Michaelskirche★

This church, built around an early-9C rotunda, with a stout, square tower, overlooks the cathedral forecourt. The crypt, in which the vaulting rests on a single pillar, is Carolingian. The rotunda itself is supported on eight columns marking the outline of an impressive well-head.

Excursions

Probsteikirche St Peter

4km/2.5mi, plus 30min walking and sightseeing. Leave Fulda by the Petersberger Strasse and road no 458. Follow the Petersberg signposts to the foot of the rock on which the church is built, and leave the car there.

A vast **panorama**★ is commanded from the summit: to the east is the Rhön massif *(see below)*, the Milseburg spur and the rounded dome of the Wasserkuppe; southwest, behind Fulda, lies the Vogelsberg. The Romanesque sanctuary built on this impressive **site**★ was largely remodelled in the 15C. It contains five 12C **low-relief sculptures**★★: Christ in Glory and the Virgin flanking a triumphal arch, St Boniface, Carloman and Pepin the Short (Charlemagne's brother and father). Mural paintings from the 9C decorate the Carolingian crypt.

Driving Tour

The Rhön

Round tour of 104km/65mi southeast of Fulda – allow 4hr.

The remnants of an enormous extinct volcano, the Rhön massif's craggy summits tower above its bleak moorlands, up to a height of 1 000m/3 280ft. These heights, swept by strong winds, have made the area a favourite among gliding clubs.

Gersfeld
The most central resort in the Rhön district, Gersfeld has a Protestant **church** (1785) with interestingly placed furnishings: the grouping of organ, altar and pulpit in a single compact ensemble symbolises liturgically the Lutheran reform.

Kreuzberg★
From the Calvary at 928m/3 044ft after a steep uphill climb is a splendid **view**★ of the massif. The Wasserkuppe can be seen to the north.

Wasserkuppe★★
From the gliding centre, climb to the summit (950m/3 116ft), following the fencing. The **panorama**★★ extends as far as Fulda and the Vogelsberg.

GARMISCH-PARTENKIRCHEN★★★

POPULATION: 26 000

This is Germany's great winter sports resort, famed as the site of the fourth Winter Olympics in 1936 and the World Alpine Ski Championships in 1978. The resort lies in a basin at the foot of the Wetterstein range, from which the massive peaks of the Alpspitze, the Waxenstein, and the Zugspitze, Germany's highest peak, stand out. *🖪 Dr.-Richard-Strauß-Platz, 82467 Garmisch-Partenkirchen. ☎ (088 21) 18 06.*

▶ **Orient Yourself:** The many surrounding peaks of more than 2 000 m make an impressive setting for the adjacent towns of Garmisch and Partenkirchen. They are also on the Deutsche Alpenstrasse, less than 15km/9mi from Austria.

🕲 **Don't Miss:** Winter sports in the surrounding mountains.

Kids Especially for Kids: Snow sports, cable-car ride up the Wank.

👌 **Also See:** *Deutsche ALPENSTRASSE, Schloss LINDERHOF (26km/16mi west), WIESKIRCHE (45km/28mi west).*

Sights

St-Martin Alte Kirche
Garmisch. The parish church stands on the west bank of the River Loisach, in a picturesque neighbourhood where the old chalets have been carefully preserved. A large number of 15C and 16C murals have been uncovered and restored inside (note especially a huge representation of St Christopher and scenes from the Passion).

Philosophenweg (Philosophers' Way)
Partenkirchen. The park of St Anton-Anlagen is the departure point for this panoramic walk with clear **views**★ of the surrounding massifs, including the Zugspitze visible behind the Waxenstein.

Garmisch-Partenkirchen and the Zugspitze massif

Kurverwaltung, Garmisch-Partenkirchen

Address Book

WHERE TO EAT

Postkeller und Alte Braustub'n – *Innsbrucker Straße 13, 82481 Mitten-wald.* ☎ *(08823) 17 29. www.postkel-ler-mittenwald.de.* ⏱ *Closed Mon.* The brewery next door ensures that the taps never run dry in the large dining room on the first floor. On the menu is regional cuisine washed down with local beers.

Zur Schranne – *Griesstraße 4.* ☎ *(08821) 16 99.* ⏱ *Closed Tue.* An establishment very typical of the region. Sample Bavarian cuisine, served in particularly hearty portions. A covered terrace is also available.

WHERE TO STAY

Gästehaus Brigitte – *St.-Martin-Straße 40.* ☎ *(08821) 739 38. Fax (08821) 79125. www.hotelbrigitte.de.* 🅿 ♿ *11 rooms.* 🍽 This spotlessly clean guesthouse is near the lower cable-car station. Tennis courts, footpaths, and the Olympic skating rink are just around the corner.

Gästehaus Edlhuber – *Innsbrucker Straße 33, 82481 Mittenwald.* ☎ *(08823) 13 89. Fax (08823) 94138. www.edlhuber-mittenwald.de.* 🅿 *16 rooms.* 🍽. This friendly, family-run hotel is located at the foot of the Karwendel massif, in the middle of the countryside, the ideal place to get away from it all. Comfortable guestrooms and personable reception.

TAKING A BREAK

Konditorei-Café Thron – *Marien-platz 13.* ☎ *(08821) 522 60. www.kon-ditorei-thron.de.* ⏱ *8:30am-7pm.* Just the presentation of the huge choice of pastries, tarts and chocolates will get your mouth watering. Prince Regent's cake (Prinzregententorte), wine-cream roulades (Weincremerouladen) and flaked cream (Flockensahne) are just a few of the specialities of this pastry shop cum tea room.

Excursions

Zugspitze★★★ (♿ *for access and description, see ZUGSPITZE*)

Wank★★

🅺🅸🅳🅂 *20min cable-car ride.* 🚠 *May to Sep, 8:45am-5pm; Oct and Nov, 8:45am-4:30pm. Leaves every hour.* 💶 *€16.50 round trip.* ☎ *(088 21) 79 70. www.zugspitze.de. Leaves from the Schützenhaus guesthouse, north of Partenkirchen.*

From the summit (1 780m/5 840ft) there is a comprehensive view of the Wetterstein chain and Zugspitze peak. A 3km/2mi panoramic footpath *(gentle gradients, parts cleared in winter)* with terraces eases exploration of the summit.

Partnachklamm★★

About 1hr30min there and back, of which 5min are in a cable-car. Remember to take rainwear.

From the Partenkirchen ski stadium, go to the lower terminus of the Graseck cable-car. The upper station is at the Forsthaus Graseck hotel, and from here a footpath leads up to the gorges. The route, carved from the solid rock, passes two spectacular bottlenecks amid the thunder of falling water and clouds of spray. It is possible to make the same trip in winter, when the route is decorated with icicles.

Eibsee★

8km/5mi west.

The calm waters of this lake occupy a superb forest site. It lies at the foot of the Zugspitze, at an altitude of 1 000m/3 280ft. A footpath *(2hr walk)* circles the lake.

GARMISCH-PARTENKIRCHEN		Hauptstr.	X	Rießerseestr.	X 38
		Hindenburgstr.	X 18	Von-Burg-Str.	X 46
		Mittenwalder Str.	X 27	Wildenauer Str.	X 48
Am Kurpark	X 7	Münchner Str.	X 30	Zugspitzstr.	X
Bahnhofstr.	X 10	Parkstr.	X 32		
Ferdinand-Barth-Str.	X 15	Promenadestr.	X 35		

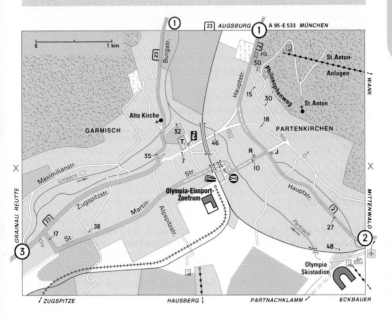

Mittenwald★

20km/12mi east.

Mittenwald, a community of violin makers on the old Augsburg-Verona trade route, still suffers from heavy traffic today. This congestion is due to the large number of excursions possible in the nearby Kranzberg and Karwendel massifs, and to the beauty of the town itself. The **painted houses**★★ lining the pavements of the main street are especially noteworthy.

Mittenwald's homage to its place in the world of music is a memorial to Matthias Klotz (1653-1743), who returned from Cremona in 1684 with a lute and, as an ex-pupil of Stradivarius, introduced the manufacture of stringed instruments to Bavaria. A dozen artisans, a technical school, and a museum, the Geigenbau-und- Heimatmuseum, carry on that tradition today. ○ *Open from end Dec to end Oct, Tue-Fri, 10am-1pm, 3pm-6pm, Sat and Sun, 10am-1pm.* ⊛ *€2.50.* ☎ *(088 23) 339 81.*

GÖRLITZ★

POPULATION: 65 000

Görlitz became extremely prosperous during the 15C and 16C through textile manufacture and trade in woad. The Second World War miraculously spared the town's 3 500 historic houses. *Obermarkt 29, 02826 Görlitz. ☎ (035 81) 475 70*

▶ **Orient Yourself:** Görlitz stretches along the west bank of the Neiße, which has formed the frontier with Poland since 1945.

🔎 **Don't Miss:** The Old Town.

🕐 **Organizing Your Time:** Görlitz can be seen in a day.

Kids Especially for Kids: Outdoor recreation in the Zittauer Gebirge (& *see Excursions*).

& **Also See:** BAUTZEN (45km/28mi west), DRESDEN (107km/67mi west), SÄCHSISCHE SCHWEIZ.

Walking Tour

Old Town★

Most of the town's sights are concentrated around two interesting squares, the Obermarkt and the Untermarkt, which dominate the historic centre of Görlitz.

Obermarkt

On the north side of this square, fine Baroque houses have been preserved between the Reichenbacher Turm, a fortified gateway to the west, and Dreifaltigkeitskirche to the east. At no 29 *(the Tourist Information Centre)*, the façade, including an entrance framed by sculpted columns, is adorned with impressive stuccowork.

Dreifaltigkeitskirche

& 🕐 *May-Sep, 10am-6pm, Sun 12pm-6pm; Oct, 10am-5pm.* ☎ *(035 81) 64 34 60.*
A high, slim tower with a Baroque cupola is a major feature of the Holy Trinity church in the Obermarkt. Note the choir **stalls**★ (1484), with the chronicle of the Franciscans above them. The Baroque high altar from 1713 was created by Caspar Gottlob von Rodewitz, a student of Permoser. The **Barbarakapelle** houses some valuable works of art, like the 16C **Maria altarpiece**★, a Late Gothic masterpiece.

Untermarkt★

Formerly the town's trading centre, the marketplace sits in the shadow of the 14C **Rathaus** (town hall). The **Alte Börse** (old exchange) occupies the middle of the market, its entrance surrounded by allegorical figures. Dating from 1706, the exchange is adjacent to the **Alte Waage** (Weigh-house).

Kulturhistorisches Museum (Museum of Cultural History)

At Neißstraße 30.
This imposing Baroque mansion (1727-29) at the southeast corner of the square houses an interesting collection of art, 16C to 19C decorative arts and beautiful Renaissance and Baroque furniture. Highlights include a collection of glassware and 18C **cupboards and cabinets**★.

"Silesian Heaven"

With a bit of luck, visitors to Görlitz will be able to sample *Schlesisches Himmelreich*: a typical Silesian sweet and sour dish prepared from pickled pork and dried fruit and served with a light lemon sauce and white bread dumplings.

St-Peterskirche★

&. ⓒ *Open May to Sep, 10.30am-5pm, Sun, 12.30pm-5pm; Oct, 10.30-4pm, Sun, 12.30-4pm; Nov to Apr, 10am-4pm, Sun, 12.30pm-4pm.* ☎ *(035 81) 40 28 58.*

This mighty place of worship, with its steep copper roof, towers high above the Neiße. It was completed by the end of the 15C. Inside is a magnificent 17C **pulpit**, with gilded acanthus leaves and angel supports. The **great organ** was built by Eugenio Casparini, Andreas Silbermann's tutor, in 1703.

Kaisertrutz

Demianiplatz. ⓒ *Open May to Nov, Tue-Sun, 10am-5pm, Fri 1pm-8pm.* ☞ *€3.50.* ☎ *(035 81) 67 13 55. www.museum-goerlitz.de.*

This solid-looking keep formed part of the town's 15C-16C fortifications. It now houses the **Museum für Stadtgeschichte und Kunst** *(Local History and Art Museum).* Opposite the Kaisertrutz stands the symbol of the town, the **Reichenbacher Turm,** recorded for the first time in 1376. 165 steps lead up to the 52m/170ft high tower;

the little room at the top offers wonderful **views**★. 🕐 *Open May to Nov,Tue-Sun. 10am-5pm, Fri, 1-8pm.* 👓 *€3.50.* ☎ *(035 81) 67 13 55. www.museum-goerlitz.de.*

Karstadt-Warenhaus

The steel-framed building faced with ashlar stone, built in 1912-13 by Potsdam architect Schmann, is the only remaining example of *Jugendstil* (Art Nouveau) department store architecture in Germany.

Excursions

Kids Zittauer Gebirge★

35km/22mi south via the B 66.
This mountain range extends for 20km/12mi, forming a towering ridge over the Zittau Basin. A favourite region for rock climbers, mountaineers and winter sports enthusiasts, it is also noted for such spas as Lückendorf, Oybin and Jonsdorf.

St-Marienthal★

15km/9mi south via B 66 in Ostritz.
The Bohemian queen Kunigunde founded this Cistercian convent in 1234, which is still run by the Cistercian Order today. Picturesquely situated on a bend in the Lausitz Neiße, the convent bears unmistakable Bohemian influences, such as the west façade with its central projection. Germany's most easterly vineyard is on the convent's estate.
The **Klosterkirche's** church tower is unusual for Cistercian architecture. The interior was painted in the narrative Romanesque style in 1850 by Nazarenes.

Karstadt-Warenhaus, Görlitz

R. Chéret/MICHELIN

GOSLAR★★

POPULATION: 43 000

A popular weekend destination among Germans, Goslar was once part of the Hanseatic League. The town exhibits its long, rich history in a large grouping of half-timbered houses and monuments around its medieval centre. The old town and the Rammelsberg mines became a UNESCO World Heritage Site in 1992. ℹ
Markt 7, 38640 Goslar, ☎ *(053 21) 780 60; www.goslar.de*

▶ **Orient Yourself:** Goslar lies on the northwestern rim of the Harz National Park and makes an ideal starting point for exploring the massif.
🌀 **Don't Miss:** The Old Town.
🕐 **Organizing Your Time:** Allow three hours for a walking tour of the Old City.
Kids **Especially for Kids:** Rammelsberg Mine.
👍 **Also See:** *HARZ, WOLFENBÜTTEL (36km/22mi north), BRANSCHWEIG (46km/29mi north), HILDESHEIM (51km/32mi west).*

WHERE TO EAT

⌐⊜⊟ **Les petites maisonnettes** – *Am Siechenhof 12.* 🕐 *Closed 1-7 Jan, Tue and Sat noon.* ☎ *(05321) 188 88.* This restaurant has a country feel and is set in a half-timbered house. The cosy décor gives this place a warm ambience and the terraced garden makes the restaurant particularly pleasant in the summer months.

WHERE TO STAY

⌐⊜⊟ **Hotel Die Tanne** – *Bäringer Strasse 10* ☎ *(05321) 343 90. Fax (05321) 343934. www.die-tanne.de.* 🅿 ⇆ *25 rooms.* 🖵 The shale frontage of this establishment (classified a historic monument) conceals comfortable rooms. Explore the little backstreets nearby.

A Bit of History

The mines – A former Free Imperial City, Goslar owed its prosperity to the mineral wealth of the Harz, particularly the **Rammelsberg** mines, worked during the Middle Ages for lead and silver. The city's commercial importance reached its height in the 15C and 16C, with profits from the mines and the surrounding forests. It was during this period that the fine houses of the city centre were built.

Walking Tour

The Old Town★★★ (Altstadt)

The old town of Goslar is largely a pedestrian zone, making it a pleasant place to wander round.

▶ *Begin on Marktplatz (see town plan).*

Marktplatz★

The market square is surrounded by slate-clad houses. Two Gothic buildings, the Kaiserworth and the Rathaus, stand before the spires of the 12C **Marktkirche**. In the centre of the square is a **fountain** *(Marktbrunnen)* with two bronze basins (1230) . The square also features a chiming **animated clock** with four different scenes *(at 9am, noon, 3pm and 6pm)* representing the history of mining in the Harz mountains.

Rathaus★ (Town Hall)

Following the medieval custom, this 15C building was designed with an open hall at street level, an arcaded gallery opening onto the Marktplatz. On the south side, an exterior staircase leads to the first floor **State Room** *(Diele)*.

Huldigungssaal★★ (Chamber of Allegiance)

🕐 *Open daily, 11am-4pm.* 🕐 *Closed 24 and 31 Dec.* ⊜ *€3.50.* ☎ *(053 21) 780 60.*

This room, transformed into the **Municipal Council Chamber** in 1490, was magnificently decorated ca 1520. Along the walls, Roman emperors alternate with sibyls in Renaissance costume; on the ceiling, scenes of Christ, the Prophets

Restaurant opposite the Marktkirche

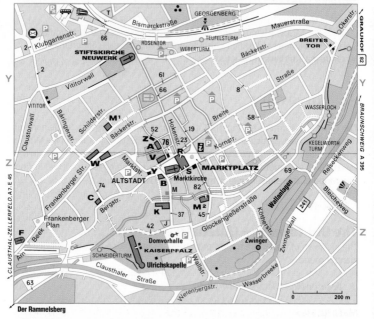

GOSLAR			Hoher Weg	Z	37	Rammelsberger Str.	Z	63
			Hokenstr.	Y		Rosenorstr.	Y	66
Astfelder Str.	Y	2	Kaiserbleek	Z	42	Schielenstr.	Y	71
Breite Str.	Y		Königstr.	Z	45	Schreiberstr.	Z	74
Brüggemannstr.	Y	8	Marktstr.	Z		Schuhhof	Y	76
Fischemäkerstr	Y	19	Münzstr.	Y	52	St-Annenhöhe	Z	69
Fleischscharren	Y	23	Obere Kirchstr.	Y	58	Worthstr.	Z	82
			Petersilienstr.	Y	61			

Alte Münze	Y	Z	Eckhaus-Münz			Rathaus	YZ	R
Alter Gasthof Am Weißen			Marktstraße	Z	V	Renaissancehäuser	YZ	W
Scwan	Y	A	Goslarer Museum	Z	M²	Siemenshaus	Z	C
Bäckergildehaus	Z	Y	Kaiserworth	Z	S	Stift zum Großen		
Brusttuch	Z	B	Mönchehaus	Z	M¹	Heiligen Kreuz	Z	K
			Pfarrkirche Peter und Paul	Z	F			

and Evangelists. Behind a door is a tiny chapel with an arm-reliquary (c 1300) of St Margaret.

Hotel Kaiserworth

Built in 1494, this Gothic edifice features a grotesque figure of **The Ducat Man** *(Dukatenmännchen),* illustrating Goslar's ancient right to mint coins.

Carved Half-timbered Houses★★ (Fachwerkhäuser)

The Schuhhof, a small square northwest of the Rathaus, is entirely surrounded by half-timbered buildings. Further on, a passageway on the left leads to the narrow Münzstraße, which in turn passes an old inn, **Am Weißen Schwan**, and then the **Alte Münze** (Old Mint). Transformed today into a restaurant, this timbered building dates from 1500. The fine house on the corner of the Münzstraße and the Marktstraße was constructed in 1526.

Facing the Marktkirche is the **Brusttuch** (1526), built for a rich mine owner and decorated with biblical, mythological and legendary characters. Not far away is the tall gable of the **Bäckergildehaus** (Bakers' Guild Hall, 1501-1557).

The **Renaissance houses** at the Marktstraße-Bäckerstraße crossroads are adorned with friezes of the fan motif, often found in Lower Saxony *(no 2 Bäckerstraße)*.

▶ *Turn into Bergstraße which leads to the Marktkirche.*

Siemenshaus

♿ 🕐 *Open Thu and Fri, 9am-12noon.* 🕐 *Closed bank holidays.* ☎ *(053 21) 238 37.*
An impressive half-timbered house built in 1693 by Hans Siemens, ancestor of the founder of the celebrated industrial firm of the same name. Note the tiled entrance (Däle) and picturesque inner courtyard.

Sights

Stiftskirche Neuwerk★

This former collegiate church was built in 12C-13C. The tall polygonal towers are among the most elegant ever built for a Romanesque church.
Heavily ribbed, pointed vaulting characterises the interior. The former 13C rood screen, with six sculptures of figures (Christ, the Virgin, the four Apostles) whose clothing and artistic design appear manifestly Gothic, is used as an organ loft in the west.

Pfarrkirche Peter und Paul★

Entrance on the Frankenberger Plan.
Later modifications had minimal impact on the Romanesque character of this 12C basilica. The pillars and vaults of the interior are richly decorated with stone carvings. Over the choir and upper loft are murals painted in the early 13C. The 12C altar bears a splendid Baroque retable dating to 1675, which, like the 1698 chancel, originated in the Goslar woodcarving workshop of Heinrich and Jobst Lessen.

Kaiserpfalz (Imperial Palace)

♿ 🕐 *Open Apr to Oct: 10am-5pm; Nov to Mar: 10am-4pm.* 🕐 *Closed 24 and 31 Dec.*
🎟 *€4.50.* ☎ *(053 21) 311 96 93.*
The 11C palace, originally built for Kaiser Heinrich III, was restored between 1868 and 1879. Historical paintings in the gigantic **Reichssaal** *(on the first floor)* chart significant Saxon events when Goslar was still an Imperial residence. Beyond the Reichssaal is the early-12C **Palatine Chapel of St Ulrich**, where the plan passes from a Greek cross to that of an octagon. Inside the chapel is the tomb of Heinrich III.

Mönchenhaus★ (Monks' House)

A **museum** of modern art (with sculpture garden) resides in this ancient half-timbered house (1528). Artists include Beuys, Hundertwasser, Serra and de Kooning.

Rammelsberg

Kids *Southwest of town, via Clausthaler Strasse and Rammelsberger Strasse.*
🚶 *Guided tour (1hr to 4hr depending on the tour) 9am-6pm.* 🕐 *Closed 24 and 31 Dec.* 🎟 *€10.* ☎ *(053 21) 75 01 22. www.rammelsberg.de.*
Over the centuries the Rammelsberg mines have been largely responsible for Goslar's prosperity. The mines were worked continuously for at least 1 000 years, giving up almost 30 million tons of ore. During the museum visit, portions of the mine can be explored on foot or in a mining train.

Excursion

Harz Mountains★★ – 👣 *See HARZ.*

GREIFSWALD ★

POPULATION: 53 000

There is evidence that Greifswald was granted municipal rights as early as 1250. Once it joined the Hanseatic League in 1281, the town flourished and continued to prosper for the next four centuries. The city boasts a decidedly Scandinavian flavor and a number of historic buildings largely spared destruction during the Second World War. ◨ *Rathaus am Markt, 17489 Greifswald. ☎ (038 34) 52 13 80.*

▶ **Orient Yourself:** On the banks of the river Ryck and the Baltic Sea, Greifswald is southeast of Stralsund. The town is halfway between Rügen and Usedom islands.

⊗ **Don't Miss:** The Marktplatz and surrounding historical buildings.

⊙ **Organizing Your Time:** One day is sufficient to enjoy Greifswald.

⚑ **Also See:** *STRALSUND (33km/20mi northwest), ROSTOCK (91km/57mi west), MECKLENBURGISCHE SEENPLATTE, Insel RÜGEN, Insel USEDOM.*

A Bit of History

Swedish Rule – Following the peace treaty of Osnabrück, West Pomerania, and with it Greifswald, passed into Swedish hands. The Swedes exercised leniency for some 200 years, granting the town an unusual degree of autonomy. From 1815, when West Pomerania became part of Prussia, a busy period of construction began, to which the numerous well-preserved burghers' houses testify.

The Greatest German Romantic Painter – **Caspar David Friedrich**, the epitome of the German Romantic artist and a revolutionary landscape painter, was born in Greifswald in 1774. Although he left Greifswald at the age of 20, he remained deeply attached to the town; Greifswald, especially the ruins of Eldena Abbey, feature in his works.

Sights

Marktplatz★

To the west of this square stands the **Rathaus** (1738). The arcades, built according to medieval model, were uncovered in 1936. Around the square stand a number of architecturally interesting houses, the most noticeable of which is **no 11**★: this early 15C building with its ornately decorated gable is one of the finest examples of north German Gothic brick architecture.

Marienkirche★

♿ ⊙ *Open May to Oct, daily, 10am-5pm, Sat 10am-12 noon, Sun, 11am-12 noon; Nov to Apr: 12 noon-3pm, Sun, 11.30am-4pm.* ⊙ *Closed Easter Mon and Pentecost, 1 May, 3 and 31 Oct. ☎ (038 34) 22 63.*

This hall-church has an elegantly structured east gable with its ornate tracery alleviates the somewhat heavy, stocky appearance of the rest of the brick church, which is known affectionately as "podgy Mary" by locals. Construction of the church began in 1280. Inside there is a beautiful carved **pulpit**★ from 1587, the work of Joachim Mekelenborg from Rostock. There are Late Gothic frescoes from the 15C.

Dom St-Nikolai★

♿ ⊙ *Open May-Oct, 11am-3pm, Sun, 11.30am-4pm; Nov to Apr, 12am-3pm, Sun 11:30am-4pm. ☎ (038 34) 26 27.*

Swing bridge at Wieck

The cathedral is dwarfed by its tower, almost 100m/328ft in height. Its crowning glory is a Dutch Baroque steeple dating from 1653. In the 14C the original hall-church was elevated to the rank of basilica, and the spaces between the flying buttresses were filled in to make a ring of 21 radiating chapels.

Klosterruine Eldena
Wolgaster Landstraße.
The original Cistercian abbey was founded in 1199, and reached its height in the mid 14C. The Thirty Years War caused large-scale destruction, and the remains were later used as a source of building materials by local people. Only fragments of the church, the cloister and the east abbey building remain; they are, nonetheless, picturesque.

Wieck★
Can be reached on foot from the Eldena Abbey ruins.
This little fishing village, now officially classified as a historical site, lies as the mouth of the River Ryck as it flows into Greifswald Bay. The shipmasters' cottages and thatched fishermen's cottages, idyllic harbour and 19C **wooden swing bridge**★ *(Zugbrücke)* are delightful scene.

HALLE★

POPULATION: 238 000

Halle is a town with a dual identity: on the one hand an important industrial centre; on the other, an intellectual enclave whose university traditions go back to the 17C. Halle is also famous as the birthplace of Georg Friedrich Händel, in 1685. The Händel Festival pays tribute to the master every year. *Roter Turm, Marktplatz, 06108 Halle. ☎ (0345) 47 23 30.*

▶ **Orient Yourself:** Halle is on the banks of the Saale, around thirty kilometres northwest of Leipzig.
🅿 **Parking:** The Händelhauskarree garage on Hallorenring is ideally located for touring Halle.
◉ **Don't Miss:** The Moritzburg National Gallery and the Händel Haus.
🕐 **Organizing Your Time:** One day is sufficient to see the sights in Halle.
🖐 **Also See:** *LEIPZIG (34km/21mi east), NAUMBURG (47km/29mi south), DESSAU (53km/33mi north).*

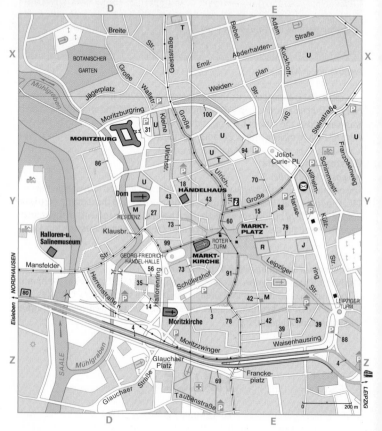

Sights

Marktplatz★

This huge square is dominated by the belfries of the Marktkirche and by the **Roter Turm** (red tower), built in the 15C and almost 80m/262ft high. An 1859 statue of Händel surveys the square from the centre.

Marktkirche★

A triple-aisle hall-church with no chancel, this building was constructed in 1529-54 between the double towers of two Romanesque churches whose naves were torn down. The pulpit dates from 1547 with a sounding board (1596) by Heinrich

Heidereiter. The **reredos**★ of the high altar carries a Virgin and Child painted by a pupil of the Cranach School. Behind the altar is Luther's death mask.

Moritzkirche
On the Hallorenring.
This triple-aisle hall-church was built between 1388 and 1511. The church's highlight is **artworks**★ by the sculptor **Conrad of Einbeck**.

Dom
Am Domplatz.
The three-naved Gothic hall-church was modified ca 1520 by Cardinal Albert of Brandenburg. The interior columns are decorated with statues of Christ, the Apostles and the saints, executed in the studios of Peter Schroh, one of the most talented sculptors of the time.

Technisches Halloren- und Salinenmuseum
52 Mansfelder Strasse. ♿ ⊘ *Open Tue-Sun, 10am-5pm.* ⊘ *Closed 1 Jan, 24, 25 and 31 Dec.* ⊜ *€2.10, no charge on Thu.* ☎ *(0345) 202 50 34.*
This museum recounts the history of the exploitation of the local salt mines and the cultural development of the "*Halloren,*" the Halle salt miners' guild. An evaporation vessel is demonstrated that still functions and produces regularly.

Staatliche Galerie Moritzburg-Halle★★
(Moritzburg National Gallery)
Friedemann-Bach-Platz. ⊘ *Open Wed-Sun, 10am-6pm, Tue, 11am-8.30pm.* ⊘ *Closed 24 and 31 Dec.* ⊜ *€5, no charge last Sunday of the month.* ☎ *(0345) 21 25 90.*
In 1484, building began on the Moritzburg, a fortress complex with four wings. Until 1541, it was the preferred residence of the archbishops of Magdeburg and Mainz. Having been destroyed during the Thirty Years War, part of the fortress was restored and converted into a museum at the beginning of the 20C. It now houses the most significant art collection in Sachsen-Anhalt.
On display are works of 1**9C and 20C German painting,** representing the periods of **Romanticism**, **Impressionism** and **Expressionism**. Works by the artists of the **Brücke** group, as well as by Kandinsky and Feininger, are also exhibited.
German sculpture of the 19C and 20C is also featured at the National Gallery. Works by Wilhelm Lehmbruck and Ernst Barlach, among others, are collected here.
The museum also displays interesting collections of glassware and ceramics from the Middle Ages to the present, as well as porcelain, goldware, coins and medals.

Händel Haus★
♿ ⊘ *Open daily, 9.30am-5.30pm, Thu, 9.30am-7pm.* ⊘ *Closed 25 Dec* ☎ *(0345) 50 09 00. www.haendelhaus.de.*

One of the world's most famous composers, Georg Friedrich Händel was born in this big half-timbered house in 1685. He left Halle in 1703 and after living elsewhere in Germany and in Italy, ended up in London. He adopted British nationality in 1727.

Excursions

Doppelkapelle Landsberg

In Landsberg, 19km/12mi east of Halle. 🚶 *From 1 May to 31 Oct: Guided tours (1hr) Sat and Sun at 11am and 3pm.* 🚗 *€2.* ☎ *(0346 02) 206 90.*

The twin chapel of **St Crucis** can be seen from way off, perched on a rocky spur. The building dates from 1195-1200. This rare chapel – there are only about 30 such buildings recorded – separated the common people, who celebrated Mass in the lower chapel, from the nobility in the upper chapel. The **capitals**★ on the columns and pillars are adorned with extraordinarily beautiful figures and plant and animal motifs. From the balcony, there is a superb **view**★ as far as Leipzig, Halle and Merseburg.

Eisleben

34km/21mi west.

Martin Luther was born – and died – in this small mining town within sight of the lower ranges of the Harz Mountains. Memories of the religious reformer are evoked in his birthplace (Luther-Geburtshaus, *Lutherstrasse 16*) and the house where he died (Luther-Sterbehaus, *Andreaskirchplatz 7*). The historic old town is also worth a quick visit. Here, too, much recalls Luther: the church of St Peter and St Paul in which he was baptised; St Andreas, with the original Luther pulpit, from which he preached for the last time; the Marktplatz with its 1883 Luther statue.

HAMBURG★★★

POPULATION: 1 744 000

Germany's second largest city after Berlin, Hamburg is one of the most important ports in Europe. Its old title of "Free and Hanseatic Town" and its status as a "City State" (Stadtstaat) testify to its eminence and influence through the centuries. Germany's publishing and media capital, renowned for its commercial dynamism and cosmopolitan atmosphere, is a city of contrasts; not far from the lively – and sometimes rowdy – St Pauli district, residential areas such as Harvestehude and Blankenesee remind the visitor that Hamburg is home to more millionaires than any other city in Germany. Take the time to explore the city, and you will soon fall under its spell. 🚉 *Hauptbahnhof, 20099 Hamburg.* ☎ *(040) 30 05 13 00. www.hamburg.de.*

▶ **Orient Yourself:** Hamburg stands at the confluence of the Bille and the Alster, on the estuary of the Elbe river, which flows into the North Sea about 100km/62mi to the northwest. The A 1 motorway links the city to Bremen, the A 7 to Hannover and the A 24 to Berlin.

🅿 **Parking:** Garages are located throughout the city. Visit http://wap.parkinfo.com for specific locations and fees.

☺ **Don't Miss:** Exploring the port and the city center.

🕐 **Organizing Your Time:** Allow one day for a walking tour of the city centre; half a day for a tour of the port (including a boat cruise); and half a day for the Altona Excursion.

Kids **Especially for Kids:** A cruise on Hamburg's port, canoeing or sailing the Außenalster basin, Tierpark Hagenbeck Zoo.

Address Book

PRACTICAL INFORMATION

TELEPHONE PREFIX: 040

TOURIST INFORMATION

For general information or room reservations: *Tourismus-Zentrale Hamburg
GmbH,* ☏ *30 05 13 00, Fax 30 05 13
33, www.hamburg-tourism.de.* Open
Mon-Sun 8am-8pm. Information offices:
Main Train Station (Hauptbahnhof),
main entrance Kirchenallee, Mon-Sat
8am-9pm, Sun 10am-6pm; Harbour,
St Pauli Landungsbrücken between
piers 4 and 5, Mon-Sun 8am-6pm (Oct-
Mar 10am-6pm). The monthly magazine
Vorschau… (followed by the month)
lists cultural events and is available
free in tourist offices, at the central
station and at the Landungsbrücken
(in St Pauli). The fortnightly magazine
Prinz, Szene Hamburg (monthly) and the
Hamburger Vorschau (at the information
offices) provide calendars of events.
Ticket sales for select events are at the
Tourismus-Zentrale Hamburg.

POST OFFICES WITH LATE HOURS

Post office at the main train station
(Hachmannplatz) is open Mon-Fri 8am-
8pm, Sat 10am-6pm.

NEWSPAPERS

*Hamburger Morgenpost, Hamburger
Abendblatt.*

INTERNET

www.hamburg.de; www.hamburg-
intern.de; www.hamburg-web.de;
www.hamburg-information.de

PUBLIC TRANSPORT

Using the buses and underground
trains of the HVV (Hamburger Verkehrsverbund) is recommended. The lines
stretch into the surrounding region of
Schleswig-Holstein, ☏ 1 94 49, www.
hvv.de, open Mon-Sun 7am-8pm.
Information at the HVV office at the
Hauptbahnhof Mon-Fri, 7am-8pm,
Sat-Sun 7am-10pm, Sat 8.30am-5pm,
Sun 11am-8pm, and in many U- and
S-Bahn stations. Tickets are available
from orange vending machines and,
for buses, from the drivers. Single
tickets for rides in the city centre from
☏ €1.50; a day ticket for one person
costs €4.90, a group day ticket for up to
five people costs from €8.10 to €9.30
(the two latter tickets are valid from
9am until the last ride). A 3-day pass
costs €14.40.

The **Hamburg Card** costs ☏ €7.80
and is valid for one person; the €11.20
version is for up to five people (card
valid on the issue date and from 6pm
onward on the day before). The three-
day version costs €17.40 (€28.30 for a
group). Besides use of the HVV network,
free entrance to 11 state-run museums
and other discounts, the card gives
discounts for water and land tours. The
Hamburg Card is available at tourist
information offices, in many hotels,
at vending machines, in the HVV cus-
tomer offices, and at many travel agents
(Reisebüros).

SIGHTSEEING

CITY TOURS

Tours by double-decker bus depart and
arrive at the Hauptbahnhof/Kirchenal-
lee, embarkation at additional stops
(including St-Pauli Landungsbrücken).
The *Top Tour Hamburg*, daily every 30
min from 9.30am to 5pm (in winter
only at 11am and 3pm) lasts about 1hr
30min and costs ☏ €12 for adults,
half price for children; the *Gala Tour*,
departs daily at 10am and 2pm, takes
in the various districts and lasts about
2hr 30min; details from ☏ 641 37 31.
Tour with the *Hummel-Bahn* train from
Hauptbahnhof/Kirchenallee, Apr-Oct
from 10.30am-4.30pm daily every 2hr
(lasts 2hr); ☏ 7 92 89 79, Fax 7 92 54 15,
www.hummelbahn.de. Walking tours
of the city under the heading of St Pauli
or the Speicherstadt, for example: *Tourismus-Zentrale Hamburg* and *Stattreisen
Hamburg* ☏ 4 30 34 81, Fax 4 30 74 29,
www.stattreisen-hamburg.de.

BOAT RIDES

Boat tours through the Hamburg
Harbour last anywhere from 1hr, begin
and end at the Landungsbrücken 1-9
in St Pauli; full price ☏ €9; Apr-Oct,
daily every hour and a half, 10.30am-

4.30pm, Nov-Mar, as required. *HADAG* (Hafen-Dampfschiffahrts-Actien-Gesellschaft), is the biggest company ☎ 3 11 70 70, www.hadag.de. Also try *Rainer Abicht*, ☎ 3 17 82 20, www.abicht. de; *Kapitän Prüsse*, ☎ 31 31 30, www.kapitaen-pruesse.de and other smaller shipping businesses offering harbour tours. Tours of the Alster and canal are also recommendable (departures from Jungfernstieg), by *Alster-Touristik GmbH*, ☎ 3 57 42 40, Fax 35 32 65, www.alstertouristik.de

WHERE TO EAT

🍽 **Kranzler – CCH Restaurant** – *Dammtor* ☎ (040) 35 69 32 00. *www.cch-gastronomie.de*. ♿ Conventioneers and tourists patronize this smart, inexpensive self-service restaurant. Located between the Alster and the *Planten un Blomen* park, it has a large terrace surrounded by greenery.

🍽🍽 **Atlas** – *Schützenstraße 9a* ☎ (040) 851 78 10. *www.atlas.at*. *Reservation necessary.* A bistro/restaurant-cum-cocktail bar with an ivy-covered terrace, set in a former factory somewhat hidden away in Phönixhof. A whole new experience.

🍽🍽 **Café Paris** – *Rathausstraße 4.* ☎ (040) 32 52 77 77. *Reservation recommended.* The main attraction of this establishment is its location, in the heart of a beautiful building right next to the town hall. The large, attractive dining room has a little balcony, and on the menu, salads, pasta and international dishes.

🍽🍽 **Gröninger Haus** – *Ost-West-Straße 47.* 🚋 *1 Messberg.* ☎ (040) 33 13 83. *www.groeninger-hamburg.de.* 🕐 *Closed Sat lunchtime and Sun.* ♿ *Reservation recommended.* This property, first documented in 1260, is the city's oldest hotel. The present Gröninger Haus comprises the Gröniger Braukeller, Anno 1750 and the Brauhaus Hanseat. Substantial dishes are washed down with beer brewed on the premises.

🍽🍽 **Warsteiner Elbspeicher** *Große Elbstraße 39.* Ⓢ *Königsstraße.* ☎ (040) 38 22 42. *www.warsteiner-elbspeicher. de.* You can choose between two floors of this old harbour-side house: the

ground floor houses a laid-back bistro with a large bar and cake buffet, while the rustic restaurant upstairs offers fish and meat dishes.

🍽🍽🍽 **Old Commercial Room** – *Englische Planke 10.* 🚋 *Stadthausbrücke.* ☎ (040) 36 63 19 *www.oldcommercial-room.de. Reservation necessary.* The Old Commercial Room was founded centuries ago by an English shipowner who left his mark. English pub decor with mahogany, copper and maritime pictures. Traditional sailors' dishes on the menu *(Labskaus)*, but also lobster, sole and knuckle of ham.

🍽🍽🍽 **Louis C. Jacob** – *Elbchaussee 401, 22609 Hamburg-Nienstedten.* ☎ (040) 82 25 50. *www.hotel-jacob. de* This Hamburg institution with its spectacular view of the Elbe, elegant upmarket interior and delicious French cuisine is a delight. The terrace with its lime trees was immortalised in a painting by Max Liebermann in 1902.

🍽🍽🍽 **Le Canard** – *Elbchaussee 139, 2763 Hamburg-Altona.* ☎ (040) 880 50 57. 🕐 *Closed Sun.* This establishment on the banks of the Elbe serves excellent classic French-style cuisine; lunchtime prices are particularly affordable. Modern, bright and elegant dining rooms. The terrace offers a remarkable view of the container terminal.

WHERE TO STAY

🛏 **Hotel Brenner Hof 1** – *Brennerstraße 70-72.* 🚋 *Lohmühlenstraße.* ☎ (040) 280 88 80. Fax (040) 28088888. *www.hotelbrennerhof.de.* 🅿 ✕ 24 *rooms.* 📶 This hotel consists of two city centre houses and offers rooms with modern furnishings. Very good public transport links.

🛏 **Hotel Etap Hamburg-City** – *Holstenkamp 3, 22525 Hamburg-Eimsbüttel* ☎ (040) 85 37 98 20. *www.etaphotel. com.* 🅿 ✕ ♿ *180 rooms.* 📶 No surprises at this chain hotel which provides inexpensive accommodation in the city centre. Well-kept and all the modern conveniences.

🛏🛏 **Hotel Schwanenwik** – *Schwanenwik 29.* ☎ (040) 220 09 18. Fax (040) 2290446. *www.hotel-schwanenwik.de.* *18 rooms.* 📶 A few offices and a charming boarding house occupy this magnificent 18C white bourgeois house on the Alster. Simple, modern rooms with a beautiful view of the lake or back garden.

⊖⊜ **Hotel Stephan** – *Schmarje-straße 31.* ⑤ *Bahnhof Altona.* ☎ *(040) 389 51 08. Fax (040) 3895195. www. hotel-stephan.de.* 🅿 ✄ *29 rooms.* ⊠ Well-kept hotel near the funicular and Altona station, with rather darkly furnished rooms. In summer, breakfast can be taken on the terrace.

⊖⊜ **Hotel Yoho** – *Moorkamp 5.* ☎ *(040) 28419191. www.yoho-ham-burg.de.* 🅿 ♿ *Reservation necessary. 30 rooms.* ⊠ ⊖⊜ *Restaurant.* The interior of this white villa was designed by a team of local architects and now houses a hotel for young people. Plain, pale decor, and a special rate for under 26-year-olds.

⊖⊜⊜ **Hotel Am Elbufer** – *Fock-sweg 40a, 21129 Hamburg-Finkenwerder* ☎ *(040) 742 19 10. Fax (040) 74219140. www.hotel-am-elbufer.de.* ⊕ *Closed 24 Dec-5 Jan.* 🅿 *14 rooms.* ⊠ Pleasant little hotel on the Elbe, with only boats to disturb the peace and quiet. Modern rooms with all conveniences and a lovely river view.

⊖⊜⊜ **Hotel Schmidt** – *Reventlow-straße 60, 22605 Hamburg-Othmarschen* ☎ *(040) 88 90 70. Fax (040) 8890715. www.hotel-schmidt.de.* 🅿 ✄ *45 rooms.* ⊠ Hotel in a leafy neighbour-hood, with rooms spread over several buildings. Wide range of rooms, from very simple to deluxe. Table service at breakfast.

⊖⊜⊜⊜ **Hotel Vier Jahreszeiten** – *Neuer Jungfernstieg 9.* ☎ *(040) 349 40 Fax (040) 34942600. www.raffles-hvj.de.* ✄ *156 rooms.* ⊠ One of the last real grand hotels, on the banks of the Alster, with luxurious Gründerzeit decor and charming, modern, comfortable rooms. Quality cuisine in the Haerlin, Doc Cheng's and Jahreszeiten Grill.

TAKING A BREAK

Destille – *Steintorplatz 1 (1st floor, Museum für Kunst und Gewerbe; entrance via Brockesstraße).* ☎ *(040) 2 80 33 54.* ⊕ *11am-5pm (buffet until 4pm).*

Roller-coaster on the Hamburg "Dom"

⊕ *Closed same as museum. Free admis-sion if visiting the museum, otherwise* ⊜ *€1.* A little café with self-service buffet (home-made salads and cakes) where the owner displays his own col-lection of 1930s decorative arts. Restful view of the leafy courtyard through the glass façade.

GOING OUT

USEFUL TIPS

Hamburg's night-life has been associ-ated with the name St Pauli since time immemorial. In addition to its old and established temples of eroticism, the area around the Reeperbahn and Große Freiheit has become the site of the "in" scene recently. 400 food outlets squeeze into these quarters. The inner city, too, between the Gänsemarkt and Millerntor (especially around Großneumarkt) offers a great number of opportunities to eat and drink; the passage quarter between Jungfernstieg and Stadthausbrücke is pleasant. The young, alternative crowd gathers around the "Schanzenviertel" west and southwest of the television tower (between Juliusstraße and Neuer Pferdemarkt).

Alex im Alsterpavillon – *Jungfernstieg 54.* ☎ *(040) 3 50 18 70 . www.alexgastro. de.* ⊕ *Fri-Sat 8am-3am, Mon-Thu 8am-1am, Sun and public holidays 9am-1am.* No doubt the best terrace in Hamburg with a panoramic view of the Binnenal-ster. People of all ages gather through-out the day for a drink or a snack.

Amphore – *Hafenstraße 140 (follows the Elbe toward the west from Landungs-brücken).* ☎ *(040) 31 79 38 80. www.*

cafe-amphore.de. ◷ *Mon-Sun from 10am*. Friendly little café with a lovely harbour view from the terrace above old blockhouses (blankets available). Breakfast served until 3pm.

Café Keese – *Reeperbahn 19-21.* ☎ *(040) 3 19 93 10.* ◷ *Mon-Fri noon-4am, Sat-Sun noon-till late ; dance hall from €5.* A café by day and dance hall by night. Low-key atmosphere and theme evenings: tango Mon, jazz Wed, soul and blues Sun.

Christiansen's Fine Drinks & Cocktails – *Pinnasberg 60 (in St Pauli, near the Fischmarkt).* ☎ *(040) 3 17 28 63. www.christiansens.de.* ◷ *Mon-Sat 8pm-3am.* 250 cocktails, 160 brands of rum and 150 varieties of whisky on offer.

Cotton Club – *Alter Steinweg 10.* ☎ *(040) 34 38 78. www.cotton-club.org.* ◷ *Mon-Sat 8pm-1am, Sun 11am-3pm, admission from €5.* Hamburg's local jazz institution was founded 1959, renamed the "Cotton Club" in 1963 and moved here in 1971. Concerts almost every day.

SHOPPING

USEFUL TIPS

Jungfernstieg, Mönckebergstraße and Spitalerstraße are the main shopping streets with department stores. The shopping arcades in Hamburg's inner city are attractive for shopping, with over 300 speciality stores and boutiques. Exclusive stores have now settled at the Neuer Wall.

Harry's Hamburger Hafenbasar – *Balduinstraße 18 (in St Pauli, at the Erichstraße crossroads).* ☎ *(040) 31 24 82. www.hafenbasar.de.* ◷ *Tue-Sun 12pm-6pm.* ◷ *Closed 2-3 weeks in Jul-Aug. Admission €2.50 (refunded if you buy).* A jumble of objects brought back by sailors from the four corners of the world, more like a museum than a shop. You will find mainly wooden sculptures in the labyrinth of little corridors which fill the two floors of this house.

Art galleries – There is no single area with an especially high concentration of galleries.

Antique dealers – Mainly in the *Quartier Satin* on ABC-Strasse and the *Antik-Center* of the market hall at Klosterwall.

Flea markets – The *Menschen & Märkte* brochure has information on the spontaneous flea markets in Hamburg (and all across northern Germany). Regular flea markets are held on Saturdays in Barmbek (Hellbrockstraße) 7am-5pm, and in Eppendorf (Nedderfeld/Parkhaus) 4:30pm-7:30pm.

Markets – The fish market is Hamburg's most famous, held every Sun, in summer 5:30am-9:30am and in winter 7am-10am. Weekly markets are held in all the city's districts. The typical market held on Mon and Fri under the U-Bahn bridge at Eppendorf is recommended.

⌔ **Also See:** *LÜNEBURG (57km/36mi southeast) and the LÜNEBURGER HEIDE, LÜBECK (67km/42mi northeast), KIEL (94km/59mi north), BREMEN (126km/78mi southwest via the A 1).*

A Bit of History

The Hanseatic Town (13C-15C) – Originally a modest settlement on the banks of the Alster, a small tributary of the Elbe, Hamburg enjoyed its first taste of prosperity when it became a member of the Hanseatic League, headed at that time by Lübeck. It was then that merchants started to organise the banks of the Elbe for warehousing and the berthing of ships.

Liberty and Neutrality – The geographic discoveries of the 16C and the sea routes they opened up destroyed the Hanseatic monopoly, so Hamburg traders set their sights on warehousing and distribution. The foundation of the first German Stock Exchange in 1558 reflected the intense business activity in Hamburg, a situation helped by the city's policy of strict neutrality, which kept it out of the Thirty Years'

The Alster basin right in the heart of the city

War. North and Latin American development greatly expanded the city. By 1913, the Hamburg-Amerika steamship line was the largest in the world, and shipbuilding became the city's key industry.

Business and Leisure – Like many big ports, Hamburg has a reputation for nightlife. This is mainly centred on the St Pauli quarter, west of the city centre, where in the side streets flanking the **Reeperbahn** and the Große Freiheit, bars, discotheques, exotic restaurants, clubs and the Eros Centre function day and night.

But there is much more to Hamburg leisure pursuits than the garish Reeperbahn district. Lake Alster lies like a jewel in the heart of the city. Between the Staatsoper (Opera House) and the Rathaus (town hall), pedestrian precincts and covered shopping centres form an almost uninterrupted labyrinth of galleries, boutiques and restaurants. The Mönckebergstraße, which links the Rathaus with the railway station, is the city's other commercial artery.

Antique shops around the Gänsemarkt specialise in Asian art. Between the Rathaus and the station, an impressive variety of old maps, prints and travel works can be found in booksellers' shops, while philatelists and tobacco lovers go to the small shops in the printing and counting house quarter.

The people of Hamburg are said to be very "British" Germans: they tend to be more reserved and serious than their lively southern compatriots. For visitors, Hamburg is among the most welcoming of German cities, and English is spoken in many of the restaurants, stores and wine cellars.

Culinary Specialities – Local dishes often mix local produce with Eastern spices, sometimes combining in one dish meat, fruit and sweet-and-sour sauces. Typical are *Aalsuppe* – eel soup – and *Labskaus*, a seaman's dish of minced meat, herring, chopped gherkins, beetroot and mashed potato, topped with fried eggs.

The Port of Hamburg

The Hamburg docks comprise 60 basins and more than 68km/43mi of quays. The overall surface area is more than 75km²/29mi². Thanks to a relatively small tidefall (3m/10ft average), no locks are necessary in the basins accessible to ocean-going traffic able to navigate the Elbe. Some 340 shipping lines call regularly (about 650 departures a month) to transport merchandise to 1 100 ports all over the world.

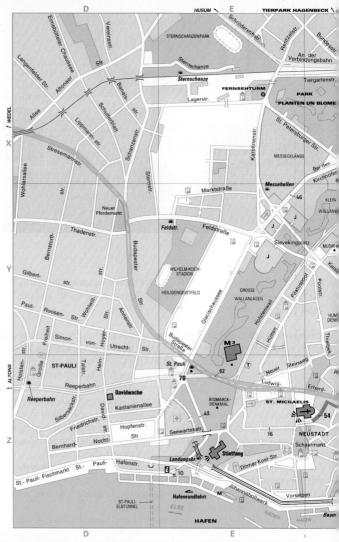

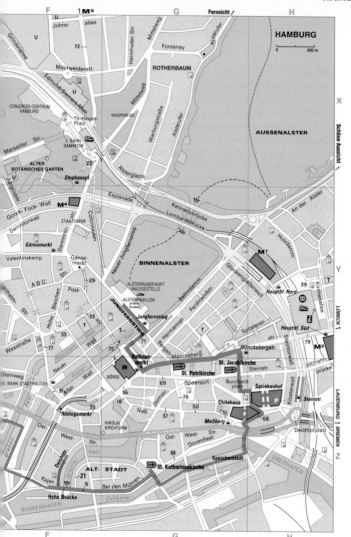

Sights

The Port★★

Exploring the port of Hamburg is one of the highlights of any trip to the city. Apart from the tower of St-Michaelis-Kirche, the best **viewpoint**★ from which to see the port is the Stintfang – a raised terrace below the youth hostel (U/S-Bahn St-Pauli Landungsbrücken).

Boat Trip Around the Port

Kids *Duration: 1hr. Boats leave from the dock near the Baumwall U-bahn station. Apr-Oct: 10am-6pm, every 30min; Nov-Mar: at 12pm and 2pm; Sat-Sun: 10.45am-4pm, every 45min.* ⏣ *€8.50.* ☏ *(040) 37 31 68. www.barkassen-centrale.de.*

Visitors will be astonished by the sheer size of the dockyards and by the extraordinary activity on either side of the Elbe, where every type of vessel is constructed. Motor ferries ply back and forth all day long, transporting south bank workers back to the city during the rush hour. The lively St Pauli Fischmarkt is held every Sun morning, and on public holidays, until 10am.

St Pauli District
North of the port and west of the new town.
St Pauli had its golden age in the 1960s when the Beatles played the Star Club in **Große Freiheit**. Its image was later considerably tarnished by prostitution and drug trafficking, but over the last few years, this district, which has the city's biggest police station **(Davidwache),** has undergone a renaissance. Although the sex industry is still prevalent, the area is full of bars, cafés and restaurants, many with a genuinely warm atmosphere and popular with locals and non-locals alike. St Pauli spreads out around the **Reeperbahn**, the main thoroughfare, which runs parallel to the port.

Walking Tour

City Centre *allow one day*

Kids Binnenalster and Aussenalster★★★
Lake Alster, north of the old town, is a beautiful stretch of water. It consists of two basins, the Binnenalster and the Aussenalster, the latter (the larger of the two) offering sailing and canoeing in the centre of the city. A fleet of Alsterschiffahrt motorboats ferries passengers regularly between a series of docks. A boat trip (Alsterrundfahrt) on the lake allows the visitor to get far enough away to appreciate the city skyline. It is also possible to sail on the Alster canals (beautifully kept parks and villas interspersed with wild areas) and on the canals in the old town and port (two locks allow access to the port area from the Binnenalster).
Departures from the Jungfernstieg dock (50min), end of Mar to end of Oct: 10am-6pm, every 30min; from end of Oct to end of Mar: "Punch Cruises" at 10.30am, 12pm, 1.30pm and 3pm. ☜ *€10. Alster-Kreuz-Fahrt (a choice of 9 docks), end of Mar to end of Sep: 10.15am-5.15pm, every hour.* ☜ *€1.30 per dock,* ☜ *€8.50 return.* ☏ *(040) 35 74 24 19. www.alstertouristik.de.*
Those with transportation can drive clockwise around the Alster, bordered by luxury apartments on one side and immaculate parks on the other.

Jungfernstieg★
Bordering the southern end of the Binnenalster (Inner Alster), this famous street is perhaps the city's most cosmopolitan thoroughfare: the crowded terraces of the waterfront Alsterpavillon café-restaurant, the boats crossing and recrossing the basin, the presence nearby of one of the world's most famous hotels (Vier Jahreszeiten), and the imposing new office blocks lining the Ballindamm all contribute to the general animation.

▸ *Leave Jungfernstieg and walk along-side the Alsterfleet to the town hall square.*

Rathausmarkt
This square, replanned after the fire of 1842, is dominated by the high campanile of the Rathaus, built in the neo-Renaissance style in 1897. The bridge (Schleusenbrücke), which forms part of the Alster's lock system, crosses the Alsterfleet, a final

The Fish Market
The Hamburg fish market originated in the early 18C and has become a veritable institution. It is held every Sunday morning in the south of the St Pauli district along the Elbe from 5.30am to 9.30am. The cheerful fishmongers, crowds of people of all ages who come to buy or simply to have a look, and musical entertainment in the *Fischauktionhalle* have made it part of living Hamburg folklore.

Speicherstadt warehouses

Hamburg Tourismus GmbH

relic of the city's former canal system. On the far bank the colonnade of the Alster-arkaden shelters elegant shops.

▶ *Turn into Mönckebergstraße.*

St-Petrikirche
In Mönckebergstraße.
This 12C church was rebuilt in neo-Gothic style after the great fire of 1842.

St-Jakobikirche
Among the treasures of this 14C-15C hall-church are the reredos of St Luke and the Fishers' Guild; a triptych of the Coopers' Guild on the high altar; Georg Bauman's alabaster and marble pulpit (1610); and the famous 1693 organ by Arp Schnitger.

▶ *Cross Steinstraße heading south to Burchardplatz.*

Kontorhäuser (Counting House Buildings)
Massively constructed of sombre brick, these stand in the printing, press and business quarter around the Burchard-platz.
Of particular interest is the **Chilehaus** (*Between Burgstraße and Meßberg*). Built in 1924 by Expressionist architect Fritz Höger, this building stands against the sky like the prow of a ship. It was built for a rich local merchant who made his fortune mainly through trade relations with Chile.
The **Sprinkenhof** (1931) is a town within the town, an office complex complete with roadways that can be used by motor cars.

▶ *Continue southwards and cross the Auf dem Sande canal to explore Speichers-tadt.*

Speicherstadt★
After Hamburg joined the German Customs Federation, a free trade zone became necessary. A whole district was destroyed along the Zoll Canal and its secondary channels to make room for the Speicherstadt warehouses in 1885. They still store in their 373 000m²/447 000sq yd of floor space (the world's largest continuous warehouse complex) such valuable merchandise as coffee, tobacco, spices, raw silk and

oriental carpets. With its rows of gabled brick buildings with green copper roofs, Speicherstadt is an original place for a pleasant stroll.

Altstadt

The old town is bounded by the Nikolaifleet, the Binnenhafen (docks reserved for river craft and tugboats) and the Zoll Canal.

Highlights of the old town begin with the **St-Katharinenkirche,** a 14C-15C Gothic brick church featuring a bulbous openwork tower above the narrow streets of the old port. **Cremon** street, from no. 33 to no. 36, is lined by warehouses and lodging houses, each with dual entrances, one from the street, one from the canal.

It was farther along on the **Deichstraße** that the great fire of 1842 started. The 17C-18C merchants' houses have today been converted into bars and taverns. The restored façades of warehouses opposite, lining the curve of the Nikolaifleet Canal, recall the Hamburg of yesteryear.

The best view is from the **Hohe Brücke**, which crosses the Nikolaifleet and lies parallel with the Binnenhafen.

St-Michaelis-Kirche★

A brick church, designed in 1762 by Ernst Georg Sonnin, this is one of the finest examples of the Baroque tradition in northern Germany. Its famous tower (1786), rising high above the Elbe, has become the emblem of the city. The **view**★ from the platform takes in the town centre; most people love the river views, crisscrossed with the wakes of ships.

Near the east end of the church, pass through the porch at no 10 Am Krayenkamp. The blind alley beyond is lined with 17C brick and timber houses, built as almshouses (Krameramtswohnungen); today they are art galleries.

Sights

Hamburger Kunsthalle★★ (Fine Arts Museum)

&. ○ *Open daily except Mon, 10am-6pm, Thu 10am-9pm.* ○ *Closed 24 Dec.* ⊜ *€8.50.* ☎ *(040) 428 13 12 00. www.hamburger-kunsthalle.de.*

This museum houses one of the largest art collections in Germany. Medieval works include religious artworks, as well as 17C Dutch Masters and land- and seascapes (Rembrandt, Van Goyen, Ruysdael and Van de Velde).

A particular strength of the exhibition is the section of 19C-20C German painting. Prominently displayed are works by Caspar David Friedrich, Phiilipp Otto Runge, Feuerbach, Von Marées, Böcklin, Menzel and Wilhelm Leibl, whose famous painting *Three Women in Church* can be found hanging here. There is a dazzling display of work by Max Liebermann, Lovis Corinth and Edvard Munch, and works by Max Beckmann, Oskar Kokoschka, Paul Klee and members of the *Brücke* and *Blaue Reiter* groups.

The Galerie der Gegenwart is devoted to post-1960 art. Look for works by Richard Serra, Claes Oldenburg, Jenny Holzer, Bruce Naumann and Andy Warho. German art is also well represented by artists like Sigmar Polke, Georg Baselitz, Markus Lüpertz, Mario Merz, Gerhard Richter, Rosemarie Trockel and Joseph Beuys.

Museum für Kunst und Gewerbe★ (Museum of Decorative Arts)

Steintorplatz 1, opposite the central station. &. ○ *Open daily except Mon, 10am-6pm, Thu 10am-9pm.* ○ *Closed 1 Jan, 1 May, 24 and 31 Dec.* ⊜ *€8.* ☎ *(040) 428 134 27 32. www.mkg-hamburg.de.*

In a 19C neo-Renaissance palace, this vast museum houses collections of sculptures, ceramics, furniture, jewelry and musical instruments. The exhibition covers periods from Antiquity to the present, including a remarkable Art Nouveau gallery.

Museum für Hamburgische Geschichte★ (History Museum)

  ♿ ⏱ *Open daily except Mon, 10am-5pm, Sun 10am-6pm.* ⏱ *Closed 1 Jan, 1 May, 24 and 31 Dec.* ✆ *€7.50.* ☎ *(040) 428 132 23 80. www.hamburgmuseum.de.*
Exhibits include models of historic Hamburg: a scale model of the city and the harbour; a shipping section (over 100 models); and a model of the railway system.

Tierpark Hagenbeck★★ (Zoo)

Kids *Leave by the Grindelallee.* ♿ ⏱ *Apr-Oct: 9am-5pm (later in good weather); Nov-Mar: 9am-4.30pm.* ✆ *€14.50.* ☎ *(040) 540 00 10. www.hagenbeck.de.*
This wonderful park founded in 1907, with ancient trees, artificial lakes and crags, is a delightful place for a stroll. Some 2 500 creatures of 360 species from five continents live in open corrals. The zoo is especially proud of its Asian elephants.

Excursions

Altona; Klein Flottbek; Wedel
22km/14mi

Altonaer Museum in Hamburg und Norddeutsches Landesmuseum★★ (Altona and North German Museum)

Leave on the Reeperbahn. ♿ ⏱ *Open daily except Mon, 10am-6pm (10pm Thur).* ⏱ *Closed 1st May, 24 and 31 Dec.* ✆ *€6.* ☎ *(040) 428 11 35 82.*

Art, culture and day-to-day life in the lower Elbe valley and Schleswig-Holstein are illustrated here. Note the exceptional collection of ships' figureheads from the 18C-19C, the models of North Sea boats, the ceramics, fine Frisian embroidery and old toys. There is also a gallery with paintings of north German landscapes.

Altonaer Museum in Hamburg – Norddeutsches Landesmuseum

"Terpsichore" ship's figurehead, Altona Museum

Altonaer Balkon (Altona Balcony)
The terrace south of Altona's town hall affords a **view**★ of the Köhlbrandbrücke and confluence of the two branches of the Elbe, a busy shipping lane. Follow the **Elbchaussee**★, a spacious avenue bordered by great houses since the early 19C.

▷ *At Klein Flottbek, turn right and drive along the Baron-Voght-Strasse as far as house no. 50.*

Jenisch-Haus, in Klein Flottbek
⏱ *Open daily except Mon, 11am-6pm.* ⏱ *Closed 1st May, 24 and 31 Dec.* ✆ *€4.* ☎ *(040) 82 87 90.*
A landscaped park with exotic trees surrounds this pleasant 19C neo-Classical villa. The luxurious rooms illustrate the style of German bourgeois interiors from the Late Renaissance to the beginning of the Jugendstil period.

Ernst-Barlach-Haus, in Klein Flottbek
Baron-Voght-Strasse 50 A. ⏱ *Open daily except Mon, 11am-6pm.* ⏱ *Closed 24 and 31 Dec.* ✆ *€5.* ☎ *(040) 82 60 85. www.barlach-haus.de.*
Designed to house cigarette mogul Hermann F Reemtsma's private collection, the Ernst-Barlach-Haus contains sculptures, wood engravings and drawings by this artist, born in Wedel.

▶ *Continue along the Elbchaussee, then head for Wedel after driving through the pleasant suburban resort of Blankenese.*

Wedel

▶ *Follow the Willkomm-Höft signposts to the café-restaurant beside the Elbe known as the Schulauer Fährhaus.*

Above the terrace is a saluting base for passing ships *(Schiffsbegrüßungsanlage)*. The ceremony involves saluting the colours according to the maritime code, and playing the national anthem of the country represented by the passing ship.

An Ernst-Barlach-Museum is located in the house where the artist was born *(Mühlenstraße 1)*. The works on display range from drawings and lithographs to bronzes. ○ *Open daily except Mon, 10am-6pm.* ⊙ €5. ☎ *(041 03) 91 82 91.*

Stade★

This town over 1 000 years old lies on the banks of the navigable stretch of the Schwinge, which flows into the Elbe. In the Middle Ages, Stade was a port of the size of Hamburg. The Swedes occupied the town during the Thirty Years' War and transformed it into a garrison stronghold and administrative centre.

Old Town★★

Most buildings in the beautiful old town were built after 1659, the date of a great fire. Among the picturesque half-timbered houses, note Hökerhaus *(Hökerstraße 27)*, Doppelhaus *(Bäckerstraße 1-3)* and Haus Knechthausen *(Bungenstraße 20)*.

Old Port

The meticulously restored houses reveal some sense of how this 17C port looked in its day. The most magnificent home is the **Bürgermeister-Hintze-Haus** *(Wasser West)*.

Schwedenspeicher-Museum★

Am Wasser West. ○ *Open daily except Mon, 10am-5pm, Sat-Sun 10am-6pm.* ○ *Closed 1 Jan, 25 and 31 Dec.* ⊙ €1. ☎ *(041 41) 32 22. www.schwedenspeicher.de.*
Built between 1692 and 1705, this Swedish brick granary houses a history museum. There is also a prehistoric department with four **bronze wheels★** (c 700 BC) from a funerary carriage, as well as antique jewellery, weapons and pots.

HAMELN★

POPULATION: 59 000

This town is the setting for the Tale of the Pied Piper, as told by the Brothers Grimm in the 19C. Hameln glories in fine old houses, of which many belong to the Weser Renaissance. 🔲 *Deisterallee 1, 31785 Hameln.* ☎ *(051 51) 20 26 17.*

▶ **Orient Yourself:** Built on the banks of the Weser, Hameln is located at the crossroads of 217 (Hannover-Paderborn) and 1 (Minden-Hildesheim). The town extends into the Weserbergland, a hilly expanse that becomes a nature park.

🔄 **Don't Miss:** The unique Weser Renaissance architecture, best seen on foot.

○ **Organizing Your Time:** Allow one hour to see the Altstadt.

🧒 **Especially for Kids:** Weekly fairy tale reenactments.

🔦 **Also See:** *LEMGO (41km/26mi southwest), HILDESHEIM (49km/30mi east), HANNOVER (45km/28mi northeast).*

Address Book

WHERE TO EAT

🍽️🍽️ **Grüner Reiter** – *Kastanienwall 62* ☎ *(05151) 92 62 00. www.gruenerreiter. de.* 🕐 *Mon-Fri. 9am-11:30pm.* ♿ This building was built in 1713 as a chapel for the soldiers of the Hameln Fortress. A bistro-style restaurant is located in a glass extension in the courtyard.

WHERE TO STAY

🍽️🍽️🍽️ **An der Altstadt** – *Deisterallee 16.* ☎ *(05151) 402 40. Fax (05151) 402444. www.hotel-an-der-altstadt.de.* 🕐 *Closed end Dec to mid-Jan.* 🅿 🛏️ *19 rooms.*

🛏️ This Jugendstil hotel in the heart of the legendary "rat catcher's town" has guestrooms furnished in cherrywood.

TAKING A BREAK

Museumscafé – *Osterstraße 8.* ☎ *(05151) 215 53. www.museumscafe.de* 🕐 *Closed Christmas and 1 Jan.* The Museumscafé of the Canons' House *(Stiftsherrnhaus)* built in 1562 has without doubt one of the most beautiful half-timbered facades in town. Delicious cakes and tarts are on the menu, as are substantial meals. Try the rat catcher's tart *(Rattenfängertorte)!*

A Bit of History

A Jewel of the Weser Renaissance – The Weser Renaissance style (late 16-early 17C) so well displayed in Hameln is distinguished architecturally by ram's-horn scrollwork and pinnacled gables. Other characteristics include delicately worked stone bands encircling the building, forward projecting pavilions *(Utluchten)*, and large, well-developed dormers *(Zwerchhäuser)* with decorated gables at the base of the roof.

The Pied Piper of Hameln – In 1284, a mysterious man in multicoloured clothes promised the townspeople that, for a substantial reward, he would free Hameln from a plague of rats and mice. He played his pipe, and all the rodents emerged to follow him to the banks of the Weser, where they drowned.

When the townspeople didn't pay him, the piper returned and played again in revenge. This time it was the children who emerged from their houses. There were 130 of them, and they too followed him, never to be seen again. Only two escaped; one was mute, the other blind. The rather less romantic but more accurate version of this tale is that 13C overpopulation led to a troop of young people being sent by the authorities to colonise territories to the east. But it is the former 🧒**Kids** **Grimm fairytale** that is acted out every Sunday at midday on the terrace of the Hochzeitshaus.

Walking Tour

Altstadt★ (Old Town)

Rattenfängerhaus★ (The Rat Catcher's House)

This large, 1603 building has little to do with rats, but is a fine example of Weser Renaissance building. The symmetrical façade features sculpted bands of stonework, adorned with carved busts and masks.

▶ *Take the Osterstraße, one of the most well-known streets in Hameln. It is here on 26 July 1284, that the children followed the Pied Piper. Stop at the top of the Kleine Strasse to look at the splendid Renaissance houses (Haus Osterstrasse 12, Leithaus and Stiftherrenhaus).*

Stiftsherrenhaus (Canons' House)

Osterstraße 8.
Another remarkable house, this one half-timbered and built in 1558, features sculpted consoles representing biblical figures. This and the Leisthaus next door house the local museum.

Demptersches Haus

In the market place.
An outstanding building from 1607, note its fine Weser Renaissance projecting pavilion *(Utlucht).*

Hochzeitshaus★

On the Markt.
The building, constructed between 1610 and 1617, acted as a reception centre for burghers' weddings. Three elegant gables break the horizontals of the façade.

▶ *Take the Fischpfortenstraße and pass in front of Wilhelm-Busch-Haus. From there, continue until you reach the Weser. Retrace your steps until you reach the Wendenstraße where the Burgerhus and the Lückingsches Haus are found.*

Haus Lücking

Wendenstraße 8.
This rich, half-timbered house of 1638 features a rounded doorway and is lavishly adorned with inscriptions and ornamentation.

▶ *At the end of the road, turn right into Bäckerstraße.*

Rattenkrug

Bäckerstraße 16.
A projecting pavilion *(Utlucht)* and a tall gable of five floors distinguish this 1568 building, an early Gothic building dating from 1250.

▶ *Continue until the Münsterkirchhof.*

Münsterkirchhof (Collegiate Church)

From the gardens to the south, the church appears to cower beneath the protection of the massive polygonal tower, once part of a 12C Romanesque basilica. Inside, the layout of the columns and their capitals draws attention to the raised transept.

▶ *Finish the tour by coming back along Alte Markt-Strasse, noticing the Kürie Jérusalem passageway.*

HANNOVER

POPULATION: 520 000

Hannover is one of northern Germany's main economic centres, and is also at the forefront of national politics. But leisure travelers will find plenty of pleasant pastimes in this city, most notably, its gardens. *Ernst-August-Platz 8, 30159 Hannover. ☎ (0511) 12 34 51 11. Open Mon-Fri 9am-7pm and Sat 9:30am-3pm.*

▶ **Orient Yourself:** Set on a plain on the banks of the Leine and the Mittelandkanal, Hannover is halfway between the Baltic Sea and the North Sea. The A2 (Dortmund-Berlin) and A7 (Kassel-Hamburg) motorways intersect here.

P **Parking:** Garages are located throughout Hannover; many are located just north of the Hauptbahnhof (main train station).

Don't Miss: Hannover's terrific gardens.

Organizing Your Time: Allow two hours to see the Herrenhäuser Gardens.

Kids **Especially for Kids:** The Hannover Zoo.

Address Book

WHERE TO EAT

Der Gartensaal – *Trammplatz 2. ☎ (0511) 16 84 88 88. www.gartensaal-hannover.de.* Open 11am-6pm, mid May to mid Sep: 11am-10pm. This bistro's unusual location is the southern entrance of the historic town hall. Arched floor-to-ceiling windows offer superb views.

Broyhan-Haus – *Kramerstraße 24 ☎ (0511) 32 39 19 www.broyhanhaus.de.* Closed public holidays. Reservation necessary. This 14C building, one of the city's oldest bourgeois houses, was bought in 1537 by master brewer Cord Broyhan. The Urbock beer bars and cellars inside cover three floors.

WHERE TO STAY

CVJM City Hotel – *Limburgstraße 3 ☎ (0511) 360 70 Fax (0511) 3607177. www.cityhotelhannover.de.* 47 rooms. A comfortable, impeccably-run hotel in the pedestrian zone. The breakfast room has a Mediterranean feel.

Kastens Hotel Luisenhof – *Luisenstraße 1. ☎ (0511) 304 40. Fax (0511) 3044807. www.kastens-luisenhof.de.* P 152 rooms Restaurant. Comfort reigns in the oldest hotel in Hannover (1856). Elegant furnishings and a tower suite with a superb city views.

TAKING A BREAK

Holländische Kakao-Stube – *Ständehausstraße 2-3 (Luisenstraße to the southwest). ☎ (0511) 30 41 00.* Open Mon-Fri 9am-7:30pm, Sat 8:30am-6pm. Closed Sun, public holidays. If you like hot chocolate check out this establishment decorated with Dutch ceramics. Homemade pastries and other dishes are also on the menu.

GOING OUT

heimW – *Theaterstraße 6. ☎ (0511) 2 35 23 03. www.heim-w.de.* Fri-Sat 9am-2am, Mon-Thu 9am-1am, Sun 10am-1am. 1970s café-bar with a casual feel. Even if you're not prone to nostalgia (*Heimweh* in German), the family welcome and seasonal dishes make it worth a visit. The back room with its aquarium resembles an old sitting room.

Oscar's – *Georgstraße 54. ☎ (0511) 32 04 08. www.oscarsbar.de.* Sun-Thu 4pm-1am, Fri-Sat 4pm-3am. Traditional cocktail bar with dark wooden decor. In summer, enjoy the pavement terrace and sample one of the 200 whiskies or other drinks (alcoholic or non-alcoholic). An ideal place to stop after exploring the city. Happy hour 4-8pm.

👣 **Also See:** *HILDESHEIM (33km/20.5mi south via the A7), CELLE (41km/25.5mi north-east), HAMELN (45km/28mi southwest), BRAUNSCHWEIG (63km/39mi east via the A2), BREMEN (129km/80mi northwest).*

Sights

Herrenhäuser Gärten★★ (Herrenhausen Gardens)

This 17C development comprises four separate and varied gardens. They are linked by the Herrenhäuser Allee, laid out in 1726.

Großer Garten★★

Creation of the garden started in 1666, and continued 15 years later under Princess Sophia. The oldest section, a French pleasure garden, features statues of allegorical figures and Roman gods. The paths in the southern section spread out around water features.

😊 **A Bit of Advice** 😊

Over a distance of around 4km/3mi, the "Red Line" leads you through the city from the new town hall (check out the view from the dome), where you can admire models of Hannover in different periods, to the Herren-hausen gardens. ♿ 🕐 *Open from the end of Mar to the beginning of Nov: 9.30am-6.30pm, Sat-Sun 10am-6.30pm; all other days 11am-4pm.* 🎫 *€3.* ☎ *(0511) 12 34 51 11.*

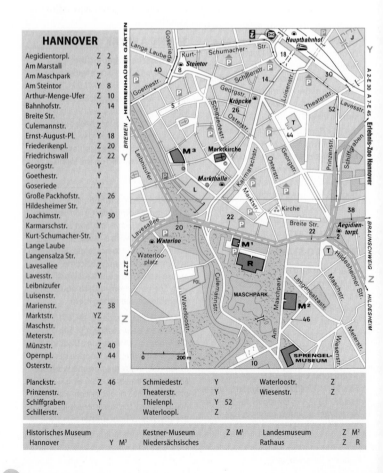

HANNOVER

Aegidientorpl.	Z	2
Am Marstall	Y	5
Am Maschpark	Z	
Am Steintor	Y	8
Arthur-Menge-Ufer	Z	10
Bahnhofstr.	Y	14
Breite Str.	Z	
Culemannstr.	Z	
Ernst-August-Pl.	Y	18
Friederikenpl.	Z	20
Friedrichswall	Z	22
Georgstr.	Y	
Goethestr.	Y	
Goseriede	Y	
Große Packhofstr.	Y	26
Hildesheimer Str.	Z	
Joachimstr.	Y	30
Karmarschstr.	Y	
Kurt-Schumacher-Str.	Y	
Lange Laube	Y	
Langensalza Str.	Z	
Lavesallee	Z	
Lavesstr.	Y	
Leibnizufer	Y	
Luisenstr.	Y	
Marienstr.	Z	38
Marktstr.	YZ	
Maschstr.	Z	
Meterstr.	Z	
Münzstr.	Z	40
Opernpl.	Y	44
Osterstr.	Y	

Planckstr.	Z	46	Schmiedestr.	Y		Waterloostr.	Z	
Prinzenstr.	Y		Theaterstr.	Y		Wiesenstr.	Z	
Schiffgraben	Y		Thielenpl.	Y	52			
Schillerstr.	Y		Waterloopl.	Z				

Historisches Museum			Kestner-Museum	Z	M¹	Landesmuseum	Z	M²
Hannover	Y	M³	Niedersächsisches			Rathaus	Z	R

Georgengarten

♿ 🕐 *Apr-Oct: open daily except Mon, 11am-5pm, Sun 11am-6pm; Nov-Mar: open daily except Mon, 11am-4pm, Sun 11am-6pm.* 🕐 *Closed Good Friday, 24 and 31 Dec.* 👓 *€4.50.* ☎ *(0511) 16 99 99 11.*

This romantically landscaped park was laid out between 1835 and 1841 with great expanses of lawn. In its midst is the Leibniztempel and the Wallmodenschlößchen, a pavilion housing the **Wilhelm-Busch-Museum**, dedicated to the famous poet, illustrator and humorist (1832-1908) who launched comic strips with such stories as "Max und Moritz."

Berggarten★

The greenhouses of this botanical garden display cacti as well as 2 500 orchids and flora native to the Canary Islands. At the far end of the garden's principal walk is the mausoleum of the Royal House of Hanover.

Welfengarten

The Welfenschloß (now a university) stands in the Welfengarten. In front of the building is the trademark of the state of Niedersachsen, the Saxon Steed, created in 1876 by Friedrich Wolff.

Marktkirche

A four-gabled tower crowned by a sharp pinnacle presides over this Gothic brick church, rebuilt after 1945 to mimic the 14C original. The modern 1957 bronze doors by Gerhard Marcks contrast sharply with the style of the remaining church. Inside, note the superb 15C sculpted polychrome **reredos**★★ representing the Passion.

Niedersächsisches Landesmuseum★ (Museum of Lower Saxony)

♿ 🕐 *Open daily except Mon, 10am-5pm, Thu 10am-7pm.* 🕐 *Closed Easter Sunday, Tue after Easter, 1 May, Pentecost, Tue after Pentecost, 24, 25 and 31 Dec.* 👓 *€4.* ☎ *(0511) 980 76 00. www.nlmh.de.*

This museum is divided into four departments. The **prehistoric department**★ *(Urgeschichte-Abteilung)* exhibits significant original artifacts from the prehistory and early history of Lower Saxony, including a well-preserved corpse. The **nature department** *(Naturkunde-Abteilung)* concentrates on the Lower Saxony countryside, earth's evolution and transformation. The **Lower Saxony picture gallery** *(Niedersächsische Landesgalerie)* exhibits paintings and sculptures from nine centuries, with an emphasis on German art from the Middle Ages to the Renaissance and from the 19C and 20C (Holbein, Cranach, Riemenschneider); 14C-18C Italian painting

Zoologischer Garten

Elephants at Hannover zoo

(Botticelli, Tiepolo); and 17C Dutch and Flemish painting (Rubens, Ruysdael). The **ethnography department** *(Völkerkunde-Abteilung)* features exhibits from New Guinea, Mexico and Indonesia.

Sprengel-Museum Hannover★

&. ○ *Open daily except Mon, 10am-6pm, Tue 10am-8pm.* ○ *Closed Good Friday, 1st May, 24 and 25 Dec.* ⊛ *€6.* ☏ *(0511) 16 84 38 75. www.sprengel-museum.de.*
A stabile by Calder, the *Hellebardier*, serves as a landmark for this museum of 20C art. Major exhibitions include Cubist works by Picasso, works of the Brücke (Schmidt-Rottluff) and the Blaue Reiter movements (Kandinsky, Jawlensky, Macke) and the surrealist movement (Kurt Schwitters, Hannoverian by birth). Contemporary spokesmen include Tapiès, Dubuffet and Willi Baumeister.

Zoologischer Garten (Zoological Garden)

Kids *Adenauerallee 3.* &. ○ *Open Mar-Oct, 9am-6pm; Nov-Feb, 10am-4pm.* ⊛ *€18.* ☏ *(0511) 28 07 41 63. www.zoo-hannover.de.*
The Hannover Zoo is known for its experiential installations: the gorilla mountain with its waterfall; a 12 000m²/120 000sq ft jungle palace for elephants, tigers and leopards; a Zambezi landscape with lions, giraffes and okapis; the African steppes for zebras, gazelles and ostriches; and the "evolution path" that traces the Neanderthal.

HARZ★★

The wooded heights of the Harz are a popular weekend destination for Germans. Hiking, mountain biking, canoeing, skiing and rock-climbing are among the many activities the area has to offer.

▶ **Orient Yourself:** The Harz borders the southern edge of the Germano-Polish plain, between the rivers Elbe and Weisser, and extending 100km/62mi.

☻ **Don't Miss:** The views from the Bodetal.

○ **Organizing Your Time:** Allow half a day for either the Upper or Eastern Harz driving tours (☝ *see below*).

Kids **Especially for Kids:** Outdoor recreation in general, especially Rübeland.

☝ **Also See:** *Surrounding area (distances from Goslar): see WOLFENBÜTTEL (36km/22mi north), HILDESHEIM (51km/32mi northwest), BRUNSWICK (46km/29mi north), MAGDEBURG (109km/68mi northeast).*

A Bit of History

Natural environment – The wooded heights of the Harz form the northern foothills of central Europe. Almost entirely covered in forests, they break the westerly damp winds and create a region plentiful with rivers and lakes. Dams have transformed the Harz into an exceptional reservoir supplying nearby areas. The Harz was rich in mineral resources; zinc, copper, lead and silver have all been mined here. These mines no longer function but several museums recall their history.

☻ **A Bit of Advice** ☻

The Harzquerbahn, a narrow-gauge railway with steam locomotives, penetrates the region from north to south, from Wernigerode to Nordhausen. It provides an excellent way of exploring the heart of the eastern Harz, especially between Wernigerode and the resort of Eisfelder Talmühle, but also from Schierke to the Brocken.

◎◎ **Hotel Zum Brockenbäcker** – *Lindenwarte 20, 38875 Tanne.* ☏ *(039457) 97 60. Fax (039457) 97633. www.brockenbaecker.de.* ◷ *Closed one week in Nov.* ▣ ✕ *16 rooms.* ☲ Typical of the Harz region, this 1912 hotel features rustic guestrooms and hot, fresh-baked bread at breakfast.

◎◎◎◎ **Michels Kurhotel Vier Jahreszeiten** – *Herzog-Julius-Strasse 64b, 38667. Bad Harzburg.* ☏ *(05322) 78 70. Fax (05322) 787200. www.kurhotelvierjahreszeiten. de.* ▣ ꒱ ✕ *74 rooms.* ☲ ◎◎◎ *Restaurant.* This establishment's recent renovation brings this former spa right up to date, melding historic architecture and a modern interior. The restaurant resembles an elegant tearoom.

A place of legend – The highest point of the range, the **Brocken** (1 142m/3 747ft), attracts many walkers to its windswept slopes. At the summit, according to legend, witches meet on the first night of May *(Walpurgisnacht)* for the Witches' Sabbath, a scene made famous in a chapter of Goethe's *Faust*. The shops of the Harz stock souvenirs relating to the *Walpurgis* legend.

Driving Tour

The Upper Harz ☐1

81km/50mi
This itinerary passes through vast tracts of rolling country with pine-covered hills.

Goslar★★ ♿ *See GOSLAR.*

Clausthal-Zellerfeld

Here is the former mining capital of the Harz. At Zellerfeld, the **Upper Harz Mine Museum** *(Oberharzer Bergwerksmuseum)* illustrates mining techniques used until 1930 and documents the history of the region. ◷ *Open 9am-5pm.* ◷ *Closed 24 Dec.* ⬡ *€4.* ☏ *(053 23) 989 50. www.oberharzerbergwerksmuseum.de.*
At Clausthal, in the *Hindenburgplatz*, the **Pfarrkirche zum Heiligen Geist**, built before 1642, is one of the largest wooden churches in Europe.
From the top of the **Oker Dam** *(Okertalsperre)* there is a fine **view**★ over the widely dispersed waters of the reservoir.

Harz countryside

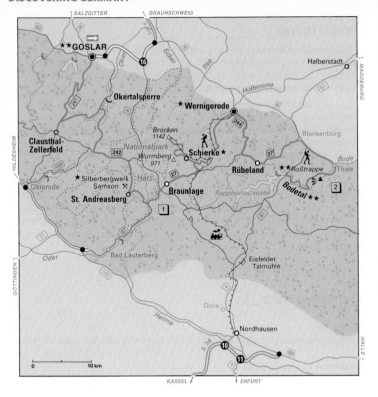

St. Andreasberg

The road leads first to an **old silver mine**★ (*Silberbergwerk Samson,* at the bottom of the valley), closed in 1910 but reopened for tourists. The *Fahrkunst,* a machine of ingenious simplicity which sent down and brought back the miners, can be seen at work. 🚶 *Guided tour (75min) 9am-4pm.* 🕐 *Closed 1 Jan and 24 Dec.* 💶 *€4.50.* ☎ *(055 82) 12 49.*

Braunlage

🅂🄿🄰 Served by the Brocken railway, this spa resort, prized for its climate and for skiing, lies high up on a plateau overlooked by the wooded slopes of the **Wurmberg** (971m/3 186ft).

Schierke

If you want to climb the summit of the **Brocken** – or at least have a go at it – the Schierke station on the Brocken railway is the place to start. Many hiking paths begin at this site, and most of them lead up.

Wernigerode★

Wernigerode is one of the most delightful small towns in this region. The 16C **Town Hall**★★ (*on the Markplatz*) is considered one of the finest half-timbered buildings in Germany. The town's narrow streets are bordered by **half-timbered houses**★★. The most picturesque group ranges from the 16C-18C and lines the Breite Straße as it leaves Marktplatz. The wooden sections and joists are often decorated with masks or carved patterns – as for instance the 1674 house at no 72 known as the "Krummelsches Haus".

The Eastern Harz ②

89km/55mi
In the Eastern Harz, forests are deciduous and the landscape is simply spectacular.

Wernigerode★ (👣 *see above*)

Rübeland

Kids Limestone caving is the chief pastime in Rübeland, with grottoes formed by erosion. In **Hermann's Grotto**★ *(Hermannshöhle)*, note particularly the Chamber of Crystals and the small pool stocked with "cave fish" *(Grottenolmen)* – blind creatures, living out their whole lives in darkness. 👁‍🗨 *Guided tour (45min),*🕐 *Jul to Aug, 9am-5:30pm; Feb to Oct, 9am-4.30pm; Nov to Jan, 9am-3:30pm.* 🕐 *Closed 24 Dec.* 👓 €5. ☎ (0394 54) 491 32.

▶ *Continue via Blankenburg and Thale to reach the Bode Valley.*

Bodetal★★

The river here has gouged a passage through a maze of rock masses and now flows along the foot of impressive cliffs. The most spectacular site is the **Roßtrappe**★★ (The Charger's Hoofmark), a 10min walk from the parking lot. From the look-out point, which juts out dizzyingly above the river far below, there is an incredible **view**★★★ of sheer cliffs, a tumbling stream, a steep gorge and the distant woods. The place owes its name to the legend that a horse, ridden by a princess and chased by a giant, leapt with such force across the gulf that it left an imprint in the rock.
Following the course of the river, the scenic stretch of road twists and turns through the rugged forest landscape as far as the junction with Route 81.

HEIDELBERG★★

POPULATION: 140 000

A source of inspiration for many a poet, each charmed by the town's natural beauty and its castle, Heidelberg symbolizes German Romanticism. Hölderlin wrote a famous ode to Heidelberg, and Brentano, Eichendorff and Von Arnim were among the Romantics who gathered here in the early 19C. But this jewel of the Neckar is also a lively university town with a vibrant cultural scene. ℹ *Willy-Brandt-Platz 1 (central station), 69115 Heidelberg.* ☎ *(062 21) 194 33.*

▶ **Orient Yourself:** Heidelberg is 20km/12mi east of Mannheim and reached via the A 5 motorway (Frankfurt-Freiburg). From the right bank of the Neckar, on either side of the bridge (Alte Brücke or Karl-Theodor Brücke), are **views**★★ of the castle ruins and the old town clustered around the Heiliggeistkirche. Further views of the castle and the town can be seen from the Philosophenweg (Philosophers' Walk), reached by crossing the Alte Brücke and climbing the Schlangenweg.

🅿 **Parking:** Heidelberg has several garages in the Old City. Especially convenient are those on Neue Schloßstraße, near the castle, and under Karlsplatz, near the Rathaus.

👁 **Don't Miss:** The hallmark Heidelberg Castle, a walking tour of the Old City and a panoramic stroll along the Philosophers' Walk (👣 Philosophenweg, *see above*).

🕐 **Organizing Your Time:** Allow half a day for a tour of the castle.

🕐 **Also See:** *MANNHEIM (20km/12.5mi northwest via the A 656), SPEYER (27km/17mi southwest), BRUCHSAL (38km/24mi south), WORMS (50km/31mi northwest) or Bad WIMPFEN (57km/36mi east).*

A Bit of History

The Political Capital of the Palatinate – The Rhineland Palatinate, of which Heidelberg was the political centre, owes its name to the "palatines," the highest officers in the Holy Roman Emqire. These functions no longer existed in the 14C, but their vestiges remained with the hereditary family. The governing prowess of these palatine-electors *(Kurfürsten)* made the Palatinate *(Kurpfalz)* one of the most advanced states of Europe.

The "Orléans War" (1688-97) – In the 16C, Elector Karl-Ludwig, hoping to ensure peace, married his daughter **Liselotte** (Elisabeth-Charlotte) to Duke Philip of Orléans,

Address Book

WHERE TO EAT

🍴🍷 **Kulturbrauerei Heidelberg**
– *Leyergasse 6 (between Hauptstraße and Am Hachteufel).* ☎ *(06221) 50 29 80. www.heidelberger-kulturbrauerei. de.* 🕐 *11am-1am (food until 11pm, beer garden until 10pm).* 🚭 ♿ 🍷🍷*20 rooms.* This restaurant, renovated in 2000, keeps its old-style charm with coffered ceilings and cast iron chandeliers. Beer brewed on-site, regional specialities on the menu. Spacious rooms in the hotel next door.

🍷🍷🍷 **Schlossweinstube** – *(in Heidelberg Castle).* ☎ *(06221) 979 70. www. schoenmehl.de.* 🕐 *Closed 23 Dec-15 Jan and Wed.* Modern black chairs provide a charming contrast with the princely setting: wooden floors and valuable paintings.

WHERE TO STAY

🍷 **Hotel-Restaurant Schnookeloch** – *Haspelgasse 8.* ☎ *(06221) 13 80 80. Fax (06221) 1380813. www. schnookeloch.de. Reservation necessary. 11 rooms.* 🛏 🍷🍷*Restaurant.* The Schnookeloch's history is intertwined with the history of this university town, the restaurant being the traditional student bistro.

🍷🍷🍷 **Hotel Backmulde**
– *Schiffgasse 11.* ☎ *(06221) 536 60. Fax (06221) 536660. www.gasthausbackmulde-hotel.de.* 🅿 ♿ *12 rooms.* 🛏 🍷🍷🍷*Restaurant.* This old sailors' lodging has pleasant rooms with distinctive carpets and blue upholstery. Dark wood and red fabrics add coziness to the dining room.

🍷🍷🍷🍷 **Romantik Hotel Zum Ritter St. Georg** – *Hauptstraße 178.* ☎ *(06221) 13 50. Fax (06221) 135230. www.ritter-heidelberg.de. 39 rooms.* 🛏 🍷🍷🍷🍷 *Restaurant.* St George the dragon-slayer is patron saint of this hotel set in a superb Renaissance-style house built in 1592. The sandstone façade is typical of the region. The lounge-style of the Belier restaurant is a bit pompous; the Knights' Room comfortable.

TAKING A BREAK

Strohauer's Café Alt-Heidelberg
– *Hauptstraße 49.* ☎ *(06221) 18 90 24.* 🕐 *Open summer: 9am-midnight; winter: 9am-7pm (food 11am until 1hr before closing).* A good place for a snack, with a selection of over 20 homemade pastries. The menu varies with the season.

GOING OUT

Zum Roten Ochsen – *Hauptstraße 217.* ☎ *(06221) 2 09 77. www.roterochsen. de.* 🕐*Mon-Fri 5pm-midnight (Apr-Oct: also 11am-2pm).* 🕐 *Closed Sun, public holidays and 3 weeks after Christmas.* Once frequented by figures like Bismarck, Mark Twain and Marilyn Monroe, this student café-restaurant offers simple cuisine on tables carved with autographs. The place becomes a pianobar from 8pm, a pleasant place to enjoy a beer or glass of wine.

Heidelberg and its legendary castle

brother of Louis XIV. The marriage alliance proved disastrous to the Palatinate and to Heidelberg. Political infighting resulted in the town's destruction and the sacking of the castle; total disaster followed in 1693, when the town was completely destroyed by fire. Before long the electors abandoned the ruined castle, but it is precisely those ruins that renders Heidelberg so romantic.

Sights

Schloss★★★ (Castle)

🕐 *Open Mar-Nov: 9.30am-6pm, Dec-Feb:10am-5pm.* 📷 *€3.* ☎ *(062 21) 65 44 29. www.heidelberg-schloss.de.*

Upon entering the castle walls, visit the Rondell promontory for **views**★ of the town, the Neckar Valley and the Rhineland. Enter the castle through the **Elisabethentor**, a gate built by Friedrich V in a single night in 1615, as a surprise for his wife Elizabeth Stuart. Two gates separated by a moat lead to the inner courtyard. The **gardens**★ were laid out under Friedrich V in the 17C. The east face of the castle, with its three towers, is visible from the Scheffel terrace.

The Feudal Courtyard and Buildings

The courtyard is on the far side of a fortified bridge guarded by the Torturm. The simple residential building, the **Ruprecht**, was built by Ruprecht III who became German king in 1400; above the crown are two little angels, thought to be the architect's twins who died just before completion of the works.

The **Apothekerturm** (Apothecary's Tower) is even older. The 14C tower forms part of the **Deutsches Apothekenmuseum**★ **(German Pharmaceutical Museum),** with 18C-19C apothecaries' equipment and an alchemist's laboratory complete with instruments. *Open Apr-Oct 10.15am-6pm, Nov-Mar 10am-5.30pm. Closed 25 Dec.* 📷 *€3, including courtyard and Vat tour.* ☎ *(062 21) 258 80.*

The Gothic and Renaissance Additions

Immediatly off the courtyard is the Gothic **Brunnenhalle** (Well Wing), whose granite Roman columns came from Charlemagne's palace at Ingelheim. The **Library (6)**, set back from the west wing, is awash with light, once home to the royals' personal library, art collections and treasure. Only slightly more modern is the **Hall of Mirrors Wing** *(Gläserner Saalbau)* (8). Following a fire, only a shell remains of this tiered, Italian Renaissance building. The **Ottheinrich Wing** *(Ottheinrichsbau)* (9), built by the

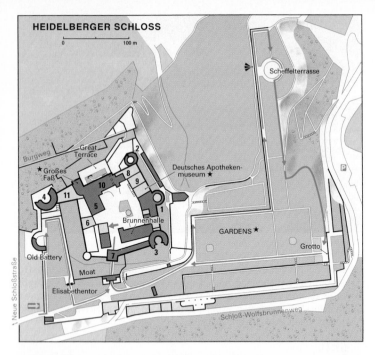

HEIDELBERGER SCHLOSS

0   100 m

Scheffelterrasse

Burgweg

Great Terrace

★ Großes Faß

Deutsches Apotheken-museum ★

10

8

9

4

11

5

1

6

Brunnenhalle

GARDENS ★

Grotto

Old Battery

7

3

Moat

Elisabethentor

Neue Schloßstraße

Schloß-Wolfsbrunnenweg

P

End of Feudal Period (and subsequent alterations)
1) Apothekerturm (14c)   2) Glockenturm (14c)   3) Gesprengter Turm (15c)

Gothic-Renaissance Transitional Period (Ludwig V – 1508-1544)
4) Dicker Turm (1533)   5) Ladles' Wing   6) Library   7) Torturm

Renaissance
8) Hall of Mirrors Wing (1549)   9) Otto-Heinrich Wing (1566)

Renaissance-Baroque Transitional Period
10) Friedrich Wing (Friedrich IV – 1592-1610), and below, Great terrace (Altan)
11) English Wing (Friedrich V – 1610-1632)

Elector Otto-Heinrich (Ottheinrich), an enlightened Renaissance ruler, inaugurated the Late Renaissance period in German architecture. Horizontals predominate in the façade, bearing biblical and mythological ornamentation. The famous sculptor Alexander Colin of Mechelen (1526-1612) helped design the entrance, a triumphal arch displaying the elector's coat of arms.

Transitional Renaissance-Baroque Additions
The **Friedrich Wing**★★ *(Friedrichsbau)* (10), whose façade retains the classical Renaissance design, also bears elements pointing toward the coming Baroque. The statues represent the ancestors of Friedrich IV, who added the wing. The rear of the building and views over Heidelberg are best seen from the **Great Terrace** *(Altan)*, accessed via a passageway to the right of the Friedrich wing.

Interior
☞ *Guided tours only.*
Two architectural models allow a comparison between the 17C castle and its modern remains.

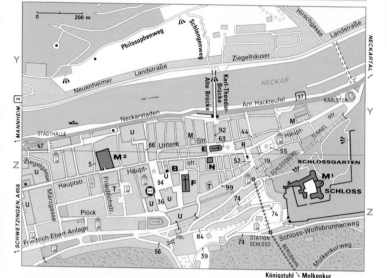

Großes Fass★ (Great Vat)

This colossal 18C cask, with a capacity of 221 726l/48 780gal, still serves up wine to visiting customers. The platform above the Fass hosts the tastings, as well as a little dancing. The guardian of this extravagance, today an idol of local folklore, was the dwarf court jester **Perkeo**, celebrated for his astonishing drinking feats.

Walking Tour

Old Town

Nestling between the Neckar and the hillside, the old town is small and traversed by the Hauptstraße, running parallel to the river.

▸ *Walk down from the castle via the western steps, then continue to the Kornmarkt. On the far side of the square is the Marktplatz with the Gothic Heiliggeistkirche at its centre.*

Heiliggeistkirche (Church of the Holy Spirit)

An example of Late Gothic style, this church is distinguished for its covered market stalls that lie between the building's buttresses as they have for centuries. The galleries in the apses were used for the Biblioteca Palatina, once Europe's finest library, which ended up as war booty in the Vatican's possession in 1623. The chancel was formerly the sepulchre of the palatine electors, but only the tomb of Ruprecht III and his wife remains.

Haus zum Ritter★ (The Knight's House)

This magnificent bourgeois house owes its name to a bust of St George in knightly armour on a richly-scrolled pediment. Built in 1592 for the Huguenot merchant Charles Bélier, it was the only Late Renaissance masterpiece spared the devastating Orléans War.

▶ *Go along Hauptstraße to Universitätplatz and the Baroque Old University (Alte Universität). The square marks the former St Augustine monastery where Martin Luther was called before his superiors to defend his doctrine in 1518.*

Studentenkarzer (Students' Prison)

🕐 *Apr-Oct: open daily except Mon, 10am-4pm; Nov-Mar: open daily except Mon and Sat-Sun, 10am-2pm.* 🕐 *Closed public holidays.* 🎟 *€2.50* ☎ *(062 21) 54 35 54.*
From 1712 to 1914, rowdy students ran the risk of incarceration. Many of them left inscriptions hailing their deeds.

Jesuitenkirche

This 18C Baroque church bears a façade based on the Gesù Church in Rome. The luminous triple nave is supported by pillars decorated with Rococo stuccowork. The **Museum of Sacred and Liturgical Art** *(Museum für sakrale Kunst und Liturgie)*, which is reached through this church, houses religious artifacts from the 17C-19C. 🕐 *Jul-Oct: open daily except Mon, 10am-5pm, Sun 1-5pm; Nov-Jun: Sat 10am-5pm, Sun 1-5pm.* 🕐 *Closed 1st Jan, Easter Monday, Pentecost, Christmas.* 🎟 *€2.* ☎ *(062 21) 16 63 91.*

> ### "Homo Heidelbergensis"
>
> In 1907, the jaw of a man who had lived in the early middle Pleistocene period, i.e. over 500 000 years ago, was found in Mauer, not far from Heidelberg. This Mauer Jaw, also known as **Heidelberg** Man *(Homo heidelbergensis)*, is considered to be the European variety of *Homo erectus*.

▶ *Go west on Hauptstraße to the Electoral Palatinate Museum in the Moraz palace.*

Kurpfälzisches Museum★ (Electoral Palatinate Museum)

Hauptstraße 97. 🕐 *Open daily except Mon, 10am-6pm.* 🕐 *Closed 1 Jan, Shrove Tuesday, 24, 25 and 31 Dec.* 🎟 *€3.* ☎ *(062 21) 58 34 000. www.museum-heidelberg.de.*
A highlight of the Electoral Palatinate museum is the jaw of the prehistoric "Heidelberg Man" (500 000 BC). Other interesting displays include the **Altarpiece of the Twelve Apostles**★★ (1509 – *Windsheimer Zwölfbotenaltar*) by Tilman Riemenschneider and the **Works from the Romantic Period**★★.

Excursions

Königstuhl

5km/3mi southeast, via Neue Schloßstraße, Molkenkurweg, and then Gaiberger Weg; or take the funicular. Funicular: summer: 9am-7:20pm, every 10min; winter: 10:50am-5:40pm, Sun 10:10am-5:40pm, every 20min. 🎟 *€5.10 round-trip (from Heidelberg-Kornmarkt station).* ☎ *(062 21) 227 96. www.hvv-heidelberg.de.*
The television tower on the summit permits a sweeping view of the Neckar Valley.

Schwetzingen★

10km/6mi west via the Friedrich-Ebert-Anlage.
During the asparagus season, gourmets flock to Schwetzingen, while in May and June music lovers come for the festivals.

Schwetzingen's **Schloss**★★, destroyed in the 17C, was rebuilt in 1700-17 as a Baroque palace. About forty of the palace rooms are open to the public. The charming 18C **rococo theatre**★ (*Rokokotheater*), is open throughout the summer. During the Schwetzingen Festival it makes an ideal setting for concerts and plays. ○ *Mid-Jun to early Sep, information ☎ (06202) 12 88 28.*

The 72ha/178 acre **Schlossgarten**★★ is undoubtedly one of the finest 18C parks in Europe. There are formal French and English gardens, ornamented with the mock ancient temples and ruins so beloved in the Late Rococo period.

INSEL HELGOLAND★★

POPULATION: 1 700

Helgoland was for ages a possession of the Danish before becoming British in 1814. The island was exchanged with the Germans for Zanzibar in 1890. Thousands of tourists each year head for the red-sandstone cliffs of the island. ▪ *Rathaus, 27498 Helgoland. ☎ (047 25) 813 70.*

▶ **Orient Yourself:** The island of Helgoland is about 60km/37mi from the coast of Schleswig-Holstein in an area of the North Sea well-known for its powerful currents and unpredictable climate. A daily car ferry runs out of Cuxhaven *(122km/76mi northwest of Hamburg)* and from the Frisian Islands.

○ **Don't Miss:** Hiking, swimming and other outdoor pastimes.

○ **Organizing Your Time:** Helgoland can be visited in a single day.

Kids Especially for Kids: The sea voyage to the island, outdoor recreation.

○ **Also See:** *NORDFRIESISCHE INSELN, Insel SYLT, HUSUM on the mainland (ferry links are subject to change; information available locally).*

Sights

An Unusual Rock

Buffeted for centuries by the sea, Helgoland covers an area of just 2km²/0.8sq mi. An aquarium, an ornithological observatory and a marine biology station appeal to serious scientists. The island attracts leisure travelers with its **outdoor pursuits**★★: cliff walks, swimming among the sheltered sands of Düne Beach and hiking. The tax-free chocolates, cigarettes and spirits are added benefits.

Access: From Cuxhaven (2hr30min), 10.30am. From Hamburg/St. Pauli-Landungs-brücken, Apr to Oct, 9am. Same-day round-trip ticket from ☎ €56.50. Information from Reederei Seetouristik: ☎ (0180) 320 20 25. www.helgolandreisen.de.

HILDESHEIM★

POPULATION: 103 000

Over the centuries Hildesheim managed to preserve its beautiful medieval buildings until an Allied attack in 1945. After concerted efforts, part of the old town was rebuilt, with focus on the historical market square. Today the town has developed an economy based largely on earth-friendly industries. ▪ *Rathausstraße 18-20, 31134 Hildesheim. ☎ (051 21) 179 80.*

▶ **Orient Yourself:** Hildesheim is 30km/19mi south of Hannover between Bruges and Novgorod.

⊘ **Don't Miss:** The Marktplatz, the Cathedral and the Pelizaeus-Museum.

🕓 **Organizing Your Time:** Allow a day to see Hildesheim's historic sites: the Markt-platz, the Cathedral and the historic churches

⚬ **Also See:** *HANNOVER (33km/21mi north) HAMELN (49km/31mi west), GOSLAR (51km/32mi southeast), HARZ (tour leaves from Goslar).*

A Bit of History

The Thousand-year-old Rose Tree – Legend has it that Louis I the Pious, exhausted after a day's hunting, hid his personal reliquary in a rose bush before laying down to sleep. When he awoke, the casket was missing. Interpreting this as a sign, he founded a chapel, and later a bishopric, on the spot, around which Hildesheim grew. The rose bush survived the 1945 air raid; it blooms every year.

HILDESHEIM						
		Gelber Stern	Z	28	Mühlenstr.	Z 61
		Godehardspl.	Z	31	Neue Str.	Z 64
Almsstr.	Y	Hannoversche Str.	Y	33	Osterstr.	Y
Bahnhofsallee	Y	Hoher Weg	Z	36	Pfaffenstieg	Z 69
Bergsteinweg	Z 8	Hohnsen	Z	39	Rathausstr.	Y 72
Bernwardstr.	Y	Jakobistr.	Y	41	Scheelenstr.	Z 80
Bischof-Janssen-Str.	Y 12	Judenstr.	YZ	44	Schuhstr.	Z 83
Domhof	Z 20	Kardinal-Bertram-Str.	Y	47	Theaterstr.	Y 91
Eckemekerstr.	YZ 23	Kläperhagen	Z	49	Zingel	YZ

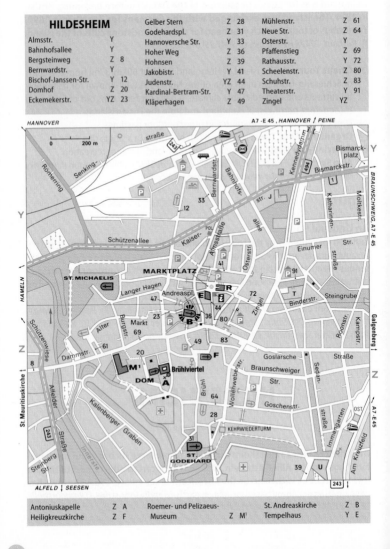

Antoniuskapelle	Z A	Roemer- und Pelizaeus-		St. Andreaskirche	Z B
Heiligkreuzkirche	Z F	Museum	Z M¹	Tempelhaus	Y E

WHERE TO EAT

◎◎🖳 **Kupferschmiede** – *Am Steinberg 6 31139 Hildesheim-Ochtersum (5km/3mi southwest via Schützenwiese and the Kurt-Schumacher-Straße, bear right 1km/0.5mi after Ochtersum).* ☎ *(05121) 26 30 25.* 🕐 *Closed Sun and Mon.* This establishment is located in the heart of the forest and was built at the turn of the 19th century. Various dishes are served in the elegant country-style house. Terrace.

WHERE TO STAY

◎◎ **Gästehaus Klocke** – *Humboldtstraße 11.* ☎ *(05121) 17 92 13. Fax (05121) 1792140. www.gaestehaus-klocke.de.* 🖪 🛦 *20 rooms.* ⊠ Built over 100 years ago, this establishment is still run by the same family. The guestrooms are individually designed, but all are quiet, simply and pleasantly decorated.

Sights

Marktplatz★

The historical market square has been beautifully restored. Visitors are greeted by eight centuries of buildings.

Rathaus

The east side of the square is lined with Gothic buildings in the 13C. Over the years, the Rathaus underwent numerous modifications and extensions, resulting in three different architectural styles. It was rebuilt after 1945 in a simplified form of the original. *A carillon rings at noon, 1pm and 5pm.*

Medieval Architectural Gems

The unusual, early-14C, Oriental-looking **Tempelhaus** stands on the south side of the Marktplatz. The gable and round turrets are probably 16C additions. The most distinctive feature is the ornate 16C Renaissance **oriel**★ which depicts the parable of the Prodigal Son. The nearby 16C half-timbered **Wedekindhaus** has bay windows projecting from ground level up to the roof, a typical feature of the Lower Saxon Renaissance. Not far off is the **Lüntzelhaus** (1755), now a local bank, and the 14C Gothic **Rolandstift** with a Baroque porch (c 1730).

The **Bakers' and Butchers' Guilds** occupy the square's west side. The original **Bäckeramtshaus** dated from 1451 but, like the **Knochenhaueramtshaus**★ (1529) next door, it is a faithful reproduction. The Knochenhaueramtshaus is known as the "most beautiful half-timbered house in the world," the pride of its citizens. The five upper floors house the **Municipal Museum** *(Stadtmuseum)*. The **Rokokohaus** on the north side of the square stands between the **Stadtschänke,** a local restaurant, and the **Weavers' Guild House** *(Wollenwebergildehaus)*.

Dom★ (Cathedral)

🛦 🕐 *Mid-Mar to end Oct: 9.30am-5pm, Sun, 12 noon-5pm; from Nov to mid-Mar: 10am-4pm, Sat, 9.30am-3pm, Sun, 12 noon-5pm.* 🕐 *Closed Good Fri and 24 Dec.* ◎ *€0.50.* ☎ *(051 21) 179 17 60.*

The present cathedral is a reconstruction of its 11C Romanesque predecessor. Fine works of **art**★ can be seen inside, including a huge 11C chandelier and a rare 13C baptismal font supported by figures representing the rivers of Paradise. The Romanesque **cloister**★ is the location of the legendary rose, trained along an outer wall.

Roemer- und Pelizaeus-Museum★

🛦 🕐 *Open daily, 10am-6pm.* ◎ *€8.* ☎ *(051 21) 936 90. www.rpmuseum.de.*

The **Pelizaeus-Museum** houses one of Germany's richest collections of Egyptian antiquities. Highlights include the life-size figure of Heimunu, and the statue of the scribe Heti from excavations near Giza. The **Roemer-Museum** exhibits natural and cultural history collections.

Medieval Churches

Hildesheim is home to several medieval churches of note. Dating from the 11C, **St-Michaelis-Kirche**★ exemplifies typical Ottonian architecture of Old Saxony. Note the 13C painted ceiling depicting the Tree of Jesse. The 12C **St-Godehardikirche**★ has an elegant silhouette marked by the slender spires of its three towers. The church's Romanesque architecture has survived almost intact. Andreaskirche, built by the citizens in the 14C and 15C, is a massive Gothic church destroyed during the Second World War and then rebuilt. It contains the west end of its 12C Romanesque predecessor. Its tower rises 114m/355ft, Niedersachsen's highest. Fronted by a Baroque façade, the **Heiligkreuzkirche** is built on an 11C Early Romanesque church refashioned from a fortified gateway. Gothic, Baroque and Ottonian elements jostle each other within. Finally, **St-Mauritiuskirche**, an 11C church, with a 12C cloister, lies in the Moritzberg quarter, on the west side of Hildesheim. The interior was outfitted with a great deal of stuccowork in the 18C.

BURG HOHENZOLLERN★

Built on a hill bordering the Swabian Jura, Hohenzollern Castle stands tall and turreted; from any angle, it looks like a fortress out of a fairytale. The site★★★ and the history of its residents are impressive enough to merit a visit.

▶ **Orient Yourself:** 25km/16mi south of Tübingen, the castle is unmissable. Perched on the Zollern hill *(Zollernberg)*, it is reached via route 27 or the A 81 (exit 31).

⊚ **Don't Miss:** The panorama from atop the castle ramparts.

🕑 **Organizing Your Time:** Allow two hours to tour the castle and its grounds.

👣 **Also See:** *SCHWÄBISCHE ALB* (🐾 *tour includes the castle), SIGMARINGEN (45km/28mi southeast), HAIGERLOCH (16km/10mi west), ZWIEFALTEN (50km/31mi east), TÜBINGEN (26km/16mi north).*

A Bit of History

The Cradle of the Hohenzollerns

– The Hohenzollern dynasty goes back to the counts of Zollern, overlords of Hechingen and subsequently divided into several branches. In 1415, the Hohenzollerns of Franconia became Margraves, and thus elector-princes, of Brandenburg. In 1618 they succeeded to the Duchy of Prussia. In the 18C the kingdom of Prussia became a leading power in Europe, and so it was a Hohenzollern, Wilhelm I, who became head of the German Empire, founded in 1871 at the instigation of Prussia. Less than 50 years later, military defeat in the First World War ended the domination of the Hohenzollern dynasty: on 9 November 1918, Kaiser Wilhelm II was forced to abdicate.

Burg Hohenzollern

The sumptuous interior of Hohenzollern

Visit

The Castle

     Guided tour (40min).   *Mid-Mar to end Oct: 9am-5.30pm; Nov to mid-Mar: 10am-4:30pm.*   *Closed 24 and 31 Dec.*   *€5.*   *(074 71) 24 28. www.burg-hohen-zollern.com.*

The castle as it is today was reconstructed from the original 19C plans of Prussian architects Von Prittwitz and Stüler. All that remains of the ancient fortress built by the counts of Zollern is the Roman Catholic chapel of **St Michael** *(Michaeliskapelle),* whose stained-glass windows are said to be the oldest in southern Germany. The neo-Gothic Protestant chapel, in the castle's north wing, has housed the tombs of the Friedrich-Wilhelm I, the Soldier-King, and his son Frederick the Great since 1952, when they were moved there from Potsdam. Mementoes of the latter, including uniforms, decorations, snuffboxes and flutes, are in the castle **treasury** *(Schatzkammer).*

Before leaving the castle, tour the ramparts *(start on the left, after the drawbridge)* and enjoy the **panorama**★ of the Swabian Jura and the Upper Neckar Valley.

HUSUM

POPULATION: 21 000

The birthplace of writer Theodor Storm (1817-88) has survived the battering of the North Sea. Today, this "grey city on the sea," as Storm described it, is the commercial hub of North Friesland as well as a modern holiday region with abundant cultural offerings. ▯ *Großstraße 27, 25813 Husum.* ☎ *(048 41) 898 70.*

▶ **Orient Yourself:** Husum is one of the last coastal towns before the border with Denmark. The A 23 motorway links the city with Hamburg and Schleswig-Holstein's western coast.

   Don't Miss: The port and the North Frisian Museum.

   Organizing Your Time: The sights of Husum can be visited in a single day.

   Also See: *SCHLESWIG (36km/22mi northeast), KIEL (85km/53mi east), HAMBURG (144km/90mi south), OSTFRIESISCHE INSELN, NORDFRIESISCHE INSELN, Insel HELGO-LAND.*

Sights

The Port

Husum's harbour is always full of boats; sometimes they float, and sometimes they lie in the sand, depending upon the tide. Some of the old merchants' houses still stand in the Großstraße.

Nordfriesisches Museum★
(North Frisian Museum)

Herzog-Adolf-Strasse 25.   *Open Apr to Oct: 10am-5pm; Nov to Mar: 10am-4pm.*   *Closed Sat, Mon, 1 Jan, 24, 25 and 31 Dec.*   *€3.* ☎ *(048 41) 25 45.*

The ground floor of this museum explores the variety of German coastal landscape as well as the life and culture of its inhabitants. The catastrophic con-

> ### Theodor Storm
>
> Born in Husum in 1817, Storm regarded his birth town with great affection throughout his life. A deeply sensitive character, Storm contributed to German literature such original works as *Immensee* (1849), a real poetic jewel which integrates song and narrative.

sequences of floods are explored, as are the construction of dikes and reclamation of land by polders.

Storm-Haus

Wasserreihe 31. 🕐 *Open Apr to Oct: 10am-12 noon, 2-5pm, Mon, Sat and Sun, 2-5pm; Nov-Mar: Tue, Thu and Sat 2-5pm.* 🕐 *Closed 24 and 31 Dec.* ⊜ *€2.* ☎ *(048 41) 66 62 70.*
This typical merchant's home was occupied by Theodor Storm from 1866 to 1880; it has furniture from the Biedermeier age and paintings and documents from the writer's estate.

Schloss vor Husum (Castle before Husum)

This 16C castle of Duke Adolf von Schleswig-Holstein-Gottdorf was originally of Dutch Renaissance style and was renovated in the Baroque in the 18C.

Excursions

Friedrichstadt

15km/9mi south.
Dutch refugees, Remonstrants, exiled for religious reasons, were given sanctuary by Friedrich III of Schleswig-Holstein-Gottorf. The Dutchmen founded Friedrichstadt in 1621, parts of which still look distinctly Dutch: canals are lined by stepped-gable houses.

Eidersperrwerk★ (Eider Dam)

35km/22mi south.
Skirting a bird sanctuary, the road arrives at the mouth of the River Eider, closed off by a **dam** built between 1967 and 1972. The five colossal steel sluice gates remain open when conditions are normal, but close when the coast is threatened by high seas.

View of Friedrichstadt

Nolde-Museum★ at Seebüll

56km/35mi north. 🕐 *Open Mar-Oct, 10am-6pm; Nov, 10am-5pm.* ⊜ *€4.* ☎ *(046 64) 364. www.nolde-museum.de.*
Known under the pseudonym of **Nolde**, the painter Emil Nansen (1867-1956), one of the most important representatives of the Expressionist School built himself a house of his own design in the solitude of the Seebüll marshes in the early 20C. Nolde's works are exhibited on a rotating basis.

IDAR-OBERSTEIN

POPULATION: 32 000

Since the Middle Ages, the history of Idar-Oberstein has been linked to the production and sale of precious stones. The abundance in earlier times of nearby agate, jasper and amethyst deposits has made the town a centre for the cutting and polishing of the gems. The many jewellery museums, workshops and boutiques bear witness to this trade. ▣ *Georg-Maus-Strasse 2, 55743 Idar-Oberstein.* ☎ *(067 81) 644 21.*

▶ **Orient Yourself:** Twin towns form this municipality: picturesque Oberstein at the foot of a gorge carved by the River Nahe and Idar on the river's tributary.

🐾 **Don't Miss:** The German Precious Stone Museum.

🕓 **Organizing Your Time:** Allow five hours for the suggested driving tour (👣 *see below*).

👣 **Also See:** *BERNKASTEL-KUES (37km/23mi northwest), MOSELTAL (tour includes Bernkastel Kues), RHEINTAL (Bingen is 60km/37.5mi east), TRIER (64km/40mi west).*

Sights

Deutsches Edelsteinmuseum★★ (German Precious Stone Museum)

In the Idar-Zentrum (Diamond Exchange), Hauptstraße 118. 🕓 *Open May-Oct 10am-6pm, Nov-Apr 10am-5pm.* 🕓 *Closed Mon in Nov-Feb, 1 Dec-25 Dec.* 👓 *€4.20. 06781-90 09 80. www.edelsteinmuseum.de.*

The museum houses precious stones from around the world, from agates to diamonds: 7 000 cut and polished stones and 1 000 precious stones delight the eye.

Felsenkirche★

30min on foot round-trip. Access via stairs (214 steps) from the Oberstein Marktplatz. Framed by a rock overhang above the river, this church, restored several times, is worth a visit for the 15C winged altarpiece alone. The scenes of the Passion represented depict the event with a ferocious realism.

Museum Idar-Oberstein

In the Oberstein Marktplatz (below the Felsenkirche stairway). 🕓 *Open Apr to Oct, 9am-5.30pm; Nov to Mar, 11am-4.30pm.* 🕓 *Closed 1 Jan, 24, 25 and 31 Dec.* 👓 *€3.60, no charge last Sun in Oct.* ☎ *(067 81) 246 19. www.museum-idar-oberstein.de.*

This museum emphasizes the region's minerals and precious stones.

Weiherschleife (Old Stonecutting Centre)

Tiefenstein district. ♿ 🐾 *Guided tour (40min).* 🕓 *From mid-Mar to mid-Nov, 10am-6pm.* 👓 *€3.* ☎ *(067 81) 315 13.*

The facetting and polishing of gems is demonstrated here, from the crude stone to the fine jewel. Skilled craftsmen still utilize traditional grindstones powered by a water-wheel.

Driving Tour

The Hunsrück

Excursion 141km/88mi

The Hunsrück forms the southern rim of the Rhine schist massif, a region of low mountains and game-stocked forests gashed by deep and steep valleys.

Erbeskopf

At 818m/2 660ft, this is the highest summit of the massif. The wooden tower affords memorable views of the undulating countryside. **Hunsrückhöhenstraße**★ offers fine views as well. The road passes the Stumpfer Turm, an old Roman watchtower.

Kirchberg

Perched on a hillside, this village boasts half-timbered houses, especially around the Marktplatz, and the pre-Romanesque St Michaelskirche.

Simmern

The farming centre of the Hunsrück, Simmern is home to the parish church of St Stephan (15C). The church's **tombs**★ of the Dukes of Pfalz-Simmern feature some of the finest Renaissance sculptures in the middle Rhineland.

Ravengiersburg

Hidden away at the bottom of a valley, this village boasts a Romanesque church with an imposing west front. Above the porch: Christ in Majesty.

Daun

The castle here is built atop a sheer rock outcrop, offering views of the countryside.

JENA

POPULATION: 102 000

Jena has developed steadily since the foundation of its university in 1548. Since then, numerous scientists and intellectuals have graced its streets: political thinker Wilhelm von Humboldt, Goethe, Schiller and Hegel, who worked on his philosphical treatise while French and Prussian armies battled outside the gates in 1806. The town is also famous for its optics, established in the mid-19C by Carl Zeiss and Ernst Abbe, inventors of the microscope. *Johannisstraße 23, 07743 Jena. ☎ (036 41) 80 64 00.*

▸ **Orient Yourself:** Jena is northeast of the forest of Thuringia.
☺ **Don't Miss:** German culture lovers should make time for the Goethe and Schiller houses.
🕐 **Organizing Your Time:** Allow two hours to see the Goethe and Schiller sites.
Especially for Kids: Zeiss Planetarium.
☝ **Also See:** *WEIMAR (22km/14mi west), NAUMBURG (31km/19mi north), THÜRINGER WALD (Ilmenau is 92km/57mi southwest).*

WHERE TO EAT

😊😊 **Ratszeise** – *Markt 1. ☎ (03641) 42 18 00. www.ratszeise.net.* 🚻 This restaurant is in Jena's historic town hall. The interior is rustic in style, perfectly matching the exterior. Enjoy views of the market place (Marktplatz) over traditional cuisine.

WHERE TO STAY

😊😊 **Hotel Jenaer Hof** – *Bachstraße 24. ☎ (03641) 44 38 55 Fax (03641) 443866.* 🅿 ✚ *Reservation recommended. 11 rooms.* ☕ A simple, practical hotel located in the heart of town and set in a *Jugendstil* building. Varied guestrooms are available.

Sights

Stadtmuseum Göhre

🕐 *Open Tue-Sun, 10am-5pm (2pm-10pm Wed), Sat-Sun, 11am-6pm.* 🕐 *Closed 1 Jan, 24 and 31 Dec.* 🎟 *€4.* ☎ *(036 41) 359 80. www.stadtmuseum.jena.de.*

This local museum, which highlight's Jena from its founding, is housed in one of the town's most beautiful buildings, built around 1500.

Stadtkirche St-Michaelis

This ancient collegiate church of the Cistercians was completely transformed in the Gothic mode in the 15C. Note, on the south side, the canopied porch.

Goethe-Gedenkstätte

🕐 *Open from Apr to end Oct: Tue-Sun, 11am-3pm.* 🕐 *Closed 1 May, Ascension, 3 and 31 Oct.* 🎟 *€1.* ☎ *(036 41) 93 11 88.*

The famous writer always said that it was in Jena that he found the tranquillity essential for literary creation. The garden house where he lived contains documents recalling his work in the field of natural science.

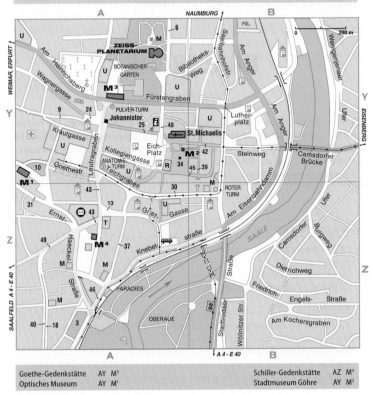

Schillers Gartenhaus (Schiller Museum)

Kids 🔍 *Guided tour (20min).* 🕐 *Apr-Oct: Tue-Sun, 11am-5pm; Nov-Mar: Tue-Sat 11am-5pm.* 🕐 *Closed public holidays.* 👓 *€2.50.* ☎ *(036 41) 93 11 88. www.uni-jena.de/Gartenhaus.html.*

Schiller lived in this summer house from 1797 to 1799 and wrote *Wallenstein* here. It now contains a display of memorabilia from Schiller's "Jena years".

Zeiss Planetarium★ (Zeiss-Planetarium der Ernst-Abbe-Stiftung Jena)

♿ 🕐 *Closed 1 Jan and 6-8 Jan.* 👓 *€6-8 varying by monthly program. For current information:* ☎ *(036 41) 88 54 88; www. planetarium-jena.de.*

This planetarium is built next to the botanical gardens by the Zeiss firm.

Statue of the Kurfürst on the Markt

Optisches Museum★

♿ 🕐 *Open Tue-Sun, 10am-4.30pm, Sat, 11am-5pm.* 🕐 *Closed bank holidays.* 👓 *€5.* ☎ *(036 41) 44 31 65.*

The museum retraces 500 years of the history of optics with a collection of spectacles, telescopes, photographic equipment and cameras.

KARLSRUHE★

POPULATION: 284 000

It is Karlsruhe's three museums which make the town worth a visit. The former seat of the grand dukes today houses Germany's supreme courts as well as the country's oldest School of Technology (1825). Among the eminent graduates of the latter are Hertz, who discovered electromagnetic waves, and Benz, the motorcar pioneer. ℹ *Bahnhofplatz 6, 76137 Karlsruhe.* ☎ *(0721) 37 20 53 83.*

WHERE TO EAT

🍴 **Lehners Wirtshaus zum Goldenen Kreuz** – *Karlstraße 21a, 76133 Karlsruhe.* ☎ *(0721) 249 57 20.* 🚭 ♿ Those who appreciate good simple food will love this convivial brasserie in the town centre. The wooden tables and large bar give a rustic feel. In summer a pleasant, 300-seat Biergarten opens.

WHERE TO STAY

🛏 **Hotel Betzler** – *Amalienstraße 3, 76133 Karlsruhe.* ☎ *(0721) 91 33 60. Fax (0721) 9133625. www.hotel-betzler.de.* 🅿 🛏 *34 rooms.* Located in the heart of Karlsruhe this establishment is equipped with clean and functional guestrooms and well-placed for access to public transport. The pedestrian zone and most sights of interest are also within walking distance.

▷ **Orient Yourself:** Only a few kilometres from the Rhine, Karlsruhe has used the river for its industrial development. The proximity of the Black Forest makes excursions into the countryside easy.

⊘ **Don't Miss:** Art lovers should head for the Fine Arts Museum and the ZKM.

🕐 **Organizing Your Time:** Allow half a day for Karlsruhe's museums.

🖑 **Also See:** *Schloss BRUCHSAL (22km/14mi northeast), Kloster MAULBRONN (34km/21mi east), SCHWARZWALD (starting with BADEN-BADEN, 38km/24mi to the south), PFALZ (Bad Bergzabern is 35km/22mi west).*

A Bit of History

A star is born – Karlsruhe is one of the "new towns" designed on a geometric plan in the 18C by the princely building enthusiasts of southern Germany. The Margrave of Baden created a town with the palace as centre and a network of streets radiating from it. Karlsruhe became the capital of the Grand Duchy of Baden (1806).

Sights

Staatliche Kunsthalle★★ (Fine Arts Museum)

⚸ 🕐 *Open Tue-Sun, 10am-5pm, Sat-Sun, 10am-6pm.* 🕐 *Closed Shrove Tue, 24 and 31 Dec.* ⊜ *€6.* ☎ *(0721) 926 33 59. www.kunsthalle-karlsruhe.de.*

The 19C building houses a remarkable collection of **German Primitives**★★ *(Gemälde Altdeutscher Meister)*, including numerous works by Grünewald. The Golden Age of Flemish and Dutch painting is represented by Rubens, Jordaens and Rembrandt. Still-life pictures by Chardin are highlights of a collection of 17C and 18C French works.

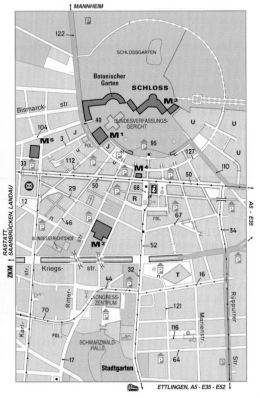

The **Hans Thoma Collection**★ includes German paintings of the 19C, part of an exhibition of German and French painters from Caspar David Friedrich to Cézanne.
The adjacent **Orangery** houses an outstanding **collection**★ of Classical modern and contemporary art. Paintings by German Expressionists (Marc), artists influenced by Cubism (Léger, Delaunay), and also works by Max Ernst and Otto Dix stand alongside sculptures by Barlach, Lehmbruck and Henry Moore. Contemporary artists include Arnulf Rainer, Gerhard Richter, Yves Klein and Antoni Tàpies.

Schloss★ (Palace)

Of the original palace building only the tall octagonal tower marking the centre of the city's radiating road system now remains. It was the grand-ducal residence up to 1918. The **tower** (Schloßturm, ⏰ *Open Tue-Sun, 10am-5pm, Fri-Sun, 10am-6pm.* €4. ☎ (0721) 926 65 14) is open to the public, offering views of Karlsruhe and the Black Forest. From the palace park is access to the **Botanical Gardens** (Botanischer Garten). ⏰ *Greenhouses: Tue-Sun, 9am-noon, 1-4pm, Sat-Sun, 10am-noon, 1-4pm.* €2. ☎ (0721) 926 30 08.

Badisches Landesmuseum★ (Baden Regional Museum)

♿ ⏰ *Open Tue-Sun, 10am-5pm, Fri-Sun, 10am-6pm.* ⏰ *Closed 24 and 31 Dec.* €4. ☎ (0721) 926 65 14. www.landesmuseum.de.
This palace museum features significant displays of the region's prehistory and early history and regional history from the Middle Ages to the present.

Museum beim Markt

♿ ⏰ *Open Tue-Sun, 11am-5pm, Fri-Sun, 10am-6pm.* ⏰ *Closed 24 and 31 Dec.* €4, no charge Fri. ☎ (0721) 926 65 78. www.landesmuseum.de. Between Marktplatz and the palace.
In another building of the Landesmuseum are collections of art from **Jugendstil**★ (Art Nouveau) and Art Deco to contemporary craft and design.

ZKM★ (Zentrum für Kunst und Medientechnologie)

Access via Kriegsstraße. ♿ ⏰ *Open Wed-Fri, 10am-6pm, Sat-Sun, 11am-6pm.* €5, no charge 3 Oct (Museumsfest). ☎ (0721) 81 00 0. www.mnk.zkm.de.
This former weapons and ammunition factory from the early 20C now unites research, teaching, workshops and museums revolving around media art.
In the **Museum für Neue Kunst (Museum for New Art),** European and American art since 1960 includes paintings, graphics, sculpture, photography and installations. *Access from Stirnseite, towards Lessingstraße.*
The **Medienmuseum** featuring interactive exhibits allows a look at media of the future. *Access at the level of the blue cube (ZKM music studio).* ♿ ⏰ *Open Wed-Fri, 10am-6pm, Sat-Sun, 11am-6pm.* €5. ☎ (0721) 8100 1990.

T. Krieger/MICHELIN

The former seat of the grand dukes of Baden now houses Germany's supreme courts

KASSEL★

POPULATION: 194 000

Once the seat of the Landgraves, Kassel is renowned for the Wilhelmshöhe park, with its grottoes, waterfalls and palace. Kassel's post-war reconstruction has not always been done in the best taste, but the town's various sights make it an interesting visit nonetheless. ▯ *Obere Königstrasse 15. ☎ 0561-7077 07.*

▶ **Orient Yourself:** Kassel sits on the banks of the River Fulda *(boat trips from Fuldabrücke)*, in the heart of a lush, wooded countryside, between the Habichtswald and Meißner-Kaufungen Natural Parks. The A 7 (Fulda-Hannover) and A 44 (to Dortmund) motorways cross in Kassel.

🕐 **Organizing Your Time:** Allow half a day for a visit of the Wilhelmshöhe park.

🔥 **Also See:** *HANN. MÜNDEN (23km/14mi northeast), GÖTTINGEN (87km/54mi northeast), EISENACH (87km/54mi southeast), THÜRINGER WALD (tour leaves from Eisenach).*

A Bit of History

The Brothers Grimm – Jakob (1785-1863) and Wilhelm Grimm (1786-1859) lived in Kassel from 1805 to 1830, both employed as Court Librarians. Fascinated by legends and folklore, the brothers collected a wealth of stories published under the title *Kinder und Hausmärchen* (Stories for Children and the Home), known in English as *Grimms' Fairy Tales.*

Documenta – Famous for its musical and dramatic activities, Kassel is nevertheless known best of all for the Documenta, an international exhibition of contemporary art held every five years since 1955 in the **Fredericianum**, in the Friedrichsplatz.

Wilhelmshöhe★★

Park★★

The landscaping of this huge 350ha/865-acre park was started in 1701, a Baroque park with almost 800 tree species. In the late 18C the the gardens were transformed into an English style. **Löwenburg**, a fantasy castle ruin of ca 1800, is an excellent example of the period's sentimental Romanticism.

The vast – and still very romantic – Wilhelmshöhe park

KASSEL

Baunsbergstr.	X 2	Hugo-Preuß-Str.	X 18	Schönfelder Str.	X 29
Brüder-Grimm-Pl.	Z 3	Kölnische Str.	X 20	Schützenstr.	X 32
Bürgerm.-Brunner-Str.	Z 5	Königspl.	Z 21	Ständepl.	Z
Dag-Hammarskjöld-Str.	X 6	Kurfürstenstr.	Y 22	Treppenstr.	Z
Dresdener Str.	X 8	Landgraf-Karl-Str.	X 23	Tulpenallee	X 33
Fuldabrücke	Z 13	Neue Fahrt	Z 25	Untere Königsstr.	Y
Fünffensterstr.	Z 12	Obere Königsstr.	Z	Werner-Hilpert-Str.	Y 3
Harleshäuser Str.	X 16	Rudolf-Schwander-Str.	Y 27	Wilhelmsstr.	Z 35
		Scharnhorststr.	X 26	Ysenburgstr.	X 38
		Scheidemannpl.	Z 28		

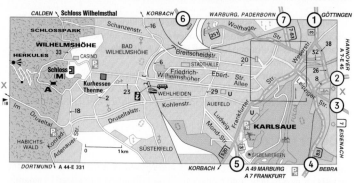

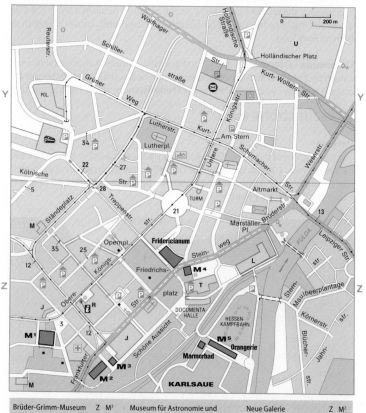

Brüder-Grimm-Museum	Z M³	Museum für Astronomie und		Neue Galerie	Z M²
Hessisches Landesmuseum	Z M¹	Technikgeschichte	Z M⁵	Schloss Löwenburg	X A
		Naturkundemuseum	Z M⁴		

At the highest point of the park stands **Hercules**★ *(Herkules)*, emblem of Kassel and highlight of the park. This gigantic statue (a copy 1717) stands atop a pyramid, itself on an eight-sided "Oktogon." The total height of the monument reaches 72m/236ft; from the statue's base is a fine **view**★★ of the park and surroundings.

Below the Oktogon the great **Water Staircase** *(Kaskadentreppe)* shoots an enormous **cascade**★ of water into the Neptune and Fountain pools.

Schloss (Castle)

  Open Tue-Sun, 10am-5pm.   *Closed Wed before Ascension, 24, 25 and 31 Dec.* €3.50. ☎ (0561) 316 800. www.museum-kassel.de.

This Classical building was completed in 1803. The museum's **Antiquities**★ section features 5C-6C vases in the entrance hall evocative of the Classical Greek era. The Roman Empire is represented by the 2C **Kassel Apollo**, a series of busts, a sarcophagus and some urns.

The **Old Masters Gallery**★★★ features world-class exhibits derived from collections amassed by the Landgraves. German Primitives are represented by some important works: Altdorfer's *Crucifixion*, a triptych *(Reisealtar)* by Cranach the Elder, Dürer's *Portrait of Elizabeth Tucher*, *Hercules at Antioch* by Hans Baldung Grien. Dutch works on display include: Rembrandt's *Portrait of Saskia van Uylenburgh* and various self-portraits; Rubens' *Crowning of a Hero*, and Jordaens' *The Painter's Betrothal*. Also on display here are landscapes by Jan Brueghel, Jacob van Ruisdael, and Jan Steen. Italian (Tintoretto, Titian, Bassano), Spanish (Ribera, Murillo) and French (Poussin) complete the collection.

Sights

Karlsaue Park★

The most popular parts of this 18C riverside park are the gardens below the Schöne Aussicht terrace, and the Siebenbergen, an artificial island on the Fulda.

In the park's northern corner is the **orangery** (1710), home to the **Museum für Astronomie und Technikgeschichte mit Planetarium**. This museum's rich **collections**★★ of old astronomical instruments and clocks are the result of Landgrave Wilhelm IV's interest in astronomy, which led to his founding modern Europe's first observatory in Kassel in 1560. Models demonstrate observable scientific phenomena and a display explains the evolution of technology from Antiquity to the present.

  Open Tue-Sun, 10am-5pm.   *Closed Wed before Ascension, 24, 25 and 31 Dec.* €3.50. ☎ (0561) 316 805 00.

Hessisches Landesmuseum★

  Open Tue-Sun, 10am-5pm.   *Closed Wed before Ascension, 24, 25 and 31 Dec.* €3.50 ☎ (0561) 316 805 00. www.museum-kassel.de.

Prehistory displays ranging from the Stone Age through the Hallstatt and La Tène periods mark the beginning of the Hessian Regional Museum. But there is a sizeable display of medieval items, including the **German Tapestry Museum**★★ *(Deutsches Tapetenmuseum)* with more than 600 wallcoverings from the 18C-20C, including tapestries and extending into wallpapers. The second floor covers sculptures and porcelain from the manufacturers of Kassel and Fulda, and decorative art from the Middle Ages to the 19C.

Excursions

Schloss Wilhelmsthal★

12km/8mi north on Rasenallee.   *Guided tour (1hr).*   *Open Mar to Oct: Tue-Sun, 10am-5pm; Nov to Feb: Tue-Sun, 10am-4pm.*   *Closed 1 Jan, 24-26 and 31 Dec.* €3.50. ☎ (056 74) 68 98.

This Rococo palace (1747-61), surrounded by an English park, features interior decoration with Chinese porcelain and a gallery by JH Tischbein the Elder.

Göttingen

47km/29mi north on the A 7

Along with Heidelberg, Tübingen and Marburg, Göttingen is one of four German towns deeply imbued with the university tradition. The streets of the old town, bustling with students on bicycles and filled with Gothic churches and neo-Classical university buildings, are charming.

The 14C-15C **Rathaus** *(Town hall)* is perhaps best known for what lies beneath it: The market place and wine cellars *(Ratskeller)* below mark the centre of social life in Göttingen. Out front is the Goosegirl **Fountain** *(Gänselieselbrunnen).* Newly anointed PhDs traditionally give the girl a kiss.

One of the city's most impressive views is the **Vierkirchenblick,** where a church lies on each point of the compass from the south-east corner of the market: east, the dome of St Albanikirche; south, St Michaelskirche; west, the towers of St Johannis; and north, the lofty belfry of St Jakobi, the tallest tower in town.

Half-timbered Houses *(Fachwerkhäuser)* lie in the eastern part of the old town. Note particularly the ancient **Junkernschänke inn**★ (at Barfüßerstraße and Judenstraße).

Finally, a visit to Göttingen should include a stop at the **Städtisches Museum (Municipal Museum),** housed in a Renaissance building and devoted to the historical and cultural development of Göttingen, both town and university. It also exhibits an interesting collection of religious art. ◷ *Open Tue-Sun, 10am (11am, Sat-Sun)-5pm.* ◷ *Closed 1 Jan, 1 May, Whitsun, 3 Oct, 24, 25 and 31 Dec.* ⊗ *€1.50.* ☎ *(0551) 400 28 43.*

KIEL★

POPULATION: 233 000

Kiel plays an important role as a gateway to Scandinavia. The city's post-war reconstruction has been largely in the modern style, its functional urbanism hiding some of its character. But dig a little and you'll find a city with plenty of charm and atmosphere. ▯ *Andreas-Gayk-Strasse 31, 24103 Kiel.* ☎ *(0431) 67 91 00.*

Office de Tourisme de Kiel

Kiel Week

▶ **Orient Yourself:** Kiel is at the end of a 17km/10mi deep inlet in the Baltic Sea at the eastern end of the North Sea-Baltic Sea canal.

☺ **Don't Miss:** A leisurely stroll along the picturesque Hindenburgufer.

🕓 **Organizing Your Time:** Allow two and a half hours for a visit of Kiel's "Little Switzerland" (☝ see Excursions).

Kids Especially for Kids: The Baltic coast resort of Laboe (☝ see Excursions).

☝ **Also See:** SCHLESWIG (56km/35mi north), LÜBECK (76km/48mi south), HAMBURG (94km/59mi south).

A Bit of History

A maritime city – Kiel, founded in the 13C, was always a seafaring town, even if this Hanseatic city never achieved more than regional importance. For centuries Kiel led a tranquil existence, until 1871, when Kiel was selected as Germany's main navy base. Within a few years, the little harbour city grew into a metropolis.

Address Book

WHERE TO EAT

Alte Mühle – *An der Holsatiamühle 8 (east bank of the Kieler Förde, follow signs for "Schwentinetal").* ☎ *(0431) 2 05 90 01. www.altemuehle-kiel.de* 🕓 *daily, 11.30am-midnight.* Located in a former 19C mill on the banks of the river Schwentine, this fish restaurant serves traditional, seasonal food. Reasonably-priced set menus are served Mon to Fri at lunchtime.

Lüneburg-Haus – Zum Hirschen – *Dänische Straße 22* ☎ *(0431) 982 60 00. www.lueneburghaus.com.* 🕓 *Closed Sun and 4 weeks in July and Aug.* On the first floor of the building, modern, bistro-style food is served on elegantly set tables in a relaxed atmosphere. Lengthy wine list and attentive staff.

WHERE TO STAY

Consul – *Walkerdamm 11.* ☎ *(0431) 53 53 70. Fax (0431) 5353770. www.hotel-consul-kiel.de 40 rooms.* *Restaurant.* Located near Kiel's port, this hotel is well-served by public transport. Every guestroom is different, but all are clean and well-equipped. Well-decorated dining rooms.

Parkhotel Kiel Kaufmann – *Niemannsweg 102.* ☎ *(0431) 881 10. Fax (0431) 8811135. www.kieler-kaufmann.de* 📇 *43 rooms.* *Restaurant.* The comfortable entrance hall of this fomer

banker's villa welcomes with its elegant fireplace. Set upstream from the port in a park, the guestrooms are modern and have internet access. Classically-styled restaurant.

TAKING A BREAK

Werkstatt-Café – *Falckstr. 16 (in the town centre).* ☎ *(0431) 9 18 65.* 🕓 *Mon-Sat, 10am-8pm* 🕓 *Closed Sun and bank holidays.* Pleasant tea room next to a goldsmith's workshop ("Werkstatt"). Try the delicious homemade cakes or one of the dishes of the day. The café also regularly exhibits the work of local artists. Beautiful garden.

GOING OUT

Café-Restaurant Schöne Aussichten – *Düsternbrooker Weg 16 (north of the town centre, west bank of the Kieler Förde).* ☎ *(0431) 2 10 85 85.* 🕓 *from 11:30am (food until 10.30pm), Sun, from 10:30am (brunch).* This establishment lives up to its name: the view over the Förde is superb especially from the terrace in summer months. Mediterranean-inspired food (mainly fish) is on the menu. But you're welcome to stop for just a cake or a beer.

Kieler Brauerei – *Alter Markt 9 (town centre)* ☎ *(0431) 90 62 90. www.kieler-brauerei.de.* 🕓 *Mon-Sat, 10-2am, Sun, 10am-midnight.* Micro-brewery with salad bar, hot dishes, and well-priced set menus for four people, drinks included (not served Mon).

Walking Tour

Hindenburgufer★★

This promenade extends for almost 4km/2mi along the shore, with shady parks on one side and extended **views**★ on the other.

Rathaus (Town Hall)

Built between 1907 and 1911, the Rathaus mixes Baroque and Art Nouveau architectural styles. From the upper gallery of its 106m/348ft tower there is a splendid **view**★. *Guided tours on request, ☎ (0431) 90 10.*

Excursions

Schleswig-Holsteinisches Freilichtmuseum★★ (Schleswig-Holstein Open-Air Museum)

6km/4mi south in Molfsee. ☐ ☐ Open Apr to Oct, 9am-6pm; Nov to Mar, Sun, 11am-4pm. ☐ €6. ☎ (0431) 65 96 60; www.freilichtmuseum-sh.de.
Sixty rural buildings typical of the north Elbe are reconstructed and arranged geographically. A forge, potter's workshop, old-fashioned bakehouse and weavers' looms are operated by local craftsmen in traditional manner.

Kids Laboe★

20km/12mi north. This Baltic resort has a picturesque harbour and is popular with families for its sandy dunes and calm waters. The memorial tower, 85m/279ft high, offers a wide **view**★★ of the landscape and, on a clear day, the Danish archipelago. The tower and underground galleries constitute the **German Naval War Memorial**★ *(Marine-Ehrenmal)*. On display is the U-995, a submarine launched in Hamburg in 1943. ☐ ☐ *Nov-Mar, 9.30am-5pm; Apr-Oct, 9.30am-7pm. ☐ €4. ☎ (043 43) 427 10; www.deutscher-marinebund.de/ehrenmal.*

Nord-Ostsee-Kanal (Kiel Canal)

This link between the Baltic and the North Sea, inaugurated by Wilhelm II in 1895, is today, at 100km/62mi, one of the world's busiest waterway: more than 38 000 vessels pass through annually, not counting sports boats. From the second viaduct from Kiel to Holtenau *(Olympiabrücke, reached from Kiel via Holtenauer Straße and Prinz-Heinrich-Straße)* is a good view of the **Holtenau** locks. Also worth seeing are the **Rendsburg Railway Viaduct**★, the **Grünental Bridge** on B 204, and the **Hochdonn Railway Bridge**.

Holstein's "Little Switzerland"★ (Holsteinische Schweiz)

51km/32mi. Between Kiel and the Bay of Lübeck, not far from the Baltic Sea, Holstein's "Little Switzerland" is scattered with lakes among wooded hills of glacial moraine. Its highest point is Bungsberg at 168m/550ft. Worthwhile stops in this region include the largest of the lakes, **Großer Plöner See**, and its accompanying town of **Plön**; **Eutin**, birthplace of the composer Carl Maria von Weber, with its 17C town centre; and **Malente-Gremsmühlen**, a small isthmus resort, which is a departure point for boating trips.

Liebfrauenkirche

This Romanesque church was remodelled in the 13C and given a Late Gothic chancel in the 15C. The belfries were crowned with Baroque roofs late in the 17C. The interesting windows in the chancel are the work of HG Stockhausen in 1992.

Jesuitenplatz

In the courtyard of a 17C Jesuit College, now serving as town hall, is the *Schängelbrunnen,* a fountain evoking the mischief perpetrated by the street urchins of the city.

Mittelrheinmuseum

Florinsmarkt 15-17. Closer to the Moselle than the Rhine, this museum retraces the history of the town and environs through paintings, religious artifacts and everyday items dating from the Middle Ages.

Excursions

Festung Ehrenbreitstein★(Citadel)

4.5km/3mi. Cross the Rhine on Pfaffendorfer Brücke then turn left. This strategic stronghold, commanding the confluence of the two rivers, was the possession of the archbishops of Trier from the 10C until 1799, when it was destroyed by the French. Between 1816 and 1832 the Prussians constructed the existing fortress. From the terrace is a **view**★ of Koblenz, Schloss Stolzenfels to the south, the wooded Hunsrück and the volcanic massif of the Eifel.

Kloster Maria Laach★

20km/12mi west. The vast crater lake beside this abbey adds a sense of calm and quiet to the abbey buildings. The 12C abbey church is a Romanesque basilica with three naves, its exterior similar to those in Worms, Speyer and Mainz. The cloister-style **entrance portico**★, added in the early 13C, has intricately worked capitals. An unusual hexagonal baldaquin over the altar suggests a possible Moorish influence.

Rheintal★★★ (👓 *see RHEINTAL)*

Moseltal★★★ (👓 *see MOSELTAL)*

KÖLN★★★

COLOGNE
POPULATION: 976 000

The city of Cologne likes to have a good time. Case in point: Kölsch – a word synonymous for the local dialect and the local beer. This pleasant Rhineland city did, however, go through a bleak period after nearly being levelled during the Second World War. But it has managed to rebuild itself with remarkable vigour. Visitors will enjoy the city's elegant churches, colourful riverside houses and numerous museums. ⓘ *Opposite the cathedral, Unter Fettenhennen 19, 50667 Köln, ☎ (0221) 30 40 0.* ⓒ *Open July-Oct, Mon-Fri 9am-10pm, Sat-Sun 10am-6pm; Oct-Jun, Mon-Fri 9am-9pm, Sat-Sun 10am-6pm. www.koeln.de; www.koeln.org.*

▸ **Orient Yourself:** A real hub of European business, Cologne stands at the intersection of old Roman roads and medieval trade routes. The ring road encircling the city today links up with ten motorways, the A 3 (Frankfurt-Essen), A 4 (Aachen), the A 59 (Düsseldorf) and the A 555 (Bonn) chief among them.

⊘ **Don't Miss:** Cologne's Cathedral, the Römisch-Germanisches Museum

ⓒ **Organizing Your Time:** Allow a minimum of one hour to fully appreciate Cologne's cathedral, and two hours for the suggested walking tour.

Kids **Especially for Kids:** The Chocolate Museum, The Rheingarten

♿ **Also See:** *BRÜHL (13km/8mi south), BONN (29km/18mi south), DÜSSELDORF (39km/24mi north) and EIFEL (Bad Münstereifel is 49km/31mi southwest).*

A Bit of History

Cologne in Roman Times – Once the Roman legions extended the Empire as far as the Rhine, General Agrippa, coloniser of the region, named the local settlement Oppidum Ubiorum, after the Germanic Ubii who lived there. But by AD 50, the town had adopted the name which would stick, at least in part: *Colonia Claudia*

Cologne

Rudolph/Köln Tourismus Office

Ara Agrippinensium (CCAA) and "Colonia's" first defensive walls were built. Roman ruins still exist in the (restored) Zeughausstraße, at the north gate of the town in front of the cathedral, and at the Praetorium, beneath the present town hall. From its official recognition onwards, the town flourished: it was the start of an era, rich in craftwork, trade and architecture, which did not end until the time of the Great Invasions, in the 5C.

The Holy City beside the Rhine – Cologne's political power in the Middle Ages derived from the Church. Until 1288, the archbishops of Cologne exercised powers both spiritual and temporal. In the 13C and early 14C, the city became the enlightened religious, intellectual and artistic centre of the Rhine Valley. Eminent men came to preach: the Dominican **Albertus Magnus** (teacher of Thomas Aquinas) and **Master Eckhart**, as well as the Scottish Franciscan, **Duns Scotus**. It was the work of such religious scholars that led in 1388 to the creation of Cologne University by local lay burghers.

Trade and Commerce – Because of its favoured position on the Rhine and on important trade routes, Cologne soon became a power in the commercial world, imposing its own system of weights and measures over the whole of northern Germany. The town's first fair was held in 1360. Its elevation to the status of Free City in 1475 did no more than set an official seal on the preponderant role Cologne had in fact been playing since the 13C.

The Modern City – Industrialisation in the late 19C quickly expanded the city of Cologne. After the Second World War, **Konrad Adenauer** continued the process of modernisation begun while he was mayor of the city between 1917 and 1933. It was due to the efforts of the man destined to become the Federal Republic's first Chancellor that the university, shut down under French occupation in 1798, was re-opened (1919); that the Deutz exhibition halls *(Messehallen)* were built; and that green belts were added throughout the city.

Art and Culture – Diversity, above all, marks cultural life in Cologne today. Apart from music and drama, the fine arts hold pride of place: no fewer than 120 galleries are devoted to contemporary art exhibitions. Two highly regarded annual international fairs include the *Westdeutsche Kunstmesse* and "Art Cologne", devoted to modern art. Beside the Schnütgen Museum, the **Josef-Haubrich-Halle** mounts important exhibitions.
Heinrich Böll (1917-85), one of the preeminent German post-war writers and winner of the Nobel Prize for Literature in 1972, was born in Cologne. His work, sparing neither the Church nor society, is inseparable from his birthplace.
Publishing houses and printers have occupied Cologne for centuries. Building on this history has been the recent push into electronic media. Cologne, the media city, is currently Germany's TV capital, with eight television stations, recording studios, a media park and an Academy of Media Arts.

Town Life – There is a strong sense of neighbourhood in Cologne. Each locality centres on its individual parish church, and each preserves its own traditions. St Severin is the oldest and most typical. But all Cologne citizens appreciate the old town bordering the Rhine. Remodelled in the 1980s, the old town is now, night and day, one of the liveliest parts of the city. Since the riverside highway has been diverted underground between the Hohenzollern and Deutzer bridges, land has been transformed into attractive gardens *(Rheingarten)* where inhabitants walk and relax. Boat excursions leave from this point.

Address Book

PUBLIC TRANSPORT

The main local transport network in Cologne is the *Kölner Verkehrsbetriebe* (KVB), which runs most buses, underground trains (U-Bahn) and trams (Straßenbahn). The KVB is linked with the Rhein-Sieg transport authority (VRS), which covers the area as far as Bonn, among other places.

Cologne is divided into price zones; the cost of single journeys *(Einzelfahrt)* is €1.30, €2.20 or €4. A *Minigruppenticket* costs €9 and covers up to five people after 9am for unlimited travel on public transport for one day. The 24hr ticket for one costs €6, the one-week ticket €17.30. For 24hr information ☎ (01803) 50 40 30 (€0.093/min). There are KVB information booths *(Informationsstellen)* all over Cologne, the main ones on the east side of the main railway station *(Hauptbahnhof Ostseite)*, Mon-Sat 7am-8pm, Sun noon-8pm; and at Neumarkt 25, open Mon-Fri 7am-7pm, Sat 8:30am-4pm, and Ehrenfeldgürtel 14, open Mon-Fri 7am-7pm, Sat 8:30am-2pm.

Internet – www.kvb-koeln.de

The **KölnTourismus Card**, available in hotels for €19 (valid 72hr), allows the use of all public transport facilities, including a coach tour of the city, free entry to some museums and discounts on tickets for the opera, boat trips, ascent of the cathedral tower, etc.

SIGHTSEEING

CITY TOURS

Coach trip with guide, including a museum visit, available from the *Köln Tourismus* office opposite the cathedral, (0221) 233 32; Apr-Oct, daily at 10am, 12:30pm, 3pm, Sat also at 5:30pm; Nov-Mar at 11am and 2pm. The tour lasts 2hr and costs €13. Meeting point for cathedral tours is the main door, Mon-Sat at 11am, 12:30pm, 2pm and 3:30pm, Sun at 2pm and 3:30pm.

City walking tours organised by *Statt-Reisen Köln*, ☎ 732 51 13, and *Inside Cologne-City Tours*, ☎ 52 19 77, www. stattreisen-koeln.de, www.inside-cologne.de.

BOAT TRIPS

The *Köln-Düsseldorfer Deutsche Rheinschiffahrt (KD)* has the largest fleet of excursion boats on the Rhine, ☎ 208 83 18; www.k-d.com. Other companies include *Dampfschiffahrt Colonia*, ☎ 257 42 25, and *KölnTourist Personenschiffahrt*, ☎ 12 16 00, www. koelntourist.net.

DATES FOR YOUR CALENDAR

Carnival in Feb (although the season traditionally begins on 11 Nov) with the great Rosenmontag (Mon before Lent) parade; **Ringfest der PopKomm** in Aug; **Art Cologne** in Nov.

WHERE TO EAT

Brauhaus Goldener Pflug – Olpener Strasse 421, 51109 Köln-Merheim. ☎ (0221) 310 56 31. www.brauhaus-goldener-pflug.de. A typical Cologne restaurant with a rustic, comfortable decor. Several bars, a brasserie section, a dining room and 240-seat summer beer garden.

Brasserie Liège – Lütticher Straße 30. ☎ (0221) 952 05 50. www. liege.de. Ⓒ *Closed Sun and public holidays.* A brasserie typical of the Belgian quarter, serving good French cuisine. Simple, modern decor.

Hase – St.-Apern-Strasse 17. ☎ (0221) 25 43 75. Ⓒ *Closed Sun.* The pale wooden tables of this restaurant-café add to its rustic charm. A few traditional dishes, marked on a board.

Heising und Adelmann – Friesenstraße 58-60 ☎ (0221) 130 94 24. www.heising-und-adelmann.de. Ⓒ *Mon-Thu 6pm-1am, Fri-Sat 6pm-3am* Ⓒ *closed Sun and public holidays.* A fashionable restaurant with a relaxed atmosphere. 50 cocktails to choose from at the bar. Lovely terrace out back.

Em Krützche – Am Frankenturm 1. ☎ (0221) 258 08 39. info@ em-kruetzche.de. Ⓒ *Closed Holy Week and Mon.* This family-run restaurant in the old town was founded over 400 years ago.

Le Moissonnier – *Krefelder Straße 25* ☎ *(0221) 72 94 79* 🕐 *closed 24 Dec-3 Jan, 1 week at Easter and 3 weeks in Aug/Sept.* 🍴 A typical Art Nouveau (*Jugendstil*) bistro in an old house in the city centre that pampers its patrons. Creative French cuisine.

Paul's Restaurant – *Bülowstraße 2, 50733 Köln-Nippes.* ☎ *(0221) 76 68 39* *www.pauls-restaurant.de* 🕐 *Closed Mon, 1 week during Carnival, 2 weeks in July.* A restored house in a residential area with smart rustic interior and well-laid tables. A choice of several original dishes.

Hanse Stube – *Dompropst-Ketzer-Straße 2.* ☎ *(0221) 270 34 02.* *ehe@excelsiorhotelernst.de.* An elegant restaurant in the Excelsior Hotel Ernst. A well-trained staff and French cuisine.

WHERE TO STAY

Hotel Im Kupferkessel – *Probsteigasse 6 (north of Christophstraße near St Gereon's Church)* ☎ *(0221) 2 70 79 60* *Fax (0221) 270 79 629* *www.im-kupfer-kessel.de 13 rooms* 📶 Small, well-kept hotel with a warm welcome on the edge of the old town. The rooms are small and basic (some with bathroom on the landing). Pleasant breakfast room.

Hotel Brandenburger Hof – *Brandenburger Straße 2* ☎ *(0221) 12 28 89 Fax (0221) 135304.* *www.brandenburgerhof.de.* 🍴 📶 *31 rooms.* 📶 North of the old town, this hotel has plain, simple rooms with a small garden and reasonable prices. The main train station and cathedral are nearby.

Haus an den sieben Wegen – *Grafenmühlenweg 220, 51069 Köln-Dellbrück.* ☎ *(0221) 689 30 00.* *Fax (0221) 68930020. www.hotel-7-wege.de.* 🕐 *Closed Christmas to early Jan.* 📶 *15 rooms.* 📶 Neat, well-appointed and well-run hotel at the heart of a small park in a residential area. Variously decorated rooms, some of them quite spacious.

Wippenbekk – *Karlstraße 7, 50996 Köln-Rodenkirchen.* ☎ *(0221) 935 31 50. Fax (0221) 93531599. www.wippenbekk.de. 11 rooms.* 📶 Restaurant. This hotel has an ideal riverfront location, with simple, modern rooms with Italian furniture. The restaurant with winter garden has a delightful view, and the hotel has a beer garden.

Das kleine Hotel – *Wichheimer Straße 200, 51067 Köln-Holweide* ☎ *(0221) 691 05 91.   Fax (0221) 6910592.* 🅿 *Reservation necessary. 7 rooms* 📶 Restaurant. A small well-kept establishment with a boarding-house atmosphere. Cosy rooms with pale wooden furniture and wood floors. The Stadtbahn station is nearby.

Hotel Trost – *Vogelsanger Straße 60-62, 50823 Köln-Ehrenfeld* ☎ *(0221) 51 66 47 Fax (0221) 512151. www.hotel-trost.de* 🍴 *18 rooms.* 📶 This well-kept family-run hotel occupies an old renovated house. Modern, welcoming rooms.

Hotel Im Wasserturm – *Kaygasse 2.* ☎ *(0221) 200 80 Fax (0221) 2008888.   info@hotel-im-wasserturm.de.* 🔑 *88 rooms* 📶 Restaurant. Houseed in an imposing brick building, once the largest water tower in Europe, this unforgettable hotel impresses immediately with its lobby. Enjoy magnificent views from the 11th-floor restaurant.

Excelsior Hotel Ernst – *Domplatz.* ☎ *(0221) 27 01 Fax (0221) 270 3333. www.excelsiorhotelernst.de. 152 rooms.* 📶 The best address in Cologne, opposite the cathedral. Access is via a beautiful marble lobby. Refined rooms and grand suites, along with a sauna and fitness facilities.

Cologne – Hohe Strasse

F. Damm/Köln Tourismus Office

TAKING A BREAK

Café Eigel – *Brückenstraße 1-3 (Glockengasse to the east).* ☎ (0221) 2 57 58 58 🕐 *Mon-Fri 9am-7pm, Sat 9am-6pm, Sun 2-6pm.* This traditional yet modern café serves homemade praline and pastries, and exhibits and sells works by modern artists.

Café Reichard – *Unter Fettenhennen 11 (opposite the cathedral).* ☎ (0221) 2 57 85 42. *www.cafe-reichard.de.* 🕐 *8:30am-8pm.* Enjoy this cafe's classic interior, a winter garden and a large terrace, as well as great views of the cathedral. The veranda is perfect for people-watching.

Käse-Pavillon – *Breite Strasse 29 (access via Opernpassagen or Neue Langgasse).* ☎ (0221) 2 58 01 30. 🕐 *Mon-Fri 7am-7pm, Sat 7am-4pm.* This unusual fast-food restaurant is a temple to cheese. In winter expect a selection of over 300 varieties (150 in summer) to choose from. Make your own sandwich or choose from the menu. Small selection of wines to accompany your snack.

GOING OUT

USEFUL TIPS

The old city offers a wealth of possibilities when it comes to dining, having a drink or finding entertainment. Areas with lots of bars include the Belgian district (between Aachener and Venloer Straße), the university district (around Zülpicher Straße), around Chlodwigplatz and the around Friesenstraße. The traditional beer is "Kölsch", served in 0.2l glasses.

Früh am Dom – *Am Hof 12-14* ☎ (0221) 2 61 32 13. *www.frueh.de.* 🕐 *8am-12:30am.* 🕐 *Closed 24 Dec.* A casual restaurant with varying cuisine on each of its three floors. No need to order your Kölsch – it will be already waiting for you. For peace and quiet, try the 1st floor restaurant.

Päffgen – *Friesenstraße 64-66 (between Friesenplatz and Römerturm).* ☎ (0221) 13 54 61. *www.paeffgen-koelsch.de.* 🕐 *10am-12:30am.* Traditional restaurant, Kölsch and regional dishes, best enjoyed in the beer garden in summer.

Papa Joe's Biersalon "Klimperkasten" *Alter Markt 50-52.* ☎ (0221) 2 58 21 32. *www.papajoes.de.* 🕐 *11am-1am, Fri-Sat until 3am.* Retro atmosphere in this restaurant whose walls and ceiling are covered in old photos. A trip down memory lane, to the sounds of piano music or musical automatons.

Papa Joe's Jazzlokal "Em Streckstrump" – *Buttermarkt 37 (street parallel to the Rhine, starting from Groß St-Martin).* ☎ (0221) 2 57 79 31 *www.papajoes.de.* 🕐 *8pm-3am, Sun from 3:30pm.* Jazz reigns supreme here as it has evenings for over 25 years. The drinks are expensive but the concerts free and the atmosphere good. "Four O'Clock Jazz" Sun.

Hyatt-Biergarten – *Kennedyufer 2a (across the Hohenzollernbrücke from the cathedral) 50679 Köln-Deutz.* ☎ (0221) 82 812 34. *www.cologne.regency.hyatt.de.* 🕐 *end Apr to early Oct, Mon-Sat noon-midnight, Sun 11am-midnight (closed in bad weather).* The beer garden of this luxury hotel on the Rhine's east bank offers magnificent views of the cathedral and historic centre. From early May to late Aug, crowds gather to hear jazz Sun (noon-3pm, free).

CULTURE

USEFUL TIPS

Cultural calendars of events can be found in the monthly publication *Köln im...* (followed by the month) at tourist information offices (👓 €1). Other monthly magazines like *StadtRevue* and *Prinz* are valuable resources and sold at bookshops and newspaper kiosks.

SHOPPING

USEFUL TIPS

The cathedral is the best point of departure for any shopping trip in Cologne, near the main shopping street, Hohe Strasse. This street is crossed by Schildergasse, which is lined with department stores. Not far from the Neumarkt are shopping arcades, such as Neumarktpassage and Neumarktgalerie. Exclusive boutiques line Breite Strasse, Mittelstraße and Pfeilstraße. There is also shopping around Chlodwigplatz, and in Bonnerstraße and Severinstraße.

Antique shops and **art galleries** are concentrated in St-Apern-Straße; more galleries lie north of Neumarkt (Albertusstraße) and around the cathedral.

4711 Echt Kölnisch Wasser – *Glockengasse 4711.* ☎ *(0221) 9 25 04 50* *www.4711.com.* 🕐 *Mon-Fri 9am-7pm, Sat 9am-6pm.* The traditional home of

the famous Eau de Cologne. Here you will find a fountain of *aqua mirabile* where you can freshen up, a historical exhibition, souvenirs and a range of beauty products. The carillon on the southern façade of the building plays the *Marseillaise* every hour from 9am to 9pm.

Dom★★★

♿ 🕐 *6am-7:30pm.* ☎ *(0221) 17 94 05 55; www.koelnerdom.de.*
It took over 600 years to complete this huge edifice. In 1164, when Frederick I Barbarossa donated relics of the Magi to the city, an influx of pilgrims precipitated the need for a larger church. Thus began construction of the cathedral, the first Gothic church in the Rhineland, its original design based on those in Paris, Amiens and Reims, although Cologne's far exceeds theirs in size. The chancel was completed ca 1320; the south tower by 1410. Finally, in 1880 the cathedral was consecrated before Emperor Wilhelm I. UNESCO has declared the cathedral a cultural heritage site.

Exterior

The twin-towered western façade marks a high point in the Flamboyant Gothic style. Embellished gables and slender buttresses burst ever upward, in line with tapering spires 157m/515ft high. The bronze doors **(1)** in the south transept entrance (1948-54) are by Ewald Mataré.

Interior

The building's colossal proportions are only fully appreciated from the nave, 144m/472ft long, 45m/148ft wide, and 43.5m/143ft high. The five Late Gothic **stained-glass windows**★ in the north aisle (1507-08) depict the lives of The Virgin and St Peter. The Kreuzkapelle, a chapel off the north ambulatory, houses the **Cross of Gero**★ *(Gerokreuz)* **(3)**, an example of 10C Ottonian art. In the axial chapel *(Dreikönigskapelle)* the stained-glass window, the *Älteres Bibelfenster* **(4)**, was installed in 1265. Behind the high altar is the shrine with relics of the Three Magi, the **Dreikönigenschrein**★★★, a 12C masterpiece in gold. The last chapel in the south ambulatory *(Marienka-*

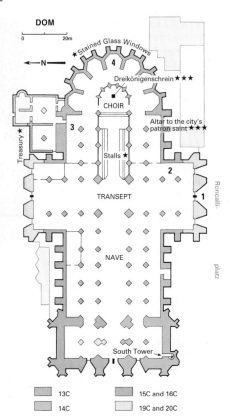

DOM

0   20m

←—N—

★ *Stained Glass Windows*

4

Dreikönigenschrein ★★★

CHOIR

3

Altar to the city's patron saint ★★★

Treasury ★

Stalls ★

2

TRANSEPT

1

Roncalli-

NAVE

South Tower

platz

	13C		15C and 16C
	14C		19C and 20C

pelle) contains the altarpiece of the city's patrons, the **Altar der Stadtpatrone**★★★, painted ca 1440 by **Stefan Lochner** illustrating The Adoration of the Magi, St Ursula and St Gereon.

The south transept houses a Flemish polyptych of 1521 with double side panels known as the **Altarpiece of the Five Moors (2)** *(Agilolphusaltar)*. Finally, the finely carved **choir stalls**★ (14C) *(Chorgestühl)*, the most extensive in Germany, contain 104 places. 🕐 *Same hours as the cathedral. The ambulatory is not accessible during services.* ☎ *(0221) 92 58 47 30.*

The **South Tower** *(Südturm)* is reached via a steep stairway. A platform at 97m/318ft reveals a panorama of Cologne and the surrounding countryside. The belfry *(Glockenstube)* houses the world's largest swinging church bell: St Peter's Bell *(Petersglocke)* was cast in 1923 at a weight of 24t.

Finally, the **Treasury**★ *(Domschatzkammer)* of the cathedral contains a wealth of religious art: gold and silver liturgical plate, the shrine to St Engelbert, and a reliquary monstrance with St Peter's chain. ♿ 🕐 *10am-6pm.* 💶 €4. ☎ *(0221) 17 94 05 55.*

Romanesque Churches

The Romanesque period in Cologne saw the construction of numerous churches; 12 remain in the old town alone. Strolling through its old streets, visitors can acquaint themselves with varying Rhineland Romanesque architecture. Certain design elements, like the trefoil chancel, originated in the city (👁 *see Art in the Introduction*).

St-Maria-im-Kapitol★

This late Ottonian church (11C) features the oldest **trefoil chancel**★ (clover-leaf) in Cologne. The crypt extends beneath almost the entire body of the chancel, the largest in Germany after the crypt in Speyer Cathedral. On the left side of the east clover-leaf is the Madonna of St Hermann-Joseph altarpiece (c 1180). The **Renaissance choir screen** is richly decorated with sculpture (c 1525). At the west end of the south side aisle are Romanesque **wooden doors**★ from 1065.

St Severin

St Severin is the oldest Christian foundation in Cologne, dating to the 4C, built on a Roman-Frankish burial ground. The present building dates from the 13C (chancel) and 15C (west tower and

St-Maria-im-Kapitol

Skyline/Köln Tourismus Office

nave). There is a fine Gothic nave in the **interior**★. Note, in the chancel, paintings by the Master of St Severinus. The tomb of St Severinus, Bishop of Cologne ca 400 and one of the city's patron saints, is in the crypt.

St Pantaleon★

The nave and impressive Westwerk are examples of Ottonian architecture (10C). The **rood screen**★ at the chancel is Late Gothic.

Carnival

Celebrations in Cologne start at 11 minutes past 11 on the 11th day of the 11th month, gradually climaxing during the three days preceding Ash Wednesday. Things get under way beforehand with Weiberfastnacht, the Women's Carnival (the Thursday before Shrove Tuesday – women throughout town indiscriminately cut off men's neckties). Then there is the People's Carnival the Sunday before Shrove Tuesday with the Veedelszöch and the Schullzöch (dialect words); Rosenmontag, the day before Shrove Tuesday, features a procession with elaborately decorated floats, bands and a cavalcade of giant current events caricatures; and finally Shrove Tuesday (Fastnachtsdienstag), which ends at midnight with the burning of straw dolls ("Nubbel"). Carnival associations meet on the evening of Ash Wednesday for a meal of fish. During the carnival season, the inhabitants of Cologne and its visitors go wild; peace and quiet are out of the question.

A brochure and leaflet detailing the procession routes and other important information, such as traffic direction and room reservation, are at the Cologne tourist office.

Gereonskirche★ (St Gereon)
The originality of this church lies in its elliptical plan and the addition in 1220 of a **decagon**★ between its towers. The crypt with its 11C mosaic floor contains the tomb of St. Gereon. The frescoes date from the 13C.

St Andreas
This Late Romanesque church was built in the early 13C with a trefoil apse and features remarkable architectural sculpture. At the beginning of the 15C, the chancel was replaced with a Gothic chancel, modelled on that in Aachen (1414-20).

St Ursula
In the north aisle are 30 plates (1456) by Stefan Lochner depicting the martyrdom of St Ursula. The daughter of a British king, St Ursula was murdered by Huns along with 10 of her companions in the 5C. In the south transept is the **Goldene Kammer**★ (Golden Chamber), which contains 120 reliquary busts. ☎ (0221) 13 34 00.

Walking Tour

Old Town

The cultural heart of Cologne lies in teh immediate vicinity of the central station and the Hohenzollernbrücke, the busiest railway bridge in the world, with a train crossing every two minutes, day and night.
Not far from Germany's best-known church, Cologne Cathedral, are several outstanding museums. The Römisch-Germanisches Museum and Diözesanmuseum rub shoulders with the Museum Ludwig, a 1986, modern edifice whose whose saw-tooth roofing contrasts with the Gothic spires of the cathedral. The complex also includes, at basement level, the **Philharmonia** auditorium. From the Heinrich-Böll-Platz, where the museums are located, a series of terraces leads down to the northern part of Rheingarten.

▶ *At the riverside, take the Frankenwerft which offers lovely views of the Rhine. The church of Groß St-Martin towers over the Fisch-Market with its reconstructed houses. Between the Rhine and the Alter Markt lies the Martinsviertel, a district famous for its tourist cafés and bars. Leave the river via Lintgasse, which leads to the Alter Markt, the site of the old Roman port.*

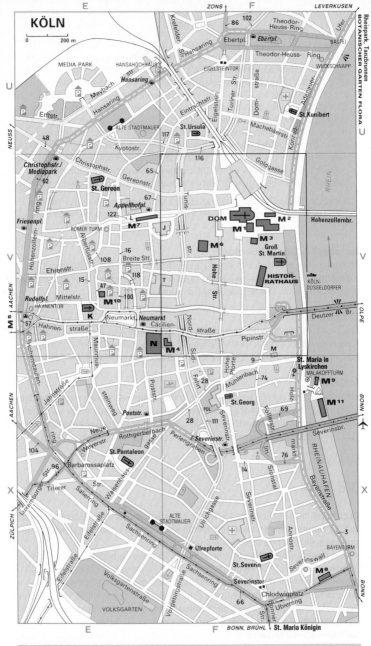

KÖLN

0 200 m

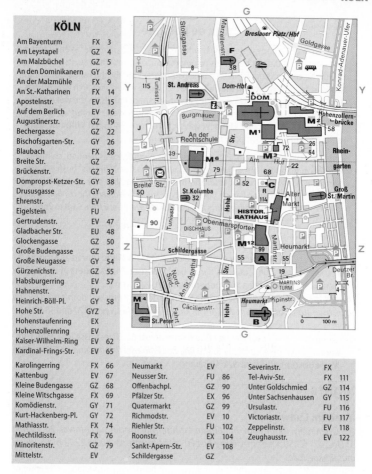

Altes Rathaus★ (Old Town Hall)

This building with its reconstructed 15C Gothic tower (carillon at noon and 5pm) and the Flemish Renaissance pavilion (1569-73) lies at the heart of the old Jewish quarter. In 1349, the ghetto was stormed, its inhabitants murdered and their homes torched. Beside the town hall part of the Jewish baths, or **Mikwe** (c 1170), are preserved under a glass pyramid *(Mon to Fri; key is held by the town hall porter.)*

Prätorium

The entrance is hidden near the underground garage in Kleine Budengasse. ⏱ *Open Tue-Sun, 10am (11am, Sat-Sun)-4pm.* ☎ *(0221) 22 12 304.*

The foundations of the Roman governor's palace (1C-4C) were excavated after the Second World War and are largely preserved. In the antechamber are small sculptures, bricks and receptacles from Roman times. Visitors can also view the Roman sewer, which was used as an air-raid shelter during the Second World War.

▶ *Head back toward the Alter Markt and follow Martinstraße to the dance hall.*

Eau de Cologne

The people of Cologne were familiar with Cologne's *"aqua mirabile"* as early as the 16C, although it did not become a commercial success until the 18C. Its success is due to the enterprising spirit of an Italian immigrant family, the Farinas, of whom the most famous is **Johann Maria Farina**. "Cologne water" *(Kölnisch Wasser)* was thought to have medicinal properties to cure a number of ills. In the wake of the Farina family's success, other producers of the wonder-water sprang up, making "Eau de Cologne" famous. The new wave of producers included **Wilhelm Mühlens**, who founded a company in Glockengasse in 1792.

Under Napoleon, the use of Eau de Cologne as medicine was banned, so manufacturers began marketing their cure-all as toilet water. Mühlens' business was located at no. 4711 Glockengasse, and in 1875 this number was registered as a trade mark for authentic Eau de Cologne *(Echt Kölnisch Wasser)*. The carillon in the gable of no 4711 Glockengasse plays the Marseillaise every hour from 9am to 9pm.

Gürzenich Dance Hall

This was one of the first secular Gothic buildings (1441-44) and served as a model for many townhouses. The "council's dance hall" was used for banquets in the Middle Ages and, in the 19C, when the modern carnival was born.

Toward the banks of the Rhine lies the **Heumarkt** *(hay market) dominated by the equestrian statue of Frederick William III, king of Prussia between 1770 and 1840.*

▶ *Continuing south over Deutzer Brücke and across Cäcilienstrasse is St-Maria-im-Kapitol. From here, continue to the Rheinauhalbinsel (island) and its* **Chocolate Museum** *(Imhoff-Stollwerck-Museum).*

Sights

Museum Ludwig★★

🕙 *Open daily 10am-6pm.* 🕙 *Closed 1st Jan, Thu-Tue during carnival, 24, 25 and 31 Dec.* 🎫 *€7.50. Free entry every first Fri of the month.* ☎ *(0221) 22 12 61 65; www.museenkoeln.de*

The spacious museum with its distinctive roof houses an important collection of 20C art, emphasizing particularly well the Expressionist movement and works by the Brücke and Blaue Reiter groups. There is also a good display of art from between the two World Wars: Constructivism, the Bauhaus and New Objectivity.

One of the museum's strong points is a collection of **Russian Avant-Garde** art. The Surrealist department reveals Dadaism's birth in Cologne, and a variety of works by **Max Ernst** are on display (he was born nearby in Brühl), along with works by Miró, Dalí and Magritte.

Cubist artworks include Gris, Léger and Delaunay, and **Nouveau Réalisme** as practised by Klein, Tàpies, Burri and Dubuffet. A highlight is **Picasso**'s work, displayed in one of the world's most comprehensive collections.

German post-war and contemporary art includes works by the **Gruppe Zero**, but mainly by **Joseph Beuys**, Baselitz, Richter, Penck and Kiefer. American abstract painting is represented (Rothko, de Kooning), as is **Pop Art** (Rauschenberg, Warhol and Segal).

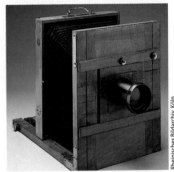

Travelling camera (c 1880)

Rheinisches Bildarchiv, Köln

Works by contemporary artists from Europe, America, Japan and China, complete with a series of installations, illustrate the most recent artistic trends.

Museum Ludwig / Agfa Foto-Historama (Museum of Photography)
🕐 *Open only during temporary exhibitions.* ☎ *(0221) 22 12 24 11.*
Compiled from various private collections), this exhibition presents an overall view of over 150 years of photography, from the magic lantern to daguerreotype, calotype, spooled film, and modern microfilm and digital cameras.

Römisch-Germanisches Museum
🐾 *Visit afternoons or weekends to avoid school groups.* ♿ 🕐 *Open daily, 10am-5pm.*
🕐 *Closed 1 Jan, Thu-Tue during carnival, 24, 25 and 31 Dec.* 🎫 *€6.45.* ☎ *(0221) 22 12 44 38; www.museenkoeln.de.*
Capital of the Roman province of Lower Germania, Cologne enjoyed immense prosperity between the 1C and the 4C, due largely to trade between the Roman colonizers and the Germanic Ubii. Evidence of these exchanges is displayed in this modern museum.

In the basement is the **Dionysius Mosaic**★, an exceptionally well-preserved Roman mosaic made of one and a half million fragments of stone (measuring 14.5x7m/ 48x23ft). The banqueting hall (part of a Roman villa) was uncovered during the construction of an air-raid bunker in 1941 and preserved on its original site. Adjacent rooms evoke funerary rites and the daily lives of the Ancient Romans.

Exhibits also include the **Mausoleum of Lucius Poblicius**, an officer of the Roman Legion; the **Philosophers' Mosaic**; and an array of Roman **glassware**★★.

Diözesanmuseum★ (Diocesan Museum)
♿ 🕐 *Open daily except Thu, 11am-6pm.* 🕐 *Closed Carnival Monday, 24 and 25 Dec.*
🎫 *Free admission.* ☎ *(0221) 257 76 72; www.kolumba.de.*
Precious religious objects and artworks from the Middle Ages make up the collection of this museum. The most famous work is Lochner's **Virgin with Violets**.

Wallraf-Richartz-Museum★★
🕐 *Open daily except Mon, 10am-6pm, Tues 10am-8pm, Sat-Sun 11am-6pm.*
🕐 *Closed 1 Jan, Carnival, 24, 25 and 31 Dec.* 🎫 *€8.* ☎ *(0221) 22 12 11 19; www.museenkoeln.de.*

The Wallraf-Richartz-Museum, which once shared space with Museum Ludwig, exhibits its own display of priceless artworks emphasizing local artists.

The Medieval Painters of Cologne collection culminates with the Late Gothic work of Stefan Lochner. Also of note are the **Master of St Veronica** and the **Master of Life of the Virgin**. Among the **German Old Masters** on view are **Dürer** and **Lucas Cranach the Elder** (*Virgin and Child*).

Numerous additional works are on display representing various genres: Baroque art by Rubens, Ruisdael, Hals and **Rembrandt**, with the famous late self-portrait; Spanish, Italian and French artists Murillo, Tiepolo and Boucher; 18C-19C French and German artists CD

Chocolate-vending machine

Imhoff-Stollwerck-Museum, Köln

The School of Cologne

Manuscript illumination and altar ornamentation were blossoming arts in Cologne in the early 14C. Painting attained its summit in the early 15C, with the works of **The Master of St Veronica** and **Stefan Lochner**, a native of Meersburg. From 1450 on, under the influence of the Dutch schools, the artists of Cologne abandoned the idealistic mysticism of the Gothic period for the gracious realism of the Renaissance. This later work is characterised by delicate colours and a tender treatment of subjects. Religious sculpture in Cologne peaked between the 14C and 15C. Many **Madonnas** display this style of tenderness sweeping Europe around 1400: the hinted smile, draping fabrics and a relaxed stance.

Friedrich, Cologne-born **Wilhelm Leibl,** and Klinger; and French Impressionists Renoir, Monet, Sisley, Cézanne, Van Gogh and Gauguin.

Schnütgen-Museum★★

🕓 *Open daily except Mon, 10am-5pm, Sat-Sun 11am-5pm.* 🕓 *Closed 1st Jan, carnival, 24, 25 and 31 Dec.* ⊜ *€4.20.* ☎ *(0221) 22 12 36 20; www.museenkoeln.de.*
The 12C former Cäcilienkirche, one of the dozen Romanesque churches still standing in the city, makes a suitable site for this museum of sacred art from the 6C to the 19C. Numerous **Madonnas in wood** illustrate the local "tender" style in statuary. A collection of medieval items in ivory, most of them from Byzantium, France or other parts of Germany, is of particularly fine workmanship, as are works in gold, silver and bronze and Medieval textiles.

Museum für Ostasiatische Kunst★★ (Museum of Far Eastern Art)

Universitätsstraße 100. ♿ 🕓 *Open daily except Mon, 11am-5pm, Thu 11am-8pm.* 🕓 *Closed 1st Jan, Thu-Tue during carnival, 24, 25 and 31 Dec.* ⊜ *€6.50.* ☎ *(0221) 940 51 80; www.museenkoeln.de.*
Germany's oldest museum of Far Eastern art (founded in 1909) is surrounded by a Japanese garden laid out by Masayuki Nagare (b 1923). The permanent exhibition displays works of Chinese, Japanese and Korean art, from the Neolithic Age to the present. Among the oldest exhibits are Chinese vessels (16C-12C BC). Other highlights include Buddhist art from China and Japan; Chinese ceramics from all phases of its evolution; 17C Chinese furniture and writing equipment and Japanese screens.

Museum für Ostasiatische Kunst, Köln

Ceremonial urn, Museum für Ostasiastische Kunst

Museum für Angewandte Kunst★ (Museum of Applied Arts)

♿ 🕓 *Open daily except Mon, 11am-5pm.* 🕓 *Closed 1st Jan, Thu-Tue during carnival, 24, 25 and 31 Dec.* ⊜ *€3.* ☎ *(0221) 22 12 67 35; www.museenkoeln.de.*
This museum contains an extensive collection of furniture, ceramics, glassware, metalwork, jewelry and textiles from the Middle Ages to the present. Of particular interest are 16C-17C pewter, German "Waldglas," Baroque and Jugendstil glassware.

Rautenstrauch-Joest-Museum für Völkerkunde (Ethnographic Museum)

🕐 *Open daily except Mon, 10am-4pm, Sat 11am-4pm, Sun 11am-6pm.* 🕐 *Closed 1st Jan, Thu-Tue during carnival, 24, 25 and 31 Dec.* ⊕ *€4.* ☎ *(0221) 336 94 0.*
This museum offers displays of Thai and Khmer ceramics and sculpture from the 8C to the 16C, and a collection of Ancient Egyptian art, Native American and Inuit art.

Imhoff-Stollwerck-Museum★ (Chocolate Museum)

Kids *Rheinauhafen.* ♿ 🕐 *Open daily except Mon, 10am-6pm, Sat-Sun 11am-7pm.* 🕐 *Closed 1st Jan, Thu-Wed during carnival, 24, 25 and 31 Dec.* ⊕ *€6.* ☎ *(0221) 931 88 80.*
This highly original museum takes as its subject that most fascinating of foodstuffs, chocolate. After arriving at the museum – visitors enter a Gründerzeit customs warehouse and then a modern glass building by way of a historical swing bridge over the Rhine – guests view displays about the 3 000-year history and production of chocolate, a miniature chocolate factory and the history of the 19C Cologne-born chocolate firm Stollwerck. Delicious chocolate treats complete the visit.

Excursions

Schloss Augustusburg★★ – *13km/8mi south.* ♿ *See BRÜHL.*

Altenberger Dom★

20km/12mi northeast. This former Cistercian abbey church (still known locally as the Bergischer Dom, lies in a lush green valley. The pure Gothic building (1255-1379) has celebrated Roman Catholic and Protestant rites alternately since 1857. Note especially the huge (18x8m/59x26ft) coloured glass canopy (c 1400) above the west entrance, considered the largest stained-glass window in Germany.

Zons★

24km/15mi north. This picturesque Rhineland fortified village, a suburb of Dormagen since 1975, had a toll-house added in the 14C, a good example of a medieval fortification. Its walls and numerous towers lend particular charm to the site.

KONSTANZ★

CONSTANCE
POPULATION: 82 000

The foundation of Konstanz, a German enclave on the Swiss shore of Lake Constance, has long been attributed to the Roman emperor Constantius Chlorus (292-306). Konstanz is now a lively holiday town with a large student population. If you wish to further explore the pleasures of the lake, the two tranquil islands of Mainau and Reichenau are perfect for walks away from it all. 🛈 *Bahnhofplatz 13, 78462 Konstanz,* ☎ *(075 31) 13 30 30.*

▶ **Orient Yourself:** Konstanz occupies an agreeable **site**★ opposite the narrows separating the lake proper ("Bodensee" in German) from its picturesque prolongation (Untersee). The islands of Mainau *(to the north)* and Reichenau *(to the west)* are each linked to the town by a bridge.

🕐 **Don't Miss:** The beautiful islands of Mainau and Reichenau.

🕐 **Organizing Your Time:** Allow two hours to tour Mainau Island.

Kids **Especially for Kids:** Outdoor activities on Mainau and Reichenau Islands *(♿ see Excursions).*

Also See: *BODENSEE, SALEM (54km/34mi northeast), SCHWÄBISCHE ALB, SIGMARIN-GEN (72km/45mi north), SCHWARZWALD (our tour includes Titisee, 96km/60mi west).*

A Bit of History

Constance, Capital of Christianity – From 1414 to 1418, a council convened in the town to attempt reunification of the Church following years of competing claims to the papal throne by three rival dignitaries. In 1417, the election of Martin V, who was universally recognised as true the Pope, put an end temporarily to the schism. Three years earlier this same council had summoned before it the religious reformer **Jan Hus**, Rector of the University of Prague. Hus expounded his Reformist theses before the Council of Constance, was declared a heretic and burned alive. This precursor of Protestantism was hailed as a national hero in his native Bohemia.

Sights

The Lake Shore★(Seeufer)

The charm and ambience of Konstanz is particularly apparent along its lakeside. Just beyond the boat dock *(near the tourist office)* is the **Konzilgebäude**, a 14C warehouse used by the Council of Constance of 1417, today a concert hall. At the bottom of the jetty is **Imperia** by contemporary sculptor Peter Lenk commemorating the 16C Italian courtier that Balzac immortalised as Constance in his novel *Ribald Tales (Contes drôlatiques)*. Across the road, in the municipal gardens *(Stadtgarten)*, is a monument to native son Count Zeppelin (1838-1917), the celebrated airship inventor. Farther down the *Konizilstraße* is a bridge leading to the Insel. Across the *Rheinbrücke* and along the *Rheinsteig* are the old **defensive towers** (Rheinturturm, Pulverturm). On the opposite bank, the Seestraße *(to the right)* is lined with Jugendstil villas. The lake itself offers numerous opportunities for excursions.

Address Book

WHERE TO EAT

Osteria Passatempo – *Markt-stätte 2* ☎ *(07531) 91 79 27* This restaurant is located where the pedestrian zone begins, in an underground passage leading to the port. The establishment is a youthful, modern place, with a relaxed atmosphere and displays of brightly coloured paintings. The menu features Italian cuisine.

WHERE TO STAY

Seehotel Siber – *Seestraße 25* ☎ *(07531) 996 69 90. seehotel.siber@t-online.de.* A tastefully decorated, Jugendstil villa, the restaurant and terrace offer beautiful views over the lake. Temptingly refined cuisine, presented with excellent service.

Hotel Barleben am See – *Seestraße 15, 78464 Konstanz-Staad.* ☎ *(07531) 942 330 Fax (07531) 66973* *www.hotel-barleben.de.* Reservation recommended 9 rooms Restaurant. This villa was built in 1872 and now serves as a small hotel with lovely, personalised guestrooms. The establishment is particularly well-located, in the heart of parkland directly adjacent to the lakeside promenade.

Steigenberger Inselhotel – *Auf der Insel 1.* ☎ *(07531) 12 50 Fax (07531) 125250 www.konstanz. steigenberger.de* 102 rooms. Set in an old Dominican monastery not far from the old town, this hotel charms guests with its tasteful, upscale ambience. Dine in the elegant restaurant or on the splendid terrace with lake views.

Münster★

Since its construction spanned the 11C to the 17C, this former **cathedral** lacks any artistic unity. The **panels**★ *(Türflügel)* of the porch doors in the main façade are decorated with bas-relief sculptures representing scenes from the life of Christ (1470). The 13C Mauritiuskapelle houses the Münster's most priceless piece of sculpture, the **Holy Tomb**★, a vaulted dodecagon containing three statuary groups. It is one of the few examples of its kind from the High Middle Ages, bearing a stylistic resemblance to the sculpture of Bamberg and Naumburg. In the crypt four gilded 11C-13C plaques represent Christ in Majesty, the Eagle of St John, and St Conrad and St Pelagius, patrons of the diocese. They are known as the **Konstanzer Goldscheiben** (gilded plaques of Constance).

Rathaus

The façade of this Renaissance building is embellished with paintings illustrating the history of Constance.

Archäologisches Landesmuseum

 ♿ ⏰ *Open Tue–Sun, 10am–6pm.* ⏰ *Closed 1 Jan, 24, 25 and 31 Dec.* ◸ *€3. (no charge on 1st Sat of month).* ☎ *(075 31) 980 40; www.konstanz.alm-bw.de.*

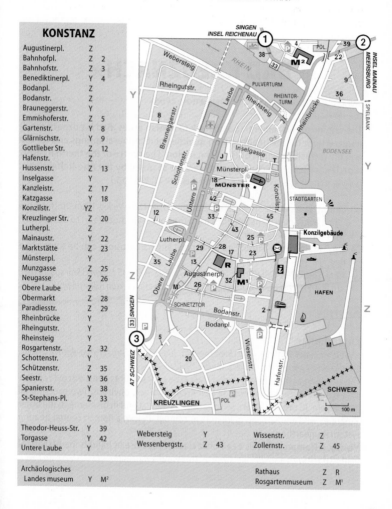

This museum is housed in an old convent building of the Peterhausen Abbey. History comes to life in 3 000m²/32 280sq ft of exhibition space, beginning with the buildings on stilts from 4000 BC and continuing to the recent industrial past.

Excursions

Mainau Island★★ (Insel Mainau)

7km/4.5mi north. Exit by ② on the town plan. ♿ ○ *Island accessible mid-March to mid-Oct: 7am-8pm; mid-Oct to mid-Mar: 9am-6pm.* ⊜ *€10.50.* ☎ *(075 31) 30 30.*
The grand dukes of Baden laid out a large park on this 45ha/110-acre island on Lake Constance. The island's palace, Baroque church and colourful plantings contribute to the island's magic. Exotic plants thrive in the mild climate; further attractions include Germany's largest butterfly house and seasonal floral displays.

Reichenau Island★ (Insel Reichenau)

7km/4.5mi west. Exit by ① on the town plan.
St Pirmin founded the first German Benedictine monastery east of the Rhine on Reichenau Island in 724. An arts and science centre flourished for centuries on the island. Some quite outstanding book illuminations were produced here during the Ottonian period.

BAD KREUZNACH★

POPULATION: 44 000

The origins of this mineral spa go back to Roman times. Bad Kreuznach is celebrated both for the health-giving qualities of its mineral springs and for the equally refreshing wines of the Nahe region. The centre of the thermal resort is on Badewörth Island, its downstream tip spanned by the Alte Nahebrücke.
🚹 *Kurhausstraße 23, 55543 Bad Kreuznach,* ☎ *(0671) 836 00 50.*

▶ **Orient Yourself:** Bad Kreuznach lies in the Lower Nahe Valley, 15km/9mi from the Rhine, where the Nahe emerges from the Palatinate mountains to the north.
☻ **Don't Miss:** The Römerhalle.
○ **Organizing Your Time:** Bad Kreuznach and its Excusions can be toured in a day.
♿ **Also See:** IDAR-OBERSTEIN (47km/29mi west), WORMS (56km/35mi southeast), RÜDESHEIM (67km/42mi north), RHEINTAL (tour leaves from Rüdesheim).

Sights

Römerhalle★

11 Hüffelsheimer Straße. ♿ ○ *Open Tue-Sun, 10am-5pm (6pm Jul-Aug, 4pm Nov-Dec).* ○ *Closed 24 and 31 Dec.* ⊜ *€2.* ☎ *(0671) 92 07 77.*
This museum at the western end of the castle park features items discovered during archaeological excavations in Bad Kreuznach and environs. Two exceptional exhibits are 3C **mosaic floors**★★: one depicts the sea god in his element; the other illustrates wild animals and gladiators in combat. Below, a Roman central heating system is unearthed.
Nearby, a **Roman villa** has been uncovered. Also close at hand is the **historical Schloßpark** with a small lake, tropical trees and a museum.

Excursion

Bad Münster am Stein-Ebernburg★

By car, 4.5km/3mi. Leave the car near the Kurhaus; then 1hr round-trip on foot.
Go into the **thermal park**★ and walk through the gardens to the Nahe. On the far side of the river is the **Rheingrafenstein**★★, a 136m/446ft rock face surmounted by the ruins of an ancient castle.

▶ *Take the ferry across and, from the Hüttental café-restaurant, climb to the panoramic platform on top.*

From here, there is a fine **view**★ of the Bad Münster basin and, downstream, the Rotenfels, whose sheer cliffs tower 214m/700ft above the river.

LAHNTAL

The winding course of the lower Lahn is characterised by wild scenery and steeply wooded banks. The valley makes a charming setting for excursions to a number of castles and the delightful historic towns of Weilburg and Limburg.

▶ **Orient Yourself:** The Lahn valley cuts through the Taunus-Rhine massif and meanders through the forests of the Naussau natural park east of Koblenz.
🙂 **Don't Miss:** The suggested driving tour *(see below).*
🕐 **Organizing Your Time:** Allow four hours for the driving tour *(🕐 see below).*
🖐 **Also See:** *KOBLENZ (18km/11mi west of Bad Ems), RHEINTAL (tour includes Koblenz), MARBURG (44km/28mi north of Wetzlar), FRANKFURT AM MAIN (66km/41mi south of Wetzlar).*

Driving Tour

From Bad Ems to Wetzlar *89km/55mi*

Bad Ems
The Lahn valley, separating the Westerwald and the Taunus-Rhine schist massif, is rich in mineral springs. Opposite the assembly rooms is a flagstone with the date 13 July 1870, commemorating the meeting of Wilhelm and the French Ambassador, Benedetti. The meeting contributed to the outbreak of the Franco-Prussian War of 1870-71.

Nassau
This health resort in the Lahn Valley was the cradle of the counts of Laurenburg, from whom Dutch royalty, including William of Orange, William III of England and the current Dutch royalty, is descended. Points of interest include the Adelsheimer Hof (town hall), the Stammburg (ancestral castle) and the Steinisches Schloss.

Kloster Arnstein
1km/0.6mi by a steep uphill road from the Obernhof bridge. The Premonstratensian church bears one Romanesque chancel (west) and one Gothic (the east).

Verwalt. D. Staatl. Schlösser u. Gärten, Bad Homburg v. d. H.

The Baroque town of Weilburg

Balduinstein

These are the ruins of a 1320 castle of Baudouin of Luxembourg, Archbishop of Trier, built to rival that of nearby **Schloss Schaumburg,** a neo-Gothic reconstitution after the English manner. There is a fine view from the tallest of the crenellated towers overlooking the valley. ⏱ *Schaumburg open May-Sept, Tue-Sun, 10am-5pm (Sat-Sun only in May).* ≋ *€2.* ☎ *(064 32) 501 275; www.schloss-schaumburg.de.*

Diez

Dominating the small town is the 17C **Schloss Oranienstein**. The castle was built as an ancestral castle of the Nassau-Orange house. In 1811, Napoleon dissolved the principality of Orange. The modern castle serves as a barracks for an armoured brigade and houses the **Oranien-Nassau-Museum**. 🔍 *Apply to the guard for the guided (1hr) tour.* ≋ *€3. Apr to Oct, Tue-Sun at 9am, 10:30am, 2pm and 3:30pm, Sat-Sun at 10.30am, 2pm and 3pm; Nov to Mar, Tue-Fri at 9am, 10:30am, 2pm and 3:30pm.* ☎ *(064 32) 940 16 66.*

Limburg an der Lahn★ 👣 See LIMBURG.

Burg Runkel★

The picturesque **setting**★★ of the castle, built into the rock face, and the ancient village below it can best be appreciated from the 15C bridge over the river.

Weilburg

Once the residence of the Counts of Nassau, this Baroque town boasts a **castle** bearing a turreted clock tower. (30 rooms are open to visitors). 🔍 *Guided tours (45min), Mar to Oct, Tue-Sun, 10am-4pm; Nov to Feb, Tue-Sun 10am-3pm.* ⏱ *Closed 1 Jan, 24-16 and 31 Dec.* ≋ *€3.50.* ☎ *(064 71) 22 36.* The **museum** is devoted to the history of the local mining industry. ⏱ *Open Apr-Oct, Tue-Fri, 10am-12pm, 2-5pm, Sat-Sun, 10am-5pm; Nov-Mar, Mon-Fri, 10am-12pm, 2-5pm.* ⏱ *Closed Jan, Good Fri and at the end of Dec.* ≋ *€3.* ☎ *(064 71) 37 94 47.*

Schloss Braunfels

This massive castle, built over 800 years, pierces the sky with its many towers. The perimeter wall encloses the whole village.

LANDSHUT★

POPULATION: 61 000

Once capital of Lower Bavaria, Landshut has kept its medieval centre intact. Memories of the Ingoldstadt and Landshut branches of the House of Wittelsbach remain much alive. ▯ *Altstadt 315, 84028 Landshut, ☎ (0871) 92 20 50.*

▶ **Orient Yourself:** Landshut is in the rolling countryside of the Isar, a tributary of the Danube.
🅿 **Parking:** Garages are located throughout the Altstadt, on Altstadt Str., Innere Münchener Str., and Bindergasse.
🕲 **Don't Miss:** The Altstadt and St. Martinskirche.
🕔 **Organizing Your Time:** The sights in Landshut can easily be seen in one day.
🜄 **Also See:** REGENSBURG (75km/47mi north), STRAUBING (58km/36mi northeast), MÜNCHEN (72km/45mi southwest).

Sights

St-Martinskirche★
Designed by Master Hans von Burghausen, this 14C-15C church features a **tower**★★ whose height is 131m/430ft, making it the world's tallest brick construction. The outside of the building is adorned with tombstones; its interior houses choir stalls and a delicate Virgin and Child by Leinberger (1518).

Princely marriage
Every four years, Landshut commemorates with great pomp the marriage in 1475 of the son of Duke Ludwig the Rich with Hedwige, daughter of the king of Poland. Don't miss it if you're in Bavaria at the beginning of summer 2009.

Altstadt★
The town's most important monuments are found in this wide, curving main street with its arcaded 15C and 16C houses, between the *Rathaus* and the Martinskirche. Note especially the variety and inventiveness of the gables.

Stadtresidenz (Town Palace)
👝 *Guided tours (45min), Apr to Sep: Tue-Sun, 9am-6pm; Oct to Mar, Tue-Sun, 10am-4pm.* 🕲 *€3. ☎ (0871) 924 11 0.*

Address Book

WHERE TO EAT
🥢🥢 **Bernlochner** – *Ländtorstr. 3.* ☎ *(0871) 899 90 www.bernlochner.com.* 🍴 Simple, well-prepared, regional cuisine in a modern restaurant. Rustic interior touches maintain a charming atmosphere.

WHERE TO STAY
🥢🥢 **Gästehaus Elisabeth** – *Bern-qteinstraße 40.* ☎ *(0871) 93 25 00. Fax (0871) 93 25 040. www.hotel-elisa-beth-altdorf.de.* 🅿 ⤢ ♿ *33 rooms*

🍽 🥢 *Restaurant.* Situated on the edge of a business park, provides its guests with access to the gym across the street.

TAKING A BREAK
Café Belstner – *Altstadt 295.* ☎ *(0871) 221 90* 🕔 *Closed on Sun.* This classic tea room is near the St. Martinskirche in the heart of the old town. Choose from a wide selection of home-made cakes, tarts and chocolates (to eat in or take out), or have lunch.

Two main blocks linked by narrow wings comprise this charming palace (1536-43) arranged around an arcaded courtyard, which faces the town hall. The German building faces the Altstadt (18C furniture, decorations etc); the 16C Italian Renaissance structure looks onto the courtyard (large rooms with painted, coffered ceilings).

Burg Trausnitz

Guided tours (45min), Apr to Sep, 9am-6pm; Oct to Mar, 10am-4pm. €2.50. (0871) 92 41 10.

The fortress founded in 1204 was decorated during the Renaissance with fine arcaded galleries (1579). Interesting features include the chapel, the Gothic hall known as the Alte Dürnitz. Several rooms embellished in 16C style are open to the public. The chapel is remarkable for its Early Gothic statuary. Note also the Jesters' Staircase *(Narrentreppe)*, painted in the 16C with scenes from the Commedia dell'Arte.

From an upper loggia *(Söller)*, there is an exceptional **view** across the town to the spire of the Martinskirche.

LEIPZIG★

POPULATION: 502 000

Leipzig is renowned as a trade and conference centre, but it is also an artistic city proud of its musical heritage; Bach, Wagner and Mendelssohn all lived here, and the city is still at the forefront of the German music scene. Leipzig has also, at times, been a centre of revolution: Liebknecht's Social Democratic Party was founded here, and it was also here, in 1989, that the silent, peaceful protests – the biggest the German Democratic Republic had ever seen – took place.
Richard-Wagner-Straße 1, 04109 Leipzig, (0341) 710 40.

▶ **Orient Yourself:** Leipzig is in the far west of Saxony, at the confluence of the River Weiße Elster and River Pleiße.

🅿 **Parking:** Garages are plentiful, especially near the main train station.

👁 **Don't Miss:** The Bach Museum, St. Thomas Church and the Musical Instrument Museum, followed by a concert at the Gewandhaus in the evening.

🕐 **Organizing Your Time:** Allow a full day to explore the musical heritage of Leipzig.

👣 **Also See:** *HALLE (34km/21mi west), NAUMBURG (63km/39mi south) or DRESDEN (113km/70mi east via the A 14 motorway).*

A Bit of History

The Leipzig Fairs – The first mention of Leipzig was in the Chronicle of Bishop Thietmar of Merseburg (975-1018), who noted the death of the Bishop of Meißen in "Urbs Lipzi". The township of "Lipzk" was granted a city charter ca 1165. Leipzig quickly became a commercial center of some influence. The famous spring and autumn international trade fairs have been held since 1896.

City of Books and Music – One of the world's earliest books, the *Glossa Super Apocalipsim*, was printed in Leipzig in 1481. The tradition of publishing continues today: More than 35 established publishers are based in Leipzig, among them Kiepenheuer, Brockhaus and Reclam. The city also enjoys a fine reputation musically, thanks to the Choir of St Thomas *(Thomanerchor)*, the Gewandhaus Orchestra, and the Mendelssohn-Bartholdy National College of Music.

A prosperous city – The discovery in the 16C of silver in the Erzgebirge mountains ensured Leipzig's prosperity. The city is still an important economic centre with corporate investors like Porsche and BMW.

Walking Tour

Old Town★

The historic centre of Leipzig, south of the impressive central station *(Haupt-banof)*, is clearly defined by a ring road which follows the town's medieval fortifications.

Augustusplatz

Formerly Karl-Marx-Platz, this renovated square boasts some of the city's most remarkable monuments. On the north side stands the 20C opera house, while toward central station is a pleasant park *(Schwanenteich)* with a statue of Wagner.

On the square's west is Leipzig's first skyscraper, **Krochhaus**, built in 1928-29, as well as Leipzig University with an bronze diorama of Karl Marx, a remnant of the city's socialist era. This remnant of socialist times was to have been removed following reunification, but the sculpture's great weight has impeded those plans.

Statue of Leibniz, born in Leipzig in 1646.

J. Bouraly/MICHELIN

Neues Gewandhaus

This auditorium south of the square was inaugurated in 1981. More than 1 900 enthusiasts can enjoy the famous Gewandhaus Orchestra at once. The bust of Beethoven (1902) in the foyer is the work of Leipzig-born Max Klinger.

▶ *Skirt the Neues Gewandhaus and turn in to Schillerstraße. South of the university stands the **Leibniz monument**, a stone's throw from the Egyptian Museum.*

Leipziger Gewandhaus Orchestra

Many orchestras were founded as court orchestras, as was Dresden's *Staatskapelle*. Not so the Leipziger Gewandhaus, founded through donations by wealthy burghers in 1743. In 1781, the Clothworkers' Guildhall was made into a concert hall, and the orchestra got its name. Famous composers and performers have appeared here over the centuries: Beethoven's *Triple Concerto*, Schubert's *Symphony in C major*, Mendelssohn's *"Scottish" Symphony*, and Brahms' *Violin Concerto in D major* all premiered here. In 1884, the city built the orchestra its own concert hall; that 19C building was bombed in 1944, and rebuilt in 1981, but "Gewandhaus" has always stuck. Since 1998, Swedish conductor Helmut Blomstedt has joined the ranks of such illustrious Gewandhaus directors as Felix Mendelssohn, Arthur Nikisch and Kurt Masur.

Address Book

WHERE TO EAT

"Zill's Tunnel" Restaurant – Barfußgässchen 9. ☎ (0341) 960 20 78 www.zillstunnel.de. ♿ A restaurant-cum-tavern since 1841 with a menu serving Saxon regional dishes. Two reasonably-priced, charming rooms are also available, all in a central location.

Barthels Hof – Hainstraße 1. ☎ (0341) 14 13 10. www.barthels-hof.de. This hotel, built between 1747 and 1750 for the merchant Gottlieb Barthel, has housed a restaurant for over one hundred years. Simple Saxon specialities.

Auerbachs Keller – Historische Weinstuben – Grimmaische Straße 2 (Mädler-Passage) ☎ (0341) 21 61 00 www.auerbachs-keller-leipzig. de. ⏰ evenings only. ⏰ closed Sun. This Weinstube has existed since 1525; Goethe frequented the place which is said to have provided inspiration for Faust: The magician Faust is said to have ridden upon a cask from this tavern. Classic, traditional cuisine.

WHERE TO STAY

Hotel Am Bayrischen Platz – Paul-List-Straße 5 ☎ (0341) 14 08 60. Fax (0341) 1408648. 🅿 ✕ 32 rooms. 🛏 In September 1874, Karl Marx and his daughter Eleanor stayed in this villa-style hotel. If you so wish, you can stay in the same room. Like the others, it is tastefully furnished.

Hotel Michaelis – Paul-Gruner-Strasse 44. ☎ (0341) 267 80. Fax (0341) 2678100. www.hotel. michaelis.de. ✕ ♿ 59 rooms. 🛏 Restaurant. Built in 1907 and now a listed building, this hotel has been renovated with an eye for detail. Harmonious and elegant individually-styled rooms. Modern, tastefully decorated restaurant.

Hotel Fürstenhof – Tröndlinring 8 ☎ (0341) 14 00 Fax (0341) 1403700. fuerstenhof.leipzig@ arabellasheraton.com 🛁 ✕ ♿ 92 rooms. 🛏 🍽 Restaurant. The façade of this classic mansion (1770) conceals a luxuriously elegant interior. Impeccable service and Mediterranean-style spa complex. Refined restaurant.

TAKING A BREAK

USEFUL TIPS

"Leipziger Lerchen" (Leipzig larks) are a local speciality found in all cake shops. The authentic bird once contributed to the town's culinary reputation, so when the king of Saxony banned lark hunting in 1876, pastry chefs transferred the name to a new pastry, made of short-bread and almond paste.

Kaffeehaus Riquet – Schumachergässchen 1-3. ☎ (0341) 9 61 00 00. www. riquethaus.de. ⏰ Open Fri-Sat 9am-midnight, Sun-Thu 9am-10pm. Easy to spot thanks to the two elephant heads on its façade, this former 19C trading house has been modelled on a Viennese coffee house since 1996.

Zum Arabischen Coffe Baum – Kleine Fleischergasse 4 (at Barfußgässchen and Kleine Fleischergasse) ☎ (0341) 9 61 00 60 www.coffe-baum.de . ⏰ ground floor: 11am-midnight, 1st floor: Mon-Sat 12pm-3pm, 6pm-midnight, 2nd floor and museum: 11am-7pm. One of the oldest coffee houses in Europe. On the ground floor is a café with terrace, on the 1st floor a restaurant, and on the 2nd floor an oriental tea room, Viennese-and Parisian-style cafés.

GOING OUT

USEFUL TIPS

A number of lively bars are found in the city centre between Brühl and the Neues Rathaus. The most animated is the Barfußgässchen, an alleyway in the pedestrian zone lined exclusively with bars, restaurants and cafés. Gottsched-strasse, west of the city centre, is another haunt for night owls and students. This street leads to Dittrichring, level with the Thomaskirche.

Gasthaus & Gosebrauerei Bayerischer Bahnhof – Bayrischer Platz 1 (at Windmühlenstraße and Nürnberger Strasse). ☎ (0341) 1 24 57 60. www. bayerischer-bahnhof.de. ⏰ 11am-1am. ⏰ Closed 1 Jan and 25 Dec. A former station where the traditional beer of Leipzig, Gose, is brewed (in addition to the usual ingredients: salt, lactic acid and coriander). Other beers are also available. Rustic setting, lovely self-serve beer garden and copious dishes.

Kümmel-Apotheke – *Grimmaische Straße 2-4 (in Mädlerpassage).* ☎ *(0341) 9 60 87 05 www.kuemmel-apotheke. de.* ◷ *Open Mon-Sat 9:30am-1am, Sun 10:30am-9pm.* A pleasant place to come any time for a drink or meal and watch the world go by.

Vinothek 1770 – *Tröndlinring 8 (in the Fürstenhof hotel)* ☎ *(0341) 1 40 33 33 www.arabellasheraton.com/fuerstenhof* ◷ *12pm-1am.* With over 170 wines, this place is popular with wine drinkers. The bottles on the wall behind the bar hint at the wine list. To accompany your bottle: cheese, antipasti, a few seasonal dishes and some good cigars.

CULTURE

USEFUL TIPS

The monthly calendar of events, "Leipzig im…" is available from Leipzig Tourist Service, €0.50. The monthly magazine *Prinz* can be bought at kiosks. For information: www.leipzig.de/tour-istservice.

SHOPPING

USEFUL TIPS

Leipzig is a pleasant place to shop. Glass-roofed arcades house shops and cafés. Try the Mädlerpassage (AZ 24), Specks Hof (ABY 38), Strohsack (BY), Steibs Hof (BY 39) or Jägerhofpassage (AY).

Aegyptisches Museum★ (Egyptian Museum)

Schillerstraße 6. ♿ ◷ *Open daily except Mon, 1pm-5pm, Sun 10am-1pm.* ◷ *Closed 1st Jan, 1st May, 24 and 31 Dec.* ⊜ *€2, free admission 2nd Sun of Sep.* ☎ *(0341) 973 70 10; www.uni-leipzig.de/~egypt.*
The 9 000 exhibits in this museum range range from antiquity to the Christian era.

▶ *Continue west along Schillerstraße to the Neues Rathaus*

Neues Rathaus (New Town Hall)

Built on the foundations of Pleißenburg Castle the 19C town hall is best known as the scene of a famous argument between Luther and Eick in 1519.

Thomaskirche★

Documented for the first time in 1212, this Late Gothic triple-aisle church took on its present appearance toward the end of the 15C. The church became famous through **Johann Sebastian Bach**, who was cantor for 27 years and buried opposite the altar (since 1950). The church is also renowned for the **St Thomas children's choir,** once directed by Bach. Founded after 1212, this choir began with only 12 singers. It now has 80 and performs Fridays at 6pm, Saturdays at 3pm (sacred choral music and Bach cantatas) and Sundays at 9:30am (main service).

Bachmuseum

Opposite the Thomaskirche, Thomaskirch-hof 16. ♿ ◷ *Open 10am-5pm.* ◷ *Closed 24, 25 and 31 Dec.* ⊜ *€4.* ☎ *(0341) 913 72 00; www.bach-leipzig.de.*
The Bach museum is housed in the former home of the Boses, a merchant family who befriended Bach. It was built in 1586 and converted in the 18C. Instruments, manuscripts and documents

Thomaskirche where Bach was cantor

J. Bouraly/MICHELIN

It Started with Prayer Group on Mondays…

From 1982, Christians and non-Christians met at the Nikolaikirche every Monday to pray for peace. By 1989 emigration to the DDR began climbing. The People's Police began guarding the streets leading to the Nikolaikirche. Still a growing number attended, filling the 2 000-seat church to overflowing. Many were arrested following the prayer meetings, and tensions rose. After uniformed troops attacked unarmed civilians in Leipzig on 7 October, people feared the worst: 1 000 members of the socialist unity party (SED) had been summoned for the upcoming 9 October prayer meeting. But when the prayer meeting participants left the church, a crowd of at least 10 000 awaited them holding candles. The peaceful revolution worked; a breach of the Wall followed just one month later. "We were ready for anything," said an SED member, "But not for candles and prayers."

trace the life and legacy of the great composer, with an emphasis on his years in Leipzig (1723-1750).

▶ *Take Thomasgasse eastward.*

Altes Rathaus★ (Old Town Hall)
This long, low building typifies the German Renaissance in its façade and dwarf gables. It was completed in 1556 after plans by architect and burgomaster Hieronymous Lotter. The tower above the main doorway features a balcony for town pipers or heralds. Today the building houses the local history museum, the Stadtgeschichtliches Museum. ♿ ⏰ *Open daily except Mon, 10am-6pm.* ⏰ *Closed 24, 25 and 31 Dec.* 🎫 *€4, free admission on 1st Sun of each month.* ☎ *(0341) 96 51 320.*

Alte Börse★ (Former Produce Exchange)
On the Naschmarkt. Built between 1678 and 1687, this former commodity market was Leipzig's first Baroque edifice. It is used today for fairs and festivals. The statue outside (Carl Seffner, 1903) represents Goethe as a student.

Katharinenstraße
North of the Alte Börse, Katharinenstaße runs alongside Sachsenplatz.
Of the Baroque houses on the west of Katharinenstraße, the finest is the Romanushaus *(at Brühl)*, built in 1701 by Johann Gregor Fuchs. The neighbouring houses *(nos 21 and 19)* were built in the mid 18C. The Fregehaus *(no 11)*, also built by Fuchs, belonged to the wealthy banker Christian Gottlob Frege, the Fugger (♿ *see AUGSBURG)* of Leipzig, whose trade emporium stretched across Europe and to America.

▶ *Skirt Sachsenplatz and head back towards the Alte Börse via Reichsstraße.*

Nikolaikirche
Nikolaistraße. At the junction of two major trade routes, this 12C church was dedicated to the patron saint of merchants, Saint Nicholas. Originally Romanesque in

Musicians in Leipzig

Johann Sebastian Bach worked and composed in Leipzig from 1723-1750. As director at St Thomas he was responsible for the musical life of the entire city. Bach had faded into obscurity when **Felix Mendelssohn-Bartholdy** became director of the Gewandhaus orchestra in 1835. He turned Leipzig into a city of musical renown, established Germany's first musical conservatory and composed a number of original musical works. **Clara Wieck** and **Robert Schumann** lived in a neo-Classical house in Leipzig's 16 Inselstraße, now memorialized to them. Their *'Spring' Symphony* was composed here.

style, the church has since seen several Gothic modifications: 14C chancel and west towers, and 16C triple nave and central tower.

The church's classical **interior**★ (1784-97) by Carl Dauthe is particularly impressive. Pale, fluted pillars end in light green palm leaves. The vaulting is coffered in old rose with stucco flowers. 30 paintings hang in the narthex and chancel. The Late Romanesque wooden crucifix in the chancel is believed to be the oldest surviving work of art in Leipzig.

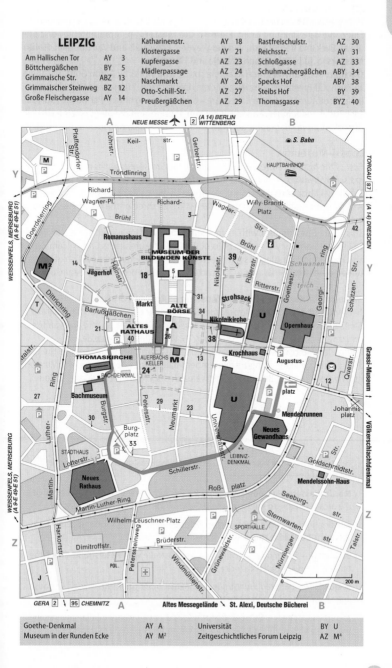

LEIPZIG			Katharinenstr.	AY	18	Rastfreischulstr.	AZ	30
			Klostergasse	AY	21	Reichsstr.	AY	31
Am Hallischen Tor	AY	3	Kupfergasse	AZ	23	Schloßgasse	AZ	33
Böttchergäßchen	BY	5	Mädlerpassage	AZ	24	Schuhmachergäßchen	ABY	34
Grimmaische Str.	ABZ	13	Naschmarkt	AY	26	Specks Hof	ABY	38
Grimmaischer Steinweg	BZ	12	Otto-Schill-Str.	AY	27	Steibs Hof	BY	39
Große Fleischergasse	AY	14	Preußergäßchen	AZ	29	Thomasgasse	BYZ	40

Goethe-Denkmal	AY	A	Universität	BY	U
Museum in der Runden Ecke	AY	M²	Zeitgeschichtliches Forum Leipzig	AZ	M⁴

Sights

Museum der Bildenden Künste★★ (Fine Arts Museum)

Katharinenstraße 10 ♿ 🕐 *Open daily except Mon, 10am-6pm, Wed noon-8pm.*
🕐 *Closed 24 and 31 Dec.* ⌨ *€5.* ☎ *(0341) 21 69 90; www.mdbk.de.*

One of Europe's most important art collections, with works from the Late Middle Ages to the present, moved to a new facility in 2006, a modernistic, 34m/112ft high glass cube designed by a firm of architects from Berlin.

Notable **German Primitives** include works by Master Francke, Lucas Cranach the Elder and Hans Baldung Grien. **Flemish Old Masters** are represented by disciples of van Eyck and Rembrandt, van der Weyden, Frans Hals and Van Ruisdael. **Italian Masters** include Conegliano, Francia and Tintoretto.

German 19C painters receive ample space, with works by Anton Graff, Tischbein, JA Koch, CD Friedrich, Spitzweg, Böcklin, Liebermann, Klinger and Wilhelm Leibl.

In the Sculpture Department there are works by, among others, Permoser, Thorvald-sen, Rodin and Klinger. And the collection of prints and drawings offers a virtually unbroken survey of graphic art from medieval times (Schongauer) to the present.

Grassi-Museum★

East of the historic centre, on Johannisplatz, the Grassi-Museum is reached via Grimmaischer Steinweg. ⚏ *Currently closed for renovation.*

The Grassi Museum is currently undergoing an extensive renovation of its facilities. A 2007 completion is anticipated, after which all three of the following museums will reopen.

This impressive complex with its four inner courtyards was built in 1925 to 1929 in the Expressionist style, with echoes of Art Deco, by architects Carl William Zweck and Hans Voigt. Funding has now been found for the urgent renovation of this fine building, so that British architect David Chipperfield's project may begin in 2005.

Museum für Kunsthandwerk★ (Museum of Arts and Crafts)

Neumarkt 20. ⚏ *Currently closed for renovation.* ♿ 🕐 *Formerly open daily except Mon, 10am-6pm, Wed 10am-8pm.* 🕐 *Closed 24 and 31 Dec.* ⌨ *€4, free admission on 1st Sun of each month.* ☎ *(0341) 213 37 19; www.grassimuseum.de.*

This collection covers European arts and crafts from the Middle Ages to the early 20C. Exhibits include furniture (Nuremberg hall cabinet, 16C), porcelain (Meissen), glassware (Venetian, Bohemian), and valuable Jugendstil pieces (Gallé, Lalique).

Arcades

Leipzig's glass-roofed arcades are remarkably well restored and offer a variety of colorful shops and bars.

Mädlerpassage – *Opposite Naschmarkt.* This is the grandest and best-known of the arcades, home to Auerbachs Keller, where Goethe set scenes in *Faust*.

Specks Hof – *Schuhmachergäßchen.* The restoration of this 1911 trade hall preserved its best old features while modernizing the whole.

Strohsack – This modern arcade links Nikolaistraße with Ritterstraße. Check the time on the glass-covered clock in the floor.

Steibs Hof – *Between Brühlstraße and Nikolaistraße.* This 1907 trade fair house appeals with its blue and white tiled courtyards.

Jägerhofpassage – *Between Hainstraße and Grosse Fleischergaße.* This arcade with ivory tiled walls is a Jugendstil work from 1913-14 housing a cinema.

Railway Station Renovation

Leipzig rail station, which had deteriorated badly in spite of being Europe's largest railway terminus, was given a major facelift in 1995. Within two years, the station lobbies had been renovated and a three-storey 30 000m²/322 800sq ft shopping centre installed. Travellers arriving in Leipzig by train today are overwhelmed: The original 1915 building is impressive with its huge 267m/876ft long by 32m/105ft wide hall, two entrance lobbies and 130 business concerns. Art is also prominently displayed, with Jean Tinguely's *Luminator* making a striking impression.

Museum für Völkerkunde★ (Museum of Ethnography)
Berliner Straße 11-13. ⚬⊸ *Currently closed for renovation.* 🚹 🕐 *Formerly open daily except Mon, 10am-6pm, Thur 10am-8pm.* 🕐 *Closed Easter and Pentecost, 1 May, 24 and 31 Dec.* 🎫 *€2, free admission on 1st Sun of each month.* ☎ *(0341) 97 31 900; www.mvl-grassimuseum.de.*
One of the oldest, most important such museum in Europe, this institution explores the history and culture of the peoples of Asia, Africa, America and Oceania.

Musikinstrumenten-Museum★ (Museum of Musical Instruments)
Thomaskirchhof 20. ⚬⊸ *Currently closed for renovation.* 🕐 *Formerly open daily except Mon, 10am-6pm.* 🕐 *Closed 1st Jan, Good Friday, 24, 25 and 31 Dec.* 🎫 *€3.* ☎ *(0341) 973 07 50; www.mfm.uni-leipzig.de.*
One of Europe's finest, Leipzig's Museum of Musical Instruments features 5 000 instruments spanning five centuries of music.

Völkerschlachtdenkmal (Battle of the Nations Monument)
Via Johannisplatz. 🕐 *Apr-Oct: 10am-6pm; Nov-Mar: 10am-4pm.* 🕐 *Closed 1st Jan, 24, 25 and 31 Dec.* 🎫 *€3.* ☎ *(0341) 878 04 71; www.voelkerschlachtdenkmal.de.*
This memorial commemorates the Allied victory over Napoleon in 1813.

St-Alexi-Gedächtniskirche
Philipp-Rosenthal-Straße. This former tsarist-style church now stands as a memorial to the 22 000 Russian soldiers who died in the Battle of the Nations in 1813.

Deutsche Bücherei (German National Library)
Deutscher Platz. Founded in 1912, this huge library groups all known German language books, a collection currently comprising 7.5 million titles. On the same premises, the German Museum of Books and Literature is open to the public.

Museum in der Runden Ecke (Stasi Museum)
Northwest of the historic centre, Dittrichring 24, documents in German only. 🚹 🕐 *10am-6pm.* 🕐 *Closed 1 Jan, 23-26 and 31 Dec.* ☎ *(0341) 961 24 43; www.runde-ecke-leipzig.de.*
This contemporary exhibition reveals the methods used by the infamous East German Ministry for State Security, the *"Stasi,"* in the very quarters that once housed them.

LEMGO★

POPULATION: 43 000

This town, founded shortly before 1200 by the Count of Lippe, was surrounded in 1365 by a town wall which still survives. The Late Gothic and Renaissance town houses testify to the grandeur of the once-wealthy Hanseatic city.

- ▶ **Orient Yourself:** Lemgo is east of Nordrhein-Westphalia, a few kilometres from the A 2 (Hannover-Dortmund).
- **Don't Miss:** A walk through the Old Town.
- **Organizing Your Time:** Allow two hours for the Walking Tour.
- **Also See:** *HAMELN (41km/26mi northeast), HILDESHEIM (91km/57mi east), HAN-NOVER (92km/58mi northeast), MÜNSTER (107km/67mi west).*

Walking Tour

The Old Town★

▶ *From the Ostertor east, approach Mittelstraße with its grand half-timbered houses. Note the fine façades of no 17 and no 36, the House of Planets (Planetenhaus).*

Rathaus★★

The town hall comprises eight buildings side by side. The elegantly worked façade of the old apothecary's shop on the Marktplatz displays sculpted portraits of 10 famous philosopher-physicians, from Aristotle to Paracelsus. Beneath the central arcades, brutal witchcraft trials were held ca 1670.

▶ *Bear left into Breite Straße.*

Hexenbürgermeisterhaus (Witch Finder's House)

⌐ *Temporarily closed. 19 Breite Strasse.* This splendid 16C Weser Renaissance house houses the city museum, focusing on everyday culture, trade and witch-hunting.

Marienkirche

A Renaissance 16C organ, among the oldest in German, adorns this triple-aisle Gothic church. Admire, too, the baptismal font (1592), the pulpit (1644) and the Cross Triumphant (c 1500).

▶ *Return to Papenstraße, following it to the right.*

St-Nicolaikirche

Dedicated to the patron saint of merchants, the 13C church combines Romanesque (three-figure tympanum), Gothic (frescoes) and Renaissance (pulpit) elements.

▶ *Papenstraße leads back to the starting point.*

Witch-Hunting in Lemgo

During the Inquisition, death was the penalty for heresy and sorcery. Great waves of persecution ran through the country. The town of Lemgo became the focus of a "witch-hunt" by inquisitor J Sprenger. From 1564-1681, more than 200 were persecuted as witches, tortured to the point of false confessions.

The persecutions finally came to an end when a young woman withstood the torture, was banished from the region and then sued her torturers before the Imperial supreme court.

Sights

Junkerhaus★
Hamelner Strasse 36. ◷ *Open Apr-Oct, Tue-Sun, 10am-5pm, Nov-Mar, Fri-Sun, 11am-5pm.* ☞ *Guided tour (90min) Sun at 3pm.* ☎ *(052 61) 21 32 76; www.junkerhaus.de.*
Karl Junker (1850-1912), painter, sculptor and architect, a contemporary of the blossoming Jugendstil, left his memorial in his own house. The house's design organizes around a spiral, and its interior views seem to change with every perspective.

Schloss Brake
Schloßstrasse 18. ♿ ◷ *Open Tue-Sun, 10am-6pm.* ◷ *Closed 1 Jan, 24, 25 and 31 Dec.* ☞ *€3.* ☎ *(052 61) 945 00; www.wrm.lemgo.de.*
This mighty castle was built between the 12C and 19C, although its predominant style is Weser Renaissance. How appropriate, then, the **Weserrenaissance-Museum** within the building, exploring art and culture between the Reformation and the Thirty Years War.

Excursions

Herford
20km/12.5mi west. Town plan in the Michelin Guide Deutschland.
This town between Teutoburger Wald and the Weser was a Hanseatic town until the 17C. The historic centre has numerous 16C-18C half-timbered houses. Herford is home to two interesting churches. The Romanesque **Münsterkirche** (1220-1280) is one of the oldest in Westphalia. The Protestant **Johanniskirche** bears fine 17C wood **carving★**, both sculpted and painted. Galleries, stalls and pulpit were donated by city institutions, whose shields and emblems can be recognised in the design.

LIMBURG AN DER LAHN★

POPULATION: 34 000

The powerful yet elegant silhouette of the cathedral dominates the Limburg skyline. The town centre consists largely of half-timbered houses dating from the 13C to the 18C. ▯ *Hospitalstraße 2, 65549 Limburg,* ☎ *(064 31) 61 66.*

▶ **Orient Yourself:** Bordering Hessen and Rheinland-Pfalz, Limburg is reached via the A 3 linking the town to Wiesbaden and Frankfurt to the south and Koblenz to the north.
◉ **Don't Miss:** Limburg's cathedral.
◷ **Organizing Your Time:** Allow half an hour for a tour of the cathedral.
◉ **Also See:** *WIESBADEN (39km/24mi south), LAHNTAL (Bad Ems is 41km/26mi west), KOBLENZ (54km/34mi west), FRANKFURT AM MAIN (69km/43mi southeast).*

Cathedral★ (Dom)

Built on a rocky spur, St Georgsdom is in a picturesque **setting★★**. It is also striking for its architecture: a classic example of Romanesque-Gothic Transitional prevalent in Germany between 1210 and 1250.
The outside remains Romanesque and closely resembles the Rhineland cathedrals (◉ *see Introduction: Architecture*), but its interior is already Gothic. Look for Gothic hallmarks: galleries, arcades, a triforium and clerestory windows. From the cemetery terrace (Friedhofsterrasse) is a good **view★** of the river.

WHERE TO STAY

⊜⊜ **Martin** – *Holzheimer Strasse 2.* ☎ *(06431) 948 40. Fax (06431) 43185. www. hotel-martin.de.* ▣ *30 rooms.* ⊠ ⊜⊜ *Restaurant.* This family-run hotel is located in the town centre opposite the station, and offers tidy, functionally-equipped guestrooms.

⊜⊜⊜ **Romantik Hotel Zimmermann** – *Blumenröder Strasse 1.* ☎ *(06431) 46 11. Fax (06431) 41314 www.romantik-hotel-zimmermann.de.* ◔ *Closed 20 Dec-5 Jan.* ▣ ⤧ *24 rooms.* ⊠ With English-inspired furnishings, the rooms have an air of luxury about them. Expect huge breakfasts.

Diözesanmuseum★
Domstraße 12. ♿ ◔ *Open from mid-Mar to mid-Nov, Tue-Sun, 10am-1pm, 2pm-5pm, Sun 11am-5pm.* ⊛ *€2.* ☎ *(064 31) 29 54 82; www.staurothek.de.*
The 10C Byzantine reliquary cross known as the Limburger Staurothek is the jewel of the religious art collection displayed in this museum. Another highlight is the sheath encasing the reliquary Staff of St Peter, completed in 980.

Sights

Old Town★ (Alstadt)
In the old town, whole streets are preserved with their original buildings, some of which have fine half-timbering *(Domplatz, Fischmarkt, Brückengasse, Römer, Rütsche, Bischofsplatz)*. Walderdorffer Hof (Fahrgasse) is a Renaissance construction with four wings. Take time to discover the beautiful old houses in Limburg's winding alleys.

LINDAU IM BODENSEE★★

POPULATION: 24 000

Lindau boasts a number of fine gabled burghers' houses in the old town, testifying to its prosperous history as a trading partner with Italy. An almost Mediterranean quality permeates life in this island resort. ▯ *Am Hauptbahnhof, 88131 Lindau,* ☎ *(083 82) 26 00 30.*

▸ **Orient Yourself:** Lindau lies in Bavaria, on the eastern extreme of Lake Constance. Ferries link the town to Konstanz or Bregenz, Austria, several times daily.
⊛ **Don't Miss:** A stroll through the old town.
◔ **Organizing Your Time:** Allow one hour for a walking tour of the Old Town.
⚲ **Also See:** *BODENSEE, KONSTANZ (94km/59mi in 1hr 30min by road or 3hr15min by boat), Deutsch ALPENSTRASSE (tours leaves from Lindau).*

Walking Tour

The Old Town★★

Marktplatz
The marketplace surrounds a large circular fountain, its eastern side dominated by the façades of the Protestant and Collegiate *(Stiftkirche)* churches. On the square's west side, in the Baroque **Haus zum Cavazzen**★, the **town museum** *(Stadtmuseum)* has exhibits focusing on home décor. ◔ *Open early Apr to end Oct, Tue-Sun, 11am-5pm, Sat, 2-5pm.* ◔ *Closed Easter Sun and Pentecost, 1 May.* ⊛ *€2.50.* ☎ *(083 82) 77 56 514.*

Maximilianstraße★★

This is the main artery through the old town, a picturesque street lined with old houses and narrow, half-timbered façades.

▶ *Turn right into the Zeppelinstraße.*

Address Book

WHERE TO STAY

Schachener Hof – *Schachener Straße 76, 88131 Lindau-Bad Schachen ☎ (08382) 31 16 www.schachenerhof-lindau.de* *Closed 2 Jan-7 Feb* Classically decorated restaurant with dark wood furniture offering regional and foreign cuisine. Welcoming staff.

Hoyerberg Schlössle – *Hoyerbergstraße 64 (sur la Hoyerberg) 88131 Lindau-Hoyren* *Closed Feb, Mon-Tue lunchtimes ☎ (08382) 252 95 www.hoyerbergschloessle.de* Pleasant décor and elegance characterise the renovated rooms of this little castle. There are views over Lindau, the Alps and the lake from the terrace.

WHERE TO STAY

Hotel Köchlin – *Kemptener Straße 41 ☎ (08382) 966 00 Fax (08382) 966043 www.hotel-koechlin.de* *Closed 3 weeks in Nov* *21 rooms* *Restaurant* A small country hotel with a shingle roof and flowery façade. Inside, lots of wood and rustic décor. In summer there is a Biergarten behind the establishment, pleasantly shaded by old trees.

Hotel Lindauer Hof – *Seepromenade ☎ (08382) 40 64 Fax (08382) 24203 www.lindauer-hof.de* *30 rooms* *Restaurant* Modern hotel with particularly comfortable guestrooms. Pleasantly close to the lake. Meals are served on the first floor or on the pretty terrace.

Hotel Bayerischer Hof – *Seepromenade ☎ (08382) 91 50 Fax (08382) 915591 www.bayerischer-hof-lindau.de* *100 rooms* *Restaurant* This elegant hotel is comfortable and chic. The restaurant offers good classical cuisine with varied menu and good views.

Lindau Tourismus

Lindau, an island resort on the Bodensee.

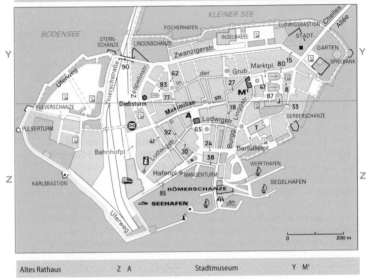

LINDAU IM BODENSEE						
B.d. Heidenmauer	Y 15	Cramergasse	Y 27	Reichspl.	Z 65
Bäckergässele	Y 8	Dammgasse	Z 30	Schafgasse	YZ 77
Bahnhofpl.	Z	Fischergasse	Z 33	Schmiedgasse	Y 80
Bindergasse	Z 18	Hafenpl.	Z 38	Schrannenpl.	Y 83
Brettermarkt	Z 24	In der Grub	Y	Seepromenade	Z 85
		Kirchpl.	Y 47	Stiftspl.	YZ 87
		Maximilianstr.	YZ	Thierschbrücke	Y 90
		Paradiespl.	Y 62	Vordere Metzgerg	Z 92

Altes Rathaus Z A   Stadtmuseum Y M¹

Schrannenplatz

The Brigands' Tower *(Diebsturm)*, a well-known Lindau silhouette, was the most westerly point of the Medieval fortifications. At the tower's base is **Peterskirche**, the oldest church in town (1000 AD), with **frescoes** (15C) by Hans Holbein the Elder.

▶ *Go back down Zeppelinstraße towards the port.*

Hafen★ (Port)

Lindau's port is a gathering point for tourists, many of them waiting to embark on one of Lake Constance's pleasure boats.

Excursion

Wangen im Allgäu★

22 km north. Lying within sight of the Allgäu Alps, the colorful houses of this small Swabian town lie in a simple cruciform plan, the two main streets crossing at right angles in **Marktplatz**★. Herrenstraße is lined with attractive houses, many with decorative shop signs.

SCHLOSS LINDERHOF★★

Deep in the forest, in one of the most secluded valleys of the Ammergau Alps, this small villa-style palace was built by Ludwig II. Designed according to 18C style, it served as a backdrop for the romantic fancies of the young king.

▶ **Orient Yourself:** The Ammergau Alps serve as a backdrop to the little Ammer valley. Linderhof Palace is slightly removed from the village of the same name *(follows the signs for "Schloss" after you enter the village),* and is framed by majestic mountains.

☺ **Don't Miss:** The palace and its surrounding park.

◷ **Organizing Your Time:** Allow two hours for a tour of the palace, more in high season when lines may be lengthy.

☝ **Also See:** *Deutsche ALPENSTRASSE (the tour passes through Linderhof), WIESKIRCHE (38km/24mi northwest), GARMISCH-PARTENKIRCHEN (26km/16mi southeast), Ludwig II's two other palaces (NEUSCHWANSTEIN is 58km/36mi away, and Herrenchiemsee (CHIEMSEE) is 137km/86mi away).*

Visit

Palace★

◷ *Open daily Apr-Sept, guided tours 9am-6pm; Oct-Mar, 10am-4pm.* ◷ *Closed 1 Jan, Shrove Tue, 24, 25 and 31 Dec. Park and grotto closed in winter.* ☞ *Summer €7, winter €6.* ☎ *(088 22) 920 30; www.linderhof.de.*

Ludwig II had the castle built between 1874 and 1879, in a style intermingling the second Italian Renaissance and the Baroque. His intention was to achieve a familiar atmosphere. Nonetheless, inside, one finds a **state bedchamber** surpassing even the luxury of Versailles.

Park★★

◷ *Open daily 8:30am to 6pm. Admission fee for grotto only (tickets available from the palace).*

The terraced gardens, in the style of an Italian villa, are designed to complement the natural slopes of the surrounding natural features. Climb to the **Temple of Venus** rotunda for a fine view, especially when the fountains play. Then climb the opposite slope for the Moorish pavilion and grotto. It is here that the skill of the landscape gardener, Karl von Effner, is most evident, with tree plantings artistically placed.

The park was designed by the architect Karl von Effner.

LÜBECK★★★

POPULATION: 214 000

Lübeck has retained much of its medieval Hanseatic character: Many of its buildings and monuments still bear the telltale signs of alternating red and black brick bands. Since 1987 the town has been on the UNESCO World Heritage list. Today the city remains the busiest German port on the Baltic Sea and a focal point for shipbuilding and heavy industry. Don't miss the city's marzipan, one of the town's gastronomic specialities. ⓘ *Beckergrube 95, 23552 Lübeck,* ☎ *(0451) 122 54 06.*

▸ **Orient Yourself:** 60km/37mi northeast of Hamburg, Lübeck has long occupied the position of trade intermediary between the Baltic and western Europe. The river Trave intersects the town. To reach the town from Hamburg, take the A 1 motorway.

▣ **Parking:** Garages are plentiful in the Old Town.

⊘ **Don't Miss:** A relaxed stroll through the Old Town.

⏱ **Organizing Your Time:** Allow three hours to tour the Old Town.

⚲ **Also See:** *WISMAR (61km/38mi east), HAMBURG (67km/42mi southwest), KIEL (94km/59mi north), SCHWERIN (110km/69mi southeast).*

A Bit of History

At the Head of the League – The 14C marked the summit of Lübeck's power as Hanseatic capital. In the 16C, the business acumen of merchants and shipowners combined to extricate the port from a long period of decline, thanks largely to the establishment of new relations with Holland and France. For a long time, Dutch architecture was the preferred style for the rich burghers on the banks of the Trave.

Contested supremacy – In the 19C, Lübeck's status as a seaport was rivalled by the Prussian port of Stettin (now Szczecin in Poland) and the opening of the Kiel canal. But the construction of a canal linking the Trave with the Elbe and an influx of almost 100 000 refugees in 1945 have combined to retain the city's importance today. Among other assets Lübeck is Germany's chief importer of French red wines, which are matured in the celebrated Lübeck Cellars beneath the River Trave.

Walking Tour

The Old Town★★★ (Altstadt)

Girdled with canals, crowned by belfries and towers, the old town of Lübeck is on a largely pedestrianized island. The west side of the old town is reached through the Holstentor, a national symbol in Germany.

▸ *Leave from the Holstentor (follow the itinerary marked on the town plan)*

Holstentor★★
This fortified gate was built between 1466 and 1478, before the construction of the city's perimeter wall, more as a matter of prestige than protection. The building houses the **Local History**

The Rathaus at Lübeck.

J. Bouraly/MICHELIN

The Holstentor used to appear on the 50 Deutschmark note.

Museum *(Stadtgeschichtliche Museum).* ◷ *Open Tue-Fri, 10am-5pm; Sat-Sun, 11am-6pm.* ◷ *Closed 25, 26 and 31 Dec.* ⊕ *€4.* ☎ *(451) 122 41 29.*

Rathaus★

Begun in 1250, on two sides of the Marktplatz, the town hall is an elegant edifice in dark glazed brick, supported on a gallery of arcades. Note the high protective walls sometimes pierced with blind arcades. The building at the extremity of the east wing, the Neues Gemach (1440), is interesting for the heightened effect lent to it by an imaginative openwork wall.

Pass beneath the arcades to see, on the Breite Strasse, a stone staircase (1594) in Dutch Renaissance style.

▶ *Continuing the circuit of the Rathaus, arrive at the foot of the north façade.*

Marienkirche★★

One of the finest brick-built Gothic churches in Germany. The original designers in 1250 planned a hall-type church without a transept, but the concept was changed while work was in progress. Composer Dietrich Buxtehude (1637-1707) was the church's official organist. The interior, audacious in design, has grandiose proportions. A fire in 1942 exposed the original 13C and 14C decoration.

▶ *Outside, go through the arcade of the Chancellery (15C-16C) to the Mengstraße.*

Buddenbrookhaus

Mengstraße 4. ♿ ◷ *Apr to Dec, 10am-6pm; Jan-Mar, 11am-5pm.* ⊕ *€5.* ☎ *(0451) 122 41 40; www.buddenbrookhaus.de.*

However attractive the concept may be, Heinrich and Thomas Mann were unfortunately not born in Buddenbrookhaus. However, it is true that in 1841 their grandfather Johann Siegmund Mann bought the 18C Baroque house, and the brothers were frequently guests there during their childhood and adolescence. Thomas Mann used the house in his world-renowned book *Buddenbrooks*, in which he described the decline of a patrician family in Lübeck.

▶ *Follow the Mengstraße until the Schabbelhaus and then retrace your steps. Take the BreiteStraße north.*

Haus der Schiffergesellschaft★ (House of the Seamen's Guild)

Behind the stepped Renaissance gable, the **interior**★★ (ⓒ *now a restaurant, see Where to Eat above*) still preserves the picturesque furnishings of a seamen's tavern, with rough wooden tables, copper lamps and model ships hanging from the beams.

Jakobikirche★

Opposite the Haus der Schiffergesellschaft. The magnificent woodwork of the two organ **lofts**★★ (16C-17C) in this small Gothic hall-church is noteworthy. Larger than life-size representations of apostles and saints adorn the pillars of the central nave. The chapel north of the tower is now a memorial to the shipwrecked, and displays a lifeboat from the *Pamir*, the full-rigged Lübeck ship lost with all hands in 1957.

▷ *Follow the promenade to the northern part of the old town and its Burgtor.*

Address Book

WHERE TO EAT

🍴 **Paulaner's** – *Breite Straße 1-5* ☎ *(0451) 707 94 50 www.paulaners.de.* ♿ *Reservations recommended.* It's quite a novelty to get Munich-brewed beer and Bavarian specialties this far north. Northern specialities are also served. Pleasant Biergarten in the churchyard of the Jakobikirchhof.

🍴🍴 **Schiffergesellschaft** – *Breite Straße 2* ☎ *(0451) 767 76 www.schiffer-gesellschaft.de.* An impressively preserved tavern, built as a sailors' meeting-house, guildhouse and almshouse back in 1535. The interior features reminders of Lübeck's maritime past.

WHERE TO STAY

🛏️🛏️ **Hotel Jensen** – *An der Obertrave 4* ☎ *(0451) 70 24 90 Fax (0451) 73386 www.ringhotel-jensen.de 42 rooms* 🍴🍴 *Restaurant.* Located within the historic triangle formed by the Trave, the Holstentor and the *Salzspeicher*, this comfortably appointed, gabled house built in 1307 has modern guestroooms with a mari-time dining room.

🛏️🛏️ **Hotel Kaiserhof** – *Krons-forder Allee 11* ☎ *(0451) 70 33 01 Fax (0451) 795083 www.kaiserhof-lue-beck.de 60 rooms* 🍴🍴 *Restaurant.* Two fine patrician houses were united to form this pleasantly decorated hotel only a few minutes on foot from the town centre. Roman-style steam bath and sound-proofed room available for musicians.

TAKING A BREAK

Café Niederegger – *Breite Str. 89.* ☎ *(0451) 5 30 11 26 www.niederegger.de* ⏱ *Mon-Fri 9am-7pm, Sat 9am-6pm, Sun 10am-6pm.* This café is *the* place to buy marzipan. The shop on the ground floor serves it in all shapes and sizes, while the tea room on the ground and 1st floors serves it in cake form. A marzipan museum is on the 2nd floor.

Café Utspann – *Wahmstr. 35-37 (in the Hansehof court)* ☎ *(0451) 7 07 06 77* ⏱ *Mon-Sat, 9am-6pm* ⏱ *Closed Sun and bank holidays.* Friesian-style décor distinguishes this inviting tea room. Homemade cakes are served, their appetising smell lingering in the air. In summer a few tables are available outside on the old Hansehof court.

GOING OUT

Brauberger – *Alfstr. 36 (parallel with Meng- and Fischstr.)* ☎ *(0451) 7 14 44 www.brauberger.de.* ⏱ *Mon-Fri from 5pm, Sat from 11am.* ⏱ *Closed Sun, 1 week in Jan.* This microbrewery opened in 1988, but its cellar dates from 1225. On the 1st floor is a small outdoor terrace. Light snacks and regional specialties are served.

Metro – *Mühlenbrücke 11 (cont. of Mühlenstr.)* ☎ *(0451) 7 02 06 98 www.metrocafe.de* ⏱ *Mon-Thu noon-1am, Fri noon-2am, Sat 10-2am, Sun 10-1am.* This café's décor was inspired by Parisian metro stations. Light snacks are inside or on the beautiful waterfront terrace and Biergarten.

LÜBECK						
		Holstenstr.	Y 36	Pferdemarkt	Y 59
Balauerfohr	Y 10	Hüxstr.	Y	Rehderbrücke	Y 61
Beckergrube	Y	Klingenberg	Y	Rosengarten	Y 63
Breite Str.	Y	Kohlmarkt	Y 42	Sandstr.	Y 64
Fleischhauerstr.	Y	Königstr.	XY	Schlumacherstr.	Y 66
Fünfhausen	Y 23	Langer Lohberg	X 48	Schmiedestr.	Y 67
Große Burgstr.	X 28	Marktpl.	Y 53	St-Annen-Str.	Z 65
Große Petersgrube	Y 31	Mühlenstr.	Z	Tünkenhagen	Y 81
		Mühlentorbrücke	Z 56	Wahmstr.	Y

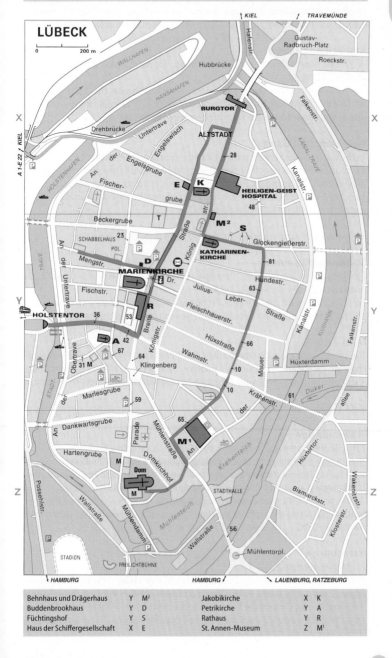

Behnhaus und Drägerhaus	Y	M²	Jakobikirche	X	K
Buddenbrookhaus	Y	D	Petrikirche	Y	A
Füchtingshof	Y	S	Rathaus	Y	R
Haus der Schiffergesellschaft	X	E	St. Annen-Museum	Z	M¹

Burgtor★

This fortified gateway defended the narrow isthmus, once the only land approach to Lübeck. The structure is a fine example of 13C-15C military architecture.

▶ *Return towards the centre of the old town along Große Burgstraße.*

Heiligen-Geist-Hospital★ (Hospice of the Holy Spirit)

Since the end of the 13C, the three turret-bordered gables of this almshouse have stood above the Koberg. The chapel, a large Gothic hall embellished with 13C and 14C paintings, is just outside the even bigger Great Hall of the hospice (Langes Haus).

Katharinenkirche★

&🕑 *Open Apr to Sep Tue-Sun, 10am-5pm.* ☞ *€1, no charge first Fri of the month.* ☎ *(0451) 122 41 80.*

The lower niches of the 14C façade contain modern **statues★**, the first three on the left being by Ernst Barlach. Inside the church, which is a museum, note, on the right side as you enter, *The Resurrection of Lazarus* by Tintoretto.

The "Höfe und Gänge"

At the corner of the church, turn left into the Glockengießerstraße, on which open the courts *(Höfe)* set back from the street in typical Lübeck style. Note, successively, the delightful **Füchtingshof★** (no 25 – Y S), with its Baroque doorway dating from 1639; the *Glandorps-Gang*, a simple alignment of small houses along an alley (no 41); and, from nos 49 to 51, the *Glandorps-Hof*.

▶ *Explore this picturesque district, then go south to the cathedral district.*

St-Annen-Museum★

🕑 *Open Apr to Sep, Tue-Sun, 10am-5pm; Oct to Mar, 10am-4pm.* 🕑 *Closed 25, 26 and 31 Dec.* ☞ *€4.* ☎ *(0451) 122 41 37.*

This former convent has a large collection of 15C and 16C paintings and sculpture originating from the churches of Lübeck. German modern art is also on display.

Dom

The 14C Gothic expansion transformed this Romanesque church. Inside there is an imposing monumental Late Gothic **Crucifix★** made between 1470-77 by Bernt Notke. A stone screen (early 14C) with a wooden tracery balustrade closes off the choir.

Excursions

Travemünde★

20km/12.5mi northeast. Town plan in the Michelin Guide Deutschland.

This smart Baltic health resort boasts a fine sandy beach, a 2.5km/1.5mi-long promenade and a casino. **Travemünde week** is an annual event for German and foreign yachtsmen. Travemünde is also a well-known port, with links to Scandinavia and Estonia.

The old town, with its half-timbered houses and the fishermen's church of St Lorenz, is charming. Along the seafront are some typical local gabled houses dating from the 18C and 19C.

Ratzeburg★

23 km/14mi southeast.

The island town of Ratzeburg is built in the middle of a **lake★**, the biggest of many in the morainal hills between the Elbe and Lübeck. The Schöne Aussicht viewpoint in Bäk on the east shore of the lake provides the best **view★** of the town. &🕑 *Open Apr to Sep, 10am-noon, 2-6pm, Sun, 2-6pm; Oct to Mar, Tue-Sun, 10am-noon, 2-4pm, Sun, 2-4pm.* ☞ *€2.* ☎ *(045 41) 34 06.*

LÜNEBURG★★

POPULATION: 71 600

The town of Lüneburg is built on a salt deposit from which brine was extracted as recently as 1980. Salt has been the source of Lüneburg's prosperity since the 10C. In the Middle Ages the town was the principal supplier of the mineral to many places. The town was spared during the Second World War and today is a colourful university town. ⓘ *Am Markt, 21335 Lüneburg, ☎ (041 31) 207 66 20.*

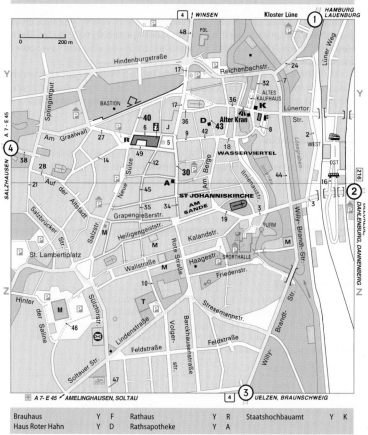

▷ **Orient Yourself:** 50km/31mi southeast of Hamburg is the entry point for the vast wild expanse of the Lüneburg heath. The town is reached via the A 7 motorway (Hannover-Hamburg); from Hamburg take the A 250.

🅿 **Parking:** Garages are located near the main train station and the Rathaus on Graalwall.

🚫 **Don't Miss:** The Rathaus and the rest of the old town.

🕐 **Organizing Your Time:** The listed sights of the old town.

👶 **Also See:** HAMBURG (57km/36mi northwest), LÜBECK (89km/56mi north), CELLE (89km/56mi south), HANNOVER (127km/79mi south), BREMEN (139km/87mi west), LÜNEBURGER HEIDE.

Sights

Rathaus★★

🎧 Guided tours Jan-Mar, Tue-Sat 10am-3:30pm; Apr-Dec daily. 🕐 Closed 1 Jan, 24-26 and 31 Dec. 🎫 €4.50. ☎ (041 31) 30 92 30.

The municipal headquarters is an assembly of different buildings from the 13C-18C. The **Great Council Chamber★★** (Große Ratsstube), right of the entrance hall, is a Renaissance masterpiece (1566-84). Panelled throughout, it is adorned with intricate wood sculptures by Albert von Soest. The **Princes' Apartment** (Fürstensaal) is equally rewarding. It is Gothic, with lamps fashioned from stags' antlers and a superbly beamed and painted ceiling.

Old Town★

The houses here are characterised by traditional brick architecture. Typical are those lining the long, narrow square known as **Am Sande★**, especially no 1, the 16C **Black House** (Schwarzes Haus or Schütting), which was once a brewery and now houses the International Chamber of Commerce.

In the Große Bäckerstraße (no 10) stands the Rathsapotheke (pharmacy), which dates, with its fine twisted brick gables, from 1598. The Reitende-Diener-Straße comprises a double row of identical low houses, each embellished with medallions and twisted brick cornices.

St-Johanniskirche

The most valuable furnishing of this 15C church is the sculpted reredos of the high altar, which has painted panels depicting scenes from the lives of St John the Baptist, St Cecilia, St Ursula and St George (late 15C).

Old Port Quarter★ (Wasserviertel)

There is a particularly fine view of this district from the bridge across the Ilmenau. To the left is the Alter Kran, a crane dating from the 14C, converted in the 18C. Look-

---

WHERE TO EAT

🍽🍽 **Zum Heidkrug** – Am Berge 5. ☎ (04131) 241 60. www.zumheidkrug.de. 🕐 Closed 1-22 Jan and for 2 weeks in Aug. 🎫 €34.50/42.50. This brick Gothic building was built in the 15C and now houses a comfortable, well-presented restaurant. Classic dishes show the talents of the chefs to perfection. A few guestrooms decorated in country house style are available.

WHERE TO STAY

🛏 **Herz der Heide** – Ernst-August-Strasse 7, 29614 Soltau. ☎ (05191) 967 50 – fax (05191) 17765 – herzdheide@aol.com – 🍴 – 16rm: 🎫 €39/80 🛏. Well-kept and reasonably quiet guesthouse with a garden located in a residential district. Each guestroom has its own character; some come with their own kitchette.

ing upstream, there is a good view of the Lüner Mühle, a grand half-timbered mill building dating from the 16C, of the *Abtswasserturm* (water-tower)

Excursions

Kloster Lüne
2km/1.2mi via ① on the plan.
This 15C **abbey** makes a harmonious complex among its conventual buildings. It has housed a community of Protestant nuns since the Reformation. Particularly fine features include the Gothic cloister and fountain, the nuns' choir, the refectory and the summer refectory. Inside there is an interesting little tapestry **museum**★ with Gothic tapestries and finely worked embroidery.

Lauenburg an der Elbe
25km/15.5mi north via ① (B 209) on the plan.
A sleepy township today, Lauenburg commands a point where the ancient salt route from Lüneburg to Lübeck crossed the Elbe. At the foot of a steep, wooded slope, lie old **half-timbered houses** clustered along Elbstraße. These were built from the 16C to the 19C.

LÜNEBURGER HEIDE

LÜNEBURG HEATH

To preserve the heath from the encroachment of agriculture and forestry, a 200km²/77sq mi nature reserve, the Lüneburg Heath, was created, where flora and fauna are protected and cars are only permitted on primary roads.

▶ **Orient Yourself:** The great expanse of Lüneburg Heath stretches between the glacial valleys of the Aller to the south and the Elbe to the north.

☺ **Don't Miss:** The stark natural beauty of the Lüneburg Heath.

◔ **Organizing Your Time:** Allow a day to see all of the sights listed in the heath.

Kids **Especially for Kids:** Heide-Park Soltau amusement park.

⚑ **Also See:** *LÜNEBURG (37km/23mi east), BREMEN (99km/62mi west), HAMBURG (53km/33mi north).*

Sights

Bergen-Belsen
7km/4mi southwest of Bergen.
The **memorial** *(Gedenkstätte)* to the victims of Bergen-Belsen concentration camp was erected in 1946 and stands in solitude in a clearing on Lüneburg Heath. There is a **documentation centre** *(Dokumentenhaus)* at the entrance, with a permanent exhibition retracing the history of the camp. The **monument,** a 45min walk from the parking lot, is beyond

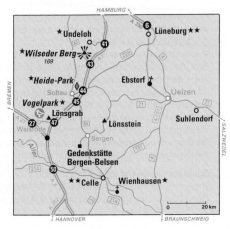

the tumulus marking the site of the mass graves. It is a simple obelisk with inscriptions in 13 languages honouring the memory of those who fell victim to the Nazis' "extermination" policy.

Celle★★ – ♿ *See CELLE.*

Kloster Ebstorf
26km/16mi south of Luneburg. 🚍 *Guided visit (75min).* 🕐 *Apr to mid-Oct, Tue-Sat, 10-11am, 2-5pm, Sun at 11.15am, 2-5pm; mid-Oct to end Oct, Tue-Sun, 2pm.* 🕐 *Closed Good Fri.* 🎟 *€3.* ☎ *(058 22) 23 04.*

Do not miss the former Benedictine abbey in the small town of Ebstorf, where the 14C and 15C cloister and nuns' gallery are the most impressive features among the ruins. A life-size wooden statue of St Maurice (1300) and several Romanesque and Gothic Virgins can be seen in the gallery.

Handwerksmuseum am Mühlenberg, in Suhlendorf
♿🕐 *Open Apr-Oct, Tue-Thur 11am-4pm, Fri-Sun 10.30am-5pm.*🕐 *€2.50.* ☎ *(058 20) 370.*

The location of this craft museum is indicated by a tall windmill visible from some way off. The museum, which has a sizeable collection of mills and documents the work of a miller as well as that of a saddler, a smith and a cobbler.

Heide-Park Soltau
🅺🇮🇩🇸 ♿🕐 *Open from Apr to end Oct, 9am-6pm (8pm Jul-Aug).* 🎟 *€26.* ☎ *(051 91) 91 91; www.heide-park.de.*

This well-maintained leisure park offers 40 different kinds of rides. It is organised into themes, such as Lüneburg Heath, a Dutch village, or Little America, and some of the attractions include roller-coasters, cable railways and water flumes.

The Heath

In the Middle Ages, the name "Heide" signified the boundary of a village; only later did it come to mean the common heather (*Calluna vulgaris*) which carpets the ground in August and September. The bell-heather (*Erica tetralix*) blooms in July, if rarely, preferring marshy areas.

The heath is actually a man-made shrubland. 5 000 years ago Lüneburg Heath was covered in forest which eventually was uprooted by farmers. To keep the forest at bay, farmers burned, grazed cattle and sheep or lifted the turf with hoes. Only then was the light-hungry heath able to spread.

Flora and Fauna – Juniper (*Juniperus communis*) thrives in the Lüneburg Heath as well, as do birch, mountain ash, pine and oak, gorse, broom, silver grass, crowberries, bilberries and cranberries.

Moorland sheep serve as living mowers. They maintain the heather at a height of 20cm/8in. Both genders have horns; those of the male are spectacularly coiled. There were one million moorland sheep on Lüneburg Heath around 1800, when it was much larger, but only a few thousand left today.

Bees are also an intrinsic feature of the heath. They frequently come with travelling beekeepers who bring their swarms in baskets called "Lüneburg Bogenstülpern". The largest bird on the heath is the nearly extinct blackcock or capercaillie. There are plenty of buzzards, red kites, hobbies and kestrels, with herons and snipes in the lowlands and high moors. Autumn sees flocks of fieldfares.

Boulders – Large and small granite boulders are scattered over Lüneburg Heath. They came from Scandinavia as boulder clay and were left behind when the glaciers of the last Ice Age retreated over 18 000 years ago.

Undeloh★

The charming village of Undeloh, with its old houses sheltered beneath huge oak trees, is the departure point for the 4km/2.5mi trip to Wilsede, a nature reserve left untouched by civilization. *Cars are prohibited; horse-drawn service is available.*

Vogelpark Walsrode

  Open Mar to Oct, 9am-7pm; Nov to Feb, 9am-6pm. €13. (051 61) 604 40; www.vogelpark-walsrode.de.

Almost 5 000 birds from all parts of the world live in this fine 22ha/54-acre **ornithological park**, most of them in their natural habitat and at semi-liberty. Also on site is the **German Birdcage Museum** *(Deutsches Vogelbauermuseum)*, where an incredible number of birdcages are on display.

Kloster Wienhausen★ *See CELLE: Excursions.*

Wilseder Berg★

From the summit (169m/554ft), there's a vast **panorama★** of heath and woodlands. On a clear day, the spires of the Hamburg's churches can be seen.

MAGDEBURG★★

POPULATION: 228 500

Magdeburg grew up on an important trade crossroads and to this day is a thriving cultural and economic centre. The town became known as the "pearl of Europe" around the turn of the 19C. *Julius-Bremer-Straße 10, 39104 Magdeburg, (0391) 540 49 03.*

▸ **Orient Yourself:** Magdeburg is in the heart of Sachsen-Anhalt, mid-way along the course of the Elbe. The town is easily reached, situated at the crossroads of the A 2 (Berlin-Hannover) and A 14 motorways (to Leipzig).

P Parking: Look for garages near the Johanniskirche and on the Elbuferprom.

Don't Miss: A walk through the Old Town.

Especially for Kids: Elbauenpark

M. Hertlein/MICHELIN

Since 1974 the Kloster Unser Lieben Frauen has been an art museum

🕐 **Organizing Your Time:** Magdeburg can be appreciated in one day's time.

🕐 **Also See:** *DESSAU (63km/39mi southeast), WÖRLITZER PARK (79km/49mi southeast), WITTENBERG (85km/53mi southeast), WOLFENBÜTTEL (96km/60mi west).*

A Bit of History

A steadfast merchant city – Magdeburg was founded by Emperor Otto I, who built his favourite Imperial palace here and raised the town to the status of archbishopric in 968. The early success of this commercial centre, which declared its support for Martin Luther in 1524, was brought to an end in 1631 when Imperial troops laid siege to the town before destroying it. Famous local figures include Baroque composer Georg Philipp Telemann (1681-1767).

Address Book

WHERE TO EAT

🍽️ **St. Immanuel** – *Alt-Prester 86 (on the right bank of the Elbe along Cracauerstr., Genthinerstr. and Pechauerstr. to the south)* ☎ *(0172) 305 40 02* 🕐 *Mon-Fri from 6pm, Sat-Sun from noon* 🍴 *Reservations recommended.* This restaurant's exceptional location and building are among its highlights. Set in a former neo-Gothic church, refined, seasonal cuisine is served in a hushed atmosphere. In summer there is a beautiful, shady, waterside terrace.

WHERE TO STAY

🍽️ **Hotel Bördehof** – *Magdeburger Straße 42, 39179 Magdeburg-Ebendorf* ☎ *(039203) 515 10 Fax (039203) 515125 www.boerdehof.de* 🅿 ✕ *42 rooms.* Located near the motorway, this former farmhouse has been extended to create a popular hotel. Some rooms have been renovated; other older rooms remain untouched and are more basic. Dinner is served in a winter garden.

🍽️ **Plaza Hotel** – *Halberstädter Straße 146* ☎ *(0391) 605 10 Fax (0391) 6051100 www.12plaza.de* 🅿 ✕ ♿ *103 rooms* 🛏 🍽️ *Restaurant.* This hotel is on the outskirts of town, well served by public transport. Behind its modern, white façade is a comfortable, tastefully-decorated hotel with a bistro restaurant and courtyard terrace.

🍽️ **Residenz Joop** – *Jean-Burger-Str. 16* ☎ *(0391) 6 26 20 Fax (0391) 6262100 www.residenzjoop.de* 🅿 ✕ *25 rooms.* 🛏 This villa hotel is in a quiet residential district. From 1903 until the Second World War it was the Swedish consulate. Spacious and comfortable guestrooms, tastefully furnished.

TAKING A BREAK

Klostercafé – *Regierungsstr. 4-6 (in the Kloster Unser Lieben Frauen)* ☎ *(0391) 5 65 02 33. www.klostercafe-magdeburg. de.* 🕐 *Tue-Sun, 10am-6pm.* 🕐 *Closed at Christmas.* A tea room has been set up in the former refectory of the abbey.

GOING OUT

Alex – *Ulrichplatz 2 (southeast of the roundabout btn. Ernst-Reuter-Allee and Otto-von-Guericke-Str.)* ☎ *(0391) 5 97 49 0 www.alexgastro.de* 🕐 *Mon-Thu, 8-1am, Fri-Sat, 8-3am, Sun, 9-1am.* Young, modern café over two floors and near the town centre. A good place to end the evening or watch the sun set over the Ulrichplatz fountain. Early risers will enjoy the breakfast set menus.

Le Frog – Brasserie am See – *Heinrich-Heine-Platz 1 (in the Rotehorn public park on the right bank of the Elbe)* ☎ *(0391) 5 31 35 56 www.lefrog-md.de* 🕐 *Mon-Sat 11am-midnight, Sun, 10am-midnight.* This glass pavillion is on the waterfront in the pretty Rotehorn park. Whether it's coffee and cake, a mediterranean-inspired meal or a late-night cocktail, there's something for everyone here. When weather allows, there is a pleasant Biergarten.

Dom St Mauritius and St Katharina★★★

South of the old town. Entrance through the north doorway.
At a time when the Romanesque style in Germany was losing its impetus, the construction of Magdeburg Cathedral at the beginning of the 13C marked the first attempt to impose a Gothic style from the architecture of the great French cathedrals. Magdeburg Cathedral's interior houses the 1495 **bronze tomb**★ of Archbishop Ernst of Saxony *(between the towers)*.

Sights

Old Town★

The historic centre and cathedral of Magdeburg lie west of the Elbe.

Kloster Unser Lieben Frauen★★

Regierungstraße. 🕐 *Open Tue-Sun, 10am-5pm.* ☎ *(0391) 56 50 20; www.kunstmuseum-magdeburg.de.*
This abbey was consecrated in the early 11C and taken over by the Premonstratensian Order, who then gave it up in 1632 during the Thirty Years War. After they moved out the abbey was used as a seminary and school until 1945; since 1974 it has been an art museum housing a collection of sculpture from Antiquity to the present. The **abbey church**★ has been used as a concert venue since 1977.

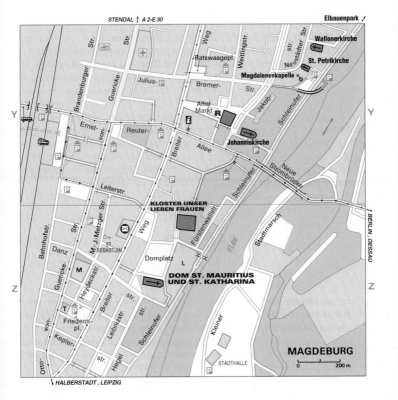

Rathaus

In front of the two-storey Baroque town hall (1691-98) stands a gilded copy of the famous statue of The Magdeburg Knight, one of the oldest equestrian sculptures in Germany (the c 1240 original is in the Kulturhistorisches Museum).

Johanniskirche

🕐 *Open Tue-Sun, May to Sep, 10am-7pm; Nov to Feb, 10am-5pm, Mar-Apr and Oct, 10am-6pm.* 🕐 *Closed 24 and 31 Dec.* 🎟 *€1, no charge on 3 Oct.* ☎ *(0391) 593 45 48.*

Magdeburg's oldest parish church (941), in which Martin Luther preached (memorial in front of church), was all but destroyed during the Second World War. It is now used as a venue for various events and exhibitions.

Petriberg

North of the town hall, on the banks of the Elbe. Three churches adorn this riverside hill: the **Magdalenenkapelle** (built 1315), with a single Gothic nave; **St Petrikirche**, a Gothic hall-church (14-15C); and the **Wallonenkirche**, a former abbey church (founded 1285) used by the Flemish Reformed from 1694-1945.

Elbauenpark★

Kids *Northeast of the old town, east of the Elbe.* 🚗🕐 *Open Summer, 9am-8pm; Winter, 10am-4pm.* 🎟 *€2.50.* ☎ *(018 05) 25 19 99; www.elbauenpark.de.*

This 140ha/345 acre park features themed gardens and a butterfly house. There are child-care facilities in an imaginatively decorated playhouse. The highlight is the **Millennium Tower★★**, at 60m/200ft the world's tallest wooden tower.

Excursion

Halberstadt

45km/28mi southwest. Halberstadt's highlight is **Dom St-Stephanus★★**, recalling the Gothic cathedrals of France. Note the finely-worked **rood screen★** (ca 1510). Above it, a group representing the **Triumphal Cross★** is a splendid example of Late Romanesque sculpture. (🕐 *Open May-Oct, 10am-5pm, Sat, 10am-5pm, Sun, 11am-5pm; Nov to Apr, Tue-Sun, 11am-4pm.* ☎ *(039 41) 242 37; www.dom-und-dom-schatz.de)*

Rare liturgical vestments and religious vessels from the 12C-16C are displayed in the **Domschatz★★ (Treasury)** with a precious collection of altar paintings, manuscripts, and 12C tapestries. 🔍 *Guided visit (75min).* 🕐 *Apr-Oct, Mon 11:30am, 2:30pm; Tue-Fri at 10am, 11:30am, 2pm and 3:30pm; Sat at 11:30am, 2:30pm, 4pm; Sun at 11:30am, 1pm and 2:30pm; Nov to Mar, Mon to Sun, at 11:30am and 2:30pm, additional weekend visit at 1pm.* 🎟 *€3.50.* ☎ *(039 41) 242 37; www.dom-und-domschatz.de.*

MAINZ★

POPULATION: 192 000

Mainz was elevated in 1949 to the capital of the Rheinland-Pfalz. It is Germany's largest and most important wine market. Although 80 per cent of the old town was destroyed during the Second World War, a large part has been reconstructed. The city is also the site of a famous annual carnival, which draws hundreds of visitors to its procession on the Monday before Shrove Tuesday (🕐 *see Calendar of events).* 🅸 *Brückenturm, 55116 Mainz, ☎ (061 31) 28 62 10.*

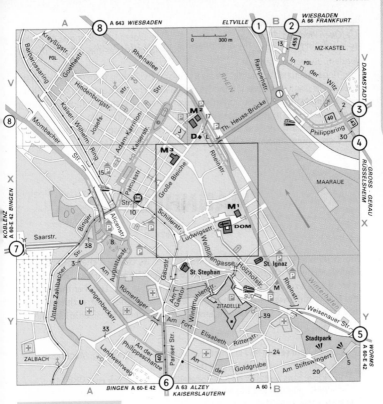

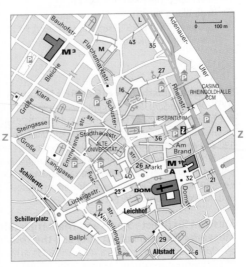

Landesmuseum Mainz★

ⓞ *Open Wed–Sun, 10am–5pm, Tue, 10am–8pm.* ⓞ *Closed 1 Jan, Carnival, Ascension, Pentecost, 3 Oct, 24, 25 and 31 Dec.* ⚭ *€2, no charge on Sat.* ☎ *(061 31) 285 70; www.landesmuseum-mainz.rlp.de.*

The Department of Antiquities traces Rhineland civilisation from prehistory to the present. Of particular interest is the Steinhalle which houses some 300 stone memorials dating from the Roman colonisation of Germany, including Jupiter's Column (*Jupitersäule*). The museum's medieval and Baroque sections and its extensive collections of Höchst porcelain and Jugendstil glassware are also well worth seeing. The 20C Department houses the largest collection of works by Tàpies in Germany.

MANNHEIM

POPULATION: 307 600

Mannheim is a rarity among European towns, its centre a chessboard of 142 identical blocks (Quadratstadt), each identified by a letter and number. But it would be wrong to think this is a staid, inflexible city. Local enthusiasm for the arts is and always has been strong, especially in the theatre, this being the site where Schiller's works premiered. 🛈 *Willy-Brandt-Platz 3, 68161 Mannheim,* ☎ *(0190) 77 00 20.*

▶ **Orient Yourself:** A few kilometres northwest of Heidelberg, Mannheim sits at the confluence of the Rhine and the Neckar.

🅿 **Parking:** Lots and garages are located throughout the city. Visit http://wap.parkinfo.com for fees and locations.

☺ **Don't Miss:** The Fine Arts Museum,

ⓞ **Organizing Your Time:** Plan two hours to view the Fine Arts Museum.

👆 **Also See:** *HEIDELBERG (20km/16mi southeast), SPEYER (22km/14mi south), WORMS (23km/14mi northwest).*

Sights

Städtische Kunsthalle★★ (Fine Arts Museum)

♿ⓞ *Open Tue–Sun, 10am–5pm, Thur noon–5pm.* ⓞ *Closed Carnival, Good Fri, 1 May, first Tue in May, 24 and 31 Dec.* ⚭ *€2.10.* ☎ *(0621) 293 64 30.*

Installed in a Jugendstil building of 1907, the museum concentrates on works of the 19C and 20C. **Sculpture**, including works by Rodin, Lehmbruck, Barlach, Brancusi, Giacometti, Moore, Nam June Paik, Richard Long and Mario Merz, form the focal point of the art collection. **French Impressionists** are also on display (Manet, Monet, Cézanne) as are the **German Secession** artists, represented by Slevogt and Corinth, and the **Expressionists** by Beckman and Heckel.

Museum für Kunst-, Stadt- und Theatergeschichte im Reiß-Museum★ (Museum of Art, City and the Theatre)

ⓞ *Open Tue–Sun, 11am–6pm.* ☎ *(0621) 293 31 51. In the Arsenal (Zeughaus).*

The Art History department houses mainly sculpture and painting of the Palatinate electorate from the 18C, as well as Baroque and Rococo furniture. There is an outstanding collection of **European porcelain and faience**★, with the highlight being a comprehensive display of Frankenthal porcelain from the Palatinate. The **local history collections** chronicle the development of the town.

Museum für Archäologie, Völker- und Naturkunde★
(Museum of Archaeology, Ethnology and Natural History)

&⏱ *Open Tue-Sun, 11am-6pm.* ⏱ *Closed 1 May, 24 and 31 Dec.* 🎫 *€2.10.* ☎ *(0621) 293 31 51. In the Mutschler-Bau opposite the arsenal.*

The archaeology collections include important artifacts from the Paleolithic and Mesolithic eras, the Carolingian period, and from ancient Greece and Rome. The Middle Ages are represented with town centre excavations. The exhibition of **folklore**★ includes a fine **Benin collection**★, of international significance.

Schloss (Palace)

🔒 *Temporarily closed until 2007.*

The building of this Baroque palace, the biggest in all of Germany (400 rooms, 2 000 windows), lasted from 1720 to 1760. Restored after the Second World War, the palace is now occupied by departments of the university.

MANNHEIM							
		Kaiserring	DZ		Reichskanzler-		
		Konrad-Adenauer-			Müller-Str.	DZ	49
Bismarckpl.	DZ 10	Brücke	CZ	30	Schanzestr.	CY	53
Dalbergstr.	CY 15	Kurpfalzbrücke	DY	31	Schloßgartenstr.	CZ	56
Freherstr.	CY 20	Kurpfalzstr.	CDYZ		Seilerstr.	CY	61
Friedrichspl.	DZ 23	Moltkestr.	DZ	38	Spatzenbrücke	CY	62
Goethestr.	DY 25	Planken	CDYZ		Willy-Brandt-Pl.	DZ	67
Heidelberger Str.	DZ						

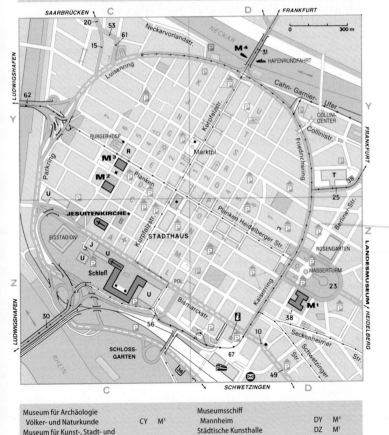

Museum für Archäologie			Museumsschiff		
Völker- und Naturkunde	CY	M³	Mannheim	DY	M⁴
Museum für Kunst-, Stadt- und			Städtische Kunsthalle	DZ	M¹
Theatergeschichte im Reiss-Museum	CY	M²			

WHERE TO EAT

🍽️🍴🍷 **Martin** – *Lange Rötterstraße 53* ☎ *(0621) 33 38 14* 🕐 *Closed 25 Aug-17 Sep, Mon, Sat lunch.* A family-run establishment, this well-managed restaurant was constructed in the old German style and offers fish specialities. Attention and service beyond compare.

WHERE TO STAY

🍽️🍴🍷 **Mack** – *Mozartstraße 14* ☎ *(0621) 124 20* Fax *(0621) 1242399* *www. hotelmack.de* ⤫ *50 rooms* ☕. From the outside, this former town house doesn't look like much. Once inside, however, the well-kept, personalised guestrooms and succulent breakfast ensure a pleasant stay.

From the staircase inside there is a view of Kurpfalzstraße, the street that bisects the chessboard centre from one end to the other, as far as the Neckar. The painted ceilings are restored works by Cosmas Damian Asam, as are the ceilings of the church *(Schlosskirche)* and the Knights' Hall *(Rittersaal)*.

Jesuitenkirche

Founded at the same time as the palace, this massive edifice is said to be the biggest Baroque church in southwest Germany. The façade is Classical.

Landesmuseum für Technik und Arbeit in Mannheim (Regional Museum of Industrial Techniques)

At Museumsstraße 1. ♿🕐 *Open Tue-Fri, 9am-5pm, Wed, 9am-8pm, Sat-Sun, 10am-6pm.* 🕐 *Closed Good Fri, 24, 25 and 30 Dec.* 🎫 *€3, no charge on Wed from 12 noon.* ☎ *(0621) 429 89; www.landesmuseum-mannheim.de.*

Two hundred and fifty years of industrial development in southwest Germany are retraced in this modernistic building, which impresses with the elegance, lightness and transparency of its architecture. The museum illustrates the effect of industrialisation on people's lives. History is presented in a chronological spiral, from enlightened absolutism on the fifth floor to the 20C in the basement. Visitors can be carried around the grounds on a steam railway.

MARBURG★★

POPULATION: 79 000

Built on the side of a hill, this charming town was once a great pilgrimage centre, with crowds drawn to venerate the relics of St Elizabeth of Hungary. Since the Reformation, Marburg has become a centre of Protestant scholarship and theology, largely due to its prestigious 16C university. 🚹 *Pilgrimstein 26, 35037 Marburg,* ☎ *(064 21) 991 20; www.marburg.de.*

▶ **Orient Yourself:** Marburg is on a rocky outcrop on the edge of the Lahn. The town occupies the centre of a triangle formed by Frankfurt, Kassel and Cologne.

😊 **Don't Miss:** The walking tour of Old Marburg and St. Elizabeth's Church.

🕐 **Organizing Your Time:** Allow two hours for the suggested tour of Old Marburg.

🖐️ **Also See:** LAHNTAL (*Wetzlar is 44km/28mi southwest*), SAUERLAND (*Bad Berleburg is 49km/31mi north*).

A Bit of History

St Elizabeth (1207-31) – Princess Elizabeth, daughter of the King of Hungary and intended bride of the Landgrave Ludwig of Thuringia, was brought to the Thuringian court at Wartburg Castle near Eisenach at the age of four. Early in her life she became known for her kindness to the sick and unfortunate. She married Ludwig in 1221, but in 1227 he died of the plague, and Elizabeth withdrew to Marburg to leave a life of service. Elizabeth died of exhaustion at the age of 24.

A place of pilgrimage – Elizabeth was canonised only four years later (1235). Her remains were exhumed the following year to be immortalised in the superb Gothic church built for her. So many pilgrims attended that it became one of the largest centres of pilgrimage in Western Christianity.

Seat of the Reformation – In 1529 Elizabeth's descendant, **Philip the Magnanimous**, abolished the cult of relics and buried Elizabeth's relics in a local cemetery. Philip later invited Reformers Luther and Zwingli to the famous "Marburg Religious Discussion" (1529).

Old Marburg and the Elisabethkirche★★

Elisabethkirche★★

&○ *Open Apr to Sep, 9am-6pm; Oct, 9am-5pm; Nov-Mar, 10am-4pm. Shrine:* ⊜ €2. ☎ *(064 21) 654 97; www.elisabethkirche.de.*

The first truly Gothic church in Germany, this church was built between 1235 and 1283. The building was also Germany's first hall-church. In the church's **interior,** note the following artworks: **(1)** A statue of St Elizabeth (c 1470) wearing an elegant court gown in the nave; **(2)** an openwork Gothic rood as well as a modern Crucifix by Ernst Barlach; **(3)** an altarpiece of the Pietà (1360); **(4)** the tomb of St Elizabeth (after 1250); **(5)** the remains of 14C-15C frescoes in the niches; and **(6)** **St Elizabeth's Shrine**★★ *(Elisabethschrein)* in the old sacristy. This masterpiece in golds was completed by craftsmen from the Rhineland ca 1250. Also worthy of note: **(7)** St. Elizabeth's Window assembled from 13C medallions; **(8)** 1510 statue of St. Elizabeth personifying Charity by Ludwig Juppe; **(9)** *The Landgraves' Chancel,* necropolis of the descendants of St. Elizabeth.

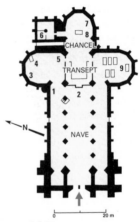

WHERE TO EAT

⊜⊜ **Zur Sonne** – *Markt 14* ☎ *(064 21) 171 90* This 16C building houses various dining rooms, all with immaculately-set tables, low ceilings and rustic decor. A variety of dishes are on offer.

WHERE TO STAY

⊜⊜⊜ **Dammühle** – *Dammühlenstraße 1, 35041 Marburg-Wehrshausen-Dammühle (5km west along Barfüßertor)* ☎ *(064 21) 935 60 Fax (064 21) 36118 www.hotel-dammuehle.de* 🅿 ⇥ *21 rooms* ⊜⊜ *Restaurant* This small half-timbered 14C mill, in a charming location has prettily-decorated, comfortable guestrooms. There is also a dining room with country-style decor, a Biergarten, mini-golf and games area.

> *Leaving the church, climb up into the old town by way of the Steinweg – an unusual ramp with three different levels, which continues as the Neustadt and then the Wettergasse. Turn right into the Marktgasse.*

Marktplatz★

Only the upper market, the Obermarkt, has retained its original houses. Particularly outstanding examples include nos 14 and 21, from 1560; no 23; and no 18, a stone house of 1323, the oldest preserved house still inhabited. The market fountain, dedicated to St George, is a popular meeting place.

Rathaus

A Gothic 16C building, the town hall's door is beloved for its mechanical cock crowing the hours from the gable.

> *The Nikolaistraße leads to the forecourt of the Marienkirche.*

This late-13C church is preceded to the right by the Gothic building of the former ossuary (Karner). From the terrace, there is a fine view over the roofs of the old town to the valley beyond. Past the church façade, at the top of a steep slope, there is a glimpse of the castle above.

At the end of the esplanade, a passage leads down to the Kugelkirche, a fine small church in the Late Gothic (end of the 15C) style.

> *Climb again, this time to the top of the Kugelgasse. Before the Kalbstor fortified gate, turn right into Ritterstraße.*

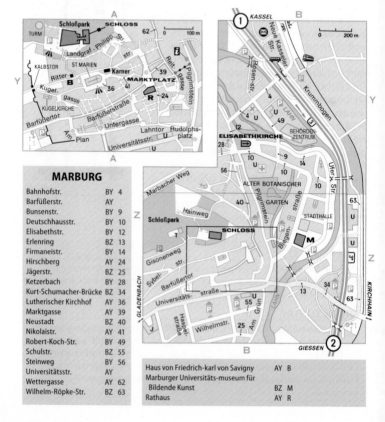

MARBURG

In Ritterstraße, at no 15, is the house which belonged to the famous legal historian Friedrich Karl von Savigny (1779-1861), one of the founders of the "historical school" of the study of law and a man who was the nucleus of the Marburg Romantics (Clemens von Brentano, Achim and Bettina von Arnim, Jakob and Wilhelm Grimm).

Sights

Schloss★ (Castle)

🕐 *Open Apr to Oct, Tue-Sun, 10am-6pm; Nov to Mar, Tue-Sun, 11am-5pm.* 🕐 *Closed 1 Jan, 24, 25 and 31 Dec.* 🎟 *€3.* ☎ *(064 21) 282 23 55.*
From the 13C to the 17C, the castle was the home of the Landgraves of Hessen. From the terrace there is a view along the Lahn Valley.

The historic buildings (13C-15C) on top of the spur include the Gothic Princes' Hall with its double nave, the west hall which gives reveals excavations of the previous fortress (9C and 11C), the south hall with its memorials of the founding of the university (1527) and of the religious debates that took place in Marburg in 1529, and finally the castle chapel with its medieval ceramic floor.

The **Regional and Art History Museum**★ (Museum für Kulturgeschichte), housed in the 15C Wilhelmsbau wing, displays among other things precious artefacts from the Elisabethkirche (fragments of stained glass, a 15C tapestry depicting the story of the Prodigal Son). There is also an exhibition of medieval shields.

There is a pleasant walk through the **park** at the foot of the buttress.

Marburger Universitätsmuseum für bildende Kunst (Fine Arts Museum)

🕐 *Open Tue-Sun, 11am-1pm, 2-5pm.* 🕐 *Closed 1 Jan, 24-25 and 31 Dec* ☎ *(064 21/2) 82 23 55.* Mainly German paintings from the 16C to the present are on view here, including Carl Spitzweg's *Der Briefbote*.

KLOSTER MAULBRONN★★

One of the earliest Cistercian foundations in Germany, this enormous abbey remains well preserved with all its outbuildings inside a perimeter wall. The school established here in 1557 has seen the flowering of such diverse talents as Johannes Kepler, Friedrich Hölderlin, Justinus Kerner and Hermann Hesse. The abbey was added to the UNESCO World Heritage List in 1993.

▶ **Orient Yourself:** The abbey is in the heart of the Salzach valley, in a small, fortified medieval village, approached by a rampart walk.
🖈 **Don't Miss:** The Monk's Refectory in the Cloister
🕐 **Organizing Your Time:** Allow two hours for your visit.
🖈 **Also See:** *Schloss BRUCHSAL (24km/15mi west), BAD WIMPFEN (53km/33mi north), STUTTGART (47km/29mi southeast) SCHWARZWALD (BADEN-BADEN is 69km/43mi southwest).*

A Bit of History

The Cistercians – This Benedictine order derives its name from the monastery of Cîteaux in Burgundy, France, founded by Robert of Molesmes in 1098. The order expanded rapidly, until by the 12C and 13C, 742 monasteries lay between Ireland and Syria. In Germany, early foundations include the abbeys of Camp in the Rhineland, Ebrach in Bavaria, Altenberg near Cologne and Maulbronn in Württemberg. Among the monasteries still extant, those in the Roman Catholic regions of Germany were transformed by the Baroque style, whereas those in Protestant regions, such as Maulbronn, survived unaltered.

Visit

🕐 Open Mar-Oct, 9am-5.30pm; Nov-Feb, Tue-Sun, 9.30am-5pm. 🕐 Closed 24, 25 and 31 Dec. ✍ €5. ☎ (070 43) 92 66 10; www.schloesser-und-gaerten.de.

Abbey Church★

Consecrated in 1178, the church houses a 13C Paradise Porch **(1)**, the first German example of the Romanesque-Gothic transition. Inside, the nave is separated into two sections, one for the monks, the other for lay brothers, by a Romanesque rood screen **(2)** topped by a dog-tooth frieze. A large Crucifix (1473) sculpted from a single stone stands before the screen. Note the richly carved monks' choir stalls (behind the choir screen), made ca 1450, Note and the beautiful 14C **Virgin** *(to the left of the high altar)* **(3)**, probably from the Cologne school.

Cloister★★

The west gallery leads to the **lay brothers' refectory (A)** (rebuilt 1869-70), and to the Romanesque **storeroom (B)**, now a *lapidarium*. The **monks' refectory**★, completed ca 1220-30, is flanked by the *calefactory* **(C)** and the kitchens **(D)** to the north. With its tall columns, featuring an annulet halfway up, and its early Gothic vaulting, the refectory is one of the most impressive rooms in the abbey complex. Off the east gallery are the **chapterhouse** and **connecting building (E)**.

Scarlet Traces

The red crayon sketches that can be seen here and there on the vaulted ceilings of the monks' refectory are in fact the outlines of a fresco that was never painted. Jörg Ratgeb, the artist who sketched them, was taken away in 1526 for having led a peasants' revolt.

Monastery Buildings★

Behind the cloister stands a three-storey Gothic palace, in spite of its having been built during the Renaissance. The picturesque **Faustturm** (Faust Tower), with its curved roof, dominates the southeast corner of the medieval fortifications. The famous doctor Faust, who inspired Goethe, Wagner and many others, was supposedly summoned here in 1516 for alchemy experiments.

Back in the monastery's main courtyard, the **museum** is housed in the Frühmesserhaus and on the first floor of the former cooperage (now an information centre).

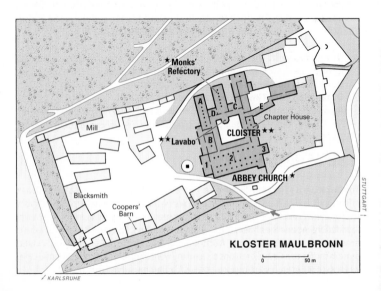

KLOSTER MAULBRONN

0   50 m

KARLSRUHE

MECKLENBURGISCHE
SEENPLATTE★★★

This unique region contains over 1 000 lakes, most of which are linked by natural or artificially created canals, making it a paradise for water sports enthusiasts. The area has not yet been particularly developed as a tourist attraction, nor has it yet been taken over by motor boats. Only a few lakes have roads along their shores. If you want to see the water, you'll have to get out of your car.

▶ **Orient Yourself:** The Mecklenburg lake district was formed during the last Ice Age and lies in the area between the Elbe-Lübeck canal and the Ucker march.

🐾 **Don't Miss:** Müritz National Park

🕐 **Organizing Your Time:** Allow one full day for the suggested Driving Tour.

Kids **Especially for Kids:** Outdoor activities at Müritz National Park.

🌲 **Also See:** NEUBRANDENBURG (43km/27mi east of Waren), SCHWERIN, ROSTOCK (89km/55mi north of Waren).

Driving Tour

From Schwerin to the Müritz Lake 150km/94mi – One day.

The **Schweriner See** forms an idyllic backdrop to the provincial capital **Schwerin**★ (🌲 see SCHWERIN) and its castle. The **Krakower See** is home to the Mecklenburg poet Fritz Reuter, who dreamt of paradise on its peaceful wooded shores. The area is a paradise for bird-watchers.

The **Plauer See**, the third largest lake in Mecklenburg-Vorpommern, offers flat shores to the north and thick forest to the south. Together with the **Müritz**, it forms the heart of the Mecklenburg lake district.

Northeast of these lies **Mecklenburg's "Switzerland"**, a mountainous stretch running north of the **Malchiner See** and the **Kummerower See**. To the west of the

---

Address Book

WHERE TO STAY

◙◙ **Hotel Paulshöhe** – Falken-häger Weg, 17192 Waren ☎ (03991) 171 40 Fax (03991) 171444 www. hotel-paulshoehe.de ▯ 14 rooms ⊠ ◙◙ Restaurant This hotel and its 7 bungalows are in a pleasant location 200m from the Müritz Lake. Hotel has all modern conveniences with a warm, well-presented restaurant.

◙◙ **Hotel Seestern** – Müritzprom-enade, 17207 Röbel ☎ (039931) 580 30 Fax (039931) 580339 🕐 Closed mid-Jan to end Feb ▯ 27 rooms ⊠ ◙◙ Res-taurant This hotel is on a small tongue of land jutting onto the lake. Ask for one of the larger rooms with superb views. The restaurant is in a welcoming

annex of the hotel with a winter garden. Pleasant terrace.

◙◙ **Insel-Hotel** – An der Drehbrücke, 17213 Malchow ☎ (039932) 86 00 Fax (039932) 86030 www.inselho-tel-malchow.de ⇆ ▯ 16 rooms ⊠ ◙◙Restaurant Situated in the old town of Malchow and on the edge of a swinging bridge (Drehbrücke). Well turned-out guestrooms, some of them with lake views. The restaurant serves traditional dishes served on wooden tables.

◙◙◙ **Hotel Kleines Meer** – Alter Markt 7, 17192 Waren ☎ (03991) 64 80 Fax (03991) 648222 www.kleinesmeer. com ⇆ 30 rooms ⊠ ◙◙◙ Restau-rant Contemporary hotel on the former marketplace, not far from the port.

Lakeside houses on piles, Müritzsee

Malchiner See *(on the B 108)* stands Mecklenburg's **Burg Schlitz**, set in a wonderful park. The road leads through the town of **Malchin**, with its fine brick basilica, to the Kummerower See.

The pearl of the Mecklenburg district is **Müritz**, the second largest lake in Germany, 110km²/42sq mi in size. The name comes from the Slavonic word *"morcze"* meaning small sea. The town of **Waren**, the main tourist centre of the region, lies on its northern shores. In addition to the two parish churches of St Georg and St Maria, the old and new town halls and the Löwenapotheke (pharmacy) draw the eye. **Röbel** is developing into a pretty marina, with attractive lakeside boathouses.

Müritz-Nationalpark★

Kids This 310km²/194mi² nature reserve stretches eastwards from the east bank of the Müritz. This park, 25 000ha/61 775 acres of which were state hunting grounds under the socialist regime, is now the realm of hikers and cyclists. With a pair of binoculars you may be able to spot a rare osprey; the high-voltage pylons are favorite nesting grounds (parking is prohibited near nests). The sea eagle, Germany's heraldic bird of prey, can also be spotted near the fish pools at Boek. White storks nest at Kargow, and the nature reserve is also home to a number of black storks and cranes. The dry areas of ground are covered mainly by pines with some beech trees.

MEISSEN★

POPULATION: 28 500

Meissen is famous for its porcelain, distinguished by a pair of crossed swords in blue. From the vineyards in the river valley it also produces a pleasantly fruity dry white wine. Meissen's historic centre is remarkably well preserved, dominated by the flamboyant Albrechtsburg and the cathedral. *Markt 3, 01662 Meissen, ☏ (035 21) 419 40.*

▸ **Orient Yourself:** Located near Dresden, the town of Meissen lies in the picturesque Elbe valley.

▸ **Don't Miss:** The Burgberg and the National Porcelain Factory.

🕐 **Organizing Your Time:** Plan to spend half a day seeing the Burgberg and the porcelain factory.

💧 **Also See:** *DRESDEN (23km/14mi east), LEIPZIG (100km/63mi west).*

A Bit of History

The porcelain of Saxony – It was in the reign of Augustus the Strong that the alchemist **Johann Friedrich Böttger** (1682-1719) revealed the formula for creating the white hard-paste porcelain until then made only in China. The formula is based on kaolin (china clay), large quantities of which still are mined only a short distance northwest of Meissen. Böttger made the discovery in 1708. In 1710 Augustus, Elector of Saxony and King of Poland, founded the Royal Saxon Porcelain Manufactory, which he installed in the castle, a well-guarded site ideal for the protection of secrets. Böttger was its first director.

Walking Tour

Old Meissen

The old town has plenty of Gothic and Renaissance charm. On **Marktplatz** stand the Late Gothic *Rathaus* (town hall, 1470-86), the *Bennohaus* from late 15C, the *Marktapotheke*, a Renaissance building from 1555-60, and the *Hirschhaus* with a fine 1642 doorway.

Frauenkirche

Also standing on the Marktplatz is this Late Gothic hall-church with its fine star-vaulting dating from the late 15C. The carillon bells are made of Meissen porcelain.

Burgberg★★

The castle and cathedral all cluster on this hill, the original site of the town. The **Albrechtsburg**★ was designed by Arnold von Westfalen, one of the most esteemed architects of late medieval times, who was commissioned in 1471 by the Margrave Albert. The finished work (1521-24) is one of the finest civic examples of the Late Gothic style. 🕐 *Open Mar to Oct, 10am-6pm; Nov-Feb, 10am-5pm.* 🕐 *Closed 1 Jan, last 3 weeks of Jan, 24, 25 and 31 Dec.* 👁 *€3.50.* ☎ *(035 21) 470 70; www.albrechtsburg-meissen.de*

The Burgberg's **Dom**★, another Gothic hall, was built from 1250 on the remains of a Romanesque sanctuary and not completed until the late 15C. Early 16C sketches for bronze **funerary plaques**★ in the Dukes' Chapel (Fürstenkapelle) are said to be due in part to Albrecht Dürer and Lucas Cranach the Elder. In front of the rood screen is the **Lay Brothers' Altar**★ (Laienaltar), which is again due to Cranach the Elder, with crucifix and altar candlesticks in Meissen porcelain (1760). The **Benefactors' Statues**★★

WHERE TO EAT

🍽🍽 **Romantik Restaurant Vincenz Richter** – *An der Frauenkirche 12* ☎ *(03521) 45 32 85 www.vincenz-richter.de* 🕐 *Closed 4 Jan-22 Jan, Sun evenings and Mon* 🍴 It's easy to be charmed by this restaurant in a former draper's house built in 1523. Numerous utensils and paintings decorate the dining room of this rustic-style restaurant. In the summer, the interior courtyard is a pleasant place to enjoy a meal.

WHERE TO STAY

🍽 **Hotel Am Talkenberger Hof** – *Am Talkenberger Hof 15, 01640 Coswig Kreis Meissen* ☎ *(03523) 743 17 Fax (03523) 74379 www.talkenberger-hof.de* 📧 📱 *Reservations recommended 9 rooms* 🍽 *Restaurant* Pleasant little guesthouse nestling among the vineyards. The clean, well-cared-for guestrooms have country-style furnishings. Superb view over the local area from the terrace.

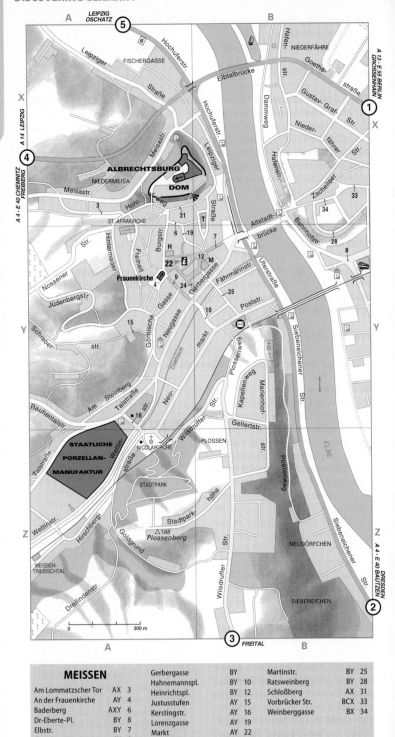

(Stifterfiguren) in the chancel, from the same studio, represent Emperor Otto I and his second wife, Empress Adelaide.

Sights

Staatliche Porzellanmanufaktur★ (National Porcelain Factory)

Talstrasse 9. 🕐 *Open May-Oct, 9am-6pm; Nov-Apr, 9am-5pm.* 🕐 *Closed 24-26 Dec.* 📷 *€8.* ☎ *(035 21) 46 82 08; www.meissen.com*

In 1865, the studios and workshops of the Meissen factory were transferred from the castle *(Albrechtsburg)*, where they had been for 150 years, to the southwest of the town centre. Today the history of the industry is retraced here via exhibits. In a demonstration workshop, the processes of manufacturing, decorating and firing porcelain can be observed *(expect long queues to the workshop)*.

BAD MERGENTHEIM★

POPULATION: 22 500

The old town of Bad Mergentheim, chosen as a base for the Knights of the Teutonic Order in the 16C, owes its popularity as a health and leisure resort to its position on the "Romantic Road," its historic old town, its castle and grounds, and its spa. ⛊ *Marktplatz 3, 97980 Bad Mergentheim,* ☎ *(079 31) 571 31.*

▶ **Orient Yourself:** Lying in the charming valley of the Tauber, between the popular towns of Wurtzburg and Rothenburg, this town is set among forested hills.
🐴 **Don't Miss:** The Castle of the Teutonic Order
🕐 **Organizing Your Time:** Allow two hours to see Bad Mergentheim.
🐴 **Also See:** *ROMANTISCHE STRASSE, HOHENLOHER LAND (15km/9mi south).*

Sights

Deutschordensschloss (Castle of the Teutonic Order)

♿🕐 *Open Apr-Oct, Tue-Sun, 10am-5pm; Nov-Mar, Tue-Sat, 2pm-5pm, Sun 10.30am-5pm.* 🕐 *Closed 24, 25 and 31 Dec.* 📷 *€3.80.* ☎ *(079 31) 522 12; www.deutschordens-museum.de.*

The Teutonic Order

The Teutonic Order was founded as a Germanic hospitaller community in the Holy Land; it became a religious order in 1198 after the fall of Jerusalem, when the knights returned home. They became princes of sizeable territories and estates, either by conquering them or by accepting them as gifts.

In 1525 the Grand Master of the order, Albrecht von Brandenburg-Ansbach, adopted Luther's teaching and suppressed the order's religious role. The community's territory of Prussia also became secular.

Dispossessed of its seat, the Teutonic Order elected as its new headquarters Schloss Mergentheim, which the order had controlled since 1219. The castle remained the Teutonic residence for three centuries. In 1809 Napoleon abolished the order.

Today the order has reconstituted itself as a religious and charitable body, with its headquarters in Vienna.

This 12C castle was extended in the mid-16C to become the residence of the Teutonic Order and its Grand Master. The museum of the Teutonic Order occupies three floors of the castle. On the second floor, the Baroque royal apartments form the setting for a presentation on the history of the order.

Excursion

Stuppach

6km/4mi on the Schwäbisch Hall road.
The parish church of this village boasts the central panel of the celebrated altarpiece from the Chapel of Our Lady of the Snow in Aschaffenburg. The panel, known as the **Stuppacher Madonna**★★ (1519), is the work of Matthias Grünewald. ₺○ *Open Mar to Apr, Tue-Sun, 10am-5pm; May to Oct, Tue-Sun, 9:30am-5:30pm; Nov, Tue-Sun, 11am-4pm.* ▭ *€1.50.* ☏ *(079 31) 26 05.*

Castle of the Teutonic Order

MONSCHAU★★

POPULATION: 12 600

Before 1919, the small town of Monschau was called Montjoie. This ancient Eifel village, with its tall, narrow, slate-roofed houses clustered in a winding river gorge, is famous for its Montjoier Düttchen (Montjoie croissants). ▯ *Stadtstraße 1, 52156 Monschau,* ☏ *(024 72) 194 33; www.monschau.de.*

▸ **Orient Yourself:** Monschau is west of the Eifel massif, only a few kilometres from the Belgian border. From Bundesstraße 258, coming from Aachen, there is a superb **view**★★ of the town.

☺ **Don't Miss:** A walking tour of the old town.

○ **Organizing Your Time:** Allow half a day for the North Eifel excursion.

℅ **Also See:** *AACHEN (38km/24mi north), EIFEL (Bad Münstereifel, our tour's departure point, is 56km/35mi to the east).*

A Bit of History

Drapers' town – Monschau owes its wealth to the clothmaking industry brought by Protestants from Aachen ca 1600. The town flourished in the 18C and its buildings are therefore predominantly Baroque in style. Visitors should watch for the wonderful Baroque doors which adorn even the most modest houses.

Walking Tour

▷ *Leaving the market place via the Unterer Mühlenberg slope, turn right along the Knieberg and climb to the chapel (Friedhofkapelle) beyond the cemetery. From here is a good* **view**★ *of the town. The oldest part of Monschau is the Kirchstraße quarter.*

Rotes Haus★ (Red House)

🕐 *Open from Good Fri to the end of Nov, Tue-Sun, at 10am, 11am, 2pm, 3pm and 4pm.*
🎟 *€2.50.* ☎ *(024 72) 50 71.*
The draper and merchant Johann Heinrich Scheibler had this house built in 1762-65 as his residence and business. The remarkable interior **decor**★ is an exceptional example of middle-class home decor in the 18C and 19C. A highlight is the magnificent **Rococo staircase**★, free-standing and three storeys high.

Haus Troistorff

Laufenstraße 18. This magnificent house was built by a cloth manufacturer in 1783. In comparison with the Rotes Haus, it is much more like a town house while standing apart from the more rustic architecture of the rest of the town.

Excursions

The North Eifel Lakes

85km/53mi Leave Monschau on B 258. The road rises rapidly, and after a mile there is a **look-out point**★ giving a good view of the village. Leaving the town of Schmidt, the Nideggen ruin lies straight ahead.

Burg Nideggen

Until the 15C the rose-coloured sandstone castle was the residence of the counts and dukes of Jülich. The restored 12C church has a Romanesque chancel with frescoes.

Rurtalsperre★ (Rur Dam)

In a wild stretch of country, the reservoir here, known also as the "Stausee Schwammenauel", forms with the Urft reservoir to the south the largest stretch of water in the Eifel. Motor boat services operate on each of them.
The road crosses the dam to enter the Kermeter forest.

MOSELTAL★★★

MOSELLE VALLEY

Dotted with picturesque villages and renowned for its wines, the Moselle Valley is an enchanting region. Castles, vineyards and cruises are regular occurrences.

▷ **Orient Yourself:** The wide, peaceful curves of the River Moselle flow between the Eifel to the northwest and the Hunsrück to the southeast.

🖈 **Don't Miss:** Stopping to sample the famous white wines along the Moselle.

🕐 **Organizing Your Time:** Allow one day for the suggested driving tour.

🕯 **Also See:** *EIFEL (Manderscheid is 56km/35mi north of Trier), IDAR-OBERSTEIN (37km/23mi south of Bernkastel-Kues), RHEINTAL (our suggested touring programme includes Koblenz).*

Driving Tour

From Tier to Koblenz *195km/121mi*

Trier★★ – 🕯 *See TRIER.*

Neumagen-Dhron

This town is known for its Roman discoveries, which have been transported to the Rhineland Museum at Trier. A copy of the famous *Wine Ship* can be seen beside the chapel opposite the Am Römerweinschiff café.

Bernkastel-Kues★– 🕯 *See BERNKASTEL-KUES.*

▶ *The road passes through typical wine-growing villages: Ürzig, Kröv, Enkirch and Pünderich among them. From Enkirch, make a 5km/3mi detour to Starkenburg. One magnificent vineyard follows another.*
Some 3km/2mi after the bridge at Zell, take the left turn toward Marienburg.

Marienburg

The old convent here enjoyed an exceptional **setting**★★. From the restaurant terrace and the wooden "Prinzenkopf" look-out tower *(follow the footpath: 45min round-trip)* there are impressive **views**★★ of the Moselle and its environs.

Address Book

CRUISES

Cruises between Koblenz and Cochem, from late April to mid-Oct: Mon, Fri, Sat-Sun from Koblenz 9.45am and from Cochem 3.40pm (end of June to early Oct). 🕐 Closed 11-19 June 🚢 €23.60 round-trip. Information from the offices at thedocks or from Köln-Düsseldorfer, Frankenwerft 35, 50667 Köln, ☎ (0221) 208 83 18; www.k-d.com

WHERE TO STAY

🍽 **Wein- und Gästehaus Port** – *Wein-gartenstraße 57, 54470 Bernkastel-Kues* ☎ (06531) 911 73 Fax (06531) 91175 *www.ferienweingut-port.de* 🛏 🅿 5 *rooms, 4 apts* 🚭. Peace and quiet reign in this establishment surrounded by vineyards. Comfortable rooms and holiday apartments available. Guests start the day with a hearty breakfast and end it with wine and *Schwenkbraten*.

🍽🍽 **Reichsschenke "Zum Ritter Götz"** – *Robert-Schuman-Strasse 57, 54536 Kröv* ☎ (06541) 816 60

Fax (06541) 8166105 www.reichsschenke. de 🕐 Closed 2 weeks in Feb and 3 weeks in Nov 16 rooms 🚭 🍽 Restaurant. This old inn with its smart, simply furnished rooms is set in the heart of the vineyards. The small, low-ceilinged dining rooms, decorated with dark wood and some wood carvings, give it a rustic air.

🍽🍽**Hotel Bären** – *Gestade 4, 54470 Bernkastel-Kues* ☎ (06531) 25 52 Fax (06531) 915547 *www.hotel-baeren. de* 🕐 *closed Nov-Mar Sun-Tue* 🍽 33 *rooms* 🚭🍽 *Restaurant.* Rooms furnished with care, offering magnificent views. The rustic restaurant next door has an elegant terrace with a river view.

🍽🍽 **Steigenberger Esprix** – *Am Flughafen Hahn, Gebäude 1380, 55483 Hahn* ☎ (06543) 50 98 00 Fax (06543) 509820 www.hahn.esprix-hotels.de 🅿 🍽 35 rooms: €61/81 🚭. This hotel next to Hahn airport is convenient to travelers. Rooms are simple but well-equipped.

Address Book

PRACTICAL INFORMATION

TELEPHONE PREFIX 089

TOURIST INFORMATION

Fremdenverkehrsamt München, ☎ *233 03 00, Fax 23 33 02 33, Mon-Thu 9am-3pm, Fri 9am-12.30pm. Information points: The Hauptbahnhof, Mon-Sat 9.30am-6.30pm, Sun 10am-6pm,* ☎ *23 33 02 57/58;* the Neues Rathaus (Marienplatz), *Mon-Fri 10am-8pm, Sat 10am-4pm,* ☎ *23 33 02 72/73.*

You can find listings of current events in a number of places throughout Munich. Newspaper listings include *Münchner* and the Thursday "SZ-extra" supplement of the *Süddeutsche Zeitung*"newspaper, all on sale at news kiosks. Events magazines include "München im…" (followed by the month), published by the tourist office, *Go!* and *Prinz,* on sale in kiosks and bookshops and in the city's tourist centres. Book tickets well in advance through the information office in the Neues Rathaus or at the numerous advance tickets booths.

Internet sites: www.muenchenticket.de, www.ticketbox.de, www.muenchen-beinacht.de, www.prinz.de, www.kunstpark.de

POST OFFICES WITH LATE HOURS

Postfiliale 32, Bahnhofsplatz, Mon-Fri 7am-8pm, Sat 9am-4pm, Sun 10am-3pm. Postfiliale 24 at the airport (central area level 3) in McPaper, Mon-Sat 7.30am-9pm.

DAILY NEWSPAPERS

Süddeutsche Zeitung, Münchner Merkur

INTERNET SITES

www.intermunich.de; www.munich-online.de; www.munich-info.de; www.muenchen.de

GETTING AROUND

Much of central Munich is a pedestrian and bicycle zone. Many sights are within walking distance; the city's main museums can be reached by tram from Karlsplatz *(lines 17, 18 and 27 stop at Nationalmuseum, Deutsches Museum and Pinakotheken).* Munich's railway station *(Hauptbahnhof),* a 10min walk from the centre, is the main public transport hub.

AIRPORT

☎ *975 00.* The FJ Strauss Flughafen, 34km/21mi north, is linked to the city by S-Bahn lines S1 and S8 *(departure every 20min from 4am to 1am,* ☎ *€8),* and by the Lufthansa shuttle *(departure every 20min from 5am to 8pm, €9).*

PUBLIC TRANSPORT

Munich and its surroundings are divided into four ring-shaped price zones. The local transport and fare association MVV (Münchner Verkehrs- und Tarifverbund) covers underground trains (U-Bahn), SWM (Stadtwerke München) buses and trams (Straßenbahn), rail (S-Bahn) and the transport authorities for the surrounding area; ☎ 41 42 43 44. Information at the tourist information office or railway station *(Hauptbahnhof)* on the mezzanine level, Mon-Sat 9am-6pm. Tickets are available from any underground or rail station and in trams, from ticket machines or from bus drivers.

TICKETS

Tickets for the central zone (Münchner Innenraum), which includes Munich city centre: Single tickets *(Einzelfahrt)* ☎ €2.20, 10-trip tickets: €10 *(10er Streifenkarte)* can be used by more than one person, in Munich city centre two strips on this ticket must be validated); travellers can transfer with these tickets. Single day tickets *(Single-Tageskarte),* ☎ €4.80, and "Partner" day tickets *(Partner-Tageskarte,* for up to five people), €8.50, are valid from when they are stamped to 6am the following day. There is also a three-day ticket costing ☎ €11.80 for one person, €20 for two to five people.

Internet – www.mvv-muenchen.de

Combination ticket – There are four varieties of **München Welcome Card**: one-day single *(Single 1 Tag)* ☎ €7.50, three-day single *(Single 3 Tage)* €17.50, one-day "Partner" (for five adults – two children between 6 and 14 years old equal one adult) *(Partner 1 Tag)* €12.50; three-day "Partner" *(Partner 3 Tage)* €25.50. The ticket is valid for use of public transport in Munich city centre and gives discounts of up to 50% for more than 30 sights, museums, castles, tourist attractions, city tours and bicycle hire. It is available from tourist information offices, in many hotels, and at the airport (where it will cost €10 more but includes a return to the centre).

BICYCLE HIRE

Radius Bike Tours, ☎ 55 02 93 74, www.radius-munich.com rents out bicycles for ☞ €14 per day. Munich is a very bicycle-friendly city.

SIGHTSEEING

THEME TOURS

The tourist office organises tours with English-speaking guides for groups, on request, ☎ 23 33 234. *Stattreisen* also offers 60 various themed tours (beer, architecture, via foot, tram or bike), ☎ 54 40 42 30, www.stattreisen-muenchen.de. Regular guided tours in English are also available from *Munich Walks*, ☎ 55 02 93 74, www.munichwalks.com.

COACH TOURS

Münchner Stadt-Rundfahrten – Panorama Tours, ☎ 55 02 89 95, www.muenchenerstadtrundfahrten.de: *Höhepunkte Münchens* (1hr, €11), daily at 10am, 11am, 12pm, 1pm, 2pm, 2.30pm, 3pm and 4pm (1 Apr to 31 Oct, 9.30am-5pm every 30 min); the city centre and Schloss Nymphenburg (2hr 30min, €19), daily at 2.30pm; departure from Bahnhofplatz (in front of Hertie dept. store), all tours with guide. Tickets also available from hotels.

FINDING YOUR WAY

The most animated part of Munich is in the pedestrian precincts of Neuhauser Straße and Kaufingerstraße, between Karlsplatz (or "Stachus") and Marienplatz. Elegant boutiques are mainly found in Maffeistraße, Pacellistraße, Maximilianstraße and Brienner Straße; antique dealers in Ottostraße near Maximilianplatz; art galleries under the arcades of Hofgartenstraße. Schwabing, around Leopoldstraße, enjoyed its fame as the city's artistic and intellectual hub at the turn of the 20C, but it remains one of Germany's most lively after-hours destinations.

REGIONAL SPECIALITIES

The most famous local specialities include the white sausages known as *Weißwurst*, roast knuckle of pork *(Schweinshaxe)* and *Leberkäs*, a meat pâté available any time after 11am. At beer festivals, a favourite offering is *Steckerlfisch*, small fish grilled on a skewer. *Bretzels*, *Salzstangen* (small salt rolls) and white radishes *(Radi)* are often served with beer.

Munich is also the capital of beer: Five and a half million hectolitres (110 000 000 gal) of beer are brewed every year, most of it drunk in the beer cellars, taverns and beer gardens *(Biergarten)* within Munich.

DATES FOR YOUR DIARY

The origins of the famous autumn *Oktoberfest*, which is held on the **Theresienwiese** *(via Mozartstraße)*, stem from the marriage of Prince Ludwig I of Bavaria and Princess Theresa in 1810. Six and a half million visitors flock to Munich each year for this huge public fair, from the second to last Saturday in September to the first Sunday in October. Although there are street parades the first two days, the festivities focus around beer-drinking: Under canvas marquees and in stands are served some five million tankards of *Wiesenbier*, brewed especially for the event and delivered by horse-drawn drays. The party is complemented by roasted poultry and beef (two oxen are cooked on a spit each day). Hotels will surely fill up, so book a year in advance.

The **Fasching** carnival is celebrated with high spirits and much merriment and ends with the traditional market women's dance at the Viktualienmarkt. The religious festival of Corpus Christi *(Fronleichnam)* involves a procession of clergy, Roman Catholic personalities, Catholic student organisations and guild representatives through streets garlanded with young birch branches. Other festivals include *Starkbierzeit* (Stark beer festival) in March; *Auer Dult* (local festival) from late April to early May, late July and mid October; *TollWood Sommerfestival* (music and theatre) from mid June to mid July and in December; *Opernfestspiele* (opera festival) in July; and the *Christkindlmarkt* (Christmas market) in December. All the cultural activities in Munich are listed in *Offizielles Monatsprogramm* (in

German, €1.55) and *Munich Found (in English, €3)*, both available from the tourist office.

WHERE TO EAT

🍴 **Dürnbräu** – *Dürnbräugasse 2* ☎ *(089) 22 21 95.* A brasserie in a little street near the city centre. Dark wood and long tables give the room a rustic look. In summer, patrons can enjoy the terrace or the courtyard garden.

🍴🍴 **Gasthaus zur Alten Schule** – *Rathausstraße 3 , 82194 Olching-Gröbenzell* ☎ *(08142) 50 46 60* 🕐 *closed Mon* 🚻 *Reservations required.* As its name suggests, this simple restaurant opposite the town hall is in an old school *(alte Schule)*. Meals are served in a former classroom. In summer you can also enjoy the garden.

🍴🍴 **Karawanserei** – *Pettenkoferstraße 1* ☎ *(089) 54 54 19 54 www.karawanserei-muenchen.de* 🕐 *11.30am-3pm and 5pm-midnight. Reservations required.* This Persian restaurant is in a little palace in the city centre. Persian cuisine and decor.

🍴🍴🍴 **Metzgerbräu** – *Klammergasse 4, 83646 Bad Tölz* ☎ *(08041) 706 11 www. augustiner-wirtschaft.de* 🕐 *closed Thu.* 🍽 An introduction to Bavaria, enjoy a large choice of traditional dishes, including calf's head, tripe and oxtail.

🍴🍴🍴 **Bogenhauser Hof** – *Ismaninger Straße 85, 81675 München-Bogenhausen* ☎ *(089) 98 55 86 bogenhauserhof@t-online.de* 🕐 *closed 24 Dec-8 Jan, Sun and public holidays.* This former 19C hunting lodge is now a traditional gourmet restaurant. In an elegant decor, or an idyllic summer garden, attentive waiters serve delicious classic cuisine.

🍴🍴🍴 **Käfer Schänke** – *Prinzregentenstraße 73, 81675 München-Bogenhausen* ☎ *(089) 416 82 47 www.feinkost-kaefer.de* 🕐 *closed Sun and public holidays* A pleasant restaurant with small, variously decorated rooms. The Meissen room is adorned with some 300 pieces of porcelain. The establishment also has a large delicatessen.

🍴🍴🍴 **Lenbach** – *Ottostraße 6* ☎ *(089) 549 13 00 www.lenbach.de* 🕐 *closed Sun.* The interior of this restaurant in the Lenbach palace is the work of famous designer Sir Terence Conran. The concept: modern cuisine on a vast scale (the restaurant covers a surface area of 2 200m²/2 630yd²!) A glass walkway leads to the restaurant.

🍴🍴🍴 **Tantris** – *Johann-Fichte-Straße 7 80805 München-Schwabing* ☎ *(089) 361 95 90 www.tantris.de* 🕐 *closed 1 week in Jan, Sun-Mon and public holidays.* Guarded by mythical monsters, this temple of delight with its avant-garde black and orange decoration is the best restaurant in Munich. Hans Haas charms the palate with his classical and innovative dishes.

WHERE TO STAY

🛏🛏 **Hotel Lutter** – *Eversbuschstraße 109, 80999 München-Allach* ☎ *(089) 812 70 04 Fax (089) 8129584 hotel-lutter@t-online.de* 🕐 *closed 20 Dec-7 Jan* 🅿 *26 rooms.* 🍽 A very well-run, inexpensive hotel in the northwest of Munich. Rooms are functional and breakfast is served in a bright and charming winter garden.

🛏🛏 **Drei Löwen Hotel** – *Schillerstraße 8* ☎ *(089) 55 10 40 Fax (089) 55104905 www.hotel3loewen. de* 🍽 *97 rooms.* 🛏 A welcoming hotel in the heart of the city centre, near the main railway station *(Hauptbahnhof)*. Access is through a vast panelled lobby. The rooms are bright and modern.

🛏🛏🛏 **Hotel Platzl** – *Sparkassenstraße 10* ☎ *(089) 23 70 30 Fax (089) 23703800 www.platzl.de* 🍽 🚻 *167 rooms.* 🛏 Comfortable rooms

Nationaltheater

in traditional Bavarian style right in the heart of the historic old town. Marienplatz with its famous carillon and the food market *(Viktualienmarkt)* can be easily reached on foot. The vaulting of the Pfistermühle restaurant gives the place an air of "old Munich", while the smart Ayingers restaurant is more a bistro.

Hotel Schlicker – *Tal 8* ☎ *(089) 242 88 70 Fax (089) 296059 www.hotel-schlicker.de* ◷ *closed 23 Dec-7 Jan* 🅿 *69 rooms.* In the heart of the old town, this hotel in a 16C building offers personalised rooms, some of them with great style. Views take in the new town hall *(Neues Rathaus)* and its world-famous carillon.

Hotel Uhland – *Uhlandstraße 1* ☎ *(089) 54 33 50 Fax (089) 54335250 www.hotel-uhland.de* 🅿 *25 rooms.* This hotel with its hundred-year-old neo-Renaissance façade on the Theresienwiese has rooms to suit all tastes, some with modern water beds, some with rustic furniture.

Müller – *Fliegenstraße 4* ☎ *(089) 232 38 60 Fax (089) 268624 www.hotel-mueller-muenchen.de* ◷ *closed 23 Dec- 6 Jan* 🅿 ⤫ *44 rooms* A hotel with refurbished rooms, attentive service and a pleasant setting near the Sendlinger Tor, directly opposite Matthäuskirche.

Hotel Bayerischer Hof – *Promenadenplatz 2* ☎ *(089) 212 00 Fax (089) 2120906 www.bayerischer-hof.de* ⤫ 👶 *395 rooms* A luxurious, traditional grand hotel with personalised rooms. The elegant Garden-Restaurant serves gastronomic specialities, and you can enjoy a South Pacific ambience in the Trader Vic's.

Mandarin Oriental Hotel – *Neuturmstraße 1* ☎ *(089) 29 09 80 Fax (089) 222539 www.mandarinoriental.com/munich 73 rooms.* This luxury hotel has retained the past splendour of the temple of dance it once was. The view from the covered terrace with swimming pool stretches as far as the Alps. A marble staircase leads to the elegant Mark's restaurant.

TAKING A BREAK

Café Arzmiller – *Theatinerstraße 22* ☎ *(089) 29 42 73* ◷ *8:30am-6:30pm.*

Arzmiller café and confectioner's

A good place to relax and forget the stress of the city. Coffee, cakes and daily specials are served in the lovely, peaceful Theatinerhof. The house speciality, *Strudel*, is not to be missed.

Café Luitpold Palmengarten – *Brienner Straße 11* ☎ *(089) 24 28 750 www.cafe-luitpold.de* ◷ *Mon-Fri 9am-8pm, Sat 9am-7pm* ◷ *closed Sun and public holidays.* Over the year, this café offers a choice of more than 300 different tarts. The house speciality is Luitpold tart, which can eaten under the glass dome in the palm-filled inner courtyard or on the terrace on Maximilianplatz and in Brienner Strasse.

Confiserie Rottenhöfer – *Residenzstraße 25/26* ☎ *(089) 22 29 15 www.rottenhoefer.de* ◷ *Mon-Fri 8:45am-7pm, Sat 8am-6pm* ◷ *closed Sun and public holidays.* A chocolate boutique (over 160 kinds) and tea room on the ground floor, non-smoking room upstairs. Founded in 1825, this shop was once official supplier to the kings of Bavaria.

Viktualienmarkt – *Viktualienmarkt* ☎ *(089) 23 39 65 00 www.viktualienmarkt.de* ◷ *Mon-Fri 10am-6pm, Sat 10am-3pm.* This traditional market dates back to 1807 and offers a wide variety of goods, including beer, wine, sausages and oysters. The beer garden in the centre is popular in good weather.

GOING OUT

USEFUL TIPS

Beer gardens are an integral part of Bavarian life, especially in Munich. Many of these shaded gardens and terraces are open even in winter; the slightest ray of sunshine will bring the regulars out. Although prices can be high and the service limited, people enjoy the unique atmosphere.

Munich's best-known café and bar scene is Schwabing. Around the university is a plethora of student bars, and along Leopoldstraße south of Münchner Freiheit a range of nice establishments where people go to "see and be seen". Other parts of town with good nightlife are Haidhausen (around Pariser and Weißenburger Platz) and Gärtnerplatz. For online information: www.where2go. de, www.nightlife-munich.de

Alter Simpl – *Türkenstraße 57* ☎ *(089) 2 72 30 83 www.altersimpl.de* 🕐 *Sun-Thu 11am-3am, Fri-Sat 11am-4am.* This casual bar with its stuccoed ceilings has been a student haunt for over 100 years. Mainly Bavarian specialities served (up to 1hr before closing).

Brasserie Tresznjewski – *Theresien-straße 72* ☎ *(089) 28 23 49 www. tresznjewski.de* 🕐 *Sun-Thu 8am-3am, Fri-Sat 8am-4am.* Opposite the Neue Pinakothek, this restaurant offers a wide choice of hot and cold drinks and Mediterranean cuisine.

Hirschgarten – *Hirschgarten 1* 🚊 *16, 17 Romanplatz* ☎ *(089) 17 25 91 www. hirschgarten.de* 🕐 *9am-midnight (beer garden from Mar to Oct)* This beer garden (with rustic restaurant next door) near Schloss Nymphenburg is probably the biggest in all of Bavaria. 8 000 outside seats include 1 200 with table service.

Hofbräuhaus – *Am Platzl 9* ☎ *(089) 2 90 13 60 www.hofbraeuhaus.de* 🕐 *Sun-Thu 9am-midnight, Fri-Sat 9am-1.30am (1st-floor restaurant until 11.30pm).* This place is so famous that it attracts tons of tourists, but its unique atmosphere makes it fun anyway. Music (wind instruments) in the noisy *Schwemme* on the ground floor *(Mon-Fri 12-4pm and 6-11pm, Sat-Sun 11:30am-3pm and 6-11pm).* It is quieter on the first floor *(Trinkstube, music 6-11:30pm)* and in the beer garden in the courtyard.

L-Opera – *Maximilianstraße 2* ☎ *(089) 54 44 46 44 www.l-opera.de* 🕐 *8am-1am.* Opposite the Residenz under the arcades of a 19C building, this place is open from breakfast to late-night. An ideal spot on one of Munich's prettiest squares.

Seehaus – *Kleinhesselohe 3 (in the Englischer Garten)* 🚇 *Münchner Freiheit (follow Haidhauser Straße)* ☎ *(089) 3 81 61 30 www.kuffler.de Beer garden, weather permitting 11am-midnight, restaurant 11:30am-midnight.* A dream location for this idyllic beer garden (self-service) and restaurant, on the shores of Lake Kleinhesselohe in the English Garden. Boat hire nearby.

SHOPPING

USEFUL TIPS

Many consider Munich Germany's best city for shopping. The old town has numerous arcades and boutiques to cater to all budgets. *Beck am Rathauseck* and other department stores are between Marienplatz and Stachus. Another good shopping district is Schwabing (on and to the west of Leopoldstraße). Exclusive boutiques are found in Residenzstraße, Brienner Straße and Maximilianstraße. The *Fünf Höfe* shopping centre is in stylish Theatinerstraße.

Art galleries – Most of Munich's galleries are in Maximilianstraße and the nearby streets, in Residenzstraße and on Odeonsplatz. In the old artists' district of Schwabing, the most interesting gallery areas are Türken-, Schelling- and Franz-Joseph-Straße.

Antiques – Munich antiques range from the elegant, exclusive dealers to inexpensive bric-à-brac shops. Schwabing boasts a wealth of antique shops in Amalien-, Türken-, Barer-, Kurfürsten- and Hohenzollernstraße, as does the city centre around Maximiliansplatz, Lenbachplatz and Promenadenplatz.

Maypole at the Viktualienmarkt

R. Chéret/MICHELIN

MÜNCHEN

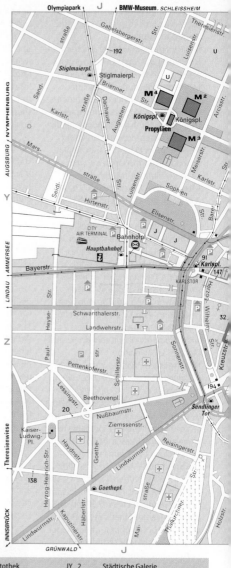

Glyptothek and the Propylaea. **Maximilian II** (1848-64) continued the artistic traditions of his father, founding in 1855 the Bavarian National Museum.

In the history of the Wittelsbach dynasty, a special place must be reserved for **Ludwig II** (1864-86). This tormented romantic, a passionate admirer of Wagner, succeeded to the throne at the age of 18. Beloved by his subjects, he was nevertheless restless and unpredictable, a young man prey to extreme depression. Craving

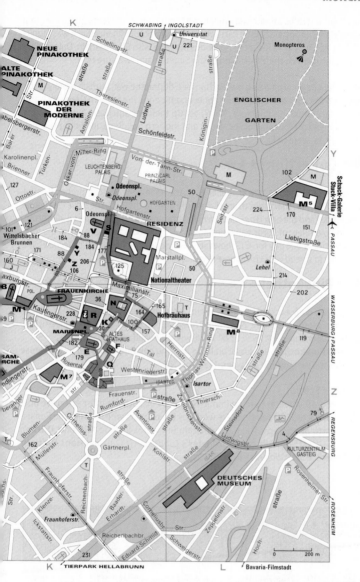

solitude and living in a fantasy world, Ludwig largely withdrew from society and built himself the three extravagant, isolated castles of Neuschwanstein, Linderhof and Herrenchiemsee. Mentally unstable, Ludwig II was deposed in 1886 and confined to Schloss Berg, on the shores of Lake Starnberg. He was found drowned there shortly afterwards.

Prince Luitpold's son, **Ludwig III** (1912-18), was the last king of Bavaria: under pressure from a workers' revolutionary movement after the First World War, he was forced to abdicate.

Between Two Wars – In 1919, **Adolf Hitler**'s German Workers' party was formed and its aims announced by the leader at the Munich Hofbräuhaus. In 1923, Hitler fomented a popular uprising (the Munich Putsch). It was unsuccessful, the party was dissolved and Hitler imprisoned. Once freed from prison, Hitler reorganised the group as the National Socialist (Nazi) Party. After he had become Chancellor, it was Munich that Hitler chose in 1938 for the notorious meeting with Chamberlain, Daladier and Mussolini at which the annexation of the Sudetenland was agreed.

Munich today – After being heavily bombed during the war, Munich rapidly recovered and became the most important economic zone in southern Germany. Large industrial companies (Siemens, BMW) set up their headquarters in the city, congress-goers and tourists flocked there, and modern buildings, including two new art galleries, were built.

Art Collections★★★

The state of Bavaria's three art galleries house an impressive, comprehensive collection. The *Alte Pinakothek* (from the Middle Ages to the 18C), the *Neue Pinakothek* (19C works) and the new *Pinakothek der Moderne* (modern works) offer an all-encompassing overview of European painting. *A combined ticket allows entry to the three art galleries in one day for €12; however, considering the size of the collections, it is advisable to spread your visit over several days.*

Alte Pinakothek★★★

&◔ *Open daily except Mon, 10am-5pm; Tue 10am-8pm.* ◔ *Closed 1 Jan, Shrove Tuesday, Easter Sun, 1ˢᵗ May, 24, 25 and 31 Dec.* ⊗ *€5.50, €1 on Sundays. Free audio guide recommended.* ☎ *(089) 23 80 52 16; www.pinakothek.de.*
The **Alte Pinakothek**, a colossal building housing paintings amassed by the House of Wittelsbach, was built between 1826 and 1836.

German School
The section devoted to German Primitives is the Pinakothek's most extensive one. Alongside sacred 15C paintings are works by the painters who brought the Renaissance north of the Alps. The most outstanding works include **Albrecht Dürer**'s *Four Apostles* (1526); **Albrecht Altdorfer's** *Landscape* (1528); and **Hans Holbein the Elder**'s *St Sebastian Altarpiece* (1516).

St Sebastian Altarpiece by Hans Holbein the Elder

Bayerische Staatsgemäldesammlung, Alte Pinakothek Munich

The Collection

The Pinakothek collection was started in the 16C by Duke Wilhelm IV, who commissioned historical scenes from the most eminent painters of his time, Altdorfer and Burgkmair. In the 17C, the Elector Maximilian I founded the Kammergalerie which, under King Ludwig I, developed into the finest exhibition of art in the whole of Europe. The building suffered severe damage in 1943, but the paintings had already been moved to a safe location.

Dutch and Flemish Schools

Among the most important works in this section are *The Land of Milk and Honey* (1566) by **Pieter Bruegel the Elder; Sir Anthony Van Dyck** and his master, **Peter Paul Rubens**, whose *The Great Last Judgement* (c 1614-16) is on display. Early Dutch masterpieces include the *Altarpiece of the Three Magi* (1455) by **Rogier Van der Weyden;** *Seven Joys of Mary* (c 1480) by **Hans Memling;** and *Last Judgement* by **Jérôme Bosch**. Finally, **Rembrandt**'s Passion cycle constitutes the heart of the collection of 17C Dutch paintings.

Italian School

Here the spotlight is on the great Renaissance masters: **Sandro Botticelli**'s *Lamentation of Christ* (post 1490); three major works by **Raphael** including the *Madonna Tempi* (1507); *The Crowning of Thorns* (1560) by **Titian; Tiepolo**'s *Veneration of the Holy Trinity by Pope Clemens* (1739) and the *Adoration of the Magi* (1753); and several works by **Antonio Canaletto** and **Francesco Guardi**.

French School

French classicism is illustrated by **Claude Lorrain**'s *Sea Port at Sunrise* (1674) and paintings by **Nicolas Poussin**, who takes his subjects from Ovid's *Metamorphoses* (1627). Among the 18C painters, **François Boucher**'s *Madame Pompadour* is on display, executed at her request and by her favourite painter in 1756.

Spanish School

This school is notably represented by **Murillo**'s lively genre paintings; the Alte Pinakothek alone has five of them. **El Greco** and **Velazquez** are also displayed.

Neue Pinakothek★★

⌚ Open daily except Tue, 10am-5pm; Wed 10am-8pm. Closed 1ˢᵗ Jan, Shrove Tuesday, Easter Sunday, 1ˢᵗ May, 24, 25 and 31 Dec. €5.50. €1 on Sundays. Plan available at the entrance, free audio guide recommended. ☎ (089) 23 80 51 95; www.neue-pinakothek.de.

The Post-Modernist style **Neue Pinakothek** building, completed in 1981, is well-proportioned. The building replaces the museum erected under Ludwig I, which had to be demolished due to serious war damage.

Early 19C

Galleries **1, 2 and 2a** are devoted to international art ca 1800. **Thomas Gainsborough**'s portraits and landscapes are displayed, as are works by **Jacques-Louis David,** the *Marquise de Sorcy ;* **Joshua Reynolds** *(Captain Pownall);* **William Turner** *(Ostend)* and **Francisco Goya** *(Marquesa de Caballero*, 1807).

German painters from the first half of the 19C

On display in Galleries **3 and 3a** are early Romantic works from Dresden, Berlin and Munich, with highly spiritual symbolic landscapes by **Caspar David Friedrich.** Johann Christian Dahl *(Frederiksholm Canal in Copenhagen*, 1817) and Karl Blechen

(*View of Assisi*, 1830) are also represented. Ludwig I of Bavaria was a great patron of the arts who commissioned many paintings, including those on display in Galleries **4 and 4a.** Galleries **5 and 5a** are devoted to the German neo-Classicists in Rome, including a well-known landscape by **Ludwig Richter**, *The Night-Watchman* (*Watzmann,* 1824).

The following galleries focus on two early 19C trends: the spiritual Nazarenes, who sought to reconcile northern and southern painting by studying Raphael and Dürer; and artists of the **Biedermeier** style.

From Romanticism to Realism

Pride of place is given to French painters in Galleries **10 and 10a**. The Romantics are represented by **Théodore Géricault** and his admirer **Eugène Delacroix**. In Galleries **11 and 11a, Andreas Achenbach** and **Carl Spitzweg** (*The Hussar, The Poor Poet,* 1839, *The Writer,* 1850) represent late German Romanticism.

German painters from the second half of the 19C

Gallery **15** is entirely devoted to **Hans von Marées** (1837-87), a great portrait painter inspired by Renaissance art. Gallery **16** contains works by a group of German painters who went to live and work in Rome: Arnold Böcklin, Hans Thoma, **Anselm Feuerbach** and **Leib.**

Impressionists, post-Impressionists and Symbolists

Galleries **18 and 19 contain** paintings by German Impressionists, notably *Summer Holiday* by Friedrich von Uhde and *Portrait of the Writer Eduard Graf von Keyserling* (1901) by Lovis Corinth.

Symbolism and Jugendstil provide the theme of Galleries **20 and 21a**. *Margarethe Stonborough-Wittgenstein,* the philosopher's sister, appears in **Gustav Klimt**'s portrait (1905). **Auguste Rodin**'s marble bust of *Helene von Nostitz* is surrounded by works by Ferdinand Hodler (*Disappointed,* five old men with resigned expressions), Egon Schiele (*Agony,* 1912) and Giovanni Segantini (*Ploughing,* 1890).

Post-Impressionists Toulouse-Lautrec, Vuillard and Ensor share Gallery **21** with a large painting of *Waterlilies* by **Claude Monet** (1918). Galleries **22** and **22a** are occupied by **French Impressionists: Paul Gauguin**'s, **Édouard Manet**. Also on display is a painting by **Vincent Van Gogh's** *Sunflowers* series (1888), **Camille Pissarro, Edgar Degas** and **Paul Cézanne.**

Pinakothek der Moderne★★

Barer Straße 40. &© *Open daily except Mon, 10am-5pm, Thu-Fri 10am-8pm.* © *Closed Shrove Tuesday, 1st May, 24 and 31 Dec.* ⊛ *€9.50, €1 on Sundays.* ☎ *(089) 23 80 53 60; www.pinakothek-der-moderne.de.*

The building, designed by Munich architect Stephan Braunfels, is known as the "Cathedral of Light" because of its glass rotunda and glazed saw-tooth roofs. It houses four museums *(the entrance ticket allows access to all departments)* focusing on 20C art, with paintings, sculptures, photographs, drawings, models and design objects.

Staatsgalerie moderner Kunst (Modern Art Collection)

3rd floor. The question of form and content in modern art is the underlying theme of the permanent exhibition, arranged in chronological order and by cross-influence.

"Classic" Modern Art (Galleries 1-17) – A large section is devoted to German Expressionism, which took aestheticism to a new height, and to the Expressionist movements: "Die Brücke" *(The Bridge,* whose tortured subjects set them apart from the Fauves) with **Ernst Ludwig Kirchner**; and "Der Blaue Reiter" *(The Blue Rider,* focusing on abstraction and spiritualisation of form) with Franz Marc and **Wassily Kandinsky**. Works by another Expressionist, **Max Beckmann**, is represented by *Temptation of St Anthony. T*he Cubists and Futurists moved towards autonomous art, as illustrated in numerous works by **Pablo Picasso** (including *Madame Soler*) and **Georges Braque**. Surrealism is represented by Max Ernst, René Magritte and Salvador Dali, and Bauhaus by Feininger and Paul Klee.

Modern Art (Galleries 20-36) – Important themes in art during the second half of the 20C – informal art, celebration of the trivial, rise of pop culture etc – are broached in artists' monographs. One can thus follow the works of **Joseph Beuys, Francis Bacon** (*Crucifixion*) and Willem de Kooning. The museum also displays some remarkable works by American artists, with paintings by **Andy Warhol**, photographs by Jeff Wall and videos by Bruce Nauman.

Other Departments

Neue Sammlung (Craft and Design, basement) – In addition to objects of industrial design, sports accessories, cars and computer equipment, the museum presents prototypes of objects designed since the industrial revolution up to the 1960s, including Bahaus and Art Nouveau. The collections of the Graphic Art department (*Grafische Sammlung*) and Architecture **Museum** (*Architekturmuseum der Technischen Universität*) are shown in temporary exhibitions on the ground floor owing to their great sensitivity to light.

Deutsches Museum★★★

🔲 *In view of the huge scope of subjects covered – 16 000 exhibits displayed over 46 000m²/495 150sq ft – visitors are advised to be selective. An English brochure and a plan of the museum's layout are available at the entrance.* 🕐 *Open 9am-5pm.* 🕐 *Closed 1st Jan, Shrove Tuesday, Good Friday, 1st May, 1st Nov, 24, 25 and 31 Dec.* 🎫 *€8.50.* ☎ *(089) 21 791; www.deutsches-museum.de.*

Founded in 1903, this museum – one of the most important in the world for scientific and technical matters – is built on an isle in the Isar *(Museumsinsel)*. It traces the history of science and technology from the beginning of time to the present and explains physical processes and phenomena. Around 1.3 million people visit it each year. Besides a large number of original items and reconstructions are dioramas and scale models. According to the wishes of founder and Bavarian electricity pioneer **Oskar von Miller**, the displays invite visitors to inquire, touch and discover.

Ground Floor

Environment, metallurgy, transportation, electricity, and civil engineering are a few of the subjects addressed in the museum's ground floor. In the Railway Hall are famous steam engines, including the 1912 S-3/6 which powered the Bavarian Express, and the first electric locomotive *(Siemens, 1879)*. The Aeronautical Section exhibits early jet planes, including the Messerschmitt Me-262, the first jet fighter made on a production line, helicopters, gliders and vertical take-off machines.

An Elbe sailing ship (1880) and an Italian steam tug (1932) stand at the entrance to the Navigation Department *(continued in the basement)*.

Basement

Among many other displays, the Navigation Section highlights naval construction, warships (including U-1, the first

😊 A Bit of Advice 😊

Two other museums near Munich described in this guide exhibit works by German Expressionists: the Lenbach Collections (*Blaue Reiter* movement) and the Buchheim Museum in Bernried (*Die Brücke* movement).

First electric locomotive (1879)

German submarine, built in 1906), methods of navigation, fishing techniques, and Jacques Picard's 1958 bathysphere.

A section on mining follows and includes a model salt mine.

The Automobile Department shows an 1885 carriage with a Benz engine, an 1891 steam-driven Serpollet, luxury cars of the 1920s and 1930s (Daimler, Opel, Horch, Bugatti) and racing cars (1936 Auto-Union Grand Prix Type-C), an among others.

First Floor

The most interesting section here is perhaps Aeronautics. Gliders built by the engineer Lilienthal (c 1885), the pioneer of this form of flight, can be seen. Also a 1917 Fokker Dr I Triplane, made famous by Baron von Richthofen's "circus" in the First World War. Note also the Wright Brothers' Type-A Standard (USA, 1909), a Blériot Type XI (1909) and a Junkers F-13 (the first true airliner, 1919).

From this most recent gallery devoted to aeronautics, there is direct access *(by escalator)* to the second floor section on space flights.

Department of Physics

Physical laws and their application feature in the Department of Physics: optics, mechanics, electronics, thermology, nuclear physics, alchemy, musical instruments and much more.

Second Floor

Manufacture of glass and ceramics, printing; photography (Daguerre's apparatus, 1839) and textiles fill this floor.

Third Floor

Weights and measures, climatology, agriculture, data processing and computer science are a few of the displays featured. There is also access to the fourth floor observatory *(visits must be booked in advance)*.

Fifth Floor

Astronomy is the chief focus, including ancient astronomical equipment. The planetarium is featured upstairs, on the Sixth Floor.

Residenz★★

🕐 *Early Apr to mid Oct: 9am-6pm; mid Oct to Mar: 10am-4pm. Open until 8pm on Thu. Combined ticket for the Residenzmuseum and Schatzkammer. ☞ €9. ☎ (089) 29 06 71; www.residenz-muenchen.de.*

In 1385, the Wittelsbachs began construction of this new royal palace *(Neuveste)*, which, with the passing of time, expanded considerably around seven courtyards. This tremendous building now houses the municipal collection of Egyptian art and the municipal numismatic collection. Visitors who are pressed for time, however, should direct their attentions first to the treasury and palace museum.

Schatzkammer★★ (Treasury)

🕐 *Same opening times as the Residenz. ☞ €6. Free audio guide recommended.*

This is one of the most fascinating collections of its kind in Europe, a testimony to three centuries of Bavarian rulers' passion for collecting things. The magnificent displays of gold work, enamels, crystal ware and carved ivories are guaranteed to fascinate. Among the highlights are the superb cross executed for Queen Gisela of Hungary (after 1006), Heinrich's crown from 1280 and a dazzling example of the goldsmith's art inlaid with precious stones.

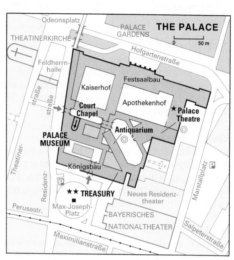

Residenzmuseum★★

☞ *€6. The tour changes at 1:30pm. Plan available at the entrance.*

Visitors who want to see all the museum's exhibits should take both morning and afternoon guided tours (which are different). Both include the most important rooms: the Ancestors' Gallery or Antiquarium.

The **Morning Tour** includes the enormous **Antiquarium** (c 1570) inlaid with marble, the oldest part of the palace, impresses with its painted ceilings and innumerable Antique busts. The **State Rooms** *(Die Reichen Zimmer – 1730-37)* illustrate with great flair early Rococo style. A highlight of the tour is the **Royal Apartments** in the Königsbau (King's Wing), which Ludwig I had built between 1826 and 1835.

The **Afternoon Tour** includes masterpieces from the workshops of Meissen, Nymphenburg, Frankenthal and Sèvres are on display in the **Porcelain Rooms**. The 17C **Hofkapelle** (Court Chapel) is dedicated to the Virgin Mary, patron saint of Bavaria. The **Reiche Kapelle**, severely damaged in 1944 but whose furnishings were saved, now lives up to its name.

Altes Residenztheater★

Access from outside the Residenz. 🕐 *Same opening times as the Treasury.* 🕐 *Closed during rehearsals. ☞ €2.*

This enchanting red and gold Rococo theatre was built by **François de Cuvilliés** between 1751 and 1753 (and is alternately known as Cuvilliéstheater). The prince-elector's box is set apart by the elegance of its hangings, marble and stuccowork.

Walking Tour

Old Town★★ (Altstadt) 👣 *See itinerary on the city map.*

Marienplatz★

This square is the heart of Munich. In the centre rises the **Mariensäule**, a column erected by the Prince-Elector Maximilian in 1638, in honour of Mary, patron saint of Bavaria. The north side is occupied by the neo-Gothic **Neues Rathaus** (1867-1908), whose **carillon** *(Glockenspiel)* installed in the tower's oriel window, is a favourite tourist attraction. When the mechanism is activated *(at 11am, noon and 5pm)*, brightly coloured figures in enamelled copper emerge and enact the Dance of the Coopers *(Schäfflertanz, below)* and the Tournament which accompanied royal weddings in the 16C *(above)*. The façade of the **Altes Rathaus**, with its stepped gables and bell turrets, occupies the eastern side of the square; a toy museum *(Spielzeugmuseum)* occupies the tower.

Peterskirche

Baroque vaulting remodelled this 13C, three-aisle Gothic church in the 17C and 18C. The centre section of the high altar is occupied by an Erasmus Grasser statue of St Peter (1492). The church's 1386 bell-tower is affectionately nicknamed "Old Pete" by Müncheners. Visitors braving the climb to the top *(306 steps)* are rewarded with a splendid view of the city.

Viktualienmarkt (Food Market)★

This market claims two centuries of tradition. It has been held here since 1807. Fresh fruit and vegetables, meat and fish are sold every day. The market stalls, kiosks and beer garden (in warm weather) ensure a lively atmosphere and a great lunch. Two of the six fountains recall local comedian Karl Valentin and his partner Liesl Karlstadt.

Heiliggeistkirche

Another Gothic original, this hall-church was completely transformed between 1723 and 1730. The façade, however, is neo-Baroque and dates from 1888. The mid-15C Virgin in the north aisle, said to be by Hammerthal, was once in the Benedictine abbey at Tegernsee.

▶ *Cross the Talstraße, take the passage beneath the old town hall, and turn right into Burgstraße.*

Weinstadel

Burgstraße 5. This is the oldest house (1552) in Munich, in days gone by the municipal office of the Clerk of the Court. The façade is decorated in *trompe-l'œil*.

▶ *At no 10 Burgstraße opposite the Weinstadel, take the vaulted passageway to Ledererstraße, then cross diagonally into Orlandostraße.*

Karl Valentin

The comedic talent of Valentin Ludwig Fey (1882-1948), nurtured since his childhood in Munich's suburbs, rapidly brought him international acclaim. This nonconformist actor, author and friend of Brecht produced sketches that were both grotesque and tragic, earning him the nickname of "metaphysical clown". A trip to the Valentin-Karlstadt museum (Tal 50, near the Isartor) will take you into the world of this local star.

Hofbräuhaus

The best-known of the famous Munich beer halls stands on Platzl and dates from 1589. Every day, in this great beer temple waiters serve 100 hectolitres (17 500 pints) of beer in one-litre (1.75 pints) tankards *(Maßkrug)*. In many of the rooms orchestras perform popular songs. The huge vaulted **Bierschwemme**, on the ground floor, is the rowdiest part of the building; here tourists and locals out with their families sit around large wooden tables eating sausages and drinking beer.

▶ *At the far end of the square, turn left into Pfisterstraße.*

March Beer

The March "strong beer" season originates with 17C Franciscan monks, traditional brewers who, in order to get through Lent, invented a high-alcohol beer thought to be more energizing. Drinking was permitted during Lent, but to be safe they took a barrel to the Pope for approval. He readily assented, believing that such a bad beer (it was very strong and probably damaged by the journey) was punishment enough. These spring beers traditionally end in "ator".

Alter Hof (Old Castle)

This building, a quadrilateral opening onto an inner courtyard, was the official Wittelsbach residence from 1253 to 1474. The south wing has an elegant tower with half-timbered corbelling (late 15C), known locally as the *Affenturm* (monkey tower).

▶ *The Hofgraben leads to Max-Joseph-Platz, enclosed on the north and east by the palace.*

Nationaltheater

Built between 1811 and 1818, the national theatre, home to the Bavarian State Opera, was endowed with one of the largest stages in the world, with space for 2 100.

Residenz★★ (See above)

▶ *Continue to the left of the Residenz via Residenzstraße.*

Odeonsplatz

On the westside of this square stands the 19C Leuchtenberg-Palais, built for Eugène de Beauharnais, Count of Leuchtenberg, now the Bavarian Finance Ministry. To the south, the **Feldherrnhalle** portico completes Ludwigstraße; the northern end leads to a triumphal arch *(Siegestor)*.

Theatinerkirche★

A fine example of Baroque ecclesiastical architecture, this church was built between 1663 and 1688, first under the direction of the Italian Barelli and later by Zuccalli, who came from Graubünden, Switzerland. Inside, the stuccowork is particularly rich, the Italian stuccodore having paid special attention to the smaller load-bearing arches and the pendentives. The wreathed double colonnade of the high altar is also embellished.

▶ *From Salvatorstraße, go to Kardinal-Faulhaber-Straße.*

Erzbischöfliches Palais (Episcopal Palace)

Kardinal-Faulhaber-Straße 7. **François de Cuvilliés** built his finest palace between 1733-37. Now an Archbishop's Palace, it boasts a magnificent pink and white façade with a rounded balcony supported by cherubs.

Frauenkirche and Neues Rathaus on Marienplatz

Palais Portia
Kardinal-Faulhaber-Straße 12. This pink and grey mansion, designed in 1694, was transformed in the Rococo in 1735, for one of Karl Albrecht's favourites, Countess Portia.

▶ *Take the alley at the end of Kardinal-Faulhaber-Straße.*

Frauenkirche★
The architect of this vast Late Gothic hall-church (1468-88) was **Jörg von Halspach**, who also designed the old town hall. The exterior of the church, in dark-red brick, is sober; the onion domes, which since 1525 have crowned the two towers at the west end, have become the symbol of the city.

In striking contrast to the exterior, the brilliant white **interior** makes an immediate impression. Eleven pairs of octagonal pillars support the reticulated vaulting. Seen from the entrance, the perspective of these columns forms a continuous line, effectively hiding the aisles.

The south side aisle contains the lavishly built monumental **cenotaph**★ to Emperor Ludwig of Bavaria, worked in black marble by Hans Krumper (1619-22). All the chapels contain high quality paintings and altarpieces. The chapels off the ambulatory contain extraordinary 15C **stained-glass windows**. In the south tower is an elevator taking visitors to the **viewing platform** ★ (🕒 *Apr-Oct*).

▶ *Take the busy shopping street Neuhauser Straße towards the Karlstor.*

Michaelskirche★
This 16C Jesuit sanctuary was the first Renaissance church north of the Alps. The façade is decorated with pilasters and bands of script. The 15 statues are of sovereigns descended from the church's patron, the Archangel Michael, who is depicted between the two entrances.

The single nave inspired many builders of the Baroque School in south Germany. The pulpit and seven side altars date from 1697. Thirty of the Wittelsbach princes, including Ludwig II of Bavaria, are buried in the crypt *(Fürstengruft)*.

Richard-Strauss-Brunnen

Bas-relief sculptures on the central column of this fountain illustrate scenes from the opera *Salome*, which the famous Munich composer wrote in 1905.

▶ *Take Eisenmannstraße which turns into Damenstiftstraße, then the first alley on the left after Brunnstraße to Sendlingerstraße.*

Asamkirche★ (St Johannes Nepomuk)

The church, built in 1733, is always referred to locally under the name of the men who constructed it, the **Asam Brothers**: Cosmas Damian Asam, who specialised in the painting of frescoes, and Egid Quirin Asam, sculptor and stuccoworker. The church's remarkable unity of style is due to the fact that the two brothers drew up the plans themselves, and both executed and supervised every stage of the work. The church's interior is a work of Rococo artistry run amok. Color, stuccowork, gilding, statuary and embellishment of every sort leave no blank spaces.

▶ *Return to Marienplatz via Sendligerstraße and Rosenstraße.*

Sights

Central District

Schack-Galerie★

Prinzregentenstraße 9. ⏲ *Open daily except Mon-Tue, 10am-5pm.* ⏲ *Closed 1st Jan, Shrove Tuesday, 1st May, Ascension Day, Corpus Christi, Assumption. 3 Oct, 24, 25 and 31 Dec.* ⊜ *€3, €1 on Sundays.* ☎ *(089) 23 80 52 24; www.pinakothek.de/schack-galerie.*

Those interested in 19C German painting must visit this collection, which is exceptionally comprehensive. The collection, assembled by Count Adolf Friedrich von Schack (1815-94), spans Early to Late Romanticism and includes numerous works by lpainters Carl Rottmann, Moritz von Schwind, Carl Spitzweg, Arnold Böckliin and Anselm Feuerbach.

Münchner Stadtmuseum★ (City Historical Museum)

St.-Jacobs-Platz 1, in the stables of the old Arsenal. ♿⏲ *Open daily except Mon, 10am-6pm.* ⏲ *Closed Shrove Tuesday, 24 and 31 Dec.* ⊜ *€4, free admission on Sundays.* ☎ *(089) 23 32 23 70; www.stadtmuseum-online.de.*

This museum houses comprehensive collections on local history, including a display of home decor in Munich, paintings, musical instruments, marionette theatres, photography and film.

Deutsches Jagd- und Fischereimuseum (German Hunting and Fishing Museum)

Neuhauserstraße 2. ⏲ *Open 9:30am-5pm, Thu 9.30am-9pm.* ⏲ *Closed Shrove Tuesday, 24 and 31 Dec.* ⊜ *€3.50.* ☎ *(089) 22 05 22.*

The museum, housed in a former Augustinian church, displays on three levels a splendid collection of ancient and modern arms, trophies, paintings and drawings of hunting scenes, and stuffed animals.

Wittelsbacher Brunnen (Wilttelsbach Fountain)

Between Lenbachplatz and Maximiliansplatz.

Adolf von Hildebrand built this fountain in 1895 to mark the completion of a water canal, serving the city with clean drinking water.

Pinakothek Quarter

Propyläen
West side of Königsplatz.
This imposing gateway by Leo von Klenze (1784-1864) was completed two years before the Munich architect died. Inspired by the Propylaea of the Acropolis, it stands on the west side of the Königsplatz. The frieze represents the Greek war of liberation against the Turks.

Glyptothek★ (Sculpture Museum)
Open daily except Mon, 10am-5pm,Thu 10am-8pm. €3.50, €1 on Sun. (089) 28 61 00.
One thousand years of Greek and Roman sculpture are gathered under the roof of this museum, built with its Classical porch and Ionic colonnade. The scarcity of Greek statues makes the original marble statues here even more remarkable. The **Tenea Apollo** *(Gallery I)*, with his handsome, smiling face, is memorable; the **Barberini Faun** (c 220 BC) *(Gallery II)*, which appears sated with drink and half asleep, dates from the Hellenistic epoque. Note the **bas-relief by Mnesarete** *(Gallery IV)*, which is said to have adorned the tomb of Socrates' daughter, and the statue of *Irene*, the Goddess of Peace *(Gallery V)*.

A Cultural Centre
Ludwig I wanted **Königsplatz** to be the cultural heart of his "Athens on the Isar". The ancient model provided architect Leo von Klenze with inspiration (1816-30) for the "orders" of the buildings bordering the square: Doric for the Propylaea, Ionic for the Glypthothek, and Corinthian for the collection of antiquities.

Staatliche Antikensammlungen★ (State Collection of Antiquities)
Opposite the Glypthothek. Open daily except Mon, 10am-5pm (Wed 10am-8pm). €3.50, €1 on Sun. (089) 59 98 88 30; www.antike-am-koenigsplatz.mwn.de.
An important display of ceramics on the ground floor of this museum traces the evolution of pottery in Greece, which reached its zenith during the 6C and 5C BC. Geometric decoration was succeeded by the representation of black figures on a red background (illustrated by an amphora and a goblet by the painter Exekias). The transition toward the use of red figures against a background of varnished black can be seen on another amphora, where a single subject – Hercules' banquet in the presence of Athena – is treated in the two styles *(Gallery III, showcase 6)*. Certain vases (*loutrophora* and *lecythus* on a white ground) were destined for funerary worship; others for domestic use.
Bronzes on the first floor and **Etruscan jewellery** in the basement *(Galleries VII and X)* testify to the enormous craftsmanship enjoyed by these metalworkers.

Städtische Galerie im Lenbachhaus★ (Lenbach Collections)
Open daily except Mon, 10am-6pm. Closed Shrove Tuesday and 24 Dec. €5. (089) 23 33 20 00; www.lenbachhaus.de.
This 19C house containing the Lenbach collections is devoted mainly to the works of **Munich painters of the 19C**. Among these are the landscapes of EB Morgenstern and portraits by FA von Kaulbach and F von Defregger. There is also a set of powerful portraits by **Franz von Lenbach** himself *(King Ludwig I, Bismarck, Wagner)*.
But the gallery's international reputation is built above all on the avant-garde **Blaue Reiter** collection. Born in the tumultuous period just before the First World War, the movement is represented by its founder members, Kandinsky, Marc and Kubin, as well as by paintings of Jawlensky, Klee and Macke.

Englischer Garten Quarter

Englischer Garten★ (English Garden)

Not far from the city centre, this park, with its broad, tree-bordered lawn, streams and lake, was designed in the late 18C. It is particularly popular in summer, when a beer garden seating 7 000 people is open near the **Chinese Tower** (*Chinesischer Turm*). From the **Monopteros**, a circular temple built by Leo von Klenze, is a **view**★ of Munich's old town.

Bayerisches Nationalmuseum★★ (Bavarian National Museum)

Plan (in German) available at reception. ○ *Open daily except Mon, 10am-5pm, Thu 10am-8pm.* ○ *Closed Shrove Tuesday, 1st May, Pentecost, 1st Nov, 24, 25 and 31 Dec.* ☞ *€5.* ☎ *(089) 211 24 01; www. bayerisches-nationalmuseum.de*

Chinese Tower in the English Garden

M. Hertlein/MICHELIN

Maximilian II created this museum in 1885 with the aim of preserving Bavaria's artistic heritage. The rooms on the ground floor offer a survey of Bavarian arts and crafts from **Romanesque to Renaissance** (Galleries 1-19), including silver and gold plate and religious statuary. The interior of an **Augsburg weaver**'s studio is in Gallery 9; the **Renaissance and Baroque** periods are represented by tapestries (Gallery 22), medieval town representations and Italian bronzes (Gallery 25). The first floor houses musical instruments, silverware and porcelain.

Museum Villa Stuck

Prinzregentenstraße 60. Professor at the Munich Academy of Fine Arts from 1895 and a founding member of the Munich Secession, **Franz Stuck** (1863-1928) built this Jugendstil villa after his own plans. It was Stuck himself who made the furniture, the panelling, the bas-reliefs, sculptures and coffered ceilings.

A Little Exercise

The people of Munich practise all kinds of sports in the English Garden: besides joggers, cyclists and basketball players, you may even see surfers on the large artificial wave which starts from one of the bridges on Prinzregentenstraße.

Excursions

Schloss Nymphenburg★★

6km/4mi west of the city centre, leaving Munich on Marsstraße. ○ *Apr to mid Oct: 9am-6pm; from mid Oct to end of Mar: 10am-4pm.* ☞ *€5.* ☎ *(089) 17 90 80; www. schloesser.bayern.de.*

The oldest part of this palace, once the summer residence of the Bavarian sovereigns, is the 17C five-storey central pavilion, built in the style of an Italian palazzo. The Prince-Elector Max Emmanuel, who reigned from 1679 to 1726, added two lateral pavilions; his successors, Karl-Albrecht (1726-45) and Max III Josef (1745-77), then constructed outbuildings underlined the palace's resemblance to Versailles.

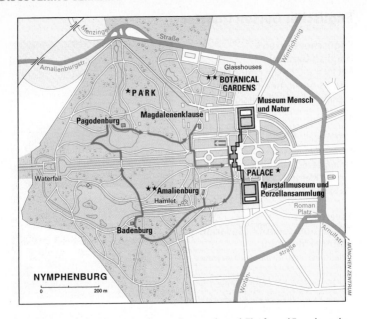

From 1701 onwards, the surrounding park was enlarged. The formal French gardens date from this period, as do the various park pavilions: Pagodenburg (1719), Badenburg (1721), Magdalenenklause (1728) and Amalienburg (1739).

Palace★

The splendid **banqueting hall**, a symphony of white, gold and pale green, was richly adorned with coloured stuccowork and frescoes by Johann Baptist Zimmermann and his son Franz. The rooms in the north wing are panelled, with tapestry hangings and paintings.

The most fascinating room in the main block's south wing is the one devoted to **Chinese lacquer**. In the south pavilion, the apartments of Queen Carolina contain the famous **Gallery of Beauties** conceived by King Ludwig I. Commissioned by the King to immortalise the most beautiful women of the epoch, these paintings were executed by the portraitist Joseph Karl Stieler (1781-1858).

Park★

See itinerary on Nymphenburg map. Most of the park can be seen from the top of the steps in front of the palace's main entrance. Below the steps, beyond the formal flower gardens, the Grand Canal, which ends in a waterfall, flows straight into the distance.

Amalienburg★★

🕐 *Same opening times as Schloss Nymphenburg.* 🚭 *€2.* ☎ *(089) 17 90 80.*
This charming hunting lodge by **Cuvilliés** is one of his most accomplished designs, a model for the Rococo country pavilions which so delighted the courts of 18C Germany. The simplicity and sobriety of the exterior contrasts vividly with the extraordinary richness of the interior. The **Hall of Mirrors** is a case in point: The combination of blue walls and ceiling, silver-plated stucco and wood-framed glass forms a marvellous ensemble.

Badenburg

A luxurious heated swimming pool, its ceiling decorated by mythological motifs, is the centrepiece of this 18C bathhouse.

Pagodenburg

The 18C taste for the Far East is exemplified in the design of this octagonal tea house. A drawing room, a Chinese room and a boudoir occupy the first floor.

Magdalenenklause

A "hermitage" built in the popular style of "artificial ruins", this pavilion is dedicated to St Mary Magdalene.

Marstallmuseum und Porzellansammlung
(Carriage Museum and Porcelain Collection)

🕐 *Same opening times as Schloss Nymphenburg.* 🎫 *€10.* ☎ *(089) 17 90 80.*

The museum is housed in the castle's former stables. Besides superb 18C and 19C harnesses, the Wittelsbachs' broughams, coaches, sledges and sedan chairs are on display. Note especially the coronation coach of Emperor Karl VII, and the state coach and personal sleigh of Ludwig II, all equipped with incredible luxury.

Above the old stables, a series of rooms houses the **Bäuml Collection of Nymphenburg Porcelain**. Painted figurines by Franz Anton Bustelli, factory master from 1754 to 1763, are particularly fine. The **reproductions in porcelain**★ – miniature copies of paintings in the Alte Pinakothek – were commissioned by King Ludwig I.

Museum "Mensch und Natur"
("Man and Nature" Natural History Museum)

Kids 👤🕐 *Open daily except Mon, 9am-5pm.* 🕐 *Closed Shrove Tuesday, 24, 25 and 31 Dec.* 🎫 *€2.50, €1 on Sundays.* ☎ *(089) 17 95 890; www.musmn.de. North wing of Nymphenburg Palace.*

Rarely is a natural history museum so interesting and accessible, especially to younger visitors. The museum provides information on the origins and internal structure of planet Earth, and on the evolution of life forms during the Earth's history. Informative interactive games encourage visitors to get involved.

Botanischer Garten★★ (Botanical Gardens)

👤🕐 *Open daily May-Aug, 9am-7pm; Apr and Sep, 9am-6pm; Feb-Mar and Oct, 9am-5pm; Jan, Nov-Dec, 9am-4.30pm.* 🕐 *Closed 24 and 31 Dec.* 🎫 *€3.* ☎ *(089) 17 86 13 10.*

Reputed to be among the finest in Europe, the Botanical Gardens' Schmuckhof *(opposite the main building)*, Spring Garden and Rose Garden make for an unforgettable pastime, even for the most casual of plant lovers. Rhododendrons brighten the Alpine Garden; orchids and sub-tropical species bloom in the greenhouses.

Dachau Concentration Camp★

19km/12mi northwest. Follow signposting "KZ-Gedenkstätte". 👤🕐 *Open daily except Mon, 9am-5pm. Free (donations appreciated). Audio guide recommended (€3).* ☎ *(081 31) 66 99 70; www.kz-gedenkstaette-dachau.de.*

Nazi Germany's first concentration camp was organised near the pleasant, terraced town of Dachau on the orders of Heinrich Himmler in March 1933. Originally designed for the detention of German political opponents of the Nazi regime, the camp was soon flooded by tens of thousands of deportees, the majority of them Jews of diverse nationalities. More than 32 000 died there, excluding several thousand Russian prisoners-of-war shot dead on the nearby SS firing range. A tour of the site provides a better account of the Nazi concentration camp system than any book or television documentary, and is highly recommended.

Whether on a guided tour or independent, visitors are sobered by the **Ruins and Commemorative Monuments** replete in Dachau. Original huts were razed, but two have been faithfully reconstructed. Foundations of 32 others are still visible, offering a glimpse at the camp designed for 5 000 prisoners but home to 30 000 by 1944. At the rear camp entrance one can still read the inscription *"Arbeit macht frei" ("Freedom Through Work")*. A Jewish memorial, a Protestant commemorative sanctuary and a

Catholic chapel have been built within the precincts of the old camp. Land surrounding the cremation ovens has been turned into a park-necropolis. Outside the camp perimeter, is a Carmelite convent with a chapel which may be visited.

A **museum** housed in the former administration buildings outlines the penal system established there by the Nazis. The recently refurbished exhibition is sober and comprehensive *(in English and German),.* outlining the organisation of the concentration camps in Germany and Europe, looking closely at their model, Dachau. Statements, photographs and documents dating from that time illustrate the thematic descriptions of the camp's history, the prisoners' daily life, hard labour, "medical" experiments, mass executions and the liberation of the camp.

Other Sights

Olympiapark
5km/3mi northwest of the centre, via Dachauer Straße. &. ⏱ *Apr to early Oct,* ⬟. *guided tour at 11am (Fußballtour, €5) and 2pm (Erlebnistour, €7). Olympiaturm: 9am-midnight.* ⬟ *€4.* ☎ *(089) 30 67 24 14; www.olympiapark-muenchen.de.*

Munich was host to the 20th Olympic Games in 1972. The many sports and leisure facilities continue to be used for international events. There is a museum on the Olympic Games in the old cycling stadium. The 1968 Olympiaturm (television tower), 290m/951ft high, features a scenic **panorama**★★ at the 190m/623ft level with exceptional views as far as the Alps.

BMW-Museum7
Petuelring 130. 5km/3mi north of the centre, via Schleißheimer Straße and Lerchenauer Straße. ⬟ *Closed for renovations until 2007.* &. ☎ *(089) 38 22 56 57.*

This cup-shaped silver building retraces the technical developments and social history of the 20C. Examples from BMW illustrate each of these themes, including aircraft engines (1916), motorcycles (1923) and motor cars (1928). Explanatory films, videos and slide shows accompany the exhibits.

Tierpark Hellabrunn★ (Hellabrunn Zoological Gardens)
Kids *6km/4mi from the city centre, leaving via Wittelsbacherstraße.* &. ⏱ *Apr-Sep, 8am-6pm; Oct-Mar, 9am-5pm.* ⬟ *€9.* ☎ *(089) 62 50 80; www.zoo-munich.de.*

Munich's zoo was founded as the world's first combined nature reserve and zoo in 1911, occupying an idyllic site on the banks of the Isar. Generous enclosures house 5 000 animals; highlights include the giant aviary, elephant house, jungle pavilion, tortoise house, polar zone and children's zoo.

Bavaria-Filmstadt (Bavaria Film Studios)
10km/6mi south of the centre via Hochstraße, Grünwalderstraße and Geiselgasteigstraße. &. ⬟ *Guided tour (1hr 30min). Mar to early Nov, 9am-5pm; early Nov to end of Feb: 10am-4pm.* ⏱ *Closed 24 and 25 Dec.* ⬟ *€10.* ☎ *(089) 64 99 20 00; www.filmstadt.de.*

Visitors learn about film and television and admire the original sets for features such as *The Boat* and *Neverending Story*. During the studio tour visitors are shown behind-the-scenes activities. Stuntspeople demonstrate their moves in the Action Show.

Schloss Schleißheim★
15km/9mi north. Leave via Schleißheimer Straße. &. ⏱ *Open daily except Mon, Apr-Sep, 9am-6pm; Oct-Mar, 10am-4pm.* ⏱ *Closed 1st Jan, Shrove Tuesday, 24 and 25 Dec.* ⬟ *€4.* ☎ *(089) 315 87 20; www.schloesser.bayern.de.*

Neues Schloss, the so-called "new" palace was built between 1701 and 1727 under Elector Max II Emanuel. The grand staircase leads to the State Apartments on the upper floor, the highlight being the huge banqueting hall in dazzling white. The princely apartments and **galleries**, adorned with European Baroque painting and works by 16C and 17C Dutch and Flemish masters, is impressive.

The palace **grounds** are laid out in formal French style by Carbonet and Girard, with a central canal as their main axis. At the far end of the park stands the 17C **Lustheim**; it houses a collection of Meissen porcelain.

Flugwerft Schleißheim★

Next to Schloss Schleißheim. 🅿🕐 *9am-5pm. Closed 1 Jan, Shrove Tuesday, Good Friday, 1 May, 1 Nov, 24, 25 and 31 Dec.* 🎫 *€3.50.* ☏ *(089) 315 71 40; www.deutsches-museum.de.* This Bavarian air corps hangar was built between 1912 and 1919. The Deutsches Museum has set up a new branch in the historic hangar, the **Museum of Air and Space Travel** *(Museum für Luft- und Raumfahrt)*. It houses a wealth of historic aircraft of all kinds.

Buchheim Museum★

45km/28mi southwest, in Bernried. Take the A95 to Starnberg then the lakeside road. 🅿🕐 *Open daily except Mon, Apr-Oct, 10am-6pm; Nov-Mar, 10am-5pm.* 🎫 *€8.50.* ☏ *(081 58) 99 70 20; www.buchheimmuseum.de.* This museum, founded by Günter Behnisch on the shores of the Starnberger See, houses the vast private collection of the German writer and painter Lothar-Günther Buchheim (author of *Das Boot*). Highlights of the collection are German Expressionism, in particular painters of the *Die Brücke* movement such as Kirchner, Heckel, Pechstein and Schmidt-Rottluff.

Driving Tour

Around Ammersee

Round trip of 116km/72mi

Ammersee★

Lying at an altitude of 533m/1 749ft, this glacial lake sits in a landscape of wooded hills. Swimming, sailing and boating can be had at small resorts like Dießen and Herrsching. Enthusiasts of the Rococo style should visit the abbey church at Andechs.

▶ *Follow the western lake shore to reach Dießen.*

Dießen

The **church**★ *(Marienmünster)* was built between 1732 and 1739 to replace a former monastery collegiate. The architect was Johann Michael Fischer, one of the most celebrated of the late, south German Baroque. The Asam brothers and François de Cuvilliés also contributed to the design.

▶ *The climb from Fischen to Andechs offers fine views of the lake.*

Andechs★

Crowning the Heiliger Berg (holy hill), this abbey *(Kloster Andechs)* overlooks the Ammersee from more than 200m/656ft. Its **church**★★, erected on a Gothic base, was remodelled as a Rococo building between 1751 and 1755. The architect JB Zimmermann (1680-1758) was responsible both for the frescoes and the stuccowork. Bavarian composer Carl Orff, famous for the *Carmina Burana*, is buried in the Chapel of Suffering. About 1.5 million visitors come to Andechs every year to visit the church and sample the famous local beer. Only the abbey church and brewery are open to the public. 🚶 *Guided tour (1hr): daily except Sat-Sun, at 3pm.* 🎫 *€2.50.* ☏ *(081 52) 37 60.*

▶ *Return to Munich via Herrsching and Seefeld.*

Exploring the Foothills of the Bavarian Alps

172km/107mi-tour. This route links up with the German Alpine Road (⛄ see Deutsche ALPENSTRASSE) at Wallgau.

▶ *Head south on the A8 until you reach exit 97, then join the B13 at Holzkirchen.*

Bad Tölz

The discovery of pure iodine springs, the richest in Germany, in 1845 transformed Tölz into a spa town famous throughout Europe. The wide curve and steep slope of the **Marktstraße**★, bordered by multicoloured façades, give the old town its special charm. At the top of the path which climbs up **Calvary Hill** *(Kalvarienberg)* stands a small chapel (1743) dedicated to St Leonard, whose powers are still widely revered among the peasants of Bavaria and Austria. The saint's anniversary, 6 November, is celebrated each year by a parade of rustic wagons and carts and drawn by teams of brilliantly harnessed horses *(see Events and Festivals)*. The Blomberg peak (1 248m/4 095ft) is a favourite day-trip destination *(chair-lift)*.

▶ *Head westwards on the B472 for 13km/8mi, then take the left fork to join the B11.*

Benediktbeuern

Built on the lower slopes of the Bavarian Alps foothills, the monastery *(Kloster)*, founded in 739, has been the home of St John Bosco's Salesians since 1930. The **abbey church** was remodelled between 1681 and 1686. On those parts of the vaulting without stuccowork, Georg Asam (father of the famous Asam Brothers) painted the first complete cycle of frescoes from the beginning of the Bavarian Baroque period: the Birth, Baptism, Transfiguration and Resurrection of the Saviour, the Descent of the Holy Spirit and the Last Judgement.

Elegant frescoes and stucco work make the **Anastasiakapelle**★ (1751-53), north of the old church, one of the most charming examples of Rococo art.

▶ *Continue south on the B11 for 21km/13mi.*

Walchensee★

40km/25mi southwest. Framed by dense woods, this deep blue reservoir lake is one of the beauties of the Bavarian Alps. A chair-lift rises to the Fahrenberg, from which a path leads in 30min to the summit of the **Herzogstand** (1 731m/5 679ft). From the observation deck, there is a superb **view**★★ taking in the Walchensee, the Kochelsee, the Karwendel massif and the rock wall of the Wetterstein, which culminates in the Zugspitze.

▶ *Head north on the B11 and return to Munich via the A95 at Sindelsdorf.*

Landsberg am Lech★

62km/39mi east via the A 96. A fortified frontier town between Swabia and Bavaria in the Middle Ages, Landsberg, on the old road from Salzburg to Memmingen, prospered through trade and the levying of tolls. Fortress gates, towers and perimeter walls still preserve an attractive medieval atmosphere.

There is a fine view of the **site**★ from the shady riverside promenade on the west bank of the Lech, where it meets the Karolinenbrücke *(the best place to park if the Marktplatz below is full)*.

Marktplatz★

Triangular in shape, the market place is surrounded by a remarkable group of coloured roughcast town houses. The **fountain** *(Marienbrunnen)*, in the centre, falls into a marble basin surmounted by a statue of the Virgin Mary.

Rathaus

The façade of this building was executed ca 1720 by Dominikus Zimmermann, one of the greatest artists of the Wessobrunn School, who built the Wies church and went on to be burgomaster of Landsberg (1749-54). The gable of the elegant structure is ornamented with finely worked stucco. The rest of the town hall was built between 1699 and 1702.

In the far corner of the square stands the **Schmalztor**, through which the upper town can be reached. Hemmed in on all sides by old houses, the 14C tower-gate is topped by a lantern turret roofed with glazed tiles.

▶ *The Alte Bergstraße climbs steeply to the "Bavarian Gate".*

Bayertor (Bavarian Gate)

With its projecting porch flanked by turrets and sculptures, this 1425 town gateway is one of the best preserved of its period in Germany. Outside the ramparts, the gateway is embellished with carved and painted coats of arms and with a Crucifixion.

▶ *Landsberg is on the Romantic Road (see ROMANTISCHE STRASSE) which continues northwards.*

MÜNSTERLÄNDER WASSERBURGEN★

MOATED CASTLES OF THE MÜNSTER REGION

There are some 100 moated castles found all over the Münster region, an area of low-relief. Most of them are privately-owned and can only be viewed from the outside, but some are open to visitors.

▶ **Orient Yourself:** The castles are spread over about 100km/63mi around the town of Münster. Few can be reached by public transport. The best ways of getting to them are by car or bicycle.

▣ **Don't Miss:** Anhalt is still in excellent condition and houses an interesting art museum.

◔ **Organizing Your Time:** Allow one hour to tour Anholt.

◔ **Also See:** *MÜNSTER, ESSEN (85km/53mi southwest), SAUERLAND (Soest is 63km/39mi southeast).*

A Bit of History

Remains of Medieval wars – The charming **Wasserburgen** – literally "water castles" – are found all over the Münster region. Witness to the incessant defensive battles between rival nobles, they are built on the sites of temporary encampments set up by the Teutons. The castles first appeared in the 12C in the form of wooden strongholds erected on artificial hills ("Motten") protected at the base by a surrounding defensive wall and a moat of water. The invention of firearms in the early 16C made this system of defence precarious, and it was replaced over time with proper fortifications isolated still more by moats or lagoons.

Many of these fortresses spread over two islands, joined by a bridge. The first isle, or "Vorburg", was used for outbuildings; the second, or "Hauptburg" for the dwelling. Their defensive character became less distinct over the centuries, and especially

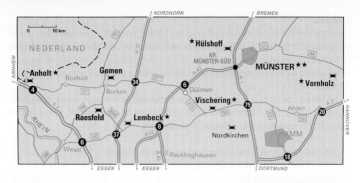

after the Thirty Years War (1618-48). After that, virtual palaces set in formal gardens began to appear.

Sights

Anholt★

🚶 *Guided tour (1hr). May to Sep, Tue-Sun, 11am-5pm; Oct to Apr, Sun, 1pm-5pm.* 🕐 *Closed 1 Jan, 24-26 and 31 Dec.* 🎟 *€6, combined ticket for guided tour and park, €8.* ☎ *(028 74) 453 53; www.fuerst-salm.de.*

Surrounded by a 34ha/84-acre landscaped park and restored Baroque garden, this moated castle (Hauptburg and Vorburg 12C-17C, converted into a Baroque palace ca 1700) is built around a square inner courtyard. The museum contains evidence of three centuries of royal home decor: paintings (Rembrandt, Brueghel, Murillo), tapestries, furniture, porcelain and weapons.

Gemen

This castle is a training centre; visits on request only: ☎ *(028 61) 922 00.*

The towers, battlements and buildings of this castle (15C, remodelled in the 17C) are grouped on a fortified islet arising from beautiful, shaded stretches of water. Today, the moated castle is a youth centre.

Hülshoff★

🕐 *Open from mid-Mar to mid-Dec, 9.30am-6pm.* 🎟 *€3.* ☎ *(025 34) 10 52.*

The massive square towers of the outbuildings (first island) complement a manor-house (second island) built in 1545. The brick and stone manor features gable ends and a turret with cupola and lantern. The poet **Annette von Droste-Hülshoff** was born here in 1797; there is a small museum recalling her life and work.

Lembeck★

🚶 *Guided visit (45min). From Mar to end Oct, 10am-6pm.* 🎟 *€4.* ☎ *(023 69) 71 67; www.schlosslembeck.de.*

The approach to this castle is impressive, a long perspective of driveway punctuated by Baroque gateways and flanked by arched entrances. The monumental edifice spread over two islands was built late in the 17C on the site of a 14C fortress. Huge towers with Baroque roofs stand at every corner. A few rooms inside can be visited. The biggest (Großer Saal) is embellished with fine panelling and stuccowork.

Raesfeld

🚶 *Guided tour (1hr) by appointment with the Tourist Office only.* ☎ *(028 65) 95 51 27.*

Raesfeld castle, built between 1643 and 1658 by Alexander von Velen, now consists only of a building with two wings, the Vorburg and the castle chapel. The tower (49.5m/162ft) and onion dome are visible from afar.

Vischering★

🕐 *Open Apr-Oct, Tue-Sun, 10am-12.30pm, 1.30-5.30pm; Nov-Mar, Tue-Sun, 10am-12.30pm, 1.30-4.30pm.* 🕐 *Closed 1 Jan and 24-26 Dec.* 🎫 *€2.50.* ☎ *(025 91) 79 90 11.*

Built on two islands and protected by a double fortified wall, Vischering is still one of the most formidable **fortresses** in the Münster region. A Renaissance building has been constructed on the medieval foundations of the Rundburg. The fortress houses a museum with special emphasis on furniture from various eras. The wall and ceiling paintings and splendid sandstone fireplaces are particularly impressive.

The Vorburg, which stands on a separate island, used to house the fortress' farm outbuildings. Today visitors can see an exhibition of life and work in the rural environment. There is also a richly decorated carriage house.

Not far from Vischering, 8km/5mi south-east of Lündinghausen, is the impressive 18C moated castle of **Nordkirchen**, known as "Westphalia's miniature Versailles."

Vornholz★   🖋   *see MÜNSTER: Excursions*

MÜNSTER★★

POPULATION: 271 000

Münster, the historical capital of Westphalia, lies amid a wooded plain studded with castles and manor houses. The city, one of Germany's most important university centres, has been restored to reveal many fine Gothic, Baroque and Renaissance façades. 🛈 *Klemensstraße 9, 48127 Münster,* ☎ *(0251) 492 27 10.*

▸ **Orient Yourself:** Münster can be reached via the A 1 (Dortmund-Bremen), and is one hour by car from the big towns of the Ruhr.

🅿 **Parking:** Garages are located throughout the Old City, near the main train station, near the Residenzschloß and near the theatre on Wasserstraße.

🏛 **Don't Miss:** The cathedral and the Prinzipalmarkt.

🕐 **Organizing Your Time:** Allow one full day to see the sights of Münster.

🖋 **Also See:** *MÜNSTERLÄNDER WASSERBURGEN, OSNABRÜCK (56km/35mi north via the A 1), RUHRGEBIET (Dortmund is 67km/42mi south via the A 1).*

A Bit of History

The Peace of Westphalia – This treaty, signed on 24 October 1648, ended the Thirty Years War. During the five years of negotiations, the Emperor shuttled between Protestant Osnabrück and Catholic Münster, where the treaty was finally signed. The

WHERE TO EAT

🍴🍴🍴 **Kleines Restaurant im Oer'schen Hof** – *Königsstraße 42* ☎ *(0251) 484 10 83* 🕐 *Closed Sun-Mon* 🍴 This establishment is spread over three floors of an old glazed brick house. Pleasant ambience, where rustic furniture is mixed with modern paintings.

WHERE TO STAY

🛏🛏 **Hotel-Restaurant Hiltruper Hof** – *Westfalenstraße 148, 48165 Münster-Hiltrup* ☎ *(0251) 278 80 Fax (0251) 7878 www.hiltruper-hof.de* 🅿 ⊷ *17 rooms* 🛏 🍴🍴 *Restaurant.* For 150 years this little family-run hotel has welcomed guests into well-cared for guestrooms. Sports and leisure equipment is available locally and the hotel is a good departure point for bike trips.

treaty recognised and confirmed the cession to France of Alsace, guaranteed the independence of Switzerland and the Netherlands, and favoured the development of Prussia. Three religious faiths were recognised, the Calvinists receiving the same rights as the Lutherans and Roman Catholics.

Sights

Dom★★

A squat building with two towers, this church is in the transitional style typical of Westphalia in the 13C.

Entering via the 16C south porch, the visitor sees an inner door surrounded by 13C statues and overlooked by a Christ in Judgement. A 16C statue of St Paul looks down from the pier. and its bays lie beneath rounded vaulting. The side aisles are very low. In the ambulatory there is a 1540 **astronomical clock**★ in which the hours are struck by metal figurines wielding hammers.

MÜNSTER						
Alter Fischmarkt	Y	2	Hammer Str.	Z	30	Salzstr.	YZ	72
Alter Steinweg	Y	5	Johannisstr.	Z	39	Spiekerhof	Y	78
An der Apostelkirche	Y	8	Ludgeristr.	Z		Steinfurter Str.	Y	80
Bahnhofstr.	Z		Mauritzstr.	Y	48	Überwasserstr.	Y	83
Bogenstr.	Y	12	Mauritztor	Y	51	Universitätsstr.	YZ	86
Drubbel	Y	16	Pferdegasse	Y	63	Verspoel	Z	89
Eisenbahnstraße	Z	20	Prinzipalmarkt	YZ		Wasserstr.	Y	92
			Rothenburg	Z	69	Wolbecker Str.	Z	96

| Domkammer | Y | M² | Westfälisches Landes-museum | | |
| Rathaus | YZ | R | für Kunst und Kulturgeschichte | YZ | M¹ |

The Chapel of the Holy Sacrament is richly **furnished**★ (note the an 18C silver tabernacle by an Augsburg craftsman).

The cathedral's modern **Treasury**★★ **(Domkammer)** blends with the cathedral to which it is indirectly attached. On the ground floor, fourteen 15C reliquary busts of the Prophets in copper and silver, the 11C head-reliquary of St Paul, and a 13C Virgin surround the **Processional Cross** of the Chapter, which is the focal point of the whole treasure house. *Off the cloister.* ♿🕐 *Open Tue-Sun, 11am-4pm.* 🕐 *Closed 1 Jan, Good Fri-Easter Sun, 1 May, Pentecost, 24-26 and 31 Dec.* ✎ *€1.* ☎ *(0251) 49 53 33.*

Westfälisches Landesmuseum für Kunst und Kulturgeschichte★ (Fine Arts Museum)

♿🕐 *Open Tue-Sun, 10am-6pm.* 🕐 *Closed 24, 25 and 31 Dec.* ✎ *€3.50.* ☎ *(0251) 59 07 01; www.landesmuseum-muenster.de*

The medieval art of Westphalia lives on through the statuary of the churches of Münster. There is a collection of **altarpieces**★★ by von Soest, Koerbecke and the Masters of Liesborn and Schöppingen.

Prinzipalmarkt★

The Principal Market is the busiest and most historic street in town with elegant houses that were once the homes of rich burghers. Under the arcades, attractive shops compete for space with restaurants and beer halls.

Rathaus

♿🕐 *Open Tue-Sun, 10am-5pm, Sat-Sun, 10am-4pm.* ✎ *€1.50.* ☎ *(0251) 492 27 24.*
The late-14C town hall is an impressive example of Gothic civic architecture.

Friedenssaal★ (Peace Hall)

The wood-panelled council chamber, now named after the peace treaty, dates from the second half of the 12C. In 1648 it was the backdrop to the peace between Spain and the Netherlands, which heralded the whole Treaty of Westphalia.

Lambertikirche

Groined vaulting over the centre nave and star vaults above the side aisles are the striking features of this Gothic hall-church. The neo-Gothic tower with its openwork **spire**★ was added in the 19C. Still visible from the tower are the iron cages that held the bodies of the Anabaptist rebel leaders displayed to the public following the defeat of their uprising in 1536.

Residenzschloss★

This Baroque palace is now part of the university. The red brick of the elegant three-part façade designed by Johann Conrad Schlaun is variegated with sandstone facings. At the back, surrounded by water, lies a park *(Schlossgarten)* with an adjoining botanical garden.

The Anabaptists

This Reform movement out of Zürich refused to acknowledge infant baptism, reserving the rite for believing adults. What began as a peaceful movement for change evolved into a revolution under the pressure of savage persecution once they dared voice criticism of the state. The group achieved supremacy in Münster, leading a reign of terror in 1534. The era was brought to an end after a 16-month siege ending with the hanging of its leaders. The Anabaptists, or Rebaptists, were spiritual forerunners of the Mennonites and the Amish.

Excursions

Telgte
12km/8mi east on B 51.
In the centre of Telgte, next to the Baroque pilgrimage chapel with a Pietà from 1370, is the local museum, Heimathaus Münsterland. One of its prize exhibits is a folk art textile, the **Lenten Veil**★ (1623), which measures 32m²/344sq ft.

Freckenhorst
26km/16mi east on B 51.
The Collegiate Church★ (Stiftskirche) is a fine example of pre-Romanesque German architecture (♿ *see Introduction*).

Ostenfelde
36km/22mi east on B 51. The graceful **Vornholz Castle**★ (1666) stands in a rolling landscape forested with ancient oaks. Built on two islets, this is a typical Münsterland "water castle" (♿ Münsterländer Wasserburg – *see below*).

Münsterländer Wasserburgen – ♿ *see MÜNSTERLÄNDER WASSERBURGEN*

NAUMBURG★

POPULATION: 29 700

The pretty town of Naumburg lies on the edge of the Thuringian basin, surrounded by vineyards and wooded hillsides. The town's exceptional cathedral marries Roman and Gothic architecture. The philosopher Friedrich Nietzsche spent a lot of time in the town at various stages of his life. The last weekend in June marks the kirsch festival. 🛈 *Markt 6, 06618 Namburg, ☎ (034 45) 20 16 14.*

▶ **Orient Yourself:** Naumburg is in the middle of the "Saale-Unstrut-Triasland" National Park and makes a pleasant and practical base for exploring the region.
👁 **Don't Miss:** Cathedral Sts. Peter and Paul.
🕐 **Organizing Your Time:** Allow half a day to see Naumburg.
♿ **Also See:** *HALLE (47km/29mi north), WEIMAR (50km/31mi southwest), LEIPZIG (63km/39mi northeast).*

A Bit of History

Important trading centre – The seat of a bishopric since 1028, by the 12C Naumburg was already developing as a civic entity independent of its cathedral. The city was an important trading centre in the Late Middle Ages and Renaissance period. The "Peter-Pauls-Messe" held here was a serious rival to the trade fair in Leipzig.

A model town – Largely spared damage during the Second World War, in 1991 Naumburg was one of five cities in the nine new Federal German states selected as a model for restoring old city centres.

Sights

Dom St. Peter und Paul★★
Access via Domplatz. This double-chancel church is a perfect example of the evolution from Late Romanesque to Early Gothic. The Romanesque nave was built in the

early 13C; by the late 13C the western section was completed with Early Gothic features. The eastern chancel is separated from the central nave by a rood screen, the only remaining hall-church rood screen in Germany.

The West Chancel features a magnificent **rood screen**★★ by the Master of Naumburg. The partition wall depicts poignant, life-like scenes of the Passion as a human tragedy. The splendid central portal depicts a Crucifixion group, surmounted by the Majesty of God as a fresco in a quatrefoil. The same master also created the famous **statues**★★★ of the cathedral's benefactors.

View of Naumburg with the Cathedral in the background

Marktplatz

The large **market square** is edged with 16C-17C houses. The **town hall**, a Late Gothic building, has a beautiful portal from 1612 and boasts six transverse gables with tracery decoration. The same façade design is repeated on the *Schlößchen* (1543), behind which towers the church of St Wenzel. The *Hohe Lilie* (municipal museum), with its Late Gothic corbie gable and traced transom, stands at the entrance to Herrenstraße.

St-Wenzel★

The original church on this site was first recorded in 1228. The present building was constructed as a Late Gothic hall-church with an unusual floor plan in the 15C. Between 1610 and 1618, five Renaissance tribunes were added, and up to the mid-18C the interior was transformed into the Baroque style with a mirror-vaulted ceiling, magnificent carved altar, pulpit and organ. This instrument is one of the largest surviving works by **Zacharias Hildebrand**. It was put through its paces by Johann Sebastian Bach, no less. Inside are also two fine paintings by **Lucas Cranach the Elder**: *The Adoration of the Magi* (1522) and *The Blessing of the Children* (1529).

Town houses

In Jakobstraße note the Alte Post (1574) with its three-storey oriel. In **Marienstraße** there are plenty of interesting old houses to look at. The extravagantly ornate portals testify to the town's prosperity. **Herrenstraße** features some fine oriels; the oldest in Naumburg at house no 1. The *Lorbeerapotheke*, chemist's shop adjacent to it, also boasts a splendid oriel, as does the house at no 8 (1525).

Marientor

This is the only one of the five original town gates to have survived. It is a rare example of a double gate with gatehouses, a courtyard with a bend in it to trap intruders, and a watchpath. Its nucleus dates from the 14C, but it was extended in the 15C.

Nietzsche-Haus

(Am Weingarten) From 1890 until 1897, during his collapse into mental and physical decline, Nietzsche was cared for in this house by his mother. Photos and documents (in German) evoke the intellectual life and works of the traveller-philosopher.

Excursions

Freyburg

7km/4.5mi north. This wine-growing centre stands in a picturesque location on the banks of the Unstrut, dominated by the Neuenburghigh above the town. Visitors can travel by steamer along the river as far as the Naumburg flower fields.

Shloss Neuenburg★

🕐 *Open Apr to Oct, Tue-Sun, 10am-6pm; Nov to Mar, Tue-Sun, 10am-5pm.* ⊛ €3.50. ☎ *(0344 64) 355 30; www.schloss-neuenburg.de.*

The Neuenburg was founded in 1090 by Ludwig der Springer, the Landgrave of Thuringia. It represented the eastern counterpart to the Wartburg fortress in the west. The 13C double **chapel**★, an extremely unusual type of building, is unusual, its lower floor reserved for the people and the upper floor for the higher nobility. The two floors are linked by a small grille in the ceiling. There are about a dozen beautifully furnished rooms to visit in the royal apartments.

Schulpforta, near Bad Kösen

On B 87, just before Bad Kösen, around 6km/3.5mi west. 🕐 *Cistercian abbey church and estate, open Apr to Aug, 10am-6pm; Sep to Mar, 10am-4pm.* 🕐 *Closed 24 Dec-6 Jan.* *Guided tours only of historic buildings (75min), Apr to early Oct, Sat at 10:30am and 2pm.* ⊛ €2.50. ☎ *(0344 63) 351 10.*

The **Cistercian monastery**, which was founded in 1137, was closed in 1540. Since then it has been the home of the renowned provincial school, whose famous scholars include Schlegel, Fichte, Klopstock and Friedrich Nietzsche, who joined the school in 1858. The **monastery church**, with its imposing west façade from ca 1300, has been under restoration for some considerable time.

Bad Kösen★

On B 87, around 7km/4.25mi west. This attractive little health resort on the Saale boasts a unique **technical monument,** the **brine extraction unit**★.

The **Romanesque house** *(by the double set of brine extraction rods)*, now used as a museum, was first recorded in 1138 as the Schulpforte monastery guesthouse. 🕐 *Open May to Oct, Tue-Sun, 10am-noon, 1-5pm, Sat-Sun, 10am-5pm; Nov to Apr, Wed, 10am-12 noon, 1-4pm, Sat-Sun, 10am-4pm.* 🕐 *Closed from mid-Dec to mid-Jan.* ⊛ €2. ☎ *(0344 63) 276 68.*

The ruined fortresses of **Rudelsburg** and **Burg Saaleck**, which were destroyed during the Thirty Years War, lie in an attractive 12C **site**★ high above the Saale 3km/2mi to the south of Bad Kösen. They are a popular tourist destination.

NEUBRANDENBURG

POPULATION: 68 600

This town, founded in 1248 at the behest of Margrave Johann von Brandenburg, is built on an almost circular ground plan, criss-crossed by a grid-like network of streets. When 80% of the old town was destroyed in 1945, the fortifications with their four unique gates were quite remarkably spared any damage, making them a principal point of attraction to tourists. 🚹 *Marktplatz 1, 17033 Neubrandenburg,* ☎ *(0395) 194 33.*

▶ **Orient Yourself:** Mid-way between Berlin and the Baltic coast, Neubrandenburg is to the northeast of the pretty lake of Tollensesee.

🅿 **Parking:** There is a garage in the heart of the old city, on Neutorstr. and Stargarder Straße.

🕙 **Don't Miss:** Neubrandenburg's medieval wall.

🕐 **Organizing Your Time:** Plan at least an hour to explore the town wall.

Especially for Kids: Climbing the old wall and towers, and outdoor recreation in the Feldberger Seenlandschaft.

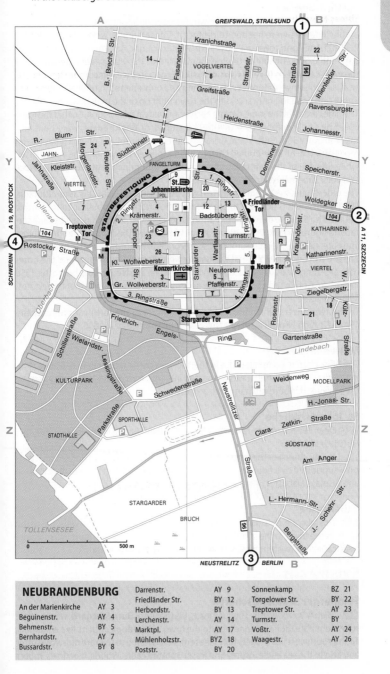

⚐ **Also See:** *MECKLEMBURGISCHE SEENPLATTE (Waren is 43km/27mi west via the 192 road), GREIFSWALD (66km/41mi north), Insel USEDOM (Mellenthin is 79km/49mi northeast).*

Sights

Fortifications★★

Kids Some 50 years after the town was founded, it became obvious that considerable defences were needed to protect it. Consequently, work was begun on a 2.3km/1.4mi-long town wall, over 7m/23 ft in height, 1.40m/4ft 7in wide at the base and 0.60m/1ft 10in at the top. Boulders from the vicinity were used to build the wall, capped by several rows of bricks. Four gates were incorporated into the wall, and these were closed every evening and only opened in return for payment. These remained the only access to the town right up to the mid-19C.

The gates are all of the same design, each an individual fortification. So that the town could be safely defended, 3- to 4-floor bastions, or **Wiekhäuser**, were built into the wall every 30m/98ft. There were 56 of them in the 16C, 25 of which have been reconstructed. All able-bodied citizens were expected to maintain the Wiekhäuser, while defence of the gates was the duty of the four principal guilds: Bakers, Wool Weavers, Shoemakers and Blacksmiths.

The oldest gate, the **Friedländer Tor,** was built just after 1300. It is 19m/62ft high. On the outside it is possible to see the transition from the Romantic to the Gothic period. The **Stargarder Tor,** built during the early 14C, is emphasised by nine terracotta figures in long stiffly-pleated robes, known as "Die Jungfrauen" *(the maids).* The outer gate is especially sumptuously decorated. The **Treptower Tor,** built ca 1400, at 32m/105ft, is the highest of the gate towers. Both the main gate and the outer gate are sumptuously decorated with brick tracery. The **Neues Tor,** built after 1550 in the Late Gothic style, combines the decorative elements of the other three gates. The outer gate no longer exists.

Of the two towers which provided reinforcement to the fortifications, only the 19m/62ft-high **Fangelturm** remains. The spire was added in 1845.

Marienkirche

The brick church, completed late in the 13C, was partly rebuilt in neo-Gothic style in the mid-19C. The church was renovated into a concert hall in 1996 and is used by the Neubrandenburg philharmonic orchestra.

St. Johanniskirche

♿🕐 *Open Tue-Sat, 10am-12 noon, 1-6pm, Sat, 10am-4pm.* 🕐 *Closed bank holidays.* ☎ *(0395) 582 22 88.*

The 13C-14C church of the former Franciscan monastery features a Renaissance **pulpit**★ supported by a figure of Moses, which dates from 1598. It is made of limestone and displays alabaster reliefs of Christ and the Evangelists.

Tollensesee

Kids This lake, which is 10.4km/6.5mi in length and almost 3km/2mi wide, lies to the south of the town, in the middle of an extremely attractive glacial (terminal moraine) landscape. The western bank slopes steeply up to Brodaer woods.

Excursions

Feldberger Seenlandschaft★

Kids *75km/47mi round trip.* The road leads, via the site of **Burg Stargard**, whose castle ruins dominate their surroundings, to the town of **Woldegk** with its five windmills. To the southwest lies a lovely hilly lake region. It is home to the rare old-world otter and also to the sea eagle, osprey and lesser-spotted eagle. Woods, meadows, moors and lakes alternate attractively between **Fürstenwerder** and **Feldberg**. The former house of the writer **Hans Fallada** in **Carwitz**, which stands in an idyllic lakeside location, is now a memorial.

Neustrelitz

27km/17mi south. The former residence of the dukes of Mecklenburg-Strelitz still bears witness today to their proud past. Visitors can admire the **Schlossgarten**★ with its graceful buildings and monuments, part of which was laid out in the 19C as an English country park. The orangerie with its remarkable Pompeii-style **paintings**★, the Baroque town **church** (1768-78), the classical **Rathaus** dating from 1841, and the neo-Gothic **Schloßkirche** (1855-59) are all worth seeing.

Ravensbrück

19km/11mi south of Neustrelitz, 1km/0.6mi from Fürstenberg. Ravensbrück concentration camp was built on the shores of Lake Schwedtsee after 1938. It was Germany's largest camp for the detention of women. Up until 1945, 132 000 women and 20 000 men from over 40 nations were deported here. Tens of thousands died here. Evidence of the camp, such as the crematorium and the cell block, has been included in the **Mahn- und Gedenkstätte Ravensbrück** memorial. A permanent exhibition in the old SS camp commander's headquarters documents the history of the camp and the lives and deaths of its victims. ◷ *Open Tue-Sun, 9am-5pm.* ◷ *Closed 24-26 and 31 Dec.* ☎ *(0330 93) 60 80; www.ravensbrueck.de.*

SCHLOSS NEUSCHWANSTEIN★★★

Neuschwanstein castle, with its countless towers and light limestone merlons, is a fairy-tale castle come true and a product of the imagination of King Ludwig II of Bavaria (1845-86). The young ruler was an ardent admirer of the composer Richard Wagner, whose theatrical world he wished to re-create in this castle. Neuschwanstein is the most popular tourist sight in Bavaria and visitors should be prepared to queue for several hours in high season. However, the many footpaths near the castle will allow visitors to escape the crowds and find some tranquillity.

- ▶ **Orient Yourself:** Five kilometres east of Füssen, the castle is on a rocky ridge 200m above the Pöllat gorge, making an impressive **site**★★. The windows of the castle or the surrounding walkway permit arresting panoramic views of the Alpes, the Allgäu plain, the Alpsee lake and the deep gorges of the Pöllat.
- **Don't Miss:** The view of the castle from the Marienbrücke.
- ◷ **Organizing Your Time:** Allow half a day for your visit, including waiting time.
- **Especially for Kids:** The royal bed chambers.
- **Also See:** *ROMANTISCHE STRASSE, Deutsche ALPENSTRASSE, FÜSSEN (5km/3mi east), WIESKIRCHE (25km/16mi northeast).*

A Bit of History

The construction – **King Ludwig** (*see MÜNCHEN*) found the ideal location for "Neu-Hohenschwangau" (the name "Neuschwanstein" came in 1890) not far from Hohenschwangau castle *(see below)*, where he had spent part of his childhood and youth. He was unquestionably inspired, when planning Neuschwanstein, by the **Wartburg**, which he had seen in 1867.

The end of a dream – Ludwig II only lived at Neuschwanstein for 170 days. The work on the castle had emptied the royal coffers and the king's increasingly unpredictable behaviour led a government commission from Munich to bring him news of his dethronement on 10 June 1886. The king was found dead three days later in Lake Starnberg. The circumstances of his death, and that of his doctor, who had accompanied him on a walk that fateful night, have never been explained.

Visit

Guided tour (35min, commentary available in English). Apr to Sep, 9am-6pm; *Oct to Mar, 10am-4pm.* Closed 1 Jan, Shrove Tue, 24, 25 and 31 Dec. Ticket booths *open at 7.30am in season.* €9. (083 62) 93 98 80; www.neuschwanstein.com. *Combined ticket with Hohenschwangau:* €15. *Tickets are purchased before going up to the castle: 30min walk up gentle slope; by bus (10min, leaves every 30min, €1.80); on horseback (30min, stops mid-way, €5).* Visitors should be prepared to queue for *several hours in high season.*

The castle's interior, with its profusion of gilded panelling and wall paintings, seems almost unreal. The most distinctive rooms are, on the third floor: the **throne room**★ (unfinished), the **bed chamber**★ furnished with Gothic pieces, the **sitting room**★, with its Lohengrin-inspired decor, and the artificial stalactite cave with the adjacent winter garden, evoking the Tannhäuser legend. The design of the **minstrels' room**★★ *(Sängersaal)* is based on the Wartburg (*see EISENACH*), where the legendary poetry contest featured in Wagner's opera *Tannhäuser* was said to have taken place in the early 13C.

Visitors can also watch a film (20min, in English or German) on the king's life.

After the tour, visitors should take the opportunity to go up to Mary's bridge *(Marienbrücke, 10min on foot, steep slope)* to watch the Pöllat river cascade down a deep gorge and admire a splendid **view**★★ of the castle.

Excursions

Schloss Hohenschwangau★

Guided visit (35min). Apr to Sep, 9am-6pm; Oct to Mar, 10am-4pm. Closed *24 Dec.* €9. (083 62) 93 08 30; www.ticket-center-hohenschwangau.de.

Maximilian II of Bavaria, who was at the time still the Crown Prince, had this 19C castle built on the remains of a 12C fortress. The neo-Gothic style was in accordance with current taste, which tended to be medieval, and the Prince's predilection for

The wonderful Neuschwanstein castle of Ludwig II of Bavaria

F. Zaninotto/MICHELIN

Gothic with All Mod Cons

Ludwig II's plans for a home recreating Germanic mythology through Gothic architecture also took into account the latest scientific developments. The cranes used to build the castle were steam powered, a steel frame was used in the throne room, and the windows held broad panes of glass that were uncommon even in the 19C. Other features included a floor-based central heating system, flushing toilets, an elevator, electric bells to summon servants, and telephones on the third and fourth floors. Not so much the "Fairytale King" *(Märchenkönig)* as a man with his own private theme park.

chivalric romance. It was in these surroundings that the unfortunate King Ludwig II of Bavaria spent most of his youth.

The **castle** stands in a picturesque setting on a wooded hill. It is best to skirt this, following the road to a beautiful **viewpoint**★ on a shaded rocky spur of the **Pindarplatz** on the Alpsee. Enjoy the view, then cross the avenue to reach the castle.

In comparison to Neuschwanstein and in spite of the almost compulsive repetition of the etymological swan – *Schwan* – motif, Hohenschwangau has retained a comfortable feel. The length of time spent here by Queen Maria, Ludwig II's mother, explains the relatively personal atmosphere.

After viewing the maniacal over-decoration of the former rooms, visitors will welcome the clean lines of the maple and cherrywood Biedermeier furniture.

The old **music room** on the second floor contains evidence of the high esteem Ludwig II held for Richard Wagner, including the grand piano on which they both played. Don't miss the King's bedchamber, where the ceiling is painted to represent night stars.

NÖRDLINGEN★

POPULATION: 20 000

The former Free Imperial Town of Nördlingen lies in the middle of the Ries basin along the Romantic Road. It is first recorded in 898, and its development continued in concentric circles, witnessed by the street pattern and ring of fortifications.
Marktplatz 2, 86720 Nördlingen, ☎ (090 81) 43 80.

▶ **Orient Yourself:** Nördlingen occupies an important position at the gates of the Bavarian Plateau, in the centre of the Ries basin, a crater 25km/16mi in diameter and formed by a meteorite.

Don't Miss: The Rieskrater-Museum.

Organizing Your Time: Allow half a day to see the primary sights of this city.

Especially for Kids: The Rieskrater-Museum.

Also See: *ROMANTISCHE STRASSE, EICHSTÄTT (65km/41mi northeast), ULM (73km/46mi southwest).*

Sights

St-Georgskirche★

This late-15C hall-church is surmounted by a majestic, 90m/295ft-high bell-tower, known as Daniel, on which a look-out still keeps watch. Climbing the 350 steps to the top of the tower allows visitors a view of the Ries crater. Fan vaulting covers the interior in style. The pulpit (1499) is reached via a corbelled staircase with only three steps. Note the curious little **organ** on the finely worked baldaquin *(on the right side)*. The **Crucifixion group**★ and the statues of St George and Mary Magdalene, created by Niclaus Gerhaert von Leyden, still remain on the Baroque altar replacement.

Stadtmauer★ (Town Walls)

The Nördlingen town walls are the only remaining fully accessible walls of their kind in Germany. Access to the historic, picturesque old town is possible through just one of the five gates, and a walk right around the town walls, which are for the most part covered, reveals 11 watchtowers. One of the most attractive parts of the walk is along the battlements from the Berger Gate via the Alte Bastei, or old bastion, to the Reimlinger Gate. The history of the town wall is documented in the Löpsinger gate tower.

Stadtmuseum★ (Local Museum)

🕐 *Mar to early Nov, Tue-Sun, 1:30pm-4:30pm.* 🕐 *Closed Good Fri.* 👓 *€3.* ☎ *(090 81) 273 82 30; www.stadtmuseum-noerdlingen.de.*
The museum displays cover the pre- and early history of the Ries basin, along with the history of the Imperial Town of Nördlingen. There is a collection of 19C painting, and altar panels by Old German masters, such as the wings (1462-77) of the altarpiece from St Georgskirche by Friedrich Herlin.

Rieskrater-Museum★

Ⓚ *Next to the Stadtmuseum.* 🕐 *Tue-Sun, 10am-noon, 1:30-4:30pm.* 🕐 *Closed 1 Jan, Shrove Tue, Good Fri, 24-26 and 31 Dec.* 👓 *€3.* ☎ *(090 81) 273 82 20.*

The Nördlingen Giant Crater was formed approximately 15 million years ago when a meteorite hit the earth. Just imagine it – a giant stone sphere, 1km/0.6mi in diameter, hits the earth at a speed of 70 000kph/44 000mph, penetrating up to 1km/0.6mi into the rock! The energy of 250 000 Hiroshima atom bombs is released, and a wave of pressure and heat extinguishes all life within a range of 100km/62mi. A crater 14km/9mi in diameter is formed, which eventually spreads to 25km/16mi due to all the rock that subsequently falls in. The crater, which was originally 4km/2.5mi deep, is gradually filled in over the course of millions of years, but later partially excavated and opened out again. The Rieskrater-Museum, which is housed in a carefully restored barn (1503), attempts to give the layperson an understanding of this scarcely imaginable phenomenon.

WHERE TO EAT

🍴🍴🍴 **Meyer's Keller** – *Marien-höhe 8* ☎ *(090 81) 44 93 www.meyerskeller.de* 🕐 *Closed for 2 weeks in Feb and Mon and Tue lunchtimes* Parquet flooring, modern artworks and contemporary decor set the tone here. Sit out on the pleasant terrace under the old trees. Tasty regional dishes are served in the brasserie.

WHERE TO STAY

🛏🛏🛏**Hotel Sonne** – *Marktplatz 3* ☎ *(090 81) 50 67 Fax (090 81) 23999 www.kaiserhof-hotel-sonne.de* 🕐 *Closed 2 weeks in Nov* 🅿 *29 rooms* 🍴🍴🍴 *Restaurant* This traditional hotel in the heart of Nördlingen dates from 1477. Behind its façade are comfortable guestrooms and higgledy-piggledy original corridors and stairways. Rural decor with vaulted ceiling in the dining room.

Excursion

Neresheim Abbey★

19km/12mi southwest. The abbey church (Klosterkirche), started in 1745 under the direction of Balthasar Neumann, was the last work of the great Baroque architect. It was not finished until 1792. Inside, the seemingly weightless ceiling decoration was painted between 1771 and 1775 by Martin Knoller.

NORDFRIESISCHE INSELN★

This group of wild islands, in perpetual battle against marine erosion, makes up part of the Schleswig-Holsteinisches Wattenmeer National Park which was created in 1985. The islands' fragile dunes are protected from the ravages of the North Sea by dykes and artificial banks.

▶ **Orient Yourself:** The Northern Frisians face the west coast of Schleswig-Holstein, in the North Sea, next to the border with Denmark. The islands are reached by ferry, departure points being determined by final destination. For the islands of Föhr and Amrun, ferries leave from Dagebüll-Hafen (43km/27mi north of Husum). For Pellworm, ferries leave from Nordstrand. Ferries for the Halligen islands leave from Husum and Nordstrand

⊛ **Don't Miss:** The tiny villages that dot each of these North Sea islands.

🕐 **Organizing Your Time:** Allow 45 minutes each way for ferries to Föhr; two and a half hours to Amrun; 35 minutes to Pellworm.

Kids **Especially for Kids:** Island cruising and exploration.

⤷ **Also See:** *HUSUM on the mainland (ferries for Dagebüll from Amrum and the Halligen islands), Insel HELGOLAND (ferries from Dagebüll, Husum and Hörnum on the isle of Sylt, among others).*

Sights

Sylt★★ (⤷ *see Insel SYLT*)

Föhr

Ferries to Föhr: Dagebüll-Föhr (45min): 9 to 12 ferries a day. ⊛ €9.70 round-trip. Dagebüll-Amrum (90min): 6 to 10 ferries a day. ⊛ €14.40 round-trip. Timetables vary. Information and car reservations from Wyker Dampfschiffs-Reederei Föhr-Amrum GmbH, in Wyk, on Föhr. ☎ 018 05 08 01 40.

Föhr is a peaceful island boasting a mild climate. The island is largely marshland, dotted with pretty villages (Nieblum, Süderende or Oldsum). The beaches lie on the island's south; its north has a windswept forest rich with birdlife.

The port of **Wyk** is in the southeast, featuring well-tended narrow streets that beg exploring. Visitors interested in local nature, history and culture should visit the **Friesenmuseum** (🕐 *Open Jul to Aug, 10am-5pm; Mar to Oct, Tue-Sun, 10am-5pm; Nov-Feb, Tue-Sun, 2-5pm.* 🕐 *Closed 24 and 31 Dec. ⊛ €2.50. ☎ (046 81) 25 71).* **Dunsum** is the departure point for a walk across the mudflats to Amrum.

Amrum

Ferries to Amrum: Schlüttsiel-Amrum (2hr 30min): 1 to 2 ferries daily. ⊛ €14.40 there and back. Timetable varies. Information and car reservations from Wyker Dampfschiffs-Reederei Föhr-Amrum GmbH, in Wyk, on Föhr. ☎ 018 05 08 01 40; www.faehre.de.

Amrum's west coast is home to sand dunes, heaths, woods, farmland and mudflats, a rich habitat for sea birds. **Nebel** grew up around the **medieval church of St Clemens** in the 16C. The town also features the **Öömrang Hüs**, an 19C sea captain's house. The far north of the island, in the bird sanctuary **Amrum Odde**, is the departure point for walks across the mudflats to Föhr.

Halligen★

These tiny islands are all that remains of mainland marshes once part of the coastal region. In 1600 there were more than 25 documented islands here; the number has fallen to 10 thanks to storm floods or merging. Most of the Halligens are unprotected by sea dikes, resulting in total island submersions up to 50 times a year. At these times only the houses on manmade mounds (terps) are visible above water. **Langeneß** is the largest with 18 mounds. Various shipping companies offer boat trips to the Halligens.

Pellworm

Ferries for Pellworm: Leaving Nordstrand/Strucklahnungshörn, Pellworm. Ferries (35min): 3 to 7 ferries daily according to the tide. ⊜ *€9 per person, €45 per car not including passengers there and back.* ☎ *(048 44) 753; www.pellworm.de.*
This island is enclosed by a 25km/15mi-long and 8m/20ft-high dike, without which Pellworm would be inundated, lying as it does below sea level. The island's main feature is the ruined tower of the **Alte Kirche St Salvator**, whose origins date back to the 11C-12C. Nearby lies the **Friedhof der Heimatlosen** (Cemetery of the Homeless), where the bodies of strangers washed up on the island's shores are buried.

Nordstrand

This marshy island is linked to the mainland by a 4km/2mi causeway. Nordstrand is formed of reclaimed farmland (polders) and villages on man-made mounds terps.

NÜRNBERG★★

NUREMBERG
POPULATION: 500 000

Before the Second World War, the capital of Franconia was so typically "Germanic" that the city was chosen by the Nazi party for its huge annual rallies each September. In the medieval centre are still some half-timbered burghers' houses with embellished gables, the remains of what was once one of the most beautiful medieval cities in Germany. From the Friday before the first Sunday in Advent until Christmas Eve the marketplace is still dominated by its famous Christkindlesmarkt. ⓘ *Hauptmarkt 18, 90403 Nürnberg,* ☎ *(0911) 233 61 35.*

▸ **Orient Yourself:** The second largest city in Bavaria after Munich, Nuremberg stands in the centre of the Franconian plateau. The major north-south (A 9) and east-west (A 3) motorways make it an obligatory stop on tourist itineraries.
Ⓟ **Parking:** Garages are located throughout the city. Visit http://wap.parkinfo.com for fees and locations.
Ⓐ **Don't Miss:** The German National Museum and the old town.
Ⓒ **Organizing Your Time:** Allow half a day for the German National Museum and for the suggested walking and driving tours.
Ⓚ **Especially for Kids:** A walk along the city's medieval ramparts.
Ⓐ **Also See:** *BAYREUTH (82km/51mi northeast), BAMBERG (63km/39mi northwest), ROTHENBURG (83km/51.5mi west), REGENSBURG (103km/64mi southeast).*

A Bit of History

The Golden Age – Nuremberg reached its peak of fame during the 15C and 16C. On the crossroads of major trade routes and a mainstay for Franconian craftsmanship, the city once rivalled Augsburg. The first German science university was founded in Nuremberg in 1526. Sculptors **Veit Stoß** (c 1445-1533) and **Adam Krafft** (c 1460-1508/09); bronze caster **Peter Vischer the Elder** (c 1460-1529); **Michael Wolgemut** (1434-1519), painter of altarpieces, and above all his pupil **Albrecht Dürer** (1471-1528) all profoundly influenced Germany from this city. From the 13C, **Hans Sachs** and the

Meistersinger (mastersingers) brought new life to German poetic form; they provided the inspiration for Wagner's opera *The Mastersingers of Nuremberg* in 1868.

The Nuremberg Trials – It was in Hitler's "ideological capital" of the Third Reich that the notorious anti-Semitic laws were promulgated in 1935; and it was here that the Allies brought 24 high-ranking officials and eight Nazi organisations before an international military tribunal to face charges of war crimes. The trials took place between November 1945 and October 1946 in the Palace of Justice on Fürther Straße, now a Civil Court.

Germanisches Nationalmuseum★★★

&.Ⓒ *Open daily except Mon, 10am-6pm, Wed 10am-9pm.* Ⓒ *Closed Shrove Tuesday, 24, 25 and 31 Dec.* ⚌ *€5, free admission on Wed 6-9pm.* ☎ *(0911) 133 10; www.gnm.de.* The museum, founded in 1852, houses the largest collection of art and antiquities in Germany, with 20 000 of its millions of exhibits on permanent display. The heart of the collection is a former 14C Carthusian monastery; the museum then spread to the neighbouring Augustinian monastery and across the Kartäusergasse.

▶ *In view of the extent of the collections, visitors are advised to be selective in their visit. Don't be put off by a closed door: all the museum rooms are open unless otherwise indicated.*

Upper Floors
The **picture gallery** *(first floor, Section B)* displays works by **Albrecht Dürer**, Hans Baldung Grien, Hans Holbein the Elder, Albrecht Altdorfer and Lucas Cranach the Elder. There are also some later works, including a *Self-portrait* by Rembrandt. Works by **Veit Stoß**, Tilman Riemenschneider and Ignaz Günther are especially outstanding within the sculpture collection. The most noteworthy of the **scientific instruments** *(Section A)* is the so-called **Behaim terrestrial globe** of 1492 to 1493, the oldest surviving depiction of the earth in globe form. The second-floor galleries include an excellent exhibition of 19C and 20C art and design *(Section E)*, notably including Ernst Ludwig Kirchner's Expressionist *Self-portrait* (1914).

Ground Floor
The impressive collection of medieval religious art treasures *(Section C)* illustrates the work of craftsmen from the Carolingians to the early Renaissance. Many types of decorative arts are represented, including glass, ceramics, furniture and textiles.

M. Hertlein/MICHELIN

The Pegnitz river and Heilig-Geist-Spital, in the heart of old Nuremberg

Address Book

WHERE TO EAT

USEFUL TIPS

The city's culinary speciality, *Nürnberger Rostbratwürste* can be sampled at booths in the city centre (often sold as *Drei in an Weckla*: three sausages in a roll) and in most restaurants serving traditional fare.

🍴 **Historische Bratwurstküche Zum Gulden Stern** – *Zirkelschmiedsgasse 26* 🕿 *(0911) 205 92 88 www.bratwurstkueche.de.* The oldest *Bratwurstküche* is set in this historic house of 1419, with country-style and wooden decor. Nuremberg sausage grilled over beechwood charcoal is the specialty.

🍴🍴🍴 **Sebald** – *Weinmarkt 14* 🕿 *(09101) 38 13 03 www.restaurant-sebald.de* 🕓 *Closed Sun.* ✂ This charming house in the old town harbours a modern restaurant and bistro. Yellow marble walls and warm shades give the place a Tuscan atmosphere.

🍴🍴🍴 **Essigbrätlein** – *Weinmarkt 3 Closed 24 Dec-1 Jan, Easter, 1 week in Aug and Sun-Mon* 🕿 *(0911) 22 51 31.* This inn of 1550, preserved in its original state, exudes a certain air of nostalgia. Andree Koethe serves ambitious dishes of his own invention.

WHERE TO STAY

🍴🍴 **Hotel Am Jakobsmarkt** – *Schottengasse 5* 🕿 *(0911) 200 70 Fax (0911) 2007200 www.hotel-am-jakobsmarkt.de* 🕓 *Closed 24 Dec-2 Jan* 🅿 ✖ *77 rooms* ⬜ The functional, modern rooms of this smart hotel are spread over two buildings: the main building and a half-timbered annex reached via an inner courtyard.

🍴🍴 **Hotel-Restaurant Jägerheim** – *Valznerweiherstraße 75, 90480 Nürnberg-Zerzabelshof* 🕿 *(0911) 94 08 50 Fax (0911) 9408585 www.hotel-jaegerheim.de* 🅿 *33 rooms* ⬜ 🍴🍴 *Restaurant.* A quiet hotel near the exhibition grounds, well served by public transport. Smart rooms with pale wooden furniture and traditional restaurant.

🍴🍴🍴 **Le Méridien Grand-Hotel** – *Bahnhofstraße 1* 🕿 *(0911) 2 32 20 Fax (0911) 2 32 24 44 www.grand-hotel.de* ✖ *186 rooms* ⬜ 🍴🍴 *Restaurant* The hotel is next to the central station, a stone's throw away from the old town. A luxurious setting, with refined Art Nouveau rooms.

GOING OUT

Altstadthof – Braustüberl "Schwarzer Bauer" – *Bergstraße 19-21* 🕿 *(0911) 22 72 17 www.altstadthof.de* 🕓 *Open 11am-1am (terrace until 10pm).* Different beers brewed on the premises and home-made brandy are served here. They can be sampled in the small bar itself, in the beer garden in the rear courtyard, or you can take them away.

Blauer Adler – *Bahnhofsplatz 5 (in west wing of the central station)* 🕿 *(0911) 2 42 62 90 www.blaueradler.com* 🕓 *Open Sun-Thur 9am-1am, Fri-Sat 9am-4am.* The modern design of this immense bar, tastefully laid out over various levels, presents an interesting contrast with the station's historic architecture. The house speciality is brochettes.

CULTURE

Events are listed in the monthly magazines *Plärrer* and *Prinz*, available from the city's bookshops and newspaper kiosks. The free monthly listings magazine *doppelpunkt* can be found in bars, cinemas and shops. Online information: www.kubiss.de, www.events-nuernberg.de, www.congressing.de.

SHOPPING

Karolinenstraße, Breite Gasse and Königsstraße are the city's busiest shopping streets, with department stores and a wide variety of specialist shops. If you're looking for small gifts, *Lebkuchen* are ideal; traditionally made during Advent, this gingerbread is now available year round and is often packaged in attractive metal boxes.

Handwerkerhof – *Königstor (opposite central station, near the Frauentorturm)* 🕿 *(0911) 8 60 70 www.handwerkerhof.de* – *Mar-Dec: boutiques: Mon-Fri 10am-6.30pm, Sat 10am-4pm, Restaurant: Mon-Sat 10:30am-10pm.* Small crafts shops and traditional restaurants in a picturesque walled-in courtyard. Ideal for souvenir-hunting (gingerbread) and a pleasant place for a short break.

The gold and silversmith's work should not be missed. The section on ancient musical instruments *(Section D)* boasts the world's largest collection of historical pianos. There is also an extensive prints and drawings section and a numismatic collection *(Section F)*.

Walking Tour

Old Town★★

Hauptmarkt (Marketplace) and Schöner Brunnen★ (Beautiful Fountain)

The 14C Gothic **fountain,** comprising 40 figures (copies) over four levels, dominates the marketplace. At the top of the 19m/62ft-high pyramid-shaped structure, Moses is surrounded by the Prophets; around the base are the seven Electors and a series of nine Old Testament and medieval heroes: three forefathers, three Jews and three Christians. A seamless gold ring is held captive in the railing *(on the upper part)*, where an apprentice locksmith is said to have placed it in the 17C. The hustle and bustle of the square, particularly during the Christmas market, masks the grisly origins of this place: the Jewish quarter stood there until 1349, when it was razed to the ground and its occupants burnt to death by the local inhabitants.

Frauenkirche★

A Gothic church on the east side of the market, built on the site of a destroyed synagogue; it was a gift from Karl IV and was built between 1350 and 1358. The gable, with its pinnacles and niches, was designed by Adam Krafft (early 16C) and crowns the beautiful façade, one of the only original parts. The 1509 clock above the balcony attracts visitors each day at noon, when a series of jacks appear to strike the hour. These colourful metal figures *(Männleinlaufen)* represent the seven Electors swearing allegiance to the Emperor after the Golden Bull in Nuremberg in 1356.

Inside, the **Tucher Altar** in the chancel is a masterpiece of the pre-Albrecht Dürer Nuremberg school of painting: the triptych (ca 1445-50) depicts the Crucifixion, Annunciation and Resurrection. Note the depiction of Jesus on his way to school, in the chancel.

Sebalduskirche★

This 13C church was enlarged in the 14C in honour of a clergyman from Nuremberg who was canonised in 1425. To the right of the entrance, at the far end of the first chancel, the **St Peter Altarpiece** (1485) takes pride of place, painted on a gold background in Michael Wolgemut's studio. In the centre, the richly decorated bronze **baptismal font★** (ca 1430) is the oldest bronze religious work in Nuremberg. In the nave, on the inner side of the great left pillar, is the painted statue of St Sebald (1390) and on the next column, the **Virgin Mary in Glory★** made of pear-tree wood.

The magnificent **tomb of St Sebald★★** stands in the centre of the west chancel. The Gothic shrine is part of a bronze display shelf by Peter Vischer (1519), supported by dolphins and snails and adorned with a host of statuettes.

Adam Krafft

Born in Nuremberg around 1460, Krafft left his mark on every church in the city. His early works – typical of the Late Gothic style – portrayed very expressive figures with tumultuous draperies, and rich decorative reliefs. He then moved towards greater clarity and his later, more monumental works, assume more rounded and restrained poses (see the Stations of the Cross from St John's cemetery, dating from 1505, in the Germanisches Nationalmuseum).

Stadtmuseum Fembohaus (Fembo Municipal Museum)

♿ 🕐 *Open daily except Mon, 10am-5pm, Sat-Sun, 10am-6pm.* 🕐 *Closed 1st Jan, Shrove Tuesday, Good Friday, 24-26 and 31 Dec.* ✎ *€5.* ☎ *(0911) 231 25 95.*

The **museum** is housed in a sandstone Renaissance mansion, the only patrician mansion in the city to survive in its entirety. The museum covers the history of Nuremberg.

Burg (Castle)

🔍 *Guided tour (1hr 30min).* 🕐 *Apr-Sep, 9am-6pm; Oct-Mar, 10am-4pm.* ✎ *€4.50.* ☎ *(0911) 22 57 26.*

Symbol of the city, the castle stands on a sandstone outcrop. The original **castle of the Burgraves** (*Burggrafenburg*), almost entirely destroyed in 1420, was completed in the 12C; its present appearance dates from the 15C.

Tiergärtnertorplatz

The half-timbered houses around the picturesque Tiergärtnertor square suffered the least damage during the Second World War.

Albrecht-Dürer-Haus★ (Dürer's House)

🕐 *Open daily except Mon, 10am-5pm, Thur 10am-8pm.* 🕐 *Closed 1st Jan, Shrove Tuesday, Good Friday, 24-26 and 31 Dec.* ✎ *€5.* ☎ *(0911) 231 25 68.*

Dürer bought this house in 1509 and lived here until his death in 1528. The interior explores the life and work of the artist through films, printing demonstrations and reproductions of works by the artist and his disciples, both past and present.

Stadtbefestigung★ (Fortifications)

Kids Completed in the mid 15C, these fortifications have remained practically intact. They comprised an inner and an outer ring (*Zwingermauer*), the ramparts of the former with a covered parapet walk. A wide dry moat (in which modern avenues now run) lay outside the latter. No less than 67 defensive towers still exist, including the four 16C **Great Towers** (Frauentor, Spittlertor, Neutor, Laufertor).

The most interesting sector lies between the Kaiserburg and the Spittlertor (*west side*). A 30min walk starts from the castle gardens (*Burggarten, below the Kaiserburg*). From the ramparts walk to the watch-path, which can be followed as far as the Neutorzwinger. Continue inside the ramparts. Cross the River Pegnitz via a suspension footbridge before concluding the promenade.

Heilig-Geist-Spital (Hospital)

This 14C-15C building, spread over two wide arches, spans a branch of the Pegnitz. The covered part of the bridge, known as the **Crucifixion Courtyard** on account of the Krafft's *Crucifixion Group*, used to be a home for the elderly.

Lorenzkirche★

A magnificent rose window enlivens the west face of this 13C-14C Gothic church. Inside (*enter via the south door*) is Veit Stoß's 16C masterpiece **Annunciation**★★ of carved wood. The **tabernacle**★★ (1493-96) by Krafft stands left of the main altar.

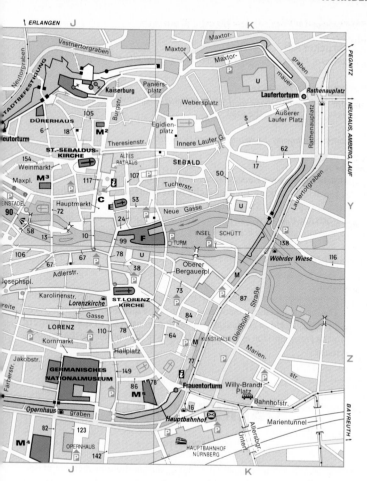

Driving Tour

Hersbrucker Alb
Round-trip of 109km/68mi. Follow Sulzbacher Str., then take the A9 toward Bayreuth.

Neuhaus an der Pegnitz★
This charming locality, dominated by the tower of Burg Veldenstein, comes suddenly into view after a bend in the road.

▶ *Continue following the Pegnitz toward Hersbruck.*

Hersbruck
An attractive little town, Hersbruck has stately burghers' houses and the remains of medieval fortifications. The **Deutsche Hirtenmuseum** (German Shepherds' Museum, *Eishüttlein 7*) in a fine half-timbered building (1524) contains collections of popular arts and traditions. Continue toward Happurg over the Pegnitz bridge, from which, looking back, there is a fine view of the Wassertor (fortified gate).

▶ *Return to Nuremberg, taking the B14.*

Erlangen
17km/10.5mi north. This residential Baroque town was a French Huguenot settlement. The Protestant church marks the centre of the quarter built for them. In an early-18C English **garden** (*Schlossgarten*) stands the **Fountain of the Huguenots**, built by the French in 1706 as a gesture of thanks to their protector, the Margrave of Bayreuth.

OBERSTDORF★★

POPULATION: 11 000

A well-known mountain and skiing village in the southernmost corner of Germany, this charming resort is also the departure point for walking tours. Motor traffic is banned from the centre of town. ▯ *Marktplatz 7, 87561 Oberstdorf,* ☎ *(083 22) 70 00.*

▶ **Orient Yourself:** Midway between Lake Constance and the castles of Ludwig II, deeply incised into the Allgäu Alps, and seven other valleys, the town lies at the junction of the valley of the Iller.
- ⌾ **Don't Miss:** A trip to the Nebelhorn or the Fellhorn.
- ⏱ **Organizing Your Time:** Allow a full day to explore this lovely Alpine resort.
- **Kids Especially for Kids:** A cable-car ride and climb up the Nebelhorn or Fellhorn.
- ⌀ **Also See:** *Deutsche ALPENSTRASSE (15km/9mi north), LINDAU (76km/48mi west), FÜSSEN (60km/38mi east) or the paths around GARMISCH-PARTENKIRCHEN (105km/66mi east).*

Walking Tour

Kids Nebelhorn★★
1hr 30min round-trip, of which 20min are by cable-car (3 stages to the trip). Operates every 10min. ⏱ *First departure 8.30am, last trip down from Höfatsblick at 4:50pm (summer) or 4:30pm (winter).* ⏱ *Closed 4-24 May, and 3 Nov to mid-Dec. Summer:* ☞ *€18 return trip, winter: €28.50 return trip.* ☎ *(083 22) 960 00.*

The highest cable railway in the Allgäu leads to the 2 224m/7 296ft-high summit of the Nebelhorn, from where, in clear weather, there is a **panoramic view**★★ over more than 400 Alpine summits, from the Zugspitze in the east to the Säntis in the west. The destination of numerous hikes, the Nebelhorn is also the point of departure for the demanding "Hindelang climb".

Fellhorn★★

Kids *Take the Fellhorn cable-car in two stages up to the summit (1 967m/6 452ft).* ① *Operates early May to late Oct, 8:20am-4:50pm; mid-Dec to mid-late Apr (depending on snow) 8:30am-4:30pm.* ◉ *Summer: €16 return trip, winter: €29.50 return trip.* ☎ *(083 22) 960 00.*
There is a wonderful **view**★★ over the Allgäu, the Austrian and Swiss Alps, from the 2 037m/6 683ft-high summit of the Fellhorn. The mountain has an easily accessible network of hiking paths, including an interesting flower walk *(Blumen- und Wanderlehrpfad)* with rare Alpine blooms all the way to the summit.

Excursions

Breitachklamm★★

6.5km/4mi southwest, plus a 1hr 30min walk there and back. ① *Accessible May to Sep daily 8am-5pm; Oct to Apr daily 9am-4pm.* ① *Closed from beginning Nov to mid-Dec.* ◉ *€2.50.* ☎ *(083 22) 48 87.*
In the lower gorge, galleries lead into sheer, polished walls, where the turbulent mountain stream has carved a course 100m/300ft deep into the bedrock. It is possible to return by a long series of stairways. From there hikers will arrive at the Walserschanze, on the Kleinwalsertal road, from which there is frequent bus service.

The Kleinwalsertal

17km/11mi – allow 30min. A high valley of the River Breitach, this mountain area was settled in the 13C by the **Walsers**, emigrants of Germanic origin from the Upper Valais. Today the Kleinwalsertal has Austrian police, German customs, a German postal service and Austrian stamps. (Adopting the Euro simplified money matters.) **Riezlern**, **Hirschegg** and **Mittelberg** are the most popular resorts of the Kleinwalsertal.

Address Book

WHERE TO EAT

◒◒ **Oberstdorfer Einkehr**
– *Pfarrstraße 9* ☎ *(083 22) 97 78 50 www.oberstdorf.net/einkehr Recommendations recommended.* The Oberstdorfer Einkehr is popular with locals and visitors. A traditional establishment with comfortable, panelled dining rooms and local specialities on the menu.

◒◒◒ **Maximilians** – *Freibergstraße 21* ☎ *(083 22) 967 80 www.maximilians-restaurant.de* ① *Closed 3 weeks in May and Jun, 3 weeks in Nov and Sun.* ⌿ Elegant restaurant furnished in country-house style typical of the region. Seasonal food is served with delicious refinement.

WHERE TO STAY

◒◒ **Hotel Traube** – *Hauptstraße 6* ☎ *(083 22) 80 99 40 Fax (083 22) 3168 www.hotel-traube.de* P *20 rooms* ⌸ ◒◒ *Restaurant.* Situated in the centre of town this traditional hotel has comfortable guestrooms furnished in country style. A sauna and a solarium are available for use and in the restaurant, a large choice of regional and foreign dishes are on offer. In summer months, check out the pleasant Biergarten.

◒◒◒ **Hotel Scheibenhaus**
– *Scheibenstraße 1* ☎ *(083 22) 95 93 02 Fax (083 22) 959360 www.scheibenhaus-oberstdorf.de* ① *Closed Apr and Nov* ⌿ P ✕ *8 rooms.* ⌸ Hospitality in the proper sense of the word, with minute attention to detail, including complimentary refreshments and homemade cakes, make this place stand out. Beautiful view of the Trettachtal and surrounding mountains.

OLDENBURG

POPULATION: 158 000

Steeped in tradition, this lively university city is the cultural and economic hub of the region. Seat of government for the Weser-Ems region, Oldenburg is becoming an increasingly popular commercial centre. ▯ *Wallstraße 14, 26122 Oldenburg,* ☎ *(0441) 157 44*

▸ **Orient Yourself:** Oldenburg is about 70km/44 mi west of the Dutch border. Its river port is linked to the Weser and the North Sea by the Hunte, and to the Benelux countries by a coastal canal *(Küstenkanal).*

▣ **Parking:** You'll find parking on the Schloßplatz and near the main train station on Willy Brandtplatz.

◉ **Don't Miss:** The Schlossgarten

◉ **Organizing Your Time:** Allow half a day to see the main sights of Oldenburg.

◔ **Also See:** *BREMEN (48km/30mi east), EMDEN (84km/53mi northwest), OSNABRÜCK (110km/69mi south).*

Walking Tour

Town Centre

The old city, which includes Germany's oldest pedestrian zone, also houses monumental buildings from five centuries, generous parkland and its former ramparts.

Schlossgarten★ (Castle Park)

A mild coastal climate has favoured the growth of magnificent trees and shrubs in this landscaped garden. From the weeping willows on the lakeshore there is a nice view of the Lambertikirche.

Schloss (Castle) – Landesmuseum für Kunst und Kulturgeschichte (Regional Art and History Museum)

♿ *Open Tue-Sun, 9am-5pm, Thu, 9am-8pm, Sat-Sun, 10am-5pm.* ◉ *Closed 1 Jan, Good Fri, Easter Sun, 1 May, Pentecost, 24, 25 and 31 Dec.* ▥ *€3.* ☎ *(0441) 220 73 00 www.landesmuseum-oldenburg.niedersachsen.de.*

The museum was built in the 17C and remodelled in the 18C and 19C. The first floor houses the Old Masters' gallery, with 16C-18C Italian and Dutch masters and 18C-19C European paintings. The series of miniature idyllic scenes by Tischbein (1751-1829) is particularly interesting. Items relating to Oldenburg's provincial history and culture are exhibited with commentaries on several floors.

Stadtmuseum★

♿◉ *Tue-Sun, 10am-6pm.* ▥ *€1.50.* ☎ *(0441) 235 28 81; www.stadtmuseum.oldenburg.de.*

Of interest are rooms from the villas Francksen (1877), Jürgens and Ballin, with paintings, furnishings and decor dating from the 17C to the early 20C. There are also departments on local history and an antiques collection.

Next door is the **Horsst-Janssen-Museum.** The illustrator and graphic artist was born and buried in Oldenburg. ♿◉ *Tue-Sun, 10am-6pm.* ◉ *Closed Good Fri, 1 May, 24 and 31 Dec.* ▥ *€1.50.* ☎ *(0441) 235 28 81.*

Augusteum

Elisabethstraße 1. ♿◉ *Open Tue-Sun, 9am-5pm, Thu, 9am-8pm, Sat-Sun, 10am-5pm.* ◉ *Closed 1 Jan, Good Fri, Easter Sun, 1 May, Pentecost, 24, 25 and 31 Dec.* ▥ *€3.* ☎ *(0441) 220 73 00.*

Landesmuseum Oldenburg

The former seat of the counts and dukes of Oldenburg, now home to the Regional Art and History Museum

Works by painters from the Worpswede colony are on show here along with such German Expressionists as Erich Heckel. Among the Surrealists, note Franz Radziwill.

Landesmuseum für Natur und Mensch Oldenburg

Damm 40-44. &. ○ *Open Tue-Sun, 9am-5pm, Fri, 9am-3pm, Sat-Sun, 10am-5pm.* ○ *Closed 1 Jan, 1 May, Pentecost, 24, 25 and 31 Dec.* ∞ *€2.* ☎ *(0441) 924 43 00; www.naturundmensch.de*

These exhibitions are focused on the northwest region of Germany with its varied landscapes and traces of pre- and early historic settlements. Natural, archeological and cultural aspects are presented in a display entitled "Neither sea nor land – the peat bogs, a lost landscape". A huge block of peat, in which ancient bodies were found buried, always attracts attention.

Excursions

Museumsdorf Cloppenburg★

31km/19mi south. &. ○ *Open Mar to Oct, 9am-6pm; Nov to Feb, 9am-4:30pm.* ○ *Closed 24 and 31 Dec.* ∞ *€4.10.* ☎ *(044 71) 948 40.*

In an area of about 20ha/50 acres, 53 historic buildings from the 15C to the 19C have been constructed around a lake and a church. Most of the buildings come from the region between the Rivers Weser and Ems. Large farmsteads, mills, peasants' and tenants' houses illustrate aspects of the history of Lower Saxony.

Steindenkmäler von Visbek (Megalithic Monuments)

38km/24mi south. In this group collectively known as **"The Intended"**, the Bride *(Visbeker Braut)* is a collection of granite blocks arranged in a rectangular pattern in a clearing that measures 80x7m/262x23ft. The Groom *(Visbeker Bräutigam)* comprises a dolmen, considered a sacrificial altar *(Opfertisch)*, and an alignment of 80 blocks in a rectangle 108x10m/354x33ft. At the western extremity of the site a funerary chamber recalls the dwellings of this period. *The site is a 30min round-trip walk from the Engelmannsbäke inn.*

OSNABRÜCK

POPULATION: 164 000

Preliminaries to the Peace of Westphalia started in Osnabrück and in neighbouring Münster. A member of the Hanseatic League, the town specialised in the textile and linen trade. 🖫 *Krahnstrasse 58, 49074 Osnabrück, ☎ (0541) 323 22 02.*

▶ **Orient Yourself:** Lying between the Teutoburger Wald and the Wiehengebirge heights, Osnabrück developed around two separate centres: the 9C town market; and the 11C Johanniskirche.

🅿 **Parking:** Garages are located throughout the city. The lot near the main train station is especially convenient.

🕭 **Don't Miss:** A visit to Tecklenburg.

🕓 **Organizing Your Time:** Allow half a day to see Osnabrück's sights.

👣 **Also See:** *MÜNSTER (56km south via the A 1), MÜNSTERLÄNDER WASSERBURGEN.*

Sights

Rathaus (Town Hall)
🕓 *8am-6pm, Sat 9am-4pm, Sun 10am-4pm.* 🕓 *Closed 1 Jan, 24 and 31 Dec ☎ (0541) 323 21 52.*
This early-16C building had to be restored after the Second World War, but still retains its Gothic look. The peace of 1648 was announced from its steps. The statue of Charlemagne stands above the entrance.

Friedenssaal (The Peace Chamber)
The hall in which peace negotiations were held is adorned with portraits of the heads of state and their delegates. The floor and ceiling have been rebuilt; the 16C wooden seats and chandelier are authentic. In the **Treasury** is the priceless 14C *Kaiserpokal* (Imperial goblet).

Felix-Nussbaum-Haus
Lotter Strasse 2. 👣🕓 *Open Tue-Sun 11am-6pm, Sat-Sun 10am-6pm.* 🕓 *Closed 1 Jan, Good Fri, 1 May, 1 Nov, 24 and 31 Dec.* 🕭 *€4. ☎ (0541) 323 22 07.*
This Deconstructivist museum building (1998) was designed by **Daniel Libeskind** to house 160 of Nussbaum's works. Its broken architectural lines and non-standard details combine to disorientate the visitor, a technique thought to mimic the turmoil of the Jewish painter **Felix Nussbaum**. The artist was born in Osnabrück in 1904. His work ranks him under Neue Sachlichkeit (New Objectivity).

Excursion

Tecklenburg★
23km/14mi southwest – around 90min. Leave the car in the lot at the town entrance.
Famous for its half-timbered houses and its position on the crest of the Teutoburger Wald, this is a popular small town. We recommend heading for the main square and then west, through the Legge gateway, to the oldest part, at the foot of the castle.

Before the Peace in 1648
Preliminaries to the **Peace of Westphalia** started in Osnabrück between the Emperor and the Protestant belligerents (Sweden and the Lutheran princes of Germany) five years before the end of the Thirty Years War. On the other side, the Roman Catholic powers negotiated with the Emperor in Münster. News of the treaties' final signature was announced in Osnabrück on 25 October 1648 to a crowd, at first incredulous and then bursting into a spontaneous hymn of thanksgiving.

OSTFRIESISCHE INSELN★

EASTERN FRISIAN ISLANDS

Due to the prevailing northwesterly tides and winds, the East Frisians are drifting ever farther southeast. To the north and east of the islands stretch sandy beaches covered with wicker-hooded deck chairs and windbreaks in summer.

▷ **Orient Yourself:** The seven inhabited Eastern Frisian islands lie between the Ems and the Weser deltas off the North Sea coast of Germany. Between the islands and the mainland are the mudflats, declared a national park in 1986. The islands are reached by ferry; departure points vary depending on the destination.

🕭 **Don't Miss:** Quiet exploration of these islands. Take your time.

🕘 **Organizing Your Time:** Allow 30min to two hours for ferry service, depending upon the destination.

🄺🄸🄳🅂 **Especially for Kids:** North sea cruises and island exploration.

👣 **Also See:** EMDEM (ferry from Borkum), BREMEN (98km/61mi from Wilhelmshaven, 131km/82mi from Emden).

Sights

Borkum

3 ferries a day (about 2hr) from Emden. 🚢 *€13.50 there and back.* ☎ *(049 21) 890 70.*

The largest of the Eastern Frisians boasts an impressive beach promenade with hotel façades from the turn of the century. There is a good view of the mainland and the "Hohes Riff" (high reef) seal bank from the 60m/200ft **Neuer Leuchtturm**, a lighthouse from 1879 *(315 steps).*

Juist

From Norddeich (around 75min). 🚢 *€16 there and back. Timetable information from* ☎ *(049 31) 98 70.*

This island (17km/11mi long) is home to an interesting **Küstenmuseum** *(Coastal Museum)* in the attractive village of Loog. The museum documents local coastal living, the history of the lifeboat service and the importance of dike building. At the exit of the village of Loog is the start of the nature conservation zone of **Bill**.

Fremdenverkehrsbüro, Hallig Langeness

Langeness: Sand undulations on the North Sea coast

The Local Brew

Statistics show that the Eastern Frisians drink 14 times more tea per capita than the inhabitants of the whole rest of Germany. Tea-drinking is a way of life here. The beverage was introduced to the region by the Dutch ca 1670 and soon caught on. Frederick the Great attempted to ban tea in 1777 but was forced to reconsider when so many disgruntled people left the region. Even during the Second World War the Eastern Frisians were allocated a more generous tea ration than others.

Eastern Frisian "tea ceremonies" are full of ritual. First warm the teapot. Then pour boiling water onto the tea leaves in the pot and leave to draw for 5min. Place a piece of white sugar crystal into a porcelain cup and pour on the strong, hot tea, which crackles pleasantly as it hits the sugar. Finally, add the merest splash of cream over the back of a special curved spoon made for this purpose. On no account should the tea be stirred; in Eastern Frisian circles this would be a grave breach of etiquette.

Norderney

From Norddeich (around 1hr). Daily ferries with variable timetables. €13 *round-trip. Timetable information from* ☎ *(049 31) 98 70.*
The most urbanised of the Eastern Frisians was once the summer residence of the House of Hanover. Its main town still has much of its old charm with the spa rooms on the Kurplatz, well-tended spa gardens and 19C houses.

Baltrum

Boat docks: Neßmersiel and Baltrum. 2 to 3 ferries (30min) according to the tide. €15 *round-trip.* ☎ *(049 33) 99 16 06.*
On the smallest of the Eastern Frisians, the water is usually calm. The main sight here is the **old church** in Westdorf, built one year after the great floods of 1826. The church bell was originally a ship's bell, washed up as jetsam on the coast of Baltrum. On the island's east side are impressive **sand dunes** *(Großes Dünental).*

Langeoog

From Bensersiel (around 1hr): 9:30am-5:30pm. €19 *round-trip (day ticket).* ☎ *(049 72) 69 30.*
The **Schiffahrtsmuseum** (Museum of Seafaring) on this island features Langeoog's lifeboat, in service from 1945 to 1980. From the raised promenade along the chain of sand dunes, near Ebbe, there is a fine view of 14km/9mi of beach and sand banks.

Spiekeroog

Spa Boat docks: Neuharlingersiel and Spiekeroog. 1 to 4 ferries daily (allow 45min). €20 *round-trip.* ☎ *(049 76) 919 31 01.*
In spite of this island's spa facilities, the traditional village infrastructure has remained virtually intact. The **Alte Inselkirche** of 1696 is the oldest surviving place of worship in the Eastern Frisians. A Pietà made of wood and fragments of a pulpit are said to have come from a ship in the Spanish Armada that sank in 1588. One of the island's more unusual sights is the **Muschelmuseum** (Mussel Museum) in the basement of the seaside hall.

Wangerooge

From Harlesiel (around 80min). Timetable information from ☎ *(044 64) 94 94 11.*
Over the course of history, the most easterly of the Eastern Frisians has belonged to Holland, France, Russia (twice) and since 1818 to the Grand Duchy of Oldenburg. This much sought after island is now a peaceful family holiday destination. The colourful island train runs from the isolated southwest point past lagoons rich in bird life straight to the centre of the village.

OTTOBEUREN★★★

POPULATION: 8 000

The Benedictine abbey of Ottobeuren, founded in 764 under the patronage of Charlemagne, was transformed into the Baroque style in the 18C. The abbey church is without doubt one of the most stunning churches in Germany.

▶ **Orient Yourself:** Ottobeuren is a charming village surrounded by forests and pasture land. The A 96 motorway (Memmingen-Munich) is 11km/7mi north.

⊙ **Don't Miss:** The Abbey Church

🕐 **Organizing Your Time:** Plan at least two hours to view the church and buildings.

🕭 **Also See:** Deutsche ALPENSTRASSE (Füssen is 67km/42mi south), ULM (69km/43mi north), WIESKIRCHE (71km/44mi south).

Sights

Abbey Church★★★

Brochure available at the entrance (€2.30). 🕭🕐 *Daily 7.30am-noon, 1.30pm-6.30pm;* 🕐 *Closed 1 week in Jun, Jul and Sep.* ☎ *(083 32) 79 80; www.abtei-ottobeuren.de.*

In 1748, **Johann Michael Fischer**, the great architect of southern Germany, put the finishing touches on this jewel of German Baroque, which was to be his masterpiece. He was assisted by equally gifted Rococo masters when it came to the church's interior ornamentation: Johann Jakob Zeiller and Franz Anton Zeiller for the frescoes, Johann Michael Feichtmayr for the stuccowork, and Johann Joseph Christian for the figurative sculptures.

The church's astonishing dimensions are only evident once inside. The impression of space is enhanced by the unusual amount of light, a result of the church's north-south orientation. The architecture of the entire church is focused on the flattened central dome, amid a proliferation of paintings, stuccowork and sculptures with wonderfully depicted cherubs, draperies, and lighting.

The four altars, of St Michael – patron saint of the Ottobeuren area and the Empire – of the Holy Guardian Angels, of St Joseph and of St John the Baptist, are remarkable features, as are the outstanding **pulpit** and, opposite, the representation of the **Baptism of Christ** in red and marble stucco.

On the altar of the Holy Sacrament stands a much venerated **crucifix** dating from 1220, the Ottobeurer Gnadenheiland (Merciful Redeemer). The **high altar**, with paintings of the Holy Trinity by Zeiller and larger than life figures of the Apostles

The church and abbey buildings

T. Krieger/MICHELIN

Interior view of Ottobeuren abbey church

and saints is outstanding. The walnut **choir stalls**★★ (1764) are a masterpiece of the woodcarver's art. The high backs to the stalls are decorated with gilded lime-wood reliefs by Joseph Christian. Karl Joseph Riepp, a pupil of the famous organ builder Silbermann, built both the **chancel organs**★★ in 1766.

Abbey buildings

🕐 *Daily 10am-12pm, 2-5pm.* 🕐 *Closed Good Friday and Holy Saturday, 24 and 31 Dec.* ⊛ *€3.* ☏ *(083 32) 79 80.*

The abbey's buildings were constructed between 1711 and 1725. Inside the **museum**★ admire the superb decoration of the rooms, in keeping with the architecture of the church. Note the abbatial palace *(Prälatur)*, magnificent **library**, theatre and **Emperor's Hall** *(Kaisersaal)*, with a frescoed ceiling depicting the coronation of Emperor Charlemagne. The museum also houses interesting medieval artworks and 15C-17C paintings.

Excursion

Memmingen

11km/7mi northwest. In the **old town**, surrounded by a preserved fortified wall, the characteristic appearance of a medieval trading centre remains. On either side of the stream through the city centre stand such ancient buildings as the **Siebendächerhaus** (House with Seven Roofs), once the tanners' headquarters. Interesting buildings also surround the **Marktplatz**: the **Steuerhaus** (1495), with its ground floor opened by arcades; and the 1589 **Rathaus**, which was remodelled in the Rococo style in 1765. A further highlight is the Late Gothic Antonierhaus, housing a museum of local painter Bernhard Strigel (1460-1528) works, and a museum on the Antonine Order.

The Gothic basilica **Martinskirche** dates from the 14C and 15C. It has a fine chancel (1496-1500), a masterpiece by architect of the Münster at Ulm, Matthias Böblinger. The **choir stalls**★ *(Chorgestühl)*, dating from 1501 to 1507, are intricately carved with 68 figures of the Prophets, sibyls and church benefactors.

On Hallhof square, the 1617 belfry of the **Kreuzherrenkirche** surpasses the town's other towers in its beauty and ornamentation.

PASSAU★★

POPULATION: 50 000

Passau lies in a marvellous **setting**★★ at the junction of the Inn, the Danube (Donau) and the small River Ilz. The old town, with its Baroque churches and patrician houses, lies crowded onto the narrow tongue of land separating the Inn and the Danube. Northwards, on the far bank of the Danube, rises the wooded bluff on which the Oberhaus fortress is built. ▯ *Rathausplatz 3, 94032 Passau, ☎ (0851) 95 59 80.*

▶ **Orient Yourself:** Situated in eastern Bavaria, Passau is actually made up of 3 towns: Ilzstadt to the north, Innstadt to the south, and the peninsula of Altstadt. The A 3 passes near Passau, and the Czech Republic is only 50km/31mi away.

▣ **Parking:** Parking is available on the Domplatz and south of the Schanzl-brücke.

⊗ **Don't Miss:** The Glass Museum and the Three Rivers Walk.

⊙ **Organizing Your Time:** Allow three hours for the suggested driving tour.

Address Book

WHERE TO EAT

⊖⊜ **Heilig-Geist-Stift-Schenke** – *Heiliggeistgasse 4* ☎ *(0851) 26 07* ⊙ *Closed 9 Jan-1 Feb and Wed.* This establishment built in 1358 has a cosy, rustic atmosphere. Expect beautiful, vaulted ceilings, open fires and charming vine-covered garden.

WHERE TO STAY

⊖ **Rotel Inn** – *Donauufer, 50m/55yds from the main station (Hauptbahnhof)* ☎ *(0851) 951 60 Fax (0851) 9516100 www.rotel-inn.de* ⊙ *May-Sep* ⤧ ▣ *96 rooms* ⊴ This hotel on the bank of the Danube offers a choice of double or single guestrooms. Bathrooms are off the corridor.

⊖⊜ **Euro-Hotel Passau** – *Neuburger Straße 128* ☎ *(0851) 98 84 20 Fax (0851) 98842111 www.euro-hotel-passau.de* ▣ ⤧ ⅙ *Reservations recommended 73 rooms* ⊴ This multi-storied hotel is close to the conference hall and the A3 motorway (Passau-Süd exit). Modern and functional guestrooms.

⊖⊜⊜ **Hotel Passauer Wolf** – *Rindermarkt 6* ☎ *(0851) 931 51 10 Fax (0851) 9315150 40 rooms* ⊴ ⊖⊜⊜ *Restaurant.* A traditional establishment is mid-way between the Danube and the town's pedestrian zone. Each guestroom is furnished uniquely. Rustic restaurant with beautiful river views.

TAKING A BREAK

Atelier Café – *Ort 2 (between Schaiblingsturm and Dreiflüsseeck)* ☎ *(0851) 9 34 66 11 www.ort2.de* ⊙ *Mar-Oct, Wed-Sun, 11.30am-7pm; Nov-Feb, Sat-Sun, 11.30am-6pm.* The Austrian proprietor of this cafe prepares cakes and cold dishes, many of which are Austrian specialities. Everything can be enjoyed in the idyllic garden.

Café Greindl – *Wittgasse 8* ☎ *(0851) 3 56 77* ⊙ *Mon-Sat, 6.30am-6pm, Sun, 11am-6pm.* Tea room offering tarts, cakes, ice-creams, and home-made chocolates. In good weather, there is a little terrace outside. Another branch of this cafe is in the pedestrian zone *(Theresienstr. 8).*

GOING OUT

Café Duft – *Theresienstr. 22* ☎ *(0851) 3 46 66 www.cafeduft.de* ⊙ *Mon-Sat, 9am-1am, Sun and bank holidays, 10am-1am.* A former stable, this cafe also features a terrace on the pedestrian zone. Regional and *tapas* dishes also served. Cosy candlelit atmosphere at night.

Passau and its cathedral

🔆 **Also See:** *BURGHAUSEN (80km/50mi south), STRAUBING (80km/50mi northwest), LANDSHUT (120km/75mi southwest).*

A Bit of History

A Powerful Bishopric – The see was founded in the 8C by St Boniface, the English-born "Apostle of Germany" (🔆 *see FULDA).* By the late 10C this see had become extraordinarily powerful. Until the 15C the diocese was so huge that it encompassed the entire Danube Valley, including Vienna.

A Commercial Base – The arrival of the Inn waters at Passau almost doubles the volume of the Danube. From the Middle Ages, river trade played an important role in the town's prosperity. Today, the "Town of Three Rivers" enjoys commercial and leisure traffic to Vienna and Budapest.

Sights

Veste Oberhaus (Fortress)
This imposing citadel was started in 1219 as a refuge for the bishops against rebellious burghers. It is linked with the Veste Niederhaus by a fortified road. From the belvedere marked Zur Aussicht, near the car park, or from atop a tower inside the compound *(142 steps),* there are magnificent **views**★★ over the Inn, the Danube and Passau itself. The town's history, art and religious roots, including some paintings of the Danube School, are traced in a small **museum**.

Dom St. Stephan
Most of this Late Gothic **cathedral** was destroyed by fire in the 17C, and was rebuilt in the Baroque style. The huge interior is richly decorated with frescoes and stuccowork. Four **lateral chapels** feature paintings by the Austrian artist JM Rottmayr (1654-1730). From the Residenzplatz, visitors can admire the cathedral's **east end**★★, a remarkable Late Gothic work. The cathedral's **organ**★★, with 17 774 pipes and 233 stops, is the largest in the world *(organ recitals).*

Residenzplatz
The square is bordered on the south by the bishops' **New Residence**, which dates from the beginning of the neo-Classical period. The surrounding streets are still

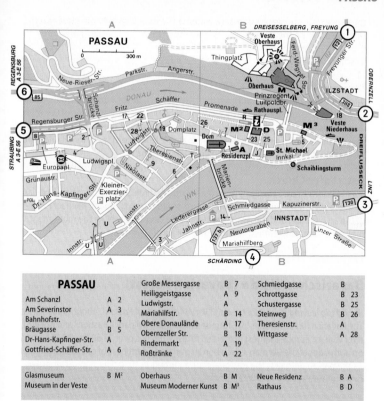

lined with many old houses above arcades, with corbelling and concealed Inn valley ridge roofs.

Rathausplatz

One of the town's most picturesque squares. The painted façade of the Rathaus (D) dates from the 14C; the building's tower was built in the late 18C.

Glasmuseum★★

In the "Wilder Mann" hotel on Rathausplatz. ◷ *Daily 1pm-5pm.* ● €5. ☎ (0851) 350 71; www.glasmuseum.de.

Glassware from Bohemia, Bavaria and Austria, from the late 18C to the 1930s, makes up most of this collection of 20 000 pieces encompassing 250 years of glassmaking history. The most important display comes from **Bohemia** (Biedermeier, Historicism, Jugendstil); note especially the Lobmeyr state goblet created in 1878-81 and depicting the *Marriage of Neptune with Amphitrite*. It is considered the most significant glass work of the 19C.

St-Michaels-Kirche

This 17C Jesuit **church** overlooks the north bank of the Inn. The rich gilding and stuccowork date from ca 1670.

Dreiflusseck★ (Three Rivers Walk)

From St Michaels-Kirche, go down to the Inn quayside. The fast-flowing, almost torrential Inn River runs at the foot of the Schaiblingsturm (1481), once used to store salt. At the confluence, the green current of the Inn can be seen running alongside the brown Danube waters and dark water of the Ilz before they mingle. From the Danube bank, on the far side of the promontory, there is a fine viewpoint.

Excursions

Dreisesselberg★

48km/30mi northeast, 3km/2mi from the Czech border. The drive to this curious group of granite rocks, eroded into flat, saucer-like shapes, runs through some of the wildest regions of the Bavarian forest. Green triangles waymark the path leading to the lowest rock outcrop. From there, steps rise to the **Hochstein** (1 332m/4 370ft). The viewpoint at the summit affords a splendid **panorama**★.

Osterhofen Church

36km/22mi NW. Leave Passau by ⑥ on the town plan. Three great names of the Bavarian Baroque style left their mark in this suburb of Altenmarkt: Johann Michael Fischer in the architecture and the Asam brothers in the decoration. Note the monumental high altar with its wreathed columns and enraptured angels.

Driving Tour

Bayerischer Wald★ (Bavarian Forest)

Round trip leaving from Bodenmais (70km/44mi north of Passau). About 65km/41mi . The Bavarian forest includes low, rounded mountains, wild rock bastions and isolated, river valleys. Europe's largest protected forest stretches over 13 300ha/32 865 acres on both sides of the German-Czech border over an ancient base of gneiss and granite. At the centre of it all is the National Park founded in 1970. The natural woodland draws a wide variety of animal species.

▶ *To get to Bodenmais from Passau, take the B 85 (Bayerische Ostmarkstr) to Regen, then fork to the right.*

Bodenmais★

This unique town with a healing climate lies in a pastureland at the southern foot of the Großer Arber.

▶ *Travel 23km/14mi toward Kötzting, where the road mounts the pastoral Weißer Regen Valley within sight of the peaks of the Osser.*

Continue climbing as far as the Lamer Winkel, a hollow of woods and upland meadows at the head of the valley. A panoramic drive across the mountainside, including a closer view of the Großer Arber, terminates this part of the journey (highest point: Brennes-Sattel, at 1 030m/3 380ft).

> ## Danube School
>
> The German painters working in the Danube Valley in the 16C were among the first to depict landscape for its own sake. The best masters of this so-called school were Albrecht Altdorfer, Lucas Cranach the Elder, Wolf Huber and Jörg Breu the Elder.

Hindenburg-Kanzel★

A **look-out point**★ offers a fine view of the Lamer Winkel and the Arber.

Großer Arber★★

From the lower cable railway terminal, 1hr there and back, including 20min on foot. ⓞ *Summer: 8.30am-4.45pm; Winter: 8.30am-4.30pm.* ⓞ *Closed 2 weeks in Apr and from Nov to early Dec.* ⬮ *€8 round trip.* ☎ *(099 25) 941 40.*

From the upper terminal, a path leads to two rocky crags, one overlooking the **Schwarzer Regen depression**★★, and one (surmounted by a cross) with views of the Lamer Winkel and the forest to the north. The **Großer Arbersee**★, a lake, sits to the right as the road winds down through the forest. On the way are several **views**★ of the Zwiesel basin, the Falkenstein and the Großer Rachel.

PFALZ★

One of the largest wooded areas of Germany, the Palatinate massif is also a protected botanical and zoological park. The northern part of the massif is popular with walkers; to the east, the mild climate encourages the growth of exotic fruit.

▶ **Orient Yourself:** The Palatinate mountains stretch from the Rhine plains to the Vosges. The massif is reached via the A 65 motorway from Mannheim, or from Karlsruhe, farther south. The German Wine Road starts 15km/9mi to the west of Worms, at Bockenheim *(B 271)* and winds 80km/50mi south toward France.

 Don't Miss: The suggested driving tour, which meanders through some of Germany's finest wine country.

🕐 **Organizing Your Time:** Allow one day for the suggested driving tour.

👃 **Also See:** *MANNHEIM (23km/14mi east of Bad Dürkheim), HEIDELBERG (42km/26mi east of Bad Dürkheim), KARLSRUHE (35km/22mi south of Bad Bergzabern).*

Address Book

WHERE TO EAT

🍷🍽 **Weinstube Ester** – *Triftweg 21, 67098 Bad Dürkheim* ☎ *(06322) 98 90 65 www.ester24.de* 🕐 *Closed 2 weeks in Sep, Mon and Tue* Many regulars come to this rustic tavern typical of the Palatinate region. Regional dishes, mostly the establishment's meat and sausage specialities, are on the menu. The wines mostly come from the vineyards which surround the restaurant.

🍷🍽🍽 **Reuters Holzappel** – *Hauptstraße 11, 76889 Bad Bergzabern* ☎ *(06343) 42 45 www.reuters-holzappel.de* 🍴 Traditional wine cellar in a 250-year-old farmhouse with courtyard. Wooden furniture and collections of objets make this place cosy and comfortable. Local and international dishes are on the menu.

WHERE TO STAY

🍷🍽🍽 **Hotel Zum Lam** – *Winzergasse 37, 76889 Bad Bergzabern* ☎ *(06343) 93 92 12 Fax (06343) 939213 www.zum-lam.de* 🕐 *Closed Wed, 2-23 Jan* 🅿 *11 rooms* 🍽🍷🍽Restaurant As well as being a charming resort, Bad Bergzabern is known for its 18C half-timbered houses. This hotel is one of them. Enjoy the pleasant garden terrace in a wine-growing community.

🍷🍽🍽🍽 **Hotel Deidesheimer Hof** – *Am Marktplatz 1, 67146 Deidesheim* ☎ *(06326) 968 70 Fax (06326) 7685 www.deidesheimerhof.de* 🕐 *Closed 1-3 Jan* 🅿 🍽 *28 rooms* Elegant inn with tastefully furnished rooms. Gourmet restaurant on the premises as well as lounge offering regional specialities. Chancellor Helmut Kohl often received official guests at this establishment.

A Bit of History

The Wines of the Palatinate – The most extensive wine-growing region of Germany, the Palatinate produces almost one-third of Germany's total output. The region's most famous vintages come from the villages of Bad Dürkheim, Forst, Deidesheim and Wachenheim. The itinerary suggested below follows part of the celebrated Deutsche Weinstraße (German Wine Road), which begins at Schweigen, on the French frontier, and ends at Bockenheim, west of Worms.

Driving Tour

From Worms to Bad Bergzabern *151km/91mi*

Worms★ ♿ *see WORMS*
South of Worms, the Rhine plain becomes progressively devoted to viticulture.

Freinsheim
A large wine town, encircled by ramparts. The town hall, beside a 15C church, occupies an elegant Baroque house with an overhanging roof that protects an outside staircase.

Bad Dürkheim
Sheltered by the Pfälzer Wald, this thermal cure town enjoys a mild climate in which fig, almond and chestnut trees in the Spa Park flower early. A couple of miles west *(via Schillerstraße and Luitpoldweg)* are the ruins of Limburg abbey.

Deidesheim
This is one of the most typical and prosperous towns on the German Wine Road with its market and half-timbered houses.

Neustadt an der Weinstraße
Narrow, picturesque lanes in this small town surround a pretty market with 18C town hall. The **old town**★ boasts the largest number of old houses in the region.

Hambacher Schloss
On the outskirts of Hambach. 🕐 *From Mar to end Nov, 10am-6pm.* 🎫 *€4.50.* ☎ *(063 21) 308 81.*
Founded by the Salian Franks in the 11C, this castle was the summer residence of the Speyer bishops before being destroyed in 1688. These ruins are famous in Germany because it was here, in 1832, that militant patriots first raised the black, red and gold flag adopted as the German national emblem in 1919, and again in 1949. An exhibition commemorates this event, the first major rally in German history.

Kalmit
8km/5mi, leaving from Maikammer, then 15min on foot there and back. At 673m/2 208ft above sea level, the Kalmit is the highest outcrop in the Rhineland Palatinate. It is a good departure point for woodland walks. From the Kalmithaus terrace, there is a **view**★★ of the Rhine plain and Speyer cathedral. Return to the Wine Road via the charming village of **St Martin**★.

Schloss-Villa Ludwigshöhe★
2km/1mi from Edenkoben. Guided tours of historic rooms only. 🕐 *From holy week until the end of Sep, 10am-6pm; Oct-Nov and Jan-Palm Sun, 10am-5pm. The Max-Slevogt-Galerie can be visited independently of the guided tour.* 🎫 *€2.60.* ☎ *(063 23) 930 16.*
Built by Ludwig I of Bavaria in the "Italian villa" style, this stately home houses a **gallery**★ devoted to the works of the German Impressionist painter Max Slevogt

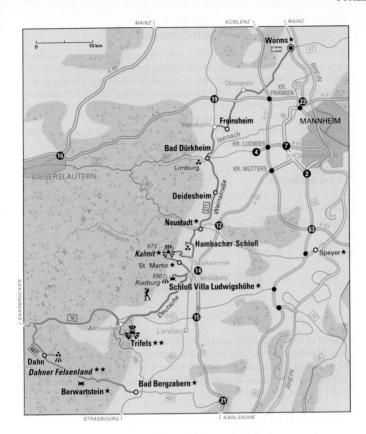

(1868-1932). The apartments are also open to the public. From here a chair-lift carries sightseers to the Rietburg (550m/1 804ft), departure point for forest walks.

Trifels★

7km/4.5mi from Annweiler, plus 1hr 30min walking and sightseeing. ◐ *From holy week until end Sep, 9am-6pm; Oct-Nov and Palm Sun, 9am-5pm.* ⊜ *€2.60.* ☎ *(063 46) 84 70.*

Trifels makes an imposing sight even from a distance. The castle was the Hohenstaufen stronghold at one time, and in the 12C and 13C, the temporary residence of the crown jewels. Legend has it that the Holy Grail was found here. It is proven fact, however, that Emperor Henry IV held **Richard the Lionheart** prisoner in the fort upon his return from the Third Crusade in 1193.

Dahner Felsenland★★

The resort of **Dahn** is surrounded by one of the best hiking areas in Germany, with breathtaking mountains and outcroppings of red sandstone. The **castle ruins**★ of Altdahn dominate the town. Flights of steps and guard rooms hewn into the rocks add to the charm of the castle, the heart of which dates from ca 1100.

Burg Berwartstein★

Turn off toward Erlenbach (B 427). ◐ *Open Mar to Oct, 9am-6pm; Nov to Feb, Sat-Sun, 1pm-5pm.* ⊜ *€2.50.* ☎ *(063 98) 210; www.burgberwartstein.de.*

This former robber baron's lair is perched 100m/330ft above the village of Erlenbach. Much of the castle is open to the public, including subterranean passages.

Rhine-Main-Danube Canal

Ever since Roman times emperors, kings, engineers and visionaries have dreamed of linking the Rhine and Danube waterways. Charlemagne began the great enterprise, called Charlemagne's Ditch (Fossa Carolina). Bavaria's Ludwig I made another attempt 1000 years later when he began the Ludwig Canal. But it would be some 12 centuries after its conception that the canal would finally be completed. In 1992, the 177km/110mi canal began transporting vessels through hundreds of locks, bridging a difference of 245m/800ft. A barge load of 20C dignitaries finally closed the link between the North Sea and the Black on September 25, 1992.

Bad Bergzabern★

This charming health resort features numerous half-timbered houses. Among the ornate 17C-18C residences note the **Gasthaus zum Engel**★ (1579), said to be the finest Renaissance building in the region.

POTSDAM★★★

POPULATION: 146 600

Just west of Berlin, Potsdam was chosen in the 17C as the residence of the electors of Brandenburg because of its ideal setting – a natural woodland dotted with lakes and crisscrossed by canals and the River Havel. It is to Frederick the Great that Potsdam owes its renown as "rococo jewel". *Friedrich-Ebert-Straße 5, 14467 Potsdam, ☎ (0331) 27 55 80.*

▶ **Orient Yourself:** The capital of Brandenburg is a few kilometres west of Berlin, in the heart of the Havelland, an area of canals and lakes.

Parking: Garages are located throughout the city, including near the main train station and near Sanssouci Palace.

Don't Miss: Sanssouci Palace

Organizing Your Time: Allow four hours for a tour of the Sanssouci complex.

Also See: *BERLIN (30km/19mi), WITTENBERG (78km/49mi southwest), WÖRLITZ (85km/53mi southwest), DESSAU (95km/59mi southwest).*

Sanssouci Palace and terraced gardens, dear to the heart of Frederick the Great

J. Malburet/MICHELIN

WHERE TO EAT

⊜⊜⊜ **La Maison du Chocolat** – *Benkertstraße 20* ☎ *(0331) 237 07 30* 🍴 ♿
After dinner, this restaurant conveniently has a boutique attached where customers can buy all manner of succulent cakes and chocolate truffles. A little corner of France in the Dutch quarter of Potsdam.

WHERE TO STAY

⊜⊜ **Bed and Breakfast am Luisenplatz** – *Zimmerstraße 1* ☎ *(0331) 971 90 20*
Fax (0331) 9719019 www.bed-breakfast-potsdam.de 🍴 *15 rooms* �! The relatively central situation and reasonable prices makes this little hotel a real find. The welcoming guestrooms are modern and furnished in light wood; breakfast is served on the Luisenplatz.

A Bit of History

A Prussian Versailles – Under Friedrich Wilhelm (1713-40), Potsdam became an administrative centre and a garrison town. The King's son, **Frederick the Great** (Friedrich II) was in contrast a patron of the arts. Most of the monuments for which the city is famous today were due to him, notably Sanssouci and the Neues Palais. Frederick, as eloquent in French as in German, welcomed many eminent Frenchmen to his court, among them **Voltaire**, who lived in Potsdam for three years.

The Potsdam Conference – The treaty defining the occupation and future of Germany after the Second World War was signed at Cecilienhof Palace on 2 August 1945 by the leaders of the Allied powers (Churchill, Truman and Stalin).

Sanssouci Palace and Park★★★

▶ *Follow the itinerary suggested on the map.*

This huge complex marries architecture with landscape better than any of its kind in Germany. Wandering here and there it is easy to understand why Frederick the Great took such delight in coming here.

Friedenskirche

Modelled on Rome's basilica of San Clemente, the church contains a fine **mosaic★** made on the island of Murano in the 18C. The mausoleum houses the recumbent statues of Emperor Friedrich III and his wife, and the sarcophagus of Friedrich Wilhelm I, the King-Sergeant.

Bildergalerie★ (Paintings Gallery)

🕐 *From mid-May to mid-Oct, Tue-Sun, 10am-5pm.* ⊕ *€2.* ☎ *(0331) 969 41 81.*
Amid the rich 18C Rococo of the great rooms visitors can admire works mainly from the Italian (Bassano, Tintoretto and Caravaggio), Flemish (Van Dyck, Rubens and Terbrugghen) and French (Simon Vouet and Van Loo) schools, all acquired by Friedrich II.

The historic mill

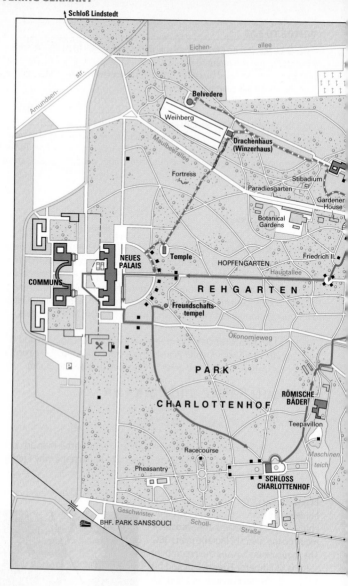

Schloß Lindstedt
Eichen- allee
Amundsen- str.
Belvedere
Weinberg
Maulbeerallee
Drachenhaus (Winzerhaus)
Fortress
Stibadium
Paradiesgarten
Gardener House
Botanical Gardens
NEUES PALAIS
Temple
Friedrich II.
HOPFENGARTEN
Hauptallee
COMMUNS
REHGARTEN
Freundschafts-tempel
Ökonomieweg
PARK
RÖMISCHE BÄDER
CHARLOTTENHOF
Teepavillon
Maschinen-teich
Racecourse
Pheasantry
SCHLOSS CHARLOTTENHOF
Geschwister-
BHF. PARK SANSSOUCI
Scholl-
Straße

Schloss Sanssouci★★★

Expect a wait due to limits on the number of allowed visitors. ☜ Guided visit (40min). 🕐 *Open Apr to Oct, Tue-Sun, 9am-5pm; Nov to Mar, Tue-Sun, 9am-4pm.* 🕐 *Closed 24, 25 and 31 Dec. ☜ €8. ☎ (0331) 969 42 02; www.spsg.de.*

It is impossible to remain unmoved by the progressive appearance of this majestic façade as one climbs the great staircase leading to the palace. The original idea of the architect (Knobelsdorff again) was for the façade, adorned with 36 atlantes, to encompass the entire terrace area. But the king preferred a generous proportion of space which indeed became one of his favourite places to relax in. On the far side of the palace the state entrance is flanked by an elegant semicircular colonnade.

A walk through the rooms inside reveals the enormous skill and artistry of the Rococo craftsmen who decorated them. In the study and bedchamber are the desk and

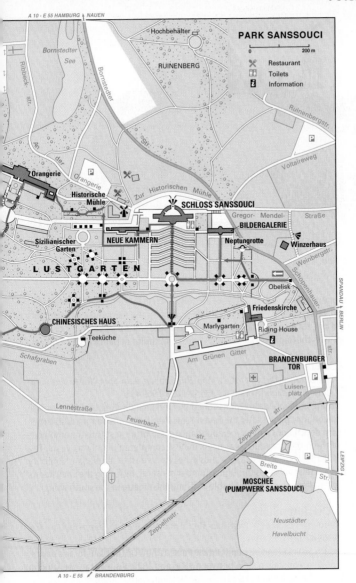

chair at which Frederick the Great died. The monarch's favourite room was the Music Room, a masterpiece of Prussian Rococo.

Neue Kammern★ (New Rooms)

♿ Ⓧ *Open Apr to mid-May, Sat-Sun, 10am-5pm; mid-May to mid-Oct, Tue-Sun, 10am-5pm.* €3. ☎ (0331) 969 42 06.

Designed in 1747 by Knobelsdorff in the form of an orangery, this block was soon transformed into the palace guesthouse. The Rococo interior is captivating. Note the **Ovid-Galerie★**, decorated with scenes from Ovid's *Metamorphoses*.

Neue Orangerie

♿ *Guided visit from mid-May to mid-Oct, Tue-Sun. 10am-5pm.* €3. ☎ (0331) 969 42 80.

Neues Palais

The orangery was built in the style of an Italian Renaissance palace between 1851 and 1860, after plans by Friedrich Wilhelm IV. Among the magnificent apartments occupied by Czar Nicolas I and his wife, the malachite hall is particularly impressive. Even better is the Raphael Hall★, which houses 47 copies of paintings by Raphael.

Neues Palais★★

🐾⊙ *Guided tours (1hr), Apr to Oct, Mon-Thu, Sat-Sun, 9am-5pm; Nov to Mar, 9am-4pm.* ⊙ *Closed 24, 25 and 31 Dec.* ⊜ *€6.* ☎ *(0331) 969 43 61.*

This imposing building was commissioned by Frederick the Great to demonstrate Prussia's economic power after the Seven Years War. Some 400 rooms, with excessively lavish decorations and a superabundance of sculpture, testify to the ambitious nature of the project – which was nevertheless completed in only six years. The unrestrained Baroque architecture stands in heavy contrast to the elegant simplicity of Sanssouci. The tour leads through a number of rooms, including the Shell Room, the Marble Gallery, the elegant Marble Hall, and the theatre in the south wing.

Schloss Charlottenhof★

🐾⊙ *Guided tour (45min).* ⊙ *From mid-May to mid-Oct, Tue-Sun, 10am-5pm.* ⊜ *€4.* ☎ *(0331) 969 42 28.*

Karl-Friedrich Schinkel and his pupil Ludwig Perseus drew up the plans for this palace, built in the Classical Italian style between 1826 and 1829. Visitors can see, among other things, the bedchamber and office of Alexander von Humboldt.

Römische Bäder (Roman Baths)

Schinkel, Perseus and landscaper Lenné designed these baths with an eye toward harmonizing them with their natural setting. The **interior decor**★ of the baths is tastefully done.

A pergola leads to the Tea Pavilion, not unlike a temple, with a single room decorated all in blue, which has a good view of the lake and gardens.

Chinesisches Teehaus★★ (Chinese Tea House)

A circular pavilion decorated with gilded statues, this structure arose from the "Sino-mania" so popular in 18C Germany. There is an exhibition of Chinese porcelain inside.

Sights

The Town

Brandenburger Tor★

Luisenplatz. This monumental gateway was built in the Baroque fashion in 1770 but takes the form of a Roman triumphal arch.

Dampfmaschinenhaus★ (Steam-powered pumping station)

Take Schopenhauerstraße, then Breite Straße. 🚶 *Guided tour (30min). From mid-May to mid-Oct, Sat-Sun, 10am-5pm.* ⊚ *€2.* ☎ *(0331) 969 42 02.*
Installed in an unusual replica of a mosque, complete with minarets, this 19C pumping station supplies water to the fountains, pools and cascades in Sanssouci Park.

Marstall (Old Stables)

Breite Straße. Dating from 1685 and modified by Knobelsdorff in 1746, these stables mark the unlikely setting for a **film museum**★ with reconstructions of Marlene Dietrich's and Lilian Harvey's dressing-rooms. The museum also contains literature on German Expressionist films and émigré film directors.

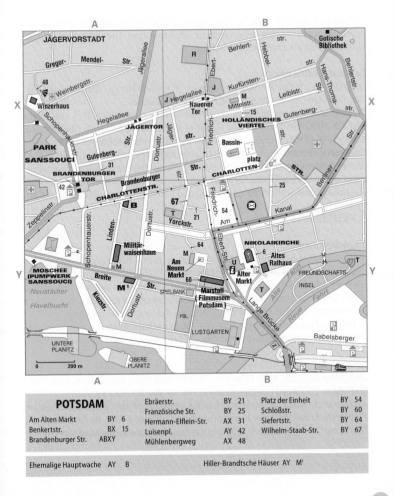

POTSDAM			Ebräerstr.	BY	21	Platz der Einheit	BY	54
			Französische Str.	BY	25	Schloßstr.	BY	60
Am Alten Markt	BY	6	Hermann-Elflein-Str.	AX	31	Siefertstr.	BY	64
Benkertstr.	BX	15	Luisenpl.	AY	42	Wilhelm-Staab-Str.	BY	67
Brandenburger Str.	ABXY		Mühlenbergweg	AX	48			

Ehemalige Hauptwache	AY	B		Hiller-Brandtsche Häuser	AY	M¹

Nikolaikirche★

Built on the site of an old Baroque church destroyed by fire in 1795, this early 19C church is the perfect example of German Classicism as conceived by Karl Friedrich Schinkel.

Holländisches Viertel★ (Dutch Quarter)

Along the Mittelstraße are the gabled houses of the Dutch Quarter, built by the Dutch architect Boumann around 1740 for Netherlands artisans in Potsdam.

Le Nouveau Parc★★

This park was laid out in the late 18C by Peter Lenné on the shore of Heiliger See for Frederick the Great, who was a great fan of English-style landscaped gardens. Interesting features in the park include the orangery, the pyramid, the kitchens and the marble palace.

Marmorpalais

&🕐 *Open Apr to Oct, Tue-Sun, 10am-5pm,* ☞ *€5; Nov to Mar (guided tour only), Sat-Sun, 10am-4pm.* 🕐 *Closed 24, 25 and 31 Dec.* ☞ *€4.* ☎ *(0331) 969 42 00; www. spsg.de*
This marble palace was built by Karl von Gontard and converted into a summer residence for Friedrich Wilhelm II by Langhans (1744-97). The king's beautiful, private apartments and the state apartments are open to visitors. The concert hall,and the Oriental Room are particularly delightful.

Schloss Cecilienhof★

&🕐 *Open Apr to Oct, Tue-Sun, 9am-5pm,* ☞ *€5; Nov to Mar (guided tours only), Tue-Sun, 9am-4pm.* ☞ *€4.* ☎ *(0331) 969 42 44; www.spsg.de.*
This English-style country residence built during the First World War for Crown Prince Wilhelm (1882-1951) and his wife Cecilia of Mecklenburg-Schwerin (1886-1954) is worth seeing for its own sake. But it is the historic **meeting rooms of the Potsdam Conference** (Historische Stätte der Potsdamer Konferenz) of 1945 that draw the most attention. Members of the Allied delegations asigned the Potsdam Agreements here on 2 August 1945, outlining Germany's occupation and future development.
The luxury hotel Schloßhotel Cecilienhof also occupies space in this castle.

Excursions

Brandenburg

38km/24mi west. It was in the 14C that this small town in the heart of the Havelland (an area of scattered lakes fed by the River Havel) began to prosper, mainly through the cloth trade. The **Dom St Peter und St Paul**★, founded in 1165 and remodelled in the 14C, is furnished with several Gothic altarpieces. In the two-aisle crypt is a mausoleum memorializing the clergy murdered during the Nazi regime.
Rich exterior decoration distinguishes the 15C **St Katharinenkirche**★, which boasts a hall chancel with an ambulatory typical of brick-built Gothic churches.

Kloster Lehnin★ (Abbey)

28km/17m southwest. &🕐 *Open Mon-Fri, 9am-noon and 1-4pm, Sat-Sun, 11am-noon and 1-5pm.* 🕐 *Closed 1 Jan, 24-26 and 31 Dec.* ☎ *(033 82) 76 88 55.*
Another brick church, this three-aisle basilica, commissioned by Otto I and occupied in 1180 by the Cistercian Order, has all the hallmarks of Early Gothic. Worth seeing are a Triumphal Cross dating from 1225 and the funerary stone of the Margrave Otto IV.

QUEDLINBURG★

POPULATION: 23 000

Nestling at the foot of a rock pinnacle crowned by a castle and an abbey church, the half-timbered town of Quedlinburg fits the ideal of a 17C German town. The old town, in which no less than 770 houses are classified as historical monuments, has been listed on UNESCO's World Heritage List since 1994. 🔲 Markt 2, 06484 Quedlinburg, ☎ (039 46) 90 56 24.

▸ **Orient Yourself:** Quedlinburg is a few kilometres north of the Harz massif. The town is near the A 14 motorway (Leipzig-Magdeburg), making it an ideal base for exploring the Harz mountains.

🞱 **Don't Miss:** The Schloßberg

🕐 **Organizing Your Time:** Allow two hours for a casual tour of the Old Town and the Schloßberg.

🞱 **Also See:** HARZ (Wernigerode is 32km/20mi west), HALLE (75km/47mi southeast), DESSAU (85km/53mi east), MAGDEBURG (56km/35mi northeast).

The Old Town★

Markt★ (Market Place)
The early-17C Renaissance **Rathaus** borders the northern side of the market place. On the left of the façade is a statue of Roland (c 1440). Houses built in the 17C and 18C line the other three sides of the square.

Old Streets★
Circle St Benediktkirche via Marktstraße and Kornmarkt to explore the cobbled lanes behind the Rathaus, then return to the Markt along Breitstraße, with several picturesque alleyways opening off it. On the far side of the square, stroll to the toward the castle by way of Wordgasse, Hohe Straße and Blasiistraße. On one side of the charming **Schloßbergplatz**★ stands the late-16C house (Klopstock-Haus, no 12) in which the poet **Friedrich Gottlieb Klopstock** was born in 1724. The house contains exhibits recalling the poet's life and work. 🕐 Open Apr-Oct, Tue-Sun, 10am-5pm; Nov-Mar, Wed-Sun, 10am-4pm. 🕐 Closed 24 and 31 Dec. 🞱 €3. ☎ (039 46) 26 10.

Feininger-Galerie
Behind the Klopstock Museum, entry at no 5A, Finkenherd. 🞱🕐 Open Apr to Oct, Tue-Sun, 10am-6pm; Nov to Mar, Tue-Sun, 10am-5pm. 🕐 Closed 1 Jan, 24 and 31 Dec. 🞱 €6. ☎ (039 46) 23 84; www.feininger-galerie.de.
This gallery houses works by Expressionist painter Lyonel Feininger. Born in New York City, Feininger trained in France and Germany, where he exhibited with the Blaue Reiter group in 1913. After the First World War he joined the Bauhaus.

WHERE TO STAY

🞱🞱🞱 **Romantik Hotel Theophano** – Markt 14 ☎ (039 46) 963 00 Fax (039 46) 963036 www.hoteltheophano.de 🅿 🞱 22 rooms 🞱 The guestrooms in this hotel are particularly charming, with tasteful pastel tones and a number of four-poster beds. The restaurant is in the vaulted wine-cellar of the half-timbered building.

🞱🞱🞱🞱 **Schlosshotel Zum Markgrafen** – Weingarten 30 ☎ (039 46) 811 40 Fax (039 46) 811444 www.schlosshotel-zum-markgrafen.de 🞱 🅿 🞱 12 rooms 🞱 Built in 1898, this beautiful villa with a turbulent past is in the centre of a small park. All the elegant guestrooms feature Italian furnishings.

Lyonel Feininger (1871-1956)

Born in New York to musicians, Feininger was fascinated from a young age by the visual universe of the American metropolis. At the age of 16 he was sent to Germany to study music, but quickly became interested in sculpture and started a career drawing picture books. Over time, Feininger became a painter known for melding Expressionism and Cubism, and focusing on apparently banal subjects (factories, boats, ports and buildings). In 1919 Walter Gropius invited Feininger to join the Bauhaus, where he taught until the closure of the school by the Nazis.

Schlossberg★

Stiftskirche St-Servatius★★

On the site of the original 9C church, the present basilica was begun in 1070. Beneath the chancel, the **crypt**★★ is divided by three aisles with diagonal rib vaulting decorated by **frescoes**★ depicting scenes from the Bible. The **treasury**★★ (Domschatz) – manuscripts, 10C Gospel, and, above all, the **Quedlinburg Knotted Carpet**★ – is kept in the sacristy.

Schloss

The 16C-17C castle formed part of the abbey, and took on its irregular floor plan due to the the rocky base on which the castle was built. The **Schloßmuseum**★ presents the history of Quedlinburg. The Abbess' Reception Room, the Throne Room and the Princes' Hall (mid-18C) can be visited. ◷ *Open Apr-Oct, daily 10am-6pm, Nov-Mar, Sat-Thu, 10am-4pm.* ◷ *Closed 24 and 31 Dec.* ⊛ *€2.50.* ☎ *(039 46) 27 30.*

Excursion

Gernrode

7km/4.5mi south. Here, the collegiate church of **St Cyriacus**★, first documented in 961, was designed with the three-aisle nave, flat ceiling and upper galleries characteristic of the Ottonian basilica. The hall crypt is among the earliest of its type in Germany. The late-12C baptismal font is in the Romanesque style. Upstairs is the **Holy Sepulchre group**★, a rare example of Romanesque sculpture.

The interior of the Stiftskirche St-Servatius

H. Champollion/MICHELIN

RASTATT★

POPULATION: 48 000.

The Margrave Ludwig of Baden (1665-1707), known as Ludwig the Turk, turned Rastatt into a stronghold while simultaneously building a castle to replace his seat at Baden-Baden. To this day, the town retains traces of its prestigious past, which lasted until this line of margraves died out in 1771. 🗎 *Herrenstraße 18, 76437 Rastatt,* ☎ *(072 22) 97 24 62.*

- ▶ **Orient Yourself:** Less than 10 kilometres from the French border, Rastatt straddles the Murg just before it enters the Rhine, and is the harbour for the Black Forest region.
- **Don't Miss:** A trip to Schloss Favorite (👆 *see Excursion*).
- **Organizing Your Time:** Allow two hours for a tour of the Schloss.
- **Also See:** *KARLSRUHE (21km/13mi north), BADEN-BADEN (8km/5mi south), SCHWARZWALD.*

Sights

Schloss★

👣 *Guided tour (45min).* 🕐 *Apr-Oct, Tue-Sun, 10am-5pm; Nov to Mar, Tue-Sun, 10am-4pm.* 🕐 *Closed 24, 25 and 31 Dec.* 👝 *€4.50.* ☎ *(072 22) 97 83 85.*

This harmonious palace complex with three wings and a vast courtyard facing the town was built 1698-1707 by Italian master architect Domenico Egidio Rossi. After Ludwig the Turk's death in 1707, his widow Sibylla Augusta dismissed the architect and summoned as his successor **Michael Ludwig Rohrer** from her Bohemian homeland who thereafter took charge of the construction of the palace.

The Margraves

Germany's Margraves began with Charlemagne, who set up border marches *(Mark)* as defensive measures, a contrast from the internal Carolingian counties. These hostile borders were overseen by a *marchione* (military governor), a term derived from the words margrave *(Markgraf)* and marquis. In time this title became honorific and hereditary.

Royal Apartments

The nucleus of the central block is the tall, sumptuous Hall of Ancestors (Ahnensaal), with the column capitals decorated with stucco figures representing Turkish prisoners. The Margrave's apartments are in the south wing, those of his wife in the north. Both are richly embellished with frescoes and stuccowork. The Collection of Porcelain (Porzellankabinett) is worth seeing.

Wehrgeschichtliches Museum (Military Museum)

Access via the south wing. ♿🕐 *Open May-Oct, Tue-Sun, 9.30am-5pm; Nov-Apr, Fri-Sun, 9.30am-5pm.* 🕐 *Closed 24 and 31 Dec.* 👝 *€3.* ☎ *(072 22) 342 44; www.wgm-rastatt.de.*
German military and general history from 1500 to the end of the First World War is displayed here. The exhibits include weapons, uniforms and pictures.

Erinnerungsstätte für die Freiheitsbewegungen in der deutschen Geschichte (German Freedom Movements Memorial Museum)

Access via the north wing. ♿🕐 *Tue-Sun, 9.30am-5pm.* 🕐 *Closed 1 Jan, 24, 25 and 31 Dec.* ☎ *(072 22) 77 13 90; www.erinnerungsstaette-rastatt.de.*
The displays here follow freedom movements in Germany from ca 1500 to the resistance in former East Germany up to 1990.

Excursions

Schloss Favorite★★

5km/3mi southeast. 🚶 *Guided visit (1hr).* 🕐 *From mid-Mar to end Sep, Tue-Sun, 10am-5pm; Oct to mid-Nov, Tue-Sun, 10am-4pm.* 🎫 *€5.* ☎ *(072 22) 412 07.*

The exterior of this charming 18C Baroque palace is coated with an unusual matrix of gravel and granite chips. The **interior**★★ is particularly fine: floors of brilliant scagliola (stucco imitating encrusted marble); mirrors, mosaics and chinoiserie.

REGENSBURG★★

POPULATION: 129 000

Walk through Regensburg's medieval town centre to discover remarkably well-preserved treasures and a host of religious buildings. Nowadays Regensburg is the economic and cultural hub of eastern Bavaria, but its situation off the beaten track lends it a relaxed air. 🛈 *Altes Rathaus, 93047 Regensburg,* ☎ *(0941) 507 44 10.*

- ▶ **Orient Yourself:** Regensburg is located in eastern Bavaria and spans the Danube at the crossroads of the A 3 and A 93.
- 🅿 **Parking:** Garages are located throughout Regensburg. Visit http://wap.parkinfo.com for fees and locations.
- 🐝 **Don't Miss:** The suggested walking tour of the old city.
- 🕐 **Organizing Your Time:** Allow half a day for the suggested walking tour.
- ⛄ **Also See:** *STRAUBING (41km/25mi east), EICHSTÄTT (100km/63mi west), NUREMBERG (100km/63mi northwest).*

A Bit of History

Preserved by time – Regensburg began as a Roman garrison guarding the natural frontier of the Danube at its most northerly point. The town was converted to Christianity in the 7C, and St Boniface founded a bishopric there in 739, making it a centre for religious life in the Middle Ages. As the seat of the Bavarian dukes (6C-13C), the town developed into an important trading post. The town became part of Bavaria in the 19C and lost influence to Munich, which saved it from bombardment during the Second World War. Today its city centre remains miraculously intact.

The City of Diets – Once a Free Imperial City, Regensburg hosted plenary sessions of the Royal Diet (Reichstag), charged with responsibility for the internal peace and external security of the federation of the Holy Roman Empire. From 1663 to 1806 the city was the seat of a Permanent Diet – the first indication of a broad German government. The Diet drew representatives from 70 other states to Regensburg.

Walking Tour

The Old Quarter

Dom St. Peter★

🕐 *Open Apr to Oct, 6:30am-6pm; Nov to Mar, 6:30am-5pm.* ☎ *(0941) 586 55 00.*
Construction on this cathedral began after 1260 but was essentially brought to a halt in 1525; the spires were not added until the 19C. The **Donkey Tower** *(Eselsturm)*, above the northern transept is all that remains of the original Romanesque sanctuary. The **west front**, richly decorated, is the work of a local family of sculptors named Roritzer. The main entrance, flanked by two neo-Gothic towers, is unusual, with a triangular, jutting porch. A statue of St Peter can be seen on the pier.
Inside the huge Late Gothic nave houses two 13C masterpieces of local Gothic statuary: the Archangel Gabriel, and Mary at the Annunciation. The three chancel windows are adorned with beautiful 14C stained **glass**★★.

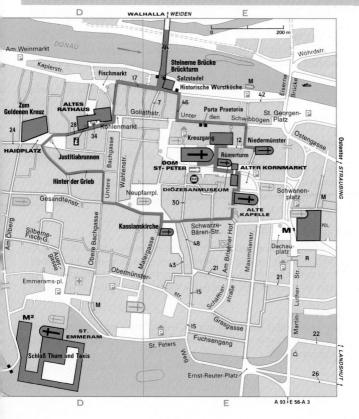

M. Herlien/MICHELIN

Detail of Dom St Peter.

Domschatz

In the south wing of the bishops' residence (Bischofshof), entrance via the courtyard. ⓞ *Open, Tue-Sat, 10am-5pm, Sun, noon-5pm.* ⓞ *Closed 1 Jan, Nov, 24 Dec.* ⊗ €2. ☎ *(0941) 595 32 25 30.*
The cathedral's treasury displays liturgical items, reliquaries and vestments from the 11C to the 18C.

Kreuzgang (Cloister)

Access via the cathedral garden. ⊷ *Guided tour (75min, cathedral visit included).* ⓞ *May to Oct, at 10am, 11am and 2pm, Sun, at 12 noon and 2pm; Nov to Apr, Mon-Sat, at 11am, Sun at 12 noon.* ⊗ €3. ☎ *(0941) 586 55 00.*
Inside the cloister are traces of ancient frescoes adorning the walls of the Romanesque *Allerheiligenkapelle*. The Alter Dom, the old 11C Stefanskapelle, is another highlight with an altar reliquary thought to date from the 5C-8C.

Diözesanmuseum

ⓞ *Open Apr to Oct, Tue-Sun, 10am-5pm.* ⊗ €2. ☎ *(0941) 595 32 25 30; www.bistumsmuseen-regensburg.de*
The museum is installed in the **Ulrichskirche**, an Early Gothic 13C church with 1 571 murals. Among other exhibits, visitors can see antique bishops' crosses, reliquaries and religious paintings.

Alte Kapelle★

The Basilica of Our Lady associated with this chapel stands on the south side of Alter Kornmarkt. Originally Carolingian, the Alte Kapelle was completely transformed in the Rococo style in the 18C. The splendid reredos, the painted ceiling and the gilded stuccowork are beautifully accented by the light penetrating the tall windows.

Kassianskirche

A Romanesque basilica with pillars and 18C Rococo decoration, the church's chief highlight is an altar in the south aisle. *Schöne Maria* (Lovely Mary) was sculpted by Hans Leinberger (1520).

Address Book

WHERE TO EAT

🍽 **Haus Heuport** – *Domplatz 7* ☎ *(941) 599 92 97 www.heuport. de* 🕐 *Closed 2 weeks in Jan.* This 13C mansion is located in the centre of the old town, opposite the cathedral. Behind the beautiful façade is a small restaurant and cocktail bar. Simple cuisine is served in the dining room or on the terrace.

🍽🍽 **David** – *Watmarkt 5 (5th floor)* ☎ *(0941) 56 18 58* 🕐 *Closed Sun and Mon.* Accessed by elevator, this 5th-floor restaurant is located in a historic mansion. French and Italian-influenced cuisine is served in a romantic atmosphere. A beautiful covered terrace offers views of the town.

WHERE TO STAY

🍽 **Hotel Wiendl** – *Universitäts-straße 9* ☎ *(0941) 92 02 70 Fax (0941) 9202728 www.hotelwiendl.de* 🅿 ⚡ *35 rooms* 🍽🍽 *Restaurant.* This small, unpretentious hotel has simple guestrooms furnished in pale chestnut wood. Country-style restaurant.

🍽🍽 **Hotel Kaiserhof** – *Kramgasse 10* ☎ *(0941) 58 53 50 Fax (0941) 58*

53 595 *www.kaiserhof-am-dom.de. 30 rooms.* ☒ Welcoming guestrooms all offer views of the cathedral's twin towers. A high vaulted ceiling overhangs the breakfast room set in a former 14C chapel.

TAKING A BREAK

Café Goldenes Kreuz – *Haidplatz 7* ☎ *(0941) 5 72 32* 🕐 *Mon-Sat, 7am-7pm, Sun and bank holidays, 9am-7pm.* This elegant tea room is in a historic building with abundant Gothic architecture. In summer months enjoy the vibrant terrace on the Haidplatz.

GOING OUT

Brauhaus Joh. Albrecht – *Schwarze-Bären-Str. 6* ☎ *(0941) 5 10 55 www. brauhaus-joh-albrecht.de* 🕐 *12pm-1am.* Convivial micro-brewery on 2 floors. Try home-brewed beers in a pleasant ambience with hearty regional dishes.

Félix – *Fröhliche-Türken-Str. 6* ☎ *(0941) 59 0 59 www.cafefelix.de* 🕐 *Sun-Thur, 9am-2am, Fri-Sat and bank holidays, 10am-3am.* This posh café is always lively. Service includes breakfast (until 3pm) through evening cocktails.

Haidplatz★

This square is surrounded by historic buildings, among which is an inn, Zum Goldenen Kreuz (no 7), with a stone tower and façade. In the centre of the square is the 1656 **Justitiabrunnen** (Fountain of Justice).

Altes Rathaus★

The eight-storey tower of the old town hall dates from 1250. The Gothic western section (Reichssaalbau) was built ca 1360. The façade includes a gabled doorway and a pedestal supporting a charming oriel window.

Inside, the **Reichstagsmuseum** is set in the splendid Gothic hall where the "Permanent Diet" used to meet. In the same building the Reichsstädtisches Kollegium houses an exhibition tracing the history of all the Regensburg Diets. 👟 *Guided tour, Apr to Oct, 9.30am-12 noon, 2-4pm, Sun, 10am-12 noon, 2-4pm, every half hour; Nov to Mar, 9.30,10.30am, 2pm, 3pm; Sun, 12 noon.* 🕐 *Closed 1 Jan and 24 Dec.* 👟 *€6.* ☎ *(0941) 507 44 10.*

Fischmarkt (Fish Market)

This is one of Regensburg's oldest market squares, built in 1529 in Italian style.

Steinerne Brücke

This 12C 310m/1 017ft bridge rests on 16 arches. From the middle, there is a fine **view**★ of the old town. In the foreground is the 14C Brückturm gateway, flanked by

The Gorges of the "Donaudurchbruch"

Between Kelheim and Weltenburg, the Danube narrows as it "breaks through" steep, narrow limestone cliffs in a series of meanders. The best way to view these gorges is to take a boat between the two towns. Excursions leave from Kelheim from mid-March to October and timetables are available from the Tourist Office. €7 round trip.

the huge roof of the 17C Salzstadel (salt loft). Beside this building, on the quayside, is the **Historische Wurstküche**, the oldest cooked sausage kitchen in Germany.

Sights

St Emmeram★

This was once the abbey church of an 8C Benedictine monastery. A Gothic gateway on **Emmeramsplatz** leads to the huge Romanesque porch (12C) and the double doors at the church entrance. The 11C sculptures by these doors (Jesus Christ, St Emmeram and St Dionysius) are among the oldest in Germany.

Schloss Thurn und Taxis

Guided visit (90min). ○ *Open Apr to Oct, at 11am, 2pm, 3pm and 4pm, and Sat-Sun at 10am; Nov to Mar, Sat-Sun, at 10am, 11am, 2pm and 3pm; 26 Dec-6 Jan, Mon-Fri at 2pm and 3pm.* ○ *Closed 24 and 25 Dec.* ○ *€11.50, Castle and Cloister.* ☎ *(0941) 504 81 33; www.thurnundtaxis.de.*

The Thurn and Taxis princes held the German postal monopoly until the 19C. As compensation for losing the monopoly, they were given the St Emmeram abbey buildings, which they occupied from 1816 and converted into a noteworthy Historicist style. Visitors can visit the state apartments as part of a guided tour.

Marstallmuseum

&○ *Open Apr to Oct, 11am-5pm, Sat-Sun, 10am-5pm; Nov to Mar, guided visit only, Sat-Sun, at 11.30am and 2pm; 26 Dec-6 Jan, additionally Mon-Fri at 2pm.* ○ *Closed 24 and 25 Dec.* ○ *€4.50.* ☎ *(0941) 504 81 33.*

The museum houses a fine collection of coaches, sleighs and sedan chairs. In the north wing of the coach house is the **Thurn und Taxis Museum,** a branch of the Bavarian Nationalmuseum. Displays include handcraft items from the royal family's possessions. ○ *Apr to Oct, 11am-5pm, Sat-Sun, 10am-5pm; Nov to Mar, Sat-Sun, 10am-5pm. Apr to Oct:* ○ *€4.50 (combined ticket with the Marstallmuseum); Nov to Mar:* ○ *€3.50.* ☎ *(0941) 504 81 33.*

☺ A Bit of Advice ☺

Nothing goes better with Bavarian *Bratwurst* than *Händlmaier's süßer Hausmachersenf*, the sweet, smoky mustard which is the speciality of Regensburg. Johanna Haendlmaier concocted it in 1914 to sell in her butcher's shop as the perfect accompaniment to her husband's sausages.

Excursions

Walhalla★

11km/7mi east – Leave Regensburg on the Steinerne Brücke, then turn left after Donaustauf. ○ *Open Apr to Sep: 9am-6pm; Oct, 9am-5pm; Nov to Mar, 10am-12 noon, 1-4pm.* ○ *Closed Shrove Tue, 24, 25 and 31 Dec.* ○ *€3.* ☎ *(094 03) 96 16 80; www.walhalla-regensburg.de.*

Built between 1830 and 1842 by Ludwig I of Bavaria, this Doric temple, strangely out of place in the Danube Valley, was intended to honour all the great men in German history. Inside are 124 busts of famous soldiers, artists and scientists.

Befreiungshalle★ (Liberation Monument)

28km/18mi southwest, just outside Kelheim. ○ *From mid-Mar to end Oct, 9am-6pm; from Nov to mid-Mar, 9am-4pm.* €2.50. ☎ *(094 41) 68 20 70.*
Celebrating Germany's liberation from Napoleonic rule, this 19C memorial was conceived by Ludwig I and modeled after Greek architecture. It takes the form of a huge rotunda, its central hall supported by 18 buttresses, each bearing an allegorical statue representing a Germanic people.

Kloster Weltenburg★

33km/21mi southwest. ♿○ *Visit to the abbey church only, 8am-6pm. .* ☎ *(094 41) 20 40.*
Set on the banks of the Danube, Weltenburg Abbey has a truly majestic appearance. The abbey church was built by Cosmas Damian Asam in 1718, with a narthex and a nave, both of them oval. A statue of St George is the church's centerpiece; the dome bears a *trompe-l'œil* Asam composition on the theme of the Church Triumphant.

RHEINTAL★★★

RHINE VALLEY

The Rhine is 1 320km/820mi long and flows through four different countries. Since the Middle Ages, it has been a unique highway for the exchange of commercial, intellectual and artistic ideas. Modern visitors will find its vineyards, escarpments, and hilltop castles just as attractive as did those Medieval merchants and travelers.

▶ **Orient Yourself:** Roads run along both river banks, allowing travellers to admire the scenery from the water's edge. There are no bridges between Koblenz and Mainz; ferries are the only way to cross the river. Shipping companies organise cruises and regular services on the Rhine, leaving from most of the larger towns.

Don't Miss: A relaxing cruise or drive along the river, if only for a short while.

○ **Organizing Your Time:** Allow four hours for suggested driving tour **1** and one day for driving tour **2**.

Especially for Kids: The fabulous legends associated with each of the Rhine's castles, fortresses and geological features.

Also See: *Bad KREUZNACH (16km/10mi south of Bingen), MAINZ (44km/27mi east of Rüdesheim), BONN (61km/38mi north of Koblenz), MOSELTAL (our suggested touring programme includes Koblenz).*

A Bit of History

The Rhine Legends – There is not, along the whole length of the Rhine, a castle, an island, even a rock without its tale of chivalry or legend. **Lohengrin**, the Knight of the Swan, appeared at the foot of the castle of Kleve (Cleves); at the **Loreley**, a beautiful enchantress bewitched boatmen with her song, leading their vessels to disaster.
But the single outstanding Rhine legend is the story of the Nibelungen, an inexhaustible source of inspiration from which Wagner borrowed for his opera tetralogy *The Ring Cycle*. Inspired by Germanic and Scandinavian myths, the **Song of the**

The treacherous Loreley and the Goethe pleasure boat

Nibelungen was probably composed late in the 12C. It tells of the splendours of the 5C Burgundian court at Worms, and of the passions inflaming the hearts of its heroes, known also under the name of Nibelungen.

From the Alps to the North Sea – The Rhine rises in the Swiss Alps. Gushing down the mountains, it quickly reaches Lake Constance *(Bodensee)* which it crosses at a sluggish pace. After the exit from Lake Constance, rock outcrops from the Black Forest and the foothills of the Jura produce the famous Rhine Falls at Schaffhausen (🕭 *see The Green Guide Switzerland)*. Farther downstream, limestone strata cause rapids *(Laufen)*. At Basle, the Rhine abruptly changes direction, veering north to fertilise the land of the Vosges and the Black Forest.

From Bingen to Neuwied, north of Koblenz, the Rhine cuts its way through the Rhineland schist massif, where the rock can foment dangerous whirlpools. This "romantic" stretch of river valley, with its alternation of vineyards, woods, escarpments and castle ruins, is the most picturesque part of the Rhine Gorge. Later, having passed through the industrial region around Duisburg, the river turns west and curls slowly across the plain toward the sea.

An Exceptional Shipping Lane – The Rhine has always been an important means of European transport. Today, the Rhine, navigable over almost 1 000km/620mi between Rotterdam and Rheinfelden, handles annual traffic of 265 million tons. The Rhine also boasts in Duisburg-Ruhrort the world's largest river port (18 million tons annually).

Driving Tours

1 The Loreley★★ – from Rüdesheim to Koblenz

75km/47mi. This route, following the Rhine's east bank, passes through the wildest and steepest part of the valley, with splendid views of the castles and fortresses on the river's far side.

After **Rüdesheim**★ (🕭 *see entry)*, the road runs beneath terraced vineyards overlooked by the ruins of Burg Ehrenfels. This fortress was built by the archbishops of Mainz at the same time as the Mäuseturm on the opposite bank, which served as a toll booth.

The Mäuseturm

According to legend, Hatto, Archbishop of Mainz, built this tower to collect tolls from boatmen. When famine hit the local peasants, they fled to Mainz to demand wheat. Hatto sent them to the granary, locked them inside and set fire to the building. Soon nothing remained but a few mice who managed to escape. They scampered to the archbishop's palace and ate everything they could find. Hatto headed to his Rhine tower for refuge. But the mice followed him, and when his boat landed, they polished him off.

After Assmannshausen, silhouetted high up on the opposite bank, the crenellated towers of Rheinstein, Reichenstein and Sooneck appear one after the other. The tower of Fürstenberg, on the wooded slopes facing Lorch, marks the start of an open stretch of vineyards and the towers of Bacharach, followed by the fortified isle of Pfalz.

Pfalz bei Kaub★ (Pfalzgrafenstein)

Opposite Kaub. ⊙ *Apr-Sep: open daily except Mon, 9am-1pm, 2-6pm; Oct-Nov and Jan-Mar: open daily except Mon, 9am-1pm, 2-5pm. Last admission 1hr before closing.* ⊙ *Closed Dec.* ⊛ *€4.10.*
The massive five-sided keep of this toll fortress rises from the centre of the river, encircled by a turreted fortified wall. Before a sharp bend in the river, admire the **setting**★★ of the towers of Oberwesel at the foot of the Schönburg on the far side of the river. The sharp bend leads to the most untamed stretch on this part of the Rhine.

The Loreley★★★

This legendary spur, 132m/433ft high, symbolizes the Romantic Rhine and enjoys a special place in German literature. The outcropping reduces the river's width by one quarter. According to legend, the Loreley was a water sprite who bewitched boatmen with her beauty and melodious songs at the river's most dangerous spot.

St Goarshausen

The town, strung out along the river bank (a pleasant spot for a walk), is dominated by the **Katz** (Cat) stronghold, said to have been built to neutralise the **Maus** (Mouse), a little farther downstream.

Burg Gutenfels and the fortified island of Pfalz on the Rhine

D. Scherf/MICHELIN

Loreley viewpoint★★

▶ *From St Goarshausen take the road signposted "Loreley-Burgenstraße". During high season there are shuttle buses between St Goarshausen/Schiffsanleger and the Loreley Plateau.*

There are impressive **views**★★ plunging down into the romantic gorge from several accessible spurs here. On the plateau a landscape garden with waymarked footpaths is laid out and a Loreley centre set up, in which interactive displays cover the Loreley legend, and local geology, flora and fauna. ⅋⏱ *From Apr to end of Oct: 10am-6pm.* ⊚ €1. ☎ *(067 71) 59 90 93; www.loreley-touristik.de.*

Address Book

WHERE TO EAT

⊝⊜ **Gasthaus Hirsch** – *Rhein-straße 17, 56154 Boppard-Hirzenach* ☎ *(06741) 26 01 www.gasthaus-hirsch. net* ⏱ *Closed 2 weeks after Easter and mid- to 25 Nov.* A tasteful, rustic establishment. The panelled dining room is adorned with paintings. Tasty dishes made with market produce.

⊝⊜ **Tannenheim** – *Bahnhof Buch-holz 3 (B 327), 56154 Boppard-Buchholz* ☎ *(06742) 22 81 www.hotel-tannen-heim.de* ⏱ *Closed 1st-18 Jan, Sat lunch-time, Thur, Sun and public holidays.* This charming restaurant has been run by the Fuchs family for four generations. It also has a few rooms and a pretty garden. Expect varied seasonal dishes.

⊝⊜⊟ **Zum Turm** – *Zollstraße 50, 56349 Kaub* ☎ *(06774) 922 00 www. rhein-hotel-turm.com* ⏱ *Closed 1 week in early Jan, 1 week late July, and mid- to late Nov.* This establishment near the old tower was founded over 300 years ago and has housed a small family-run restaurant for over a century.

WHERE TO STAY

⊝⊜ **Hotel Altkölnischer Hof** – *Blücherstraße 2, 55422 Bacharach* ☎ *(06743) 13 39 Fax (06743) 2793 www. altkoelnischer-hof.de* ⏱ *Open Apr-Oct* 20 rooms ⊠ ⊝⊜ Restaurant. This family-run hotel is in an old, restored half-timbered house. Charming rooms have wooden furniture and Rhineland specialties are served in the panelled dining room or tavern.

⊝⊜ **Hotel Zum Goldenen Löwen** – *Heerstraße 82, 56329 St. Goar* ☎ *(06741) 16 74 Fax (06741) 2852* ⊁ *12 rooms* ⊠ ⊝⊜⊟ Restaurant. A convenient little hotel with well-kept rooms of varying size and furnishings. Old German-style rustic restaurant.

⊝⊜⊟ **Hotel Ebertor** – *Heer-straße 172, 56154 Boppard* ☎ *(06742) 80 70 Fax (06742) 807100 www.ebertor. de* ▣ ⊁ ⅋ *66 rooms* ⊠ ⊝⊜ Restaurant. This hotel offers simple rooms and an extra bed on request. The "Brasserie Eberbach" serves wild boar specialities from the Boppard forest.

⊝⊜⊟ **Hotel Landsknecht** – *An der Rheinufer-Straße (B 9), 56329 St. Goar-Fellen* ☎ *(06741) 20 11 Fax (06741) 7499 www.hotel-landsknecht.de* ⏱ *Closed Jan-Feb* ▣ *15 rooms* ⊠ ⊝⊜ Res-taurant. A pleasant, modern hotel with comfortable rooms and an adjoining garden. The rustic restaurant offers Rhine River views from its terrace.

⊝⊜⊟ **Park-Hotel** – *Marktstraße 8, 55422 Bacharach* ☎ *(06743) 14 22 Fax (06743) 1541 park-hotel-bachar-ach@t-online.de* ⏱ *Open mid Mar to mid Nov* ▣ ⌇ *25 rooms* ⊠ ⊝⊜⊟ Restaurant. This establishment has been run by the same family for years, offering comfortable rooms, some with Rhine River views. Regional dishes served in the *Pfalzgrafen* room.

⊝⊜⊟⊟ **Schloßhotel und Villa Rheinfels** – *Schloßberg 47, 56329 St. Goar* ☎ *(06741) 80 20 Fax (06741) 802802 www.burgrheinfels. de* ▣ ⌇ *56 rooms* ⊠ ⊝⊜⊟ Res-taurant. In the Loreley Valley, in front of the impressive castle, the Schloß-hotel und Villa Rheinfels offers pleasant accommodation in comfortable rooms. Lovely view from the classic restaurant.

The Rival Brothers

▷ *At Kamp-Bornhofen, turn right toward Dahlheim, then right again at the sign "Zu den Burgen".*

The hill slopes become wild again. Beyond Kestert there is a fine **panorama**★★; from the ruins of **Liebenstein Fortress** care seen **Sterrenberg** and the valley below. The two castles are traditionally linked to a legend concerning two rival brothers. From Boppard on, where the Rhine swings into a huge double loop, the landscape becomes densely cultivated by vines. Soon the fortress of Marksburg emerges on its promontory.

▷ *At Braubach, take the road to Nastätten.*

Marksburg★

Guided tour (50min). ⏰ *From Easter to Oct: 10am-5pm; from Nov to Easter: 11am-4pm.* ⏰ *Closed 24-31 Dec.* ⊕ *€4.50.* ☎ *(026 27) 206; www.marksburg.de.*
The **castle**, the only one in the whole Rhine Valley never to have been destroyed, is built on an almost aerial **site**★★. Noteworthy are the medieval garden and collection of armor from 600 BC to the 15C.

Burg Lahneck

3km/2mi from Lahnstein, near the confluence of the Rhine and the Lahn. *Guided tour (40min).* ⏰ *Apr-Oct: 10am-5pm.* ⊕ *€3.* ☎ *(026 21) 91 41 71; www.burg-lahneck.de.*
The ruins of this fortress, originally built in the 13C to protect neighbouring silver mines, were reconstructed in neo-Gothic style in the 19C. From the keep is a **view** of the junction of the two rivers and the troubadour castle of Stolzenfels, on the far side of the Rhine.

2 The Rhine Castles★★★ – from Koblenz to Bingen

63km/39mi This itinerary retraces the previous one, in the opposite direction, on the other side of the river. Soon after leaving Koblenz, Lahneck comes into view again, its tower overlooking the river confluence. Above, on the right, is Stolzenfels.

Stolzenfels

Guided tour (45min). ⏰ *Apr-Sep: open daily except Mon, 10am-6pm; Oct-Mar: open daily except Mon, 10am-5pm* ⊕ *€2.60.* ⏰ *Closed Dec* ☎ *(0261) 516 56; www.schloss-stolzenfels.de.*
This enormous **castle** was reconstructed in 1842. The style is now neo-Gothic, and the sumptuous **interior**★ is a museum. From the slope against which Stolzenfels is built, the terrace offers a view of Koblenz and the citadel of Ehrenbreitstein.

Gedeonseck

1hr round trip, including 20min on a chair-lift. ⏰ *Late Mar to early Apr: 10am-5pm, Sat-Sun 10am-5.30pm; Apr: 10am-5.30pm, Sat-Sun 10am-6pm; 1 May and mid-Jun to late Aug: 9.30am-6.30pm; 2 May to mid-Jun and Sep: 10am-6pm, Sat-Sun 10am-6.30pm; early to mid-Oct: 10am-5.30pm; mid- to late Oct: 10am-5pm.* ⊕ *€6.20 round trip.* ☎ *(067 42) 25 10.*
Southward is a superb **view**★ of the great convex loop of the Rhine as it flows around the Boppard curve.

The Rhine Valley Castles

The Rhine Valley boasts an impressive number of castles. Stately residences, defensive forts, toll gates, travelers' refuges for travellers, each served a purpose. While many were severely damaged in fighting during the 17C and 18C, many castles were rebuilt in following the creation of the German Confederation in 1815.

Boppard

Originally a Roman camp, Boppard became a Free Imperial City in the Middle Ages. Interesting sights include the Late Romanesque Severuskirche and the Gothic Carmelite church with its rich interior fittings: 15C choir stalls and Renaissance tombs. The museum in the 14C fortress displays, among other things, wooden furniture by local artist Michael Thonet. There is also a pleasant riverside walk.

The beginning of the "romantic" Rhine Gorge is marked by the two Rival Brothers fortresses (& *see above*) on the opposite slopes. After Hirzenach, the Cat and Mouse towers are visible, standing above St Goarshausen.

St-Goar

The village, clinging to the hillside at the foot of the impressive **Rheinfels Castle**★★, *(Burg Rheinfels:* ◷ *Mar-Sep 9am-6pm; Oct 9am-5pm; Nov-Mar, sat-Sun, 11am-5pm.* ◌ €4. ☏ *(067 41) 7753)* commands with St Goarshausen the Loreley passage. The river here, obstructed and narrowed by the legendary rock, swirls and eddies dangerously. Rheinfels was, until it fell to the French in 1797, the most powerful fortress in the whole valley. It is worth climbing the clock tower to get an overall view of the turbulent Rhine, the Cat and Mouse towers, and the maze of towers, gates and courts comprising Rheinfels.

The banks of the river remain steep and heavily wooded until Oberwesel.

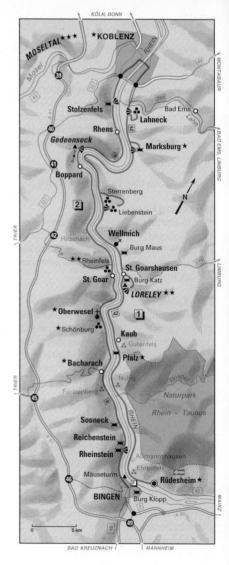

Oberwesel

Sixteen towers survive of the original fortifications around this idyllic wine-growing village. It is possible to walk along part of the medieval wall, from where there is a good view of the Rhine. South of the town, the Gothic **Liebfrauenkirche**★ has a fine 14C altarpiece, one of the oldest in Germany, a Gothic rood screen and an unusual 1510 triptych illustrating the 15 cataclysms presaging the end of the world.

From the terrace of **Schönberg Castle**★, a little farther on, is a view of Kaub, on the far side of the river, and the fortified isle of Pfalz. Schönberg is a block of three forts sheltered by a common defensive wall.

Bacharach★

Once the property of the counts of the Palatinate, Bacharach, a town of vineyards and ancient towers, is one of the most popular resorts in the Rhine Valley. The houses in Marktplatz and Oberstraße, decked with flowers, are a delight. One of the last Romanesque naves built in Germany can be seen in Peterskirche.

The ruined towers of Nollig and Fürstenberg mark the end of the valley's most grandiose stretch; from here on are fewer bends, the river running between the steep eastern bank and the cliffs on the opposite shore.

The road on this side passes below castles whose sites are ever more audacious, from Sooneck to Reichenstein and finally Rheinstein.

Burg Sooneck

Guided tour (45min). Mid Apr-Sep: open daily except Mon, 10am-6pm; Oct-mid-Apr, daily except Mon, 10am-5pm. Closed Dec. €2.60. (067 43) 60 64.

This **fortress** is restored and tiered to suit the terrain with a maze of staircases, platforms and terraced gardens beneath the turrets. It clings to a steep slope of the Soonwald outcrop.

Burg Reichenstein

From Mar to mid Nov: open daily except Mon, 10am-6pm. €3.40. (067 21) 61 17.

Well-situated at the mouth of a rural valley, this 10C neo-feudal **castle** has a collection of arms and hunting trophies. After serving as an imperial tollhouse, it was converted into a summer residence in the 19C.

Burg Rheinstein

From mid Mar to mid Nov: 9.30am-5.30pm; from mid Nov to mid Mar: open daily except Fri-Sat, 2-5pm, Sun 10am-5pm. Closed 20 Dec-5 Jan. €9. (067 21) 63 48.

The **castle** is perched on a perpendicular rock spur, in a commanding position above the Rhine. From the foremost watchtower there is a bird's-eye **view**★★ of the valley. Rheinstein was the first of the Rhine castles to be rebuilt by the Hohenzollerns (after 1823).

Once past the **Mäuseturm**, balanced on its tiny islet in the middle of the river, the valley widens out and the east bank becomes covered with terraced vines.

Bingen

Bingen was founded by the Romans at the confluence of the Rhine and the Nahe (*Castel Bingium*). Nowadays, tourism and wine-growing are the town's main sources of income.

Burg Klopp, an ancient stronghold built by the bishops of Mainz, has been razed to the ground more than once. From the terrace there is a **view**★ of the Binger Loch.

ROMANTISCHE STRASSE★★

By way of river valleys and an idyllic, rolling countryside, the "Romantic Road" itinerary recalls at every stage some aspect of uniquely German history. As the route unfolds, it evokes medieval city life (Rothenburg), the religious sensibility of artists like Tilman Riemenschneider, German chivalry (Bad Mergentheim), Baroque episcopal courts and Imperial towns like Würzburg. ▪ *Waaggässlein 1, 91550 Dinkelsbühl, ☎ (09851) 902 71. Internet site: www.romantischestrasse.com.*

▶ **Orient Yourself:** From the Main Valley to the foot of the Bavarian Alps stretches Germany's most popular tourist itinerary, crossing river valleys, prairies, forests and orchards, as well as pretty little towns, most of them with car-free town centres. The entire route is signposted "Romantische Straße." From April to October, the Europabus travels the route in both directions once a day. Deutsche Touring,(069) 790 32 56; www.deutsche-touring.com.

⊙ **Don't Miss:** Rothenburg o.d. Tauber, Dinkelsbühl

⏱ **Organizing Your Time:** Allow four hours for suggested driving tour ①; five hours for driving tour ②; and a full day for driving tour ③.

⛰ **Also See:** *Deutsche ALPENSTRASSE, MÜNCHEN (66km/41mi east of AUGSBURG).*

Driving Tours

① From Würzburg to Rothenburg o. d. T.

100km/62mi

▶ *Leaving* **Würzburg**★★ *(⛰ see entry), B 27 descends toward the valley of the Tauber.*

Address Book

WHERE TO STAY

⊜⊜ **Hotel Goldener Anker** – *Untere Schmiedgasse 22, 91550 Dinkelsbühl* ☎ *(09851) 578 00 Fax (09851) 578080 www.goldener-anker-dkb.de 25 rooms* ⊑ ⊜⊜ *Restaurant* This old inn has a neat façade and good, spacious rooms decorated in a rustic style. Traditional Franconian cooking.

⊜⊜ **Hotel Kunst-Stuben** – *Segringer Straße 52, 91550 Dinkelsbühl* ☎ *(09851) 67 50 Fax (09851) 553527 www.kunst-stuben.de* ⏱ *Closed Feb* ✝✝ *5 rooms* ⊑ A friendly small hotel incorporating an artist's workshop. Immaculate rooms and a library guarantee a restful stay.

⊜⊜ **Laurentius** – *Marktplatz 5, 97990 Weikersheim* ☎ *(07934) 910 80 Fax (07934) 910818 www.hotel-laurentius.de* ▣ ✝✝ *11 rooms* ⊑ ⊜⊜ *Restaurant* Behind this establishment's charming yellow façade are immaculate guestrooms with Italian furnishings. The restaurant with visible kitchen is in a beautiful vaulted cellar.

⊜⊜ **Hotel Blauer Hecht** – *Schweinemarkt 1, 91550 Dinkelsbühl* ☎ *(09851) 58 10 Fax (09851) 581170* ⏱ *Closed Jan* ⚒ ✝✝ *44 rooms* ⊑ ⊜⊜ *Restaurant* Charming hotel in a former brewery inn of 1684. Beautifully furnished and personalised guestrooms. Rustic old German restaurant.

⊜⊜ **Romantik Hotel Greifen-Post** – *Marktplatz 8, 91555 Feuchtwangen* ☎ *(09852) 68 00 Fax (09852) 68068 www.greifen.de* ⚒ ✝✝ *35 rooms* ⊑ ⊜⊜ *Restaurant* This 600-year-old establishment knows the true meaning of hospitality. Guestrooms are elegantly furnished and the dining rooms reflect historic charm.

Dinkelsbühl

Bad Mergentheim★ – 🍴 *See Bad MERGENTHEIM.*

Weikersheim
♿🚶 *Guided tour (1hr).* 🕐 *Open Apr to Nov, 9am–6pm.* 🕐 *Closed 24 and 31 Dec.* 💶 *€4.50.* ☎ *(079 34) 99 29 50.*
Once the seat of the counts of Hohenlohe, this town's castle was built between 1580 and 1680 on the banks of the Tauber without Baroque influences. The magnificent **Knights' Hall**★★ *(Rittersaal)* is typical of the transition between the Renaissance and Baroque styles. **Formal gardens** (1710), peopled with grotesque statues in the Franconian style, end in a charming orangery.

▶ *The picturesque section of the route, in the narrow Tauber Valley, begins above the town of Bieberehren. The road rises and falls over slopes covered alternately by woodland, orchards and willow-fringed riverbanks.*

Creglingen
The isolated Herrgottskirche, 1.5km/1mi along the road to Blaufelden, contains the **Altarpiece of the Virgin Mary**★★ sculpted by Tilman Riemenschneider. The artist appears to have channeled his own sensitivity into the expression of the Madonna at the Assumption. Opposite the church is a **thimble museum** *(Fingerhutmuseum)*, the only one of its kind in Germany.

Detwang
In the church at Detwang another **Riemenschneider altarpiece**★ portrays the *Crucifixion.*

Rothenburg ob der Tauber★★★ – 🍴 *See ROTHENBURG OB DER TAUBER.*

② From Rothenburg o. d. T. to Donauwörth

105km/64mi

Feuchtwangen

Once a Free Imperial City, this town was also the birthplace of the troubadour Walther von der Vogelweide. An attractive market place sits surrounded by pretty houses and overlooked by a parish church with another Altarpiece of the Virgin, this time by Albrecht Dürer's teacher, Michael Wolgemut. Installed in a 17C burgher's house is a **Museum of Franconian Folklore** (Fränkisches Museum) displaying a collection of furniture and regional pottery and costumes.

Dinkelsbühl★

Ramparts and watchtowers still surround this idyllic medieval town which wakes up every July with a colourful children's festival (Kinderzeche) commemorating the relief of Dinkelsbühl in the Thirty Years War (see Calendar of events).

The **Georgskirche**★ has retained its Romanesque tower. Other historic highlights include the **Deutsches Haus**★ (Am Weinmarkt), with its richly decorated Renaissance façade; and the Hezelhof (Segringer Straße 7), remarkable for its long, flower-bedecked balconies overlooking the inner courtyard.

The undulating landscape is supplanted, after Nördlingen, by the bleak Ries basin. This treeless depression forms a symmetrical bowl 20km/12mi across and 240m/656ft deep, thought by some geologists to have been caused millions of years ago by a meteorite.

Wallerstein

From the summit of the rock, reached by a pathway cut in the strata, there is a panorama over the Ries Basin (access via the Fürstlicher Keller).

Nördlingen★ – See NÖRDLINGEN

Schloss Harburg

Guided visit (1hr). Mid-Mar to end Oct, Tue-Sun, 10am-5pm. €4.50. (090 80) 968 60.
A large fortified castle whose buildings look down on the picturesque houses of a village along the banks of the Wörnitz.

▶ Leave on the Mündlingerstraße, to the left, and take the Romantic Road to Mündling for Kaisheim.

Kaisheim

The former Cistercian abbey church (Zisterzienserkloster) was built at the end of the 14C in the full flower of the Gothic era. (The abbey itself is now a penal institution). Around the chancel is a 12-sided **ambulatory**★ (to visit, apply at the presbytery.) The 18C emperor's room in the Imperial foundation is open to the public (on request).

Donauwörth

This Free Imperial City is proud of its pastel historic buildings along the Reichsstraße; the most impressive are the town hall and Fuggerhaus (1543). The 18C Baroque pilgrimage church of Heilig Kreuz boasts Wessobrunn stuccowork. The Gothic Liebfrauenmünster has beautiful 15C murals. Parts of the town's fortifications still stand.

③ **From Donauwörth to Füssen**

148km/92mi. This drive along the ancient Via Claudia, one of the main arteries of the old Holy Roman Empire, owes its interest less to the route (which follows the Lech Valley) than to the historical souvenirs evoked by the sites on the way. These include **Augsburg**★★, **Landsberg**★, **Neuschwanstein**★★★ and **Hohenschwangau**★, and (well worth the price of a small detour) the **Wieskirche**★★ (see separate entries).

ROSTOCK★

POPULATION: 199 000

A particularly choice situation on the wide Warnow estuary favoured the development of Rostock from its earliest days: the town was a member of the Hanseatic League and the town's port still plays an important part in international maritime commerce. An intensive rehabilitation program has returned this city's historic glory, making the city more attractive than ever to tourists. 🛈 *Neuer Markt 3, 18055 Rostock, ☎ (0381) 194 33.*

▶ **Orient Yourself:** One of the most important Baltic ports, Rostock also has one the highest populations in the Mecklemburg area. The A 19 and the A 24 link the town to Berlin (allow 2hr 30min); the A 20 links the town to Lübeck.

🅿 **Parking:** Garages are located throughout Rostock. An especially convenient garage is located near the main train station.

😊 **Don't Miss:** The Baltic resorts of Warnemünde, Fischland, Darß and Zingst.

🕐 **Organizing Your Time:** Allow half a day for the suggested walking tour.

Kids **Especially for Kids:** The Baltic resorts of Warnemünde, Fischland, Darß and Zingst.

👣 **Also See:** *Bad DOBERAN (16km/10mi west), STRALSUND (75km/47mi east), MECKLEMBURGISCHE SEENPLATTE (accessible via the A 19 to the south).*

A Bit of History

Object of Desire – By the 13C, Rostock was already a member of the Hanseatic League, minting its own money and asserting independence from the princes of Mecklenburg. In 1419, Rostock founded the first Baltic university. Such a position drew the envy of powerful neighbours, with the result of substantial damage during the Thirty Years War (1618-48), the Nordic struggle for supremacy (1700-21), and the **Napoleonic Wars**. In more modern times, until German **Reunification**, Rostock was East Germany's only significant outlet to the Baltic and to the rest of the world.

Traditional wicker beach-chairs on the sands

M. Hertlein/MICHELIN

Walking Tour

The Old Town★

Marienkirche★★

The imposing cross-shaped basilica results from a 15C transformation of an existing hall-church. It is one of the biggest churches in northern Germany. The massive tower was not completed until the 18C. From the top is a **panorama**★ of the city and the docks. Inside the church, note the 1472 **astronomic clock**★★ (its face was remodelled in 1643), which comprises a calendar valid until 2017.

Address Book

TOUR OF THE HARBOUR

We recommend a tour of the harbour to fully appreciate the role of international shipping to Rostock. Boats depart from docks Stadthafen, by Schnickmannstraße, and Warnemünde/Alter und Neuer Strom. Details and fares from the tourist office: ☎ (0381) 381 22 22.

WHERE TO EAT

🍽🍽 **Seekiste zur Krim** – *Am Strom 47, 18119 Rostock-Warnemünde* ☎ *(0381) 5 21 14* 🕐 *End of May to early Oct, 11am-midnight, Oct-Apr, Mon-Fri, 5pm-midnight, Sat-Sun, 11am-midnight* ♿ 🍽*4 rooms* Before he moved to Warnemünde, the proprietor of this establishment was a sailor, collecting souvenirs now displayed here. Traditional dishes and Baltic fish are served.

🍽🍽🍽 **Zur Gartenlaube 1888** – *Anastasiastraße 24, 18119 Rostock-Warnemünde 11km/7mi northwest* ☎ *(0381) 526 61 www.zur-gartenlaube.de* 🕐 *Closed Sun* Behind its painted façade, this restaurant serves dinner in a nostalgic setting. Enjoy varied cuisine in a rustic atmosphere.

WHERE TO STAY

🍽🍽 **Hotel & Appartementhaus Fischerhus** – *Alexandrinenstr. 124, 18119 Rostock-Warnemünde* ☎ *(0381) 54 83 10 Fax (0381) 5 48 31 10 www.hotel-fischerhus.de* 🚭 🅿 ♿ *24 apartments*🛏 Modern apartments with all modern comforts, most of them in former fishermens' huts complete with kitchens. Breakfast is served on the white porcelain of the Wellenspiel Café.

🍽🍽 **InterCityHotel** – *Herweghstraße 51* ☎ *(0381) 495 00 Fax (0381) 4950999 rostock@intercityhotel.de* 🅿 🍴 ♿ *174 rooms* 🛏 🍽🍽 *Restaurant* A few feet from the main train station, functional rooms with light-coloured furniture. The hotel pass *(Hotelausweis)* entitles you to reduced fares on public transport.

TAKING A BREAK

Marientreff – *Bei der Marienkirche 27* ☎ *(0381) 4 92 23 89* 🕐 *Mon-Sat, 11.30am-5.30pm* 🕐 *Closed 25 Dec-1 Jan.* This meeting place cum tea room is a charitable concern in the former sacristan's house near the Marienkirche. Homemade cakes and drinks are served in a cosy atmosphere.

GOING OUT

USEFUL TIPS

There are plenty of restaurants on and around Kröpeliner Str. and in the Kröpeliner Tor-Vorstadt district west of the old town. Young people and students frequent the latter. There is a seaside resort at Warnemünde, located 11km/7mi north of the town centre, with promenades along the estuary of the Warnow (Am Strom) and Baltic sea beach (Seestr. and Seepromenade) edged with cafés, restaurants and bars.

Szenario – *Friedhofsweg 44a* ☎ *(0381) 5 10 84 22* 🕐 *Mon-Sat, 11am-11pm.* The proprietor's Swiss heritage shows with *röstis* on this bistro's menu. *Tapas* is served from 6pm. Contemporary art covers the walls of the former school.

Zur Kogge – *Wokrenter Str. 27* ☎ *(0381) 4 93 44 93 www.zur-kogge.m-vp.de* 🕐 *11.30am-midnight.* This restaurant's interior is reminiscent of a ship. Lifebelts are attached to the balustrade of the gallery and there is plenty of maritime bric-a-brac.

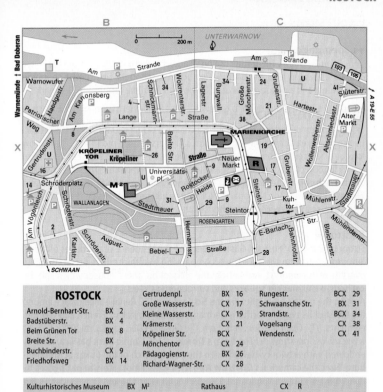

Rathaus (Town Hall)

Neuer Markt. This town hall is composed of three 13C-14C gabled houses topped by a brick gallery supporting seven towers. The Baroque façade was added in 1727.

Schiffahrtsmuseum★ (Navigational Museum)

At the corner of August-Bebel-Straße and Richard-Wagner-Straße. 🕐 *Open Tue-Sun, 10am-6pm.* 👁 *€3.* ☎ *(0381) 12 83 13 64.*
The museum charts the history of maritime travel in the Baltic region from its earliest days to the present. Models of ships, paintings, navigational instruments and photographs document maritime life and work.

Kröpeliner Straße

This pedestrian zone is Rostock's shopping and commercial centre. It is bordered by gabled houses with façades from Baroque and Renaissance times. At no 82, the brick façade of the 15C Heilig-Geist-Spital is unique for its stepped gable.

Kulturhistorisches Museum★ (Cultural history museum)

🕐 *Open Tue-Sun, 10am-6pm.* ☎ *(0381) 20 35 90.*
A former 13C Cistercian convent founded by Danish Queen Margarethe, this building, the only completely preserved convent complex in the region, houses medieval religious art, including the **Altarpiece of the Three Kings**★ (late 15C).

Excursions

Warnemünde★

Kids *11km/7mi north.* This former fishing village, bought by its citizens from the Prince of Mecklenburg in 1323, has become Rostock's most popular beach, with charming little streets and a pleasant seacoast. Ferries run from the terminal to Denmark.

Fischland, Darß and Zingst

Kids *Northeast of Rostock.* The peninsular chain of Fischland-Darß-Zingst is an attractive coastal area alternating with woods, salt-marshes and moorland. The narrow tongue of land extends north and east, parallel to the mainland and separated from it by a lagoon of brackish Baltic seawater and fresh riverwater. The artists' village of **Ahrenshoop** in the slightly hilly **Fischland** is a popular Baltic resort. **Darß** and **Zingst** form part of the National Park. The little villages and seaside resorts feature attractive, relaxing reed-covered houses and cottages.

Güstrow★

50km/31mi south of Rostock. Güstrow became the residence of the dukes of Mecklenburg-Güstrow in the 16C. The accompanying wealth continued to accumulate over the next centuries, visible from the elegant burghers' houses which line the **cathedral** and **market squares** and surrounding streets.

Among the town's highlights are the **Schloss**★, a 16C Renaissance palace among the finest of its type in northern Germany, combining Italian, French and German elements. (*Open Tue-Sun, 9am-5pm. Closed 24 Dec. €3. (038 43) 75 20; www.schloss-guestrow.de)* The town's **Dom**★, a 14C Gothic brick basilica, is richly endowed with artworks, having been the court church of the dukes of Mecklenburg. Note the cathedral's **Güstrow Apostles**★, 12 almost life-size oak figures by Claus Berg of Lübeck from ca 1530. A stark contrast to these is Ernst Barlach's *Der Schwebende.*

Ernst-Barlach Stiftung★ (Barlach Museum)

Open Apr to Oct, Tue-Sun, 10am-5pm; Nov to Mar, Tue-Sun, 11am-4pm. Closed 1 Jan, 24 and 31 Dec. €3.50. (038 43) 822 99.

This museum honoring Barlach is located in three different parts of Güstrow: his religious works are in the Late Gothic **Gertrudenkapelle**, which the artist longed in vain to use as a studio. The "Barlachweg" leads to Barlach's **Heidberg studio**, on the shores of the Inselsee just outside town. A few yards from the studio are rotating exhibitions in the first museum built in the former East Germany.

ROTHENBURG

ob der TAUBER★★★

POPULATION: 11 000

One of the oldest towns on the "Romantic Road," Rothenburg overlooks the winding course of the River Tauber from its rocky crag. Once behind the ramparts in the pedestrian-only central enclave, visitors revel in the 16C among ancient houses, fountains and narrow, cobbled lanes. *Marktplatz 2, 91541 Rothenburg, (098 61) 404 92. The tourist office offers a free booklet about the town's historic buildings.*

▶ **Orient Yourself:** The old town stands on a steep promontory overlooking a meander in the River Tauber, its sides cloaked in vineyards.

◉ **Don't Miss:** A stroll through the Old Town.

◔ **Organizing Your Time:** Allow four hours for the suggested walking tour.

Kids **Especially for Kids:** The mechanical clock on the Ratstrinkstube and a walk along the ramparts.

◔ **Also See:** *ROMANTISCHE STRASSE, HOHENLOHER LAND (Langenburg is 30km/19mi west), NUREMBERG (83km/52mi east).*

A Bit of History

A Long Drink *(Meistertrunk)* – During the Thirty Years' War, Protestant Rothenburg was unable to withstand the Catholic siege by General Tilly's army. After 40 000 victorious mercenaries had pillaged the town for three months, Tilly decided to raze it unless, he declared, some local could empty in a single draught a hanap (a 6-pint/3.4litre tankard) of wine. A man named Nusch succeeded and Rothenburg was saved. Ever since Rothenburgers have re-created the event annually at Pentecost.

Saved again – Rothenburg stagnated throughout the 17C and 18C, too poor to expand beyond its own walls. In the 19C, however, the town's steep-roofed houses with their gables, staircase turrets and corner oriels were rediscovered by Romantic painters, and Rothenburg became a tourist attraction.

Walking Tour

Old Town★★★ (Altstadt)

▶ *Starting at Marktplatz, follow the itinerary marked on the town map.*

Rathaus★ (Town Hall)
This 14C structure has seen a number of architectural additions over the centuries. Visitors can inspect the historic vaults *(Historiengewölbe)*, now a history museum, or climb the tower for a **view**★ of the fortified town.
North of Marktplatz is the gable of the Ratstrinkstube with a Kids **mechanical clock** that reenacts *(at 11am, noon, 1pm, 2pm, 3pm, 8pm, 9pm and 10pm)* the Long Drink (◔ *see above*).

Rothenburg: a striking illustration of the Middle Ages

T. Krieger/MICHELIN

Baumeisterhaus

The stepped gables of this Renaissance house support dragon motifs. Statues on the first floor represent the seven cardinal virtues, those on the second the seven deadly sins.

Mittelalterliches Kriminalmuseum (Museum of Medieval Justice)

🕐 Apr-Oct: 9.30am-6pm; Nov and Jan-Feb: 2-4pm; Mar and Dec: 10am-4pm. 👓 €3.50. ☎ (098 61) 53 59; www.kriminalmuseum.rothenburg.de

Medieval attitudes towards crime and dissidence are reflected in this museum in the former headquarters of the Knights of the Order of St John of Jerusalem. Documents and instruments of public humiliation, torture and execution are displayed.

Address Book

WHERE TO EAT

🍽🍽 **Baumeisterhaus** – *Obere Schmiedgasse 3* ☎ *(09861) 947 00* This Renaissance treasure was built opposite the town hall in 1596. In its venerable walls, a restaurant is laid out over two floors and adorned with beautiful old wall paintings. The courtyard is surrounded by half-timbered galleries.

WHERE TO STAY

🍽🍽 **Hotel-Gasthof Schwarzes Lamm** – *Detwang 21, 91541 Rothenburg-Detwang (from Rothenburg: Romantische Straße toward Bad Mergentheim)* ☎ *(09861) 6727* Fax *(09861) 86899* *www.hotelschwarzeslamm-rothenburg. de* 🕐 *Closed from mid Jan to mid Feb* 🅿 ✕ *30 rooms* 🍽🍽 *Restaurant* A charming establishment with a long family tradition, set in the oldest part of Rothenburg. The hotel has quiet, modern rooms with balconies. The lime-tree garden is plesant in good weather.

🍽🍽 **Mittermeier** – *Vorm Würzburger Tor 9* ☎ *(09861) 945 40 www.mittermeier.rothenburg.de* 🕐 *Restaurant closed Sun* 🅿 ✕ *27 rooms* 🍽🍽 *Restaurant* Guests here can sleep in "Africa" or "Spain," names of two rooms in this hotel. The restaurant reflects a youthful, fresh style.

🍽🍽 **Hotel Spitzweg** – *Paradeisgasse 2* ☎ *(09861) 942 90* Fax *(09861) 1412 www.hotel-spitzweg. de* 🅿 *10 rooms* This little 16C hotel has comfortable, rustic rooms full of souvenirs of the Rothenburg painter Spitzweg.

TAKING A BREAK

USEFUL TIPS

Almost all of the cafés in town sell *Schneeballen* (snowballs), traditional regional cakes made with shortbread pastry. Originally covered only with icing sugar or cinnamon, they now come in a variety of forms, sometimes covered or filled with chocolate.

Caféhaus – *Untere Schmiedgasse 18* ☎ *(09861) 9 39 85* 🕐 *9.30am-6pm, terrace/winter garden closed Jan-Easter.* Over one hundred speciality coffees and a wide variety of *Schneeballen* are served here. The café's glass-fronted winter garden affords a magnificent view of the green Tauber valley.

GOING OUT

Zur Höll – *Burggasse 8* ☎ *(09861) 42 29 www.romanticroad.com/hoell* 🕐 *6pm-1am.* This picturesque half-timbered house now harbours a weinstube serving mainly local wines and brandies as well as traditional dishes.

SHOPPING

Käthe Wohlfahrt – *Herrngasse 1* ☎ *(09861) 40 93 65 www.wohlfahrt. com* 🕐 *Mon-Fri 9am-6.30pm, Sat-Sun 9am-6pm* 🕐 *Closed Sun from Christmas to mid May; museum from mid Apr to beginning of Jan 10am-5.30pm (last admission 5pm) museum:* 👓 *€4.* Here it's Christmas all year round. Choose from among 65 000 by the light of the "Christmas Village" candles. The museum on the 1st floor presents the evolution of Christmas decorations.

Plönlein

A picturesque corner of half-timbered houses, often photographed: One street is level, another ascending to the Siebers tower, another descending. The fountain once fed the two fish stocks used by Tauber fishermen.

▶ *Leave the town by the Koboldzell gate, on the right, turn sharp right again, and follow the path circling the spur some way below the ramparts. In the valley below, is an arched, two-storey viaduct (Doppelbrücke) crossing the Tauber. Return to the old town via the Burggarten.*

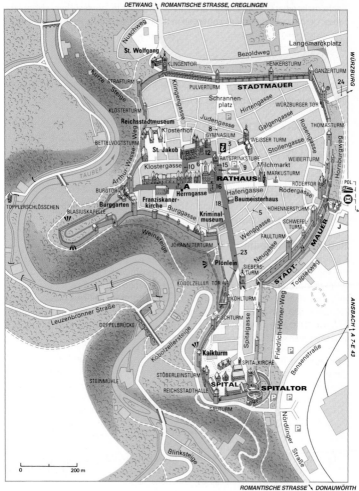

Burggarten

All that remains of the double fortress erected on this promontory is a chapel, the Blasiuskapelle, which has been turned into a war memorial, and a fortified gateway, the Burgtor. The area is now a large public garden with magnificent **views**★.

▶ *Return to the town via the Burgtor; assailants unaware of the grimacing mask above the second gate risked being drenched in boiling oil here.*

Herrngasse★

The mansions of medieval burghers line this busy commercial street. In the **Franziskanerkirche,** note the 15C and 16C sculptures and the Creglingen Madonna (1400). Back in Herrngasse, check out the hidden courtyards. No 15 features a half-timbered gallery on embossed wooden pillars.

▶ *Turn left into Kirchgasse after the round fountain.*

St Jakobskirche★

Admission charge ⊜ *€1.50.*

Building of the Gothic church started in the 14C. The works of art inside include Tilman Riemenschneider's **"Holy Blood" altarpiece**★★ (1504), in the west chancel. Note the tense, perplexed expressions conveyed in the scene, as well as Jesus' compassion.

Sights

Spital★ (Hospital)

A picturesque group of 16C-17C buildings, the Spital's Gothic chapel *(Spitalkirche)* features numerous notable works of religious art.

Stadtmauer★ (The Ramparts)

Kids Constructed in the 13C and 14C, these ramparts, complete with gates and towers, are still in a state of perfect preservation. Long stretches are open to the public.

Wolfgangskirche

North of the Klingentor, this curious 15C Gothic church, fortified and incorporated into the barbican, doubled the defences of the gateway.

Reichsstadtmuseum

🕓 *Apr-Oct, 10am-5pm; Nov-Mar, 1-4pm.* 🕓 *Closed Shrove Tuesday, 24 and 31 Dec.* ⊜ *€3.* ☎ *(098 61) 93 90 43; www.reichsstadtmuseum.rothenburg.de*

A Dominican monastery from 1258 to 1554, this building is now a local museum showing, among other collections, the Rothenburg Stations of the Cross (1494). Perhaps the most fascinating exhibit is the original hanap drained by ex-Burgomaster Nusch in front of General Tilly *(👆 see above).* The tankard's design depicts the emperor and the seven electors. It was made in 1616.

ROTTWEIL★

POPULATION: 24 000

This charming 12C town became a Free Imperial City in 1268. Traces of the Baroque era are still evident, especially in the church buildings. 🚹 *Hauptstraße 21, 78628 Rottweil, ☎ (0741) 49 42 80.*

▶ **Orient Yourself:** Rottweil occupies a pleasant site on the Upper Neckar, between the Swabian Jura and the Black Forest and near the A 81 motorway.

▣ Lots on Kriegsdamm or Nägelesgraben are 2min walk from the town centre.

◉ **Don't Miss:** Lingering in Rottweil's Old Town.

◕ **Organizing Your Time:** Allow three hours for the sights in the walking tour.

◔ **Also See:** *DONAUESCHINGEN (31km/19mi south), TÜBINGEN (56km/35mi northeast), SCHWARWALD, SCHWÄBISCHE ALP.*

Walking Tour

Old Town★
The almost fully preserved late-medieval town centre is a pleasant stop. Burghers' houses adorned with oriels *(Hauptstraße)* and fountains are as remarkable as the town's churches and museums. From Hauptstraße is a **view**★ of the Swabian Alps.

▶ *Turn left at the Rathaus.*

Heiligkreuzmünster
The 15C Late Gothic minster features a high altar adorned with a crucifix attributed to Nuremberg master Veit Stoß (1447/48-1533). Splendid 15C **altarpieces**★ decorate the side chapels, including St Peter's altarpiece in the north side aisle, St Nicholas' altarpiece in the south side aisle and the Virgin Mary and Apostles altarpieces.

▶ *Go through the Pfarrgasse, left along Schulgasse and then onto Kriegsdamm.*

> ### The Rottweiler
> The rottweiler is descended from a race of sheepdogs used by the Roman legions. The breed was particularly widespread in the region from the Middle Ages. Robust and powerful, with distinctive black and tan markings, the dogs are used by the police for their strength and intelligence.

Dominikanermuseum
♿◕ *Open Tue-Sun, 2-5pm.* ◕ *Closed on all public holidays that fall on weekdays.* ◉ *€1.50.* ☎ *(0741) 7662.*

The museum owes its name to a Dominican monastery founded on this site in 1266. Of the monastery buildings, only the Baroque church remains. The modern museum exhibits the most important local finds, including the beautiful Roman **Orpheus Mosaic**★ from the 2C AD, composed of 570 000 small stones; and a collection of 14C-16C **Swabian sculptures**★ by Hans Multscher and Michel Erhart.

▶ *Take Lorenzgasse to Lorenzkapelle.*

Lorenzkapelle
This former cemetery chapel was built ca 1580, and now houses a collection of **Rottweil stonemasonry**. It displays the best work produced by the Rottweil stonemason's lodge in late medieval Swabia.

▶ *Turn left, and take Hauptstraße back to the town's central crossroads.*

Kapellenkirche
The **tower**★ of this Gothic church, Baroque on the inside, is a splendid example of the Flamboyant style.

Excursions

Dreifaltigkeitsberg★ (Trinity Hill)
20km/12mi southeast; about 30min. A minor road leads to the pilgrimage church from Spaichingen, on the edge of the Swabian Jura. From the hill a **panorama**★ includes the Baar Depression and, in the distance, the dark outline of the Black Forest.

RÜDESHEIM AM RHEIN★

POPULATION: 10 000

The wine town of Rüdesheim lies at the Bingen Gap, gateway to the "Romantic Rhine." Rüdesheim has become the most popular tourist centre in the valley: The narrow streets, including the famous Drosselgasse, are crammed with visitors attracted by the wine bars offering the celebrated local Riesling. There are also distilleries and cellars with sparkling wine. 🖪 *Geisenheimerstraße 22, 65385 Rüdesheim,* ☎ *(067 22) 29 62.*

▶ **Orient Yourself:** Rüdesheim lies at the southern end of the Rhine Gorge, where the river, deflected by the Taunus massif, turns north again.

🏵 **Don't Miss:** A sampling of Rüdesheim's famous Riesling wine.

🕔 **Organizing Your Time:** Allow two hours for the suggested driving tour *(see below).*

👍 **Also See:** RHEINTAL *(suggested itinerary includes Rüdesheim), WIESBADEN (28km/18mi east), MAINZ (32km/20mi east), Bad KREUZNACH (67km/42mi south).*

Sights

Brömserburg
Rheinstrasse 2. Residence of 13C Mainz bishops, stronghold of the knights of Rüdesheim, meeting-place for brigands. This fortress went through many incarnations before its current role as a **wine museum**. The outstanding exhibits include old winepresses and amphorae (vases and jars for storing or transporting wine).

Niederwald Monument
Access by road (2km/1mi) or by cable-car (terminal on the Oberstraße: 20min there and back).
Built to commemorate the re-establishment of the German Empire in 1871, the monument comprises a statue of Germania (weighing 32t) on a bronze plinth featuring Bismarck, Emperor Wilhelm I, German princes and their armies.

WHERE TO STAY

🛏🛏🛏 **Hotel Trapp** – *Kirchstraße 7, 65385 Rüdesheim* ☎ *(067 22) 911 40 Fax (067 22) 47745 www.ruedesheim-trapp.de* 🕔 *Open from mid-Mar to mid-Dec* 🅿 *38 rooms* 🛌 Located in the heart of this romantic little town, this family-run establishment offers guestrooms in light wood and a welcoming atmosphere.

🛏🛏🛏 **Hotel Rüdesheimer Schloss** – *Steingasse 10, 65385 Rüdesheim* ☎ *(067 22) 905 00 Fax (067 22) 47960 www.ruedesheimer-schloss.de* 🕔 *Closed from Christmas to early Jan* 🅿 ♿ *21 rooms* 🛌 🛏🛏🛏 *Restaurant* Historic building from 1729, with pretty interior courtyard and vineyard. Designer furnishings in rooms. The restaurant is laid out along the lines of a traditional taverna.

Driving Tour

The Rheingau

23km/14mi A southern exposure allows cultivation of vines high up on the foothills of the Taunus. Note the picturesque villages of Geisenheim, Winkel and Hattenheim, surrounded by vineyards, en route to Eberbach Abbey.

Kloster Eberbach★★ – 👶 *See Kloster EBERBACH*

Kiedrich

The 15C **church** in this wine-growers' market town still bears its original, rare Flamboyant elements: carved **pews**★★ and choir stalls are still adorned with polychromatic embellishment and Gothic inscriptions. Gregorian chant in a Gothic German dialect has been practised in Kiedrich since 1333.

Eltville

The oldest town in the Rheingau always pleases with its narrow streets, 16C-17C town houses and 14C castle. The Johannes Gutenberg memorial in the castle is testimony to the printer's fame during his lifetime.

INSEL RÜGEN★

The Baltic island of Rügen, Germany's largest, offers a surprising variety of scenery. In the west, the straits widen toward the open sea. Chalk cliffs and sandy beaches in the east attract summer crowds. The southern shores are wooded; and to the north is the deep, jagged Jasmunder Bodden (gulf).

- ▶ **Orient Yourself:** Rügen can be reached by train or car via a long bridge (2.5km/1.5mi) that straddles the straits at Stralsund. Ferries to Scandinavia leave from the port of Saßnitz.
- **Don't Miss:** The vistas at Stubbenkammer and Hiddensee.
- **Organizing Your Time:** Allow half a day for the suggested driving tour. Allow five hours to visit Hiddensee (👶 *see Excursion*).
- **Especially for Kids:** Rügen's bathing resorts, Hiddensee Island.
- **Also See:** *GREIFSWALD (33km/21mi south of Stralsund), ROSTOCK (75km/47mi to the west of Stralsund), Insel USEDOM.*

WHERE TO STAY

☺☺☺ **Strandhotel Lissek** – *Strandpromenade 33, 18609 Binz* ☏ *(038393) 38 10 Fax (038393) 381430 strandhotel-lissek@t-online.de* 🅿 *40 rooms.* ☐ Carefully restored spa architecture with great attention to detail. Modern comforts, some rooms with fine views of the Baltic Sea. The marine-style restaurant carries the name of the fish market *(Fischmarkt).*

☺☺☺ **Wreecher Hof** – *Kastanienallee, 18581 Putbus-Wreechen* ☏ *(038301) 850 Fax (038301) 85100 www.wreecher-hof.de* 🅿 ⚱ *43 rooms* ☐☺☺☺ *Restaurant.* Peaceful hotel village off the beaten track, with reed-thatched buildings. Modern comfortable rooms, many with sitting rooms. The restaurant has a winter garden and beautiful terrace.

Driving Tour

From Putbus to Kap Arkona *75km/47mi*

Putbus★

The "white town" in the south-east of the island was founded in 1810 by Prince William Malte of Putbus, in imitation of Bad Doberan, as a royal seat and bathing resort. The princely castle no longer remains, but the neo-Classical town does. The town's round **circus**★ is surrounded by houses, many with neo-Classical ornamentation. Finished in dazzling white, they stand out from the green of the oaks. Nearby, the 19C **Theatre**★ *(Alleestraße)* bears a

portico of four Tuscan columns. The theatre is famous for its acoustics.

The 75ha/185-acre **Schloßpark**★ with its orangery, royal stables and parish church, is laid out in the style of an English garden.

Jagdschloss Granitz

12km/7.5mi east of Putbus, south of Binz. ◷ *Open May to Sep, 9am-6pm; Oct to Apr, Tue-Sun, 10am-4pm.* ◷ *Closed 25 Dec.* ⊛ *€3.* ☎ *(0383 93) 22 63.*

In 1837 Prince William Malte I of Putbus had built a neo-Gothic Tudor hunting lodge atop the Tempelberg, the highest point in Eastern Rügen. The four crenellated corner towers of the "castle" rise up in the middle of Granitz woods. A 19C viewing tower and platform are reached via cast-iron **spiral staircase**. From the top, the **view**★★ of Rügen Island is breathtaking. The rooms inside the house are open to the public.

Bathing Resorts★

Kids **Binz**, **Sellin**, **Baabe** and **Göhren** are in the southwest of the island, awaiting visitors with sandy beaches, beautiful resort architecture and a woodland backdrop. They can be reached via "**Rasender Roland,**" a train that connects Putbus to Göhren.

Stubbenkammer★★

The **Königsstuhl**, a 117m/384ft-high cliff, towers over an impressive chalk bluff. If you visit on a sunny day you will see the breathtaking white cliff surrounded by green foliage above the deep blue sea. This postcard idyll also inspired painter Caspar David Friedrich.

Kap Arkona★

Kap Arkona, with its 50m/164ft-high chalk cliffs, is the northernmost point of the island. The **old lighthouse** *(Alte Leuchtturm:* ◷ *Jul to Aug, 10am-7pm; May to Jun and Sep, 10am-6pm; Mar to Apr and Oct, 10am-5pm; Jan to Feb and Nov, 11am-4pm.* ⊛ *€2)* a square three-storey brick building, was built in 1826-29 on plans by Karl Friedrich Schinkel. There is a wonderful **view**★★ from here to the neighbouring island of Hiddensee.

Störtebeker

Klaus Störtebeker was a notorious pirate said to have been born in Ruschwitz on Rügen in 1370. As a young man, he drank from his master's tankard at work, and, having been seen by his boss, was promptly chained and beaten. But Störtebeker's strength was such that he broke free and thrashed his tormentors. Then he took off in a fishing boat as far as the cape of Arkona. There he joined Michael Gödecke and his band of brigands whose reputation struck terror into all who sailed the coast. Störtebeker became one of the most feared buccaneers of his age, scouring the seas until eventually being captured in Hamburg and condemned to the guillotine. As a mark of the respect he commanded, his last request was granted: mercy for the companions arrested with him.

Legend has it that Störtebeker hid his booty beneath the cliffs of the Stubbenkammer, and once a year a ship steered by phantom buccaneers is said to haunt this coast. Every summer, at Ralswiek, islanders put on a play commemorating the adventures of this anti-hero, scourge of the rich and benefactor of the poor.

Excursion

Hiddensee Island★

Kids *Ferry connections – Boat trips to the island from Wiek and Schaprode on Rügen and from Stralsund, journey time 30min-2hr 30min. Details from Reederei Hiddensee GmbH, Büro Hiddensee, Achtern Diek 4, 18565 Vitte/Hiddensee, ☎ (0383 00) 210; www.frs.de/hiddensee/start.htm. Motor traffic (except service vehicles) is forbidden on the island. We recommend the ferry from Kloster and a bicycle rental once on Hiddensee.*

Hiddensee Island, the "pearl of the Baltic", is 17km/10mi off the west coast of its larger neighbour, Rügen. It falls almost entirely within the Nationalpark Vorpommersche Boddenlandschaft. The island boasts a natural landscape, with towering cliffs, land spits, lagoons and deeply incised coastal inlets. The highest point lies in the north, at the **Dornbusch peak** (72m/236ft), site of the island's trademark **lighthouse**, put into operation in 1888 and measuring 28m/90ft in height.

Hiddensee is crisscrossed by footpaths and bicycle paths. The village of **Grieben** is famous for its thatched houses. **Kloster** has developed into a bathing resort. **Gerhart Hauptmann** (1862-1946), best-known for his Naturalist dramas, is buried in the graveyard beside the church. Hauptmann's summer residence, Haus Seedorn on Kirchweg street, is open to the public. The island's administrative centre is at **Vitte**, a fishing village turned tourist resort. South of Vitte are vast dunes interspersed with marshland *(Dünenheide)*. **Neuendorf**, the island's most southerly village, has fishermen's houses arranged east to west axis, so that living quarters face the sun.

RUHRGEBIET

RUHR BASIN

The Ruhr, Rhine and Lippe Rivers encouraged settlement in pre-Roman times. But it was the recent centuries of mining and heavy industry that left their mark most notably on the landscape of the Ruhr Basin. But there is plenty of charm and culture beneath this industrial façade. Duisburg, for example, already had a town charter by the 12C and Dortmund was a member of the Hanseatic League. The Ruhrfestspiele attracts an international crowd. Theatres, opera houses, and even local churches host performances of theatre or classical music. ⓘ *Ruhrgebiet Tourismus GmbH, service-center, Königswall 21, 44137 Dortmund ☎ 0231 18 16 186.*

▶ **Orient Yourself:** The Ruhr Basin region (4 400km²/1 700sq mi) lies among three rivers: the Ruhr, the Rhine and the Lippe. and is home to the large towns of Duisburg, Essen and Dortmund.

🅐 **Don't Miss:** Religious art lovers will be impressed by Essen's cathedral and its artworks.

🕒 **Organizing Your Time:** Allow two days to get a flavor of the Ruhr region.

Especially for Kids: Warner Bros. Movie World, the Open Air Technical Museum and the Schwebebahn.

🅒 **Also See:** *KÖLN (66km/41mi south of Duisburg via the A 3), MÜNSTER (67km/42mi north of Dortmund via the A 1).*

A Bit of History

Important Industrial Centre – The Ruhr remains one of the world's most important industrial centres. A large portion of German steel is manufactured here; Duisburg is the largest inland port in Europe and the largest river port in the world. The landscape in the region's north is shaped by the chemical industry and modern mining operations.

A New Image – The legacy of heavy industry has become an opportunity to rework the Ruhr's "Black Country" image in favor of culture and leisure activities. Large-scale projects are renovating abandoned industrial plants to create shopping centres, restaurants and bars, and venues for theatrical, film and musical performances. And in many cases, old pits and factories have been converted into industrial museums, offering insight into the production methods and social history of heavy industry.

Sights

Bochum

Kunstsammlung Museum Bochum
Kortumstrasse 147, opposite the Stadtpark. 🅷🕒 *Open Tue-Sun, 10am-5pm, (-8pm Wed; -6pm Sun).* 🚻 *€3, no charge 1st Wed of the month.* 🕒 *Closed 1 Jan, Good Fri, 1 May, 24, 25 and 31 Dec.* ☎ *(0234) 516 00 30; www.bochum.de/museum.*
The collections in this spacious, airy modern building concentrate mainly on contemporary international art.

Deutsches Bergbau-Museum★★ (German Mining Museum)
Am Bergbaumuseum 28. 🅷 🕒 *Tue-Sun, 8.30am-5pm, Sat-Sun, 10am-5pm.* 🕒 *Closed 1 Jan, 1 May, 24-26 and 31 Dec.* 🚻 *€6.* ☎ *(0234) 587 70; www.bergbau-museum.de.*
Founded in 1930, this museum borders the town centre and examines the evolution of mining from Antiquity to the present. 50 feet underground, in the **Schaubergwerk**, more than 2.5km/1.5mi of abandoned workings

German Mining Museum in Bochum

Deutsches Bergbau-Museum

illustrate methods of coal extraction and transport. The tour ends with a trip up the 71m/233ft-high mining tower.

Eisenbahnmuseum★ (Railway Museum)

At Bochum-Dahlhausen, C-Otto-Straße 191, halfway between Essen and Bochum. Car park. ◷ *Open Mar-Nov, Tue-Sun, 10am-5pm.* ✍ *€5.* ☎ *(0234) 49 25 16; www.eisenbahnmuseum-bochum.de.*

Founded by railway enthusiasts, this museum is installed in an abandoned station and repair shop on the north bank of the Ruhr. Equipment from 1914 is for the most part still in mint condition. More than 180 rail machines recall this form of transport from the beginnings to the end of the steam era, including 15 **steam locomotives**.

Bottrop

Quadrat Museum Centre

Im Stadtgarten 20 (near town centre). ♿◷ *Open Tue-Sun, 10am-6pm.* ◷ *Closed 1 Jan, 24, 25 and 31 Dec. Museum für Ur- und Ortsgeschichte and Josef Albers Museum.* ☎ *(020 41) 297 16.*

The Constructivist Bottrop painter and Bauhaus theorist Josef Albers referred to his work as *Hommage an das Quadrat* (Homage to the Square). Thus inspired, this museum is dedicated to Constructivist works. The adjoining sculpture park contains works by Max Bill, Donald Judd, Norbert Kricke etc. Next to the Quadrat is the **Museum of Pre- and Local History** *(Museum für Ur- und Ortsgeschichte).* The **Ice Age Hall**★ houses Germany's largest Quaternary Era collection.

Warner Bros. Movie World★

🧒 *In Bottrop-Kirchhellen, via A 31, exit Kirchhellen.* ◷ *Open Aug, 10am-9pm; mid-Apr to end Sep, 10am-6pm, Sat-Sun, 10am-7pm; Oct, Mon-Thu, 10am-6pm, Fri-Sun, 10am-10pm.* ◷ *Closed Mon in Apr, May, Sep and Oct.* ✍ *Day ticket €26.50.* ☎ *(020 45) 89 98 99.*

This 45ha/110-acre film and amusement park, under the motto "Hollywood in Germany", features more than 35 attractions and shows. They include the **Bermuda Triangle** with its rapids and raging waterfalls, the **Batman adventure** in the breathtaking flight simulator, the *Police Academy* Stunt Show and many more.

Visitors in need of some peace and quiet can visit the **Museum of German Film History**★, examining over 100 years of film in Germany.

Dortmund

Dortmund was first mentioned around 885 and given market rights before 900. Documents prove its status as an Imperial City since 1220, and as such it was a flourishing town during the Middle Ages. But as in many places, the Thirty Years War left deep scars.

Dortmund was reborn in the mid-19C with the Industrial Revolution, notably coal, steel and beer. Nevertheless, innovation and research were not forgotten. Trade, insurance and the service sector are also economic buttresses.

Westfalenpark★

◷ *10am-11pm (automatic ticket booths).* ✍ *€1.80.* ☎ *(0231) 502 61 00.*

The two main centres of attraction in this 70ha/173-acre park are the **Television Tower** (Fernsehturm "Florian") and the **Rose Garden** *(Deutsches Rosarium),* which cultivates some 3 200 varieties from all over the world. The tower is 220m/722ft high. At 137m/450ft is a revolving restaurant and terrace with superb **panoramas**★ of the Ruhr and the Sauerland.

Address Book

TOURIST OFFICE
Opposite Hauptbahnof Süd, Königswall 18a, 44137 Dortmund ☎ *(0231)189 99222.*

WHERE TO EAT
⊜⊜ **Pfefferkorn** – *Hoher Wall 38* ☎ *(0231) 14 36 44 www.pfefferkorn-dortmund.de Reservations recommended.* This restaurant's old German-style decor, friendly service and its pleasant atmosphere make this a good address to know about.

WHERE TO STAY
⊜⊜⊜ **Haus Überacker** – *Wittbräucker Straße 504 (B 234), 44267 Dortmund-Höchsten* ☎ *(02304) 807 06 Fax (02304) 86844* ◷ *Closed 3 weeks in Aug/Sep* ⃞ *17 rooms* ⃞ ⊜⊜⊜ *Restaurant* Good family-run hotel in a neat half-timbered house. Partly panelled guestrooms with solid wooden furnishings. A new heated winter garden and pleasant terrace complete the restaurant.

Reinoldikirche★

In the Ostenhellweg, near the market. This triple-aisle basilica houses a good deal of 14C and 15C religious works: a sculpted reredos, probably Burgundian work; the bronze eagle pulpit (Adlerpult); a wood statue of St Reynold, patron saint of the town; and a statue of Charlemagne.

Museum für Kunst und Kulturgeschichte (Museum of Art and Civilisation)

At no 3, Hansastraße. ♿◷ *Open Tue-Sun, 10am-5pm, Thu, 10am-8pm, Sat, noon-5pm.* ◷ *Closed 1 Jan, 24, 25 and 31 Dec.* ☞ *€6.* ☎ *(0231) 502 55 22; www.mkk.dortmund.de.*

The exhibits here, displayed chronologically, cover such diverse subjects as the history of Dortmund; religious art in the late Middle Ages; houses and furniture; and 19C painting. The Romanesque section contains the **Dortmund Treasure**★ *(Dortmunder Goldschatz)*, 444 gold coins, most from the 4C.

Duisburg

Wilhelm-Lehmbruck-Museum★★

In Duisburg town centre, Kantpark. ♿◷ *Tue-Sat, 11am-5pm, Sun, 10am-6pm.* ◷ *Closed 1 Jan, 1 May, 24, 25 and 31 Dec.* ☞ *€5.* ☎ *(0203) 283 26 30; www.lehmbruckmuseum.de.*

The "Centre for International Sculpture" is home to over 700 20C sculptures and objets (Barlach, Beuys, Calder, Dalí, Giacometti, Kollwitz, Magritte, Tinguely, etc). One museum wing showcases works by Duisburg sculptor **Wilhelm Lehmbruck** (1881-1919). The surrounding park (7ha/17 acre) contains outdoor sculptures by international artists against a wooded backdrop.

Museum der Deutschen Binnenschiffahrt★

Duisburg-Ruhrort, Apostelstraße 84. ♿◷ *Open Tue-Sun, 10am-5pm.* ◷ *Closed 1 Jan, 24-26 and 31 Dec.* ☞ *€3.* ☎ *(0203) 80 88 940.*

The former Jugendstil swimming pool at Ruhrort has become Germany's largest museum on the economic, technologicaly and social aspects of inland shipping. Visitors examine developments from dug-outs to modern tug boats. Two museum ships (from 1882 and 1922) are near the maritime stock exchange, 10min walk away along a path through Ruhrort port.

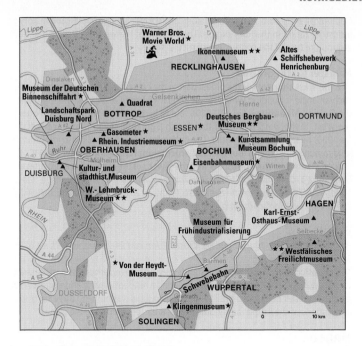

Landschaftspark Duisburg Nord

In Duisburg-Meiderich, Emscherstraße 71. Car park. Sound and light shows at dusk.
☏ *(0203) 429 19 42; www.landschaftspark.de.*

The centrepiece of the park is the abandoned iron and steel works, their blast furnaces and chimneys towering skyward. Industrial hangars now host a variety of events, including a fascinating show of light and colour in the evening.

Essen★

Essen no longer lives up to its coal-bowl image. Three-quarters of the people in what was Europe's largest mining town now work in administration, service, and retail industries. In typical Ruhr form, Essen-Katernberg: the Zollverein Colliery *(Gelsenkirchener Staße 181)* is now home to Design-Zentrum Nordrhein-Westfalen, in the old boiler house, which was rebuilt by Sir Norman Foster.

Museum Folkwang★★

Museumszentrum. ♿🕐 *Open Tue-Sun, 10am-6pm, Fri, 10am-midnight.* 🕐 *Closed 1 Jan, 1 May, 24 and 31 Dec.* ♾ *€5.* ☏ *(0201) 884 53 01; www.museum-folkwang.de.*

This museum houses a major collection of 19C and 20C painting, sculpture, graphic art and photography, particularly rich in works of art from Germany and France. Besides the German Romantics and Realists of the 19C are the French Realists and Impressionists, as well as the French Cubists and Surrealists.

Works by the artists of the Brücke group, the Blaue Reiter (Kandinsky, Macke, Marc) and the Bauhaus demonstrate the tremendous variety of German Impressionism and art of the 20C. Note also the collection of post-1945 art, with works by Baselitz, Kiefer, Lüpertz, Penck and Richter, as well as Americans Pollock, Newman and Stella.

Ruhrlandmuseum★

♿🕐 *Open Tue-Sun, 10am-6pm, Fri, 10am-midnight.* 🕐 *Closed 1 Jan, 1 May and 31 Dec.*
♾ *€5.* ☏ *(0201) 884 52 00; www.ruhrlandmuseum.de.*

Geological, archaeological and sociological displays examine the life and history of industrialization in the Ruhr region. The lifestyle of the working-class in the Ruhr around the turn of the century is a particular focus.

Münster (Cathedral)★★

The 10C **west chancel**★ is the oldest part of the cathedral, and it is only fitting that such an ancient building would house similarly ancient artworks. The highlight is the **Golden Madonna**★★★ (AD 980), said to be the oldest statue of the Virgin in the West. In the western part of the church a gigantic seven-branch candelabra (ca 1000) bears geometric motifs. The **cathedral treasury**★ *(Domschatzkammer)* holds among other things four splendid **processional crosses**★★★ (10C and 11C), the Golden Madonna's crown, gospels, and the "Sword of the Martyr-Saints Cosmas and Damian". ○ *Open Tue-Sat, 10am-5pm(7pm on Wed), Sun, 11.30am-5pm.* ○ *Closed 1 Jan, Good Fri, Easter Sun and Pentecost, 1 Nov, 24, 25 and 31 Dec.* ⊛ *€3.* ☎ *(0201) 220 42 06; www.domschatz.info.*

Villa Hügel★

♿○ *Open Tue-Sun, 10am-6pm.* ○ *Closed 1 Jan and 24-26 Dec.* ⊛ *€1.* ☎ *(0201) 188 48 23.*

This imposing Gründerzeit mansion stands in an attractive park on the north shore of Lake Baldeney. The original 19C house included a residential wing and a guest wing, and boasted 269 bedrooms. Until 1945, the Villa Hügel was home to three successive generations of the Krupp family. Since 1953, it has been open to the public.

Hagen

Karl-Ernst-Osthaus-Museum

Hochstraße 73. ○ *Open Tue-Sun, 11am-6pm, Thu, 11am-8pm.* ○ *Closed 1 Jan, 1 May, 24, 25 and 31 Dec.* ⊛ *€3.* ☎ *(023 31) 207 31 38; www.keom.de*

This museum steeped in tradition dates to industrialist Karl Ernst Osthaus, who founded the Museum Folkwang for art and crafts here in 1902 (the collections were donated to the city of Essen in 1922). The museum building was fitted out with Jugendstil interior decor designed by Henry van de Velde. The collection covers Classical Modern and contemporary works of art.

Westfälisches Freilichtmuseum★★ (Open-Air Technical Museum)

Kids *At Hagen-Selbecke, in the valley of Mäckingerbachtal. Leave Hagen heading south on the Frankfurt, then the Eilpe road. At Eilpe, turn right towards Breckerfeld-Halver and continue for just over 1.5km/1mi to Selbecke. From the museum car park (Museumsparkplatz), on the left of the road, 10min on foot.* ○ *Open Apr-Oct, Tue-Sun, 9am-6pm.* ⊛ *€5.* ☎ *(023 31) 780 70; www.freilichtmuseum-hagen.de.*

Along 2.5km/1.5mi of this valley, more than 70 installations or buildings illustrate the evolution of crafts in Westphalian industry (17C-19C). A half-timbered 18C house is now a **Blacksmith Museum** with a working forge. There are also examples of James Nasmyth's steam hammer (ca 1840) and the zinc rolling mill of Hoesch (1841), both of which marked the start of true industrialisation.

Higher up the valley an 18C **paper mill** houses a Printing Museum. Finally is a village of traditional craftsmen, where saddlers, smiths, rope makers, bakers and brewers demonstrate and sell their crafts. *Visit weekday mornings to see craftsmen in action.*

Oberhausen

Gasometer★

Oberhausen new town centre (near CentrO shopping centre). ♿○ *Panoramic view from the roof, Tue-Sun, 10am-5pm, Wed, 10am-3pm.* ☛ *Guided tour, Sat at 3pm, Sun at*

11am and 3pm. 😑 *€2. Exhibition prices vary.* ⏰ *Closed 1 Jan, Apr to mid-May and Oct, 24-26 and 31 Dec.* ☎ *(0208) 850 37 30; www.gasometer.de.*

The present exhibition hall used to be Europe's largest blast furnace gas storage tank in its heyday (117.5m/385ft high, 68m/220ft in diameter, built in 1928-29). The outside staircase has 592 steps leading up to the viewing platform, from where there is a view toward the lower Rhine. Inside, an elevator takes visitors to 106m/350ft.

Rheinisches Industriemuseum★

In Oberhausen town centre (behind the main station), Hansastraße 20. ⏰ *Tue-Sun, 10am-5pm.* ⏰ *Closed 1 Jan, 24, 25 and 31 Dec.* 😑 *€4.* ☎ *(0208) 857 92 81.*

The Altenberg zinc works was closed in 1981, after 130 years of processing zinc from Mülheim and Essen. The heavy industry museum is housed in the rolling hall, examining technological progress since the 19C, as well as the political and economic importance of iron and steel to the Rhine and Ruhr regions. Original factory components are incorporated into the exhibition.

Recklinghausen

Ikonen-Museum★★ (Icon Museum)

Kirchplatz 2a. ⏰ *Tue-Sun, 10am-6pm.* 😑 *€5.* ☎ *(023 61) 50 19 41; www.ikonen-museum.com.*

The marvellous specimens exhibited here are arranged by theme: the Holy Trinity and the Celestial Hierarchy (a theme rich in symbolism); the Virgin Mary; the Saints and their Days (a splendid calendar of all the religious feasts).

Altes Schiffshebewerk Henrichenburg

In Waltrop, Am Hebewerk 2. ♿⏰ *Open Tue-Sun, 10am-6pm.* ⏰ *Closed 1 Jan, 24, 25 and 31 Dec.* 😑 *€3.50, no charge on Fri.* ☎ *(023 63) 970 70.*

In 1899 Emperor Wilhelm II inaugurated this construction, bridging land with a 14m/46ft climb in elevation via the Dortmund-Ems canal (1892-99), the waterway to the North Sea. The Westphalian Industrial Museum illustrates the process. Also included are technical, political and economic aspects of canal building, and life along the canal. The museum ship **MS Franz Christian** gives insight into shipboard life.

Solingen

Deutsches Klingenmuseum★ (Blade Museum)

At Solingen-Gräfrath. ♿⏰ *Open Tue-Sun, 10am-5pm, Fri, 2-5pm.* ⏰ *Closed 1 Jan, 24, 25 and 31 Dec.* 😑 *€3.50.* ☎ *(0212) 25 83 60; www.solingen.de/klingenmuseum.*

Known the world over for its knives and its scissors, Solingen is the centre of fine metalwork in Germany. The museum is in the former Gräfrath Abbey, a converted, elegant Baroque building. The museum traces the history of side arms including magnificent dress swords. A further highlight is the cutlery and tableware of the 18C.

From the abbey gardens, descend the steps to the historic **Marktplatz**. The houses around the square have been restored in the traditional half-timbered style of the Bergisches Land, with slate shingle roofs and walls and green wooden shutters.

Wuppertal

Von der Heydt-Museum★

At Wuppertal-Elberfeld. ♿⏰ *Open Tue-Sun, 11am-6pm, Thu 11am-8pm.* ⏰ *Closed 1 Jan, 1 May, 24, 25 and 31 Dec.* 😑 *€3.* ☎ *(0202) 563 62 31; www.von-der-heydt-museum.de.*

This museum, housed in the old Elberfeld town hall (1827-42), has an interesting collection of paintings and sculpture. The museum is named after the Wuppertal bankers, the Von der Heydts, who were its generous patrons. The collections include

16C and 17C Flemish and Dutch painting; French and German painting from the 19C to Impressionism, Expressionism (Kirchner, Beckmann), Fauvism, Cubism (Braque) and the present. Sculptures from the 19C and 20C are also on display (Rodin, Maillol).

Museum für Frühindustrialisierung

At Wuppertal-Barmen. ○ *Open Tue-Sun, 10am-1pm, 3pm-5pm.* ◈ *€4.* ☎ *(0202) 563 64 98.*
Housed in an abandoned factory, this museum traces the economic and social history of the Wupper Valley since the mid-18C.

Schwebebahn (Cable railway)

Kids An enjoyable mode of transport for getting around Wuppertal is the cable railway (1898-1903). This is the world's oldest suspended railway for transporting passengers and also one of the safest means of public transport, carrying 22.6 million passengers a year. Most of the station buildings date from the turn of the century.

OBERES SAALETAL★

SAALE VALLEY

The winding Saale forms a natural link between towns like Jena and Halle, masterpieces of sacred architecture like Merseburg and Naumburg, and innumerable riverside castles.

▶ **Orient Yourself:** Rising on high ground at the eastern extremity of the Thüringer Wald, the River Saale flows 427km/265mi to the north before joining the Elbe upstream of Magdeburg.
◈ **Don't Miss:** The Fairy Grottoes
○ **Organizing Your Time:** Allow four hours for the suggested driving tour.
Kids Especially for Kids: The Fairy Grottoes
◔ **Also See:** *WEIMAR (37km/23mi north), JENA (38km/24mi north), THÜRINGER WALD (Ilmenau is 43km/27mi west).*

Driving Tour

From Rudolstadt to Saalburg *61km/38mi*

Rudolstadt

Once the seat of the princes of Schwarzburg-Rudolstadt, this town is dominated by the fine silhouette of 18C **Schloss Heidecksburg★**. Several magnificent Rococo **rooms★★** are open to the public. ○ *Open Tue-Sun, Apr-Oct,10am-6pm (5pm Nov-Mar).* ◈ *€6.* ☎ *(036 72) 429 00; www.heidecksburg.de.*

Saalfeld

The Renaissance **Rathaus** in Marktplatz is designed around a façade that centres on a staircase tower with two oriel windows. The historic rooms of a Francisan abbey house the local **Museum** (Stadtmuseum Saalfeld im Franziskanerkloster) with collections on local history and folklore. ♿○ *Open Tue-Sun, 10am-5pm.* ○ *Closed 24 and 31 Dec.* ◈ *€2.50.* ☎ *(036 71) 59 84 71.*

Feengrotten★ (Fairy Grottoes)

Kids *1km/0.6mi southeast of Saalfeld on B 281.* ☜☞ *Guided tour (45min).* ○ *Open Mar to Oct, 9am-5pm; Nov, Sat-Sun, 10am-3.30pm; Dec to Feb, 10am-3.30pm.* ☜ *€6.50.* ☎ *(036 71) 550 40; www.feen-grotten.de*

Stalactites and stalagmites adorn the floors and ceilings of this abandoned slate mine.

Saalfeld Fairy Grottoes.

▸ *Leave Saalfeld on B 85. Cross the Saale at the Hohenwarte Dam. The artificial lake at Hohenwarte (Hohenwarte-Talsperre) curves for 10km/6mi, in a series of wide arcs. Via Drognitz and Remptendorf, the route arrives at the Bleiloch reservoir, the largest of the five artificial lakes between Saalfeld and Blankenstein. Driving across the dam, sightseers regain the river's east bank.*

Saalburg

Now a lakeside town, Saalburg lost its outskirts when the valley was flooded. Remains of the 16C fortifications can still be seen.

SAARBRÜECKEN★

POPULATION: 179 000

Although it was seriously damaged during the Second World War, the capital of the Saarland has developed into a regional metropolis. The city's architecture owes its character a large number of preserved Baroque buildings. ⓘ *Reichstrasse 1, 66111 Saarbrüecken, ☎ (0681) 93 80 90.*

▸ **Orient Yourself:** Saarbrüecken is in the Saar valley, on the French border and at the crossroads of the A 6 motorway to Mannheim and the A 4 to Metz, France.

🅿 **Parking:** Garages in the Old City are at Tal- and Reepersbergstraßen and at Roon- and Stengelstraßen.

◉ **Don't Miss:** The Ludwigsplatz and its yellow and red Ludwigskirche.

○ **Organizing Your Time:** Allow three hours for the suggested walking tour.

⚐ **Also See:** *Unteres SAARTAL (Mettlach is 53km/33mi north), PFALZ (Dahn is 78km/49mi east), TRIER (96km/60mi north), WORMS (124km/76mi northeast via the A 6).*

Walking Tour

Alt-Saarbrücken *(on the south bank of the Saar)*

Schloss

The medieval fortress was replaced in the 17C by a Renaissance castle, demolished in 1738 to make way for a Baroque castle designed by Stengel. Wars and conversion necessitated reconstruction in 1982. The central façade was given a modern look, becoming a glass building through which the light floods.

WHERE TO EAT

⊖⊜ **Hauck – Das Weinhaus** – *St-Johanner-Markt 7* ☎ *(0681) 319 19 www. weinhaus-hauck.de* Only the first floor still retains something of the old tavern dating from 1856. A fine selection of wines, most of them also available in carafes, to accompany simple dishes, including a number of regional specialities.

WHERE TO STAY

⊖⊜ **Hotel Schlosskrug** – *Schmollerstraße 14* ☎ *(0681) 367 35 Fax (0681) 375022 www.hotel-schlosskrug.de* ◷ *Closed from Christmas to earlyf Jan* 🅿 ⊁ *20 rooms* ⌨ ⊖⊜⊜ *Restaurant* This boarding-house-hotel is set in an old town house. Functional rooms, some with their own bath, and some family rooms with several beds available.

The **Saar Historical Museum** adjoins the right wing of the castle. Its permanent exhibition deals with the First World War and National Socialism in the Saar region. ♿◷ *Tue-Sun, 10am-6pm (8pm, Thu), Sat, 12 noon-6pm.* ⊜ *€2.50, no charge Thu from 5pm.* ☎ *(0681) 506 45 01; www.historisches-museum.org.*

Museum für Vor- und Frühgeschichte

First building on the left in Schloßplatz. ♿◷ *Open Tue-Sun, 9am-5pm, Sun, 10am-6pm.* ◷ *Closed bank holidays.* ☎ *(0681) 954 05 11.*

Housed in the former Parliament house, a neo-Baroque building, this museum's highlight is the **Celtic princess's grave**★★ from Reinheim, which dates to 400 BC. The find is considered one of the most important in Central Europe from the Early Celtic period. The princess' jewellery and tomb furnishings, including a gilded bronze pitcher, are wonderfully preserved.

Altes Rathaus

To the far west of the Schloßplatz.

The old town hall, with its clock tower and imperial roof (1748-50), stands at the western end of the Schloßplatz. The Saarbrücken city coat of arms is visible on the gable end. The **Abenteuermuseum** (Museum of Adventure) on the upper floor examines foreign peoples and countries.

The Erbprinzenpalais stands on the southern side of Schloßplatz. The 18C building was converted by Stengel for the hereditary prince Ludwig von Nassau from three older houses and adapted to the style of the castle.

Ludwigsplatz★★

The square is bordered in the north, south and west by eight palaces of various sizes. All with three storeys and mansard roofs, they illustrate the transition from the Late Baroque to the neo-Classical style. Their white and silver-grey colouring enhances the effect of the Ludwigskirche, built in yellow and red sandstone in the centre of the square. The minister-president has his offices in Ludwigsplatz.

Ludwigskirche

♿◷ *Open Tue-Sun, 10am-5pm.* ◷ *Often closed on Sat for weddings.* ⊜ *€0.50.* ☎ *(0681) 525 24; www.ludwigskirche.de.*

A successful restoration project has allowed this unique Baroque Protestant church to radiate its former glory once again. The east end exhibits a degree of splendour unusual in a Protestant church, with statues of the Evangelists by Franziskus Bingh.

St Johann

St Johanner Markt★

The old city around the market is the true heart of Saarbrüecken. The focal point is the beautiful market fountain, with its obelisk and cast-iron railing, built in 1759-60. Life pulses in the crooked streets and the numerous bistros.

Basilika St. Johann★

Open daily, 9:30am-5pm. ☎ (0681) 329 64.

Built by master builder Stengel between 1754 and 1758, and consecrated to St John the Baptist and St Ludwig, this church with its onion tower and lantern is another jewel of the Late Baroque period.

Sights

Saarland Museum – Alte Sammlung

Karlstraße 1 (opposite the Moderne Galerie). Open Tue-Sun, 10am-6pm, Wed, 10am-10pm. Closed Tue after Easter and Pentecost, 24, 25 and 31 Dec. €1.50. ☎ (0681) 996 40; www.saarlandmuseum.de.

On display are paintings and decorative arts from southwestern Germany and Lorraine from the Middle Ages to early modern times.

Saarland Museum – Moderne Galerie

Bismarckstraße, on the banks of the Saar. Open Tue-Sun, 10am-6pm, Wed, 10am-10pm. Closed Tue after Easter and Pentecost, 24, 25 and 31 Dec. €1.50. ☎ (0681) 996 40; www.saarlandmuseum.de.

20C art is featured in this museum, with the emphasis on German Impressionism and **Expressionism★**. Major artists include Picasso, Léger, Tàpies and Beuys.

Stiftskirche St-Arnual★

In the district of St Arnual, via Talstraße and Saargemünder Straße.

This 13C-14C Gothic church was given a Baroque dome in 1746 based on plans by Stengel. It was named after Bishop Arnuald von Metz, who lived in the 7C. Having been the burial place of the dukes of Nassau-Saarbrücken since the 15C, the church houses 50 **tombs★★** dating from the 13C to the 18C, some of which are masterly and decorated in colour.

Excursions

Weltkulturerbe Völklinger Hütte★

In Völklingen, 10km/6mi west of Saarbrücken. Open Apr to Oct, 10am-7pm; Nov to Mar, 10am-6pm. Closed 25 and 31 Dec. €10. ☎ (068 98) 910 00; www.voe-lklinger-huette.org.

This iron and steel works was established in 1873 and became a major industrial centre. During its heyday, the monumental works employed more than 16 000 people. When the blast furnaces closed in 1986, it signalled the end of an era. In 1994 the plant became the first industrial monument included in the UNESCO world cultural heritage list. Visitors are familiarised with the various stages of pig iron manufacture. The tour's highlight is the visit to the vast gas **blower hall★**, a cathedral of industrial culture with its heavy machinery dating from the early 20C.

Homburg: Schlossberghöhlen (currently closed for repair)

20km/12mi east on the A 6 motorway. Closed for repair. ☎ (068 41) 20 64; www.homburg.de.

The largest sandstone caves in Europe are man-made, 2km/1mi-long corridors which extend over 12 levels. The caves were built between the 11C and 17C for defensive purposes. They served as munitions and food stores and were used as air raid shelters during the Second World War.

Römermuseum Schwarzenacker
2km/1mi east of Homburg, on the B 423. 🕐 *Open Mar to Oct, Tue-Sun 9am-5pm; Nov to Feb, Sat-Sun 10am-4:30pm.* 🕐 *Closed 24 Dec-1 Jan.* 🎟 *€3.* ☎ *(068 48) 875.*
The **Roman settlement of Schwarzenacker** was founded around the time of the birth of Christ and was destroyed by the Alemanni in AD 275. Excavations revealed Roman roads and building which are displayed in an open air museum.

UNTERES SAARTAL

SAAR VALLEY

The region of the Saar Valley, far from the tourist routes, remains unspoiled. Between Mettlach and Konz, where it flows into the Moselle, the River Saar cuts its way through the crystalline Hunsrück massif. Grapes, predominantly Riesling, have been cultivated here since the 18C.

▸ **Orient Yourself:** South of the Moselle Valley, the Saar valley runs along the French and Belgian borders. The B 51 road links the Saar to Saarburg and Trier.
�︎ **Don't Miss:** The breathtaking scenery at Cloef.
🕐 **Organizing Your Time:** Allow two hours for the suggested driving tour.
Kids **Especially for Kids:** The town of Saarburg, with its waterfall in the heart of the city center.
🚻 **Also See:** *MOSELTAL (suggested itinerary includes Trier), SAARBRÜECKEN (53km/33mi southeast), EIFEL (Manderscheid is 56km/35mi north).*

Driving Tour

From Mettlach to Trier *57km/35mi*

Mettlach
The Baroque, red sandstone façade of the abbey, now headquarters of Villeroy & Boch ceramics, rises above the road to Merzig. In the abbey gardens stands the 10C "Alter Turm", a ruined octagonal funerary chapel for Lutwinus, the abbey's founder.

Cloef★★
7km/4mi west of Mettlach then 15min on foot there and back. From a viewpoint high above the river is a breathtaking view of the Montclair loop, a hairpin curve enclosing a long, densely wooded promontory.
From Cloef or Orscholz it is possible to take a detour *(about 30km/18mi there and back, via L 177 and B 406)* towards the Moselle valley and the Roman villa of Nennig.

Römisches Mosaik in Nennig★★
🚻🕐 *Open Feb-Sep, Tue-Sun, 8.30am-12.30pm, 1-6pm; Oct-Nov, Tue-Sun, 9am-11:30am, 1-4:30pm.* 🕐 *Closed 1 Nov.* 🎟 *€1.50.* ☎ *(068 66) 13 29; www.nennig.de.*
In 1852 were discovered the remains of an enormous Roman villa thought to date from the 2C or 3C AD. A superb floor mosaic survives (16x10m/52x33ft), consisting of eight medallions framed by intricate geometric designs and gladiator scenes in the Trier amphitheatre.

German wines

(Deutscher) Tafelwein – Table wine with no clearly defined region of origin, perhaps a blending of other Common Market wines or of purely German ones.

Landwein – Medium quality wine with an indication of origin (e.g. Pfälzer Landwein) and made from officially approved grapes. It can be dry or medium dry.

Qualitätswein bestimmter Anbaugebiete – Wine of superior quality with an allocated control number and from an officially recognised region (Gebiet), e.g. Moselle, Baden, Rhine.

Qualitätswein mit Prädikat – Strictly regulated wine of prime quality, grown and made in a clearly defined region. These wines will be designated: Kabinett (a reserve wine), Spätlese (a late-harvest wine), Auslese (wine from selected grapes), Beerenauslese and Trockenbeerenauslese (sweet wine) or Eiswein (wine produced from grapes harvested after a minimum -7°C frost).

▶ *From Mettlach to Saarburg, the road runs through the valley, forested on the lower slopes, escarpments above, vines appearing as the valley widens.*

Saarburg

Kids This picturesque town on the banks of the Saar is dominated by its mighty ruined fortress. Dating from at least 964 and later property of the electoral princes of Trier, it was blown up by the French in 1705. There is a good view of the town and Saar valley from the site.

The **old town**, with its charming medieval alleyways, half-timbered houses and a 20m/65ft **waterfall** in the town centre, makes a delightful scene. The local museum (Amüseum am Wasserfall), the Hackenberger Mühle watermill museum and a bell-casting foundry are further attractions.

▶ *After Konz, where the Saar joins the Moselle, follow the river to Trier.*

Trier★★ 🜚 *See TRIER.*

SÄCHSISCHE SCHWEIZ★★★

SWISS SAXONY

Swiss Saxony is one of Germany's most popular natural wonders, an area of sheer sandstone cliffs, rock outcrops and pillars and deep gorges through which the Elbe flows. The valley can be explored by road, following the itinerary below, or by river on one of the "Weiße Flotte" boats linking Dresden and Bad Schandau.

▶ **Orient Yourself:** Swiss Saxony lies between Dresden and the Czech frontier, on the upper course of the Elbe.

🜚 **Don't Miss:** Bastei and Festung Königstein.

🕐 **Organizing Your Time:** Allow one day for the suggested driving tour.

Kids Especially for Kids: Festung Königstein and rock-climbing nearly anywhere.

🜚 **Also See:** *DRESDEN, MEISSEN (23km/14mi northwest), BAUTZEN (64km/40mi east), GORLITZ (107km/67mi east).*

Driving Tour

Round Trip from Dresden *78km/49mi*

Dresden★★★ ♿ *See DRESDEN.*

▶ *Leave the city to the east by Pillnitzer Landstraße on the town map.*

Schloss Pillnitz ★ ♿ *See DRESDEN: Excursions.*

Bastei★★★

The **view**★★ from this rocky spine across the Elbe Valley to the table mountains of Swiss Saxony is famous. The narrow rocky outcrop projecting furthest towards the Elbe is the Bastei itself, the top of which towers 190m/620ft above river level. The spectacular, almost lunar landscape of these unusual rock formations is all the more impressive seen close at hand, with visitors actually able to touch the rocks that make up this dramatic scenery.

▶ *A short stretch downhill leads to the 76m/250ft long Basteibrücke. There are numerous waymarked footpaths through the surrounding rocks.*

The Bastei viewpoint, Swiss Saxony

D. Scherf/MICHELIN

Bad Schandau★

Spa The main tourist centre of the region is also a spa renowned for its iron-rich waters. At the town exit, in the direction of Schmilka, an elevator and footpath lead to the Ostrauer Scheibe, with a **views**★ of the Schrammsteine – a rock massif popular with mountaineers.
The **Kirnitzsch Valley**★ *(Kirnitzschtal)*, hemmed in by steep cliffs, can be followed by railway.

▶ *Cross the Elbe at Bad Schandau and turn right along B 172 toward Königstein.*

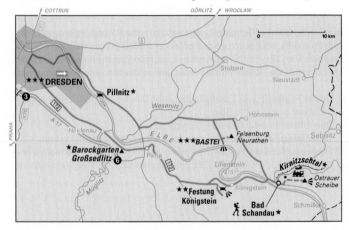

Festung Königstein★★

The great sweep of the Elbe is overlooked by the 415m/1 362ft Lilienstein on the east bank, and the **Königstein** (360m/1 181ft) on the west. The formidable **fortress** crowning the latter was built between the 13C and the 16C and served as refuge for the Court of Saxony. Prisoners here had little chance of escaping. Among the most famous were JF Böttger, inventor of porcelain (👍 *see MEISSEN*); August Bebel, co-founder of the Social Democrat party; and Fritz Heckert, co-founder of the Spartacists and prominent German Communist. From the rampart walk, which follows the Erzgebirge, are **views**★★ of the distant mountains of Bohemia.

Barockgarten Großsedlitz★

♿ 🕐 *Open Apr-Sep, 8am-8pm; Oct, 8am-6pm, Nov-Mar, 8am-4pm.* 👓 *€2.60.* ☎ *(035 29) 563 919; www.barockgarten-grosssedlitz.de*
This garden was commissioned in 1719 by Count Wackerbarth and laid out in the French style. Großsedlitz still ranks among the finest achievements of Baroque German landscape gardening.

▸ *Return to Dresden on B 172.*

BAD SÄCKINGEN★

POPULATION: 16 800

The warm springs at Bad Säckingen were already in use in the Middle Ages. There is clear evidence of Swiss architectural influence in the buildings of this Rhine River town south of the Black Forest. 🛈 *Waldshuter Straße 20, 79713 Bad Säckingen,* ☎ *(077 61) 568 30.*

▸ **Orient Yourself:** The town grew up around the 9C convent and sits on the border of the Black Forest near Switzerland.
🔎 **Don't Miss:** The Fridolinsmünster and the Roofed Bridge.
🕐 **Organizing Your Time:** Allow three hours to see all the listed sights of Bad Säckingen.
♿ **Also See:** *ST BLASIEN (40km/25mi north), BADENWEILER (46km/29mi northwest), SCHWARZWALD (Belchen is 47km/29mi north).*

Sights

Fridolinsmünster★

Named after St Fridolin, the missionary who converted the Alemanni and founded a missionary cell here in 522, this church has a crypt dating from the Carolingian era. The present Gothic basilica was built in the 14C and later had Baroque features added. The treasury houses the Shrine of St Fridolin, a superb 18C gold work from Augsburg.

Gedeckte Brücke★ (Roofed Bridge)

The stone pillars of this wooden bridge were erected in 1575. The bridge is 200m/650ft long, the longest of its kind in Europe, and spans the Rhine, leading to Stein in the Swiss canton Aargau.

Schloßpark (Palace gardens)

These pleasant grounds are the setting for the *Trompeterschloß* (Trumpeter's Palace), built ca 1600 by the lords of Schönau. The palace now houses a museum with the largest **collection of trumpets** in Europe. From the corner of the park there is a good view of the old wooden roofed bridge.

Excursion

Waldshut
26km/16mi west. Halfway up a wooded slope rising from the Rhine, this small town retains two fortified gateways, the Lower or Basle Gate to the west and the Upper or Schaffhaus Gate to the east. The heart of the historic **old town**★ is **Kaiserstraße**, a street whose orderly line of houses is broken only by overhanging eaves. Buildings of note include the 18C Late Baroque **town hall**, the **"Wilder Mann",** a 16C town house, and the 16C **"Alte Metzig"** (Butcher's Gateway), now home to the **Local Museum** (*Heimatmuseum*).

SALEM★

POPULATION: 11 000

Salem was founded in 1134 by the Cistercian Order and remained one of the the most important German foundations of this Order for over 650 years. Since 1802, it has been the property of the Margraves of Baden.

▶ **Orient Yourself:** Salem is in the extreme south of Baden-Württemberg, on the edge of a small lake, only 7km/4mi away from its larger cousin, Bodensee (Lake Constance).
- **Don't Miss:** Salem's cathedral and castle.
- **Organizing Your Time:** Allow three hours to see the sights of Salem.
- **Especially for Kids:** Salem's collection of museums.
- **Also See:** BODENSEE (tour passes through Birnau, 8km/5mi south), KONSTANZ (54km/34mi southeast), WEINGARTEN (36km/23mi east), SIGMARINGEN, SCHWÄBISCHE ALB (40km/25mi north).

Sights

Münster★
The central part of the complex is the High Gothic abbey church. Construction was begun in 1297. Inside, the design is typical Cistercian Gothic, with a large chancel and flattened chevet, soaring vaults and side aisles supporting the nave. The unusual alabaster decoration is thanks to Abbot Anselm II.

Schloss★
   Open Apr-Oct, 9.30am-6pm, Sun, 10.30am-6pm. ✆ €5.50. ☎ (075 53) 814 37; *www.salem.de*
The old abbey complex encompasses three inner courtyards. Its size and decoration testify to the tremendous wealth the abbey accumulated over the course of its history. The ceiling of the old summer refectory still boasts its Wessobrunn stucco ornamentation. Further highlights include the Bernardus passage, the Imperial Hall completed in 1707 and the Rococo study of Abbot Anselm II.

Museums
500 years of the history of firefighting is brought to life at the **Firefighting Museum** (Feuerwehr-Museum), with equipment from around the world. A **distillery museum** explains the production of spirits (*Branntwein-Museum*), while the

Cooperage Museum *(Küferei)*, housed in an old winepressing room, sheds light on this old profession. Craftsmen and women demonstrate their art in a special handicrafts village.

SAUERLAND★

The meanders of the Lenne and Ruhr Rivers cut through the forest-covered mountain range of the Sauerland. The picture-postcard countryside is popular with visitors year-round: skiers converge on the town of Wintenberg in winter, and in the summer walkers, cyclists and water sports enthusiasts flock to the area.

▸ **Orient Yourself:** The Sauerland stretches from the southeastern Rhineland to north Westfalen. The region is reached via the A 46 and the A 44 to the north and by the A 46 to the south.

⊘ **Don't Miss:** The historic town of Soest and the outdoor pursuits at the Möhnesee.

⊙ **Organizing Your Time:** Allow one day for the suggested driving tour.

Kids **Especially for Kids:** The caves of Attahöhle and water sports throughout the region.

⚲ **Also See:** *MÜNSTER (63km/39mi north of Soest), ESSEN (83km/52mi west of Soest), KÖLN (86km/54mi southwest of Attendorn), DÜSSELDORF (119km/74mi west of Attendorn), KASSEL (122km/76mi east of Soest via the A 44).*

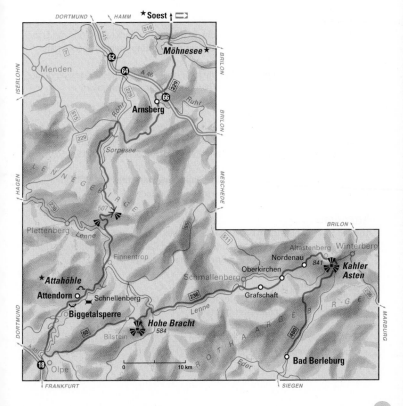

A Bit of Geology

Mountains, lakes and forests – The Sauerland, which forms the hinterland to the Ruhr Basin, is the most mountainous of the Rhineland Schist Massif. It is crowned by the **Langenberg** (843m/2 766ft), near Niedersfeld. Artificial lakes in the region supply water and hydroelectric energy to the industrial towns of the Ruhr, and serve as water sports centres. The Upper Sauerland, especially the forested Rothaargebirge, is popular with tourists.

Driving Tour

From Soest to Bad Berleburg *181km/112mi*

Soest★

The famous German **Pumpernickel**, dense black rye bread baked for 16-24 hours, is made in Soest. The town is also known for its massive 11C-12C Romanesque **Patroklidom** is interesting for its **Westwerk**★★ and its perfectly balanced square **tower**★★. Romanesque frescoes in the apse are original, having survived the Second World War; the others were restored in 1950. The perfect cube-shaped 14C Gothic hall-church **Wiesenkirche**★ includes the 1520 **stained-glass Last Supper,** its table set with local food specialties (boar's head, ham, pitchers of beer and rye bread loaves).

Möhnesee★

Kids This artificial lake on the northern edge of the Sauerland is 10km/6mi long. Its waters are dammed, and its northern lakeshore open to tourists and water sports enthusiasts. The south bank is a well-forested nature reserve known for its birdlife.

Arnsberg

The old town is built on a spur in the Ruhr. To the north, a clock tower commands the approach to the Schloßberg ruins; to the south a hunting-themed Rococo gate.

▶ *Beyond Arnsberg, the road skirts the right bank of the Sorpesee reservoir before crossing the Lennegebirge massif. There are many scenic viewpoints.*

Attahöhle★ (Grotto)

Kids *Right side of the road (signposted), just before Attendorn.* 🕊 *Guided tour (40min).* 🕐 *Open Apr-Oct, 10am-4pm; May to Sep, 9.30am-4.30pm; Nov to Mar, Tue-Sun, 10.30am-3.30pm.* 🕐 *Closed 24 and 25 Dec.* ⊛ *€5.50.* ☎ *(027 22) 937 50; www. atta-hoehle.de*
This limestone cavern extends for 3km/2mi. Many stalactites and stalagmites are visible, as are stone "draperies," some of them translucent.

Attendorn

The Old Town of Attendorn boasts a 14C town hall with stepped gable, the arcaded covered market (Alter Markt), and the **"Sauerland Cathedral"** (Sauerländer Dom). Southeast of Attendorn is the 17C **Burg Schnellenberg**.

Biggetalsperre

Kids This dam, dating from 1964, forms with the **Lister barrage** the largest reservoir in Westphalia, popular for water sports.

▶ *About 2km/1mi before Olpe, fork left on the B 55. Soon after Bilstein, on a small mountain road, turn right turn toward the Hohe Bracht.*

Hohe Bracht

Alt 584m/1 916ft. From the viewing tower (620m/2 034ft above sea level) is a fine panorama, including the Rothaargebirge massif as far as Kahler Asten.

▶ *After crossing the rural Lenne Valley, the route passes* **Grafschaft** *and* **Oberkirchen**, *with charming half-timbered houses, before the landscape becomes wilder and hillier. Beyond* **Nordenau**, *a typical slate-roofed Upper Sauerland village, is the ski station of Altastenberg. On the far side of a plateau, the road nears Kahler Asten.*

Kahler Asten

At 841m/2 759ft above sea level, this is the highest point of the Rothaargebirge. From the look-out tower is a superb view. To the northeast is the spa and winter-sports centre of Winterberg.

▶ *Slate quarries flank the road back down. There are many attractive views towards the south.*

Bad Berleburg

Spa The townscape of the Kneipp spa resort Bad Berleburg is characterised by the 13C castle of the princes of Sayn-Wittgenstein in the historic town centre.

SCHLESWIG ★

POPULATION: 27 000

Schleswig-Holstein's oldest town makes a striking impression with its bright welcoming houses. Smaller than the rival towns of Lübeck or Kiel, Schleswig has interesting sights and a relaxing, plesant atmosphere. *Plessenstraße 7, 24837 Schleswig, ☎ (046 21) 98 16 16.*

▶ **Orient Yourself:** Schleswig was built on low-lying banks at the inner end of an arm of the sea, the Schlei, which penetrates the coast for 43km/27mi.

▶ **Don't Miss:** The Viking Museum and the Nydam Boat.

▶ **Organizing Your Time:** Allow half a day at the Schloss Gottorf.

▶ **Especially for Kids:** The Viking Museum.

▶ **Also See:** *HUSUM (36km/23mi west), KIEL (56km/35mi south), HAMBURG (124km/78mi south, direct route via the A 7 motorway).*

WHERE TO EAT

Eckernförder Fischdeel – *Kattsund 22, 24340 Eckernförde (Follow the signposts to the port, Hafen)* ☎ *(04351) 56 51 www.eckernfoerder-fischdeel.de* ⊙ *Open Thu-Tue, 11:30am-2:30pm, 6-10pm,* ⊙ *Closed Wed and 1 Nov* ✁ *Reservations recommended* Specialising in fish dishes, this restaurant is in the heart of the old town of Eckernförde, near the harbour. Tasty, traditional cuisine in a comfortable setting.

WHERE TO STAY

Zollhaus – *Lollfuß 110* ☎ *(04621) 29 03 40 Fax (04621) 290373 www.zollhaus-schleswig.de* ⊙ *Closed Jan and mid-Nov to mid-Dec* P *9 rooms* ⊏ ⊝⊝⊜ *Restaurant* Set in a lively street near the Schlei, with bright, functional rooms of beechwood. Temporary art exhibitions are held in the restaurant-bistro.

A Bit of History

The Vikings – Merchants had settled on the south bank of the Schlei by the 9C . Set on major crossroads, the settlement became an important North European trade centre. The area, Haithabu, was encircled with a vast defence system of which a portion remains beside the Haddebyer Noor. More artifacts are in the Wikinger Museum Haithabu. In the 11C, Haithabu's residents, seeking better defences, crossed to the north bank of the Schlei to found Schleswig.

Schloss Gottorf

&⚲ *Open Apr to Oct, 10am-6pm; Nov to Mar, Tue-Fri, 10am-4pm, Sat-Sun, 10am-5pm.* ⚲ *Closed 1 Jan, 24, 25 and 31 Dec.* ⚐ *€6.* ☎ *(046 21) 81 32 22; www.schloss-gottorf.de*

Two large museums devoted to Schleswig-Holstein are housed in this 16C-18C palace, once the seat of the Holstein-Gottorf ducal family, which in 1762 became the Imperial House of the Czars of Russia.

Landesmuseum für Kunst und Kultur★★

This museum contains extensive cultural and historical collections (local arts, crafts and traditions). Note the **Cranach collection** and the **Renaissance chapel**★★ with its ducal loggia and oratory. Finally, visitors should not miss the remarkable **Jugendstil collection**★.

An adjacent building houses Rolf Horn's collection of works spanning Expressionism to the present. The paintings by Emil Nolde and Alexei von Jawlensky are especially striking. One room is devoted to sculptures by Ernst Barlach. Works by artists of **the Brücke** are on display on two floors in the old stable. This is the largest collection after the *Brücke-Museum* in Berlin.

Wikinger Museum Haithabu

Terslev fibula in the Viking museum

Archäologisches Landesmuseum★

This museum offers a systematic presentation of Schleswig-Holstein's pre- and early history from the Paleolithic Age to the time of the Vikings. There are spectacular finds from the 4C (bodies found perfectly preserved, fragments of clothing, shoes, weapons) rescued from the peatbogs before their decay.

Nydam-Boot (Nydam Boat)

In the Nydam Hall. This oak-hulled longship dates from ca 320 AD and was excavated in 1863 from the Nydam marshes on Danish territory. It is some 23m/75ft long by 3m/10ft wide and was powered by 36 oarsmen. It is the oldest surviving Germanic longship, and was probably sunk in the peatbogs as a sacrifice in c 350 AD. Further artefacts from Nydam and Thorsberg are on display in the hall.

Sights

Dom St-Peter★

Thanks to its graceful spire, this brick Gothic hall-church can be seen from far off. The most remarkable work of art is the 1521 **Bordesholm Altarpiece**★★, in the chancel.

The Holm★

This picturesque sailors' and fishermen's quarter with its18C-19C houses is centred around a small cemetery and chapel.

Wikinger Museum Haithabu (Viking Museum)★

Kids *Access via B 76, direction Kiel.* ⓖⓞ *Open Apr to Oct, 9am-5pm; Nov to Mar, Tue-Sun, 10am-4pm.* ⓞ *Closed 1 Jan, 24, 25 and 31 Dec.* ⓢ *€3.* ☏ *(046 21) 81 30.*

This annexe to the Archäologisches Landesmuseum is near the Haddebyer Noor lagoon, next to the old Viking site. A number of unearthed objects (jewels, weapons and domestic implements) are on display, along with models of the Viking settlement. There is a wealth of information on the lives of the Haithabu inhabitants. In the Boat Hall (Schiffshalle) is a Viking longship, reconstructed from fragments dredged from the ancient port.

SCHWÄBISCHE ALB★

SWABIAN JURA

The Swabian Jura region is a paradise for walkers, cyclists and history buffs. From the highest point at Lemberg (1 015m/3 330ft), the Jura plateaux drop 400m/1 312ft to the Neckar Basin in the northwest. Mountain outcrops form natural fortresses; some were chosen as castle sites by families who enjoyed great fame and glory, among them the Hohenstaufens and the Hohenzollerns.

▶ **Orient Yourself:** East of the Black Forest, between Stuttgart and Lake Constance, this itinerary will take you through a karst landscape punctuated by caves, dry valleys and steep-sided gorges.
⊘ **Don't Miss:** Burgruine Reißenstein and Burg Hohenzollern.
ⓞ **Organizing Your Time:** Allow one day for driving tour ① and half a day for driving tour ② (ⓖ see below).
Kids **Especially for Kids:** The Hauff Museum in Holzmaden (especially the dinosaur skeletons) and the Bärenhöhle caverns (especially the bear skeletons).
ⓖ **Also See:** *TÜBINGEN (14km/9mi from Lichtenstein), STUTTGART (31km/19mi north), ZWIEFALTEN (35km/22mi northeast of Sigmaringen), KONSTANZ (Constance is 41km/26mi south of Sigmaringen).*

Driving Tours

① From Kichheim unter Teck to Burg Hohenzollern

125km/78mi

Kirchheim unter Teck

The tower of the 18C half-timbered Rathaus overlooks the main crossroads.

Holzmaden

Kids The **Hauff Museum**★ *(Urwelt-Museum Hauff, follow the arrows)* displays dinosaurs, fish, sea lilies and ammonites found locally in the 180 million year old Jurassic slate strata. ⓒ *Open Tue-Sun, 9am-5pm.* ⓒ *Closed 1 Jan, 24, 25 and 31 Dec.* ⊛ €4.50. ☏ *(070 23) 28 73; www.urweltmuseum.de.*

Burgruine Reußenstein (Castle ruins)

45min on foot there and back. Head for the edge of the escarpment to appreciate the **setting**★★ of Reußenstein as it dominates the Neidlingen valley. From the look-out point built into the castle ruins there is a **view**★ of the whole valley and, beyond it, the plain of Teck.

▶ *After Wiesenstein, with its half-timbered houses, the route follows the* Schwäbische Albstraße, *marked by blue-green arrows.*

Bad Urach

This is a pretty town, enclosed deep in the Erms Valley, with half-timbered houses around a central Marktplatz.

Uracher Wasserfall (Urach Falls)

15min on foot there and back. Leave from the parking area marked "Aussicht 350m". Impressive **view**★ of the valley and the waterfall (flow reduced in summer).

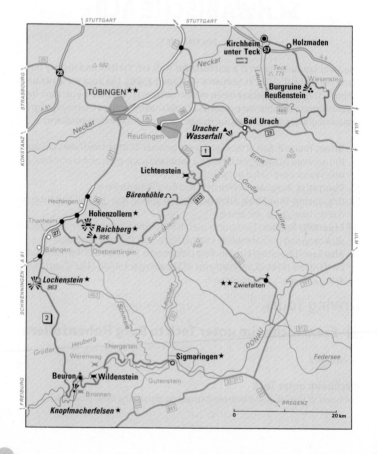

Schloss Lichtenstein

Guided tours (30min). *Open Apr to Oct, 9am-5.30pm; Nov and Feb to Mar: Sat and Sun, 9am-4pm.* *€5.* *(071 29) 41 02; www.schloss-lichtenstein.de.*

Built on a rock spur protected by a natural cleft, Lichtenstein was completely rede-signed in the Troubadour style in 1842. Before crossing the entrance bridge, turn right for two viewpoints: one overlooks the Echaz Valley, the other the castle itself.

Bärenhöhle

Kids *In Erpfingen.* *Guided tour (30min).* *Open Apr to Oct, 9am-5:30pm; Mar and Nov, Sat-Sun 9am-5pm.* *€3.* *(071 28) 925 18.*

The biggest cavern in this "Bear Grotto" contains well-preserved fossilised bear skeletons, as well as the skeleton of a bear on its feet.

▶ *At Onstmettingen, follow the signs 'Nädelehaus' and 'Raichberg'.*

Raichberg★

30min on foot there and back. Leave the car at the hotel and walk past a stone tower, across the fields to the lip of the plateau. From here there is a **view★** of the downward sweep of the Jura and, 3km/2mi away, Burg Hohenzollern.

▶ *Continue to Burg HOHENZOLLERN (* *see entry) via Tannheim and Hechingen.*

② From Hohenzollern to the Danube Gap★

89km/55mi

Burg Hohenzollern★ – *See Burg HOHENZOLLERN.*

Lochenstein★

30min on foot there and back. Leave the car at the saddle *(Lochenpaß)* and climb to the summit (alt 963m/3 160ft) of the Lochenstein, which is surmounted by a Cross. From here a **view★** of the Balingen-Hechingen depression, and, in the distance, Hohenzollern Castle is possible.

▶ *Beyond the pass, the road sweeps downhill in tight curves and then crosses the bare, rolling uplands of the Großer Heuberg plateau.*

Knopfmacherfelsen★

Below the car park, make your way to a **viewpoint★** of the Danube Valley as far as Beuron Abbey and, on the right, Schloss Bronnen.

Kloster Beuron

6am-8pm *(074 66) 170.*

A flourishing Benedictine congregation at Beuron contributed to the revival of monastic life, the liturgy and the use of the Gregorian chant in Germany. The Gnadenkapelle, added to the abbey church in 1898, is treated in the "Beuron style," derived from a 19C Byzantium-influenced school of sacred art.

Burg Wildenstein

7km/4.5mi from Beuron via Leibertingen. This small citadel commanding the Danube was designed with two moats. Its defence system comprised two towers linked by a long wall.

▶ *Below Beuron, the road follows the **Danube Valley★** past the rocky fortresses of Wildenstein and Werenwag on the way to Sigmaringen. Approaching the town,* *the cliffs give way to curious rock needles which form a fantastic ensemble between Thiergarten and Gutenstein.*

Sigmaringen★ – ⟨ *See SIGMARINGEN.*

SCHWÄBISCH HALL★★

POPULATION: 36 500

This town, built in tiers up the steep flank of the Kocher Valley, grew up around salt springs known in Celtic times. In the Middle Ages, it was famous for the Imperial silver coins, the Heller, minted there. The town's well-preserved half-timbered houses and tranquillity make this a pleasant stopping point. ▯ *Am Markt 9, 74523 Schwäbisch Hall,* ☎ *(0791) 75 12 46.*

▶ **Orient Yourself:** Schwäbisch Hall is hidden in the Kocher valley, south of the Hohenlohe plain.

⟨ **Also See:** *STUTTGART (69km/43mi southwest), ROMANTISCHE STRASSE (ROTHEN-BURG is 69km/43mi northeast).*

Sights

Marktplatz★★

Laid out on a slope, this square is dominated by the monumental stone steps of Michaelskirche (where actors, during a summer-long annual festival, perform a repertory of the world's theatre classics). The square is flanked by houses in a variety of architectural styles from Gothic to Baroque.

Dating from 1509, the **fountain** *(Marktbrunnen)* stands against a decorative wall adorned with statues of Samson, St Michael and St George *(copies, originals in the Hällisch-Fränkisches Museum)*. The rectangular design, unusual in a Gothic work, includes the old pillory post. The elegant 18C Late Baroque **town hall**★ and its beautiful clock tower stands opposite the church.

The two parallel streets of the **Obere** and the **Untere Herrengasse**, linked by stone stairways, are bordered by numerous 15C and 16C half-timbered houses.

Michaelskirche

The church occupies an imposing position atop 53 steps. The **interior**★, originally Romanesque, was transformed into a Gothic hall-church in the 15C. The Flamboyant chancel was added in the 16C.

WHERE TO EAT

⊖⊜ **Sonne** – *Gelbinger Gasse 2* ☎ *(0791) 97 08 40* ⊙ *Closed Mon Reservations recommended* Pleasant restaurant in the centre of Schwäbisch Hall, with two panelled dining rooms. Regional specialities are on the menu. Enjoy the Biergarten, weather permitting.

WHERE TO STAY

⊖⊜ **Hotel Sölch** – *Hauffstraße 14* ☎ *(0791) 518 07 Fax (0791) 54404 www.hotel-soelch.de* ⊙ *Closed 24 Dec-6 Jan* ▯ ⊱ *24 rooms* ⊐ This welcoming hotel is located fifteen-minutes' walk from the old town. Guestrooms are furnished in oak and home-made breads are served at breakfast.

Half-timbered houses on the banks of the Kocher

Hällisch-Fränkisches Museum (Regional Museum)
🕐 *Open Tue-Sun, 10am-5pm.* 🕐 *Closed Good Fri, 24, 25 and 31 Dec.* 👓 *€2.50.* ☎ *(0791) 75 12 89.*
This museum is housed in six historical buildings, one of which is an 8-storey tower. The collections cover geology, prehistory and early history from the Middle Ages to the Thirty Years War and the history of Hall until the end of its Imperial City status in 1802. Collections concentrate on the art, culture and everyday life of the townspeople, and delve into the history of the Heller and the region's salt trade.

Gräterhaus
This beautiful 1605 half-timbered house, so exquisitely decorated, stands alongside further half-timbered buildings in Gelbinger Gasse.

The banks of the Kocher★
From the Henkersbrücke bridge is an attractive view of the mass of half-timbered buildings on the opposite river bank, and their reflection in the waters of the Kocher. The view is perhaps even better from the junction of the street named Am Spitalbach and the Salinenstraße quay, from which the church of St Johann can also be seen. From Unterwöhrd island there is a **view**★ of the old town, its roofs stepped one above the other at the foot of Michaelskirche. Below, the arms of the river are spanned by attractive roofed wooden bridges.

The White Gold of Hall
The word Hala means "salt" in old German. The Celts found a salt water spring here and were using it as long ago as ca 500 BC. Rediscovered in 800 AD, the salt works quickly brought fame and fortune to the town of Hall. Green brine was pumped from a well that was dug where Haalplatz now stands, then processed by "distillers" who fed huge wood fires to evaporate the water. The resulting salt, said to be very white, very fine and of high quality, was used until 1924. The town was renamed Schwäbisch Hall in 1934.

Excursions

Benediktinerkloster Großcomburg★
3km/2mi south. 🚶 *Guided tour (30min).* 🕐 *Open from Apr to end Oct, Tue-Fri, at 11am, 1pm, 2pm, 3pm and 4pm, Sat-Sun at 2pm, 3pm and 4pm.* 👓 *€2.30.* ☎ *(0791) 93 81 85.*

Along with those of Aachen and Hildesheim, the church's chandelier is one of the most precious in the West. Dating from 1130 and designed in the shape of a crown, the **chandelier**★★★ *(Radleuchter)* is made of iron, subsequently copper-plated and then gilded. In front of the high altar is an **antependium**★ of the same period, made of gilded beaten copper representing Christ among the Apostles. The framework supporting this is treated with *cloisonné* enamel and filigree work.

Hohenloher Freilandmuseum★ (Hohenlohe Open-Air Museum)

At Wackershofen, 5km/3mi northwest. ◷ *Open May-Sep, 9am-6pm (May, Sep closed Mon); Mar-Apr, Tue-Sun, 10am-5pm; Oct-Nov, Tue-Sun, 10am-5pm.* ⊗ *€5.50.* ☎ *(0791) 97 10 10; www.wackershofen.de*

Over 50 buildings from the 16C to the 19C, which originally stood in different locations, have been moved here to faithfully recapture rural life of this area from the mid-16C to the 19C. There is an exhibition of furniture and agricultural implements.

SCHWARZWALD★★★

BLACK FOREST

Although it was named after its dark forests of conifers, the Black Forest also boasts lakes, pasture land, vineyards – a surprising variety of scenery for such a small region. Add to that picturesque villages, cuckoo clocks and unsurpassed summer hiking and winter skiing and it is easy to see why this mountainous region has become one of Germany's most popular tourist destinations.

▶ **Orient Yourself:** In the southwest corner of Germany, the Black Forest stretches for 170km/106mi from Karlsruhe to Basle. It is accessible from Stuttgart via the A81, and from Strasbourg or Freiburg via the A5.

⊗ **Don't Miss:** A drive along the Crest Road, driving tour **1** below.

◷ **Organizing Your Time:** Allow four hours to travel the Crest Road, driving tour **1**, one day each for driving tour **2** and **3** (◔ *see below*).

Kids Especially for Kids: Outdoor pursuits throughout the Schwarzwald.

◔ **Also See:** *RASTATT (to the north), ROTTWEIL and DONAUESCHINGEN (to the east), ST BLASIEN and Bad SÄCKINGEN (to the south).*

Black Forest landscape

Address Book

WHERE TO EAT

◎⊜ **Gasthof Gedächtnishaus**
– Fohrenbühl 12, 78730 Lauterbach
☎ (07422) 44 61 www.king-gastro.
de ⓒ Closed from early Jan to mid Feb
⌇ ⁂ ⅋ This guesthouse, built in
traditional style, is in an ideal moun-
taintop location. The rustic restaurant is
decorated in dark wood. Simple accommodation for tired hikers.

◎⊜ **Löffelschmiede** – Löffelschmiede
1, 79853 Lenzkirch ☎ (07653) 279 www.
sbo.de/loeffelschmiede ⓒ Closed from
Nov to mid Dec This little family-run
restaurant is set in a small valley near
Lenzkirch. Trout and simple regional
dishes are served in the bright and welcoming restaurant with its earthenware
stove. A few rooms are also available.

◎⊜⊜ **Dorfstuben** – Gärtenbühl-
weg 14, 72270 Baiersbronn-Mitteltal
☎ (07442) 470 www.bareiss.com Its
charming decor and creaking wood
make the Dorfstuben a delightful refuge. Expect Black Forest specialties.

◎⊜ **Jägerstüble** – Marktplatz 12,
72250 Freudenstadt ☎ (07441) 23 87
www.jaegerstueble-fds.de ⓒ Closed
mid Oct to early Nov The rustic setting and relaxed atmosphere of the
Jägerstüble, make it popular with locals
and visitors.

WHERE TO STAY

◎ **Berggasthaus Gisiboden** – 79674
Todtnau-Gschwend ☎ (7671) 99 98 21
Fax (07671) 999821 ⌇ ℗ 16 rooms ⌇
⊜ Restaurant Guaranteed peace and
quiet at an altitude of 1 200m/3 937ft.
This mountain hotel offers simple
rooms with showers and a pleasant
restaurant with a garden. An ideal hub
for mountain hiking and biking.

◎⊜ **Hotel Belchen-Multen** – 79677
Schönau-Aitern-Multen ☎ (07673) 209
Fax (07673) 7039 www.belchen-multen.
de ⓒ Closed mid Nov to mid Dec ⌇ ℗
⌇ ⁂ 22 rooms ⌇ ◎⊜ Restaurant
A well-kept hotel in the wilds of the
Black Forest, with simple rooms. The
covered swimming pool, solarium and
sauna are welcome in bad weather.

◎⊜ **Hotel Hirsch** – Haus Nr. 10, 72250
Freudenstadt-Zwieselberg ☎ (07441)
86 01 90 Fax (07441) 8601959 www.
zwieselhirsch.de ⓒ Closed from early
Nov to mid Dec ℗ 29 rooms ⌇ ◎⊜
Restaurant A typical Black Forest hotel
in an ideal location in the heart of
nature. Much of the interior looks brand
new. Bright, welcoming restaurant.

◎⊜ **Hotel Sonne** – Krumlinden 44,
79244 Münstertal-Obermünstertal
☎ (07636) 319 Fax (07636) 377 www.
sonne-muenstertal.de ⓒ Closed mid
Nov to mid Dec ⌇ ℗ ⁂ 13 rooms
⌇ ◎⊜ Restaurant A pleasant little
hotel with a new addition, set in the
romantic Münstertal. The comfortable
rooms in feature wooden flooring
and furniture. The restaurant with its
panelled walls is also pleasant.

◎⊜ **Schwarzwaldhaus** – Am
Kurpark 26, 79872 Bernau-Innerlehen ⓒ Closed mid Nov to mid Dec
☎ (07675) 365 Fax (07675) 1371 www.
sbo.de/schwarzwaldhaus ℗ 15 rooms
⌇ ◎⊜ Restaurant This farmhouse
covered in wooden shingles is a typical
Black Forest establishment. Well-kept
and efficiently run with rustic rooms.
The restaurant is housed in the former
stables and serves mainly regional fare.

◎⊜⊜ **Hotel Alemannenhof** – Brud-
erhalde 21, 79822 Titisee ☎ (07652)
911 80 Fax (07652) 705 www.hotel-ale-
mannenhof.de ℗ ⌇ ⅋ 22 rooms ⌇
◎⊜ Restaurant On the shores of the
Titisee, this modern Black Forest hotel
boasts a private beach and dock. In
addition to the comfortable rooms, the
establishment has a pleasant restaurant
and a lakeside terrace.

A Bit of History

Twin Sister of the Vosges – The Vosges and Black Forest ranges both rise from a crystalline base to similar altitudes (the Feldberg at 1 493m/4 899ft and the Grand Ballon at 1 424m/4 674ft). Both drop steeply in the direction of the Rhine, and less abruptly to the Swabian plateaux in one case, to Lorraine in the other.

Varied resources – The economy of this region has always been linked to the forest, wood being practically the sole construction material and the base of all crafts. The trunks of trees, often 50m/165ft long, were floated away as far as the Netherlands, where they were much in demand by boat builders. Clock-making, including the famous cuckoo clock, remains a fruitful activity. Much of the region's wealth today comes from the spa and winter sports resorts.

Driving Tours

1 Crest Road★★★ (Schwarzwald-Hochstraße)

From Baden-Baden to Freudenstadt. 80km/50mi

Amply provided with viewpoints and car parks, the Black Forest Crest Road, or Hochstraße, runs past many slopes with ski lifts. Much of the route is at heights approaching 1 000m/3 280ft.

Baden-Baden★★ – *See BADEN-BADEN.*

▶ *Follow signs 'Schwarzwald-Hochstraße/B500'.*

The road gradually climbs, passing through quiet health resorts such as Bühlerhöhe, at an altitude of 750m/2 460ft.

Mummelsee

This small, dark glacial lake at the foot of the **Hornisgrinde** (1 164m/3 819ft), the highest point of the northern Black Forest, is named after the "Mümmeln" (water sprites) that inhabit its icy depths, according to local legend. In days gone by, Black Forest breweries obtained blocks of ice chopped out of the frozen lake until well into spring.

▶ *At Ruhestein, leave the Hochstraße temporarily to plunge towards the **Allerheiligen Valley**★ then climb back from Oppenau toward Zuflucht via an extremely steep mountain road.*

Allerheiligen★

The ruins of a 13C church still stand, along with a Gothic chapel. A footpath leads from the ruins to the **Allerheiligen-Wasserfälle**★, a celebrated series of seven waterfalls with a total drop of 90m/295ft. (*45min on foot there and back from the car park to the foot of the falls, 2km/1mi beyond the abbey ruins.*)

▶ *Continue along the Hochstraße towards Freudenstadt.*

Freudenstadt★

At the crossing of several tourist routes, this 17C town was destroyed by fire in 1945. It now follows a chessboard plan centred on the **Marktplatz**★, a huge square surrounded by houses with arcades. The two naves of the 17C church (*Stadtkirche*), built at right angles, form one corner of Marktplatz. Note the carved 12C Romanesque **lectern**★★ supported by the Four Apostles. A further treasure is the 12C **font**★.

② **Central Black Forest★★**

From Freudenstadt to Freiburg. 152km/94mi

The itinerary follows the foot of the Kinzig and Elt valleys, passing through busy villages before reaching the Upper Black Forest at Freiburg.

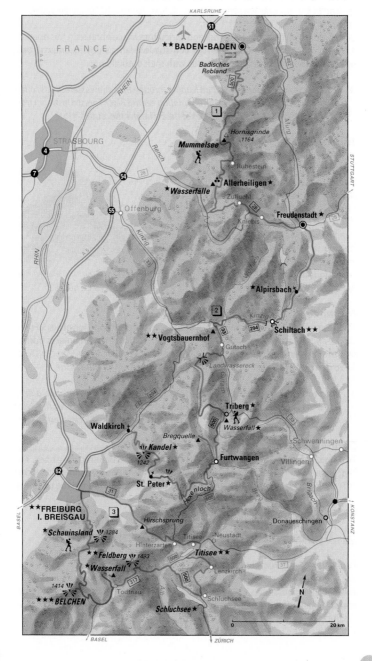

Alpirsbach★

The 12C church, joined to the old Benedictine **abbey**★, is the Black Forest's oldest Romanesque monument and has an unusual layout: the Romanesque base supports a Gothic chancel with buttresses that do not reach the ground but stand on free columns.

Freilitchtmuseum Vogtsbauernhof★★
(Black Forest Open-Air Museum), in Gutach

🕐 End of Mar to early Nov: 9am-6pm. 🕭 €5. ☎ (078 31) 935 60; www.vogtsbau-ernhof.org

Black Forest construction, craftwork and agriculture are celebrated in this open-air museum in the Gutach Valley. The 1612 Vogtsbauern farm, still in its original state, is set amid six reconstituted farmhouses with their outbuildings.

▶ *Continue towards Triberg. The road leading through the Landwassereck pass offers a number of fine **views**★ over the undulating central Black Forest. Upstream from Oberprechtal, the beautiful cascades of the Elz border the route.*

Triberg★

The **Waterfall Walk**★ *(1hr on foot round trip)* follows the Gutach rapids among boulders and tall trees. The church of **Maria der Tannen (Our Lady of the Firs)**★ is one of the most popular pilgrims' sanctuaries in the Black Forest. The **Schwarzwald Museum** exhibits traditional costumes and local craftwork, including one of Europe's largest collections of barrel-organs. (🕐 *Early Apr to mid Nov: 10am-5pm.* 🕭 *€3.90)*

A traditional Black Forest house

R. Corbel/MICHELIN

Furtwangen

The **Deutsches Uhrenmuseum** displays the world's largest collection of Black Forest clocks, and goes on to present the art, history and technology of timepieces from all over the world and every age. 🕭🕐 *Apr-Oct, 9am-6pm; Nov-Mar, 10am-5pm.* 🕐 *Closed 24-26 Dec.* 🕭 *€4.* ☎ *(077 23) 920 28 00; www.deutsches-uhrenmuseum.de*

▶ *Soon after leaving Furtwangen, turn right for Hexenloch. Pass through a deep wooded gorge enlivened by waterfalls. Between St Märgen and St Peter, the twists and turns of the road allow plenty of **views**★★ of the central Black Forest.*

St Peter★

Two onion-domed towers top the **church**★ of this 18C Benedictine abbey. The Feuchtmamayer statues inside the church represent the Dukes of Zähringen, founders of Freiburg, and date to the 11C. A variety of hiking paths leave from the car parks.

Freiburg★★ – 🕭 *See FREIBURG.*

③ Upper Black Forest★★★ (Hochschwarzwald)

Round trip leaving from Freiburg im Breisgau. 142km/88mi

This circuit, mountainous early on, passes the three principal summits of the Black Forest (Schauinsland, Belchen and Feldberg), followed by the two best-known lakes (Schluchsee and Titisee).

Schauinsland★

The mountain road, extremely twisty, leads to the upper cable-car station. From the car park, climb to the top of the viewing tower *(91 steps)* after following the signs "Rundweg" and "Schauinsland Gipfel" *(30min on foot there and back)*. The lookout point offers a **view**★ across upland meadows to the Feldberg.

▶ *Follow the road for 1km/0.5mi, and take the right-hand fork toward Stohren and the Münstertal. Winding down through the meadows, the route finally plunges once more into the forest. At Wiedener Eck, turn right toward the Belchen.*

Mount Belchen★★★

From the end of the road, walk (30min there and back) to the viewing platform.
This mountain dominates the Wiesenthal. The Belchen summit, at a height of 1 414m/4 637ft, makes a magnificent **observation point**★★★ when the skies are clear, taking in the Rhine plain, the High Vosges, and the Alps.

The Falls of Todtnau★

1.5km/1mi from Todtnau, 60min round trip.
Climbing through a wooded combe, a footpath leads to an impressive series of cascades *(Wasserfall)* gushing 97m/318ft.

Feldberg Massif★★

A chair lift *(Feldbergbahn)* conveys sightseers to Mount Seebuck (1 448m/4 750ft), which is crowned by the Bismarck monument. From here is a **view**★ of the circular bowl of the Feldsee, a small lake in the hollow of a glacial cirque. It is possible to reach the bare Feldberg summit at 1 493m/4 897ft *(1hr 30min there and back)* to enjoy a **panorama**★★ stretching as far as the Alps.

Schluchsee★

This glacial lake became the largest body of water in the Black Forest when it was dammed in 1932.

▶ *The Titisee is reached via Lenzkirch. During the final part of the descent, the road overlooks the lake.*

Titisee★★

This clear glacial lake sits at the junction of several tourist routes. It has developed into a popular tourist centre and a departure point for many Black Forest excursions.

▶ *The return to Freiburg is through the **Höllental**★ ("The Vale of Hell")*

😊 A Bit of Advice 😊

For a unique travel experience, travel the **German Clock Road** *(Deutsche Uhrenstraße)*, covering about 320km/199mi and taking in various cuckoo-clock sites: museums, factory tours, and remarkable clocks (details available from information offices in the region). For railway fans, the **Black Forest Train** *(Schwarzwaldbahn)* negotiates a 670m/2 198ft elevation change following the landscape on a route that avoids bridges. Despite the 39 tunnels required to manage the largest natural obstacles, the journey encompasses magnificent scenery, the most interesting section (27km/17mi) between Hornberg and St-Georgen.

SCHWERIN★

POPULATION: 97 000

Schwerin is one of the most pleasant towns of northern Germany. The city boasts refined architecture and a castle reigning majestically on an island opposite the old town. *Am Markt 10, 19055 Schwerin, ☏ (0385) 592 52 12.*

▸ **Orient Yourself:** The town of Schwerin is situated in a landscape of lakes and forests. The A 24 motorway (Hamburg-Berlin) is about 20km to the south.

P **Parking:** Near the Old Town you'll find garages at Reiferbahn and Wittenburger Str. and on Geschwister Scholl Str.

Don't Miss: A visit to the Schloßinsel and Ludwigslust (*see Excursion*).

Organizing Your Time: Allow two hours to visit the Schloßinsel.

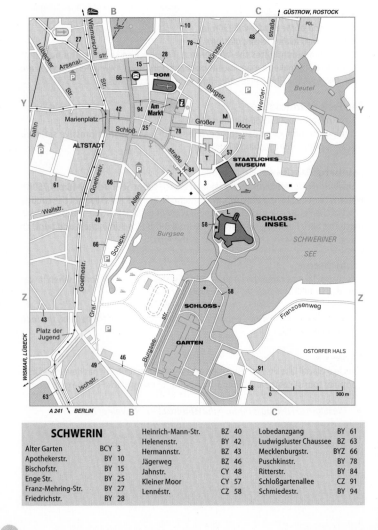

SCHWERIN		Heinrich-Mann-Str.	BZ 40	Lobedanzgang	BY 61
		Helenenstr.	BY 42	Ludwigsluster Chaussee	BZ 63
Alter Garten	BCY 3	Hermannstr.	BZ 43	Mecklenburgstr.	BYZ 66
Apothekerstr.	BY 10	Jägerweg	BZ 46	Puschkinstr.	BY 78
Bischofstr.	BY 15	Jahnstr.	CY 48	Ritterstr.	BY 84
Enge Str.	BY 25	Kleiner Moor	CY 57	Schloßgartenallee	CZ 91
Franz-Mehring-Str.	BY 27	Lennéstr.	CZ 58	Schmiedestr.	BY 94
Friedrichstr.	BY 28				

☝ **Also See:** *MECKLENBURGISCHE SEENPLATTE, WISMAR (31km/19mi north), LÜBECK (66km/41mi northwest).*

A Bit of History

The oldest town in Mecklenburg – The origins of Schwerin date to the 11C, when the Slavs built a fortress on what is now Schloßinsel. They were soon expelled by Henry the Lion, who colonized Schwerin as the first German town east of the Elbe.

Schlossinsel★★

Schloss★

🕐 *Open from mid-Apr to mid-Oct, 10am-6pm; from mid-Oct to mid-Apr, Tue-Sun, 10am-5pm.* 🎫 *€4.* ☏ *(0385) 525 29 20; www.schloss-schwerin.de*

Built as the residence of the Grand Dukes of Mecklenburg-Schwerin, the castle recalls the Château of Chambord on the Loire, a key inspiration for this building. The museum occupies the old state rooms; the **Throne Room★**, Ancestors' Gallery *(Ahnengalerie)* and Smoking Room are especially nice.

Schlosskirche★

This 16C church was the first newly built Protestant church in Mecklenburg.

Schlossgarten★

Created in the 19C, this formal Baroque garden is organised around canals, lime trees and ornamental flowerbeds. The canals feature statues by Balthazar Permoser.

The Castle

J. Bouraly/MICHELIN

Sights

Altstadt

Markt

Four 17C half-timbered houses are preserved beside the town hall. On the north side of the square, the so-called New Building (Neues Gebäude) was erected between 1783 and 1785 in the Classic style.

WHERE TO EAT

⊜⊜ **Weinhaus Uhle** – *Schusterstraße 15* ☏ *(0385) 56 29 56 www.weinhaus-uhle. de* Located near the market place, this neat town house is home to a well-run, elegant restaurant with an 18C vaulted ceiling and pretty arched windows. Huge wine list.

WHERE TO STAY

⊜⊜⊜ **Niederländischer Hof** – *Karl-Marx-Straße 12* ☏ *(0385) 59 11 00 Fax (0385) 59110999 www.niederlaendischer-hof.de* 🅿 ⤢ *33 rooms* ⊒ ⊜⊜⊜ *Restaurant* In an old building with listed façade, this hotel fits perfectly into the surrounding urban landscape. The tasteful interior is elegantly furnished and the parquet flooring and warm tones of the restaurant add up to a refined atmosphere.

Ludwigslust Cardboard Decor

Duke Friedrich's intensive building activity exhausted his funds, but he determined to decorate his palace in a manner befitting a duke. Instead, expensive material was substituted at Ludwigslust by papier mâché. Paper, glue and water were used to create a product that, after it had set, could be ground, polished and painted and was even weather resistant. The Ludwigslust workshop achieved such mastery that its products were exported as far as Russia. Production ceased in 1835 due to lack of demand. The original recipe was closely guarded, and remains a secret today.

Staatliches Museum★

Werderstraße. ♿🕐 *Open Tue-Sun, 10am-6pm (5pm mid-Oct to mid-Apr).* 🕐 *Closed 24 and 31 Dec.* ⊛ *€6.* ☎ *(0385) 595 80; www.museum-schwerin.de*
The **national museum** houses important Flemish and Dutch paintings of the 17C (Brueghel, Rembrandt, Rubens), European painting from the 16C to the 20C (Cranach, Gainsborough) and contemporary art (Cage, Polke).

Excursion

Ludwigslust★

The town was founded by Duke Friedrich von Mecklenburg in 1764.
The **Schloss★** is an E-shaped, 18C Late Baroque building with some early Classical elements. The attic parapet which crowns the roof is still adorned with the original 18 vases and 40 statues, produced by the Bohemian sculptor Rudolph Kaplunger. The figures represent the arts, sciences and virtues, special interests of the Duke.
The **Interior** is dominated by white and gold ornamentation, in German interpretations of Louis XVI style. The sumptuous **Golden Room** contains exclusively papier mâché ornamentation. The Venus Medici, in the salon just before the gallery, is also made of papier mâché although it looks deceptively like marble. 🕐 *Open from mid-Apr to mid-Oct, Tue-Sun, 10am-6pm; mid-Oct to mid-Apr, Tue-Sun, 10am-5pm.* 🕐 *Closed 24 Dec.* ⊛ *€3.* ☎ *(038 74) 571 90; www.schloss-ludwigslust.de*
The **Schloßpark**★ covers an area of 135ha/334 acres and is one of the largest of its kind in Mecklenburg-Vorpommern. Take a stroll around the park to view streams, monuments, mausoleums and a grotto.

SIGMARINGEN★

POPULATION: 16 500

Sigmaringen's castle rises in traditional style from the edge of the cliff, but the only feudal parts remaining are the site and its general appearance. 🛈 *Schwabstraße 1, 72488 Sigmaringen,* ☎ *(075 71) 10 62 23.*

▸ **Orient Yourself:** Sigmaringen castle is located on a rocky spur rising from the Danube valley.
😊 **Don't Miss:** The Schloss.
🕐 **Organizing Your Time:** Allow two hours for a visit to the Schloss.
👣 **Also See:** *SCHWÄBISCHE ALB (suggested itinerary leaves from Sigmaringen), ZWIEFALTEN (35km/22mi northeast), BODENSEE (Überlingen is only 41km/26mi south).*

Sights

Schloss

🚶 *Guided tour (1hr).* 🕐 *Feb to Apr and Nov, 9.30am-4.30pm; May to Oct, 9am-4.45pm.* 🕐 *Closed Shrove Tue.* ⊜ *€6.* ☎ *(075 71) 72 92 30; www.hohenzollern.com*

The State Apartments are adorned in the 16C style with coffered ceilings and tapestries. The weaponry boasts one of Europe's largest collection of arms and armour (15C-19C).

The **Marstallmuseum** *(under renovation; by appointment only)* houses a display of carriages and sleighs and works by 15C-16C Swabian artists.

Pfarrkirche St Johann

Luminous with Rococo stuccowork, the church clings to the castle rock. A shrine in a transept chapel contains the cradle of St Fidelio of Sigmaringen (1577-1622), first Capuchin martyr, Patron of the Order and local patron saint.

SPEYER★

POPULATION: 50 000

The old Imperial City of Speyer lies in the Rhine plain, easily distinguished by its belfries. A historic city with a prestigious past, the town boasts the largest Romanesque cathedral in Europe. 🛈 *Maximilianstraße 13, 67346 Speyer,* ☎ *(06232) 14 23 92.*

▶ **Orient Yourself:** South of Heidelberg, Speyer is located between the wooded mountains of the Odenwald and those of the Pfalz.

🅿 **Parking:** Garages are located throughout Speyer. The main train station has a garage convenient for travelers.

☺ **Don't Miss:** The Kaiserdom.

🕐 **Organizing Your Time:** Allow two hours to enjoy Speyer Cathedral.

☝ **Also See:** *HEIDELBERG (27km/17mi northeast), BRUCHSAL (35km/22mi southeast), KARLSRUHE (51km/32mi south), PFALZ (Dahn is 64km/40mi southwest).*

A Bit of History

Imperial city – Once favoured by the Salian emperors, and an episcopal seat since the 4C, Speyer enjoyed considerable attention from the 11C. It was made Imperial City in 1294, and more than 50 Imperial Diets were held here, but the city was razed in 1689 by Louis XIV's. For this reason, the only evidence of its medieval splendour is the Kaiserdom, fragments of the town wall and the *Altpörtel*, a tall tower at the west end of Maximilianstraße, once the town's main gateway.

The *Protestants*

The Edict of Worms, in fact never enacted, was confirmed by the Diet of Speyer in 1529. The Lutheran states then made a solemn protest against the Diet's decisions, from which derives the label "Protestant" to identify partisans of the Reformation. The fact is commemorated by the existence of a neo-Gothic church, Gedächtniskirche, built early in the 20C on Bartholomäus-Weltz-Platz.

Kaiserdom★★

🕐 *Open Apr to Oct, 9am-7pm; Nov to Mar, 9am-5pm. Donations requested.* ☎ *(062 32) 100 92 18.*

Founded by Konrad II in 1030 and remodelled at the end of the 11C, this Romanesque basilica is the largest Romanesque building in Europe.

There is an interesting **view**★★ of the east end from the garden approach to the 13C **Heidentürmchen** (Pagan Tower).

The most impressive way to enter is via the door in the west face. The **transept**★★ is a masterpiece of unity and balance; the **Chapel of the Holy Sacrament** *(Afrakapelle, on the left, before the north transept)* houses two 15C low-relief sculptures: the Bearing of the Cross and the Annunciation. The two-tier central rotunda houses the **baptistery** (Chapel of St Emmerammus) and, above, a chapel dedicated to St Catherine.

Speyer Cathedral

The Kaiserdom's **crypt**★★ is probably the finest and largest Romanesque crypt in Germany. Romanesque groined vaulting features transverse arches of alternately pink and white sandstone. Four Holy Roman Emperors and four German Kings are buried in the **Royal Vault**.

In the gardens south of the cathedral is the 16C **Ölberg**, once the centre of the cloister. A large stone trough, the **Domnapf**, stands in the forecourt. In days gone by, each time a bishop was enthroned, it was filled with wine and anyone who wished to could drink until he dropped.

Sights

Old Town

This stretches from the cathedral west toward the 12C-13C **Altpörtel**★, a gateway tower. Maximilianstraße is a lively street, whose crowning glory is the Late Baroque town hall. At the fork with Korngasse stands the "Alte Münze" (Old Mint) built in 1748; its name is derived from the coin minters' guildhall which stood on this spot in the Middle Ages.

Judenbad (Jewish Baths)

Access via Judengasse, southwest of the cathedral (signposted). Ritual ablutions were performed here; a changing room, a semicircular staircase and the bath remain. The building *(Judenhof)*, in the centre of the medieval Jewish quarter, was erected in the 12C, by workmen engaged in the construction of the cathedral.

Historisches Museum der Pfalz★ (Palatinate Museum)

&. ⊙ *Open Tue-Sun, 10am-6pm.* ⊙ *Closed 25 and 31 Dec.* ⊛ *€8.* ☎ *(062 32) 132 50; www.museum.speyer.de*

This museum houses the solid gold, 12C cone-shaped **Golden Hat**★ of Schifferstadt, the rarest, most valuable item in the Prehistoric Department.

The **Cathedral Treasury** *(Domschatzkammer, basement level)* houses tomb furnishings of the emperors, a prime highlight of the exhibit. Note the funerary crown of Konrad II, the first Salian emperor; the Imperial orb of Heinrich III; and the crown of the Canossa penance of Heinrich IV.

In the cellar is the **Wine Museum** *(Weinmuseum)*, presenting 2 000 years of wine history. The showpiece is the **Roman wine**★, the oldest wine in the world that remains liquid.

Technik-Museum★

&. ⊙ *Open year-round, 9am-6pm (7pm on Sat-Sun).* ⊛ *€12.* ☎ *(062 32) 670 80; www. technik-museum.de*

The Technology Museum south of the cathedral displays an impressive number of aircraft, railway engines, and classic cars. Visitors can also tour a 1966 U 9. Further attractions include a maritime display and a collection of musical instruments.

SPREEWALD★★

A network of over 300 waterways crisscrosses this lush countryside, painstakingly drained to give it the appearance of a "Venice in the Woods." Another regional interest is its Sorbian minority, western Slavs who settled in Germany's Lausitz area in the 6C, and whose language and culture remain (& *see BRANITZ*).

▸ **Orient Yourself:** Spreewald is nearly 100km/62mi to the southeast of Berlin, near the Polish border. The region covers about 260km²/100sq mi.
⊛ **Don't Miss:** A barge trip from Lübbenau.
⊙ **Organizing Your Time:** Allow at least half a day for a Spreewald barge trip.
Kids Especially for Kids: A barge trip from Lübbenau.
& **Also See:** *BRANITZ (37km/23mi southeast), FRANKFURT AN DER ODER (76km/48mi northeast, see Berlin Excursions), BERLIN (93km/58mi northwest).*

Sights

Barge Trip (Kahnfahrt)

Kids *Boat trips are available in the Spreewald, although* **Lübbenau** *has established itself as the centre for such trips. Embarkation in Lübbenau harbour. Apr to Oct (weather permitting). Duration: 2-9hr, with a stopover.* ⊛ *From €7.* ☎ *(035 42) 22 25; www.spreewaldexpress.de*

Boatmen organise excursions aboard flat-bottomed craft which ferry passengers to a garden paradise.

A stop at **Lehde**★, a tiny lagoon village of 150, boasts almost as many islands as houses. The **Open-Air Museum** (Freilandmuseum Lehde) includes three 19C farms, complete with living quarters and outbuildings, furniture, folk art,

Boating in the Spreewald

R. Chéret/MICHELIN

costumes and agricultural implements. Outdoor enthusiasts can choose between three footpaths starting from Lübbenau: one leading towards Lehde *(1hr there and back)*, another to Wotschofska and a third to Leipe *(3hr there and back)*.

Lübbenau

The 18C town church of **St Nikolai**★ is designed in the Dresden Baroque style. A highlight is the church's impressive tombs, including the high **tomb** (c 1765) of Prince Moritz Carl, Count of Lynaer. ♿⏰ *Open from May until the local Autumn school holidays, Tue-Sun, 2-4pm.* ⏰ *Closed bank holidays. Donation requested.* ☎ *(035 42) 36 68.*

Lübbenau castle and grounds are worth a trip as well for the chancellery (1745, now a museum), the neo-Classical castle (1817, now a hotel) and the orangery.

ST BLASIEN★

POPULATION: 4 000

The majestic domed church dedicated to St Blaise comes suddenly into view in the southern part of the Black Forest. It stands in the grounds of a medieval monastery founded in 835 by hermit monks. 🛈 *Am Kurgarten, 79837 St Blasien,* ☎ *(076 72) 414 30.*

▶ **Orient Yourself:** St Blasien is at the far end of a wooded valley in the Hotzenwald and is dominated by the peaks of the Feldberg.

⊙ **Don't Miss:** The Hochkopf Massif (👁 *see Excursion*).

🕐 **Organizing Your Time:** Allow half a day for the Hochkopf excursion.

👣 **Also See:** *SCHWARZWALD (Schluchsee is 15km/9mi away), Bad SÄCKINGEN (40km/25mi south), DONAUESCHINGEN (62km/39mi northeast), BODENSEE (115km/72mi east).*

Sights

Dom★★

This Baroque church is built in the old abbey complex. The French architect, Pierre-Michel d'Ixnard (1723-95), graced it with a central dome; after those of St Peter's in Rome and Les Invalides in Paris this is the third largest dome in Europe (33.5m/110ft in diameter).

Excursions

The Hochkopf Massif *45km/28mi*

▶ *Drive via Todtmoos to the Weißenbachsattel pass.*

Hochkopf

1hr on foot there and back. From the car park, a footpath leads to the look-out tower, from which are **views**★★ of the barren peaks of the Belchen and the Feldberg and, on clear days, the Alps.

T. Krieger/MICHELIN

The church and its impressive dome

Bernau★
At Bernau-Innerlehen, the **town hall** (Rathaus) houses the **Hans-Thoma-Museum**, an exhibition of paintings by this local artist.

The Alb Valley (Albtal)
30km/18.5mi south. The road runs high above the Alb gorges, tunneling through the cliffs on its way to the Rhine at Albbruck.

STENDAL

POPULATION: 37 000

Founded ca 1160 by the Margrave Albrecht the Bear, Stendal was a member of the Hanseatic League and until the mid-16C remained the most influential town in the Brandenburg March. Stendal was the birthplace of Johann Joachim Winckelmann (1717-68), founder of scientific archaeology. One of his admirers, French novelist Henri Beyle (1783-1842), liked the town's name so much he adopted it (with an extra "h") as a pseudonym: Stendhal.

▶ **Orient Yourself:** Stendal is on the B 189 road which links it to Magdeburg to the south.
- **Don't Miss:** Stendal's Uenglingen Gate and an excursion to to Tangermünde.
- **Organizing Your Time:** The main sights of Stendal can be seen in a day.
- **Also See:** *MAGDEBURG (64km/40mi south), POTSDAM (101km/63mi east) BERLIN (125km/78mi east)*.

Sights

Rathaus
Markt. The oldest part of the town hall, in exposed brick, dates from the 15C. Added at the end of that century, the main wing was later remodelled in the Renaissance style. In front of the town hall's arcade stands a statue of Roland, the third largest in Germany and a copy of the 16C original.

Marienkirche
Behind the Markt. The 15C hall-church features a chancel ambulatory separated from the nave by a delicately worked partition. The high altar is in the Flamboyant Gothic style.

Dom St Nikolaus★
The 15C cathedral St. Nikolaus supplanted an Augustinian monks' church, the square ground-plan recalling the hall-churches of Lower Saxony. The 22 stained-glass **windows**★ (1420-60) are remarkable. Note those in the chancel, which, because of their size, suggest a huge conservatory.

Uenglinger Tor★ (Uenglingen Gate)
Northwest of the old town. Dating from ca 1380, this is one of the most interesting fortified medieval gateways in the region. From the outside, the two lower storeys are purely defensive, while the upper part, added in the 15C, is more decorative.

Excursions

Tangermünde★

10km/6mi southeast. Situated at the confluence of the Rivers Tanger and Elbe, Tangermünde's remains enclosed within its 14C ramparts, its streets bordered by half-timbered houses. The brick Late Gothic (1430) **Rathaus**★ has a three-gable façade with lacework of carved decorations. Ancient gateways retain their monumental aspect, particularly the **Neustädter Tor**★, an imposing circular tower on the south side.

Havelberg★

46km North, cross the Elbe at Tangermünde. Overlooking this small town on the River Havel is the **Cathedral of St Marien**★ consecrated in 1170. The sculpturing of the chancel partition and the **rood-screen panels**★★ (1396-1411) is especially nice. Note also three **sandstone candelabra** and a **Triumphal Cross** (c 1300).

STRALSUND★

POPULATION: 58 700

Separated from the island of Rügen by a narrow sea channel and surrounded by lakes, the Baltic town of Stralsund has since its earliest days developed as a maritime navigation. Its Gothic brick buildings are a distinguishing feature of the townscape. *Alter Markt 9, 18409 Stralsund, ☎ (038 31) 246 90*

- ▶ **Orient Yourself:** Stralsund is on the Baltic at the far northeasterly point of mainland Germany. A 2.5km/1.6mi bridge links the town to the island of Rügen.
- **Don't Miss:** A walking tour of the Olt Town.
- **Organizing Your Time:** Allow two hours for the suggested walking tour.
- Kids **Especially for Kids:** The Oceanographic Museum.
- **Also See:** *Insel RÜGEN, GREIFSWALD (33km south), ROSTOCK (75km west).*

A Bit of History

A Coveted City – From the moment of its foundation in 1209, Stralsund was subjected to assaults from envious neighbours: from Lübeck, Denmark, Sweden and even Holland. Protected by its massive rampart, the town was able during the Thirty Years War to beat off its attackers.

Walking Tour

The Old Town★

Rathaus★ (Town Hall)

Alter Markt. Built in the 13C and 14C, this splendid edifice comprises two separate, parallel blocks. The magnificent **north façade**★★ was added ca 1450. The ground floor arcades open onto a covered market hall leading to the west porch of Nikolaikirche.

WHERE TO STAY

⊝⊜ **An den Bleichen** – *An den Bleichen 45* ☎ *(03831) 39 06 75 Fax (03831) 392153* 🅿 ✕ *23 rooms* 🛏 Located in a residential area, this family-run establishment is surrounded by pretty gardens. Close to the old town, port and beach. Practical and comfortable guestrooms.

⊝⊜⊜⊜ **Steigenberger Hotel Baltic** – *Frankendamm 22* ☎ *(03831) 20 40 Fax (03831) 204999 www.stralsund.steigenberger.de* ✕ *134 rooms* 🛏⊝⊜⊜ *Restaurant* This hotel is located in a former barracks renovated in an elegantly modern style. Contemporary bistro-restaurant.

Nikolaikirche★

Alter Markt, opposite the town hall. Modelled on the Marienkirche at Lübeck, this 13C hall-church features interior columns and chapels that retain Late Gothic frescoes. Among the works of art, note the six medieval carved altarpieces and a stone group depicting St Anne (ca 1290).

▶ *Leave the Alter Markt and take Mönchstrasse south.*

Deutsches Meeresmuseum★ (Oceanographic Museum)

Kids *Mönchstraße.* ◷ *Open Jun to Sep, 10am-6pm; rest of the year, 10am-5pm.* ◷ *Closed 24 and 31 Dec.* ⊕ *€6.50.* ☎ *(038 31) 26 50 210; www.meeresmuseum.de* The Germany Oceanographic Museum is set in building once part of an abbey (the Katharinenkloster). Displays include sea fishing and the flora and fauna of the Baltic Sea. Among the aquariums the 50 000l/11 000gal shark tank and the 15m/50ft long fin-back whale skeleton are highlights.

Kulturhistorisches Museum (Historical Museum)

Mönchstraße. ◷ *Open Tue-Sun, 10am-5pm.* ◷ *Closed 24 and 31 Dec.* ⊕ *€3.* ☎ *(038 31) 287 90.* Medieval sacred art, gold and silver plate from the isle of Hiddensee *(see Insel RÜGEN),* and the history of Stralsund are among the diverse exhibits on display.

▶ *Continue south until the Neuer Markt.*

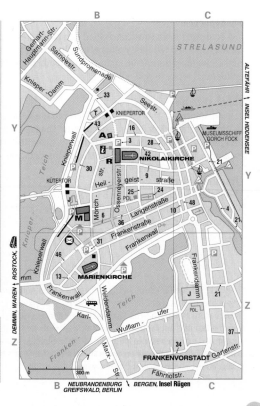

Marienkirche★

Neuer Markt. Apart from the impressive 15C 104m/340ft west tower, the church's Gothic High Altar with the Coronation of the Virgin Mary (15C) and an organ (c 1659) by organ builder Friedrich Stellwagen from Lübeck.

STRAUBING

POPULATION: 44 500

Straubing evolved from a Roman military camp, but the present town centre, the Neustadt, is a 13C Wittelsbach addition. Modern Straubing is still the economic focus of the region. ▣ *Theresienplatz 20, 94315 Straubing, ☎ (094 21) 94 43 07.*

▸ **Orient Yourself:** Embraced by a loop of the Danube, Straubing's site in the fertile Gäuboden region, the granary of Bavaria, contributed in no small terms to its prosperity.

▣ **Parking:** There's a large, free garage on Am Hagen and another garage on Theresienplatz.

⊘ **Don't Miss:** The Stadtplatz and the Ursulinenkirche.

🕓 **Organizing Your Time:** The sights of Straubing can be seen in half a day.

🖒 **Also See:** *REGENSBURG (41km/26mi west), LANDSHUT (58km/36mi south), PASSAU (80km/50mi east).*

Sights

Stadtplatz★

The elongated town square is divided into the Theresienplatz *(West)*, with a wonderfully-adorned 17C Trinity column, and the Ludwigsplatz *(East)* with the Jakobsbrunnen fountain from 1644. In the centre stands an original 14C tower, the town's emblem.

Jakobskirche

Just off Stadtplatz, this 15C brick hall-church is unusual in this part of Bavaria for its almost total lack of Baroque decoration. The panels of the high altar **reredos**, bought in 1590 from a church in Nuremberg, frame 16C statuary. Note the figure of the Virgin, in the middle, and Mary Magdalene, at the far left.

Ursulinenkirche

This is the last joint project by the Asam brothers. It was built between 1736 and 1741 during the transition from Baroque to Rococo and features a rare blend of architecture and decor.

Agnes Bernauer

Agnes, a beautiful young barber's daughter from Augsburg, was married in secret to Albrecht III, son of Duke Ernst of Bavaria. The Duke took exception to the match, for reasons of State, and had Agnes condemned as a witch. In 1435 she was drowned in the Danube not far from Straubing. The tragic fate of this beautiful country girl captured many a heart, inspiring Friedrich Hebbel to write a political tragedy (1855) and Carl Orff to compose an opera (1947). Every four years there is a festival (Agnes-Bernauer-Festspiele) in her memory (next one in 2007).

Excursion

Kirche St-Peter

1.5km/1mi. Leave town in the direction of the Danube by route 20 (signposted Cham). Turn right before the castle bridge. St Peter's is the second church.

The 12C Romanesque pillar church stands in the middle of a walled graveyard with graves from the 14C to the 19C. In the graveyard, note the Gothic chapel dedicated to Our Lady, the Agnes Bernauer chapel, and the chapel of the dead with a Dance of Death fresco by local painter Felix Hölzl (1763).

STUTTGART★

POPULATION: 591 500

The capital of Baden-Württemberg is a commercial and industrial centre whose name is often associated with automobiles. The name of the city, originally Stutengarten, derives from a seigniorial stud farm which flourished in the 10C. In the 14C the town became the home of the dukes and kings of Württemberg, and prospered during the industrial revolution. ▣ *Königstraße 1 a, 70173 Stuttgart,* ☎ *(0711) 222 82 40.*

▶ **Orient Yourself:** Stuttgart lies in a valley surrounded by vineyards and wooded hills opening onto the Neckar. The finest **view**★ of Stuttgart is from the upper platform of the **Fernsehturm** (television tower, access via the Hohenheimer Straße), which soars 400m/1 312ft on the southern side of town.

ⓟ **Parking:** There is ample parking throughout Stuttgart. Visit http://wap.parkinfo. com for fees and locations.

🅐 **Don't Miss:** Car buffs should make time for the Mercedes-Benz and Porsche museums.

🄺 **Especially for Kids:** Wilhelmina Park and Zoo.

🄲 **Also See:** *TÜBINGEN (45km/28mi south), SCHWÄBISCH ALB (at Kirchheim, 31km/19mi southeast), SCHWÄBISCH HALL (69km/43mi northeast) or MAULBRONN Abbey (47km/29mi west).*

Staatsgalerie Stuttgart

Terrace leading to the entrance of the Staatsgalerie

Address Book

WHERE TO EAT

🍴 **Jägerhaus** – *Obere Waiblinger Straße 110, 70374 Stuttgart-Bad Canstatt* ☎ *(0711) 52 60 90 www.krehl-gastronomie.de* 🕐 *Closed 1 week early Jan, and Tue* ♿ You will receive a warm welcome in this pleasant restaurant in the Canstatt quarter. Rooms are divided into alcoves where you can sample regional dishes. There is also a beer garden.

🍴 **Amici** – *Lautenschlagerstraße 2* ☎ *(0711) 227 02 92 www.amici.de* 🕐 *Mon-Thur 11am-2am, Fri and Sat 11am-4am, Sun 5pm-2am* ♿ *Reservation required* Restaurant, café, bar or lounge – the choice is yours. Spectacular architecture and lighting set this site apart. The decor includes an original race car. Mediterranean dishes prepared in the glass-fronted kitchen and live music on weekends are among the highlights of this trendy place.

🍴 **Weber's Gourmet im Turm** – *Jahnstraße 120, 70597 Stuttgart-Degerloch* ☎ *(0711) 24 89 96 10 www.bongusto.net/webers* 🕐 *Closed 2 weeks in Jan, 3 weeks in Aug, and Sun-Mon* After you get a boarding pass, you can take the elevator up to the restaurant in the television tower *(Fernsehturmrestaurant)*, 144m/472ft up. The creative cuisine and fine wines make the trip worthwhile.

WHERE TO STAY

🛏 **Hotel Geroksruhe** – *Pischekstraße 70* ☎ *(0711) 23 86 90 Fax (0711) 2360023 www.smg.nethotels.com/geroksruhe* 🅿 ⤫ *19 rooms* 🛏 Charming, functional rooms near the city centre make this a convenient place to spend the night. The breakfast room with its terrace is pleasant. Apartments are available for longer stays.

🛏 **Hotel Bergmeister** – *Rotenbergstraße 16* ☎ *(0711) 268 48 50 Fax (0711) 268485169 www.hotelbergmeister.de* 🕐 *Closed 23 Dec-6 Jan* ⤫ *46 rooms* 🛏 Bright, comfortable rooms, many with large balconies. Mahogany or cherrywood furniture and cheerful blue decor.

🛏 **Hotel Abalon** – *Zimmermannstraße 7 (access via no 79 Olgastraße)* ☎ *(0711) 217 10 Fax (0711) 2171217 www.abalon.de* ⤫ *42 rooms* 🛏 A modern building with covered terrace (which doubles as a breakfast room). Rooms are spacious. Near the city centre, but away from the hustle and bustle.

TAKING A BREAK

irma la douce – café & suppenbar – *Neue Brücke 8 (behind the Karstadt dept store in Königstraße)* ☎ *(0711) 2 84 88 21* 🕐 *Open Mon-Sat 11am-1am*. If you like soup, see what's cooking at this little self-service restaurant. In addition to delicious seasonal soups, there are homemade sandwiches and desserts to eat in or take out. Make the most of the large terrace in summer.

Weinhaus Stetter – *Rosenstraße 32 (south of and parallel to Charlottenstraße)* ☎ *(0711) 24 01 63 www.weinhaus-stetter.de* 🕐 *Weinstub: Open Mon-Fri 3-11pm, Sat 11am-3pm.* 🕐 *Wine cellar: Mon-Fri 10am-12.30pm and 2.30pm-10pm, Sat 11am-4pm;* 🕐 *Closed 25 Dec-8 Jan, 2 weeks between late Aug and early Sep* For over 100 years this rustic establishment has been offering its clients an excellent choice of mainly regional wines to accompany typical dishes. Buy a bottle to take home at the wine cellar.

GOING OUT

USEFUL TIPS

The *Bohnenviertel* between Charlotten- and Pfarrstraße offers lots of charming restaurants and bars. The mainly cobbled streets are pedestrian friendly.

Biergarten Karlshöhe – *Humboldtstraße 44 (No signposting; the path through vineyards leaves from the first bend in the street coming from Marienstraße and Mörikestraße; 10min on foot)* ☎ *(0711) 2 84 68 78* 🕐 *Mar-Oct: 11am-11.30pm (in good weather).* This self-service beer garden is not easy to find. But many people make the effort in summer to enjoy city views, particularly stunning at sunset.

Brasserie Flo – *Marktstraße 1* ☎ *(0711) 211 16 61* 🕐 *Closed Sun and public holidays*. This modern bistro is in Karl-spassage in the Breuninger department store. Serving breakfast, lunch, cakes and dinners.

Teehaus – *Im Weißenburgpark (access via Hohenheimer Straße and Bopser-waldstraße)* ☎ *(0711) 2 36 73 60 www. teehaus-stuttgart.de* 🕐 *May-Oct: 11am-11pm (opening hours weather dependent); open weekends from Mar* Set in a public park, this Art Deco pavilion with its terrace is an idyllic place to enjoy a coffee, cake, ice cream or cold drink.

CULTURE

USEFUL TIPS

Highlightbroschüre (annual) and *Highlightflyer* (bi-annual) are available from Stuttgart Marketing's offices and provide calendars of events in the city. The monthly magazines *Lift* and *Prinz* highlight current happenings and are on sale in bookshops and newspaper kiosks.

SHOPPING

USEFUL TIPS

Stuttgart's shopping centre (department stores and specialised shops) is based on Königstraße and neighbouring streets. The city's main department store is *Breuninger (Marktplatz)*. South of the *Altes Schloss* on the other side of Dorotheenstraße is the *Markthalle*, an Art-Deco covered market. Crafts shops and antique dealers are found in the *Bohnenviertel* (between Charlotten- and Pfarrstraße).

A Bit of History

Two Motor Car Pioneers – An engineer deom in Bad Cannstatt, **Gottfried Daimler** (1834-1900) pioneered the internal combustion engine to the powering of vehicles. **Carl Benz** (1844-1929) envisaged an entire motor vehicle, which he elaborated in every detail at Mannheim. Soon he was able to start manufacturing in series; in 1899 he sold his 2 000th vehicle and thus became the world's leading automobile manufacturer. In 1901, Daimler's company marketed the **Mercedes**, a name that would make a fortune. Today, above the roofs of the city, the night sky over Stuttgart blazes with the illuminated three-point-star within a circle, the firm's world-famous trademark.

Urban Landscape – The former appearance of the city is only apparent today on Schillerplatz, flanked by the Stiftskirche (Collegiate Church) and the Altes Schloss (Old Castle). The statue of Schiller in the centre of the square is the work of the Danish sculptor Thorwaldsen (1839). The Baroque Neues Schloss (New Palace) is now the home of regional ministerial departments.

Sights

Staatsgalerie★★ (Art Gallery)

🚻🕐 *Open daily except Mon, 10am-6pm; Thu 10am-9pm, 1st Sat of the month 10am-midnight.* 🕐 *Closed Good Friday, 24 and 25 Dec.* 👁 *€4.50, free admission on Wed.* ☎ *(0711) 47 04 00; www.staatsgalerie.de*

The 19C building commissioned under King Wilhelm I of Württemberg houses European painting from medieval times to Impressionism. Note the 14C-16C **Old German Masters Section★★** with an emphasis on Swabian painting. The **Herrenberg Altar** by Jerg Ratgeb (1519) portrays the Last Supper, the Crucifixion and the Resurrection.

Venetians and Florentines from the 14C dominate the Italian section. Among the Dutch Old Masters are Hans Memling, Rembrandt, Jacob van Ruisdael and Rubens.

An annexe houses the department of 20C Art. Among the modern classics on display are works by the Fauvists and French Cubists (Matisse, Braque, Juan Gris), the

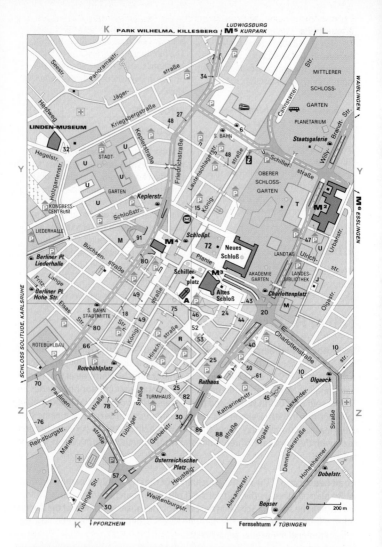

STUTTGART

Arnulf-Klett-Pl.	LY 6	Holzstr.	LZ 40	Rotebühlpl.	KZ 66
Augustenstr.	KZ 7	Karlspl.	LY 43	Rotebühlstr.	KZ 70
Blumenstr.	LZ 10	Karlstr.	LZ 44	Schloßpl.	LY 72
Bolzstr.	LY 15	Katharinenpl.	LZ 45	Schulstr.	KZ 75
Calwer Str.	KYZ 18	Kirchstr.	LZ 46	Silberburgstr.	KZ 76
Charlottenpl.	LZ 20	Königstr.	KLYZ	Sophienstr.	KZ 78
Dorotheenstr.	LZ 24	Konrad-Adenauer-Str.	LY 47	Theodor-Heuss-Str.	KYZ 80
Eberhardstr.	KLZ 25	Kronenstr.	KLY 48	Torstr.	KZ 82
Friedrichspl.	KY 27	Kronprinzstr.	KYZ 49	Wilhelmspl.	LZ 86
Hauptstätter Str.	KZ 30	Leonhardspl.	LZ 50	Wilhelmstr.	LZ 88
Hegelpl.	KY 32	Marktpl.	KLZ 52	Willi-Bleicher-Str.	KY 91
Heilbronner Str.	LY 34	Marktstr.	LZ 53		
		Österreichischer Pl.	KZ 57		
		Pfarrstr.	LZ 61		

Galerie der Stadt Stuttgart	LY M⁴	Staatsgalerie	LY M²	Württembergisches	
Mercedes-Benz Museum	LY M⁶	Stiftskirche	KY A	Landesmuseum	LY M³
Museum am Löwentor	LY M⁵				

Expressionists (Kokoschka), the artists of Neue Sachlichkeit (Dix, Grosz) and artists of the Bauhaus. The section on contemporary art covers the half century since the Second World War, starting with Dubuffet and Giacometti and ending with the latest works of Baselitz and Kiefer, including American Pop Art (Warhol, Segal) and the "installations" of Beuys.

Linden-Museum★★

♿🕐 Open daily except Mon, 10am-5pm; Wed 10am-8pm. 🕐 Closed Mon and Shrove Tuesday, Good Friday, 1st May, 24, 25 and 31 Dec. ∞ €3, free admission on Wed from 5pm. ☎ (0711) 202 23; www.lindenmuseum.de

Exhibits in this ethnographic museum are presented under six main headings. On the ground floor: America (Native Americans and Ancient Peruvian cultures) and the Pacific (Melanesia, Papua New Guinea and Australia). On the first floor: Africa and the Middle East; and on the second floor: the Far East and South Asia (Japan, China, India, Nepal and Tibet and Indonesia).

Altes Schloss (Old Castle)

Four wings flanked by round towers comprise this building, most of which dates from the 16C. The **Renaissance Courtyard**★ *(with access to the Schloßkirche)* is surrounded by three floors of arcaded galleries.

Württembergisches Landesmuseum★

Inside the Altes Schloss. 🕐 Open daily except Mon, 10am-5pm. 🕐 Closed 1st Jan, Good Friday, 24, 25 and 31 Dec. ∞ €3. ☎ (0711) 27 94 98; www.landesmuseum-stuttgart.de

The first floor displays collections from the Bronze and Iron Ages, with important finds from the excavation of the **royal tomb**★, a mid-6C BC Celtic burial site near Ludwigsburg.

On the second floor are collections of Ancient Roman artefacts, along with a section on South German **religious statuary**★★. Funerary objects (weapons, jewels and household items) are displayed in the **Franks and the Alemanni section**, revealing the civilisation that existed between the 3C and 8C.

Additional museum exhibits include a coin gallery, collections of furniture, clocks, scientific instruments, weapons, and the crown jewels of the kings of Württemberg. The collection of musical instruments is on display in the Fruchtkasten on Schillerplatz, not far from the Altes Schloss.

Stiftskirche

The collegiate church with its combination of the Romanesque (lowest floor of the south tower, 12C), Early Gothic (chancel, 14C) and Late Gothic (the nave, 15C), suffered heavy damage in 1944. The baptistery contains a rare protective cloak of Christ (Late Gothic, c 1500). A large **funerary monument**★, a memorial to the dukes of Württemberg, stands in the chancel. Eleven armoured figurines in historically accurate costume representing ancestors of the Duke are standing in front of a decor of Renaissance arcades.

Galerie der Stadt Stuttgart (City Gallery)

🕐 Open daily except Mon, 10am-6pm, Wed, Fri 10am-9pm. 🕐 Closed Good Friday, 24, 25, 31 Dec and 1 Jan. ☎ (0711) 216 21 88; www.galerie-der-stadt-stuttgart.de

The gallery owns some important works by famous artists from the Classical Modern and contemporary periods. Neue Sachlichkeit artist **Otto Dix**★ is strongly represented. Famous for the ferocity of his social critique and anti-war sentiment, the artist's Big City *(Großstadt)* triptych and anti-war *Grabenkrieg* painting well characterize his work.

Excursions

Mercedes-Benz Museum★
Leave by Schillerstraße. At Mercedesstraße 136, in a block of the company's main factory, located at Stuttgart-Untertürkheim. ⟁⟐ *Open daily except Mon, 9am-5pm.* ⟐ *Closed public holidays.* ⟐ *Free admission.* ☎ *(0711) 172 25 78.*

This museum boasts the world's largest collection of vehicles of a single marque. Beginning with the oldest Benz and Daimler vehicles up to today's models, the display retraces the company's highlights. The legendary early racing cars are a highlight, including the Silver Arrows of the 1930s and 1950s.

Porsche Museum★
Leave on Heilbronner Straße, toward the motorway. Before the motorway, take the exit signposted Zuffenhausen-Industriegebiet, and turn right into Porschestraße. The museum is at no 42. ⟁⟐ *9am-4pm, Sat-Sun 9am-5pm.* ⟐ *Closed 24 Dec-1st Jan* ☎ *(0711) 911 256 85.*

In 1934 Daimler-Benz engineer **Ferdinand Porsche** (1875-1951) successfully designed the famous "Beetle" for *Volkswagen*. From 1948 Porsche devoted himself to a sports model bearing his own name, developed from the original VW chassis and engine and subsequently manufactured at Zuffenhausen. 30 different Porsches are on show at the Porsche Musuem, along with a display of high-performance engines.

Wilhelma Park and Zoo★
Kids *4km/2.5mi northeast of the centre. Leave by Heilbronner Straße.* ⟁⟐ *May-Aug: 8.15am-6pm; Apr and Sep: 8.15am-5.30pm; Mar and Oct: 8.15am-5pm; Nov-Feb: 8.15am-4pm.* ⟐ *€10.80.* ☎ *(0711) 540 20; www.wilhelma.de.*

This botanical and zoological garden (one of Europe's finest), laid out in the 19C, houses tropical plants including orchids and cacti. The zoo is home to more than 8 000 animals. Also worth seeing are the **aquarium, terrarium** and **Amazonian house**.

Höhenpark Killesberg
4km/3mi north of the centre. Leave by Heilbronner Straße. West of the Rosenstein, this park is a continuation of the green belt encircling the inner city. The Höhenpark integrates perfectly with the undulating terrain, including terraced cascades, fountains and brilliant flower beds, as well as a **miniature train** for touring the whole park. A look-out tower *(Aussichtsturm)* takes in sweeping views of the entire city.

Schloss Solitude★
9km/5.5mi southwest. Leave by Rotebühlstraße. ⟐ *Apr-Oct: open daily except Mon, 9am-12pm, 1.30-5pm; Nov-Mar: open daily except Mon, 10am-12pm, 1.30-4pm.* ⟐ *€3.* ☎ *(0711) 69 66 99; www.schloesser-und-gaerten.de.*

The 18C former summer residence of the Württemberg court is built around an oval pavilion with a cupola, the whole being majestically raised on a base of open arcades. Around this, the lower outbuildings lie in an immense arc. The palace interior is decorated largely in the neo-Classical tradition; some apartments are French Rococo.

Esslingen am Neckar
13km/8mi southeast. The busy road linking northern Italy to Flanders passed through this 1 220-year-old Swabian town. The finest ornament to the 19C **Marktplatz★** is the Kielmeyer house. 13C and 14C **stained glass★** is a key sight within the Gothic **Stadtkirche**. The 15C and 16C **Altes Rathaus★** (old town hall) combines the charm of half-timbering with the gracefulness of Renaissance façades. And the Gothic **Frauenkirche**, which stands on a hillside *(reached from the Marktplatz via the Untere Beutau rise)*, has a beautiful ornate **church tower★**.

Schloss Ludwigsburg★

15km/9.5mi north. Built by Duke Eberhard Ludwig von Württemberg after Versailles , this 18C monumental quadrilateral has 452 rooms, 75 of them open to the public.

Tour of the Apartments

Inside, the rooms most worth visiting are the apartments of the first king of Württemberg, furnished in the Empire style. Through the Ancestors' Gallery *(Ahnengalerie)* and the Catholic church *(Schloßkirche)*, decorated with lavish Italian stucco, visitors arrive at the Fürstenbau state apartments. *Guided tour (1hr 15min).* Mid Mar to mid Nov, 10am-5pm; from Nov to mid Mar, 10am-12pm, 1-4pm. €7. (071 41) 18 64 10; www.schloss-ludwigsburg.de.

Blühendes Barock★ (Park)

Green Baroque arbours and flowered terraces have been reconstituted in the southern part of the park, in front of the newest part of the palace. The terrain to the north and east has been landscaped in the English manner. In the **Märchengarten**★★ (Fairytale Garden), German fairy tales and legends are illustrated. *From mid Mar to beginning of Nov: 7.30am-8.30pm.* €6.50. (071 41) 97 56 50; www.blueba.de.

Tiefenbronn★

38km/24mi west. This village is home to the **Pfarrkirche St Maria Magdalena**, boasting an unusually rich interior. Besides 13C and 14C murals and stained glass and numerous tombs are some particularly fine Late Gothic altarpieces. The high altar by Ulm master Hans Schüchlin (1469) depicts scenes from the life of the Virgin Mary and the Passion of Christ. On the south aisle is a magnificent **altarpiece of St Mary Magdalene**★★ (1432) by **Lucas Moser**.

Schwäbisch Gmünd

54km/34mi east. Traditionally Schwäbisch Gmünd is a centre for the working of precious metals; there are 70 gold- and silver-working firms here. The Baroque **Marktplatz** (marketplace) is surrounded by stately houses and a fountain dedicated to the Virgin Mary. The beautiful 14C **Heiligkreuzmünster**★ has a ridge turret in place of towers. The interior chapels are rich in statuary, including a Holy Sepulchre (ca 1350) and the Tree of Jesse (1520) in the Batpismal Chapel, with 40 sculpted figurines.

Hohenstaufen★

14km/9mi southwest, plus 30min on foot there and back. Park in the village square. From the two churches at the top of the town, a shady footpath leads to the summit at 684m/2 244ft. Nothing remains of the Staufer castle, but the climb is worthwhile for the **panorama**★ of the Kaiserberge and, on the horizon, the Swabian Jura.

INSEL SYLT★★

Despite its modest area (100km²/39sq mi), the landscape of this long, narrow island is quite varied: sandy beaches and dunes, marshes and mudflats, fields and meadows, open heathland and primeval burial mounds. The island's spas, North Sea bathing and health resorts make it popular with holidaymakers.

▶ **Orient Yourself:** Sylt extends north to for 40km/25mi; at its narrowest it is less than 457m/500yd across. The island is the largest of the Northern Frisian Islands and the most northerly part of Germany. Since 1927, it has been connected to the mainland via rail across the Hindenburgdamm causeway. You can reach Sylt via train-car ferry from Niebüll (Westerland, 35min: car with passagers €77 round-trip). ☎ (046 61) 93 45 67). To travel by ferry, leave from Havneby (on the Danish island of Römö – accessible by road): 5 to 7 ferries a day, up to 12 daily in July and Aug. Journey time 50min. €53 round-trip per vehicle including passengers, €6.20 round-trip for pedestrians. Information: ☎ (0180) 310 30 30.

🏛 **Don't Miss:** The megalithic graves of Denghoog near Keitum.

🕐 **Organizing Your Time:** Allow a full day to enjoy this Frisian island.

Kids Especially for Kids: Swimming and outdoor recreation on the North Sea.

🕼 **Also See:** *NORDFRIESISCHE INSELN, Insel HELGOLAND (via ferry from Hörnum).*

Sights

Westerland★

Spa This is the largest resort on the island and the most popular North Sea spa in Germany. The cure establishment boasts a boat-shaped leisure pool, the *Sylter*

Address Book

WHERE TO EAT

◯◯🍽 **Webchristel** – *Süderstraße 11, 5980 Sylt-Westerland* ☎ *(04651) 229 00* 🕐 *Closed 20 Nov-24 Dec and Wed* 🍴 Frisian house with rustic decor. This restaurant serves refined regional dishes.

◯◯🍽 **Landhaus Nösse** – *Nösistig 13, 25980 Sylt-Ost-Morsum* ☎ *(04651) 972 20 info@landhaus-noesse.de* 🕐 *Closed Mon* Reed-thatched, gourmet restaurant and bistro in a wonderfully isolated cliff-top location. Most of the neat guestrooms have a view over the Watt.

WHERE TO STAY

◯◯🍽🛏 **Parkhotel am Südwäldchen** – *Fischerweg 45, 25980 Sylt-Westerland* ☎ *(04651) 83 63 00 Fax (04651) 8363063 www.parkhotel-sylt.de* 🅿 🏊 *24 rooms* ⬡ Set in a quiet residential area, this manicured hotel has an indoor pool and sauna.

◯◯🍽🛏 **Hotel Seiler Hof** – *Gurtstig 7, 25980 Sylt-Ost-Keitum* ☎ *(04651) 933 40* *Fax (04651) 933444 www.seilerhofsylt. de* 🍴 🅿 *11 rooms* ⬡ This former captain's house dates from 1761 and has a beautiful garden and comfortable guestrooms.

TAKING A BREAK

Kupferkanne – *Stapelhooger Wai, 25999 Sylt-Kampen* ☎ *(04651) 41010 www.kupferkanne-sylt.de* 🕐 *Open 10am-6pm.* This slightly surreal everyday café in a former bunker serves excellent coffee and cakes off a small menu. Large garden with view of the mud-flats.

GOING OUT

Salon 1900 – *Süderstraße 40, 25980 Sylt-Ost-Keitum* ☎ *(04651) 93 60 00 www.salon1900.de* 🕐 *Closed mid-Jan to mid-Feb.* A café, restaurant, bar and disco are all under one thatched roof. *Jugendstil* decor and a pleasant garden are a big draw.

Welle, and a 7km/4mi-long sandy beach. The promenade is the place to see and be seen, as it is centred around a large music hall, and there is plenty of action in the bars, bistros and nightclubs. As the island's metropolis, Westerland has everything visitors desire, from window-shopping *(Strandstraße and Friedrichstraße)* and galleries to a casino (in the old *Jugendstil* spa). There are also various sports facilities and cultural events.

Keitum

This idyllic village and its craftshops is the other face of the island. Keitum's traditional thatched Frisian houses, hidden among trees and lilacs, the embankments of dog roses, and *Grünes Kliff* overlooking endless miles of water and mudflats earn it the nickname "the green heart."

South of **Kampen**, a resort favoured by VIPs and artists, the **Rotes Kliff** towers above the sea. In Wenningstedt-Braderup, the **Denghoog**★ is a 4 000-year-old megalithic grave open to the public. **Morsum-Kliff**, featuring 10 million years of geological history, is an interesting geological feature. North of Sylt, near the port of **List**, lie the **Wanderdüne**, 1 000m/3 280ft-long and 30m/10ft-high dunes of quartz sand.

THÜRINGER WALD★★

THURINGIA FOREST

The Thuringia Forest is a wooded massif orientated northwest-southeast with an average height of 1 000m/3 300ft. This is one of the most beautiful natural regions in Germany. The massif is littered with charming villages whose inhabitants retain traditional skills and craftsmanship.

▸ **Orient Yourself:** Around 100km/63mi in length, the Thuringia Forest separates the valleys of Swiss-Franconia from Thuringia.

⊘ **Don't Miss:** Literature lovers should not miss Ilmenau, closely affiliated with Wolfgang von Goethe.

🕐 **Organizing Your Time:** Allow one day for the suggested driving tour.

Kids **Especially for Kids:** Marienglashöhle cavern.

👶 **Also See:** *ERFURT (61km/38mi), WEIMAR (77km/48mi), Oberes SAALETAL.*

Driving Tour

Thüringer Hochstraße: Eisenach to Ilmenau
110km/68mi

This fascinating forest road mainly follows the **Rennsteig**, a hiking path 160km/100mi long which keeps to the highest parts of the forest and includes such major summits as the Großer Inselsberg and the Großer Beerberg.

Eisenach★ 👶 *see EISENACH*

▸ *Leave Eisenach in the direction of Gotha.*

Großer Inselsberg
1hr on foot round-trip. The **views**★★ from the summit take in much of the forest.

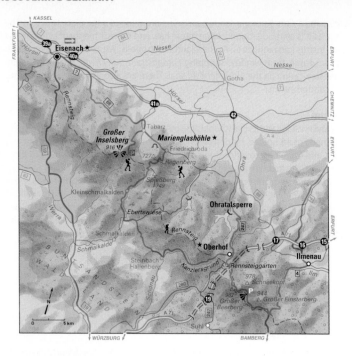

Marienglashöhle★

Kids 🚶 Guided visit (45min). 🕐 Open Apr to Oct, 9am-5pm; Nov to Mar, 9am-4pm. 🎫 €4. ☎ (036 23) 332 00.

This natural **cavern** produces crystalline gypsum, a mineral used in the decoration of church altars. (Hence its name: *Marienglas* means Glass of Mary).

▶ *The road cuts across the Rennsteig and twists between the Regenberg (727m/2 385ft) and the Spießberg (749m/2 457ft). Consider a hike through the Ebertswiese, a marsh- and meadowland. Steinbach is overlooked by the Hallenburg ruins. The road continues toward Oberhof via the grasslands of the Kanzlergrund.*

Oberhof★

At 800m/2 625ft altitude, this town is the most important leisure and winter sports centre in the Thuringia Forest, the training ground for international toboggan and bobsledding. In the **Rennsteiggarten** botanical park more than 4 000 plant species are grown.

Ohratalsperre

▶ *Follow the B 247 to the large car park.*

The reservoir dammed by this **barrage**, the surface of which extends over 88ha/218 acres, supplies water to Weimar, Jena, Gotha and the Thuringian capital, Erfurt.

▶ *Leave Oberhof in the direction of Schmücke. The country road winds again sinuously between the Großer Beerberg and the Schneekopf. From the hotel car park at Schmücke is a viewpoint overlooking the valley and the Finsterberg.*

Städtisches Museum Simeonstift

🔒 *Closed for renovation until 2007.* ☎ *(0651) 718 14 58. www.museum-trier.de.*
This municipal museum is installed in a Romanesque convent, the Simeonstift, built beside the Porta Nigra in the 11C. The history of Trier is illustrated with models, paintings, engravings, maps and sculptures. The museum also encompasses a double storey Romanesque **cloister** surrounding Germany's oldest cloister garth.

Dreikönigenhaus★ (House of the Three Kings)

This Early Gothic town house (c 1230), with arched windows, recalls the Italianate towers of the patricians of Regensburg.

Hauptmarkt★

One of the finest old squares in Germany. In the middle is the **Market Cross**★ (Marktkreuz), erected in 958. The 16C **fountain** is surrounded by figures representing the cardinal virtues. Standing by the Cross, 15 centuries of history are represented in the square's monuments: To the north is the Porta Nigra; to the east the Romanesque cathedral; to the south the Gothic **Gangolfkirche**, its 16C tower once used as a look-out post. Half-timbered houses stand to the west. The **Steipe**,

TRIER		Dietrichstr.	CX	10	Liebfrauenstr.	DXY	24
		Domfreihof	DX	12	Lindenstr.	CX	25
Ausoniusstr.	CX 3	Fahrstr.	CY	15	Nagelstr.	CY	
Bismarckstr.	DX 4	Fleischstr.	CXY		Neustr.	CY	
Brotstr.	CDY	Grabenstr.	DX	16	Simeonstr.	DX	
Bruchhausenstr.	CX 6	Hauptmarkt	DX		Stresemannstr.	CY	34
Brückenstr.	CY 7	Kornmarkt	CY		Walramsneustr.	CX	35
Deutschherrenstr.	CX 9						

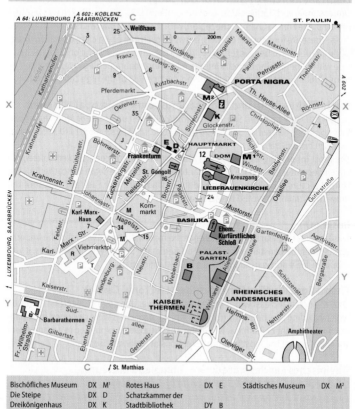

Bischöfliches Museum	DX	M¹	Rotes Haus	DX	E	Städtisches Museum	DX	M²
Die Steipe	DX	D	Schatzkammer der					
Dreikönigenhaus	DX	K	Stadtbibliothek	DY	B			

a 15C municipal building, is elegantly built over an open gallery. Beside it, the 17C **Rotes Haus** (Red House), bears the proud inscription: "There was life in Trier for 1 300 years before Rome even existed."

Frankenturm
This heavily built Romanesque tower (ca 1100) is named after one of its early owners, Franco of Senheim (14C).

Dom★ (Cathedral)
Trier Cathedral with its six towers looks more like a fortress than a church. A rounded apse projects from a massive, austere façade whichis a fine example of Early Romanesque architecture. From the north side is visible a flattened gable and rectangular plan, the 4C Roman heart of the building. West of this central block is the 11C Romanesque section; east of it the 12C polygonal chancel. A Baroque axial chapel crowned by a dome was added in the 18C.

Inside, note near the main door the fallen Roman column *(Domstein)* which supported part of the former church. Inside, the decoration is principally Baroque. A splendid **tympanum**★ in the south aisle depicts Christ between the Virgin Mary and St Peter.

Silver and gold plate, valuable ivories, and magnificently illuminated Gospels are on view in the **Treasury**★ *(Domschatz,* 🕒 *Apr-Oct: 10am-5pm, Sun 2-5pm; Nov-Mar: 11am-4pm, Sun 2-4pm.* 🕒 *Closed 1st Jan, Easter Sun, 25 Dec.* ✆ *€1.50.* ☎ *(0651) 979 07 90; www.dominformation.de)*

Liebfrauenkirche★ (Church of Our Lady)
One of the earliest Gothic sanctuaries in Germany (1235-60), this church was inspired by one in the French Champagne region, with the ground plan in the form of a Greek cross. There are four apsidal chapels, between each pair of which two smaller, three-sided chapels have been interposed, giving the whole church the original form of a rose with 12 petals. The church's interior has an incomparable elegance, enhanced by rings of foliage around each column and the richness of the high central vaulting.

Bischöfliches Dom- und Diözesanmuseum★ (Episcopal Museum)
♿🕒 *Apr-Oct: 9am-5pm, Sun 1-5pm; Nov-Mar: open daily except Mon, 9am-5pm, Sun 1-5pm.* 🕒 *Closed 1st Jan, 24-26 and 31 Dec.* ✆ *€2.* ☎ *(0651) 710 52 55; www. museum.bistum-trier.de*

The most interesting exhibits in this museum are the frescoes *(Deckenmalerei,* 4C) which decorated the Palace of Constantine, discovered beneath the cathedral. The central picture is believed to represent Constantine's wife Fausta. The rest of the museum is mainly devoted to sacred art.

Basilika★
This large rectangular building was once the main hall *(Aula Palatina)* of the Imperial palace, built by Constantine ca 310. Modified many times over the centuries, it was rebuilt in 1954 and is used today as a Protestant church.

Ehemaliges Kurfürstliches Schloss (Electorial Castle)
Only the north and east wings remain of the former Renaissance electoral castle, on which building was begun in 1615. The 18C Rococo wings were designed by Johannes Seitz, student of Balthasar Neumann. His virtuosity is expressed in a magnificent staircase, one of the most beautiful creations of its kind in Germany.

Rheinisches Landesmuseum★★ (Rhineland Museum)
🕒 *Open daily except Mon, 9.30am-5pm (May-Oct: open daily), Sat-Sun 10.30am-5pm.* 🕒 *Closed 1st Jan, carnival, 24-26 Dec.* ✆ *€2.50.* ☎ *(0651) 977 40; www.landesmuseum-trier.de*

Of particular interest in this museum is the **Paleolithic** section, featuring Stone Age implements and ceramics; objects from the Bronze Age; and jewels set in gold from Iron Age sepulchres. Another highlight is the **Roman** section, featuring marvellous mosaics. bronzes and bas-reliefs. Among the sculpture discovered at Neumagen is the representation of a ship sailing down the Moselle loaded with wine. Included in this **Neumagen ship carving** is the figure of "the jolly sailor" – a mariner with a broad grin who has passed into the folklore of the Moselle.

Kaiserthermen★★ (Imperial Roman Baths)

Same opening times as the Porta Nigra. ⊜ *€2.10.* ☎ *(0651) 460 89 65.*
Among the largest in the Roman Empire, these baths date from the time of Constantine but appear never to have been used. The construction of the rounded walls is typically Roman.

Schatzkammer der Stadtbibliothek★★ (Municipal Library Treasury)

🕐 *Open only during exhibitions.* ☎ *(0651) 718 44 26.*
Fascinating exhibits include rare illuminated manuscripts (medieval Bibles, homilies, fables etc); examples of the earliest illustrated books (Gospels, teaching manuals, legal volumes); and many treaties, letters of credit and safe conduct passes.

Karl-Marx-Haus

Brückenstraße 10. 🕐 *Open Apr-Oct: 10am-6pm, Mon 1-6pm; Nov-Mar: 10am-1pm, 2-5pm, Mon 2-5pm.* 🕐 *Closed 1st Jan, 24-26 and 31 Dec.* ⊜ *€3.* ☎ *(0651) 97 06 80; www.museum-karl-marx-haus.de*
The birthplace of the socialist theoretician Karl Marx has been turned into a museum, displaying letters, manuscripts and a first edition of the *Communist Manifesto*.

Sights

Basilika St Paulin★

Access via Thebäerstraße. Tall windows illuminate the single nave of this 18C church, the interior of which was designed by Balthasar Neumann. The martyrdom of St Paul, citizens of Trier, and of the Theban Legion (AD 286) are illustrated in ceiling paintings by Christoph Thomas Scheffler of Augsburg. The high altar was based on Neumann's designs with woodcarving by Trier artist Ferdinand Tietz.

Barbarathermen

🕐 *Same opening times as the Porta Nigra* 🕐 *Closed Mon.* ☎ *(0651) 442 62.*
Roman baths from the 2C, used for several centuries, are now in ruins.

Amphitheater (Roman Amphitheatre)

🕐 *Same opening times as the Porta Nigra.* ⊜ *€2.10.* ☎ *(0651) 730 10.*
Once seating 20 000 spectators, this hillside arena was used as a quarry in the Middle Ages, and became so damaged by the 18C that vines were grown on the terraces. The cellars below ground housed theatrical equipment and machinery. The amphitheatre now houses the Antikenfestspiele (Ancient Plays Festival) every summer.

TÜBINGEN★★

POPULATION: 83 000.

Tübingen was lucky enough to escape undamaged during the Second World War. It therefore gives an unbroken picture of its evolution from the Middle Ages to the 19C. The labyrinth of narrow sloping streets lined with ancient half-timbered houses and its animated student life create a delightful atmosphere. ⓘ *An der Eberhardsbrücke, 72072 Tübingen, ☎ (070 71) 913 60.*

▶ **Orient Yourself:** Tübingen is near Stuttgart, on the banks of the Neckar and Ammer, between the slopes of Schloßberg and Österberg.

🅿 **Parking:** Garages are located throughout Tübingen. Visit http://wap.parkinfo. com for fees and locations.

⊘ **Don't Miss:** A walking tour of the old town.

🕐 **Organizing Your Time:** Allow a full day to absorb the history of Tübingen.

⚲ **Also See:** *STUTTGART (40km/25mi north), SCHWÄBISCHE ALB (Liechtenstein is 14km/9mi away), SCHWARZWALD (60km/38mi west).*

A Bit of History

The University – They say that, rather than having a university, Tübingen is a university, so closely linked are the town and its Alma Mater. It all began in 1477, when Count Eberhard founded a university in a town of only 3 000. Tübingen University now has 16 faculties and 23 000 students registered in 74 different subjects. The university and the Protestant seminary of 1536 have educated such important figures as the poets Hölderlin, Mörike and Uhland; the philosophers Hegel and Schelling; the astronomer Kepler and theologian Melanchthon; and, in 1869, 25-year-old Friedrich Miescher, discoverer of deoxyribonucleic acid, or DNA.

Walking Tour

The Old Town★★

Eberhardsbrücke

This bridge gives a scenic **view**★ over the Neckar. Hölderlin Tower rises above weeping willows. The **Platanenallee** leads to the left, a beautiful walkway along the Neckar. From here visitors may be fortunate enough to see the gondolas of Tübingen, which make trips from Hölderlin Tower past the riverfront.

Friedrich Hölderlin in Tübingen

Friedrich Hölderlin was born at Lauffen am Neckar in 1770. He studied theology at Tübingen's Protestant seminary in preparation for the ministry where he befriended philosophers Hegel and Schelling. Poetry continued to interest him in Tübingen, a craft he began while studying in Maulbronn, finally rebelling against a career in the church, and he worked as a tutor in Frankfurt, Switzerland and Bordeaux. The first sign of mental illness (thought to be schizophrenia) manifested itself in 1802. In 1806, he returned to Tübingen where he was promised recovery under the care of medical professor Autenrieth at the residential home. When treatment failed, Hölderlin resided with the Zimmers, a family of carpenters, at no 6 Bursagasse where he resided the remainder of his life in their tower room.

Hölderlinturm

🕐 *Open Tue-Sun, 10am-12 noon, 3-5pm, Sat-Sun, 2-5pm.* 📷 *€1.50.* ☎ *(070 71) 220 40.*

Once part of the fortifications, this tower was the residence of Friedrich Hölderlin from 1807 until he died in 1843. Now a museum, it displays many souvenirs of the poet.

Schloss Hohentübingen

The present Renaissance building was constructed on the foundations of an 11C fortress built by the archdukes of Tübingen. It houses several university institutes, including a **museum**★. The pre- and early history department displays numerous exhibits. A favorite is the tiny ivory **"Vogelherdpferdchen"**★, a horse figurine named for the cave near Ulm where it was discovered in 1931. It is one of the oldest works of art from the New Paleolithic Age. There are also outstanding exhibits from Classical Antiquity, Ancient Egypt and the Ancient Orient. Note in particular the **religious chamber**★ from an

Castle Residents

Schloss Hohentübingen houses the largest bat colony in southern Germany. Disturbed by roof renovations in 1995, the bats moved to the castle cellars, making it impossible for the public to view the giant 16C vat, with a capacity of 850hl/18 700gal.

TÜBINGEN						
Am Markt	Y	Hirschgasse	Y 21	Münzgasse	Y 39
Ammergasse	Y 5	Holzmarkt	Y 27	Neckargasse	Y 42
Derendinger Str.	Z 8	Karlstr.	Z	Pfleghofstr.	Y 48
Friedrichstr.	Z 12	Kirchgasse	Y 30	Poststr.	Z 54
Froschgasse	Y 15	Kronenstr.	Y 33	Schmiedtorstr.	Y 60
		Lange Gasse	Y	Wilhelmstr.	Y
		Mühlstr.	Y		

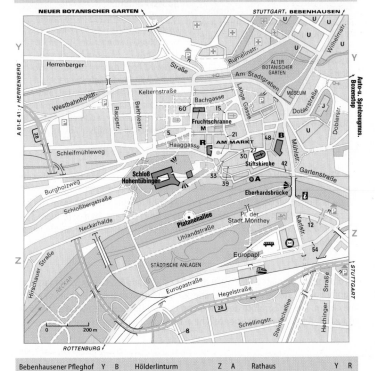

Bebenhausener Pfleghof	Y B	Hölderlinturm	Z A	Rathaus	Y R

Address Book

WHERE TO EAT

🍴 **Schwärzlocher Hof** – *Schwärzloch 1 (2.5km/1.5mi west of town, via Schwärzlocher Str. between Schleifmühleweg and Burgholzweg* ☎ *(07071) 4 33 62 www.schwaerzlocher-hof.de* 🕐 *Wed-Sun 11am-10pm* 🕐 *Closed 25 Dec to mid-Feb* The chancel of a 12C church has been incorporated into this farm inn. There is a beautiful view of the surrounding area from the terrace, shaded by lime trees. Sample the *Most* (dry cider) with traditional dishes.

🍴 **Weinstube Forelle** – *Kronenstraße 8* ☎ *(07071) 240 94 www.weinstube-forelle.de* This restaurant is popular with students and tourists in the evenings. Friendly staff serves typical Swabian dishes.

WHERE TO STAY

🛏 **Hotel Am Bad** – *Am Freibad 2* ☎ *(07071) 797 40 Fax (07071) 75336 www.hotel-am-bad.de* 🕐 *Closed 18 Dec-6 Jan* 🅿 ✕ *35 rooms* 🛏 This hotel is near Tübingen's open-air swimming pool. Some of the guestrooms have dark-wood furniture, others have a more natural look. Family rooms are available.

🛏 **Hotel Metropol** – *Reutlinger Straße 7* ☎ *(07071) 910 10 Fax (07071) 910125* 🅿 ✕ ♿ *12 rooms* 🛏 **Restaurant** 🛏 This little hotel is on the edge of town and dominates the Tübingen skyline. Guestrooms are clean and modern and the old town is easily accessible on foot.

TAKING A BREAK

Die Kelter – *Schmiedtorstr. 17* ☎ *(07071) 25 46 90 www.diekelter. de* 🕐 *Café: Mon-Fri 9.30am-11pm, Sat 9.30am-4pm, Bar: Mon-Wed until 1am, Thu-Sat until 2am, Sun, 5pm-1am* 🕐 *Closed early Jan* This half-timbered building joins a café-restaurant, bar, delicatessen and wine shop (tastings available) under the one roof.

GOING OUT

Schöne Aussichten – *Wilhelmstr. 16* ☎ *(07071) 2 28 84 www.schoene-aussichten-tuebingen.de* 🕐 *Mon-Thu, 10am-midnight, Fri and Sat, 10am-1am, Sun and bank holidays, 2pm-midnight.* This relaxed café has a selection of sweet and savoury nibbles and breakfasts (between 10am and 6pm, set menus available).

SPORT AND LEISURE

Bootsvermietung H. Märkle – *Eberhardsbrücke (behind the tourist office)* ☎ *(07071) 3 15 29 www.bootsvermietung-tuebingen.de* 🕐 *Apr-Sep: 11am-8pm* 🕐 *Closed in bad weather* – Rowing boat from 💶 €6.90, pedalo from €9.20, Stocherkahn from €45.60. Row around Neckar island (1hr) and enjoy beautiful views of the old town. A trip in *Stocherkahn*, a piloted gondola, is also fun; book 2-3 days in advance.

Old Kingdom tomb (3rd millennium BC), completely covered in bas-relief sculptures.

There is a good view of the Neckar and the roofs of the old town from the castle terrace. 🕐 *Open May-Sep, Wed-Sun, 10am-6pm; Oct-Apr, Wed-Sun, 10am-5pm.* 🕐 *Closed 24, 25 and 31 Dec.* 💶 *€4.* ☎ *(070 71) 297 73 84; www.uni-tuebingen.de/ museum-schloss*

Marktplatz★

An old square, animated on market days *(Mon, Wed and Fri)*, features a Renaissance fountain and a statue of Neptune. The surrounding half-timbered houses add to the charm. The 19C graffito decoration on the 15C **Rathaus** depicts the allegories of Justice, Agriculture and Science. The astronomic clock dates from 1511.

Neckar riverfront, Tübingen

Stiftskirche
Rood screen and Tower. ⏰ *Open from Easter to Harvest Festival (Erntedank) in early October; Fri and Sat, 11:30am-5pm, Sun, 12:45-5pm; during local school summer holidays, Tue-Sun, 11:30am-5pm.* 🎫 €1.

A 15C Gothic hall-church built in the 15Cthis church features as the burial place of the Württemberg princes. Note the funerary monument of Eberhard the Bearded, original founder of the university, and the **Renaissance tombs**★★ of Duke Ludwig and his wife, adorned with fine alabaster relief work.

At the foot of the perron leading to Stiftskirche stretches the *Holzmarkt* (woodwork market). The old Heckenhauer bookshop (now a travel agent) is where the writer and poet Hermann Hesse spent his apprenticeship from 1895 to 1899.

Excursion

Kloster Bebenhausen★
6km north via the Wilhelmstraße. ⏰ *Open Apr to Oct, 9am-6pm, Mon, 9am-12 noon, 1-6pm; Nov to Mar, Tue-Sun, 9am-12 noon, 1-5pm.* ⏰ *Closed 1 Jan, 24, 25 and 31 Dec.* 🎫 €3. ☎ *(070 71) 60 28 02.*

This 12C monastery, along with Maulbronn and Eberbach, is the best preserved Cistercian monastery in Germany. The famous roof **turret**★, which has become the monastery's trademark, dates from the monastery's most prosperous years, in the 15C.

On the monastery grounds is **Schloss Bebenhausen,** the monastery house turned hunting lodge of King Karl of Württemberg. This is where the last king of Württemberg, Wilhelm II, retired after his abdication. His widow, Charlotte, lived here until her death in 1946. 🚶 *Guided tour (45min, leaves hourly).* ⏰ *Open Apr to Oct, 9am-6pm, Mon, 9am-12 noon, 1-6pm; Nov to Mar, Tue-Sun, 9am-12 noon, 1-5pm.* ⏰ *Closed 1 Jan, 24, 25 and 31 Dec.* 🎫 €3. ☎ *(070 71) 60 28 02.*

ÜBERLINGEN★

POPULATION: 21 000

This former Imperial City on Lake Constance was founded ca 1180 by Frederick I Barbarossa. Its medieval prosperity stemmed largely from vineyard harvests and trade in salt and grain. From the mid 19C, the tourist industry played an increasingly important role. Überlingen has been an officially recognised Kneipp spa resort since 1956. *Landungsplatz 14, 88662 Überlingen, ☎ (075 51) 99 11 22.*

▶ **Orient Yourself:** The town is on the northwest bank of Lake Constance surrounded by orchards and a mild climate. West of the town there is a pleasant **moat walk** *(Stadtbefestigungsanlagen)* leading to the **Seepromenade**.

⊘ **Don't Miss:** The Münsterplatz and its Münster.

⊙ **Organizing Your Time:** Allow three hours to see the sights of Überlingen.

⟲ **Also See:** *BODENSEE, KONSTANZ (41km/26mi south), SALEM (13km/8mi east).*

Sights

Münsterplatz

The square lies between the Gothic cathedral, the north façade of the town hall, and the Renaissance municipal chancellery (Alte Kanzlei).

Münster★

The Gothic cathedral, or minster, proves its influence as a place of worship with its volume of donor altarpieces, including the High Altar by the Brothers Zürn in 1616. A 16C Swabian work, the Virgin of the Crescent Moon, stands in St Elizabeth Chapel.

Rathaus

Enter through the turret on the right and walk up to the first floor. ⊙ *Open May to Oct, Tue-Sun, 9am-12 noon, 2.30-5pm, Sat, 9am-12 noon; Nov to Apr, Mon-Fri, 9am-12 noon, 2.30-5pm.* ☎ *(075 51) 99 10 11.*

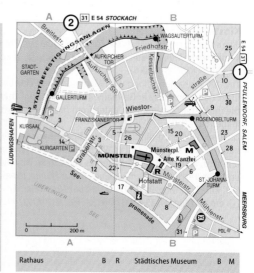

ÜBERLINGEN

Bahnhofstr.	A	2
Christophstr.	A	3
Franziskanerstr.	B	5
Gradebergstr.	B	6
Hafenstr.	B	8
Hizlerstr.	B	9
Hochbildstr.	B	10
Hofstatt	B	
Jakob-Kessenring-Str.	A	12
Klosterstr.	A	14
Krummebergstr.	B	15
Landungspl.	B	17
Lindenstr.	B	19
Luziengasse	B	20
Marktstr.	AB	22
Münsterstr.	B	
Obertorstr.	B	23
Owinger Str.	B	25
Pfarrhofstr.	B	26
Schlachthausstr.	B	30
Seestr.	B	31
St-Ulrich-Str.	B	28

Rathaus	B	R	
Städtisches Museum	B	M	

The **Council Chamber**★ *(Ratssaal)* is decorated with great finesse in the Gothic manner: panelled walls embellished with projecting arches; ribbed, slightly rounded wooden ceiling; and a series of 15C statuettes.

Städtisches Museum

🕐 *Open Tue-Sun, 9am-12.30pm, 2-5pm (Apr to Oct, additionally Sun, 10am-3pm).*
🕐 *Closed Tue after Easter and Pentecost.* ⊛ *€2.* ☎ *(075 51) 99 10 79.*
Among the exhibits in a late-15C mansion with Baroque modifications are paintings and sculpture by local artists from the Gothic period to Classicism, a collection of 18C crèches (Krippen) and 50 dollhouses from the Renaissance to Jugendstil.

ULM★★

POPULATION: 120 000

The royal palace of "Hulma", recorded for the first time in 854, was one of Europe's most important medieval cities. Blessed with an exceptional cathedral, the Old City delights visitors and walks along the Danube. Ulm's most famous local figure is Albert Einstein, born here in 1879. 🗊 *Münsterplatz, 89073 Ulm,* ☎ *(0731) 161 28 30.*

▶ **Orient Yourself:** Ulm is separated from Neu-Ulm by the river Danube, mid-way between Munich and Stuttgart on the A 8.

🅿 **Parking:** Garages can be found near the main train station and on Am Rathaus, as well as numerous sites throughout the city.

☺ **Don't Miss:** Ulm's Cathedral and the suggested walking tour.

🕐 **Organizing Your Time:** Allow at least an hour to tour Ulm's cathedral, including a climb up the world's tallest church spire.

Kids Especially for Kids: Ascending Ulm Cathedral's spire (older children).

⚲ **Also See:** ZWIEFALTEN (50km/31mi southwest), SCHWÄBISCHE ALB (50km/31mi west), ROMANTISCHE STRASSE – join it at AUGSBURG (77km/48mi east) or at NÖRDLINGEN (73km/46mi north).

M. Hertlein/MICHELIN

At 161m, the spire of Ulm cathedral is the tallest in the world

Münster★★★

At a height of 161m/528ft, Ulm cathedral spire is the tallest in the world, lifing the entire Gothic building skyward. Although the foundation stone was laid in 1377, the two towers and spire were not erected until 1890.

The Münster's **interior** also draws the eye heavenward. The chancel arch bears the largest fresco north of the Alps, a 1471 work depicting the Last Judgement. To the right on the chancel arch stands the 15C *Man of Sorrows*, an early work by native Ulmer Hans Multscher. The pulpit is surmounted by a splendid wooden sounding board from 1510, the work of Jörg Syrlin the Younger, and above this is a second pulpit in the Late Gothic style. This is intended for the Holy Spirit, the invisible preacher. The four side aisles feature fine Late Gothic fan vaulting.

Left of the entrance to the chancel is the **tabernacle**★, at 26m/85ft the tallest in Germany. The masterpiece, chiselled out of limestone and sandstone, was produced

The Iconoclasts

Konrad Sam, a virulent preacher, brought the Swiss Reformation to Ulm in 1530, advocating the destruction of religious imagery. Following a referendum approved by 87% of the population, he made the cathedral Protestant. Private donors removed their altars and sealed the cathedral's central door, the stalls and the tabernacle. Some altars were given to neighbouring villages, where they remain today. The rage of the iconoclasts was unleashed on 21 June 1531: The remaining cathedral icons (60 altars, numerous statues, altarpieces and hangings) were destroyed.

Address Book

WHERE TO EAT

⊜ **Weinkrüger** – *Weinhofberg 7* ☎ *(0731) 649 76* Enjoy regional specialities in the comfortable ambience of this former tannery. Dark wood and pleasant decor give the dining room a country feel.

⊜⊜⊜ **Zunfthaus** – *Fischergasse 31* ☎ *(0731) 644 11 www.zunfthaus-ulm. de Reservation recommended* Set in the heart of the old town this half-timbered building was built 600 years ago and has been home to fishermen and shipbuilders. Today its 3 floors house a country-style restaurant.

WHERE TO STAY

⊜⊜ **Pension Rösch** – *Schwörhausgasse 18* ☎ *(0731) 657 18 Fax (0731) 6022584 16 rooms* ⊠ This simple little hotel provides good value and clean rooms at the entrance to the fishermen's district.

⊜⊜⊜⊜ **Schiefes Haus** – *Schwörhausgasse 6* ☎ *(0731) 96 79 30 Fax (0731) 9679333 www.hotelschiefeshausulm.de* ⇥ *11 rooms* ⊠. This restored medieval house is filled with

designer furniture. Comfortable water beds in the guestrooms.

TAKING A BREAK

Café Ströbele – *Hirschstr. 4* ☎ *(0731) 6 37 79* 🕐 *Mon-Sat, 7.30am-8pm, Sun, 11am-6pm, Shop. Mon-Fri, 8am-6pm, Sat, 8am-4pm.* First floor tea room with delicious coffee, 10 different types of tart, more than 40 types of chocolate and freshly baked cakes.

GOING OUT

Alexandre – *Marktplatz 1* ☎ *(0731) 6 02 74 90 www.alexandre-welt.de* 🕐 *Mon-Wed, 9am-1am, Thu-Sat, 9am-2am, Sun, 10am-1am.* French café on the ground floor of the old town hall, recognisable by its 16C murals and *Jugendstil* interior. In good weather, enjoy the terrace on the Marktplatz.

Barfüßer – *Paulstr. 4 (northeast of Augsburger-Tor-Platz) 89231 Neu-Ulm* ☎ *(0731) 97 44 80 www.barfuesser-brauhaus.de* 🕐 *8am-1pm.* Micro-brewery with tasteful decor and enormous Biergarten on the banks of the Danube. Nibbles and traditional dishes are served to accompany the beer.

ca 1460-70. Three rows of wooden figures depict the prophets and lawbringers. Note the small figures of people and animals carved into the handrail of the banister and on which the artist has allowed his imagination to run riot.

The cathedral's **choir stalls**★★★, (Chorgestühl) are a marvellous example of wood carving, executed by Jörg Syrlin the Elder between 1469 and 1474. Two series of characters, from the Bible and from pagan antiquity, face one another. Men are grouped on the left, women on the right, the upper gables being devoted to the Church's apostles and martyrs, and the high backs of the stalls to Old Testament figures.

For many cathedral visitors the Münster's highlight is a 768-step **ascent of the spire,** the tallest in the world. The structure resembles stone lacework in its upper reaches, revealing a **panorama**★★ including the town, the Danube, the plateaux of the Swabian Jura and the Alps.

Walking Tour

Fischerviertel★

The best place to begin an exploration of Ulm is in the little alleys extending along the Blau in the quarter once inhabited by millers, fishermen and tanners. Begin with the Fischerplätzle, a small square shaded by a lime tree. Turn left into a narrow street and pass over the little bridge, which leads to the so-called **crooked house** (*Schiefes Haus*, mid-15C) on the banks of the *Blau*. The tiny alley opposite is known as the "kissing alley" *(Kußgasse)*, because the roofs of the houses touch one another. The 17C house of oaths *(Schwörhaus)* nearby is the scene every year on Oath Monday of

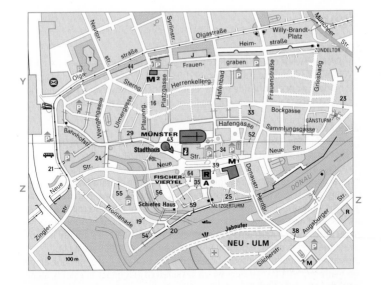

Olympic Designs

Pictograms representing each of the Olympic disciplines were designed at the Ulm School of Design by German designer Otl Aicher for the Olympic Games in Munich in 1972. They have been used at each subsequent Games and are reproduced on the medals, to the great pride of the city.

the ceremonial statement of account by the chief burgomaster and the renewal of his oath of office.

The town **walls** afford a wonderful close-up of the gables of the old houses. The crooked **butcher's tower** (Metzgerturm), erected in 1349, stands out since it stands 2.05m/nearly 7ft out of true. Go through the rose garden to reach the eagle bastion (*Adlerbastei*), where the unfortunate tailor of Ulm attempted to fly in 1811.

Baker's sign dating from 1820.

South bank of the Danube★

A walk along the Jahnufer (the south bank of the Danube) offers views of gabled houses, of the Metzgerturm and the cathedral.

Sights

Stadthaus

The gleaming white town hall with its avant-garde architecture, has been the subject of controversy since its construction in 1991-93. It was unquestionably daring to erect this modern work right beside the venerable cathedral; however it provides a link between the past and the present and lends a casual air to the Münsterplatz.

Ulmer Museum★

 Open Tue-Sun, 11am-5pm, Thu 11am-8pm. Closed 24, 25 and 31 Dec. €3, no charge on Fri. (0731) 161 43 12; www.museum.ulm.de.

Comprising four adjacent houses, the Ulmer Museum is noteworthy for its artworks by local masters, including the Virgin Mary of Bihlafingen by Hans Multscher. One of the most arresting exhibits is the charming 13C *Mary of Sorrows*, edged in blue and gold, the work of a master from the Lake Constance area. There is a collection of 20C art, including works by Klee, Kandinsky, Kirchner and Rothko as well as the **Kurt Fried collection**. And the museum's archaeological section boasts a statuette hailed as one of the world's oldest representations of man, about 32 000 years old.

The easternmost of the museum houses, the Kiechelhaus, is the only one among the many 16C-17C Ulm mansions which has survived fully intact. It features, among other things, a beautiful Renaissance coffered ceiling on the second floor. Several rooms are dedicated to the guilds, which were especially important in a rich town like Ulm.

Altes Rathaus

This elegant Gothic and Renaissance building features painted façades and an astronomic clock on its west façade. On the market square in front of the town hall is the *Fischerkasten*, a fountain thus named because fishermen would cool their wares in it. The spiral stem was fashioned by Jörg Syrlin the Elder in 1482.

Deutsches Brotmuseum★ (German Bread Museum)
&♿① *Open daily, 10am-5pm (8.30pm, Wed).* ① *Closed Good Fri and 24 Dec.* ⊗ €3.
☎ *(0731) 699 55; www.museum-brotkultur.de*
Anyone who has spent any time in Germany will recognize the appropriateness of this museum in a country so fond of its bread. 8 000 years of the cultural and social history of bread is explored in this unique museum, established in 1950. Exhibits range from ovens, models, guilds, coins and stamps, to specially selected works of art (by Brueghel, Corinth, Kollwitz, Picasso), all related to grain or bread. The world's food supply is also critically exaimined.

Excursions

Kloster Wiblingen (Abbey)
5km/3mi south. ① *Open Apr to Oct, Tue-Fri, 10am-12 noon, 2-5pm, Sat-Sun, 10am-5pm; Nov to Mar, Sat-Sun, 1-5pm.* ① *Closed 24, 25 and 31 Dec.* ⊗ €3.50. ☎ *(0731) 502 89 75; www.kloster-wiblingen.de.*
Foundation of this abbey church dates to the 11C, but its final touches were added in the 18C. As at Vierzehnheiligen (& *see Wallfahrtskirche VIERZEHNHEILIGEN*), more than a third of the church's floor plan is occupied by the transept, where pilgrims worshipped relics of the Holy Rood. The flattened domes of the Baroque building were given the illusion of height in frescoes by painter Januarius Zick, who was also responsible for the high altar.
The **abbey library**★, completed in 1760, is one of the finest examples of the Rococo in Swabia. The library gallery is supported by 32 columns, painted alternately pink and blue; they combine with the large false-relief ceiling fresco to create an ensemble rich in colour and movement.

Blaubeuren★
18km/11mi west. This village of the Swabian Jura is renowned for its setting among the rocks. Follow the signposts for Blautopf-Hochaltar, then leave the car near the monumental abbey entrance.
Blautopf (*15min on foot round-trip*) is a deep blue pool formed by a natural embankment of glacial origin. The shady approaches have been laid out as pleasant walks. Nearby is the **Benedictine Abbey** (*allow 30min, follow the "Hochaltar" signs*). The premises includes picturesque, ancient, half-timbered buildings. In the chancel of the abbey church (Klosterkirche) is a magnificent **altarpiece**★★ (Hochaltar), a masterpiece of Gothic sculpture and a collective work created by the principal studios of Ulm in the 15C. Themes treated are Christ's Birth and Passion, the life of St John the Baptist, and the Virgin Mary between the saints. The beautiful choir **stalls**★ of 1493 and the triple throne are the work of Ulm master Jörg Syrlin the Younger.

INSEL USEDOM★

Usedom displays a wonderfully unspoiled natural landscape, alternating between moors, inland seas, forest, dunes, sandy beaches and steep cliffs. The island is part of the Usedom-Oderhaff Nature Reserve, and its main industry is tourism, what with the elegant bathing resorts on the Baltic coast. For some time the island was known as "Berlin's bathtub" given the number of Berliners who came here to relax and recuperate.

▶ **Orient Yourself:** Usedom is Germany's easternmost island, although its eastern portion, with the town of Swinoujscie, belongs to Poland. The flat northwest contrasts with the hilly southeast, sometimes called Usedom's Switzerland.

- 🕙 **Don't Miss:** The 19C beach resorts in the southeast.
- 🕐 **Organizing Your Time:** Allow one day to soak up the atmosphere of Usedom
- 👶 **Especially for Kids:** Outdoor recreation on any of many sandy beaches and dunes.
- 👜 **Also See:** GREIFSWALD (30km/19mi north of Wolgast), STRALSUND (63km/39mi north of Wolgast), Insel RÜGEN.

Sights

Wolgast

On the mainland. One point of access to Usedom is in the south at Zecherin; the other lies in the northwest, from Wolgast over the River Peene. The 14C **parish church**, Pfarrkirche St Petri, is worth a visit. Its formidable octagonal tower and unadorned exterior contrast sharply with a sumptuous interior. Highlights include 15C-16C wall paintings and a 1700 danse macabre cycle painted by Caspar Sigmund Köppe based on a woodcut by Hans Holbein the Younger. 👜🕐 *Open from May to end Sep, 10am-12:30pm, 1:30pm-5pm, Sun after the church service until noon.* ☎ *(038 36) 20 22 69.*

Krummin

East of Wolgast. The most beautiful avenue of **lime trees**★ *(Lindenallee)* in Usedom leads to the right off B 111 and extends to the little fishing village on the Krummin cove. The surfaced road is just 2km long, but is marvellous; the rounded canopy of leaves overhead gives the impression of being in a high Gothic cathedral.

Peenemünde

The German army located its V2 rocket-testing center in Peenemünde in 1936, signalling the dawn of modern space travel. A rocket museum, the **Historisch-technisches Informationszentrum,** in the old power station retraces the history of rocket development and its associated perils. 👜🕐 *Open Apr to Oct, Tue-Sun, 9am-6pm; Jun to Sep, 9am-6pm; Nov to Mar, Tue-Sun, 10am-4pm.* 🕐 *Closed 24-26 Dec.* ☎ *€5.* ☎ *(0383 71) 50 50.*

The "Taille" Usedoms

👶 At the island's narrowest point, the white sandy beaches of the resorts of **Zinnowitz**, **Koserow**, **Kölpinsee** and **Ückeritz** lie side by side, protected by the steep cliff face. At Koserow, the island is barely 200m/220yd wide.

Bansin, Heringsdorf, Ahlbeck

These "three sisters" in the island's southeast are linked by a 10km/6mi-long beach promenade. During the 19C these fashionable resorts were rendezvous of the aristocratic and the wealthy. A number of these imposing and attractive beach villas and hotels remain. **Heringsdorf** was an extraordinarily fashionable resort, and Emperor Wilhelm II was a regular visitor. He resided in the Villa Staudt *(Delbrückstraße 6)*, which still stands today. At 508m/1 666ft long, the pier is the longest on mainland Europe. **Ahlbeck** is also proud of its **historical pier**★, built in 1898. A restaurant was added in 1902. With its white walls, red roof and four green-roofed corner towers, it is one of the most photographed subjects on the island.

Mellenthin

Northeast of the town of Usedom, 2km/1mi north of the B 110. This seldom-visited village and its Renaissance castle create a rural idyll. The three-winged castle surrounded by a moat is unadorned, while a colourfully mounted 17C Renaissance fireplace in the entrance hall is magnificent. The 14C village church in the town cemetery is seriously damaged, but remains a little pearl with its 17C interior **decoration**★.

WALLFAHRTSKIRCHE VIERZEHNHEILIGEN★★

This pilgrimage church dedicated to the 14 Auxiliary Saints is a marvel of Baroque architecture. The bold concepts of Balthasar Neumann, master of the Baroque, are evident in the interior.

▸ **Orient Yourself:** The church is 26km/16mi southeast of Coburg, on an open hillside overlooking the Upper Main Valley, opposite Kloster Banz (👁 *see BAMBERG: Excursions*).

🆒 **Don't Miss:** The Rococo jewel, the Nothelfer Altar.

🕐 **Organizing Your Time:** Allow one hour to see this pilgrimage church.

👁 **Also See:** BAMBERG (32km/20mi south), BAYREUTH (56km/35mi east), THÜRINGER WALD.

A Bit of History

The Pilgrimage – In 1445 and 1446, a herdsman on this hillside received a number of visions, the last of them identified as the Christ Child among the "Fourteen Holy Helpers." The worship of this group of saints, actively encouraged by German Dominicans and Cistercians, occurred at a time when mysticism prevailed, in the early 15C. Visions and voices were commonplace (those heard by Joan of Arc, born in 1412, were of St Catherine and St Margaret, themselves members of the Auxiliary Saints). Devotion to the Holy Helpers remained alive for many years among locals, attracting crowds of pilgrims to a chapel which was superseded, in the 18C, by a sumptuous Rococo church.

Visit

Exterior

The church was built in handsome yellow ochre sandstone following designs by Balthasar Neumann between 1743 and 1772. The west façade is framed by domed towers unusually tall for a Baroque building. The ornately decorated gables are adorned with a statue of Christ between allegorical figures of Faith and Charity (the statues were once gilded).

Interior

The interior layout is organised as a succession of three oval bays framed by colonnades and covered by low inner domes. The true centre of the church is the bay containing the altar to the Auxiliary Saints. The church's interior Rococo decoration features outstanding colour combinations inside the domes, delicate stuccowork, rich gold outlines defining the woodwork of the galleries, and graceful cherubs.

Nothelfer-Altar★★ (Altar to the Fourteen Auxiliary Saints)

A Rococo pyramid with a pierced baldaquin, this remarkable work was executed by Johann Michael Feuchtmayr and stuccoworkers of the Wessobrunn School in 1764. It stands where the herdsman's visions are said to have occurred. Artistic representations include:

- **Balustrade**: 1) St Denys 2) St Blaise 3) St Erasmus 4) St Cyriacus (delivery from the Devil at the final hour).
- **Altar niches**: 5) St Catherine, patron saint of the learned, of students and girls wishing to marry (signifying the model of Christian wisdom) 6) St Barbara, patron saint of miners, artillerymen and prisoners (signifying the grace of a noble death).
- **Buttresses**: 7) St Acacius (the agonies of death) 8) St Giles, the only intercessor not to suffer martyrdom 9) St Eustace (converted by the vision of a stag with a Cross between its antlers) 10) St Christopher, patron saint of travelers.
- **Atop the baldaquin**: 11) St Vitus 12) St Margaret (intercession for the forgiveness of sins) 13) St George, patron saint of peasants and their possessions 14) St Pantaleon.

Inspiring views of the Wallfahrtskirche Vierzehnheiligen, nearby Banz Abbey and the surrounding countryside should can be had from the slopes above the church.

WEIMAR★★

POPULATION: 64 000

To most non-Germans, Weimar recalls the ill-fated republic which existed uneasily between the First World War and the Hitler years. But the city's claim to a place in European history rests unshakeably on the extraordinary flowering of intellectual and artistic talent over the centuries, as it attracted names as diverse as Luther, Cranach, Bach, Wieland, Schiller and Liszt. The one genius whose traces one cannot escape in Weimar, however, is that greatest of all German classicists, Johann Wolfgang von Goethe. *Markt 10, 99423 Weimar, ☎ (036 43) 240 00.*

▶ **Orient Yourself:** Set on the banks of the Ilm, Weimar is in the heart of Thuringia, around 20km/13mi from Erfurt, the capital of the Land. The A 4 motorway links the town to Dresden to the east and Frankfurt to the southwest.

- 🅿 **Parking:** Convenient Old City parking is found in a garage near the Goethe House.
- 🚾 **Don't Miss:** The suggested walking tour.
- 🕐 **Organizing Your Time:** Allow two hours for the historic walking tour.
- 👣 **Also See:** ERFURT (20km/13mi west), JENA (22km/14mi east), NAUMBURG (50km/31mi north).

A Bit of History

An Intellectual and Cultural Phenomenon – Weimar's hour of glory coincided with the succession, in 1758, of the Duchess Anna Amalia. It was during her reign that the town's intellectual reputation grew, largely because of **Goethe** (1749-1832). He was appointed Minister of the small, provincial capital, and produced here the majority of his life's work, including his dramatic masterpiece *Faust*.

Goethe's success went hand-in-hand with that of **Friedrich von Schiller**, who moved permanently to Weimar in 1799. The work produced by these two close friends, along with the writings of the theologian **Johann Gottfried Herder** (1744-1803), a disciple of Kant, raised Weimar's literary reputation to that of "home of German classicism".

From 1552 until his death a year later, **Lucas Cranach the Elder** worked in Weimar on his final masterpiece: the altarpiece triptych for the local church of St Peter and St Paul (👣 *see Stadtkirche below*). **Johann Sebastian Bach** was organist and choirmaster there from 1708 to 1717. In 1848 **Franz Liszt** took the position, and became the driving force behind Weimar's School of Music, which still bears his name today.

In 1860, the School of Fine Arts was founded in Weimar, an establishment which would evolve into Bauhaus University, a College of Architecture and Design. It was under the influence of such celebrated graduates as **Arnold Böcklin** (1827-1901) that painters spearheading the contemporary avant-garde movement developed "the Weimar School".

The Weimar Republic (1919-33) – The constitution of the ill-fated Weimar Republic was set up in 1919 by the German National Assembly, which sat at that time in the theatre. However, the government was never really based in Weimar and returned to Berlin one week after adoption of the text. The humanist tradition of Goethe's town had merely provided the budding democracy with a welcome counterpoint to the politically oppressive atmosphere of post-war Berlin.

Walking Tour

The Historic Centre★★

Weimar's chief highlights – mostly related to heroes of the German Renaissance or Enlightenment – are found within a small area in the lively pedestrian city centre, around two large, neighbouring squares: Theaterplatz, with the National Theatre and Bauhaus Museum, and Marktplatz.

Goethes Wohnhaus und Goethe Museum★★

Frauenplan. 🕐 *Open Apr to Oct, Tue-Sun, 9am-6pm (7pm on Sat, Apr-Sep); Nov to Mar, Tue-Sun, 9am-4pm.* 🕐 *Closed 24 Dec.* ⊜ *€6.50.* ☎ *(036 43) 54 53 47; www. weimar-klassik.de.*

The dramatist-politician lived in this Baroque mansion for over 20 years, from 1809 until his death in 1832. The interior is largely the way he left it. The living rooms, workroom, library and garden can all be visited, each furnished with paintings and sculptures amassed by Goethe during his travels. The museum features manuscripts, letters and *objets d'art* that also evoke his contemporaries: Wieland, Herder, Schiller and even the Duchess Anna Amalia and her son the Duke Carl August.

▶ *Go to Haus der Frau von Stein via Ackerwand.*

Haus der Frau von Stein

Ackerwand 25. Goethe met Charlotte von Stein, lady-in-waiting to Anna Amalia, in November 1775, a young woman who profoundly influenced him and his work. Today the building is home to the Goethe Institute as well as a language school and cultural centre.

Platz der Demokratie

The equestrian statue of the Grand Duke Carl August stands in this square. On the south side, the former palace (1757-74) is occupied by the **Franz Liszt Hochs-**

Garden of Goethes Wohnhaus

J. Bouraly/MICHELIN

chule für Musik. The 16C-18C *Grünes Schloss* houses the **Duchess Anna Amalia Library,** with medieval manuscripts, early printed works, rare 16C-17C documents and 18C volumes. The museum also collects manuscripts relating to the "Age of Enlightenment" *(Aufklärung),* including those by Kant, Locke, Leibniz etc.

▶ *From Platz der Demokratie go to the neighbouring market place.*

Cranach-Haus

The famous painter spent the last year of his life in this Renaissance house (1549) adorned with scrolled gables. His studio was on the third floor.

The Rathaus, opposite, was built ca 1500 but heavily remodelled in the mid-19C.

▶ *Take Schillerstraße towards Theaterplatz.*

Schillers Wohnhaus★

Schillerstraße 12. ○ *Open Apr to Sep, Wed-Mon, 9am-6pm (7pm on Sat); Oct, Wed-Mon, 9am-6pm; Nov to Mar, Wed-Mon, 9am-4pm.* ○ *Closed 24 Dec.* ⌾ *€4.* ☎ *(036 43) 54 53 50; www.klassik-stiftung.de*

Schiller moved here in 1802 to be near his great friend Goethe, and in this house wrote *William Tell* and *The Bride of Messina.* The museum examines his life and work.

▶ *Follow Schillerstraße until Theaterplatz.*

Deutsches Nationaltheater

The present 1907 structure was built on the site of a 1779 Baroque building. It was in this previous theatre that Schiller's great plays were staged and directed by Goethe, and it was here, in 1850, that Richard Wagner's *Lohengrin* was first performed. In 1919 the Weimar Republic constitution was adopted by the German National Assembly which sat in this location. In front of the present

Goethe and Schiller, Weimar

H. Champollion/MICHELIN

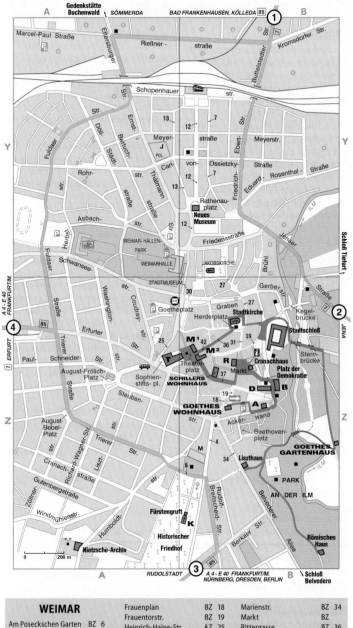

Address Book

WHERE TO EAT

Sommer's Weinstube Restaurant – *Humboldtstr. 2* ☎ *(03643) 40 06 91 www.wein-sommer.com* 🕐 *Closed Sun* This restaurant has been run for over 130 years by the Sommer family, who have managed to retain its old-fashioned charm. Thuringian specialites, often potato-based, are served as well as regional and international wines.

Bratwurstglöck'l – *Carl-August-Allee 17a* ☎ *(03643) 20 28 75* 🕐 *Closed Mon* ♿ Built in 1870, this traditional German inn is close to the station. The panelling and beautiful decor make this little town house really comfortable. Regional specialities are on the menu.

WHERE TO STAY

Hotel Zur Sonne – *Rollplatz 2* ☎ *(03643) 80 04 10 Fax (03643) 862932 hotelzursonne@web.de 21 rooms* 🍽 *Restaurant* This neat brick house is in the heart of the old town. Inside the style is modern, with practical, welcoming guestrooms. The pleasant restaurant follows the style of an old German inn.

Romantik Hotel Dorotheenhof – *Dorotheenhof 1, 99427 Weimar-Schöndorf* ☎ *(03643) 45 90 Fax (03643) 459200 www.dorotheenhof. com* 🅿 ⚡ ♿ *60 rooms* 🍽 🍴

Restaurant. Country house hotel set above the city in a quiet park location. Elegant restaurant with charming vaulted ceiling.

GOING OUT

Café Louis – *Jakobstr. 10 (courtyard of the Kirms-Krackow)* ☎ *(03643) 80 16 81 www.cafe-louis-weimar.de* 🕐 *Tue-Sun, 11am-midnight (dinner until 11pm).* Hidden away in the courtyard of an old house, this establishment features a terrace, 19C Goethe drawing room and idyllic garden. Thai cuisine and cakes are on the menu, along with local wines and cocktails.

Crêperie du palais – *Am Palais 1 (east of Wittumspalais)* ☎ *(03643) 40 15 81 www.creperie-weimar.de* 🕐 *9:30am-midnight; closed second week in Jan).* This French-style crêperie has pancakes, crêpes, cider, wine, aperitifs and a selection of French cigarettes. Small shady terrace on the other side of the road.

Residenz-Café – *Grüner Markt 4 (near Stadtschloss)* ☎ *(03643) 5 94 08 www. residenz-cafe.de* 🕐 *Mon-Fri, 8am-1am, Sat-Sun, 9am-1am.* This building dates from 1839; before it became a café, the *Goethezimmer* was Goethe's living room. Today it is a modern establishment with pleasant ambience where refreshments are served all day long.

---

building stand the **statues**★★ of Goethe and Schiller, sculpted in 1857 by Ernst Rietschel.

Bauhaus-Museum

🕐 *Open daily 10am-6pm.* 🎫 *€4.50.* ☎ *(036 43) 54 59 61; www.klassik-stiftung.de*
The Bauhaus School occupied this building from 1919 until 1925, when it moved to Dessau. The museum brings together designs and finished work from Henry Van de Velde's School of Applied Arts. The main collection is that accumulated by Walter Gropius.

Wittumspalais

🕐 *Open Apr to Oct, Tue-Sun, 9am-6pm; Nov to Mar, Tue-Sun, 10am-4pm.* 🕐 *Closed 24 Dec.* 🎫 *€4.* ☎ *(036 43) 54 53 77.*
After her husband's death, Anna Amalia moved to this Baroque palace where she organised her famous salons with Goethe, Schiller, Herder and Wieland. The life and work of Wieland are examined in the **Wielandmuseum**.

▶ *Go to Herderplatz via Zeughof then Rittergasse.*

Stadtkirche or Herderkirche

Am Herderplatz. This triple-nave Gothic hall-church *(see Art and Music in Weimar above)* was built between 1498-1500 and much remodelled in the Baroque between 1735-1745. The church is also known as the Herderkirche, in memory of the sermons preached there by the philosopher, who is buried in the church. The famous **Cranach Triptych**★★, started by Lucas Cranach the Elder and finished by his son in 1555, represents the Crucifixion on its central panel, and is surrounded by scenes from the Old and New Testmanents. On the right are Luther and Cranach the Elder.

Stadtschloß und Kunstsammlungen zu Weimar

An early-19C palace built for Duke Carl August, the Stadtschloß features some of Germany's finest neo-Classicist apartments and important Weimar artworks. Highlights include an important **Cranach collection**★★; Flemish and Italian paintings; and work by Hans Baldung Grien, Albrecht Dürer and Bartholomäus Bruyn the Elder. The Weimar School and German Impressionists and Expressionists (Max Beckmann, Max Liebermann) are also represented. ◷ *Open Apr to Oct, Tue-Sun, 10am-6pm; Nov to Mar, Tue-Sun, 10am-4pm.* ✎ *€5.* ☎ *(036 43) 54 59 60.*

Ilm Park★★

"Weimar is in fact a park in which they happened to build a town." This compliment was written by Adolf Stahr in 1851. Indeed, modern Weimar remains a city of green spaces, indissolubly linked with its riverside park. From the palace of Tiefurt to the Belvedere, a single stretch of greenery centred on the gardens extends along each side of the Ilm. The gardens are only a few yards from the city centre.

Goethes Gartenhaus★★

Duke Carl August made a present of this summer residence to Goethe, and the great man liked it so much that he lived there permanently from 1776 to 1782. It remained his favourite retreat until the end of his life. Here it was that Goethe wrote *Wilhelm Meister's Theatrical Mission*, major parts of *Iphigenia*, and early drafts of *Egmont* and *Torquato Tasso*.

▶ *Cross the park in the direction of the Belvederer Allee.*

Liszt-Haus

On the west side of the park along the Belvederer Allee. ◷ *Open Apr-Oct, Wed-Mon, 10am-6pm.* ◷ *Closed 24 Dec.* ✎ *€2.50.* ☎ *(036 43) 54 53 88; www.weimar-klassik.de*
In this former gardeners' lodge at the park entrance it is possible to visit Liszt's apartments, occupied during his second stay in Weimar, from 1869 to 1886.

Sights

Neues Museum

Rathenauplatz. ♿◷ *Open Apr to Oct, Tue-Sun, 1pm-6pm.* ✎ *€2.50.* ☎ *(036 43) 54 51 59.*
The 19C neo-Renaissance building was erected as an archducal museum. During the Third Reich it was the headquarters of Thuringia's Nazi administration. Once again a museum, the collections focus on the Avant-Garde since 1960 with emphasis on German art, Italian *Arte Povera*, and American Minimal and Conceptual Art.

Historischer Friedhof und Fürstengruft

This 19C was built as the burial place of the princely family. It is the last resting place for Goethe, Schiller and Grand Duke Carl August, who lie here side by side. The **Russian Orthodox Church** nearby was built in the 19C for Maria Pavlova, Grand

Duchess and daughter-in-law of Carl August. Goethe's muse, Frau von Stein, also lies in the cemetery.

Nietzsche Archiv

🕐 *Open Apr to Oct, Tue-Sun, 1-6pm; Nov to Mar, Tue-Sun, 1-4pm.* 🕐 *Closed 24 Dec.* 👓 *€2.* ☎ *(036 43) 54 54 01.*

The philosopher **Friedrich Nietzsche** spent the last three years of his life here, until his death in 1900. The archive houses literature on the life and work of this brilliant, although tragically misinterpreted, philosopher.

Excursions

Schloss Tiefurt

2km/1mi east. 🕐 *Open Apr to Oct, Tue-Sun, 9am-6pm; Nov to Mar, Tue-Sun, 10am-4pm.* 🕐 *Closed 24 Dec.* 👓 *€3.50.* ☎ *(036 43) 54 54 01.*

The former summer residence (18C) of Duchess Amalia is surrounded by English-style gardens. Both palace and gardens were frequently the scene of the literary gatherings she loved, including such distinguished guests as Goethe and the Humboldt brothers.

Schloss Belvedere

4km/3mi southeast. 🕐 *Open Apr-Oct, Tue-Sun, 10am-6pm.* 👓 *€4.* ☎ *(036 43) 54 69 62.*

This is one of the most delightful and the most artistically successful stately homes of Thuringia. Comprising a large central block flanked by two low wings, the mansion is completed by four outbuildings and an orangery harbouring carriages and barouches. The beautifully restored interior is open to visitors. There is an outstanding collection of 17C-19C porcelain and glassware.

Buchenwald

8km/5mi northwest. 🕐 *Open Apr-Oct, Tue-Sun, 10am-6pm; Nov-Mar, Tue-Sun, 10am-4pm.* 🕐 *Closed 24-26,31 Dec and 1 Jan.* ☎ *(036 43) 43 02 00; www.buchenwald.de*

Only a few miles from Weimar, the Ettersberg beech forests housed one of the largest concentration camps of the Hitler regime. Some 250 000 humans took the road to Buchenwald; more than 50 000 died there. The camp was liberated by the Americans on 11 April 1945.

The **Memorial Centre** (Gedenkstätte Buchenwald) shows a film tracing the history of the camp. A tour of the camp starts at the gatehouse, still bearing the chilling slogan: "Jedem das Seine" ("You get what you deserve").

Each residential hut is marked on the ground; at the far end a building used for storing the inmates' possessions and effects is now a museum. Outside the camp, a road leads to the quarry where many prisoners were essentially worked to death.

From 1945 to 1950, the Soviet occupation force set up **Special Camp 2**, in which Nazi criminals, officials and political prisoners were interned. Over 7 000 are believed to have died here. From the entrance (*1km/0.6mi toward Weimar*) the Steles' Way leads to the Avenue of Nations, which links three mass graves. The last of these brings you to the **Buchenwald Memorial** (Mahnmal Buchenwald).

In August 1943, about 100km/60mi north of Weimar near Nordhausen was an auxiliary camp called **Dora** *(see HARZ)*. Internees converted underground shafts into a manufacturing plant for V-2 rockets. The factory's unsuitable location, appalling hygiene and rigorous working conditions resulted in the deaths of some 20 000 prisoners in its 20 months of operation. Dora is now a memorial and museum; some factory shafts are open to visitors as part of a guided tour.

WIESBADEN ★

POPULATION: 274 000

Lying at the foot of the Taunus mountains and favoured by the mild climate of the Rhine Valley, the capital city of Hessen has the refined atmosphere of a spa town and the flair of an elegant city. *Marktstrasse 6, 65183 Wiesbaden, ☎ (0611) 172 97 80.*

▶ **Orient Yourself:** Located 40km west of Frankfurt and close to Mainz on the opposite bank of the Rhein, Wiesbaden is reached via the A 63 or the A 67 to the south, and via the A 3 or the A 5 to the north. Take the A 66 if you are coming from Frankfurt.

🅿 **Parking:** Old City parking garages can be found near the market on Bahnhofstraße and at Neugasse and Friedrichstraße.

👁 **Don't Miss:** A peak at the Kurhaus and its park and gardens.

🕐 **Organizing Your Time:** Allow one hour each for the Old Town and the Spa Quarter.

👍 **Also See:** *MAINZ (11km/7mi south), FRANKFURT AM MAIN (41km/26mi northeast), RHEINTAL (Rüdesheim is 48km/30mi west).*

A Bit of History

An International Spa Town – The ancient Romans were aware of the benefits of the 26 hot sodium chloride springs (46-66°C/115-150°F), and Pliny noted with surprise that the water from the springs stayed warm for three days. In the 9C, Wiesbaden was first called "Wisibada" (spa in the meadows). The middle of the 19C saw the start of Wiesbaden's heyday as a spa town, when it became a rendezvous for the crowned heads and higher nobility of the world. Modern Wiesbaden enjoys an excellent reputation as a spa resort specialising in rheumatism with a modern rehabilitation clinic.

Walking Tour

Old Town

The town centre is largely a pedestrian zone and is organised around the *Schlossplatz*. The shop-lined Landgasse and Neugasse are two particularly lively streets.

Schlossplatz

This elegant and well-proportioned square is the heart of the town. It is lined with beautiful buildings and hosts a market which takes place here twice a week.

The former residence of the dukes of Nassau, the 19C **Schloss** from which the square takes its name, was built in the unadorned Classical style. Today the palace is the seat of the Hessen Provincial Parliament.

WHERE TO EAT

🍽🍽🍽 **Käfer's Bistro** – *Kurhausplatz 1 (inside the spa complex, Kurhaus)* ☎ *(0611) 53 62 00 info@kurhaus-gastronomie.de* This restaurant offers a varied menu. The building was constructed in 1907 in Wilhelminian style. Paintings and wood dominate the decor of the beautiful dining room. Access to the casino.

WHERE TO STAY

🛏🛏🛏 **Drei Lilien** – *Spiegelgasse 3* ☎ *(0611) 99 17 80 Fax (0611) 9917888 www.dreililien.com* 🕐 *Closed Christmas until early Jan* ⚑ *15 rooms* Modern, well-presented guestrooms. *Jugendstil* features were added when the building was restored in 1905, but older historical details were preserved.

Altes Rathaus (Old town hall)

The oldest building in the city, the ground floor of this town hall retains its Late Renaissance style, built in 1609-10. The upper story dates from 1828 and bears the Romantic Historicist style.

Neues Rathaus (New town hall)

Georg Hauberisser, architect of the Munich town hall, erected this building in the German Renaissance style in 1886-87. It was destroyed in the Second World War and has been rebuilt since.

Marktkirche

This first brick-built church in the Nassau region was erected in the mid-19C. Its architect, Carl Boos, copied the Schinkel-designed Friedrichwerder church in Berlin. *Carillon rung daily at 9am, noon and 5pm.*

Spa Quarter

The spa quarter has developed west of the old town.

Kaiser-Friedrich-Bad – *Langgasse 38-42.* The early 20C Jugendstil building boasts frescoes in the entrance hall worth seeing, as is the Roman-Irish steam bath with its majolica glazed tiles.

Kochbrunnen

This fountain is made up of 15 springs. Its hot salty water contains iron, evident from the reddish deposit on the granite basin. The octangular Kochbrunnen Temple dates from 1854.

Kurhaus★ (Spa house)

A lawn as flat as a bowling green, flanked on either side by the hydro and the theatre colonnades and by lofty plane trees, leads up to what is, according to Emperor Wilhelm II, "the most beautiful spa house in the world," built in 1907. The sumptuous interior decoration was restored to its original state in 1987. Although visitors don't see the magnificent rooms unless attending an event or visiting the casino in the left wing, they should at least glimpse the splendid foyer.

Staatstheater

The impressive 19C Renaissance-style building lies south of the theatre colonnade. The taste for lavish decoration is evident in its foyer, redolent of the Rococo.

Kurpark und Kuranlagen★ *(Spa park and grounds)*

A vast park, laid out in 1852, stretches east behind the spa house. Sonnenberger Straße *(to the north)* and Parkstraße *(to the south)* feature magnificent villas from the Gründerzeit.

From Wilhelmstraße to Neroberg

Museum Wiesbaden

&♿ 🕐 *Open Tue-Sun, 10am-5pm, Tue, 10am-8pm.* 🕐 *Closed 1 Jan, Tue after Easter and Pentecost, 1 May, 24, 25 and 31 Dec.* 🚌 *€2.50, free entry Tue from 4pm.* ☎ *(0611) 335 22 50; www.museum-wiesbaden.de*

This museum comprises the **natural sciences collection**, the **collection of Nassau antiquities** and the **art collections**, which proudly boast the largest **Jawlensky collection**★ in the world. (The artist lived in Wiesbaden from 1921-41.) The exhibition includes works from the 16C-17C as well as Classical modern paintings and contemporary art.

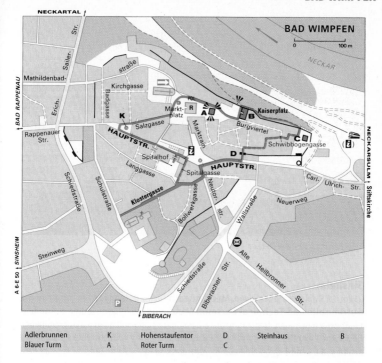

Adlerbrunnen	K	Hohenstaufentor	D	Steinhaus	B
Blauer Turm	A	Roter Turm	C		

▶ *Continue to follow the wall as far as a flight of steps, on the right, which leads to the spur on which the town is built, below the* **Roter Turm** *(Red Tower), the fortress' final defensive point.*

Old Streets

In **Klostergasse** a number of half-timbered houses stand in their own gardens. On the left are the former bathhouses, recognisable by their outside galleries. Explore more of the town's streets via Langgasse, which leads to **Hauptstraße**★ by way of a narrow alley on the right. *No 45* features the courtyard of a former hospital *(Spitalhof)*, with half-timbered houses that are among the oldest buildings in Bad Wimpfen. Return along Hauptstraße, with its picturesque, finely worked signs, and pass the 1576 Eagle Fountain *(Adlerbrunnen)* before regaining Marktplatz via Salzgasse.

Bad Wimpfen im Tal (Lower Town)

The Gothic **Stiftskirche St Peter und St Paul** (Parish Church) has retained a strikingly plain Westwerk from an earlier Romanesque building. The **cloister**★★ (Kreuzgang) shows the evolution of Gothic style. The north gallery (ca 1350), already more angular in design, marks the transition to the more sober Renaissance. ☛ *Guided tour (1hr) by written appointment.* ☎ (07063) 970 40

Excursions

Neckarsulm

10 km/6mi southeast. The former Teutonic castle experienced a radical transformation once it became the **German Cycle and Motorcycle Museum** (Deutsches Zweirad-museum). Nearby is the Audi plant, originally the NSU motor factory which produced Germany's first bicycles. ♿☀ *Open Tue-Sun, 9am-5pm (-7pm, Thu).* ☀ *Closed 24 and 31 Dec.* ⊜ €4. ☎(07132) 352 71.

View of Hirschhorn am Neckar

Sinsheim

25km/15.5mi west via Steinweg. Mechanised vehicles of many types comprise the **Automobile and Technical Museum** (Auto- und Technikmuseum). In the first building are early-20C tractors, locomotives, luxury cars and a replica of a 19C hang-glider, the Lilienthal. A second building exhibits military vehicles (tanks, motorised artillery, airplanes). ♿ ◷ *Open daily, 9am-6pm, Sat-Sun, 9am-7pm.* ⊜ *€12.* ☎ *(072 61) 929 90; www.technik-museum.de*

Driving Tour

Neckartal★ (The Neckar Valley) *74km/46mi round-trip*

Downstream from Bad Wimpfen, the Neckar cuts through the sandstone massif of the Odenwald, many of its hills crowned by castles.

Burg Guttenberg

◷ *Museum open Mar and Nov, on request; Apr to Oct, 10am-6pm.* ⊜ *€4.* ☎ *(062 66) 228.*
A massive defensive wall protects this **castle**. Inside are rare collections of **objets d'art**★ and archives. Note the odd 18C "Library-Herbarium", in which plants are encased in 92 "books" of wood.

Burg Hornberg

1.5km/1mi outside Neckarzimmern. ◷ *Open Thu-Fri from 6pm, Sat from 3pm, Sun from 11am.* ⊜ *€3.* ☎ *(062 61) 50 01; www.burg-hornberg.de.*
Crowning a vine-covered hill, this **castle,** now partly in ruins, can be recognised from afar by its tall keep. A history **museum** features the armour of Götz von Berlichingen, who died here in 1562. This knight, popularised in German folklore as a Robin Hood figure, was immortalised in a play by Goethe.

Hirschhorn am Neckar★

The castle stands on a fortified spur. From the terrace and tower *(121 steps, a difficult climb)* the **view**★ encompasses the wooded slopes of the Neckar Valley.

Neckarsteinach

Four castles stand guard on a narrow ridge overlooking the village: the Vorderburg and Mittelburg castles are privately owned. Hinterburg Castle, built shortly after 1100, is the oldest and is now in ruins. Burg Schadeck, also in ruins, is a small 13C castle known as "swallow's nest" because of its site.

Dilsberg

4.5km/3mi from Neckarsteinach. Follow the signposts "Burgruine" to reach the ruined castle. From the tower *(97 steps)* there is another **panorama**★ of the winding Neckar.

The best way to get to **Heidelberg**★★ *(see entry)* is along the east bank road, which leads straight to the castle.

WISMAR★

POPULATION 45 300

Mid-way between Rostock and Lübeck, Wismar is known for its fisheries and naval dockyards. Sweden reigned over the town in the 17C and 18C and evidence of this occupation remains in Wismar today. The historic town centre with its characteristic red-brick houses is included in the UNESCO World Heritage List.
Am Markt 11, 23966 Wismar, ☎ (038 41) 194 33.

▸ **Orient Yourself:** Wismar stands on a bay in the Baltic Sea, looking out toward the island of Poel. The A 20 links the town to Lübeck.

Don't Miss: Meandering through the Old Town.

Organizing Your Time: Allow three hours to explore the Old Town.

Especially for Kids: A visit to Poel Island.

Also See: *Bad DOBERAN (43km/27mi northwest), ROSTOCK (57km/36mi northeast), LÜBECK (61km/38mi west), SCHWERIN (31km/19mi south).*

A Bit of History

A trading town – Wismar dates back to 1229. It enjoyed its heyday as a Hanseatic city, relying principally on trade with the main countries in Europe. Breweries (Wismar was known for its excellent beer) and wool weaving were further sources of wealth. Wismar's downfall came with the **Thirty Years War**. The peace of Osnabrück meant that the town came under Swedish rule in 1648, under which it stayed until 1803.

Walking Tour

Old Town★

Remarkable houses lie throughout the old town. With a little imagination, the visitor can picture what a treasure Wismar was and promises to become again once restoration is complete.

Marktplatz★

This large square is dominated by the white silhouette of the neo-Classical 19C **Rathaus**. Gabled houses date from various eras. To the east stands the oldest upper middle-class house in town, an eye-catching red-brick building known as the "Old Swede" *(Alter Schwede)* and built around 1380. On its right stands the Reuterhaus, where the works of the Mecklenburg writer Fritz Reuter were published and on its

Wismar harbour

left, a house with charming Jugendstil ornamentation. On the southeast side of the market stands an artistic pavilion, the **waterworks**★. It was built in 1580-1602 in the Dutch Renaissance style and supplied the town with water for centuries.

Marienkirchturm

Only the 80m/262ft-high **tower** remains of the Marienkirche, built during the early 13C and destroyed during the Second World War *(carillon at noon, 3pm and 7pm).*

Fürstenhof

West of the Marienkirchturm. The building, which was erected in two phases, is thought to be the northernmost Renaissance castle in Europe. The more recent, long section, built in 1553-54 by Gabriel von Aken and Valentin von Lyra, is impressive with its pilastar ornaments and friezes. Those facing the road represent the Trojan Wars, and those facing the courtyard represent the parable of the Prodigal Son.

Grube

The "Grube" is a watercourse laid in 1255, where washing was done right up into the 20C. It is the only artificial stream of its kind still in Germany.

Schabbellhaus★

🕐 *Open May-Oct, Tue-Sun, 10am-8pm; Nov to Apr, Tue-Sun, 10am-5pm.* 🕐 *Closed Good Fri, 24 and 31 Dec.* ⬥ *€2, no charge on Fri.* ☎ *(038 41) 28 23 50.*
The sumptuously decorated red-brick Dutch Renaissance building on the corner of Schweinsbrücke and Frische Grube was erected in the 16C. It bears witness to the wealth of the owner, a respected merchant and mayor of the town (his gravestone

---

WHERE TO STAY

⊜⊜ **Willert** – *Schweriner Straße 9* ☎ *(03841) 261 20 Fax (03841) 261241 www.hotel-willert.m-vp.de* 🅿 *17 rooms.* ⬛ Built in 1910, this Jugendstil villa was meticulously restored after the fall of the Berlin Wall. Stucco ceilings in the breakfast room and stairwell are original.

⊜⊜⊜ **Reuterhaus** – *Am Markt 19* ☎ *(03841) 222 30 Fax (03841) 222324 www.hotel-reuterhaus.de 10 rooms* ⬛ ⊜⊜⊜ *Restaurant.* A small hotel in a renovated building on the market place with rather large, comfortable guestrooms and Italian furnishings.

is in the Nikolaikirche). The house is home to a **Museum of Local History** *(Stadt-geschichtliches Museum).*

Nikolaikirche★

♿🕐 *Open Apr and Oct, 10am-6pm, Sun, 11:30am-6pm; May-Sep, 8am-8pm, Sun, 11:30am-8pm; Nov to Mar, 11am-4pm, Sun, 11:30am-4pm.* 💰 *Donation requested, suggested amount: €1 per person.*

Beyond the *Grube* looms the dark mass of this, the highest brick church in the world after Lübeck's Marienkirche. The basilica was built between 1381 and 1487. The **Altar der Krämergilde**★ (Grocers' Guild Altarpiece), a 15C hinged, panelled altarpiece, is worth a closer look. A bronze font cast in 1335 depicts the Life of Christ, the Last Judgement and the Wise and Foolish Virgins.

Alter Hafen (Old Harbour)

From the Grube and the idyllic street Am Lohberg, just a few steps lead to the harbour, at the end of which stands an unadorned Baroque building, the *Baumhaus* (tree house). Here the harbour used to be locked with a tree trunk. The function of the two "Swedish heads" is unknown. They are known to date from 1672.

Excursion

Insel Poel

🧒 This little Baltic island north of Wismar makes a pleasant day trip. Poel's charming seaside villages and wild coastal stretches invite exploration. The flat relief makes a perfect cycling destination; the local tourist office has bikes for hire.

LUTHERSTADT WITTENBERG

POPULATION: 46 800

Wittenberg provided the stage for some of the major events in the Reformation, aided by long-time resident Martin Luther. In summer, thousands of "pilgrims" flock here to walk in the footsteps of the great man. Also a renowned university town, Wittenberg attracted many people of great talent, including Lucas Cranach the Elder, who lived here for 43 years. 🛈 *Schloßplatz 2, 06886 Wittenberg,* ☎ *(034 91) 49 86 10.*

▸ **Orient Yourself:** Wittenberg enjoys a pleasant location between the wooded hills of Fläming and the Elbe. To reach the town from the A 9, take exit 8 and follow B 187, toward Coswig then Wittenberg.
- **Don't Miss:** The Castle Church and the Luther House.
- **Organizing Your Time:** Protestants will want to spend at least one day in this cradle of the Reformation.
- **Also See:** *WÖRLITZER PARK (20km/13mi south), DESSAU (32km/20mi west).*

A Bit of History

A Key Town in the Reformation – Summoned by the Elector Friedrich the Wise (1502) to teach philosophy in the university he had just founded, **Martin Luther** was at the same time appointed the town preacher. After the celebrated public burning of a Papal Bull, Luther was forced to appear before the Imperial Diet at Worms. A year after Luther's death in 1546 at Eisleben, and eight years before he signed the Peace of Augsburg allowing freedom of worship to the Lutherans, **Emperor Charles V** seized

Philipp Melanchthon (1497-1560)

A gifted humanist with a perfect command of Greek and Latin, Philipp Melanchthon entered Heidelberg University at age twelve and finished his studies at the
Faculty of Philosophy in Tübingen. He became professor of Greek at Wittenberg
in 1518 and made a strong impression on Martin Luther. The two men became
close friends and Melanchthon became an ardent defender of the Reformation.
The strength of his Loci communes of 1521 contributed greatly toward the spread
of Protestantism. Melanchthon, who became head of the Lutheran church after
Luther's death, was an open and tolerant man; driven by a desire to reconcile Protestant and Catholic dogmas, he was resented by the most orthodox Lutherans.

Wittenberg and is said to have meditated over the tomb of the great Reformer. The
Lutherstadt prefix was added to Wittenberg in 1938.

Sights

Schloßkirche★ (Castle Church)
Am Schloßplatz, in the west of town. The church attached to the royal residence was
burned down in 1760 and rebuilt; hence the original doors were destroyed on which
Luther pinned his famous 95 Theses condemning the abuses of the Church (1517).
The new church contains the text, which was cast in bronze in 1855. Luther's tomb
is in this church, as is that of his dear friend and supporter, Philipp Melanchthon *(see
below)*. There is also a bronze epitaph to protector Friedrich the Wise.

Markt★
In front of the Late Gothic (1440) town hall stand statues of Luther and of his friend
and disciple Melanchthon, both erected in the mid-19C. The square is bordered by
gabled houses, that in the southwest corner *(Markt 4)* the birthplace of painter Lucas
Cranach the Elder. The artist lived and worked nearby at Schloßstraße 1 between
1513-50.

Stadtkirche St-Marien
On Kirchplatz, east of the market square. This triple-aisle Gothic (14C-15C) **church** was
redecorated in neo-Gothic style in the 18C. Luther's ministry here is celebrated in one
panel of the 1547 **Cranach Reformation Altarpiece**★. Melanchthon is depicted on
the left-hand panel. Luther married Katharina von Bora in this church in 1525.

Melanchthon-Haus
Collegienstraße 60. ○ *Open May to Oct, Sat-Thu, 9am-6pm; Nov to Apr, Sat-Thu, 9am-
5pm.* ☞ *€2.50.* ☎ *(034 91) 32 79.*
The building in which Luther's companion lived and died is a Renaissance edifice
topped by a gable of particularly elegant form. A man of moderate temperament,
more tolerant than Luther, and the author of the Confession of Augsburg worked
for most of his life trying to reconcile the different factions of the Reformation. His
study and many documents relating to his work can be seen in this house.

Luther-Haus★
At the far end of Collegienstraße. Occupied by Luther from 1524 on, this house faces
the courtyard of the Collegium Augusteum, the town's old university. The Reformation Museum, housed here since 1883, exhibits collections of antique Bibles,
manuscripts, and original editions of Luther's works. One department displays a
selection of fine arts from Luther's time: portraits of the Reformer, prints and paintings by Lucas Cranach the Elder, canvases by Hans Baldung Grien etc. ○ *Open from*

Apr to Oct, 9am-6pm; Nov to Mar, Tue-Sun, 10am-5pm. 🚫 *€5.* ☎ *(034 91) 420 30; www.martinluther.de*

Excursion

Wörlitz Park★★
18km/11mi west. Take the car ferry across the Elbe in Coswig. 👍 *See WÖRLITZER PARK.*

WOLFENBÜTTEL★★

POPULATION: 54 500

For three centuries, until the court transferred to Brunswick in 1753, Wolfenbüttel was the seat of the dukes of Brunswick and Lüneburg. The precise, spacious plan, with die-straight streets linking large symmetrical squares, makes it one of the most successful examples of Renaissance town planning in Germany. 🚩 *Stadtmarkt 3-6, 38100 Wolfenbüttel,* ☎ *(053 31) 29 83 46.*

▶ **Orient Yourself:** Built on the banks of the Oker, a few kilometres from the border between Lower-Saxony and Sachsen-Anhalt, Wolfenbüttel is the ideal base for exploring the Harz massif.
👁 **Don't Miss:** The city's half-timbered houses.
🕐 **Organizing Your Time:** Allow three hours for the suggested walking tour.
👍 **Also See:** *BRAUNSCHWEIG (11km/7mi north), GOSLAR (36km/23mi south), HARZ, HILDESHEIM (49km/30mi west).*

Walking Tour

Half-timbered Houses ★★ (Fachwerkhäuser)
The homes of High Court officials lining Kanzleistraße, Reichstraße and western Harzstraße, built ca 1600, are distinguished by majestic façades with overhangs on either side of the main entrance. At no 12 Harzstraße, note the grimacing heads above cornices carved with biblical inscriptions. The decoration of smaller houses owned by lesser dignitaries and merchants is, surprisingly, more elaborate. A single gable normally tops their wide, flat façades (Lange Herzogstraße, Brauergildenstraße, Holzmarkt, Krambuden). The simpler, two-storey houses of the less well-to-do (Krumme Straße, Stobenstraße) are ornamented with coloured fan designs. Corner houses with slightly projecting oriels are a particular characteristic of Wolfenbüttel. Note these houses around the main town square *(Stadtmarkt)*.

WHERE TO EAT

🍴🍴🍴 **Ratskeller** – *Stadtmarkt 2* ☎ *(05331) 98 47 11* 🕐 *Closed Mon* ♿ *Reservation recommended.* This pleasant establishment is in the basement of a house which is over 400 years old. Its brick façade and grey-blue half-timbered frontage is typical of the region. Charming guestrooms and beautiful library.

WHERE TO STAY

🏨🏨🏨 **Parkhotel Altes Kaffeehaus** – *Harztorwall 18* ☎ *(05331) 88 80 Fax (05331) 888100 www. parkhotel-wolfenbuettel.de* 🅿 ✂ *74 rooms* 🛏 🍴🍴 *Restaurant.* Modern hotel with attractive, comfortable guestrooms furnished in light wood. Dine in the bright restaurant or in the wine cellar *(Weingrotte).*

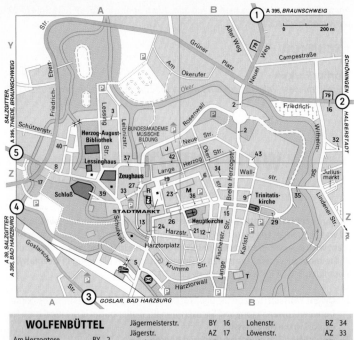

WOLFENBÜTTEL

Stadtmarkt★

The town hall (Rathaus) occupies a number of 16C and 17C buildings on the north and west of the square. The Weights and Measures Office has a distinctive arched doorway surmounted by King Solomon's Edict and the Wolfenbüttel coat of arms.

Schloss★

&Ⓒ *Open Tue-Sun, 10am-5pm.* Ⓒ *Closed 1 Jan, Good Fri, 1 May, 24, 25 and 31 Dec.* ⚏ *€3.* ☏ *(053 31) 924 60.*

The castle is reached via an attractive narrow street bordered by arcades known as the Krambuden. Originally a 12C stronghold conquered by Henry the Lion, the building experienced many transformations before it evolved into Lower Saxony's second largest palace (after the *Leineschloß* in Hannover).

The palace museum consists of the **Ducal Apartments** as they were 1690-1750. Rare furniture, tapestries, porcelain and paintings illustrate Baroque court life. Note the ivory scenes adorning the walls of the small study. *Access via the central courtyard and main stairway.*

Herzog-August-Bibliothek★ (Library)

Ⓒ *Open Tue-Sun, 10am-5pm.* Ⓒ *Closed Good Fri, 24, 25 and 31 Dec.* ⚏ *€3.* ☏ *(053 31) 80 80.*

The Town of Jägermeister

Jägermeister ("Hunt Master") first appeared in Wolfenbüttel in 1935. This unique-ly-flavored alcoholic drink is made from 56 plants, roots and extracts ripened for twelve months. The stag on the label refers to St Hubert, patron saint of hunters. Legend has it that 7C King Hubert rejected his wealth when his wife Floribana died, devoting himself to hunting. During one of his solitary outings a stag with a cross floating between its antlers appeared to him. The vision gave him his calling; he immediately forsake his wealth and title and founded several monasteries.

Founded in 1572 by Augustus the Young, this was the largest, most important library in Europe in the 17C. Still a treasure for researchers and scholars, it houses today some 860 000 volumes. Among the priceless manuscripts and illuminated documents from the Middle Ages are a rare example of the 14C *Saxon Mirror*, and the first *Helmarshausen Gospel* (12C) said to have belonged to Henry the Lion. In the Globe Room are terrestrial and celestial globes, as well as ancient maps. The Malerbuchsaal contains books illustrated by great artists of the 20C *(shown in rotation)*.

Lessinghaus
🕐 *Open Tue-Sun, 10am-5pm.* 🕐 *Closed Good Fri, 24, 25 and 31 Dec.* 🎟 *€3.* ☎ *(053 31) 80 82 14.*
Gotthold Ephraim Lessing, the great innovator of German drama, spent eleven years working as official ducal librarian in Wolfenbüttel (1770-81) and writing, among other works, *Emilia Galotti* and *Nathan the Wise*. His former home is now a museum containing an evocation of his life and works.
Beside the Lessing house is the Zeughaus (Arsenal, 1613), a distinctive Renaissance building with projecting gables, obelisks and scrolls.

Hauptkirche
Built on Kornmarkt in 1608, this Protestant church was influenced by the Late Gothic hall-church tradition. The massive tower with its Baroque roof resembles the castle tower in shape. The altar, pulpit and organ case date from the Late Renaissance.

Trinitatiskirche
The church, which closes off the east end of the *Holzmarkt*, was built in 1719. In its construction, the architects made use of an existing, twin-towered structure, thus explaining its strangely flat silhouette. Near the church is a **park**, formed from the old city walls.

WÖRLITZER PARK★★

WÖRLITZ PARK

Wörlitz Park was the first landscaped park on the European mainland. The park extends over 112 hectares/277 acres between the towns of Dessau and Wittenberg and has retained all its original magic. Visitors are free to wander the canalside pathways and to explore by boat the small islands on the lake.

▶ **Orient Yourself:** Wörlitz Park is 17km/11mi west of Dessau. From the A 9 motor-way (Leipzig-Berlin), take exit 10 and follow B 185 to Orienbaum. Take B 107 to Wörlitz.

🌿 **Don't Miss:** A leisurely stroll through the gardens.

○ **Organizing Your Time:** Allow at least half a day to see the grounds and buildings.

Kids **Especially for Kids:** Exploring the lake and small islands by boat.

ċ **Also See:** *DESSAU (17km/11mi west), WITTENBERG (20km/13mi northeast), LEIPZIG (77km/48mi south), MAGDE-BURG (79km/49mi northwest).*

A Bit of History

Prince Leopold III Friedrich Franz von Anhalt-Dessau (1740-1817), known as "Father Franz" to his subjects, was an enlightened ruler to whom the welfare of his small state was paramount (ċ *see DESSAU*). His endeavours extended far beyond material matters; he sought to

The Pantheon in Wörlitz Park

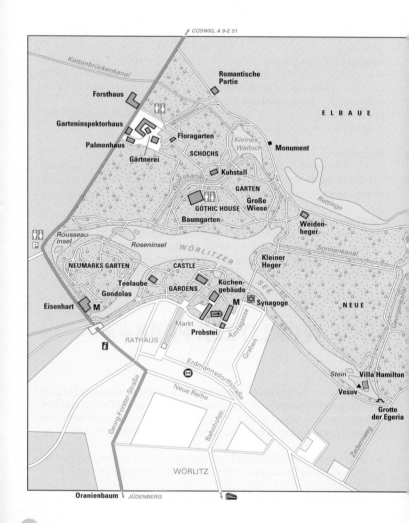

link the beautiful with the useful, promoting literature, music, architecture and garden design.

A number of trips to England provided him with food for progressive thought and paved the way for his planned reforms. It was also in England that he saw his first landscaped parks. He wanted to create such a park environment in his own kingdom. Master builder **Friedrich Wilhelm von Erdmannsdorff**, who had accompanied him on his trips, acted as his assistant and like-minded adviser. The gardens were completed around 1800.

Visit

Schloss★

🚶 *Guided tour (1hr).* 🕐 *Apr and Oct, Tue-Sun, 10am-5pm; May to Sep, Tue-Sun, 10am-6pm.* 🎟 *€4.50.* ☎ *(0340) 64 61 50; www.gartenreich.com.*

Erdmannsdorf built the 18C palace in the neo-Classical style, the earliest such architectural work in Germany. The two-storey yellow and white building stands out boldly against a backdrop of trees. Practical accoutrements, like water pipes, elevators, folding beds and cupboards, abound. All sculpture and carpentry work was undertaken by local people.

The original interior has survived virtually intact. The elegant **dining room** *(Speisesaal)* with its stucco decoration and slim Corinthian pillars, and the great **banqueting hall** *(Großer Festsaal)* are striking. The **library** is richly hung with paintings (Snyders, Van Ruysdael, Antoine Pesne) and fitted with furniture, the highlight of which is the suite of Roentgen pieces.

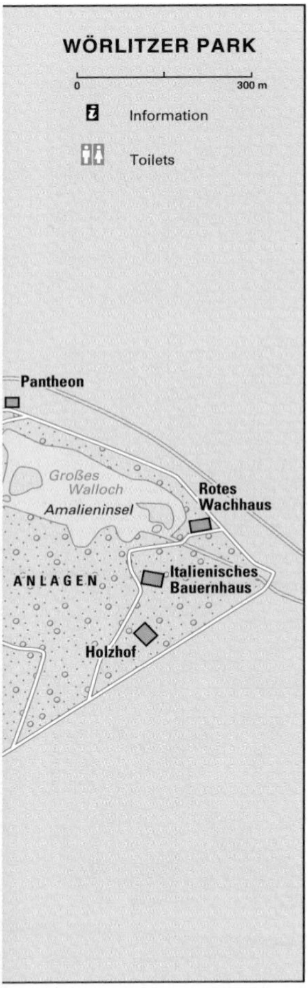

WÖRLITZER PARK

0 — 300 m

🛈 Information

🚻 Toilets

Pantheon
Großes Walloch
Amalieninsel
Rotes Wachhaus
ANLAGEN
Italienisches Bauernhaus
Holzhof

Gotisches Haus★ (Gothic House)

🚶 *Guided tour (1hr).* 🕐 *Apr and Oct, Tue-Sun, 10am-5pm; May to Sep, Tue-Sun, 10am-6pm.* 🎟 *€4.50.* ☎ *(0340) 64 61 50.*

This "Gothic house" is the first neo-Gothic building in Germany, with the exception of the Nauener Gate in Potsdam. While the palace served for official purposes, the Gothic house was a refuge for the prince, to which he could withdraw and live for a period. Through Swiss scholar Johann Caspar Lavater he acquired an outstanding **Swiss stained glass★** collection from the 15C to the 17C. This has survived intact and adorns the windows of the Gothic house. All rooms house numerous paintings, including works by Tintoretto Lucas Cranach the Elder.

WORMS★

POPULATION: 81 000

The city of Worms was, like Speyer and Mainz, an Imperial residence on the banks of the Rhine. Today Worms is a good point of departure for exploring the local vineyards and the Rhineland Palatinate region. *Neumarkt 14, 67547 Worms, ☎ (06241) 250 45.*

▶ **Orient Yourself:** Worms sits on the left bank of the Rhine, 20km/13mi north of Mannheim. The Liebfrauenkirche *(leave on Remeyerhofstraße)* has given its name to the wine sold only outside Germany as *Liebfraumilch.*

▣ **Parking:** You'll find a parking garage at Römerstraße and Paulusstraße.

⊛ **Don't Miss:** St. Peter's Cathedral

⊙ **Organizing Your Time:** Allow half an hour for a tour of St. Peter's Cathedral.

⟡ **Also See:** *PFALZ (suggested tour leaves from Worms), MANNHEIM (23km/14mi southeast), MAINZ (47km/29mi north), HEIDELBERG (50km/31mi southeast).*

WORMS					
		Hardtgasse	A 15	Neumarkt	A 30
		Heinrichstr.	B 16	Petersstr.	A 32
Adenauerring	A 2	Herzogenstr.	B 18	Pfauenpforte	A 34
Allmendgasse	B 3	Kämmererstr.	A 20	Pfauentorstr.	A 35
Am Römischen Kaiser	A 5	Karolingerstr.	B 22	Remeyerhofstr.	B 36
Bärengasse	B 6	Ludwigspl.	A 23	Stephansgasse	A 38
Bauhofgasse	B 8	Mähgasse	B 24	Valckenbergstr.	A 39
Fischmarkt	A 9	Mainzer Str.	A 25	Wilhelm-Leuschner-Str.	A 40
Folzstr.	A 12	Marktpl.	A 26		
Friedrich-Ebert-Str.	A 14	Martinsgasse	A 27		
Friedrichstr.	A 13				

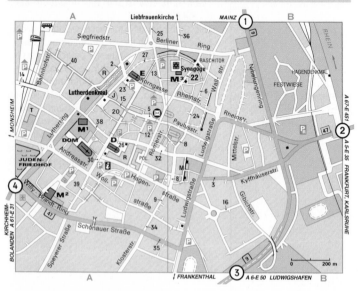

Dreifaltigkeitskirche	A	D	Raschi-Haus	B	M³	Städtisches Museum	A	M²
Museum Heylshof	A	M¹	St. Martinskirche	A	E			

Luther Before the Diet

Everyone knows the old story about Luther and the "diet of worms", bandied about in school history lessons. In fact this particular Diet had perhaps the most far-reaching consequences of any conference before the two world wars (👆 see Introduction: History – "The Reformation and the Thirty Years War: Luther"). Summoned before the Diet by Charles V in 1521 after a Papal Bull condemning everything he believed, Luther arrived in Worms "as though going to the torture chamber." He went nevertheless, troubled by the anxiety of his friends but acclaimed by enthusiastic crowds. Refusing to retract his beliefs, he was banned to the outer parts of the empire (see Introduction).

Sights

Dom St-Peter★★
Worms Cathedral, completed in 1181, is one of the finest Romanesque creations in Germany. The best way to enter the cathedral is through the south doorway. A splendid Christ In Judgement on the far side of the door dates from the 12C. Inside, the east chancel is the older of the chancels: the **high altar**★ is the work of Balthasar Neumann. The west chancel, the last to be built, is extremely elegant, with rose windows, a chequered frieze and arches added to its blind arcades. Five **Gothic relief sculptures**★ in the north aisle represent the Annunciation, the Nativity, the Entombment, the Resurrection and the Tree of Jesse.

Lutherdenkmal (Luther Monument)
Unveiled in 1868, this monument commemorates the reformer's appearance before the Diet. Luther (centre) is surrounded by precursors of the Reformation: Pietro Valdo, John Wycliffe, Jan Hus and Savonarola. At the corners are the Reformist theologians Melanchthon and Reuchlin (rear), the Landgrave of Hessen Philip the Magnanimous (👆 see MARBURG) and the Elector of Saxony who protected Luther (front).

Museum Heylshof★
🕐 Open May to Sep, Tue-Sun, 11am-5pm; Oct to Apr, Tue-Sun, 2-5pm, Sun, 11am-5pm. 🕐 Closed Jan to mid-Feb, Good Fri, 24, 25 and 31 Dec. 🎫 €2.50. ☎ (062 41) 220 00; www.museum-heylshof.de
This museum in a Gründerzeit mansion displays **paintings**★ from the 15C-19C, including works by Rubens, Van Loo and Tintoretto, among others. Also on view are ceramics, glassware, valuable porcelain, and 15C-16C stained-glass windows.

Judenfriedhof★ (Jewish Cemetery)
Worms was one of Germany's great centres of Jewish culture. This is Europe's oldest Jewish burial ground, in use since the 11C, with over 2 000 Hebrew steles.

WHERE TO EAT

🍽🍽🍽 **Rôtisserie Dubs** – Kirchstraße 6, 67550 Worms-Rheindürkheim (9km/6mi north, via the Nibelungenring) ☎ (06242) 20 23 www.dubs.de 🕐 Closed 3 weeks in Jan, Tue and Sat lunchtime Small country restaurant with elegant interior. Wolfgang Dubs, the owner, treats guests to refined and varied cooking.

WHERE TO STAY

🏨🏨 **Kriemhilde** – Hofgasse 2, ☎ (06241) 911 50 Fax (06241) 9115310 www.hotel-kriemhilde.de 19 rooms 🍴🍽🍽 Restaurant A small hotel in the town centre with friendly service and practical guestrooms, with pine or oak furniture. Rustic, tastefully-designed restaurant.

Synagogue

This is the oldest synagogue in Germany, built in the 11C and rebuilt in 1961. Nearby is the *Mikwe* (Bathhouse) and the *Raschi-Haus*, an old Jewish school that now displays archives, ceremonial items and other examples of Jewish life in the Rhineland.

Städtisches Museum

🕐 *Open Tue-Sun, 10am-5pm.* 🕐 *Closed 1 Jan, Good Fri, 1 May, 24-26 Dec and 31 Dec.* 🎫 *€2.* ☎ *(062 41) 94 63 90.*

Five thousand years of artefacts are displayed in the Romanesque buildings of a former monastery. The Ancient Roman section is a highlight, with one of the largest collections of glassware from this period in Germany. There is a lapidary museum in the picturesque cloister.

Excursion

Rhineland Palatinate★ – 🚶 *See PFALZ.*

WÜRZBURG★★

POPULATION: 133 500

Würzburg lies at the starting point of the Romantic Road; unfortunately most of the city's treasures were destroyed by bombs on 16 March 1945 in the space of just twenty-two minutes. What remains of the grandeur acquired in the 17C can be seen in the city's Baroque churches and the splendid Residenz Palace. It was in Würzburg that Wilhelm Conrad Röntgen discovered X-rays in 1895.
🏛 *Congress Centrum, 97070 Würzburg,* ☎ *(0931) 37 23 35.*

▸ **Orient Yourself:** Former capital of the Duchy of Franconia, Würzburg lies on the banks of the Main, at the northwest border of Bavaria.

🅿 **Parking:** You'll find parking garages throughout Würzburg. Visit http://wap.parkinfo.com for fees and locations.

🚫 **Don't Miss:** The Residenz.

🕐 **Organizing Your Time:** Allow one hour for the Residenz; allow one day for the suggested driving tour.

🚶 **Also See:** *ROMANTISCHE STRASSE, BAMBERG (99km/62mi east), FRANK-FURT-AM-MAIN (115km/72mi north-west), HOHENLOHER LAND (Schöntal is 72km/45mi south).*

A Bit of History

The Master of Würzburg – Flamboy-ant Gothic sculptor **Tilman Riemen-schneider** (1460-1531) came to live in Würzburg in 1483, and became mayor in 1520-21. Riemenschneider's work was never purely decorative: his interest cen-tred on humans, whose faces, hands and garments served as vehicles for express-ing emotion.

M. Hertlein/MICHELIN

The old bridge across the Main and Marienberg Fortress

Residenz★★

  Apr-Oct 9am-6pm; Nov-Mar 10am-4pm.   *Closed on Shrove Tue, 24,25,31 Dec and 1 Jan.*   *€5.*   *(0931) 35 51 70; www.schloesser.bayern.de.*

This superb 18C Baroque palace, one of the biggest in Germany, was built under the direction of **Balthasar Neumann**.

Palace★★

  Open daily except Mon, 9am-6pm from Apr to Sep, 10am-4pm from Oct to Mar.   *€5.*

The monumental **Grand Staircase**★★ *(Treppenhaus)* occupies the whole northern part of the vestibule and is one of Neumann's masterpieces. The huge **fresco**★★ (600m²/6 400sq ft) decorating the vaulted ceiling is by the Venetian, **Tiepolo** (1753). In the White Room *(Weißer Saal)*, between the Grand Staircase and the Imperial Hall, the brilliant **stuccoes**, also Italian, are the work of Antonio Bossi. The oval **Imperial Hall**★★ *(Kaisersaal)* is also splendid. Situated on the first floor, it, too, is adorned with **frescoes by Tiepolo**.

The **Imperial Apartments** *(Paradezimmer)* are a luxurious suite of restored rooms with Rococo stuccowork, tapestries and German furniture. The museum also houses

WÜRZBURG							
Am Studentenhaus	X	2	Hofstallstr.	Y	13	Sanderglacisstr.	X	40
Augustiner Str.	Z		Juliuspromenade	Y	15	Schönbornstr.	Y	42
Auverastr.	X	3	Kaiserstr.	Y	16	Schweinfurter Str.	X	43
Bahnhofstr.	Y	5	Kantstr.	X	18	Seinsheimstr.	X	45
Balthasar-Neumann-			Kürschnerhof	YZ	23	Semmelstr.	Y	46
Promenade	Z	6	Leistenstr.	X	24	Sieboldstr.	X	48
Barbarossapl.	Y	7	Ludwigsbrücke	X	25	Spiegelstr.	Y	50
Deutsche EinheitBrücke	X	8	Marienpl.	Y	27	Textorstr.	Y	52
Domstr.	Z		Marktpl.	Y	29	Theaterstr.	YZ	
Eichhornstr.	Y		Martin-Luther-Str.	X	30	Urlaubstr.	X	54
Friedensbrücke	X	9	Mergentheimer Str.	X	32	Valentin-Becker-Str.	X	55
Georg-Eydel-Str.	X	10	Nürnberger Str.	X	34	Veitshöchheimer Str.	X	58
Haugerring	X	12	Peterstr.	Z	35	Virchowstr.	X	60
			Raiffeisenstr.	X	37	Wirsbergstr.	Z	64
			Rimparer Str.	X	38			

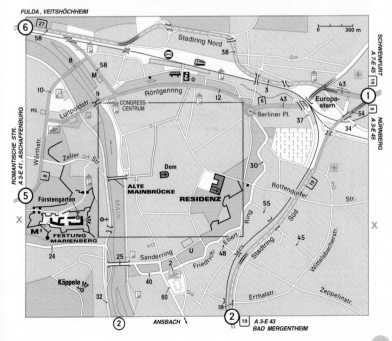

a picture gallery with some fine **17C and 18C Italian paintings**, among them works by Bellucci, Canaletto and the school of Veronese.

Hofkirche★

The Residenz church is the work of Balthasar Neumann. Marble, gilding and warm ceiling frescoes by court painter Rudolf Byss all combine to form a colourful composition. Two more **Tiepolo** paintings hang above the side altars: *The Assumption* and *The Fall of the Angels*.

Hofgarten★

Astute use of old, stepped bastions has produced a layout of terraced **gardens**. From the eastern side, the whole 167m/545ft of the palace façade, with its elegant central block, is visible. The stucco is the work of Johann Peter Wagner.

Martin-von-Wagner-Museum★

South wing. ○ *Picture gallery: open daily except Mon and Sun, 9.30am-12.30pm, collection of antiquities: open daily except Mon, 2-5pm, Sun 9.30am-12.30pm; picture gallery and collection of antiquities open alternately.* ○ *Closed 1 Jan, Good Friday, 1st May, 3 Oct, 1 Nov, 24 and 31 Dec.* ☎ *(0931) 31 28 66; www.uni-wuerzburg.de/museum.*
The museum's second floor includes a **picture gallery★** with 14C-20C German and European works. The most interesting exhibits include altar paintings by the masters of Würzburg (14C-16C) and Franconian sculpture, especially that of Riemenschneider. Dutch and Italian painters from the 16C to the 18C are well represented (Tiepolo). On the third floor is a **collection of antiquities★** displaying a series of **painted Greek vases★★** (6C-4C BC).

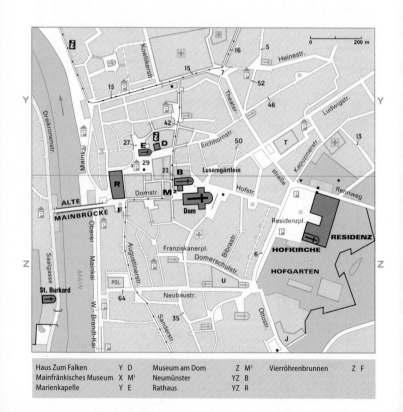

Haus Zum Falken	Y	D	Museum am Dom	Z	M²	Vierröhrenbrunnen	Z	F
Mainfränkisches Museum	X	M¹	Neumünster	YZ	B		
Marienkapelle	Y	E	Rathaus	YZ	R		

A Masterpiece in 210 Days

Disappointment with other painters led Prince-Bishop Carl Philipp von Greif-fenclau to commission the best fresco painter of the age, **Giovanni Battista Tie-polo**, to paint the palace. The painter arrived with his two sons on 12 December 1750. Tiepolo wanted for nothing; he was served eight courses at lunch and seven in the evening. In addition, he received three times the pay he earned in Venice. Tiepolo had a reputation for painting with great speed, but the artist surpassed all estimates during his short three years in Würzburg: He created frescoes in the Imperial Hall and staircase, two altars for the Würzburg court church, one for Schwarzach Abbey (now in Munich's Alte Pinakothek) and worked for other Würz-burg families. Unable to paint during the winter, Tiepolo worked day and night for the rest of the year. It took him only 210 days to complete the staircase fresco, 32x19m/105x62ft in size with a wide range of people, allegories and details.

Sights

Dom St. Kilian (Cathedral of St Kilian)

This basilica with columns and four towers, rebuilt after 1945, has retained its original 11C-13C silhouette, although the interior is marked by many other centuries. The modern **Altar of the Apostles** holds three 16C **sculptures**★ by Riemenschneider. Off the left transept is the 18C **Schönborn Chapel** by Balthasar Neumann built for the tombs of the prince-bishops of that house.

Neumünster (New Cathedral)

The imposing Baroque **west façade** of this church (1710-16) is attributed to Johann Dientzenhofer. In niches below the cupola are a Riemenschneider *Virgin and Child* and a Christ in an unusual pose with arms folded below the chest (14C). In the west crypt is the **tomb of St Kilian**, apostle, patron of Franconia and missionary, executed in Würzburg in 689. On the left of the chancel is the Lusamgärtlein, a small garden where the 13C troubadour-poet Walther von der Vogelweide is said to be buried.

Museum am Dom (Cathedral Museum)

Between the two cathedrals. ⏰ *Open daily except Mon, 10am-7pm from Apr to Oct, 10am-5pm from Nov to Mar.* 🎫 €3.
Opened in 2003, this museum houses mainly works of modern art (Joseph Beuys, Otto Dix) but also some works by masters of Romanesque, Gothic and Baroque art (Tilman Riemenschneider, Georg Anton Urlaub).

Marienkapelle

This fine Gothic chapel was built by the town burghers in the 14C and 15C and boasts an attractive *Annunciation* on the tympanum of the north doorway. Inside the west front is the 1502 tombstone of Konrad von Schaumberg, carved by Rie-menschneider and, on the north side, a **silver Madonna** made by the Master of Augsburg, J Kilian, in 1680.

Rathaus (Town Hall)

A 13C building, the town hall boasts a painted façade from the 16C. The interior courtyard is charming. The western part, the **red building** *(Roter Bau)*, is in Late Renaissance style. The Baroque **fountain** *(Vierröhrenbrunnen)* in front of the town hall dates from 1765.

Festung Marienberg★ (Marienberg Fortress)

Mid-Mar-Oct: open daily except Mon, 9am-6pm. €4. (0931) 35 51 70; www. schloesser.bayern.de

From 1253 to 1719, this stronghold was the home of the prince-bishops of Würzburg. Built above the west bank of the Main, the original 13C medieval castle was transformed into a Renaissance palace by Julius Echter ca 1600.

The prince-bishops' apartments now house a **museum** (Fürstenbaumuseum), richly furnished and hung with paintings and tapestries, including the huge Echter family tapestry from 1564. The treasury contains liturgical items from the cathedral, royal chapel and Marienberg Chapel. *Open Tue-Sun, 10am-5pm. €4. (0931) 35 51 70.*

Mainfränkisches Museum★★ (Franconian Museum of the Main)

Entrance on the right in the fortress' first courtyard. Open daily, 10am-7pm. Closed Shrove Tuesday, 24, 25 and 31 Dec. €4. (0931) 20 59 40.

Among the displays of local arts and crafts in this former arsenal (Zeughaus, 1702-12) is an important collection of **80 Riemenschneider sculptures** *(first floor)*, including Adam and Eve, Virgin Mary and Child and The Apostles. In the vaulted galleries of the **Echterbastei**, statues, gold and silver religious plate, Gothic easel paintings and examples of Franconian folk art can be seen.

Address Book

WHERE TO EAT

Bürgerspital – *Theaterstraße 19* (0931) 35 28 80 *Closed 3 weeks in Aug* This is one of Germany's major taverns, part of the Bürgerspital wine estate. Impeccable tables sit beneath a lovely groined vault, and Franconian specialities accompany local wines.

Weinhaus zum Stachel – *Gressengasse 1 (near Marktplatz)* (0931) 5 27 70 www.weinhaus-stachel. de *Reservation recommended* This traditional Weinstube with an idyllic courtyard dates to the 15C. Excellent Franconian wines and regional cuisine.

WHERE TO STAY

Hotel Alter Kranen – *Kärnergasse 11 (street parallel to Mainkai)* (0931) 3 51 80 Fax (0931) 50010 www. hotel-alter-kranen.de *14 rooms* This hotel sits on the banks of the Main, a stone's throw from the old town. Magnificent view of Marienberg Fortress from the breakfast room.

Hotel Rebstock – *Neubaustraße 7* (0931) 309 30 – Fax (0931) 3093100 www.rebstock.com *72 rooms Restaurant* Behind the Rococo façade of 1737, a range of elegant and modern rooms awaits. Charming restaurant and bistro-style winter garden.

TAKING A BREAK

Café Michel – *Marktplatz 11* (0931) 5 37 76 *Open Mon-Fri 8am-6pm, Sat 7.30am-6pm, Sun and public holidays 1.30-5.30pm; Brasilino: Mon-Tue 9am-6pm.* This café covers two floors and offers a variety of cakes, tarts and savoury dishes. You can also get a drink in the adjoining cafe-bar, the Brasilino.

GOING OUT

USEFUL TIPS

Bars frequented mainly by young people and students are along Juliuspromenade north of the city centre and in Sanderstraße south of the city centre.

Gutsschenke Schützenhof – *Mainleitenweg 48 (near the Käppele)* 35 Käppele (0931) 7 24 22 *Open 9am-1am Closed mid Dec to early Mar.* Peace and quiet and a shady terrace grace this cafe slightly outside the city. Coffee, sweets or a full meal are on tap. Produce from the garden is used to prepare the dishes.

Schönborn – *Marktplatz 30* (0931) 4 04 48 18 *Open Mon-Sat 8am-1am, Sun 10am-1am.* Always busy, whatever the hour, this café has a large terrace on Marktplatz. Choose from a wide choice of drinks, coffee to cocktails, and full meals.

Käppele (Chapel)

Atop a monumental Way of the Cross, this well-situated Baroque pilgrim sanctuary was built by Balthasar Neumann in 1748. The adjoining chapel of mercy is connected via a "miracle passage". The finest **view**★★ of Würzburg and the river is from the chapel terrace, with the fortress of Marienberg rising from the vineyards in the foreground.

Excursion

Schloss Veitshöchheim★

7km/4mi northwest via ⑥ on the town map. ⏱ *Apr-Oct: 9am-6pm.* ✎ *€3.* ☎ *(0931) 35 51 70.*

The 17C **palace**, built after plans by Balthasar Neumann, contains splendid Rococo and Empire furniture. But it was the **park**★ that received particular attention from the prince-bishops, who eventually reworked it as a Rococo creation. In the southern park, 200 statues people the shaded walks and arbours.

Driving Tour

Franconian Wine Route★ (Bocksbeutelstraße)

87km/55mi

▶ *Leave Würzburg via ③ on the town map.*

It was medieval monks who introduced viticulture to the Franconian region – an area with a mild climate and hot, dry summers. The 4 500ha/11 115 acres produce mainly dry white wines from the **Müller-Thurgau** and traditionally fruity **Silvaner** grape stock. Such wines adapt perfectly to the essentially rich Franconian cooking.

Ochsenfurt

Another town still encircled by ancient **ramparts**★, Ochsenfurt's centre features many half-timbered houses and hotels adorned with wrought-iron statuettes or signs. A mechanical clock in the lantern turret strikes the hours at the **Neues Rathaus** (15C). The **Stadtpfarrkirche St Andreas**, built between the 13C and the 15C, is noteworthy for its interior decoration.

▶ *Turn left off the B13 and drive alongside the Main on the U47.*

Sulzfeld

The fortified historic town centre in Sulzfeld features towers and gateways and numerous half-timbered houses. A highlight of this pretty wine-growing village is the Renaissance **town hall** with its scrolled gables.

▶ *Pass through Kitzingen and Mainstockheim (on the east bank of the Main), and take the road for Dettelbach.*

Dettelbach★

Dettelbach clings to the northern slopes of the Main valley. Its charm lies in its Late Gothic (ca 1500) town hall and the 15C parish church, whose principal tower is linked by a wooden bridge to the smaller staircase tower. Northeast of the upper town is the **pilgrimage church "Maria im Sand"** (1608-13).

▶ *From Dettelbach to Neuses am Berg, the road crosses an open plateau of vines, with good views of the neighbouring slopes. It then drops down again to the Main valley; follow a meander before crossing to the other bank.*

Volkach★

This delightful wine-growing town lies on the eastern side of a wide oxbow in the Main. Of the original medieval enclave only two gates remain: the **Gaibacher Tor** and the **Sommeracher Tor**, one at each end of the main street. On one side of Marktplatz is the **Renaissance town hall** *(Tourist Information Centre)*, built in the mid 16C. In front of it a 15C fountain bears a statue of the Virgin Mary. Slightly farther south is the **Bartholomäuskirche**, a Late Gothic building with Baroque and Rococo interior decor.

At the northwestern limit of the town *(about 1km/0.5mi, in the direction of Fahr)* stands the 15C **pilgrimage church "Maria im Weingarten"**, among vineyards covering the Kirchberg. Inside is the famous **Virgin with Rosary**★ *(Rosenkranzmadonna)*, a late work (1512-24) of Tilman Riemenschneider, in carved limewood.

▸ *Return to Würzburg via Schwarzach, turning right onto the B 22.*

ZUGSPITZE★★★

With a summit at 2 964m/9 724ft above sea level, the Zugspitze is the highest peak in Germany. Its matchless panorama and extensive ski slopes keep the mountain well-supplied with tourist facilities.

▸ **Orient Yourself:** The Zugspitze is the northwest pillar of the Wetterstein limestone massif, a rocky barrier enclosing the valley of the Loisach and on the border with Austria. On clear days, 4 countries can be seen from the summit, including Munich in Germany, the Dolomites in Italy, the Piz Bernina in Switzerland and the Groß Venediger in Austria.

Don't Miss: The panorama from the summit.

Organizing Your Time: Plan at least half a day to scale the Zugspitze.

Especially for Kids: A cable-car trip to the summit

Also See: *Deutsche ALPENSTRASSE, Schloss LINDERHOF and Schloss NEUSCHWAN-STEIN (to the west of Garmisch). Walks are also possible from GARMISCH-PARTEN-KIRCHEN.*

Visit

Ascent

Wear warm clothing! From Eibsee by cable-car (Journey time: 10min, departs every 30min). *8am-4.45pm.* *Closed 2 weeks in spring and autumn.* *Summer: €45 round trip, winter: €34 round trip. (088 21) 79 70; www.zugspitze.de Service is reduced in bad weather.*

The summit can be reached by cable-car *(Gletscherbahn)* from Zugspitzplatt station, the terminus of the rack railway rising from Garmisch, directly from the Eibsee, or from Ehrwald via the Tyrolean Zugspitz train. Only experienced hikers should undertake the ascent on foot.

From Garmisch-Partenkirchen

1hr15min. Departs every hour from 8:15am to 2:15pm. *€45 round trip (€34 in winter). Last train back: 4:30pm. (08821) 79 70.*

A 4.6km/2.9mi tunnel ends the rack-railway climb to Zugspitzplatt station. As long as the snow is good (from October to May), the lower Zugspitzplatt offers a skiing area of 7.5km²/almost 3sq mi, equipped with many tow ropes. The cable-car *(Gletscherbahn)* from Zugspitzplatt station climbs the last 350m/1 148ft to the summit.

From the Eibsee

🚟 *Cable-car direct to the summit in 10min. Departs every 30min from 8am to 5:15pm (4:15pm in winter).* 🔗 *Same price (👤 see above).*

From the Austrian Tyrolese side

🚟 *From Ehrwald, the Tyrolean cable-car ascends the summit from the valley station in 10min.*

Zugspitzgipfel★★★ (The Summit)

The upper terminals of the Gletscherbahn and the Eibsee cable-car are on the German side. The look-out terrace by the Gipfelbahn is 2 964m/9 724ft high. On the Austrian side is the upper station of the Tyrolean Zugspitzbahn.

The **panorama**★★★ to the east reveals the Kaisergebirge, the Dachstein and the Karwendel, the glacial peaks of the Hohe Tauern, the High Alps of the Tirol and the Ortler and the Bernina massifs. Nearer are the mountains of the Arlbergbefore the Säntis in the Appenzell Alps; further away, to the west and northwest, are the Allgäu and Ammergau ranges. To the north, the Bavarian lowlands are visible, along with the Ammersee and Starnberger See lakes.

ZWIEFALTEN★★

POPULATION: 2 300

The Upper Swabian Plateau is scattered with beautiful Baroque churches whose fluid decorations harmonise with the landscape. The prosperity and cultural influence of 18C Benedictine abbeys led to updating their churches as a priority, regardless of whether they needed it. Thanks to the abbots' patronage of the arts, artists were able to create magnificent buildings, built "so that God may be glorified in all things", according to the inscription on the Weingarten façade.

▶ **Orient Yourself:** Between Ulm and Lake Constance (Bodensee), this tour crosses the Upper Swabian Plateau with its gentle hills and soft light.

😊 **Don't Miss:** The abbey churches in Weingarten and Zwiefalten.

👤 **Also See:** *SALEM (32km/20mi southwest of Ravensburg), LINDAU IM BODENSEE (32km/20mi south of Ravensburg), ULM (50km/31mi northeast of Zwiefalten), SCHWÄBISCHE ALB (35km/22mi west of Zwiefalten).*

Driving Tour

85km/53mi

Ravensburg

This ancient Swabian town still shelters behind a city wall of towers and fortified gateways. The road from Wangen passes beneath the Obertor, a gateway with stepped gables. At the end of Marktstraße is a block of old buildings comprising the Rathaus (14C-15C) and the weigh-house with the Blaserturm,

---

The Devil to Pay

Of the 66 stops (sets of pipes) of the Weingarten organ, the 46th is called Vox Humana. Gabler's ambition was to build an organ combining man and machine in resounding praise of God. After countless attempts to recreate a human sound, he is said to have sold his soul to the devil, who supplied him with a piece of metal which he melted down to make the pipes. The monks were so enthralled by the beauty of the organ's song that they were unable to pray, whereupon the abbot ordered an inquiry. Gabler was found out, confessed and sentenced to death. But since the only sounds produced by the organ now resembled wailing, Gabler was reprieved.

a 15C-16C tower. An observation tower built to spy on Veitsburg stands on a nearby hill. The stone **Mehlsack** (Sack of Flour), originally whitewashed, towers 50m/164ft and is outfitted with 240 steps. The **view** from the tower extends as far as the church at Weingarten.

▶ *Exit via the B 30 towards Weingarten.*

Weingarten★★

Consecrated in 1724, the abbey church in Weingarten rivals Ottobeuren as the largest Baroque sanctuary in Germany, 102m/335ft long and 44m/144ft wide at the transepts. Various architectural elements betray an Italian influence transmitted by way of Salzburg. Inside, the painting and stuccowork were entrusted to the masters of the day. Scenes on the vaulting by Cosmas Damien Asam are

Interior of Zwiefalten Church

full of virtuosity, as are the choir stalls by Joseph Anton Feuchtmayer. The **organ**★★ is due to Joseph Gabler (1700-71) and fits perfectly with the rest of the decoration: Its 6 666 pipes follow the line of the windows and blend with the pink marble.

▶ *The tour continues along the Upper Swabian Baroque Road (signposted "Oberschäbische Barockstraße") via the B 30 until Bad Waldsee Turn left onto the L 275.*

Bad Schussenried

This pleasant town boasts **abbey buildings** (now a conference and exhibition centre) and an abbey church which owe their sumptuous Baroque appearance to Premonstratensian abbots. In the church, the upper panels of the intricately decorated choir stalls (1717) are separated by 28 statuettes representing men and women who founded religious orders. The **library**★ has a painted ceiling by Franz Georg Herrmann.

○ *Open Apr to Oct, Tue-Fri, 10am-1pm, 2pm-5pm, Sat-Sun and bank holidays, 10am-5pm; Nov to Mar, Sat-Sun and bank holidays, 1-4pm.*
○ *Closed 24, 25 and 31 Dec.* ⊛ *€3.*
☏ *(073 15) 02 89 75.*

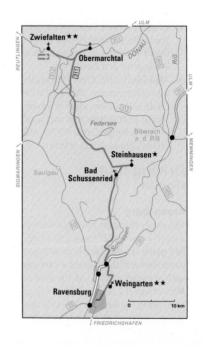

Steinhausen★

Designed by Dominikus and Johann Zimmermann, the pilgrimage church in this hamlet comprises a single nave and a small chancel, both oval. Capitals, cornices and window embrasures are adorned with birds, insects or flowers.

School of Wessobrunn

In the 17C and 18C, the little town of Wessobrunn produced a series of multi-talented architects and artists who, according to construction requirements or the dictates of their own inspiration, were able to exchange the compass at will for the paintbrush or the tools of the stuccoworker. Working in a corporate and family framework known as the Wessobrunn School, these non-specialized artists of Baroque genius beautified churches and civic buildings all over Bavaria, Swabia and the Tyrol. The names of the **Feuchtmayer** and **Schmuzer** families are eminent within the group, though the most celebrated is perhaps **Dominikus Zimmermann**, who was responsible for the church at Wies.

▶ *Follow the L 275 until Riedlingen, then join the B 312 to Zwiefalten.*

Zwiefalten★★

This village on the Danubian edge of the Swabian Jura has a remarkable **church**. Like most Baroque edifices in this region, the church's exterior conceals a lavishly decorated interior. Inside the 18C building by **Johann Michael Fischer** is a profusion of luminous colours, exuberant decoration and artistic virtuosity. The eye finally settles on the details: ceiling paintings of the Virgin Mary by Franz Joseph Spiegler, a pulpit decorated by Johann Michael Feuchtmayer (uncle of the sculptor and stuccoworker Joseph Anton Feuchtmayer), angels and cherubs galore.

▶ *Go back to Zwiefaltendorf then take the B 311 to the left.*

Obermarchtal

The 17C **abbey church** in this small town was one of the first completed by the Vorarlberg School. The rigidity of the architecture, an as yet undeveloped Baroque, and the church's heavy furnishings are lightened only by the Wessobrunn stuccowork.
🕰 *Tour on request.* ☎ *(073 75) 95 91 00.*

INDEX

INDEX

INDEX

INDEX

INDEX

ACCOMMODATIONS

INDEX

RESTAURANTS

INDEX

MAPS AND PLANS

LIST OF MAPS

COMPANION
PUBLICATIONS

MICHELIN MAP 718 GERMANY

- a practical map on a scale of 1:750 000 which shows the German road network and indicates isolated sites and monuments described in this guide;
- with index of place names.

MICHELIN TOURIST AND MOTORING ATLAS GERMANY/ AUSTRIA/BENELUX/ SWITZERLAND/CZECH REPUBLIC

- spiral-bound atlas on a scale of 1:300 000 for Germany;
- with index of place names and town maps.

MICHELIN REGIONAL MAPS (541-546)

- maps on a scale of 1:350 000 with detailed road mapping and maps of the main towns.

CITY PLANS:

- Berlin in map format (33)
- Berlin in spiral atlas format (2033)

TRAVELLING TO GERMANY

Michelin Tourist and Motoring Atlas Europe – A4 spiral (1136), A3 spiral (1129), A3 paperback (1135)

- the whole of Europe on a scale of 1:1 000 000 in one volume;
- major roads and 73 town plans and area maps;
- highway code of every country.

WWW.VIAMICHELIN.COM

Internet users can access personalised route plans, Michelin maps and town plans, and addresses of hotels and restaurants featured in The Michelin Guide Deutschland.

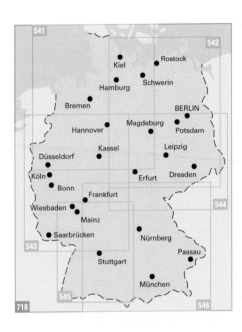

Michelin North America
One Parkway South – Greenville, SC 29615 USA
☏ 800-423-0485
www.MichelinTravel.com
michelin.guides@us.michelin.com

Manufacture française des pneumatiques Michelin

Société en commandite par actions au capital de 304 000 000 EUR
Place des Carmes-Déchaux – 63000 Clermont-Ferrand (France)
R.C.S. Clermont-Fd B 855 200 507

No part of this publication may be reproduced in any form
without the prior permission of the publisher.

© Michelin et Cie, Propriétaires-éditeurs
Dépot légal novembre 2006 – ISSN 0763-1383
Printed in France: octobre 2006
Printing and Binding: IME